Dancing with Qubits
Second Edition

From qubits to algorithms, embark on the
quantum computing journey shaping our future

Robert S. Sutor

<packt>

BIRMINGHAM – MUMBAI

Dancing with Qubits, Second Edition

Producer: Denim Pinto
Acquisitions Editor – Peer Reviews: Gaurav Gavas
Project Editor: Parvathy Nair
Content Development Editor: Rebecca Youé
Copy Editor: Safis Editing
Technical Editor: Aniket Shetty
Proof Reader: Safis Editing
Presentation Designer: Rajesh Shirsath

First published: November 2019
Second edition: March 2024

Production reference: 1250324

Published by Packt Publishing Ltd.
Grosvenor House
11 St Paul's Square
Birmingham
B3 1RB, UK

ISBN 978-1-83702-075-1

www.packt.com

To Judith, Katie, and William,
*to whom my debt is **still** beyond computation.*

Contributors

About the author

Robert S. Sutor has been a technical leader and executive in the IT industry for over 40 years. More than two decades of that were spent in IBM Research in New York. During his time there, he worked on and led efforts in symbolic mathematical computation, mathematical programming languages, optimization, AI, blockchain, and quantum computing software. He is the author of *Dancing with Qubits, First Edition: How quantum computing works and how it can change the world* and *Dancing with Python: Learn Python software development from scratch and get started with quantum computing,* also with Packt. He is the published co-author of several research papers and the book *Axiom: The Scientific Computation System* with the late Richard D. Jenks. He's a theoretical mathematician by training, has a Ph.D. from Princeton University, and an undergraduate degree from Harvard College.

I thank my wife, Judith Hunter, and children, Katie and William, for their love, patience, and humor while I wrote this book and its first edition. I also thank Franz, Ferdinand, Gus, Georgia, Sinjin, and Chester.

I thank the following for their conversations, insight, and inspiration regarding business, mathematics, machine learning, physics, and quantum technologies: Aleksandra Mojsilovic, Alex Olivas, Alex Radnaev, Alex Tingle, Andrew Cross, Anjul Loiacono, Antonio Mezzacappo, Barry Behnken, Brittany Mazin, Chester Kennedy, Chid Apte, Chris Lirakis, Chris Wood, Christina Willis, Dana Anderson, Denny Dahl, Doug McClure, Eric Copenhaver, Evan Salim, Fred Chong, Hanhee Paik, Hannah North, Ismael Faro, James Rabeau, Jay Gambetta, Jeanette Garcia, Jerry Chow, Jon Lenchner, Judith Olson, Kaitlin Smith, Laura Thomas, Lev Bishop, Mark Ritter, Mark Saffman, Markus Brink, Matthias Steffen, Max Perez, Neil Anderson, Noah Fitch, Paul Lipman, Paul Nation, Pranav Gokhale, Robert Loredo, Robert Wisnieff, Sarah Schupp, Sarah Sheldon, Sayantan Pramanik, Scott Faris, Shahram Babaie, Stefan Woerner, Teague Tomesh, Thomas Noel, Tim Ballance, Victory Omole, William Clark, and Zaira Nazario.

I particularly want to thank Jack Krupansky for his careful review of and suggestions for the newest parts of the text.

About the reviewers

Gerhard Hellstern (Prof., Dr. rer. nat, graduate physicist, *1971) is a full professor at the Faculty of Economics at the Baden-Württemberg Cooperative State University in Stuttgart. From 1990–1995, he studied physics at the University of Tübingen and the State University of New York at Stony Brook; in 1998, he graduated as Dr. rer. nat. From 1998 to 2018, he was employed by several commercial banks and then for 17 years at Deutsche Bundesbank. There, he was in charge of the banking audits division for many years.

Gerhard Hellstern has been involved in the application of data science methods (data analytics as well as machine and deep learning) in finance for many years. These methods also include quantum computing as well as quantum machine learning based on it. He is a Qiskit advocate at IBM and a member of the research network Quantum Computing of the Fraunhofer Gesellschaft, Germany. His current research focuses on applications of quantum computing and quantum machine learning in the financial sector and beyond and he has published several papers in this domain.

Prateek Jain is an inquisitive person with a lifelong passion for science. He is currently focusing and researching quantum computing technologies and algorithms, focusing on the intersection of quantum computing and AI. He leads Quantum AI research at Fractal Analytics. He has over 5 years' research experience in quantum computing and technologies and 18 years' experience in machine learning and artificial intelligence. He possesses a Master's in quantum computing technologies from the Technical University of Madrid and a Master's in innovation and entrepreneurship from HEC Paris. He is also an IBM Quantum advocate and educator and his research interests include quantum computing, quantum machine learning, machine learning, and AI because it is fascinating to ponder the greatest questions of our age and catch a glimpse of how the world would look in the future.

Contents

List of Figures

Preface

Everything we call real is made of things that cannot be regarded as real.

– Niels Bohr

When most people think about computers, they consider laptops or maybe even bigger systems such as the servers that power the web, the Internet, and the cloud. If you look around, you may start seeing computers in other places. Modern cars, for example, have anywhere from around 20 computers to more than 100 to control all the systems that allow you to move, brake, monitor the air conditioning, and control the entertainment system.

The smartphone is the computer many people use more than anything else in a typical day. A modern phone contains a 64-bit processor, whatever a "64-bit processor" is. The amount of memory used for running all those apps might be 3GB, which means 3 gigabytes.

All these computers are called *classical computers*, and the original ideas for them go back to the 1940s. Sounding more scientific, we say these computers have a *von Neumann architecture*, named after the mathematician and physicist John von Neumann.

It's not the 1940s anymore, obviously, but more than seventy years later, we still have the modern versions of these machines in so many parts of our lives. Through the years, the "thinking" components, the processors, have gotten faster and faster. The amount of memory has also gotten larger, so we can run more—and bigger—apps that do some pretty sophisticated things. The improvements in graphics processors have given us better and better games. The amount of storage has skyrocketed in the last couple of decades, so we can have more and more apps and games and photos and videos on devices we carry around. When it comes to these classical computers and how they have developed, "more is better."

We can say similar things about the computer servers that run businesses and the Internet worldwide. Do you store your photos in the cloud? Where is that exactly? How many photos can you keep there, and how much does it cost? How quickly can your photos and all the other data you need move back and forth to that nebulous place?

It's remarkable, all this computer power. It seems like every generation of computers will continue to get faster and faster and be able to do more and more for us. There's no end in sight for how powerful these small and large machines will get to entertain us, connect us to our friends and family, and solve the important problems in the world.

Except ...that's false.

While there will continue to be some improvements, we will not see anything like the doubling in processor power every two years that happened starting in the mid-1960s. This doubling went by the name of *Moore's Law* and went something like ''every two years, processors will get twice as fast, half as large, and use half as much energy.''

These proportions, such as ''double'' and ''half,'' are approximate, but physicists and engineers really did make extraordinary progress for many years. That's why you can have a computer in a watch on your wrist that is more powerful than a system that took up an entire room forty years ago.

A fundamental problem is the part where I said processors would get half as large. We can't keep making transistors and circuits smaller and smaller indefinitely. We'll start to get so small that we approach the atomic level. The electronics will get so crowded that when we try to tell part of a processor to do something, a nearby component will also get affected.

There's another more profound and more fundamental question. Just because we created an architecture over seventy years ago and have vastly improved it, does that mean all kinds of problems can eventually be successfully tackled by computers using that design? Why do we think the types of computers we have now might eventually be suitable for solving every possible problem? Will ''more is better'' run out of steam if we keep to the same kind of computer technology? Is there something wrong or limiting about our way of computing that will prevent our making the progress we need or desire?

Depending on the problem you are considering, it's reasonable to think the answer to the last question is somewhere between ''probably'' and ''yes.''

That's depressing. Well, it's only depressing if we can't come up with one or more new types of computers that have a chance of breaking through the limitations.

That's what this book is about. Quantum computing as an idea goes back to at least the early 1980s. It uses the principles of quantum mechanics to provide an entirely new kind of computer architecture. Quantum mechanics, in turn, goes back to around 1900, but especially to the 1920s, when physicists started noticing that experimental results did not match what the theories predicted.

However, this is not a book about quantum mechanics. Since 2016, tens of thousands of users have been able to use quantum computing hardware via the cloud, what we call quantum cloud services. People have started programming these new computers even though the way you do it is unlike anything done on a classical computer.

Why have so many people been drawn to quantum computing? I'm sure part of it is curiosity. There's also the science fiction angle: the word ''quantum'' gets tossed around enough in sci-fi movies that viewers wonder if there is any substance to the idea.

Once we get past the idea that quantum computing is new and intriguing, it's good to ask, ''ok, but what is it really good for?'' and ''when and how will it make a difference in my life?'' I discuss the use cases experts think are most tractable over the next few years and decades.

It's time to learn about quantum computing. It's time to stop thinking classically and to start thinking *quantumly,* though I'm pretty sure that's not really a word!

For whom did I write this book?

This book is for anyone who has a very healthy interest in mathematics and wants to start learning about the computer science, engineering, and a bit of the physics of quantum computing. I review the basic math, but things move quickly, so we can dive deeply into an exposition of how to work with qubits and quantum algorithms. There are exercises in every chapter for you to test and deepen your knowledge.

While this book contains a lot of math, it is not of the definition-theorem-proof variety. I'm more interested in presenting the topics to give you insight into the relationships between the ideas than giving you a strictly formal development of all results.

Another goal is to prepare you to read more advanced texts and articles on the subject, perhaps returning here to understand some core topic. You do not need to be a mathematician, and certainly not a physicist, to read this book, nor do you need to understand quantum mechanics beforehand.

At several places in the book, I give some code examples using Python 3. Consider these extra and not required, but if you know Python, they may help your understanding.

What does this book cover?

Before we jump into understanding how quantum computing works from the ground up, we need to take a little time to see how things are done classically. This is not only for the sake of comparison. The future, I believe, will be a hybrid of classical and quantum computers.

The best way to learn about something is to start with basic principles and then work your way up. That way, you know how to reason about it and don't rely on rote memorization or faulty analogies.

Part I – Foundations

The first part covers the mathematics you need to understand quantum computing concepts. While we will ultimately be operating in very large dimensions and using complex numbers, you can gain a lot of insight from what happens in traditional 2D and 3D.

Chapter 1 – Why Quantum Computing

In the first chapter, we ask the most basic question that applies to this book: why quantum computing? Why do we care? In what ways will our lives change? What are the use cases to which we hope to apply quantum computing and see a significant improvement? What do we even mean by "significant improvement"?

Chapter 2 – They're Not Old, They're Classics

Classical computers are pervasive, but relatively few people know what's inside them and how they work. To contrast them later with quantum computers, we look at the basics along with the reasons why they have problems doing some kinds of calculations. I introduce the simple notion of a bit, a single 0 or 1, but show that working with many bits can eventually give you all the software you use today.

Chapter 3 – More Numbers Than You Can Imagine

The numbers people use every day are called real numbers. Included in these are integers, rational numbers, and irrational numbers. Other kinds of numbers and structures have many of the same algebraic properties. We look at these to lay the groundwork for understanding the "compute" part of what a quantum computer does.

Chapter 4 – Planes and Circles and Spheres, Oh My

From algebra, we move to geometry and relate the two. What is a circle, really, and what does it have in common with a sphere when we move from two to three dimensions? Trigonometry becomes more obvious, though that is not a legally binding statement. What you thought of as a plane becomes the basis for understanding complex numbers, which are key to the definition of quantum bits, usually known as *qubits*.

Chapter 5 – Dimensions

After laying the algebraic and geometric groundwork, we move beyond the familiar two- and three-dimensional world. Vector spaces generalize to many dimensions and are essential for understanding the exponential power that quantum computers can harness. What can you do when working in many dimensions, and how should you think about such operations? This extra elbow room comes into play when we consider how quantum computing might augment AI.

Chapter 6 – What Do You Mean "Probably"?

"God does not play dice with the universe," said Albert Einstein.

This was not a religious statement but rather an expression of his lack of comfort with the idea that randomness and probability play a role in how nature operates. Well, he didn't get that quite right. Quantum mechanics, the deep and often mysterious part of physics on which quantum computing is based, very much has probability at its core. Therefore, we cover the fundamentals of probability to aid your understanding of quantum processes and behavior.

Part II – Quantum Computing

The next part is the core of how quantum computing really works. We look at quantum bits—qubits—singly and together, and then create circuits that implement algorithms. Much of this is the ideal case when we have fault-tolerant, error-corrected qubits. When we build quantum computers, we must deal with the physical realities of noise and the need to reduce errors.

Chapter 7 – One Qubit

At this point, we can finally talk about qubits in a nontrivial manner. We look at both the vector and Bloch sphere representations of the quantum states of qubits. We define superposition, which explains the common cliché about a qubit being "zero and one at the same time."

Chapter 8 – Two Qubits, Three

With two qubits, we need more math, and so we introduce the notion of the tensor product. This allows us to explain entanglement, which Einstein called "spooky action at a distance." Entanglement tightly correlates two qubits so that they no longer act independently. With superposition, entanglement gives rise to the very large spaces in which quantum computations can operate.

Chapter 9 – Wiring Up the Circuits

Given a set of qubits, how do you manipulate them to solve problems or perform calculations? The answer is you build circuits for them out of gates that correspond to reversible operations. For now, think about the classical term "circuit board." I use the quantum analog of circuits to implement algorithms, the recipes computers use for accomplishing tasks.

Chapter 10 – From Circuits to Algorithms

With several simple algorithms discussed and understood, we turn to more complicated ones that fit together to give us Peter Shor's 1995 fast integer factoring algorithm. This chapter's math is more extensive, but we have everything we need from previous discussions.

Chapter 11 – Getting Physical

When you build a physical qubit, it doesn't behave exactly like the math and textbooks say it should. There are errors, and they may come from noise in the environment of the quantum system. I don't mean someone yelling or playing loud music, I mean fluctuating temperatures, radiation, vibration, and so on. We look at several factors you must consider when you build a quantum computer, introduce Quantum Volume as a whole-system metric of the performance of your system, and conclude with a discussion of the most famous quantum feline.

Part III – Advanced Topics

The final part of this book looks at more advanced topics that may require additional physics or machine learning background.

Chapter 12 – Considering NISQ Algorithms

Noisy Intermediate-Scale Quantum, or "NISQ," computers have qubits that are not fully fault-tolerant and error-corrected. Decoherence, together with initialization, gate, and measurement errors, make calculations even more unpredictable than probability would indicate. Are there algorithms that use small quantum circuits intermixed with classical methods to approximate solutions to exponentially hard problems?

Chapter 13 – Introduction to Quantum Machine Learning

Many researchers have begun to look at whether quantum methods can augment AI and machine learning. This research has not yet shown an advantage over purely classical methods, but we survey several topics, such as neural networks and kernel methods, to understand the approaches and the issues.

Chapter 14 – Questions about the Future

This book concludes with a chapter that moves beyond today by asking motivating questions to determine how "quantum-ready" you are to work with this new technology today and as it evolves.

What conventions do I use in this book?

When I want to highlight something important that you should especially remember, I use this kind of box:

> This is very important.

This book has exercises throughout the text. We answer some in later discussions, but others, the majority, are left for you as thought experiments. They are numbered within chapters.

Exercise 0.1

Is this a sample exercise?

Exercise 0.2

Is this another sample exercise?

Try to work each exercise as you go along. If you need assistance, I recommend:

- asking your professor or instructor if you have one
- looking on Wikipedia
- checking the works cited in the References section
- performing a web search, including the words ''quantum computing'' along with your other terms
- searching the online documentation of the Qiskit and Cirq quantum software development kits
- browsing or posting a question in r/QuantumComputing on Reddit or Quantum Computing on Stack Exchange
- viewing videos on YouTube about quantum computing

Due to typographical restrictions, square roots in mathematical expressions within sentences in the eBook version of this book may not have lines over them. For example, an expression such as $\sqrt{(x+y)}$ in a sentence is the same as

$$\sqrt{x+y}$$

when it appears within a standalone centered formula.

Occasionally, you may see something such as [23]. This is a reference to a book, article, or web content. The References section provides details about the works cited.

Though this is not a book about coding, I have included some sample calculations using Python version 3.11 or later. Most of the necessary features are available in earlier Python 3 versions.

Executable Python code and its produced results are shown in a `monospace` font and we mark them off in the text in the following way:

```
2**50
```

```
1125899906842624
```

The second expression shown is indented and results from running the code.

Code can also span several lines, as in this example where we create and display a set of numbers that contains no duplicates:

```
print({1, 2, 3, 2, 4,
       1, 5, 3, 6, 7,
       1, 3, 8, 2})

  {1, 2, 3, 4, 5, 6, 7, 8}
```

When I refer to Python function, method, and property names in text, they appear like this: print. Python module and package names appear like **math** and **numpy**.

The code bundle for the book is hosted on GitHub at

https://github.com/PacktPublishing/Dancing-with-Qubits-2E.

We also have other code bundles from the rich Packt catalog of books and videos available at https://github.com/PacktPublishing/. Check them out!

Share your thoughts

Once you've read *Dancing with Qubits, Second Edition*, we'd love to hear your thoughts! Scan the QR code below to go straight to the Amazon review page for this book and share your feedback.

https://packt.link/r/1837636753

Your review is important to us and the tech community and will help us make sure we're delivering excellent quality content.

Learn more on Discord

Join the Discord community for this book, where you can share feedback, ask questions to the author, and learn about new releases:

https://discord.com/invite/9sJCQvCAAD.

Get in touch

Feedback from my readers is always welcome.

General feedback: If you have questions about any aspect of this book, mention the book title in the subject of your message and email us at `customercare@packtpub.com`.

Errata: Although we have taken every care to ensure our content's accuracy, mistakes do happen. If you have found an error in this book, we would be grateful if you report this to us. Please visit

`http://www.packt.com/submit-errata`

selecting your book, clicking on the Errata Submission Form link, and entering the details.

Piracy: If you come across any illegal copies of our works in any form on the Internet, we would be grateful if you would provide us with the location address or website name. Please contact us at `copyright@packt.com` with a link to the material.

If you are interested in becoming an author: If there is a topic that you have expertise in, and you are interested in either writing or contributing to a book, please visit

`http://authors.packtpub.com`

Download a free PDF copy of this book

Thanks for purchasing this book!

Do you like to read on the go but are unable to carry your print books everywhere?

Is your eBook purchase not compatible with the device of your choice?

Don't worry, now with every Packt book you get a DRM-free PDF version of that book at no cost.

Read anywhere, any place, on any device. Search, copy, and paste code from your favorite technical books directly into your application.

The perks don't stop there, you can get exclusive access to discounts, newsletters, and great free content in your inbox daily.

Follow these simple steps to get the benefits:

- Scan the QR code or visit the link below:

https://packt.link/free-ebook/9781837636754

- Submit your proof of purchase
- That's it! We'll send your free PDF and other benefits to your email directly

• • •

Now let's start seeing why we should look at quantum computing systems to try to solve problems that are intractable with classical systems.

I

Foundations

1

Why Quantum Computing

*Nature isn't classical, dammit, and if you want to make a
simulation of nature, you'd better make it quantum
mechanical.*

– Richard Feynman [82]

In his 1982 paper ''Simulating Physics with Computers,'' Richard Feynman, 1965 Nobel Laureate in Physics, said he wanted to ''talk about the possibility that there is to be an *exact* simulation, that the computer will do *exactly* the same as nature.'' He then made the statement above, asserting that nature doesn't especially make itself amenable to computation via classical binary computers.

In this chapter, we begin to explore how quantum computing differs from classical computing. Classical computing drives smartphones, laptops, Internet servers, mainframes, high-performance computers, and even the processors in automobiles.

We examine several use cases where quantum computing may someday help us solve today's intractable problems using classical methods on classical computers. This is to motivate you to learn about the underpinnings and details of quantum computers I discuss throughout the book.

No single book on this topic can be complete. The technology and potential use cases are moving targets as we innovate and create better hardware and software. My goal here is to prepare you to delve more deeply into the science, coding, and applications of quantum computing.

Topics covered in this chapter

1.1   The mysterious quantum bit

Suppose I am standing in a room with a single overhead light and a switch that turns the light on or off. This is a normal switch, so I can't dim the light. It is either entirely on or entirely off. I can change it at will, but this is the only thing I can do to the switch. There is a single door to the room and no windows. When the door is closed, I cannot see any light.

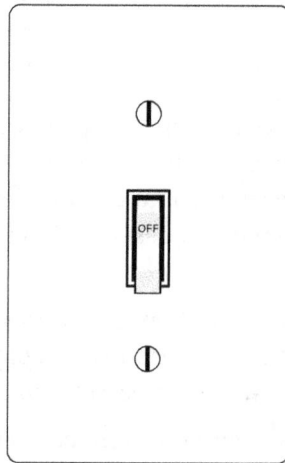

I can stay in the room, or I may leave it. The light is always on or off based on the position of the switch.

Now, I'm going to do some rewiring. I'm replacing the switch with one located in another part of the building. I can't see the light from there, but once again, whether it's on or off is determined solely by the two positions of the switch.

If I walk to the room with the light and open the door, I can see whether it is lit or dark. I can walk in and out of the room as many times as I want. The status of the light is still determined by that remote switch being on or off. This is a "classical" light.

Let's imagine a *quantum* light and switch, which I'll call a *qu-light* and *qu-switch*, respectively.

When I walk into the room with the qu-light, it is always on or off, just like before. The qu-switch is unusual in that it is shaped like a sphere, with the topmost point (the "north pole") being OFF and the bottommost (the "south pole") being ON. A line is etched around the middle, as shown in Figure 1.1.

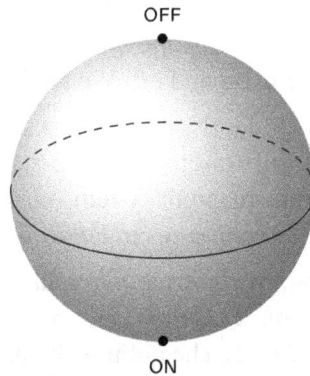

OFF

ON

Figure 1.1: The qu-switch

The interesting part happens when I cannot see the qu-light when I am in a different part of the building from the one the qu-switch.

I control the qu-switch by placing my index finger on the qu-switch sphere. If I place my finger on the north pole, the qu-light is off. If I put it on the south, the qu-light is on. You can go into the room and check. You will always get these results.

If I move my finger anywhere else on the qu-switch sphere, the qu-light may be on or off when you check. If you do not check, the qu-light is in an indeterminate state. It is not dimmed, it is not on or off; it just exists with some probability of being on or off when seen. This is unusual!

You remove the indeterminacy when you open the door and see the qu-light. It will be on or off. Moreover, the switch is forced to the north or south pole, corresponding to the state of the qu-light when you see it.

Observing the qu-light forced it into either the on or off state. I don't have to see the qu-light fixture itself. If I open the door a tiny bit, enough to see if any light is shining, that is enough.

If I place a video camera in the room with the qu-light and watch the light when I put my finger on the qu-switch, the qu-switch behaves like a normal switch. I am prevented from touching the qu-switch anywhere other than the top or bottom, just as a normal switch only has two positions.

If you or I are not observing the qu-light in any way, does it make a difference where I touch the qu-switch? Will touching it in the northern or southern hemisphere influence whether it will be on or off when I observe the qu-light?

Yes. Touching it closer to the north pole or the south pole will make the probability of the qu-light being off or on, respectively, higher. If I put my finger on the circle between the poles, the equator, the probability of the light being on or off will be exactly 50–50.

We call what I just described a *two-state quantum system*. When no one observes it, the qu-light is in a *superposition* of being on and off. We explore superposition in section 7.1.

While this may seem bizarre, evidently, nature works this way. For example, electrons have a property called "spin," and with this, they are two-state quantum systems. The photons that make up light itself are two-state quantum systems via polarization. We return to this in section 11.9.3 when we look at polarization (as in Polaroid® sunglasses).

More to the point of this book, however, a *quantum bit*, more commonly known as a *qubit*, is a two-state quantum system. It extends and complements the classical computing notion of a bit, which can only be **0** or **1**. The qubit is the basic information unit in quantum computing.

This book is about how we manipulate qubits to solve problems that currently appear intractable using just classical computing. It seems that just sticking to **0** or **1** will not be sufficient to solve some problems that would otherwise need impractical amounts of time or memory.

With a qubit, we replace the terminology and notation of on or off, **1** or **0**, with the symbols $|1\rangle$ and $|0\rangle$, respectively. Instead of qu-lights, it's qubits from now on.

In Figure 1.2, we indicate the position of your finger on the qu-switch by two angles, θ (theta) and φ (phi). The picture itself is called a Bloch sphere and is a standard representation of a qubit, as we shall see in section 7.5.

1.2　I'm awake!

What if we could do chemistry inside a computer instead of in a test tube or beaker in the laboratory? What if running a new experiment was as simple as running an app and completing it in a few seconds?

For this to work, we would want it to happen with full *fidelity*. The atoms and molecules as modeled in the computer should behave **exactly** like they do in the test tube. The chemical

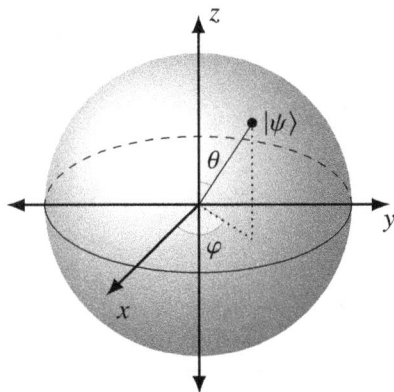

Figure 1.2: The Bloch sphere

reactions in the physical world would have precise computational analogs. We would need a fully faithful simulation.

If we could do this at scale, we might be able to compute the molecules we want and need. These might be for new materials for shampoos or even alloys for cars and airplanes. Perhaps we could more efficiently discover medicines that we customize for your exact physiology. Maybe we could get better insight into how proteins fold, thereby understanding their function and possibly creating custom enzymes to change our body chemistry positively.

Is this plausible? We have massive supercomputers that can run all kinds of simulations. Can we model molecules in the above ways today?

Let's start with $C_8H_{10}N_4O_2$ – 1,3,7-Trimethylxanthine. This is a fancy name for a molecule that millions of people worldwide enjoy every day: **caffeine**. Figure 1.3 shows its structure.

An 8-ounce cup of coffee contains approximately 95 mg of caffeine, which translates to roughly 2.95×10^{20} molecules. Written out, this is

$$295,000,000,000,000,000,000 \text{ molecules.}$$

A 12-ounce can of a popular cola drink has 32 mg of caffeine, the diet version has 42 mg, and energy drinks often have about 77 mg. [136]

Exercise 1.1

How many molecules of caffeine do you consume a day?

These numbers are large because we are counting physical objects in our universe, which we know is very big. Scientists estimate, for example, that there are between 10^{49} and 10^{50} atoms in our planet alone. [81]

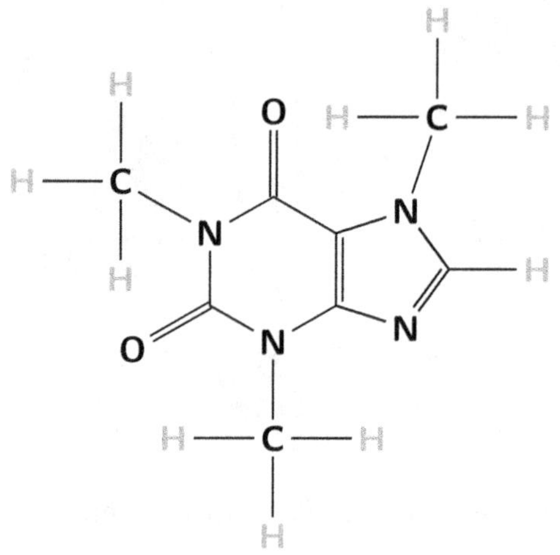

Figure 1.3: The caffeine molecule

To put these values in context, one thousand = 10^3, one million = 10^6, one billion = 10^9, and so on. A gigabyte of storage is one billion bytes, and a terabyte is 10^{12} bytes.

Returning to the question I posed at the beginning of this section, can we model caffeine exactly in a computer? We don't have to model the huge number of caffeine molecules in a cup of coffee, but can we fully represent a single molecule at a single instant?

Caffeine is a small molecule and contains protons, neutrons, and electrons. In particular, if we look at the energy configuration that determines the structure of the molecule and the bonds that hold it all together, the amount of information to describe this is staggering. In particular, the number of bits, the **0**s and **1**s, needed is approximately 10^{48}:

$$10,000,000,000,000,000,000,000,000,000,000,000,000,000,000,000,000 .$$

From what I said above, this is comparable to 1% to 10% of the number of atoms in the Earth.

This is just one molecule! Yet somehow, nature manages to deal quite effectively with all this information. It handles the single caffeine molecule, to all those in your coffee, tea, or soft drink, to every other molecule that makes up you and the world around you.

How does it do this? We don't know! Of course, there are theories, and they live at the intersection of physics and philosophy. [134] We do not need to understand it thoroughly to try to harness its capabilities.

We have no hope of providing enough traditional storage to hold this much information. Our dream of exact representation appears to be dashed. This is what Richard Feynman (Figure 1.4) meant in his quote at the beginning of this chapter: ''Nature isn't classical.''

Figure 1.4: Richard Feynman at the California Institute of Technology in 1959

However, 160 qubits (quantum bits) could hold $2^{160} \approx 1.46 \times 10^{48}$ bits while the qubits are involved in a computation. To be clear, I'm not saying how we would get all the data into those qubits, and I'm also not saying how many more we would need to do something interesting with the information. It does give us hope, however. We look at some ways of encoding data in qubits in section 13.2.

In the classical case, we will never fully represent the caffeine molecule. In the future, with enough very high-quality qubits in a powerful enough quantum computing system, we may be able to perform chemistry in a computer.

To learn more

Quantum chemistry is not an area of science in which you can say a few words and easily make clear how we might eventually use quantum computers to compute molecular properties and protein folding configurations, for example. Nevertheless, the caffeine example above is an example of *quantum simulation.*

For an excellent survey of the history and state of the art of quantum computing applied to chemistry as of 2019, see Cao et al. [35] For the specific problem of understanding how to scale quantum simulations of molecules and the crossover from High-Performance Computers (HPC), see Kandala et al. [120]

1.3   Why quantum computing is different

I can write a simple app on a classical computer that simulates a coin flip. This app might be for my phone or laptop.

Instead of heads or tails, let's use **1** and **0**. The routine, which I call **R**, starts with one of those values and randomly returns one or the other. That is, 50% of the time it returns **1**, and 50% of the time it returns **0**. We have no knowledge whatsoever of how **R** does what it does. When you see ''**R**,'' think ''random.''

This routine is a ''fair flip.'' It is not weighted to prefer one result or the other slightly. Whether we can produce a truly random result on a classical computer is another question. Let's assume our app is fair.

If I apply **R** to **1**, half the time I expect that same value and the other half **0**. The same is true if I apply **R** to **0**. I'll call these applications **R(1)** and **R(0)**, respectively.

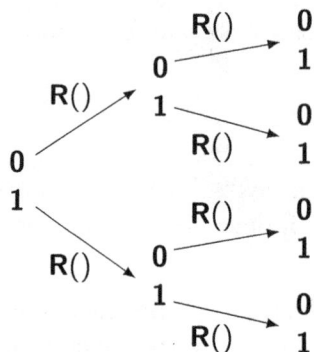

Figure 1.5: Results from a fair flip of a coin

If I look at the result of **R(1)** or **R(0)** in Figure 1.5, there is no way to tell if I started with **1** or **0**. This process is like a secret coin flip, where I can't know whether I began with heads or tails by looking at how the coin has landed. By ''secret coin flip,'' I mean that someone else does it, and I can see the result, but I have no knowledge of the mechanics of the flip itself or the starting state of the coin.

If **R(1)** and **R(0)** are randomly **1** and **0**, what happens when I apply **R** twice?

I write this as **R(R(1))** and **R(R(0))**. It's the same answer: random result with an equal split. The same thing happens no matter how many times we apply **R**. The result is random, and we can't reverse things to learn the initial value. In the language of section 4.1, **R** is not *invertible*.

Now for the quantum version. Instead of **R**, I use **H**, which we learn about in section 7.6. It, too, returns **0** or **1** with equal chance, but it has two interesting properties:

- It is reversible. Though it produces a random **1** or **0**, starting from either of them, we can always go back and see the value with which we began.
- It is its own reverse (or *inverse*) operation. Applying it twice in a row is the same as having done nothing at all.

There is a catch, though. You are not allowed to look at the result of what **H** does the first time if you want to reverse its effect.

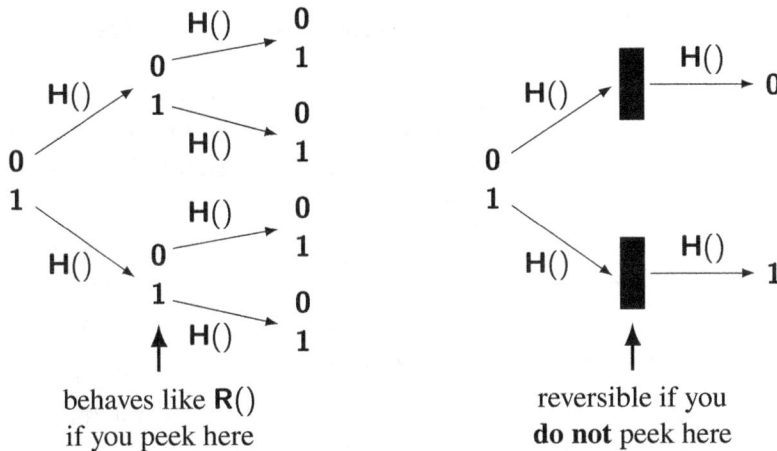

behaves like **R()**
if you peek here

reversible if you
do not peek here

Figure 1.6: A quantum "coin flip"

If you apply **H** to **0** or **1**, as shown in Figure 1.6, peek at the result, and apply **H** again to that, it is the same as if you had used **R**. If you observe what is going on in the quantum case at the wrong time, you are right back at strictly classical behavior.

To summarize, using the coin language: if you flip a quantum coin and then **don't look at it**, flipping it again will yield the heads or tails with which you started. If you do look, you get classical randomness.

Exercise 1.2

Compare this behavior with that of the qu-switch and qu-light in section 1.1.

A second area where quantum is different is in how we can work with simultaneous values. Your phone or laptop uses a byte as the individual memory or storage unit. That's where we get phrases such as "megabyte," which means one million bytes of information.

We further break down a byte into eight bits, which we've seen before. Each bit can be **0** or **1**. Doing the math, each byte can represent $2^8 = 256$ different numbers composed of eight **0**s or **1**s, but it can only hold *one value at a time*.

Eight qubits can represent all 256 values *at the same time*.

This representation is enabled not only through superposition, but also through *entanglement*, where we can tightly tie together the behavior of two or more qubits. These give us the (literally) exponential growth in the amount of working memory that we saw with a quantum representation of caffeine in section 1.2. We explore entanglement in section 8.2.

1.4   Applications to artificial intelligence

Artificial intelligence (AI) and one of its subsets, machine learning, are broad collections of data-driven techniques and models. They help find patterns in information, learn from the information, and automatically perform tasks more "intelligently." They also give humans help and insight that might have been difficult to get otherwise.

Here is a way to start thinking about how quantum computing might apply to large, complicated, computation-intensive systems of processes such as those found in AI and elsewhere. These three cases are, in some sense, the "small, medium, and large" ways quantum computing might complement classical techniques:

- There is a single mathematical computation somewhere in the middle of a software component that might be sped up via a quantum algorithm.
- There is a well-described component of a classical process that could be replaced with a quantum version.
- There is a way to avoid using some classical components entirely in the traditional method because of quantum, or we can replace the entire classical algorithm with a much faster or more effective quantum alternative.

At the time of writing, quantum computers are not "big data" machines. You cannot take millions of information records and provide them as input to a quantum calculation. Instead, quantum may be able to help where the number of inputs is modest, but the computations "blow up" as you start examining relationships or dependencies in the data. Quantum, with its exponentially growing working memory, as we saw in the caffeine example in section 1.2, may be able to control and work with the blow-up. (See section 2.7 for a discussion of exponential growth.)

In the future, however, quantum computers may be able to input, output, and process much more data. Even if it is only theoretical now, it makes sense to ask if there are quantum algorithms that can be useful in AI someday.

Let's look at some data. I'm a big baseball fan, and baseball has a lot of statistics associated with it. The analysis of this even has its own name: "sabermetrics."

Year	GP	AB	R	H	2B	3B	HR	RBI	BB	SO
2019	136	470	105	136	27	2	41	101	110	111
2018	162	587	94	156	25	1	46	114	74	173
2017	152	542	73	132	24	0	29	92	41	145
2016	140	490	84	123	26	5	27	70	50	109
2015	162	634	66	172	32	4	25	83	26	108
2014	148	545	110	153	35	1	29	79	74	144

where

GP	=	Games Played	**AB**	=	At Bats
R	=	Runs scored	**H**	=	Hits
2B	=	2 Base hits (doubles)	**3B**	=	3 Base hits (triples)
HR	=	Home Runs	**RBI**	=	Runs Batted In
BB	=	Bases on Balls (walks)	**SO**	=	Strike Outs

Figure 1.7: Baseball player statistics by year

Suppose I have a table of statistics for a baseball player given by year, as shown in Figure 1.7. We can make this look more mathematical by creating a matrix of the same data:

$$
\begin{bmatrix}
2019 & 136 & 470 & 105 & 136 & 27 & 2 & 41 & 101 & 110 & 111 \\
2018 & 162 & 587 & 94 & 156 & 25 & 1 & 46 & 114 & 74 & 173 \\
2017 & 152 & 542 & 73 & 132 & 24 & 0 & 29 & 92 & 41 & 145 \\
2016 & 140 & 490 & 84 & 123 & 26 & 5 & 27 & 70 & 50 & 109 \\
2015 & 162 & 634 & 66 & 172 & 32 & 4 & 25 & 83 & 26 & 108 \\
2014 & 148 & 545 & 110 & 153 & 35 & 1 & 29 & 79 & 74 & 144
\end{bmatrix}
$$

Given such information, we can manipulate it using machine learning techniques to predict the player's future performance or even how other similar players may do. These techniques use the matrix operations we discuss in Chapter 5, ''Dimensions.''

There are 30 teams in Major League Baseball in the United States. With their training and feeder ''minor league'' teams, each major league team may have more than 400 players throughout their systems. That would give us over 12,000 players, each with their complete player histories. There are more statistics than I have listed, so we can easily get more than 100,000 values in our matrix.

As another example, in the area of entertainment, it's hard to estimate how many movies exist, but it is well above 100,000. For each movie, we can list features such as whether it is a comedy, drama, romance, or action film, and who each actor is. We might also know all members of the directorial and production staff, the geographic locations shown in the film, the languages spoken, and so on. There are hundreds of such features and *millions of people who have watched the films!*

For each person, we can also add features such as whether they like or dislike a type of movie, actor, scene location, or director. Using all this information, which film should I recommend to you on a Saturday night in December, based on what you and people similar to you like?

Think of each feature or each baseball player or film as a dimension. While you may think of two and three dimensions in nature, we might have thousands or millions of dimensions in AI.

Matrices as above for AI can grow to millions of rows and entries. How can we make sense of them to get insights and see patterns? Aside from manipulating that much information, can we even eventually do the math on classical computers quickly and accurately enough?

While scientists initially thought that quantum algorithms might offer exponential improvements to such classical recommender systems, a 2019 algorithm showed a classical method to gain such a large improvement. [213] An example of a process being exponentially faster is doing something in 6 days instead of $10^6 = 1$ million days. That's approximately 2,740 years.

Tang's work is a fascinating example of the interplay of progress in classical and quantum algorithms. People who develop algorithms for classical computing look to quantum computing and vice versa. Also, any particular solution to a problem may include classical and quantum components.

Nevertheless, many believe that quantum computing will greatly improve some matrix computations. One such example is the HHL algorithm, whose abbreviation comes from the first letters of the last names of its authors, Aram W. Harrow, Avinatan Hassidim, and Seth Lloyd. This algorithm is an example of case number 1 above. [104] [62]

Algorithms such as these may find use in fields as diverse as economics and computational fluid dynamics. They also place requirements on the structure and density of the data and may use properties such as the condition number, which we discuss in section 5.13.

To learn more

Completing this book will equip you to read the original paper describing the **HHL** algorithm and more recent surveys about applying quantum computing to linear algebraic problems. [104]

An important problem in machine learning is classification. In its simplest form, a *binary classifier* separates items into one of two categories or buckets. Depending on the definitions of the categories, it may be more or less easy to do the classification.

Examples of binary categories include:

- book you like *or* book you don't like
- comedy movie *or* dramatic movie
- gluten-free *or* not gluten-free
- fish dish *or* chicken dish
- UK football team *or* Spanish football team
- hot sauce *or* extremely hot sauce
- cotton shirt *or* permanent press shirt
- open-source *or* proprietary
- spam email *or* valid email
- American League baseball team *or* National League team

The second example of distinguishing between comedies and dramas may not be well designed, since there are movies that are both.

Mathematically, we can imagine taking some data value as input and classifying it as $+1$ or -1. We take a reasonably large data set and label each value by hand as a $+1$ or -1. We then *learn* from this *training set* how to classify future data.

Machine learning binary classification algorithms include random forest, k-nearest neighbor, decision tree, neural networks, naive Bayes classifiers, and support vector machines.

In the training phase, we have a list of pre-classified objects (books, movies, proteins, operating systems, baseball teams, etc.). We then use the above algorithms to learn how to put a new object in one bucket or another.

The support vector machine (SVM) is a straightforward approach with a precise mathematical description. In the two-dimensional case, we try to draw a line separating the objects (represented by points in the plot in Figure 1.8) into one category or the other.

The line should maximize the gap between the sets of objects.

The plot in Figure 1.9 is an example of a line separating the dark gray points below from the light gray ones above.

Given a new point, we plot it and determine whether it is above or below the line. That will classify it as dark or or light gray, respectively.

Suppose we know we correctly classified the point with those above the line. We accept that and move on. If we misclassify the point, we add it to the training set and try to compute a new and better line. This may not be possible.

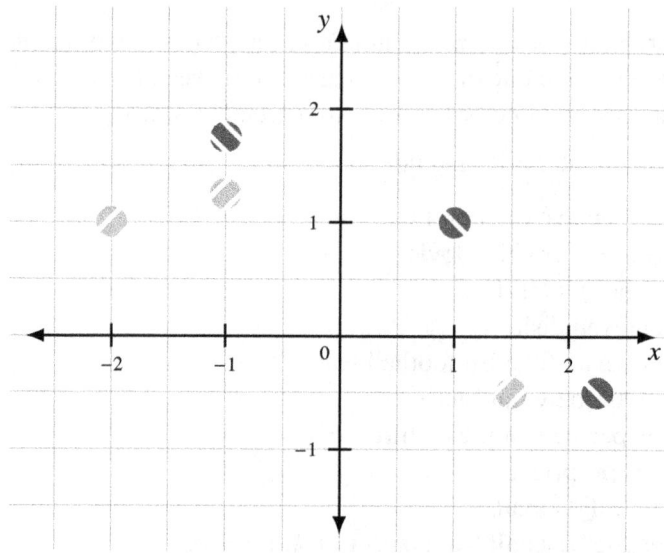

Figure 1.8: Points we wish to separate

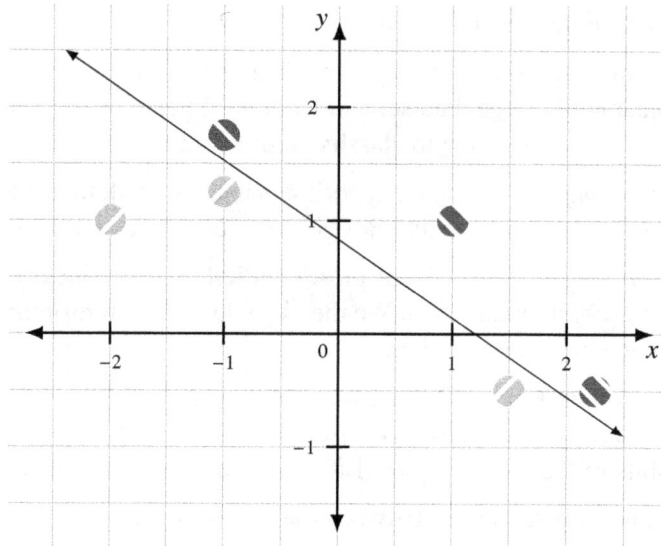

Figure 1.9: The points separated by a line

In the plot in Figure 1.10, I added a new light gray point close to 2 on the vertical axis. With this extra point, there is no line we can compute to separate the points.

Had we represented the objects in three dimensions, we would have tried to find a *plane* that separated the points with a maximum gap. We would need to compute some new amount that the points are above or below the plane. In geometric terms, if we have x and y only, we

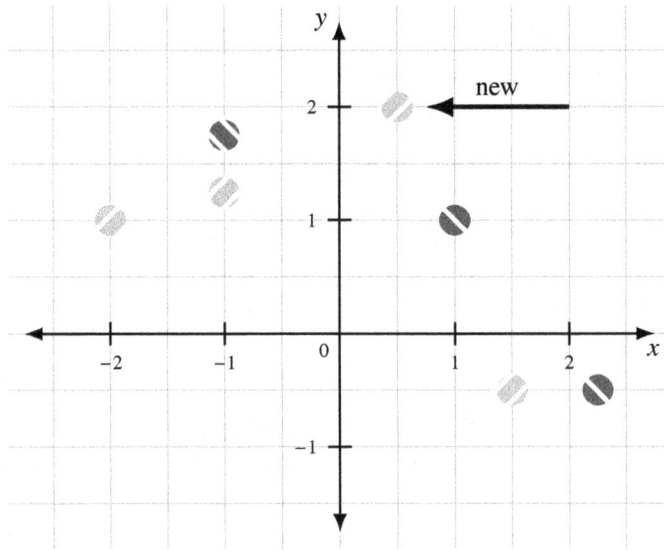

Figure 1.10: We cannot separate the points by a line

must somehow compute a z to work in that third dimension.

For a representation using n dimensions, we try to compute an $(n - 1)$-dimensional separating *hyperplane*. We look at two and three dimensions in Chapter 4, "Planes and Circles and Spheres, Oh My," and the general case in Chapter 5, "Dimensions."

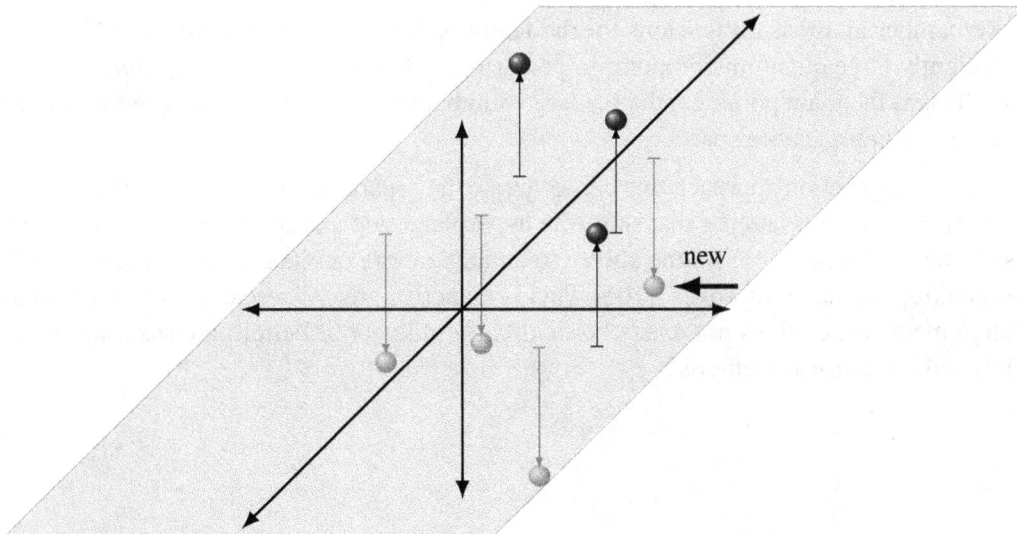

Figure 1.11: The points moved into three dimensions

In the three-dimensional plot in Figure 1.11, I take the same values from the last two-dimensional version and lay the coordinate plane flat. I then add a vertical dimension. I push the light gray points below the plane and the dark gray ones above. With this construction, the coordinate plane itself separates the values.

While we can't separate the points in two dimensions, we can in three dimensions. This kind of mapping into a higher dimension is called a *kernel trick*. While the coordinate plane might not be the ideal separating hyperplane, it gives you an idea of what we are trying to accomplish. The benefit of *kernel functions* (as part of the similarly named ''trick'') is that we can do far fewer explicit geometric computations than you might expect in these higher-dimensional spaces.

> It's worth mentioning now that we don't need to try quantum methods on small problems that we can handle quite well using traditional means. We won't see any quantum advantage until the problems are big enough to overcome the quantum circuit overhead versus classical circuits. Also, if we come up with a quantum approach that we can simulate efficiently on a classical computer, we don't need a quantum computer.

A quantum computer with 1 qubit provides us with a two-dimensional working space. Every time we add a qubit, we double the number of dimensions. This is due to the properties of superposition and entanglement that I introduce in Chapter 7, ''One Qubit.'' For 10 qubits, we get $2^{10} = 1,024$ dimensions. Similarly, for 50 qubits, we get $2^{50} = 1,125,899,906,842,624$ dimensions.

Remember all those dimensions for the features, baseball players, and films? We want a sufficiently large quantum computer to perform the AI calculations in a *quantum feature space*. This is the main point: handle the large number of dimensions coming out of the data in a large quantum feature space.

There is a quantum approach that can generate the separating hyperplane in the quantum feature space. There is another that skips the hyperplane step and produces a highly accurate classifying kernel function. As the ability to entangle more qubits increases, the successful classification rate also improves. [105] This is an active area of research: how can we use entanglement, which does not exist classically, to find new or better patterns than we can with strictly traditional methods?

To learn more

Researchers are writing an increasing number of papers connecting quantum computing with machine learning and other AI techniques, but the results are somewhat fragmented. [236] We return to this topic in Chapter 13, ''Introduction to Quantum Machine Learning.'' I warn you again that quantum computers cannot process much data now!

For an advanced application of machine learning for quantum computing and chemistry, see Torlai et al. [218] I introduce machine learning and classification methods in Chapter 15 of *Dancing with Python*. [211]

1.5   Applications to financial services

Suppose we have a circle of radius 1 inscribed in a square, as in Figure 1.12. The sides of the square have length 2, and the square's area is $4 = 2 \times 2$. What is the area A of the circle?

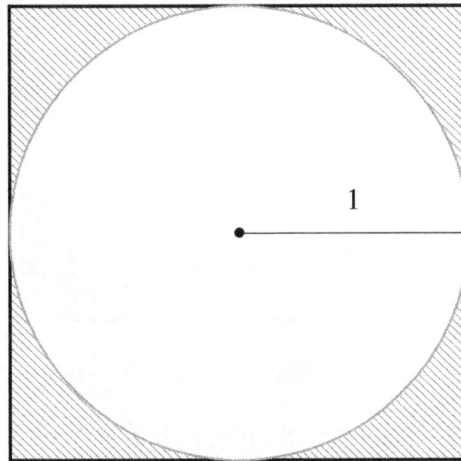

Figure 1.12: Circle in a square

Before you try to remember your geometric area formulas, let's compute the area of a circle using ratios and some experiments.

Suppose we drop some number N of coins onto the square and count how many have their centers on or inside the circle. If C is this number, then

$$\frac{\text{area of the circle}}{\text{area of the enclosing square}} = \frac{A}{4} \approx \frac{C}{N} = \frac{\text{number of coins that land in the circle}}{\text{total number of coins}}.$$

$$A \approx 4\frac{C}{N}.$$

There is randomness involved here: it's possible they all land inside the circle or, less likely, outside the circle. For $N = 1$, we do not get an accurate estimate of A because $\frac{C}{N}$ can only be 0 or 1.

Exercise 1.3

If $N = 2$, what are the possible estimates of A? What about if $N = 3$?

We will get a better estimate for A if we choose N large.

I created 10 points whose centers lie inside the square using Python and its random number generator. The plot in Figure 1.13 shows where they landed. In this case, $C = 9$, and so $A \approx 3.6$.

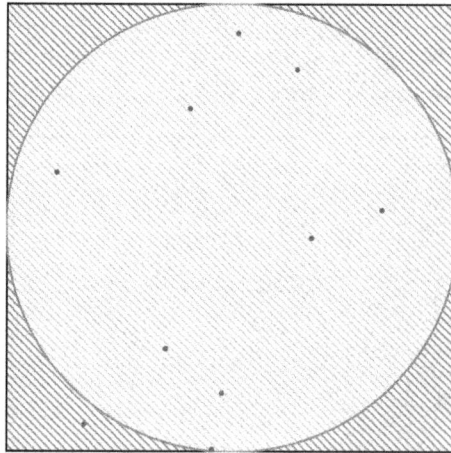

Figure 1.13: 10 points dropped in the square

For $N = 100$, we get a more interesting plot in Figure 1.14 with $C = 84$ and $A \approx 3.36$. Remember, this value would be different if I had generated other random numbers.

The final plot is in Figure 1.15 for $N = 500$. Now $C = 387$ and $A \approx 3.096$.

The real value of A is $\pi \approx 3.1415926$. We call this technique *Monte Carlo sampling*, which goes back to the 1940s.

Using the same technique, here are approximations of A for increasingly large N. Remember, we are using random numbers, so these numbers will vary based on the sequence of values used.

N	10	100	1,000	10,000	100,000	1,000,000	10,000,000
A	3.6	3.36	3.148	3.1596	3.14336	3.141884	3.1414132

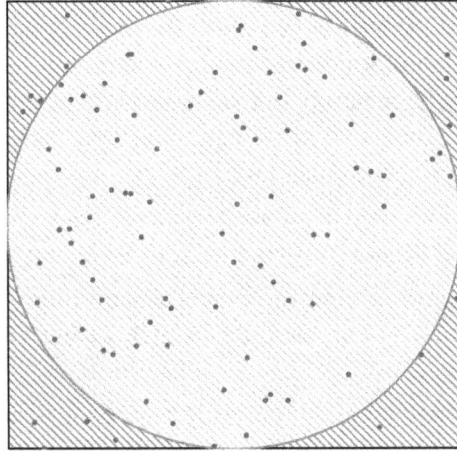

Figure 1.14: 100 points dropped in the square

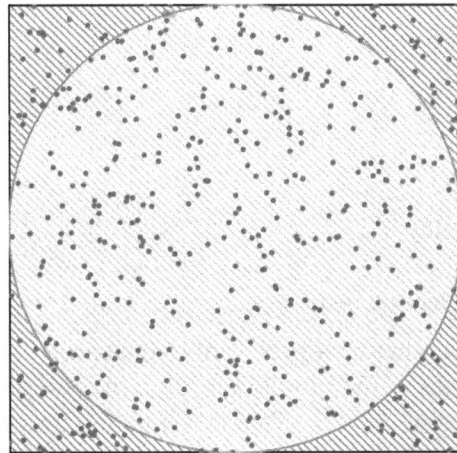

Figure 1.15: 500 points dropped in the square

That's a lot of runs, the value of N, to get close to the actual value of π. Nevertheless, this example demonstrates how we can use Monte Carlo sampling techniques to approximate the value of something when we may not have a formula. In this case, we estimated A. For the example, we ignored our knowledge that the formula for the area of a circle is πr^2, where r is the circle's radius.

In section 6.8, we work through the math and show that if we want to estimate π within 0.00001 with a probability of at least 99.9999%, we need $N \geq 82863028$. We need to use more than 82 million points! So it is possible to use a Monte Carlo method here, but it is not efficient.

In this example, we know the answer ahead of time by other means. Monte Carlo methods can be a useful tool if we do not know the answer and do not have a nice neat formula to compute. However, the very large number of samples needed to get decent accuracy makes the process computationally intensive. If we can reduce the sample count significantly, we can compute a more accurate result much faster.

Given that the title of this section mentions "finance," I now note, perhaps unsurprisingly, that quantitative analysts use Monte Carlo methods in computational finance.

The randomness we employ to calculate π translates over into ideas such as uncertainties. Uncertainties can then be related to probabilities, which we use to calculate the risk and rate of return of investments.

Instead of looking at whether a point is inside or outside a circle, for the rate of return, we might consider several factors that go into calculating the risk. For example,

- market size
- share of the market
- selling price
- fixed costs
- operating costs
- obsolescence
- inflation or deflation
- national monetary policy
- weather
- political factors and election results

For each of these or any other factor relevant to the particular investment, we quantify them and assign probabilities to the possible results. In a weighted way, we combine all possible combinations to compute risk. This is a function that we cannot calculate all at once, but we can use Monte Carlo methods to estimate. Techniques similar to, but more complicated than, the circle analysis in section 6.8, give us how many samples we need to use to get a result within the desired accuracy.

In the circle example, reasonable accuracy can require tens of millions of samples. We might need many orders of magnitude greater for an investment risk analysis. So what do we do?

We can and do use High-Performance Computers (HPC). We can consider fewer possibilities for each factor. For example, we might vary the possible selling prices by larger amounts. We can consult better experts and get more accurate probabilities. This could improve the result but not necessarily the computation time. Or, we can take fewer samples and accept less precise results.

Alternatively, we could consider quantum variations and replacements for Monte Carlo methods. In 2015, Ashley Montanaro [152] described a quadratic speedup using quantum computers. How much improvement does this give us? Instead of the 82 million samples required for the circle calculation with the above accuracy, we could do it in something closer to 9,000 samples ($9055 \approx \sqrt{82000000}$).

In 2019, Stamatopoulos *et al.* showed methods and considerations for pricing financial options using quantum computing systems. [206]

I want to stress that to do this, we need much larger, more accurate, and more powerful quantum computers than we have at the time of writing. However, like much of the algorithmic work researchers are doing on industry use cases, I believe we are getting on the right path to solve significant problems significantly faster using quantum computation.

By using Monte Carlo methods, we can vary our assumptions and do scenario analysis. If we can eventually use quantum computers to significantly reduce the number of samples, we can look at far more scenarios much faster.

To learn more

David Hertz' original 1964 paper in the Harvard Business Review is a very readable introduction to Monte Carlo methods for risk analysis without ever using the phrase ''Monte Carlo.'' [109] A more recent paper gives more of the history of these methods and applies them to marketing analytics. [86]

My goal with this book is to give you enough of an introduction to quantum computing so that you can read industry-specific quantum use cases and research papers. For example, to learn about modern quantum algorithmic approaches to risk analysis, see the articles by Woerner, Egger, et al. [237] [75] Some early results on heuristics using quantum computation for transaction settlements are covered in Braine et al. [22]

1.6   What about cryptography?

You may have seen media headlines such as

Quantum Security Apocalypse!!!
Y2K??? Get ready for Q2K!!!
Quantum Computing Will Break All Internet Security!!!

These breathless announcements grab your attention and frequently contain egregious errors about quantum computing and security. Let's look at the root of the concerns and insert some reality into the discussion.

RSA (Rivest-Shamir-Adleman) is a commonly used security protocol, and it works something like this:

- You want to allow others to send you secure communications. This means you give them what they need to encrypt their messages before sending them. You and only you can decrypt what they then give you.
- You publish a *public key* used to encrypt these messages intended for you. Anyone who has access to the key can use it.
- There is an additional key, your *private key*. You and only you have it. With it, you can decrypt and read encrypted messages. [190]

Though I phrased this in terms of messages sent to you, the scheme is adaptable for sending transaction and purchase data across the Internet and storing information securely in a database.

Indeed, if anyone steals your private key, there is a cybersecurity emergency. Quantum computing has nothing to do with physically taking your private key or convincing you to give it to a bad person.

What if I could compute your private key from the public key?

The public key for RSA looks like a pair of numbers (e, n) where n is a very large integer that is the product of two primes. We'll call these primes numbers p and q. For example, if $p = 982451653$ and $q = 899809343$, then $n = p \times q = 884019176415193979$.

Your private key looks like a pair of integers (d, n) using the very same n as in the public key. It is the d part you must keep secret.

Here's the potential problem: if someone can quickly factor n into p and q, then they can compute d. That is, fast integer factorization leads to breaking RSA encryption. [204]

Though multiplication is very easy and can be done using the method you learned early in your education, factoring can be very, very hard. For products of certain pairs of primes, factorization using known classical methods could take hundreds or thousands of **years**.

Given this, unless d is stolen or given away, you might feel pretty comfortable about security. But what if there is another way of factoring involving nonclassical computers?

In 1995, Peter Shor published a quantum algorithm for integer factorization that is almost exponentially faster than known classical methods. We analyze Shor's factoring algorithm in section 10.7.

This sounds like a major problem! Here is where many articles about quantum computing and security start to go crazy. The key question is, **how powerful and of what quality must a quantum computing system be to perform this factorization?**

At the time of writing, scientists and engineers are building quantum computers with low four-digit numbers of *physical* qubits. For example, IBM researchers have a demonstrated qubit count of 1,121. [36] A physical qubit is the hardware implementation of the *logical* qubits we start discussing in Chapter 7, "One Qubit."

Physical qubits have noise that causes errors in computation. Shor's factoring algorithm requires fully fault-tolerant, error-corrected qubits. We can detect and correct errors that occur in logical qubits. This happens today in the memory and data storage in your laptop and smartphone. We explore quantum error correction in section 11.5.

As a rule of thumb, assume it will take 1,000 very good physical qubits to make one logical qubit. This estimate varies by the researcher, the degree of marketing hype, and wishful thinking, but I believe 1,000 is reasonable. We discuss the relationship between the two kinds of qubits in Chapter 11, ''Getting Physical.'' Meanwhile, we are in the Noisy Intermediate-Scale Quantum, or NISQ, era. Physicist John Preskill coined the term NISQ in 2018. Although Preskill initially thought these systems would have between 50 and 100 qubits, or at most a few hundred, it seems apparent that the power of NISQ machines may still be limited even if they have several thousand physical qubits. [173]

Figure 1.16: It will take many physical qubits to make one logical qubit

A further estimate is that it will take $2 \times 10^7 = 20$ million physical qubits to use Shor's algorithm to factor the values of n used in RSA today. That's approximately twenty thousand logical qubits. On the one hand, we have quantum computers with two or three digits worth of physical qubits. We'll need seven digits' worth for Shor's factoring algorithm to break RSA. That's a huge difference. [91]

These numbers may be too conservative, but I don't think by much. If anyone quotes you much smaller numbers, try to understand their motivation and what data they are using.

There's a good chance we won't get quantum computers this powerful until 2035 or much later. We may never get such powerful machines. Assuming we will, what should you do now?

First, you should move to so-called ''post-quantum'' or ''quantum-proof'' encryption protocols. These are being standardized at NIST, the National Institute of Standards and Technology, in the United States by an international team of researchers. We believe these protocols can't be broken by quantum computing systems, as RSA and some of the other classical protocols might be eventually.

You may think you have plenty of time to change over your transactional systems. How long will it take to do that? Financial institutions can take ten years or more to implement new security technology.

Of greater immediate importance is your data. Will it be a problem if someone can crack your database security in 15, 30, or 50 years? For most organizations, the answer is a loud YES. Start looking at hardware and software encryption support for your data using the new post-quantum security standards.

Finally, quantum or no quantum, if you do not have good cybersecurity and encryption strategies and implementations in place now, you are exposed. Fix them. Listen to the people who make quantum computing systems to get a good idea of when hackers might use quantum algorithms to break encryption schemes. All others deal with second and third-hand knowledge.

> **To learn more**
>
> Estimates for when and if quantum computing may pose a cybersecurity threat vary significantly. Any study on the topic must be updated as technology evolves. The most complete analysis at the time of writing this book appears to be Mosca and Piani. [157]

1.7 Summary

In this first chapter, we examined what motivates the recent interest in quantum computers. The lone **1**s and **0**s of classical computing bits are extended and complemented by the infinite states of qubits, also known as quantum bits. The properties of superposition and entanglement give us access to many dimensions of working memory that are unavailable to classical computers.

Industry use cases for quantum computing are nascent, but the areas where experts believe it will be applicable sooner are chemistry, materials science, and financial services. AI is another area where quantum may boost performance for some calculations.

There has been confusion in traditional and social media about the interplay of security, information encryption, and quantum computing. The major areas of misunderstanding are the necessary performance requirements and the timeline.

In the next chapter, we look at classical bit-based computing to more precisely and technically explore how quantum computing may help us attack problems that are otherwise impossible today. In Chapter 3, ''More Numbers Than You Can Imagine,'' through Chapter 6, ''What Do You Mean ''Probably''?,'' we work through the mathematics necessary for you to see how quantum computing works. There is a lot to cover, but it is worth it to be able to go deeper than a merely superficial understanding of the ''whats,'' ''hows,'' and ''whys'' of quantum computing.

2

They're Not Old, They're Classics

No simplicity of mind, no obscurity of station, can escape
the universal duty of questioning all that we believe.

– William Kingdon Clifford

When introducing quantum computing, it's easy to say, "It's completely different from classical computing in every way!" Well, that's fine, but to what exactly are you comparing it?

We start by looking at what a classical computer is and how it works to solve problems. This sets us up to later show how quantum computing replaces even the most fundamental classical operations with ones involving qubits, superposition, and entanglement.

Topics covered in this chapter

2.1   What's inside a computer?

If I were to buy a laptop today, I would need to think about the following kinds of hardware options:

- size and weight of the machine
- quality of the display
- processor and its speed
- memory and storage capacity

Several years ago, I built a desktop gaming PC. I had to purchase, assemble, and connect:

- the case
- power supply
- motherboard
- processor
- internal memory
- video card with a graphics processing unit (GPU) and memory
- internal hard drive and solid-state storage
- internal Blu-ray drive
- wireless network USB device
- display
- speakers
- mouse and keyboard

As you can see, I had to make many choices. In the case of the laptop, I would think about why I wanted the machine and what I wanted to do, and much less about the particular hardware. I don't have to choose the parts manufacturers nor the standards that allow those parts to work together.

The same is true for smartphones. I decide on the mobile operating system, which may determine the manufacturer. I pick a phone and choose how much storage I want for apps, music, photos, and videos.

Of all the components above, I'm going to focus mainly on four of them: the storage for long-term preservation of data used and produced by applications; the memory for holding information during a computation; the processor (the "brain" for general computation); and the GPU for specialized calculations.

All these live on or are controlled by the motherboard, and a lot of electronic circuitry supports and connects them. My discussion about every possible independent or integrated component in the computer is, therefore, incomplete.

2.1.1 Data, error correction, and storage

Let's start with storage. In applications such as AI, it's common to process many megabytes or gigabytes of data to look for patterns and to perform tasks such as classification. This information is held on either hard disk drives or modern solid-state drives.

> The smallest unit of information is a bit, representing either the value **0** or **1**.

We usually measure the capacity of today's storage in terabytes, which is $1,000 = 10^3$ gigabytes. A gigabyte is 1,000 megabytes, which is 1,000 kilobytes, which is 1,000 bytes. Thus, a terabyte is $10^{12} = 1,000,000,000,000$ bytes. A *byte* is 8 bits. These are the base 10 versions of these quantities and are the standard definitions from the International System of Units.

It's not unusual to see a kilobyte given as $1,024 = 2^{10}$ bytes when specifying computer storage and memory capacity.

The data can be anything you can think of – from music, to videos, to customer records, to presentations, to financial data, to weather history and forecasts, to the source for this book, for example. The device must reliably hold this information for as long as needed. For this reason, this is sometimes called *persistent storage*. Once I put it on the drive, I expect it to be there whenever I want to use it.

The drive may be within the processing computer or somewhere across the network. Data "on the cloud" is held on drives, accessed by server processors, or pulled down to your machine for use.

What do I mean when I say that the information is reliably stored? At a high level, the information has backups somewhere else for redundancy. I can also insist that the data is encrypted so that only authorized people and processes have access. At a low level, I want the information I store, the **0**s and **1**s, always to have the values placed there.

Let's think about how plain characters are stored. Today, we often use Unicode to represent over 100,000 international characters and symbols, including relatively new ones like emojis. [215] However, many applications still use the ASCII (also known as US-ASCII) character set, which represents a few dozen characters common in the United States. It uses 7 bits (zeros or ones), and their patterns correspond to the characters. Here are some examples:

Bits	Character	Bits	Character
0100001	!	0111111	?
0110000	0	1000001	A
0110001	1	1000010	B
0110010	2	1100001	a
0111100	<	1100010	b

We number the bits from right to left, starting with 0:

$$\text{character 'a':} \quad \mathbf{1} \quad \mathbf{1} \quad \mathbf{0} \quad \mathbf{0} \quad \mathbf{0} \quad \mathbf{0} \quad \mathbf{1}$$
$$\uparrow \quad \uparrow \quad \uparrow \quad \uparrow \quad \uparrow \quad \uparrow \quad \uparrow$$
$$\text{position:} \quad 6 \quad 5 \quad 4 \quad 3 \quad 2 \quad 1 \quad 0$$

If something accidentally changes bit 5 in 'a' from **1** to **0**, I end up with an 'A'. If this happened in text, you might say it wasn't so bad because it was still readable. Nevertheless, it is not the data with which we started. If I change bit 6 in 'a' to a **0**, I get the character '!'. Data errors like this can change the spelling of text and the values of numeric quantities such as temperature, money, and driver's license numbers.

Errors may happen because of original or acquired defects in the hardware, extreme "noise" in the operating environment, or even the unlikely stray bit of cosmic radiation. Manufacturers build modern storage hardware to very tight tolerances with extensive testing. Nevertheless, software within the storage devices can often detect errors and correct them. Such software aims to detect and correct errors quickly using as little extra data as possible. This is called *fault tolerance.*

The diagram in Figure 2.1 shows how we process the information. We start with our initial data, encode it in some way with extra information that allows us to tell if errors occurred and perhaps how to fix them, do something with the data such as sending it or saving it in a database, decode and correct the data if necessary, and use it.

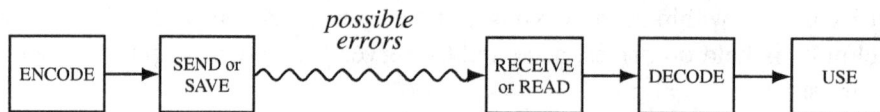

Figure 2.1: Encoding and decoding data

A *repetition code* tries to avoid errors by storing many copies of the data. Suppose I want to store an 'a'. I could save it five times:

$$\mathbf{1100001} \quad \mathbf{1100001} \quad \mathbf{1100001} \quad \mathbf{1100001} \quad \mathbf{1100001}$$

Suppose, however, the data ended up in storage as

$$\underline{\mathbf{1100001}} \quad \underline{\mathbf{0100001}} \quad \underline{\mathbf{1100001}} \quad \underline{\mathbf{1100001}} \quad \underline{\mathbf{1100001}}$$

The first and second copies differ in bit 6, so an error occurred. Since four of the five copies agree, we might "correct" the error by deciding the actual value is **1100001**. However, who's to say the other copies also don't have errors? There are more efficient ways of detecting and correcting errors than repetition, but it is a central concept underlying several other schemes.

Another way to detect an error is to use an *even parity bit*. We append one more bit to the data: if there is an odd number of **1** bits, we precede the data with a **1**. For an even number of **1**s, we place a **0** at the beginning.

$$1100001 \mapsto 11100001$$
$$1100101 \mapsto 01100101$$

If we get a piece of data with an odd number of **1**s, we know at least one bit is wrong.

If errors continue to occur within a particular storage region, the controlling software can direct the hardware to avoid using it. Three processes within our systems keep our data correct:

- *Error detection:* Discovering that an error has occurred.
- *Error correction:* Fixing an error with an understood degree of statistical confidence.
- *Error mitigation:* Preventing errors from happening in the first place through manufacturing or control.

One of the roles of an operating system is to make persistent storage available to software through file systems. There are many schemes for file systems, but you may only be aware that individual containers for data, the files, are grouped into folders or directories. Most of the work regarding file systems is very low-level code that handles moving information stored in some device onto another device, or into or out of an application.

To learn more

The terminology and many techniques of quantum error correction have their roots and analogs in classical use cases dating back to the 1940s. [102] [111] [174]

2.1.2 Memory

From persistent storage, let's move on to the memory in your computer. We'll call this "working memory" because it holds much of the information your system needs to use while processing. It stores part of the operating system, the running apps, and the data the apps use. Data or parts of the applications that are not needed immediately might be put on disk by a method called "paging." Information in memory can be obtained from disk storage, computed by a processor, or placed in memory directly in some other way.

The standard rule is "more memory is good." That sounds trite, but low-cost laptops often skimp on the amount or speed of the memory, so your apps run more slowly. Such laptops may have only 20% of the memory used by high-end desktop machines for video editing or games.

A computer accesses a memory location via an address:

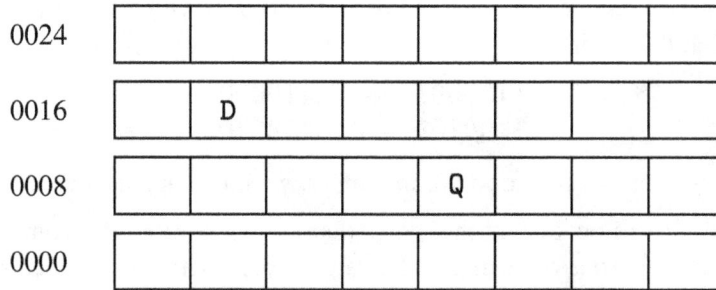

0024								
0016		D						
0008					Q			
0000								

The byte of data representing the character "Q" is at address 0012, while we have a "D" at address 0017. If your computer has a lot of memory, the system must use very large numbers as addresses.

2.1.3 Central Processing Unit (CPU)

Next, we consider a classical computer's **central processing unit**, the **CPU**. It's a cliché, but it is like the brain of the computer. It controls executing a sequence of instructions that can do arithmetic, move data in and out of memory, use designated extra-fast memory called *registers* within the processor, and conditionally jump somewhere else in the sequence. Some of the latest processors can help memory management for interpreted programming languages and generate random numbers.

Physically, CPUs are made today from transistors, capacitors, diodes, resistors, and the pathways that connect them into *integrated circuits*. We differentiate between these electronic circuits and the logic circuits we implement using them.

Within a processor, there are special units that perform particular functions. A *floating-point unit (FPU)* handles fast mathematical routines with numbers that contain decimals. An *arithmetic logic unit (ALU)* provides accelerated hardware support for integer arithmetic. A CPU is not limited to having only one FPU or ALU. The architecture may include more to optimize the chip for applications such as High-Performance Computing (HPC).

Caches within a CPU improve performance by storing data and instructions we might use soon. For example, instead of retrieving only a byte of information from storage, it's often better to pull several hundred or thousand bytes near it into fast memory. This technique assumes that if the processor currently uses some data, it will soon use other nearby data.

Engineers have developed sophisticated schemes to keep the cores busy with all the necessary data and instructions, with minimal waiting time.

You may have heard about 32- or 64-bit computers and chosen an operating system based on one or the other. These numbers represent the *word size* of the processor. This is the "natural" size of the piece of data that the computer usually handles. It determines how large a signed or unsigned integer the processor can handle for arithmetic or how big an address it can use to access memory.

In the first case, for a 32-bit word, we use only the first 31 bits to hold the number and the last to hold the sign. Although there are variations on how the number is stored, a typical scheme says that if that sign bit is **1**, the number is negative, and zero or positive if the bit is **0**.

Exercise 2.1

Suppose our computer uses 64-bit words. What happens if you add or multiply two integers and the result is larger than what can fit in a word?

For a possible software solution, see section 10.2.2.

For addressing memory, suppose that the first byte in memory has address 0. Given a 32-bit address size, the largest address is $2^{32} - 1$. This total of 4,294,967,296 addresses says that 4 gigabytes is the largest amount of memory with which the processor can work. With 64 bits, you can "talk to" much more data.

Exercise 2.2

What is the largest memory address a 64-bit processor can access?

In advanced processors today, memory data is not retrieved or placed via a simple integer address pointing to a physical location. Instead, a *memory management unit (MMU)* translates the address you give it to a memory location somewhere within your computer, via a scheme that maps to your particular hardware. We call this *virtual* memory.

2.1.4   Graphics Processing Unit (GPU)

In addition to the CPU, a computer may have a separate *graphics processing unit (GPU)* for high-speed calculations involving video, particularly games and applications such as augmented and virtual reality. The GPU may be part of the motherboard or on a separate plug-in card with 2, 4, or more gigabytes of dedicated memory. These cards can use a lot of power and generate heat, but they produce extraordinary graphics.

Because a GPU has a limited number of highly optimized functions compared to the more general-purpose CPU, it can be much faster, sometimes hundreds of times quicker, at certain operations. Those operations and the data they involve are not limited to graphics. Linear algebra and geometric-like procedures make GPUs good candidates for some AI algorithms. [219] Even cryptocurrency miners use GPUs to try to find wealth through computation.

Today, a quantum processing unit today does not have its own storage, memory, FPU, ALU, GPU, or CPU. It is most similar to a GPU in that it has its own set of operations through which it may be able to execute some algorithms significantly faster. How much faster? I don't mean twice as fast; I mean thousands of times faster.

A GPU is a variation of the classical architecture, while a quantum computer is something entirely different.

You cannot take a piece of classical software or a classical algorithm and directly run it on a quantum system. Quantum computers work together with classical ones to create new integrated systems. The trick is understanding how to meld them together to do things that have been intractable to date.

2.2 The power of two

For a system based on 0s and 1s, the number 2 frequently appears in classical computing. This is unsurprising because we use binary arithmetic, a set of operations on base 2 numbers.

Most people use base 10 for their numbers. These are also called decimal numbers. We construct such numbers from the symbols 0, 1, 2, 3, 4, 5, 6, 7, 8, and 9, which we often call *digits*. Note that the largest digit, 9, is one less than 10, the base.

A number such as 247 is shorthand for the longer $2 \times 10^2 + 4 \times 10^1 + 7 \times 10^0$. For 1,003, we expand to $1 \times 10^3 + 0 \times 10^2 + 0 \times 10^1 + 3 \times 10^0$. In these expansions, we write a sum of digits between 0 and 9 multiplied by powers of 10 in decreasing order, with no intermediate powers omitted.

We do something similar for binary. We write a binary number as a sum of bits (0 or 1) multiplied by powers of 2 in decreasing order, with no intermediate powers omitted. Here are some examples:

$$0 = 0 \times 2^0$$
$$1 = 1 \times 2^0$$
$$10 = 1 \times 2^1 + 0 \times 2^0$$
$$1101 = 1 \times 2^3 + 1 \times 2^2 + 0 \times 2^1 + 1 \times 2^0$$

The "10" is the binary number 10, not the decimal number 10. You should confirm from the above that the binary number 10 is another representation of the decimal number 2. If the context doesn't make it clear whether I am using binary or decimal, I use subscripts such as 10_2 and 2_{10}, where the first is base 2 and the second is base 10.

If I allow myself two bits, the only numbers I can write are 00, 01, 10, and 11. 11_2 is 3_{10}, which is $2^2 - 1$. If you allow me 8 bits, the numbers go from 00000000 to 11111111. The latter is $2^8 - 1$.

For 64 bits, the largest number I can write is a string of sixty-four 1s, which is

$$2^{64} - 1 = 18,446,744,073,709,551,615.$$

This is the largest positive integer a 64-bit processor can use.

We do binary addition by adding bits and carrying.

$$0 + 0 = 0$$
$$1 + 0 = 1$$
$$0 + 1 = 1$$
$$1 + 1 = 0 \text{ carry } 1$$

Thus, while $1 + 0 = 1$, $1 + 1 = 10$. Because of the carry, we had to add another bit to the left. If we were doing this on hardware and the processor did not have the space to allow us to use that extra bit, we would have an overflow. Hardware and software that do math need to check for such a condition.

2.3 True or false?

From arithmetic, let's turn to basic logic. Here, there are only two values: **True** and **False**. We want to know what we can do with one or two of these values.

The most interesting thing you can do to a single logical value is to replace it with the other. Thus, the **not** operation turns **True** into **False** and **False** into **True**:

$$\textbf{not True} = \textbf{False}$$
$$\textbf{not False} = \textbf{True}$$

For two inputs, which I call p and q, there are three primary operations, **and**, **or**, and **xor**. Consider the statement, "We will get ice cream only if you **and** your sister clean your rooms." The result is the truth or falsity of "we will get ice cream."

If neither you nor your sister cleans your rooms, or if only one of you cleans your room, the result is **False**. If both of you are tidy, the result is **True**, and you can start thinking about ice cream flavors and whether you want a cup or a cone.

Let's represent by (you, sister) the different combinations of you and your sister, respectively, having cleaned your rooms. You will not get ice cream for (**False, False**), (**True, False**), or (**False, True**). The only acceptable combination is (**True, True**). We express this as

True and True = True
True and False = False
False and True = False
False and False = False

More succinctly, we put this in a table

p = you	q = your sister	p **and** q
True	True	True
True	False	False
False	True	False
False	False	False

where the first column has the values to the left of the **and**, and the second column has the values to the right of it. The rows are the values and the results. This is a "truth table."

Another situation is where we are satisfied if at least one of the inputs is **True**. Consider, "We will go to the movie if you **or** your sister feed the dog." The result is the truth or falsity of the statement, "We will go to the movie."

p = you	q = your sister	p **or** q
True	True	True
True	False	True
False	True	True
False	False	False

Finally, think about a situation where we care about one and only one of the inputs being **True**. This is similar to **or** except in the case (**True, True**), where the result is **False**. It is an "exclusive or," and we write it **xor**. If I were to say, "I am now going to the restaurant or the library," then one of these can be **True** but not both, assuming I mean my next destination.

p = you	q = your sister	p **xor** q
True	True	False
True	False	True
False	True	True
False	False	False

There are also versions of these that include an "**n**," which means we apply **not** to the result. We apply an operation such as **and**, **or**, or **xor** and then flip **True** to **False** or **False** to **True**. "Do something and then negate it" is not common in spoken or written languages, but it is useful in computer languages. By convention, we use **xnor** instead of **nxor**.

nand is defined this way:

$$p \text{ nand } q = \text{not } (p \text{ and } q)$$

with truth table

p = you	q = your sister	p **nand** q
True	True	False
True	False	True
False	True	True
False	False	True

I leave it to you to work out what happens for **nor** and **xnor**. These **n**-versions seem baroque and excessive now, but we will see several in the next section.

Instead of **True** and **False**, we could have used **1** and **0**, which hints at some connection between logic and arithmetic.

Exercise 2.3

Fill in the following table for **nor** based on the examples and discussion above.

p = you	q = your sister	p **nor** q
True	True	
True	False	
False	True	
False	False	

Exercise 2.4

Fill in the following table for **xnor** based on the examples and discussion above.

p = you	q = your sister	p **xnor** q
True	True	
True	False	
False	True	
False	False	

2.4 Logic circuits

Now that we have a sense of how the logic works, we can look at logic circuits. The most basic logic circuits look like binary relationships, but more advanced ones implement operations for addition, multiplication, and many other mathematical operations. They also manipulate basic data. Logic circuits implement algorithms and, ultimately, the apps on your computer or device.

We begin with examples of the core operations, also called *gates*. Rather than **True** and **False**, we use **1** and **0** as the values of the bits coming into and out of gates.

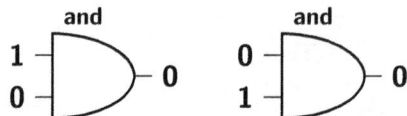

This gate has two inputs and one output. It is not reversible because it produces the same output with different inputs. Given the **0** output, we cannot know which example produced it. Here are the other gates we use, with example inputs:

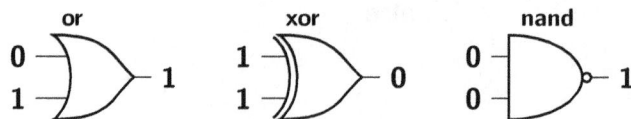

We frequently use the symbol ''⊕'' for the **xor** operation.

To me, these standard gate shapes used in the United States look like variations on spaceship designs.

The **not** gate has one input and one output. It is reversible: if you apply it twice, you get back the original value.

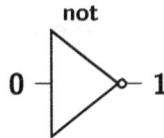

People who study electrical engineering see these gates and the logic circuits you can build from them early in their training. This is not a book about electrical engineering. Instead, I want you to think of the above as literal building blocks. We plug them together, pull them apart, and make new logic circuits. We'll experiment with them while getting comfortable with creating logic circuits that do what we want.

I connect the output of one **not** gate to the input of another to show that you get the same value you put in. x can be **0** or **1**.

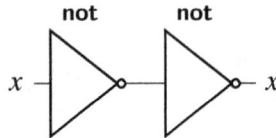

If we didn't already have a **nand** gate, we could build it.

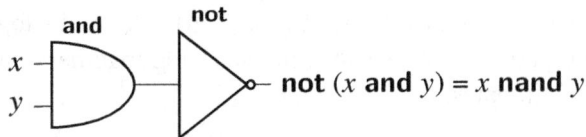

not $(x$ **and** $y) = x$ **nand** y

Note how we compose gates to get other gates. We can build **and** from **nand** and **not**. We could shrink the collection of gates we use if we desire. From this last example, it's technically redundant to have **and**, **nand**, and **not**, but it is convenient to have them all. Let's keep going to see what else we can construct.

Even though a gate such as **nand** has two inputs, we can push the same value into each input. We show it this way with a single line and a dot:

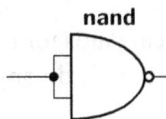

What do we get when we start with **0** or **1** and run it through this logic circuit? **0 nand 0 = 1** and **1 nand 1 = 0**. This behaves exactly like **not**! If we wanted to, we could get rid of **not**. Having only **nand**, we could drop **not** and **and**. It's starting to seem that **nand** has some essential building block property.

By stringing together four **nand** gates, we can create an **xor** gate. It takes three to make an **or** gate. It takes one more to make **xnor** and **nor** gates.

> We can construct every logic gate from a logic circuit of only **nand** gates. The same is true for **nor** gates. We call **nand** and **nor** gates *universal* gates because they have this property. [159]

Having all the basic gates replaced by multiple **nand** gates would be tedious and inefficient, but you can do it. We can build **or** this way:

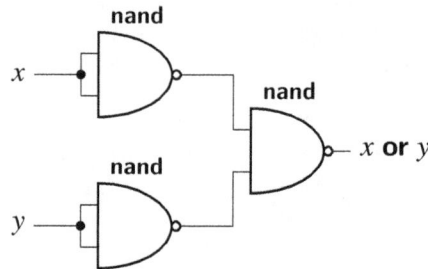

For the binary logic gates that have two inputs and one output, there are only eight possibilities: the four possible inputs, **(0, 0)**, **(0, 1)**, **(1, 0)**, and **(1, 1)**, together with an output of **0** or **1** for each input pair. Like **or** above, you can string together combinations of **nand**s to create any of these eight gates.

Exercise 2.5

Show how to create the **nor** gate only from **nand** gates.

We looked at these logic circuits to see how we do classical processing at a very low level. We return to circuits and the idea of universal gates again for quantum computing in section 9.3.

So far, this has been a study of classical gates for their own sake. The behavior, compositions, and universality are interesting but don't do anything fascinating yet. Let's do some math!

2.5   Addition, logically

We can put these logic gates together to do addition using binary arithmetic, as we discussed in section 2.2:

$$0 + 0 = 0$$
$$1 + 0 = 1$$
$$0 + 1 = 1$$
$$1 + 1 = 0 \text{ carry } 1$$

Focus on the values after the equal signs, and temporarily forget the carrying in the last case. The results are the same as what **xor** does with two inputs:

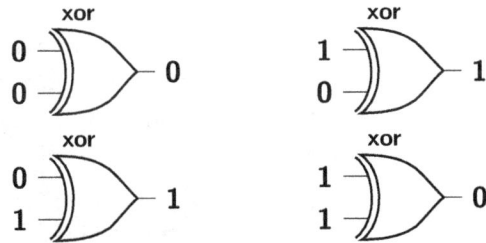

We lost the carry bit but limited ourselves to having only one output bit. What gate operation would give us that **1** carry bit only if both inputs were also **1** and otherwise return **0**? Correct, it's **and**! If we combine the **xor** and the **and**, and give ourselves two bits of output, we can do a simple addition of two bits.

> **Exercise 2.6**
>
> Try drawing a circuit that would do this before peeking at what follows. You are allowed to clone the value of a bit and send it to two different gates.

The circuit is

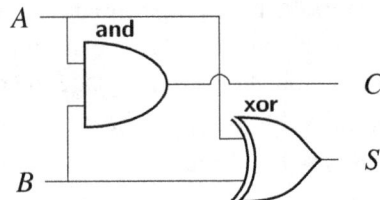

where A, B, S, and C are bits. The circuit takes two single input bits, A and B, and produces a 2-bit answer CS.

$$A + B = CS$$
$$0 + 0 = 00$$
$$1 + 0 = 01$$
$$0 + 1 = 01$$
$$1 + 1 = 10$$

We call S the *sum* bit and C the *carry-out* bit. This circuit is a "half-adder" since, as written, we cannot use it in the middle of a larger circuit. It's missing something. Can you guess what it is?

A "full-adder," as shown in Figure 2.2, has an additional input called the *carry-in*. This bit is the carry from an addition that might precede it in the overall circuit. If there is no previous addition, we set the carry-in bit to **0**. The square in the figure contains a circuit to handle the three inputs and produce the two outputs.

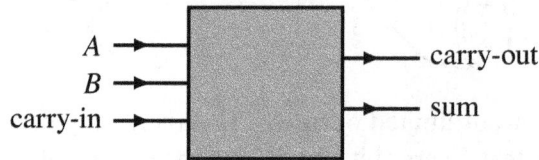

Figure 2.2: An addition operation with two inputs and a "carry-in" bit

Exercise 2.7

What does the circuit look like?

We can create classical processors that implement full addition by extending this to more bits with additional gates. We implement other arithmetic operations such as subtraction, multiplication, and division and often group them within the *arithmetic logic unit* (ALU).

For addition, the ALU takes multi-bit integer inputs and produces a multi-bit integer output sum. Other information can also be available from the ALU, such as if the final bit addition caused an *overflow*, a carry-out that had no place to go.

Modern ALUs contain circuits with hundreds or thousands of gates. A processor in a laptop or smartphone uses integers with 64 bits.

Figure 2.3 shows a schematic of an `early ALU integrated circuit`.

Modern-day programmers and software engineers rarely deal directly with logic circuits themselves. Engineers build several software library layers on top of the logic circuits so that coders can quickly do what they need to do.

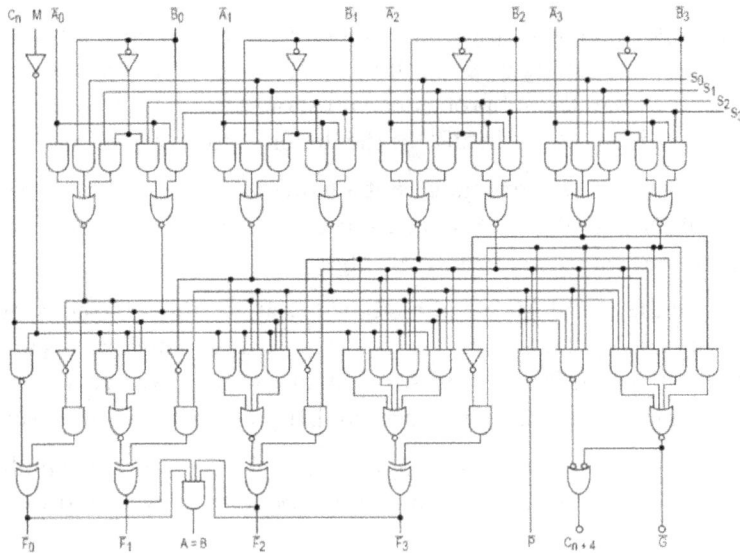

Figure 2.3: The Texas Instruments 74181 4-bit arithmetic logic unit

If I write an app for a smartphone that involves drawing a circle, I don't need to know anything today about the low-level processes and circuits that do the arithmetic and cause the graphic to appear on the screen. I use a high-level routine that takes as input the location of the circle's center, the radius, the circle's color, and the fill color inside the circle.

At some point, a person created the library implementing the high-level routine. Someone wrote the lower-level graphical operations. Someone or some design program wrote the logic circuits that implement the primitive operations under the graphical ones.

We layer software in increasing levels of abstraction. Programming languages such as C++, Python, R, Java, and Swift hide the low-level details. Libraries for these languages provide reusable code that many people can use to piece together new apps.

However, there is always a bottom layer, and logic circuits live near there.

2.6 Algorithmically speaking

We often use the word ''algorithm'' generically to mean ''something a computer does.'' Quantitative analysts employ financial market algorithms to calculate the exact moment and price to sell a stock or bond. They are used in artificial intelligence to find patterns in data to understand natural language, construct responses in human conversation, find manufacturing anomalies, detect financial fraud, and even create new spice mixtures for cooking.

Informally, an algorithm is a recipe. Like a food recipe, an algorithm states what inputs you need (water, flour, butter, eggs, etc.), the expected outcome (for example, bread), the sequence of steps you take, the subprocesses you should use (stir, knead, bake, cool), and what to do when a choice presents itself ("if the dough is too wet, add more flour").

We call each step an *operation* and give it a name as above: "stir," "bake," "cool," and so on. We want the overall process to be successful and efficient, and we construct the best possible operations for each action in the algorithm.

The recipe is not the actual baking of the bread; you are doing the cooking. In the same way, an algorithm abstractly states what you should do with a computer. It is up to the circuits and higher-level routines built on circuits to implement and execute what the algorithm describes. There can be more than one algorithm that produces the same result.

Operations in computer algorithms might, for example, add two numbers, compare whether one is larger than another, switch two numbers, or store or retrieve a value from memory.

Quantum computers do not use classical logic gates, operations, or simple bits. While quantum circuits and algorithms look and behave very differently from their classical counterparts, there is still the idea that we have data we manipulate over a series of steps to get what we hope is a valuable result.

2.7   Growth, exponential and otherwise

Many people who use the phrase "exponential growth" misuse it, somehow thinking it only means "very fast." Exponential growth involves, well, exponents. Figure 2.4 is a plot showing four kinds of growth: exponential, quadratic, linear, and logarithmic.

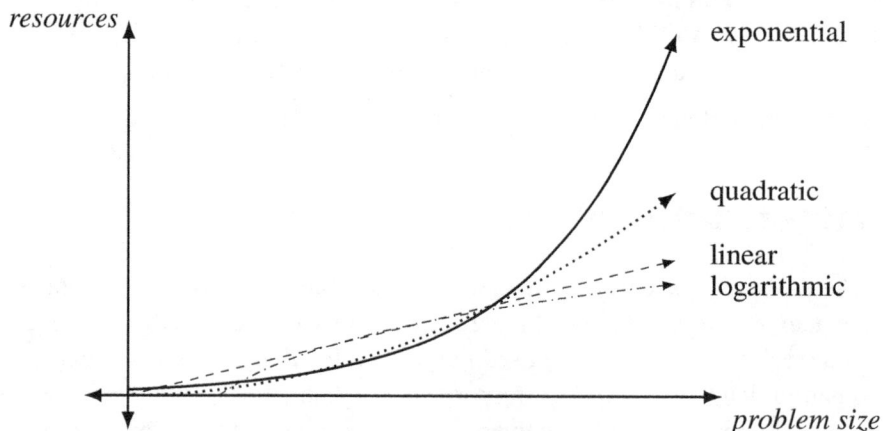

Figure 2.4: Four kinds of growth

I've drawn them so they all intersect at a point but afterward diverge. After the convergence, the logarithmic plot (dot-dashed) grows slowly, the linear plot (dashed) continues as it did, the quadratic plot (dotted) continues upward as a parabola, and the exponential one shoots up rapidly.

Look at the change in the vertical axis, the one I've labeled *resources*, versus the horizontal axis, labeled *problem size*. As the size of the problem increases, how fast does the number of resources needed increase? Here, a resource might be the time required for the algorithm, the amount of memory used during computation, or the megabytes of data storage necessary.

When we move a certain distance to the right horizontally for *problem size,* the logarithmic plot increases vertically at a rate proportional to the inverse of the size 1/*problem size*. The linear plot increases at a constant rate for *resources* that does not depend on *problem size*. The quadratic plot increases at a vertical rate proportional to *problem size*. The exponential plot increases at a rate proportional to its current *resources*. If you know calculus, these rate changes are derivatives.

We define the logarithm for a real number only when that number is positive. The function $\log_{10}(x)$ answers the question, "To what power must I raise 10 to get x?" When x is 10, the answer is 1. When x is equal to one million, the answer is 6. Another common logarithm function is $\log_2$, which substitutes 2 for 10 in these examples. Logarithmic functions grow *very* slowly.

Examples of growth are

$$resources = 2 \times \log_{10}(problem\ size)$$
$$resources = 4 \times (problem\ size)$$
$$resources = 0.3 \times (problem\ size)^2$$
$$resources = 7.2 \times 3^{problem\ size}$$

for logarithmic, linear, quadratic, and exponential, respectively. Note the variable *problem size* in the exponent in the fourth case.

For large problem size, the exponential plot goes up rapidly, then more rapidly, and so on. Things can quickly get out of hand with this kind of positive exponential growth.

If you start with 100 units of currency and get 6% interest compounded once a year, you will have $100 \times (1+0.06)$ after one year. After two, you will have $100 \times (1+0.06) \times (1+0.06) = 100 \times 1.06^2$. In general, after t years, you will have 100×1.06^t. This is exponential growth. Your money will double in approximately 12 years.

We will not fully replace classical computers with quantum computers over the next several decades. Instead, quantum computing may help make specific problems solvable in a short time instead of their being intractable. The power of a quantum computer potentially grows exponentially with the number of quantum bits, or qubits, in it.

Can we use this "good growth" to control "bad growth" in problems we are trying to solve?

Exercise 2.8

A *double exponential* function looks like

$$f(x) = a^{b^x} \text{ for constants } a > 1 \text{ and } b > 1.$$

On one graph, plot the double exponential function with $a = b = 2$ versus the exponential function

$$g(x) = 2^x$$

for $0 \le x \le 4$.

2.8 How hard can that be?

Once you decide to do something, how long does it take you? How much money or other resources does it involve? How do you compare the worst way of doing it with the best?

All these questions come to bear when you try to accomplish tasks on a computer. The point about money may not be obvious, but when running an application, you need to pay for the processing, storage, and memory you use. This is true whether you paid for a more powerful laptop or have ongoing cloud costs.

To end this chapter, we look at classical complexity. We consider sorting and searching and some algorithms for doing these procedures.

2.8.1 Sorting

Sorting involves taking multiple items and putting them in some kind of order. Consider your book collection. You can rearrange them so that the books are on the shelves in ascending alphabetic order by title. Or you can move them around so they are in descending order by the year of publication. If more than one book was published in the same year, order them alphabetically by the first author's last name.

When we ordered by title, that title was the *key* we looked at to decide where to place the book among the others. When we considered it by year and then author, the year was the *primary key*, and the author's name was the *secondary key*.

Before we sort, we need to decide how we compare the items. We might ask, "Is the first number less than the second?" or "Is the first title alphabetically before the second?". The response is either **True** or **False**.

Something that often snags new programmers is comparing things that look like numbers either numerically or *lexicographically*. In the first case, we think of the complete item as a number, while in the second, we compare the text character by character. Consider 54 and 8. Numerically, the second is less than the first. Lexicographically, the first is less because the character 5 comes before 8.

Therefore, when coding, you need to convert them to the same format. If you were to convert the characters "-34,809" into a number, what would it be? In much of Europe, people use the comma as the decimal point, while in the United States, the United Kingdom, and several other countries, people use it to separate groups of three digits.

We now look at two ways of numerically sorting a list of numbers into ascending order. The first is called a "bubble sort," and it has several nice features, including simplicity. However, it is inefficient for large collections of objects not already close to being in the correct order.

We have two operations: *compare*, which takes two numbers and returns **True** if the first is less than the second, and **False** otherwise; and *swap*, which interchanges the two numbers in the list.

The idea of the bubble sort is to make repeated passes through the list, comparing adjacent numbers. We swap them if they are out of order and continue through the list. We keep doing this until we make a complete pass where we did no swaps. At that point, the list is sorted. That's pretty elegant and straightforward to describe!

Let's begin with a case where a list of four numbers is already sorted:

$$[-2, 0, 3, 7]$$

We compare –2 and 0. They are already in the correct order, so we move on. 0 and 3 are also correct, so there is nothing to do. 3 and 7 are fine. We did three comparisons and no swaps. Because we did not have to interchange any numbers, we are finished.

Let's look at

$$[7, -2, 0, 3]$$

Comparing 7 and –2, we see the second is less than the first, so we swap them to get the new list

$$[-2, 7, 0, 3]$$

Next, we look at 7 and 0. Again, we need to swap and get

$$[-2, 0, 7, 3]$$

Comparing 7 and 3, we have two more numbers that are out of order. Swapping them, we get

$$[-2, 0, 3, 7]$$

So far, we have done three comparisons and three swaps. Since the number of swaps is not zero, we pass through the list again. This time, we do three more comparisons but no swaps, and we are done. In total, we did six comparisons and three swaps.

Now for the worst case, with the list in reverse sorted order

$$[7, 3, 0, -2]$$

First pass

$[7, 3, 0, -2]$	swap the first and second numbers
$[3, 7, 0, -2]$	swap the second and third numbers
$[3, 0, 7, -2]$	swap the third and fourth numbers
$[3, 0, -2, 7]$	

We did three comparisons and three swaps.

Second pass

$[3, 0, -2, 7]$	swap the first and second numbers
$[0, 3, -2, 7]$	swap the second and third numbers
$[0, -2, 3, 7]$	compare the third and fourth numbers, but do nothing

We did three comparisons and two swaps.

Third pass

$[0, -2, 3, 7]$	swap the first and second numbers
$[-2, 0, 3, 7]$	compare the second and third numbers, but do nothing
$[-2, 0, 3, 7]$	compare the third and fourth numbers, but do nothing

We did three comparisons and one swap.

Fourth pass

$[-2, 0, 3, 7]$	compare the first and second numbers, but do nothing
$[-2, 0, 3, 7]$	compare the second and third numbers, but do nothing
$[-2, 0, 3, 7]$	compare the third and fourth numbers, but do nothing

There's no swap, so we are done, and we did the usual three comparisons.

For this list of four numbers, we did twelve comparisons and six swaps in four passes. Can we put some formulas behind these numbers for the worst case?

We had four numbers in altogether the wrong order, so it took four full passes to sort them. For a list of length n, we must make $n - 1$ comparisons, which is three in this example.

The number of swaps is the interesting number. On the first pass, we did three, on the second we did two, on the third we did one, and on the fourth, we did none. So the number of swaps is

$$3 + 2 + 1 = (n - 1) + (n - 2) + \cdots + 1$$

where n is the length of the list. There is a pattern here.

There is a formula that can help us with this last sum. If we want to add up 1, 2, and so on through a positive integer m, we compute

$$1 + 2 + 3 + \cdots + m = \frac{m(m + 1)}{2}.$$

Exercise 2.9

Try this out for $m = 1$, $m = 2$, and $m = 3$. Now, see if the formula still holds if we add $m + 1$. That is, can you rewrite

$$\frac{m(m + 1)}{2} + m + 1$$

as

$$\frac{(m + 1)(m + 2)}{2} ?$$

If so, you have proved the formula by *induction*.

In our case, we have $m = n - 1$, so we do a total of $\frac{(n-1)n}{2}$ swaps. For $n = 4$ numbers in the list, this is none other than the six swaps we counted by hand.

It may not seem so bad that we had to do six swaps for four numbers in the worst case, but what if we had 1,000 numbers in completely reversed order? Then, the number of swaps would be

$$\frac{999 \times 1000}{2} = 499500.$$

That's almost half a million swaps for a list of 1,000 numbers.

For 1 million numbers, in the worst case it would be

$$\frac{999999 \times 1000000}{2} = 499999500000,$$

which is 499 billion, 999 million, 500 thousand swaps. This is terrible. Rewriting this as

$$\frac{(n-1)n}{2} = \frac{n^2 - n}{2} = \frac{1}{2}n^2 - \frac{1}{2}n,$$

we can see that the number of swaps grows with the *square* of the number of entries. In fact,

$$\text{number of swaps} \leq \frac{1}{2}n^2$$

for all $n \geq 1$. In this situation, we say that our algorithm is $O(n^2)$, pronounced: "big O of n squared." We also say that the algorithm has *complexity* n^2.

> More formally, we say that the number of nontrivial operations used to solve a problem on n objects is $O(f(n))$ if there is a positive real number c and an integer m, such that
>
> $$\text{number of operations} \leq c f(n)$$
>
> once $n \geq m$, for some function f.

To learn more

> In the area of computer science called *complexity theory*, researchers try to determine the best possible f, c, and m to match the growth behavior as closely as possible. [50, Chapter 3] [199, Section 1.4]

In our case, $c = \frac{1}{2}$, $f(n) = n^2$, and $m = 1$.

If an algorithm is $O(n^t)$ for some positive fixed number t, then the algorithm is *of polynomial time*. Easy examples are algorithms that run in $O(n)$, $O(n^2)$, and $O(n^3)$ time.

If the exponent t is very large, we might have a very inefficient and impractical algorithm. Being of polynomial time means that it is bounded above by something that is $O(n^t)$. Technically, we can also say that an $O(\log(n))$ algorithm is of polynomial time, since it runs faster than an $O(n)$ algorithm.

Getting back to sorting, we are looking at the worst case for this algorithm. In the best case, we do no swaps. Therefore, when looking at a process, we should examine the best, worst, and average cases. For the bubble sort, the best case is $O(n)$, while the average and worst cases are both $O(n^2)$.

If you are coding up and testing an algorithm and it seems to take a very long time to run, you likely either have a bug in your software or stumbled onto something close to a worst-case scenario.

Can we sort more efficiently than $O(n^2)$ time? How much better can we do?

By examination, we could have optimized the bubble sort algorithm slightly. Look at the last entry in the list after each pass, and consider how we could have reduced the number of comparisons. However, the number of swaps dominates the execution time, not the number of comparisons. Rather than tinkering with this kind of sort, let's examine another algorithm that takes a very different approach.

There are many sorting algorithms, and you might have fun searching the web to learn more about the main kinds of approaches. You'll also find interesting visualizations of how the objects move around during the sort. Computer science students often examine the different versions when learning algorithms and data structures.

The second sort algorithm we look at is the *merge sort* that dates back to 1945. John von Neumann, shown in Figure 2.5, discovered it. [114]

Figure 2.5: John von Neumann in the 1940s

To better see how the merge sort works, let's use a larger data set with eight objects and use names instead of numbers. Here is the initial list:

Katie   Bobby   William   Atticus   Judith   Gideon   Beatnik   Ruth

We sort this in ascending alphabetic order. This list is now neither sorted nor in reverse order, so this is an average case.

We begin by breaking the list into eight groups (because we have eight names), each containing only one item.

| Katie | Bobby | William | Atticus | Judith | Gideon | Beatnik | Ruth |

Each group is sorted within itself because there is only one name. Next, working from left to right pairwise, we create groups of two names, where we put the names in the correct order as we merge.

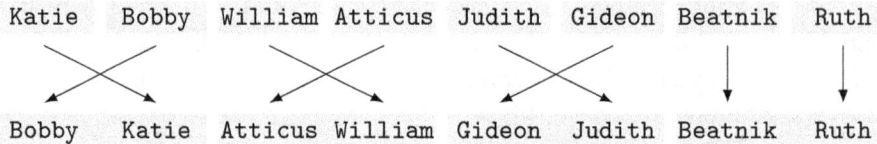

| Katie | Bobby | William | Atticus | Judith | Gideon | Beatnik | Ruth |
| Bobby | Katie | Atticus | William | Gideon | Judith | Beatnik | Ruth |

We now combine the groups of two into groups of four, again working from left to right. We know the names are sorted within the group. Begin with the first name in the first pair. If it is less than the first name in the second pair, put it at the beginning of the group of four. If not, put the first name in the second pair there.

Continue in this way. If a pair becomes empty, put all the names in the other pair at the end of the group of four in order.

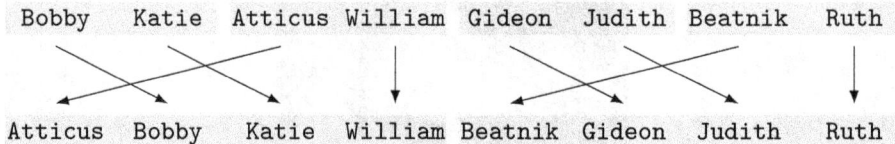

| Bobby | Katie | Atticus | William | Gideon | Judith | Beatnik | Ruth |
| Atticus | Bobby | Katie | William | Beatnik | Gideon | Judith | Ruth |

We finally create one group, merging in the names as we encounter them from left to right.

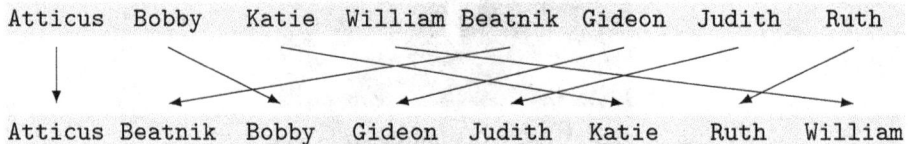

| Atticus | Bobby | Katie | William | Beatnik | Gideon | Judith | Ruth |
| Atticus | Beatnik | Bobby | Gideon | Judith | Katie | Ruth | William |

Among the variations of merge sort, this is a *bottom-up* implementation because we break the data into chunks of size one and then combine them.

We are not interested in swaps for this algorithm because we are forming new collections rather than manipulating an existing one. We need to place a name in a new group no matter what. Instead, the metric we care about is the number of comparisons. The analysis is nontrivial and is available in algorithm books and on the web. The complexity of a merge sort is $O(n \log(n))$. [50]

This is a big improvement over $O(n^2)$. Forgetting about the constant in the definition of $O()$ and using logarithms to base 10, for $n = 1000000 = 1$ million, we have $n^2 = 1000000000000 = 10^{12} = 1$ trillion, while $\log_{10}(1000000) \times 1000000 = 6 \times 10^6 = 6$ million. Would you rather perform a million times more comparisons than there are names or six times the number of names?

We end up with the same answer using both bubble and merge sorts, but the algorithms and their performance differ dramatically. Your choice of algorithm is an important decision.

For the bubble sort, we use only enough memory to hold the original list, and then we move around numbers within this list. For the merge sort in this implementation, we need the memory for the initial list of names, and then we need that much memory again when we move to groups of two. However, after that point, we can reuse the memory for the initial list to hold the groups of four in the next pass.

By reusing memory repeatedly, we can get away with using twice the initial memory to complete the sort. You can reduce this memory requirement by being extra clever, which I leave to you and your research.

Exercise 2.10

I just referred to storing data in memory. What would you do if there were so many objects to be sorted that the information could not all fit in memory? You might use persistent storage like a hard drive, but how?

Although I have focused on how many operations, such as swaps and comparisons are needed for an algorithm, you can also look at how much memory is necessary and do a $O()$ analysis of that. Memory-wise, bubble sort is $O(1)$, and merge sort is $O(n)$.

2.8.2 Searching

Here is our motivating problem: I have a collection S of n objects, and I want to find out if a particular object *target* is in S. Here are some examples:

- Somewhere in my closet, I think I have a navy blue sweater. Is it there and where? Here, *target* = ''my navy blue sweater.''
- If I keep my socks sorted by the names of their predominant colors in my dresser drawer, are my blue argyle socks clean and available?
- I have a database of 650 volunteers for my charity. How many live in my town?
- I brought my kids to a magic show, and I volunteered to go up on stage. Where is the Queen of Hearts in the deck of cards the magician holds?

With only a little thought, we can see that searching is, at worst, $O(n)$ unless you are doing something strange and questionable. Look at the first object. Is it *target*? If not, look at the second and compare. Continue if necessary until we get to the nth object. Either it is *target*, or *target* is not in S. This is a *linear search* because we go in a straight line from the beginning to the end of the collection.

If *target* is in S, we find it the first time, in the best case scenario. In the worst case scenario, it is the nth time. On average, it takes $\frac{n}{2}$ attempts.

To do better than this classically, we have to know more information:

- Is S sorted?
- Can I access any object directly, as in "give me the fourth object"? We call this *random access*.
- Is S simply a linear collection of objects, or does it have a more sophisticated data structure?

If S only has one entry, look at it. If *target* is that one entry, we have succeeded.

I can do a *binary search* if S is a sorted collection with random access. Since the word "binary" is involved, this has something to do with the number 2.

I now show this with our previously sorted list of names. The problem is seeing if *target* = Ruth is in S. There are eight names in the list. If we do a linear search, it takes seven tries to find Ruth.

```
Atticus Beatnik  Bobby  Gideon  Judith  Katie   Ruth   William
                                                  ↑
```

Let's take a different approach. Let $m = \frac{n}{2} = 4$, a position near the midpoint of the list of eight names.

In case m is not a whole number, we round up. Examine the mth = the fourth name in S. That name is Gideon. Since S is sorted and Gideon < Ruth, Ruth cannot be in the first half of the list. With this simple calculation, we have already eliminated half the names in S. We need only consider

```
Judith  Katie   Ruth   William
```

There are four names, so we divide this in half to get two. The second name is Katie. Since Katie < Ruth, Ruth is again not in the first half of this list. We repeat with the second half.

```
Ruth   William
```

The list has length 2; we divide this in half and look at the first name. Ruth! Where have you been?

We find Ruth with only three searches. If that last split and compare does not find Ruth, the remaining sublist has only one entry. That entry must be Ruth, since we assumed that name was in S. We locate our target with only $3 = \log_2(8)$ steps.

Binary search is $O(\log n)$ in the worst case scenario, but remember that we imposed the conditions that S was sorted and had random access. As with sorting, there are many searching techniques and data structures that can make finding objects quite efficient.

As an example of a data structure, look at the binary tree of our example names, as shown in Figure 2.6. The dashed lines show our route to Ruth. Implementing a binary tree in a computer requires much more attention to memory layout and bookkeeping.

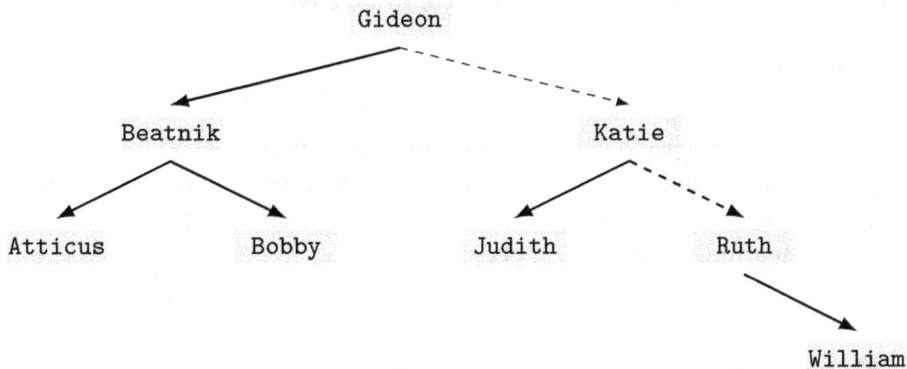

Figure 2.6: Binary tree

Exercise 2.11

I want to add two more names to this binary tree: Richard and Kristin. How would you insert the names and rearrange the tree? What about if I delete Ruth or Gideon from the original tree?

Exercise 2.12

For extra credit, look up how *hashing* works. Think about the combined performance of searching and what you must do to keep the underlying data structure of objects in a useful form.

Authors have written entire books on the related topics of sorting and searching. We return to this topic when we examine Grover's quantum search algorithm for locating an item in an unsorted list without random access in only $O(\sqrt{n})$ time, in section 9.7.

> If we replace an $O(f(n))$ algorithm with an $O\left(\sqrt{f(n)}\right)$ one, we have made a *quadratic* improvement. If we replace it with an $O(\log(f(n)))$ algorithm, we have an *exponential* improvement.

Suppose I have an algorithm that takes 1 million = 10^6 days to complete. That's almost 2,740 years! Forgetting about the constant in the $O()$ notation and using $\log_{10}$, a quadratic improvement would complete in $1,000 = 10^3$ days, which is about 2.74 years. An exponential improvement would give us a completion time of just 6 days.

To learn more

> There are many sorting and searching algorithms and, indeed, algorithms for hundreds of computational use cases. As we have just seen, deciding which algorithm to use in which situation is critical to performance. For some applications, there are algorithms to choose the algorithm to use! [127] [199]

2.9 Summary

Classical computers have been around since the 1940s and are based on using bits, **1**s and **0**s, to store and manipulate information. This is naturally connected to logic, as we can think of **1** or **0** as **True** or **False**, respectively, and vice versa. From logic operators like **and**, we created logic circuits that perform higher-level operations such as addition. Circuits implement portions of algorithms.

Since all algorithms to accomplish a goal are not equal, we saw that having some idea of measuring the time and memory complexity of what we are doing is essential. By understanding the classical case, we'll later be able to show where we can get a quantum improvement.

3

More Numbers Than You Can Imagine

*The methods of theoretical physics should be applicable to
all those branches of thought in which the essential
features are expressible with numbers.*

– Paul Dirac, 1933 Nobel Prize Banquet Speech

People use numbers for counting, percentages, ratios, prices, math homework, taxes, and other practical applications.

$$1 \qquad 0 \qquad -1 \qquad 9.99999$$

$$\sqrt{2}+1 \qquad \frac{22}{7} \qquad 3.14159265\ldots \qquad \pi$$

These are all examples of real numbers. In this chapter, we look at the properties and operations of real numbers, especially those of subsets such as the integers. We extend those properties and operations to other collections, such as the complex numbers, that are core to understanding quantum computing.

For example, we define a quantum bit, or qubit, as a pair of complex numbers with additional properties. We begin to lay the foundation for the algebraic side of quantum computing. In the next chapter, we'll turn to geometry.

Topics covered in this chapter

3.1 Natural numbers

While there are special and famous numbers such as π, the numbers we use for counting are much simpler: $1, 2, 3, \ldots$. I might say, "Look, there is 1 puppy, 2 kittens, 3 cars, and 4 apples." If you give me 2 more apples, I will have 6. If I give my sister 1 of them, I will have 5. If I buy 2 more bags of 5 apples, I will have 15 in total, which is 3×5."

The set of natural numbers is the collection of increasing values

$$\{1, 2, 3, 4, 5, 6, 7, \ldots\},$$

where we get from one number to the next by adding 1. 0 is not included. The braces "{" and "}" indicate we are talking about the entire set of these numbers.

When we want to refer to some arbitrary natural number but not any particular one specifically, we use a variable name such as n or m.

The set of natural numbers is infinite. Suppose otherwise and that some specific number n is the largest natural number. But then $n + 1$ is larger, and is a natural number, by definition. This *proof by contradiction* shows that the original premise that there is a largest natural number is false. Hence, the set is infinite.

To avoid writing out "natural numbers" repeatedly, I sometimes abbreviate the collection of all natural numbers by using **N**. What can we do if we restrict ourselves to working only with **N**?

First, we can add them via the usual arithmetic rules: $1 + 1 = 2$, $3 + 4 = 7$, $999998 + 2 = 1000000$, and so on.

Addition is so key to natural numbers that we consider it an essential part of the definition. In fact, we did: we described the values in the set, $\{1, 2, \dots\}$, but then also pointed out that we get from one value to the next by adding 1.

I've started with these basic numbers to make this point clear: we're not only concerned with a number here or a number there. We want to consider the entire collection and what we can do with the numbers via operations such as addition.

If we have two natural numbers and we add them together using "+", we always get another natural number. Hence, **N** is closed under addition. The idea of closure, or being closed with respect to some operation, means that the result is in the collection after we do it.

To choose something more exotic than basic arithmetic, consider the square root operation. The square root of 1 is still 1, and so it is a natural number, as is the square root of 4. But $\sqrt{2}$ is not a natural number and is, in fact, an irrational number.

$$\sqrt{2} = 1.41421356237\dots$$

N is not closed under the square root operation.

In **N**, addition is commutative: $4 + 11 = 11 + 4$ and $n + m = m + n$, in general. You always get the same answer no matter in which order you count things.

What about subtraction, which is, in some sense, the complement of addition? Since $3 + 4 = 7$, then $3 = 7 - 4$ and $4 = 7 - 3$. We can also state the last as "4 is 7 minus 3, or 7 take away 3, or 7 subtract 3."

For all natural numbers n and m, we always have $n + m$ in **N**. However, we have $n - m$ in **N** only if $n > m$. $24 - 17 = 7$ is a natural number, but $6 - 6$ is not a natural number because 0 is not in **N**, by definition. $17 - 24$ is not a natural number since the smallest natural number is 1.

N is not closed under subtraction.

We can use comparisons such as "<" and > to tell if one natural number is less than or greater than another, respectively, in addition to testing for equality with "=". Because we can compare any two numbers in **N**, we say that the natural numbers are ordered. Since we have comparison operations, we can sort collections of natural numbers in ascending or descending order.

Given that we have addition, we can define multiplication "×" by saying that $n \times m$ is m added to itself n times. In particular, $1 \times n = n \times 1 = n$. Multiplication distributes over addition:

$$3 \times (8 + 11) = (3 \times 8) + (3 \times 11) = 57 \,.$$

Multiplication is commutative like addition: $n \times m = m \times n$. It's just a question of how you group things for counting:

$$
\begin{aligned}
3 \times 7 &= 7 + 7 + 7 \\
&= (3 + 3 + 1) + (2 + 3 + 2) + (1 + 3 + 3) \\
&= 3 + 3 + (1 + 2) + 3 + (2 + 1) + 3 + 3 \\
&= 3 + 3 + 3 + 3 + 3 + 3 + 3 \\
&= 7 \times 3 \,.
\end{aligned}
$$

N is closed under multiplication but is not closed under division. $\frac{1}{3}$ is not a natural number, for example, even if $\frac{4}{2}$ is.

For natural numbers, the definition of multiplication follows directly from addition. For more sophisticated mathematical collections, multiplication can be much more complicated.

Let's start extending the collection to eliminate some of these problems regarding closure.

3.2   Whole numbers

If we append 0 to **N** as a new smallest value, we get the whole numbers, denoted **W**. They are both infinite sets of numbers, but **N** is a subset of **W**. We do not use the whole numbers a lot in mathematics, but let's see what we get with this additional value.

We are still closed under addition and multiplication and not closed under division. We do now have to watch out for division by 0. Expressions such as $3 - 3$ or $n - n$, in general, are in **W**, so that's a little better for subtraction, but this does not give us closure.

So far, there's not much that we've gained, it seems. Or have we?

0 is an *identity element* for addition, a new concept for us to consider. I've put it in bold to show how special it is. This element is a unique (meaning there is one and only one) number such that for any whole number w, we have $w + \mathbf{0} = \mathbf{0} + w = w$.

Thus, $14 + \mathbf{0} = \mathbf{0} + 14 = 14$. Also, $\mathbf{0} \times w = w \times \mathbf{0} = \mathbf{0}$.

For the whole numbers **W**, we have a collection of values

$$\{\mathbf{0}, 1, 2, 3, \dots\},$$

an operation "$+$", and an identity element **0** for "$+$".

You may have realized by now that when we discussed **N**, we could have also noted that **1** is an identity element for multiplication. So let's restate everything we know about **N** and **W**:

The set of natural numbers **N** is the infinite ordered collection of values $\{1, 2, 3, 4, \dots\}$ with a commutative operation "$+$" called *addition*. We get from one natural number to the next larger natural number by adding **1**. **N** is closed under addition.

We also have a commutative operation *multiplication* "$\times$" with identity element **1**. Multiplication distributes over addition. **N** is closed under multiplication.

N is not closed under subtraction or division defined in the usual manner.

The set of whole numbers **W** is the infinite ordered extension of **N** formed by adding a new smallest value **0**. **0** is an identity element for addition. **W** is closed under the commutative addition and multiplication operations but not under subtraction or division.

I hope you agree that we've come a long way from only considering the numbers $1, 2, 3, 4, \dots$. We've gone from thinking about counting and specific values to entire sets of numbers and their properties. Though I'll stop putting them in bold, 0 and 1 are not random numbers; they play very special roles. Later, we'll see other "**0**-like" and "**1**-like" objects that are more than simple numbers.

Since we have addition and multiplication, we can define exponentiation. If w and a are whole numbers and $a > 0$, w^a equals w multiplied by itself a times. Note the similarity with how we defined multiplication to addition:

$$3 \times 7 = 3 + 3 + 3 + 3 + 3 + 3 + 3$$
$$3^7 = 3 \times 3 \times 3 \times 3 \times 3 \times 3 \times 3.$$

The definition means that $w^1 = 1$. Less intuitively, $w^0 = 1$ even when $w = 0$.

What do we get when we multiply two expressions with exponents? When the base is the same (the thing we are raising to a power), we add the exponents:

$$2^3 \times 2^4 = (2 \times 2 \times 2) \times (2 \times 2 \times 2 \times 2)$$
$$= 2 \times 2 \times 2 \times 2 \times 2 \times 2 \times 2$$
$$= 2^7 = 2^{3+4}.$$

In general, $w^a \times w^b = w^{a+b}$. Also,

$$w^a \times w^0 = w^{a+0} = w^a = w^a \times 1,$$

further showing why $w^0 = 1$ makes sense.

> We omit the "×" when it is clear that the context is multiplication:
> $$2^3 \times 2^4 = 2^3 2^4 = 2^{3+4} = 2^7.$$

3.3 Integers

People are sometimes confused by negative numbers when they first encounter them. How can I have a negative amount of anything? I can't physically have fewer than no apples, can I?

To get around this, we introduce the idea that a positive number of things or amount of money means something you *have*. A negative number or amount means what you *owe* someone else.

If you have $100 and you write a check or pay a bill electronically for $120, one of two things will likely happen. The first option is for the payment to fail, and your bank may charge you a fee. The second is that the bank will pay the full amount, let you know you are overdrawn, and charge you a fee. You will then need to pay the overdrawn amount quickly or have it paid from some other account.

You started with $100 and ended up with $-20 before repayment. You owe the bank $20. If you deposit $200 in your account immediately, your balance will be $180, which is $-20 + $200.

The set of *integers*, which we denote by the letter **Z**, addresses the problem of the whole numbers not being closed under subtraction. We define an operation "−", called *negation*, for each whole number n such that $-0 = 0$ and $-n$ is a new value such that $n + (-n) = n + -n = 0$. This new, extended set of numbers with the operations and properties we will discuss is called the *integers*.

We say that integers such as 1, 12, and 345 are *positive*. More precisely, any integer that is also a natural number or a whole number greater than 0 is positive: positive integers are greater than 0.

Integers such as -4, -89, and -867253 are *negative*. Said differently, for n a natural number, an integer of the form $-n$ is negative. Negative integers are less than 0. 0 is neither positive nor negative.

Negation has the property that $--n = n$. Negation reverses the order of the values: since $4 < 7$, then $-4 > -7$, which is the same as $-7 < -4$. The set of ordered values in the integers looks like

$$\{\ldots, -4, -3, -2, -1, 0, 1, 2, 3, 4, \ldots\}.$$

Negative signs cancel out in multiplication and division: $-1 \times -1 = 1$ and $-1/-1 = 1$. For any integers n and m, we have relationships like $n \times -m = -n \times m = -(n \times m)$.

If n is a whole number, then $(-1)^n$ is 1 if n is even and is -1 if n is odd.

Given an integer n, we define the *absolute value* of n to be 0 if n is 0, n if n is positive, and $-n$ if n is negative. We use vertical bars $|n|$ to denote the absolute value of n. Therefore

$$|n| = \begin{cases} n & \text{when } n > 0 \\ 0 & \text{when } n = 0 \\ -n & \text{when } n < 0. \end{cases}$$

Here are some examples:

$$|-87| = 87 \qquad |0| = 0 \qquad |231| = 231$$

Informally, you get the absolute value by discarding the negative sign in front of an integer if it is present. We could also say that the absolute value of an integer is how far it is away from 0, where we don't worry whether it is less than or greater than 0.

For integers n and m, we always have $|n \times m| = |n| \times |m|$ and $|n + m| \leq |n| + |m|$.

Absolute value is a measurement of size or length, which generalizes to other algebraic and geometric concepts. In fact, for a qubit's quantum state, absolute values are related to the probabilities of getting one answer or another in a computation.

Examples

$n + 3$ gives us n increased by 3, and $n + -3 = n - 3$ yields n decreased by 3:

- $7 + 3$ means we increase 7 by 3 to get 10.
- $7 + -3$ means we decrease 7 by 3 to get 4.
- $-7 + 3$ means we increase -7 by 3 to get -4.
- $-7 + -3$ means we decrease -7 by 3 to get -10

Considering the usual rules for addition and the above, $n + -m = n - m$ and $n - -m = n + m$ for any two integers n and m.

With this, you can see that the integers are closed under subtraction: if you subtract one integer from another, you get another integer. Given addition and negation, we can get away with not using subtraction, but we keep it for convenience and to reduce the complexity of expressions.

You may have been first introduced to these rules and properties when you were young. I repeat them here so you think more generally about addition, subtraction, and negation operations as they apply to arbitrary integers versus simply doing some arithmetic.

Returning to negation, for any integer, there is one and only one number you can add to it and get 0. If we have 33, we would add -33 to it to get 0. If we started with -74 then adding 74 yields 0. 0 is significant here because it is the identity element for addition.

Any number with absolute value 1 is a *unit*. The integers have two units: 1 and -1.

A *prime* is a positive integer greater than 1 whose only factors under multiplication are 1 and itself. These are primes:

$$2 = 1 \times 2 \qquad 3 = 1 \times 3 \qquad 37 = 1 \times 37$$

These are not primes:

$$0 \qquad 1 \qquad 4 = 2 \times 2 \qquad -25 = -5 \times 5 \qquad 500 = 2^2 \times 5^3$$

When one number divides another evenly, we use "|" between them. Since 5 divides 500, we write 5 | 500. An integer that is the product of two or more primes (which may be the same, such as 7×7) is composite.

3×2 and 2×3 are equivalent factorizations of 6. We usually display factorizations with the individual factors going from small to large.

You can uniquely factor a nonzero integer into zero or more primes times a unit, with some primes possibly repeated. In the factorization of 500 above, we repeated the prime 2 twice and the prime 5 three times.

There are an infinite number of primes. The study of primes and their generalizations is relevant to several areas of mathematics, especially number theory.

The integers **Z** are the infinite ordered extension of **W** formed by appending the negative values $-1, -2, -3, -4, \dots$. The integers have a unique identity element 0 such that for any integer n, there exists a unique additive inverse $-n$ such that $n + -n = 0$.

Z is closed under subtraction and the commutative addition and multiplication operations. **Z** is not closed under division.

Multiplication distributes over addition.

Taking a more geometric approach to the integers, we can draw the familiar number line with the negative values to the left of 0 and positive values to the right.

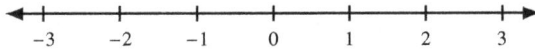

$$\xleftarrow{\hspace{0.5cm}} \underset{-3}{+} \quad \underset{-2}{+} \quad \underset{-1}{+} \quad \underset{0}{+} \quad \underset{1}{+} \quad \underset{2}{+} \quad \underset{3}{+} \xrightarrow{\hspace{0.5cm}}$$

This visualization helps you think about the integers. The number line is *not* the set of integers but connects the algebra with a geometric aid.

Negating an integer corresponds to reflecting it to the other side of 0. Negating an integer twice means moving it across 0 and back to where it started. Hence, double negation effectively does nothing. The absolute value means measuring how far to the left or right an integer is from 0.

Adding 0 does not move the position of a number on the line. Adding a positive integer n means moving n units to the right of the number. Adding a negative integer n means moving $|n|$ units to the left.

Exercise 3.1

Describe the movements on the number line when you subtract a positive or negative integer.

Exercise 3.2

Using the number line, think about why negation reverses the order of two integers. That is, if $n < m$, why is $-n > -m$?

A line is one-dimensional. It takes only one number to precisely position a point anywhere on the line. Hence, we can write (7) as the coordinate of the point 7 units to the right of 0. On this line, we call (0) the *origin*, which is another example of a special role for 0.

Mathematicians often work by taking a problem in one domain and translating it into another that they understand better or have better tools and techniques. Here I've shown some of the simple ways you can translate back and forth between the algebra and geometry of integers.

3.4 Rational numbers

The rational numbers, denoted **Q**, take care of the problem of the integers not being closed under division by nonzero values.

3.4.1 Fractions

Let's start by talking about fractions, also known as the rational numbers, in the way a teacher may have introduced them to you. We then relate this review to what we have in the big picture with $\mathbf{Q}$.

Given a loaf of bread, if we cut it right down the middle, we say we have divided it into halves. Fraction-wise, one-half $= \frac{1}{2}$. The two halves equal one whole loaf, so $\frac{1}{2} + \frac{1}{2} = 2 \times \frac{1}{2} = 1$. Two halves are $\frac{2}{2}$, which is 1. Four halves would make two loaves: $\frac{4}{2} = 2$.

Considering whole loaves, $\frac{1}{1}$ is one loaf, $\frac{2}{1}$ is two loaves, and $\frac{147}{1}$ is one hundred and forty-seven loaves. We can represent any integer n as a fraction $\frac{n}{1}$.

To multiply fractions, we multiply the tops (*numerators*) together, put those over the product (the result of multiplication) of the bottoms (*denominators*), and then simplify the result.

If we get another loaf, and this time we cut it into three equal parts or thirds, each part is $\frac{1}{3}$ of the entire loaf. The three thirds equal the whole loaf, so $\frac{1}{3} + \frac{1}{3} + \frac{1}{3} = 1$.

If we instead cut the loaf of bread so that there are two pieces, but one is one-third of the loaf, and the other is two-thirds of the loaf, the equation is

$$\frac{1}{3} + \frac{2}{3} = \frac{3}{3} = 1 \,.$$

If we cut the one-third piece in half and divide the two-thirds evenly piece in four, we get six equal pieces, all of which add up to the original loaf. If we push two of the one-sixth pieces together, we return to a third. So $\frac{1}{6} + \frac{1}{6} = 2 \times \frac{1}{6} = \frac{1}{3}$. Written another way and in more detail:

$$2 \times \frac{1}{6} = \frac{2}{6} = \frac{2 \times 1}{2 \times 3} = \frac{2}{2} \times \frac{1}{3} = 1 \times \frac{1}{3} = \frac{1}{3} \,.$$

Think of "$\times$" as meaning "of." So one-half of a one-third being one-sixth is

$$\frac{1}{2} \times \frac{1}{3} = \frac{1}{6} \,.$$

Arithmetic, notably addition and subtraction, is easy only when we are dealing with fractions that have the same denominators, such as halves (2), thirds (3), and sixths (6), as above. When the denominators differ, we need to find the least common denominator (lcd).

What do we get if we push another one-sixth of a loaf of bread onto one-third of a loaf?

$$\frac{1}{6} + \frac{1}{3} = \frac{1}{6} + 2 \times \frac{1}{6} = 3 \times \frac{1}{6} = \frac{3}{6} = \frac{1}{2} \,.$$

In this case, the least common denominator is simply 6 because we can always represent some number of thirds as twice that number of sixths.

What about $\frac{1}{3} + \frac{1}{5}$? We cannot easily represent thirds as fifths, so we have to subdivide each to have a common size. In this case, the smallest size is fifteenths: $\frac{1}{3} = \frac{5}{15}$ and $\frac{1}{5} = \frac{3}{15}$.

$$\frac{1}{3} + \frac{1}{5} = \frac{5}{15} + \frac{3}{15} = \frac{8}{15}.$$

You might not think that fifteenths are as easy as halves, thirds, fourths, or fifths, but one fraction is as good as any other. In this example, 15 is the *least common multiple* (lcm) of 3 and 5: it is the smallest nonzero positive integer divisible by 3 and 5.

An example shows you how to compute the least common multiple of two integers. Let's work with -18 and 30. Since we care only about finding a positive integer, we can forget the negative sign in front of 18.

Factor each number into primes: $18 = 2 \times 9 = 2 \times 3^2$ and $30 = 2 \times 3 \times 5$. We gather these primes into a new collection, which is initially empty.

For each prime in *either* factorization, put it in the collection with its exponent if it is not already there. Otherwise, if that prime in the factorization has a larger exponent than it does in the collection, replace it in the collection. For 18 and 30:

- The collection starts empty as { }.
- Process $18 = 2 \times 9 = 2 \times 3^2$ prime by prime. 2 is not already in the collection, so insert it, yielding $\{2\}$. 3 is not already in the collection with any exponent, so insert 3^2, yielding $\{2, 3^2\}$.
- Process $30 = 2 \times 3 \times 5$ prime by prime: 2 is already in the collection with the same exponent, so ignore it. 3 is already in the collection with the larger exponent 2, so ignore it. 5 is not in the collection, so insert it.
- The final collection is $\{2, 3^2, 5\}$.

Multiplying all the numbers in the collection yields 90, the least common multiple. We have ensured that each of the original numbers divides into 90 and that 90 is the smallest number for which this works.

When the numbers have no primes in common, the least common multiple is simply the absolute value of their product.

When the numerators are nontrivial (not equal to 1), we need to do some multiplication with them. As above, suppose we have found 15 to be the least common multiple of 3 and 5. Hence, it is the least common denominator in $\frac{2}{3} + \frac{7}{5}$.

This is how we do the addition:

$$\frac{2}{3} + \frac{7}{5} = \frac{5}{5} \times \frac{2}{3} + \frac{3}{3} \times \frac{7}{5}$$

$$= \frac{5 \times 2}{5 \times 3} + \frac{3 \times 7}{3 \times 5}$$

$$= \frac{10}{15} + \frac{21}{15}$$

$$= \frac{31}{15}.$$

Subtraction is similar.

Exercise 3.3

What is $\frac{5}{12} - \frac{7}{16}$?

To raise a rational number to a whole number exponent, raise the numerator and denominator to that exponent. For example:

$$\left(\frac{-3}{4}\right)^5 = \frac{(-3)^5}{4^5} = \frac{-243}{1024}.$$

To simplify a fraction, you express it in the lowest terms, which means you have factored out common primes from the numerator and denominator. To further normalize it, make it contain at most one negative sign and, if it is present, put it in the numerator.

Examples

$$\frac{1}{-2} = \frac{-1}{2} \qquad\qquad \frac{5}{5} = \frac{5^1}{5^1} = \frac{5^0}{5^0} = \frac{1}{1} = 1$$

$$\frac{2}{8} = \frac{2^1}{2^3} = \frac{2^0}{2^2} = \frac{1}{4} \qquad\qquad \frac{12}{30} = \frac{2^2 \times 3^1}{2^1 \times 3^1 \times 5^1} = \frac{2^1}{5^1} = \frac{2}{5}$$

If a prime is present in the numerator and denominator, we have that prime divided by itself, which is 1. That means we can remove it from both. This is *cancellation*.

There is no integer strictly between two consecutive integers, such as 3 and 4. However, you can always find a rational number between two different rational numbers. Just average them:

$$\frac{3+4}{2} = \frac{7}{2} \quad \text{or, more generally,} \quad \frac{n + (n+1)}{2} = \frac{2n+1}{2} = n + \frac{1}{2}.$$

So, while we proceed from integer to integer by adding or subtracting 1, we can't slip between an integer and its successor and find another integer.

Integers are infinite in each of the positive and negative directions, and so are the rational numbers. There are an infinite number of rational numbers between any two distinct rational numbers.

Greatest common divisor

A more direct way of calculating the least common multiple is via the greatest common divisor.

Let a and b be two nonzero integers. We can assume that they are positive. The *greatest common divisor* (gcd) g is the largest positive integer such that $g \mid a$ and $g \mid b$. Necessarily, $g \leq a$ and $g \leq b$.

An important property of the greatest common divisor g is that there are integers n and m so that $an + bm = g$.

If $g = 1$, we say that a and b are *coprime*.

Given this definition of gcd, we compute the least common multiple (lcm) by

$$\text{lcm}(a, b) = \frac{a\,b}{\gcd(a, b)}.$$

If either a or b is negative, use its absolute value.

To calculate $\gcd(a, b)$, we use quotients and remainders in *Euclid's algorithm*. By the properties of division for positive integers a and b with $a \geq b$, there exist nonnegative integers q and r such that

$$a = bq + r$$

with $0 \leq r < b$. q is the *quotient* upon dividing a by b, and r is the *remainder*. Because $r < b$, q is as large as it can be. If $r = 0$, then $b \mid a$ and $\gcd(a, b) = b$.

If $a = 11$ and $b = 2$, $q = 5$ and $r = 1$. We say, "11 divided by 2 is 5 with remainder 1."

Let's suppose n divides a and b. Then n divides $a - bq = r$ because it divides both terms in the subtract on the right-hand side. In particular, for $n = \gcd(a, b)$,

$$\gcd(a, b) = \gcd(b, r).$$

We have replaced the calculation of the gcd of a and b with that of the gcd of b and r, a smaller pair of numbers. We can keep repeating this process, getting smaller and smaller pairs. Since $r \geq 0$, we eventually stop.

Once we get an r that is 0, we take the previous remainder. That is the gcd.

Exercise 3.4

Compute gcd(15295, 38019). Factor the answer if you can.

Euclid initially used subtractions, but we can use a faster method with quotients and remainders with modern computers.

The gcd function in the Python **math** module computes the greatest common divisor:

```
import math
math.gcd(96, 2560)
```

32

3.4.2   Getting formal again

Let's rewind now and look at the rational numbers and their operations in the ways we did with the natural numbers, whole numbers, and integers.

Equality

Two expressions $\frac{a}{b}$ and $\frac{c}{d}$ with integers $a, b \neq 0, c,$ and $d \neq 0$ represent the same rational number if $a \times d = c \times b$.

Addition

Cross-multiply the numerators and denominators, add the results to get the new numerator, multiply the denominators to get the new denominator, and simplify.

For nonzero integers b and d,

$$\frac{a}{b} + \frac{c}{d} = \frac{a \times d + c \times b}{b \times d}.$$

Alternatively, convert each fraction to have the same least common denominator, add the numerators, and simplify.

Exercise 3.5

How would you express $\frac{a}{b} + c$ for the integer c?

Subtraction

Cross-multiply the numerators and denominators, subtract the results to get the new numerator, multiply the denominators to yield the new denominator, and simplify.

For nonzero integers b and d,

$$\frac{a}{b} - \frac{c}{d} = \frac{a \times d - c \times b}{b \times d}.$$

Alternatively, convert each fraction to have the same least common denominator, subtract the numerators, and simplify.

> **Exercise 3.6**
>
> How would you express $\frac{a}{b} - c$ for the integer c? $c - \frac{a}{b}$?

Negation

Negating a value is the same as multiplying it by -1. Negative signs "cancel" across the numerator and denominator.

For nonzero b,

$$-\frac{a}{b} = \frac{-a}{b} = \frac{-1 \times a}{b} = \frac{a}{-1 \times b} = \frac{a}{-b}.$$

By convention, an explicit fraction is often written with the "$-$" in the numerator if there is a sign:

$$\frac{-2}{3} \quad \text{instead of} \quad \frac{2}{-3}.$$

They are equivalent mathematically, of course.

Multiplication

Multiply the numerators to yield the new numerator, multiply the denominators to get the new denominator, and simplify.

For nonzero integers b and d,

$$\frac{a}{b} \times \frac{c}{d} = \frac{a \times c}{b \times d}.$$

> **Exercise 3.7**
>
> How would you express the multiplication of $\frac{a}{b}$ by the integer c?

Inversion

Form the inverse of a nonzero rational number by swapping the numerator and denominator.

For nonzero integers a and b,

$$\frac{1}{\left(\frac{a}{b}\right)} = \left(\frac{a}{b}\right)^{-1} = \frac{b}{a}.$$

Raising a rational number to the -1 power means computing its inverse.

Division

Divide two rational numbers by multiplying the first by the inverse of the second.

For nonzero integers b, c, and d,

$$\frac{\left(\frac{a}{b}\right)}{\left(\frac{c}{d}\right)} = \frac{a}{b} \times \frac{1}{\left(\frac{c}{d}\right)} = \frac{a}{b} \times \frac{d}{c} = \frac{a \times d}{b \times c}.$$

Exercise 3.8

How would you express the division of $\frac{a}{b}$ by the nonzero integer c?

Exponentiation

Like other numbers, raising a rational number to the 0th power yields 1. Raising it to a negative integer power means swapping the numerator and denominator and raising each to the absolute value of the exponent.

For nonzero integer b or nonzero a if n is a negative integer,

$$\left(\frac{a}{b}\right)^n = \begin{cases} \dfrac{a^n}{b^n} & \text{for integer } n > 0 \\ 1 & \text{for } n = 0 \\ \dfrac{b^{-n}}{a^{-n}} & \text{for integer } n < 0. \end{cases}$$

The rational numbers **Q** is the infinite ordered extension of **Z** formed by appending the multiplicative inverses $\frac{1}{n}$ of all nonzero integers n and then further extending by defining values

$$\frac{n}{m} = n \times \frac{1}{m}$$

for integers n and nonzero m.

The rational numbers have a unique identity element **1** such that for any nonzero r, there exists a unique multiplicative inverse $\frac{1}{r}$ such that $\frac{1}{r} \times r = 1$.

Q is closed under subtraction, the commutative addition and multiplication operations, and division by nonzero values.

3.4.3 Is $\sqrt{2}$ rational?

The rational numbers seem to finally solve most of our problems about doing arithmetic and getting a valid answer. However, even though $\sqrt{4}$ and $\sqrt{\frac{1}{25}}$ are both rational numbers, neither $\sqrt{2}$ nor $\sqrt{\frac{1}{5}}$ is.

If $\sqrt{2}$ were rational, there would exist positive integers m and n such that $\frac{m}{n} = \sqrt{2}$, meaning that

$$\frac{m^2}{n^2} = 2.$$

We can assume m and n have no factors in common. This is key!

Let's show this is not possible. Every even integer is of the form $2k$ for some other integer k. Similarly, all odd integers are of the form $2k + 1$. Therefore, the square of an even integer looks like $4k^2$, which is even, and the square of an odd integer looks like

$$(2k + 1)^2 = 4k^2 + 4k + 1 = 2(2k^2 + 2k) + 1,$$

which is odd.

This also shows that if an even integer is a square, it is the square of an even integer. If an odd integer is a square, it is the square of an odd integer.

If $\frac{m^2}{n^2} = 2$, then $m^2 = 2n^2$, and so m^2. and therefore m, are even integers. So there is some integer j such that $m = 2j$ and $m^2 = 4j^2$.

We then have

$$m^2 = 4j^2 = 2n^2$$

or

$$2j^2 = n^2 .$$

As before, this shows that n^2 and n are *even*. So both m and n are even, and they share the factor 2.

But we assumed m and n have no factors in common, a contradiction! Thus, there exist no such m and n, and $\sqrt{2}$ *is not a rational number*.

Exercise 3.9

By similar methods, show $\sqrt{3}$ is not rational.

3.5 Real numbers

In this section, we look at the real numbers, denoted **R**, to conclude our analysis of the typical numbers most people encounter. Let's begin with decimals.

3.5.1 Decimals

A *decimal* expression for a real number looks like

- an optional minus sign,
- followed a finite number of the digits 0, 1, 2, 3, 4, 5, 6, 7, 8, and 9,
- followed by a period, also called the *decimal point*,
- followed by a finite or infinite number of digits.

In many parts of the world, the decimal point is a comma instead of a period, but I use the United States and UK convention here.

You may omit the decimal point if there are no digits after the decimal point.

We usually omit trailing 0s on the right when we use the number in a general mathematical context. We may keep them when they indicate the precision of a measurement or a numeric representation in computer code.

We usually omit any leading 0s on the left. We have

$$0 = 0. = .0 = 000.00$$
$$1 = 1. = 1.0 = 000001$$
$$-3.27 = -03.27 = -3.27000000000$$

By convention, it is common to have at least a single 0 before the decimal point and a single 0 after: 0.0 and −4.0, for example. As mentioned above, the explicit inclusion of 0s may have significance in numerical analysis.

The integer 1327 is a shorthand way of writing

$$1 \times 10^3 + 3 \times 10^2 + 2 \times 10^1 + 7 \times 10^0 .$$

Similarly, the integer −340 is

$$(-1) \times \left(3 \times 10^2 + 4 \times 10^1 + 0 \times 10^0 \right) .$$

We extend to the right of the decimal point by using negative powers of 10:

$$13.27 = 1 \times 10^1 + 3 \times 10^0 + 2 \times 10^{-1} + 7 \times 10^{-2}$$

$$-0.340 = (-1) \times \left(0 \times 10^0 + 3 \times 10^{-1} \times 4 \times 10^{-2} + 0 \times 10^{-3} \right)$$

The decimal point is at the place where we move from 10^0 to 10^{-1}.

Since 10^{-1} is $\frac{1}{10}$ = one-tenth, the digit immediately after the decimal point is said to be in the "tenths position." The one after that is the "hundredths position" because it corresponds to $10^{-2} = \frac{1}{100}$ = one-hundredth. We continue this way to the thousandth, ten-thousandth, hundred-thousandth, millionth, and further positions.

To convert a fraction such as $\frac{1}{2}$ to a decimal, we try to re-express it with a denominator equal to some power of ten. In this case, it is easy because $\frac{1}{2} = \frac{5}{10}$. So five-tenths is 0.5.

For $\frac{3}{8}$, we need to go up to $\frac{375}{1000}$:

$$\frac{3}{8} = \frac{3}{2^3} \times \frac{5^3}{5^3} = \frac{3}{2^3} \times \frac{125}{125}$$

$$= \frac{375}{1000} = \frac{300}{1000} + \frac{70}{1000} + \frac{5}{1000}$$

$$= \frac{3}{10} + \frac{7}{100} + \frac{5}{1000}$$

$$= 3 \times 10^{-1} + 7 \times 10^{-2} + 5 \times 10^{-3} = .375 .$$

Since $10 = 2 \times 5$, each power of 10 is the product of the same power of 2 times the same power of 5. That's why we chose 5^3 in the above example: $10^3 = 2^3 5^3$.

Repeating decimals

This method doesn't always work to convert a fraction to a decimal. The decimal expression of $\frac{1}{7}$ is

$$0.142857142857142857142857142857142857142857\ldots$$

Notice the section "142857" that repeats over and over.

0.**142857** 142857 142857 142857 142857 142857 142857...

It goes on repeating forever, block after adjacent block. This is an infinite decimal expansion. We write the repeating block with a line over it:

$$\frac{1}{7} = 0.\overline{142857}$$

Any rational number has a finite decimal expression or an infinite one with a repeating block.

We showed above how to go from a finite decimal expansion to a fraction: express the decimal as a sum of powers of 10 and then do the rational number arithmetic.

$$2.13 = 2 \times 10^0 + 1 \times 10^{-1} + 3 \times 10^{-2}$$
$$= 2 + \frac{1}{10} + \frac{3}{100} = \frac{213}{100}.$$

This fraction is already simplified, but in general, we need to do that at the end.

The general process is slightly more complicated. Let

$$r = 0.\overline{153846}.$$

The repeating block has **6** digits immediately after the decimal point. Multiply both sides by $10^6 = 1000000$:

$$1000000\,r = 153846.\overline{153846}$$

and so

$$1000000\,r - r = 153846.\overline{153846} - 0.\overline{153846}$$

which gives

$$999999\,r = 153846$$
$$r = \frac{153846}{999999} = \frac{2}{13}.$$

Exercise 3.10

How would you adjust this if the repeating block begins more to the right of the decimal point?

If the entire decimal expression does not repeat, you can separate it into a finite expansion plus the repeating one divided by the appropriate power of 10:

$$3.2\overline{153846} = 3.2 + 0.0\overline{153846}$$

$$= \frac{32}{10} + \frac{2}{13} \times 10^{-1}$$

$$= \frac{32}{10} + \frac{2}{130}$$

$$= \frac{32}{10} \times \frac{13}{13} + \frac{2}{130}$$

$$= \frac{416}{130} + \frac{2}{130}$$

$$= \frac{418}{130} = \frac{209}{65}$$

These calculations show the relationships between rational numbers and their decimal expansions.

Exercise 3.11

What is the rational number corresponding to

$$0.\overline{9} \ ?$$

If r is a real number, then $\lfloor r \rfloor$, the *floor* of r, is the largest integer $\leq r$. Similarly, $\lceil r \rceil$, the *ceiling* of r, is the smallest integer $\geq r$.

Scientific notation

Scientific notation formats a finite decimal d as a decimal $0 \leq |a| < 10$ times a power of 10.

$$1.0 = 1.0 \times 10^0$$

$$153846 = 1.53846 \times 10^5$$

$$1538.46 = 1.53846 \times 10^3$$

$$-0.007363 = -7.363 \times 10^{-3}$$

In calculators and programming languages, it is common to replace the 10 with an uppercase or lowercase ''e'', followed by a sign. In Python, we have

```
1.6 / 100000000000000000000000000000000000000000

1.6e-41

for n in [0.0, 0.5, 1.0, 153846, 1538.46, -0.007363]:
    print(f"{n:E}")

0.000000E+00
5.000000E-01
1.000000E+00
1.538460E+05
1.538460E+03
-7.363000E-03
```

> Note that the ''e'' we use in scientific notation shows us where the exponent part of the number begins. It is not the *e* we use as the base of the natural logarithms in the next section.

Having one digit before the decimal point is a normalized notation. Programming languages such as Python allow more digits and allow you to skip the decimal point:

```
[1.2e30, 1200.e27, 1200000e24]

[1.2e+30, 1.2e+30, 1.2e+30]
```

3.5.2 Irrationals and limits

The case we have not considered is an infinite decimal expansion d that does not have an infinitely repeating block. Not being rational, d is an *irrational number*. The real numbers are the rational numbers and all the irrational numbers. Since $\sqrt{2}$ is not rational, it must be irrational.

Let's consider the approximation of a real number by a decimal.

$$\pi = 3.14159265358979323846264338327950\ldots$$

is an irrational number and so has no infinitely repeating blocks. It is not $\frac{22}{7}$, and it is not 3.14. Those are rational and decimal approximations to π, and not even good ones.

π exists as a number even though you cannot write it down as a fraction or write out the infinite number of digits that express it. π is a real number, but it is not in **Q**.

Consider

$$3.1 \to 3.14 \to 3.141 \to 3.1415 \to$$
$$3.14159 \to 3.141592 \to 3.1415926 \to \ldots$$

This sequence has rational numbers expressed as decimals that get closer and closer to the actual value of π.

Want to be within one millionth of the actual value?

$$\pi - 3.1415926 < 0.000001 \,.$$

Within one hundred-millionth?

$$\pi - 3.141592653 < 0.00000001 \,.$$

We could keep going. We have a sequence of rational numbers such that if we set a closeness threshold such as one-millionth, then one member of the sequence and all that follow it are at least that close to π. We say the irrational number π is the *limit* of the given sequence of rational numbers.

If we make the threshold smaller, we can find a possibly later sequence member so we will be at least that close from then on. We say the above sequence *converges* to π.

Think about this. All the sequence members are rational numbers, but the limit is not. Informally, if we take the rational numbers and throw in all the limits of convergent sequences of them, we get the real numbers.

Of course, there are sequences of rational numbers that converge to rational numbers.

$$\frac{1}{1}, \frac{1}{2}, \frac{1}{3}, \ldots, \frac{1}{n}, \ldots$$

converges to the limit 0. Here, we let n get larger and larger, and we write

$$\lim_{n \to \infty} \frac{1}{n} = 0 \,.$$

Similarly,

$$-\frac{2}{1}, -\frac{3}{2}, -\frac{4}{3}, \ldots, -\frac{n+1}{n}, \ldots$$

converges to -1.

For a nonobvious example, consider

$$\lim_{n \to \infty} \left(1 + \frac{1}{n}\right)^n \,.$$

Even though n is getting bigger, the expression inside the parentheses is getting closer to 1, but we are raising it to larger and larger powers. As n gets bigger, the computed values appear to converge.

```
# compute for powers of 10

for t in range(10):
    n = 10**t
    print(f"{n}: {(1.0 + 1.0/n)**n}")


    1: 2.0
    10: 2.5937424601000023
    100: 2.7048138294215285
    1000: 2.7169239322355936
    10000: 2.7181459268249255
    100000: 2.7182682371922975
    1000000: 2.7182804690957534
    10000000: 2.7182816941320818
    100000000: 2.7182817983473577
    1000000000: 2.7182820520115603
```

This sequence converges to $e = 2.718281828459045235360\ldots$, the base of the natural logarithms and an irrational number. Like π, e is a special value in mathematics and shows up ''naturally'' in many contexts.

The sequence

$$1, 2, 3, 4, 5, \ldots, n, \ldots$$

does not converge to any finite rational number. We call it a *divergent sequence*.

We define the real numbers **R** as the extension of **Q** that contains the limits of all convergent sequences of rational numbers. Furthermore, the real numbers are closed under taking the limits of convergent sequences of real numbers: a convergent sequence of real numbers has a real number as its limit.

Closure, closure, closure. The concept is fundamental to the kinds of numbers we use every day.

Limits are essential in calculus. The idea that we can have an infinite sequence of numbers that converges to a fixed and unique value is unlike anything most people have seen earlier in their mathematical studies. It can be a scary and daunting concept at first.

Remember above when I asked you to compute $0.99999\ldots$;? This is the limit of the sequence

$$0.9$$
$$0.99$$
$$0.999$$
$$0.9999$$
$$0.99999$$

$$\cdots$$

Every time we move to the next sequence member, we put another 9 on the far right. It appears the limit is 1. If you want to be within one quadrillionth of 1, 10^{-15}, then go out to 0.9999999999999999. However close you want to be to 1, you can put enough 9s at the right end so you are at least that close, and every member of the sequence after it is too. The sequence converges to 1, its limit.

We can also consider sequences where each member is a sum that builds on the previous member. This sequence

$$1$$
$$1 - \frac{1}{3}$$
$$1 - \frac{1}{3} + \frac{1}{5}$$
$$1 - \frac{1}{3} + \frac{1}{5} - \frac{1}{7}$$
$$1 - \frac{1}{3} + \frac{1}{5} - \frac{1}{7} + \frac{1}{9}$$

$$\cdots$$

converges to $\frac{\pi}{4}$, but it does so excruciatingly slowly. For use with computer calculations, it's critical to find sequences that converge quickly. [235]

Exercise 3.12

If you know Python, write code that computes the first ten members of this sequence.

3.5.3 Binary forms

Just as we can write a whole number in base 10 form using the digits 0, 1, 2, 3, 4, 5, 6, 7, 8, and 9, we can also use the bits 0 and 1 to represent it in binary form. We saw examples of this in section 2.2.

This algorithm converts from decimal to binary for w in $\mathbf{W}$:

1. If $w = 0$, the result is also 0, and we are finished.
2. Otherwise, let b be an initially empty placeholder where we put the bits.
3. If w is odd, put a 1 to the left of anything in b and set w to $w - 1$. Otherwise, put a 0 to the left of anything in b. In both cases, w is now even, and we set w to $w \div 2$.
4. If $w = 0$, we are finished, and b is the answer. Otherwise, go back to step 3.

For example, let $w = 13$. Initially, b is empty.

- w is odd, so b is now 1, and we set $w = (w - 1) \div 2 = 6$.
- w is even, so b is now 01, and we set $w = w \div 2 = 3$.
- w is odd, so b is now 101, and we set $w = (w - 1) \div 2 = 1$.
- w is odd, so b is now 1101, and we set $w = (w - 1) \div 2 = 0$.
- $w = 0$, and we are done. The representation of w in binary is $b = 1101_2$.

We put the subscript 2 at the end of the value for b to remind ourselves that we are in base 2.

Exercise 3.13

For a given initial w, how many times do we need to divide by 2 in this algorithm? Express this as $O(f(w))$ for some function f.

Suppose we start with a decimal r with $0 \leq r < 1$. We want to create a base 2 representation using just 0s and 1s to the right of the "binary point."

We expand as we usually do, but instead of using negative powers of 10, we use negative powers of 2. For example,

$$.011_2 = 0 \times 2^{-1} + 1 \times 2^{-2} + 1 \times 2^{-3}.$$

In base 10, this is $\frac{1}{4} + \frac{1}{8} = \frac{3}{8} = .375$.

Our algorithm for converting the fractional part of a real number to binary is reminiscent of the one above.

1. If $r = 0$, the result is also 0, and we are finished.
2. Otherwise, let b be a placeholder where we put the bits, initially containing only ".".
3. Multiply r by 2 to get s. Since $0 \leq r < 1$, $0 \leq s < 2$. If $s \geq 1$, put a 1 to the right of anything in b and set $r = s - 1$. Otherwise, put a 0 to the right of anything in b and set $r = s$.
4. If $r = 0$, we are finished, and b is the answer. Otherwise, go back to step 3.

This process sounds reasonable. Let's try it out with $r = .375_{10}$ to confirm our example above. r is not 0, and b starts with the binary point ".".

1. Set $s = 2r = .75$, which is less than 1. We append a 0 to the right in b and set $r = s = .75$. b is now $.0$.
2. Set $s = 2r = 1.5$, which is greater than or equal to 1. Append a 1 to the right in b and set $r = s - 1 = .5$. b is now $.01$.
3. Set $s = 2r = 1$, which is greater than or equal to 1. Append a 1 to the right in b and set $r = s - 1 = 0$. b is now $.011$.
4. Since $r = 0$, we are finished, and the answer is $.011_2$.

In a less verbose table form, this looks like

s	b	r
	$.$	.375
.75	.0	.75
1.5	.01	.5
1	.011	0

The first line holds the initial settings. The answer is b on the last line where $r = 0$.

The binary and decimal examples produce equivalent results. Let's do another with $r = .2_{10}$.

s	b	r
	$.$	.2
.4	.0	.4
.8	.00	.8
1.6	.001	.6
1.2	.0011	.2
.4	.00110	.4
$\vdots$	$\vdots$	$\vdots$

I stopped because the process started to repeat itself. Put another way, and using the notation we employed for repeating decimals,

$$.2_{10} = .\overline{0011}_2 .$$

There is no exact finite binary expansion for the decimal 0.2: it repeats in a block.

The following hold in parallel to the decimal case:

- A base 10 rational number has either a finite binary expansion or repeats in blocks.
- A repeating-block binary expansion is a base 10 rational number.
- An irrational real number has an infinite, nonrepeating-block binary expansion.
- An infinite binary expansion that has no repeating blocks is irrational.

Given a real value with the whole number part w and decimal part $0 \leq t < 1$, you create the full binary form by concatenating the binary forms of each. The binary expansion of the decimal 5.125 is 110.001_2, for example.

Exercise 3.14

What is the binary expansion of 17.0156625_{10}? Of 4/3?

3.5.4 Continued fractions

There is yet another expansion for real numbers, the *continued fraction*. Two examples are on the right-hand sides in each of the following:

$$\tfrac{15}{11} = 1\tfrac{4}{11} = 1 + \cfrac{1}{2 + \cfrac{1}{1 + \cfrac{1}{3}}} \qquad\qquad \tfrac{11}{15} = 0 + \cfrac{1}{1 + \cfrac{1}{2 + \cfrac{1}{1 + \cfrac{1}{3}}}}$$

We write the integer portion out front and then construct a recurring sequence of fractions with 1 in the numerators.

Working through the example on the left for $\tfrac{15}{11}$ shows you the algorithm. Begin with writing the integer portion out front.

First approximation:

$$1$$

What's left is $\tfrac{4}{11}$. Invert this to get $\tfrac{11}{4} = 2\tfrac{3}{4}$. Take the whole number part and use this as the second part of the expansion.

Second approximation:

$$1 + \cfrac{1}{2}$$

Invert the remaining fractional part to get $\frac{4}{3} = 1\frac{1}{3}$. The whole number part goes into the expansion.

Third approximation:

$$1 + \cfrac{1}{2 + \cfrac{1}{1}}$$

Invert the remaining fractional part $\frac{1}{3}$ to get 3 for the expansion. There is no nonzero fractional part, and we are finished.

Final expression:

$$1 + \cfrac{1}{2 + \cfrac{1}{1 + \cfrac{1}{3}}}$$

This is a finite continued fraction expansion since there are only a finite number of terms. Working through the fraction arithmetic, you end up with a rational number if you start with a finite continued fraction. We are doing a variation of Euclid's algorithm from section 3.4.1.

Even more interesting, every rational number terminates in this way when you do the expansion. We don't have to worry about repeating blocks for rational numbers converted to continued fractions as we do with decimal and binary expansions.

Exercise 3.15

What is the continued fraction expansion of $\frac{9}{7}$? Of $-\frac{97}{13}$? Of 0.375?

When we use many variables or an indeterminate number of them, we can't always use specific letter variable names such as a, b, c, x, y, and z. Therefore, we use subscripted variables such as x_0 and y_j whenever necessary. 0 and j are *subscripts*. For example, some expressions involve n constants, and we show them as $a_1, a_2, \ldots, a_n$.

Using variables, we can write a finite continued fraction as

$$b_0 + \cfrac{1}{b_1 + \cfrac{1}{b_2 + \cfrac{1}{\ddots + \cfrac{1}{b_n}}}}$$

Here, all the b_j are in **Z** and $b_j > 0$ for $j > 0$. That is, b_0 can be negative, but the rest must be positive integers. An alternative and much shorter notation for the above is

$$[b_0; b_1, b_2, \ldots, b_{n-1}, b_n] \ .$$

We can also represent a rational number using a form with one more term,

$$[b_0; b_1, b_2, \ldots, b_{n-1}, b_n - 1, 1] \ ,$$

but I prefer the shorter version. If we decide that the last term cannot be 1, there is a unique continued fraction representation for a rational number.

Exercise 3.16

Let $r > 0$ be in **R**. Is

$$r \, [b_0; b_1, b_2, \ldots, b_n] = [r b_0; r b_1, r b_2, \ldots, r b_n] \ ?$$

If not, show a counterexample.

What if we are given an infinite expansion? It can't be a rational number, but it converges to an irrational real number.

Every irrational real number has a unique infinite continued fraction expansion

$$f = [b_0; b_1, b_2, b_3, \ldots] \ .$$

Infinite continued fractions can have repeating blocks or blocks that repeat via a formula. A line over a block means that it repeats, as usual.

The first expansion in the table in Figure 3.1 is the "golden ratio," while the last is for e, the base of the natural logarithms. In the expansion for e, note how the integer between the two ones is incremented by 2 in every block.

$$\frac{1 + \sqrt{5}}{2} = [1; \overline{1}] \qquad \sqrt{19} = [4; \overline{2, 1, 3, 1, 2, 8}]$$

$$1 + \sqrt{2} = [2; \overline{2}] \qquad \tan(1) = [1; 1,\ 1, 3,\ 1, 5,\ 1, 7,\ 1, 9, \ldots]$$

$$\frac{3 + \sqrt{13}}{2} = [3; \overline{3}] \qquad e = [2; 1,\ 2, 1, 1,\ 4, 1, 1,\ 6, 1, 1, \ldots]$$

$$\sqrt{3} = [1; \overline{1, 2}] \qquad \pi = [3; 7, 15, 1, 292, 1, 1, 1, 2, 1, 3, \ldots]$$

Figure 3.1: Several continued fraction expansions

Exercise 3.17

Calculate the first 6 digits of the golden ratio from its continued fraction.

Let's revisit the first two examples, which I now write in short form:

$$\frac{15}{11} = [1; 2, 1, 3] \qquad \frac{11}{15} = [0; 1, 2, 1, 3] \,.$$

What do you notice about these? First, the numbers are reciprocals; second, they have the same expansion, except the right-hand one has a 0 at the beginning. This situation is true in general.

Let r be in **Q** with $0 < r < 1$. If its continued fraction expansion is

$$[0; b_1, b_2, \ldots, b_n] \,,$$

then the expansion for $\frac{1}{r}$ is

$$[b_1; b_2, \ldots, b_n] \,.$$

On the other hand, if $r \geq 1$ with expansion

$$[b_0; b_1, b_2, \ldots, b_n] \,,$$

then the expansion for $\frac{1}{r}$ is

$$[0; b_0, b_1, b_2, \ldots, b_n] \,.$$

Given an infinite continued fraction $f = [b_0; b_1, b_2, \ldots]$, it's natural to look at the sequence of finite fractions, the *convergents* of f,

$$f_0 = [b_0;\,] = \frac{x_0}{y_0}$$

$$f_1 = [b_0; b_1] = \frac{x_1}{y_1}$$

$$f_2 = [b_0; b_1, b_2] = \frac{x_2}{y_2}$$

$$\vdots$$

$$f_n = [b_0; b_1, b_2, b_3, \ldots, b_n] = \frac{x_n}{y_n},$$

and ask about the relationship between f and the f_j. Each x_j is an integer, and each y_j is a positive integer. We assume the f_j are in reduced form (that is, $\frac{1}{2}$ and not $\frac{3}{6}$).

The convergents f_j have the following properties with respect to a specific convergent f_n:

- $f_1 > f_3 > f_5 > \ldots > f_n$ for all f_j with odd $j < n$.
- $f_2 < f_4 < f_6 < \ldots < f_n$ for all f_j with even $j < n$.
- If $j < k < n$ then $|f_n - f_k| < |f_n - f_j|$.

The convergents oscillate above and below f_n, always getting closer. This example shows the rapid convergence to $\sqrt{3}$:

With f as above,

$$f_2 = [b_0; b_1, b_2] = b_0 + \cfrac{1}{b_1 + \cfrac{1}{b_2}}$$

$$= \frac{b_0 b_1 b_2 + b_2 + b_0}{b_1 b_2 + 1} = \frac{b_2(b_0 b_1 + 1) + b_0}{b_1 b_2 + 1}.$$

Exercise 3.18

Compute f_1, x_1, and y_1, and f_3, x_3, y_3. Establish a guess about how to compute the x_n and y_n given the values for $n-1$ and $n-2$. Confirm if this works for f_4, x_4, and y_4.

Convergence properties of continued fractions

We need the following result, which we do not prove, for our analysis of Shor's factoring algorithm in Chapter 10, "From Circuits to Algorithms": [122]

Let r in $\mathbf{R}$ be the value of the infinite continued fraction $f = [b_0; b_1, b_2, \dots]$. Let $f_j = \frac{x_j}{y_j}$ be the convergents.

- Each convergent is a reduced fraction. That is, $\gcd(x_j, y_j) = 1$.
- If $k > j$ then $y_k > y_j$.
- The denominators y_j are increasing exponentially:

$$y_j \geq 2^{\frac{j-1}{2}}.$$

- We can approximate r as closely as we wish by computing a divergent with large enough j:

$$\left| r - f_j \right| = \left| r - \frac{x_j}{y_j} \right| < \frac{1}{y_j y_{j+1}}.$$

To learn more

Continued fractions are a fascinating but somewhat specialized area of mathematics. They're not difficult, but we don't use them in every field. The topic is often covered briefly in algebra and number theory texts, but there are only a few dedicated books about them. [151, Chapter 10] [122] [167]

3.6 Structure

I took time to show the operations and the properties of $\mathbf{R}$ and its subsets such as $\mathbf{Z}$ and $\mathbf{Q}$ because these are very common in other parts of mathematics when abstracted. This structure allows us to learn and prove things and then apply them to new mathematical collections as we encounter them. We start with three: *groups*, *rings*, and *fields*.

These will come into play when we consider modular arithmetic in section 3.7, complex numbers in section 3.9, and vector spaces, linear transformations, and matrices in Chapter 5, "Dimensions."

3.6.1 Groups

Consider a collection of objects we call **G**. For example, **G** might be **Z**, **Q**, or **R**, as above. We also have some pairwise operation between elements of **G** that we denote by "$\star$". This is a placeholder for an action that operates on two objects.

This "$\star$" operation could be addition "+" or multiplication "$\times$" for numbers but might be something entirely different. Use your intuition with numbers, but understand that the general case is not always arithmetic. We call the collection together with its operation $(\mathbf{G}, \star)$.

We use "$\star$" the same way as we typically would the addition or multiplication between elements. We write $a \star b$ for a and b in **G**.

We call this *infix* notation because the operator is *in* between the objects. Negation such as -7 uses *prefix* notation. The factorial operation $n! = 1 \times 2 \times \cdots \times (n - 1 \times n)$ uses *postfix* notation. As a special case, $0! = 1$.

We say $(\mathbf{G}, \star)$ is a group if the following conditions are met:

- If a and b are in **G**, then $a \star b$ is in **G**. This is closure.
- If a, b, and c are in **G**, then $(a \star b) \star c = a \star (b \star c)$ is in **G**. This is associativity.
- There exists a unique element *id* in **G** such that $a \star id = id \star a = a$ for every a in **G**. This is the existence of a unique identity element.
- For every a in **G**, there is an element denoted a^{-1} such that $a^{-1} \star a = a \star a^{-1} = id$. This is the existence of an inverse.

The inverse is unique. Suppose there are two elements b and c that are inverses for a. Then

$$b \star a = a \star b = id \text{ and } c \star a = a \star c = id \Rightarrow (b \star a) \star c = id \star c = c$$
$$\Rightarrow b \star (a \star c) = c$$
$$\Rightarrow b \star id = c$$
$$\Rightarrow b = c .$$

So, a has only one inverse. The double right arrow "$\Rightarrow$" means "implies."

We do not require the "$\star$" operation to be commutative: $a \star b$ need not equal $b \star a$. When this is true for all a and b, we call **G** a commutative group.

Figure 3.2 shows the standard x, y, and z axes in three dimensions. We call a rotation around the x-axis *roll*, around the y-axis *pitch*, and around the z-axis *yaw*. These rotations form a noncommutative group. The group operation is performing one rotation after another. We will see rotations like these when we discuss the Bloch sphere representation of a quantum state in section 7.5.

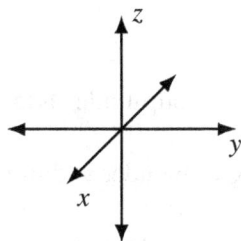

Figure 3.2: The x, y, and z axes in three dimensions

Consider any of the rotations on a Rubik's Cube. Sequences of these rotations are the elements of a noncommutative group. The composition of these elements is the group operation.

In the mathematical literature, commutative groups are called *abelian groups* in honor of the early nineteenth-century mathematician Niels Henrik Abel (Figure 3.3), but we stick to the descriptive name.

Figure 3.3: Portrait of Niels Henrik Abel

While you are likely aware of the quadratic formula for finding the roots of a polynomial such as $x^2 + x - 6$, you may not know that there are also (very messy) formulas for third- and fourth-degree polynomials. Despite others working on this for hundreds of years, Abel finally proved that there is no corresponding formula for polynomials of degree 5.

A subset of **G** that uses the same operation ''$\star$'' and is closed under it, contains *id*, and is closed under inversion is a *subgroup* of **G**.

Examples

- The natural numbers are not a group under addition because of the lack of 0 and negative numbers.
- The whole numbers are not a group under addition because all positive numbers lack their negative counterparts.
- The integers **Z**, rational numbers **Q**, and real numbers **R** are each a group under addition with identity element 0. **Z** is a subgroup of **Q**, which is a subgroup of **R**. When we want to consider **Z** as an additive group, we write $\mathbf{Z}^+$. We call a group under addition an *additive group*.
- The even integers are a group under addition with identity element 0. They are a subgroup of **Z**.
- The odd integers are not a group under addition.
- The integers **Z** are not a group under multiplication because most integers lack multiplicative inverses.
- The rational numbers **Q** are not a group under multiplication because there is no multiplicative inverse for 0.
- The rational numbers without 0 are a group under multiplication but not under addition.
- Similarly, the nonzero real numbers are a group under multiplication but not under addition.

Much of the fuss we made when we proceeded from **W** to **N** to **Z** was to examine their properties to show **Z** is a group under "+".

For another example, imagine you live on a world that is one long, straight, infinite street:

For our group elements, take movements of the form "walk 12 meters to the right" and "walk 4 meters to the left." The group operation is composition "∘" thought of as "and then." We can write

$$a = \text{``walk 12 meters to the left''}$$
$$b = \text{``walk 4 meters to the right''}$$

and so

$a \circ b =$ "walk 12 meters to the left" *and then* "walk 4 meters to the right."

The result is

$$a \circ b = \text{``walk 8 meters to the left.''}$$

Note I don't specify where on the street to start: all movements are relative. The inverse of a "walk to the right" element is the corresponding "walk to the left" element. The identity element *id* is "walk to the right 0 meters," which we take to be the same as "walk to the left 0 meters."

Verify for yourself that "∘" is associative and commutative.

You can extend this group in two dimensions by adding similar "walk forward" and "walk backward" elements. For three dimensions, you would indicate up and down movements. Think about associativity and commutativity.

Exercise 3.19

In the three-dimensional case, is it a finite or infinite group? What are some subgroups?

Rather than being on a straight line, consider being on a circle with a circumference of 4 meters, as in Figure 3.4. The elements are integer meter movements clockwise or counterclockwise. For example, "move 2 meters clockwise" and "move –1 meter counterclockwise."

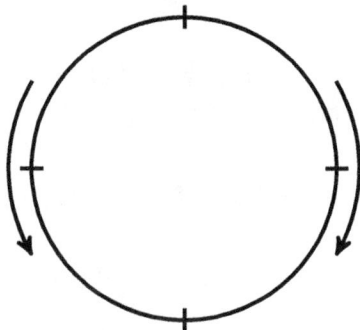

Figure 3.4: The group of integer-length movements on a circle

We equate moving 4 meters in either direction with moving 0 meters since we move all the way around the circle. Moving 5 meters counterclockwise is the same element as moving 1 meter in that direction or 3 meters in the other.

Exercise 3.20

Is this a finite or infinite group? If we allow moving clockwise or counterclockwise in any real number increments, is it a finite or infinite group?

3.6.2 Rings

When we have one more operation, we get a more sophisticated structure called a *ring* if specific requirements are met. For convenience, we call these two operations ''+'' and ''×'' but remember they can behave in very different ways from the addition and multiplication we have for numbers.

> We say $(\mathbf{S}, +, \times)$ is a *ring* if the following conditions are met:
>
> - $\mathbf{S}$ is a commutative group under ''+'' with identity element 0.
> - If a, b, and c are in $\mathbf{S}$, then $(a \times b) \times c = a \times (b \times c)$ is in $\mathbf{S}$. This is associativity for ''×''.
> - There exists an element 1 in $\mathbf{S}$ such that $a \times 1 = 1 \times a = a$ for every a in $\mathbf{S}$. This is the existence of a multiplicative identity element.
> - $0 \neq 1$.
> - Multiplication ''×'' distributes over addition ''+''. If a, b, and c are in $\mathbf{S}$, then
>
> $$a \times (b + c) = (a \times b) + (a \times c)$$
> $$(b + c) \times a = (b \times a) + (c \times a).$$

While addition is commutative in a ring, multiplication need not be. As you might guess, a *commutative ring* is one with commutative multiplication. A *noncommutative ring* has the obvious definition.

A subgroup of $\mathbf{S}$ under ''+'' is a *subring* if it also shares the same ''×'', contains 1, and is closed under ''×''.

Examples

- The integers $\mathbf{Z}$, rational numbers $\mathbf{Q}$, and real numbers $\mathbf{R}$ are each a ring under addition and multiplication with identity elements 0 and 1, respectively. $\mathbf{Z}$ is a subring of $\mathbf{Q}$, which is a subring of $\mathbf{R}$.
- The even integers are not a subring of $\mathbf{Z}$ because they do not contain 1.
- Consider all elements of $\mathbf{R}$ of the form $a + b\sqrt{2}$ for a and b integers. We call this $\mathbf{Z}[\sqrt{2}]$. It is a commutative ring that extends $\mathbf{Z}$. Other than $\mathbf{Q}$, this is the first ring we have seen that is larger than $\mathbf{Z}$ but smaller than $\mathbf{R}$ itself. We have

$$0 = 0 + 0\sqrt{2}$$
$$1 = 1 + 0\sqrt{2}$$
$$-(a + b\sqrt{2}) = -a - b\sqrt{2}$$
$$(a + b\sqrt{2}) + (c + d\sqrt{2}) = (a + c) + (b + d)\sqrt{2}$$
$$(a + b\sqrt{2}) \times (c + d\sqrt{2}) = (a \times c + 2b \times d) + (a \times d + b \times c)\sqrt{2}$$

In some commutative rings, it is possible for $a \times b = 0$ with neither a nor b being 0. We call **S** an *integral domain* if this cannot happen. Said otherwise, we must have a or b being 0 for the product to be 0 in an integral domain. All the rings we have seen so far are integral domains.

Later in this chapter, in section 3.8, we define a ring that is not an integral domain. The ring of all 2-by-2 square matrices over **R** that we define in section 5.5.2 is also not an integral domain.

3.6.3 Fields

A *field* **F** is a commutative ring where every nonzero element has a multiplicative inverse. A field is closed under division by nonzero elements.

Q and **R** are fields, but **Z** is not. **Q** is a *subfield* of **R**. Viewed from the opposite direction, **R** is an *extension* of **Q**. For example, if we look at all numbers of the form $r + s\sqrt{2}$ with r and s in **Q** and perform the arithmetic operations in the usual way, we have an extension field of **Q** that is a subfield of **R**. We denote this field by $\mathbf{Q}[\sqrt{2}]$.

Exercise 3.21

Suppose we have $r + s\sqrt{2}$ in $\mathbf{Q}[\sqrt{2}]$ with r and s not both 0. What is $(r + s\sqrt{2})^{-1}$? Express it as some $u + v\sqrt{2}$ in $\mathbf{Q}[\sqrt{2}]$ with u and v in **Q**. Begin by considering the product $(r + s\sqrt{2}) \times (r - s\sqrt{2})$.

All fields are integral domains. Suppose otherwise, and $a \times b = 0$ with neither a nor b being 0. There exists a^{-1} such that $a^{-1} \times a = 1$. Hence $a^{-1} \times (a \times b) = a^{-1} \times 0$ means $1 \times b = 0$. But we said b is not 0! We have a contradiction, and there can be no such b. So a field is an integral domain.

3.6.4 Even greater abstraction

If **Z** is a group under addition, what is **W**? It doesn't contain additive inverses such as −2, so it can't be a group.

Even worse, what is **N**? We don't even have 0, the additive identity element.

We say $(\mathbf{G}, \star)$ is a *semigroup* if the following conditions are met:

- If a and b are in **G**, then $a \star b$ is in **G**. This is closure.
- If a, b, and c are in **G**, then $(a \star b) \star c = a \star (b \star c)$ is in **G**. This is associativity.

$(\mathbf{G}, \star)$ is a *monoid* if also:

- There exists a unique element id in **G** such that $a \star id = id \star a = a$ for every a in **G**. This is the existence of a unique identity element.

With this, **N** is a semigroup and **W** is a monoid. All groups are monoids, and all monoids are semigroups.

I provide a table and a chart at the end of this chapter that show how these algebraic structures are related to each other and the collections of numbers in this chapter.

To learn more

Group theory is ubiquitous across many areas of mathematics and physics. [192] Rings, fields, and other structures are fundamental to areas of mathematics such as algebra, algebraic number theory, commutative algebra, and algebraic geometry. [73] [131]

3.7 Modular arithmetic

There are an infinite number of integers and hence rationals and real numbers. Are there sets of numbers that behave somewhat like them but are finite?

Consider the integers *modulo* 6: $\{0, 1, 2, 3, 4, 5\}$. We write 3 mod 6 when we consider the 3 in this collection. Given any integer n, we can map it into this collection by computing the remainder modulo 6. We do arithmetic in the same way:

$$7 \equiv 1 \bmod 6 \qquad (4 - 5) \equiv 5 \bmod 6 \qquad -2 \equiv 4 \bmod 6$$
$$(3 + 7) \equiv 4 \bmod 6 \qquad (5 + 4) \equiv 3 \bmod 6 \qquad (2 + 4) \equiv 0 \bmod 6$$

Instead of "=", we write "$\equiv$". We say that a is *congruent* to b mod 6 when we see $a \equiv b$ mod 6, which means $a - b$ is evenly divisible by 6: $6 \mid (a - b)$.

These six elements form a group under addition with identity 0. In the last example, 2 is the additive inverse of 4. We denote this group $\mathbf{Z}/6\mathbf{Z}$.

Exercise 3.22

What is $-1 \bmod 6$? For n a natural number greater than 1, what is $-1 \bmod n$?

Let's consider the same collection **but without the 0**. Instead of addition, use multiplication with identity 1.

Is this a group? Is it closed under multiplication? Does every element have an inverse?

Since $2 \times 3 = 6 \equiv 0 \bmod 6$, and 0 is not in the collection, it is not closed under multiplication! The elements that **do not** have multiplicative inverses are 2, 3, and 4 because each shares a factor with 6.

The multiplicative inverse of 1 is itself. $5 \times 5 \equiv 5^2 \equiv 25 \equiv 1 \bmod 6$, so 5 is also its own inverse.

If we restrict ourselves to the elements that do not have a factor in common with 6, we get a group we denote $\{1, 5\}$, though it is not a very big one. The fancy mathematical way of writing this group is $(\mathbf{Z}/6\mathbf{Z})^{\times}$.

If, instead of 6, we had chosen 15, the elements in $(\mathbf{Z}/15\mathbf{Z})^{\times}$ would be

$$\{1, 2, 4, 7, 8, 11, 13, 14\} .$$

We have a better way of expressing "does not have a factor in common" via the greatest common divisor. The integers a and b do not share a nontrivial factor if and only if $\gcd(a, b) = 1$. That is, a and b are coprime.

If this is the case, Euclid's algorithm tells us there are integers n and m such that

$$an + bm = 1 .$$

If we look at this modulo b,

$$1 \equiv an + bm \equiv an \bmod b .$$

Hence, n is congruent to $a^{-1} \bmod b$!

The integers a that are in $(\mathbf{Z}/15\mathbf{Z})^{\times}$ have $0 < a < 15$ and $\gcd(a, 15) = 1$.

The phrase "X if and only if Y" means "if X is true, then Y is true, and if Y is true, then X is true." We cannot have one of them true and the other false. We often use "iff" as a shorthand for "if and only if."

If we use 7 instead of 15, the elements in $(\mathbf{Z}/7\mathbf{Z})^\times$ are $\{1, 2, 3, 4, 5, 6\}$. Well, this case is interesting!

We got all the nonzero elements *because 7 is prime.* If p is a prime number, none of the numbers $1, 2, \ldots, p - 1$ share a factor with p. That is, they are coprime with p.

> The elements $1, 2, \ldots, p - 1$ form a multiplicative group with identity element 1 if and only if p is prime. The group has $p - 1$ elements.
>
> The elements $0, 1, 2, \ldots, p - 1$ form a field under "+" and "×" with identity elements 0 and 1, respectively, if and only if p is prime. The field has p elements, and we denote it by $\mathbf{F}_p$.

There are more finite fields than these, but any other finite field that is not formed this way is an extension of an $\mathbf{F}_p$. The number of elements in any finite field is a power of a prime number p. Any two finite fields with the same number of elements are *isomorphic*, meaning they are the same in all algebraic respects.

One way mathematicians differentiate among the kinds of fields is via their *characteristic.* For p prime, a field that is either an $\mathbf{F}_p$ or an extension has characteristic p. Otherwise, the field has characteristic 0. $\mathbf{Q}$ and $\mathbf{R}$ are examples of fields with characteristic 0.

The smallest field is $\mathbf{F}_2$, with only two elements, 0 and 1. Fields with characteristic 2 often require special handling because 2 is the only prime that is an even number.

To learn more

Finite fields have many applications in pure and applied mathematics, including computer error correction and cryptography. [115] [128] [148] [174]

3.8 Doubling down

So far, we've seen finite and infinite groups, rings, and fields, some of which are extensions of others. In this section, we look at combining them.

Consider the collection of all pairs of integers (a, b), where we define addition and multiplication component-wise.

$$\mathbf{0} = (0, 0)$$
$$\mathbf{1} = (1, 1)$$
$$-(a, b) = (-a, -b)$$
$$(a, b) + (c, d) = (a + c, b + d)$$
$$(a, b) - (c, d) = (a - c, b - d)$$
$$(a, b) \times (c, d) = (ac, bd)$$

This is a ring, denoted $\mathbf{Z}^2$, but it is not an integral domain. $(1, 0) \times (0, 1) = (0, 0)$, but neither of the factors is $\mathbf{0}$.

For the same reason, neither $\mathbf{Q}^2$ nor $\mathbf{R}^2$ can be an integral domain. In particular, they are not fields with these operations.

Let's change the definitions for $\mathbf{R}^2$ so that $\mathbf{1} = (1, 0)$ and multiplication is

$$(a, b) \times (c, d) = (ac - bd, ad + bc).$$

For $(a, b) \neq \mathbf{0}$, we define

$$(a, b)^{-1} = \left(\frac{a}{a^2 + b^2}, -\frac{b}{a^2 + b^2} \right).$$

With these unusual definitions for multiplication and inversion, we not only have an integral domain, we have a field, which we examine in the next section.

3.9 Complex numbers, algebraically

In section 3.6.2, I gave an example of extending the integers by considering elements of the form $a + b\sqrt{2}$. We can similarly extend $\mathbf{R}$.

The real numbers $\mathbf{R}$ do not contain the square roots of negative numbers. We *define* the value i as $\sqrt{-1}$, which means $i^2 = -1$.

For a and b in $\mathbf{R}$, consider all elements of the form $z = a + bi$. This is the field of *complex numbers* $\mathbf{C}$ formed as $\mathbf{R}[i] = \mathbf{R}[\sqrt{-1}]$. We call a the *real part* of z and denote it by $\text{Re}(z)$. b is the *imaginary part* $\text{Im}(z)$. a and b are real numbers. Every real number is also a complex number with a zero imaginary part.

While we can always determine if $x < y$ for two real numbers, there is no equivalent ordering for arbitrary complex ones that extends what works for the reals.

3.9.1 Arithmetic

The equations for arithmetic are

$$0 = 0 + 0i$$
$$1 = 1 + 0i$$
$$-(a + bi) = -a - bi$$
$$(a + bi) + (c + di) = (a + c) + (b + d)i$$
$$(a + bi) - (c + di) = (a - c) + (b - d)i$$

Multiplication is more complicated:

$$(a + bi) \times (c + di) = (ac - bd) + (ad + bc)i$$
$$\text{Re}((a + bi) \times (c + di)) = ac - bd$$
$$\text{Im}((a + bi) \times (c + di)) = ad + bc$$

Let's work this out:

$$
\begin{aligned}
(a + bi) \times (c + di) &= a \times (c + di) + bi\,(c + di) \\
&= ac + adi + bic + (bi)(di) \\
&= ac + (ad + bc)i + bd(ii) \\
&= ac + (ad + bc)i + bd(-1) \\
&= ac + (ad + bc)i - bd \\
&= (ac - bd) + (ad + bc)\,i\,.
\end{aligned}
$$

For example,

$$
\begin{aligned}
(2 + 3i) \times (4 + 6i) &= 2\,(4 + 6i) + 3i\,(4 + 6i) \\
&= 2 \times 4 + 2 \times 6i + 3i \times 4 + 3i \times 6i \\
&= 8 + 12i + 12i + 18 \times i \times i \\
&= 8 + 24i + 18 \times -1 \\
&= -10 + 24i\,.
\end{aligned}
$$

It's conventional to use the variable z when referring to a complex number, perhaps because "Zahl" is the German word for "number." w is a frequent choice if we need another.

3.9.2 Conjugation

Complex numbers have one operation we have not seen before: *conjugation*. For $z = a + bi$, the conjugate of z is

$$\bar{z} = a - bi\,.$$

In mathematics, using a line over the expression is common to indicate conjugation. Physicists sometimes use an asterisk superscript: conjugate of $z = z^*$.

The product of a complex number $z = a + bi$ with its conjugate is a *nonnegative* real number:

$$z\bar{z} = (a + bi)(a - bi)$$
$$= a^2 - abi + bai - b^2 i^2$$
$$= a^2 + b^2 .$$

We also have:

$$z = \bar{\bar{z}} \qquad\qquad \mathrm{Re}(z) = \mathrm{Re}(\bar{z})$$
$$z = 0 \text{ if and only if } \bar{z} = 0 \qquad\qquad \mathrm{Im}(\bar{z}) = -\mathrm{Im}(z) = -b$$

Exercise 3.23

Under what condition is z equal to its conjugate?

It's hard to overstate the importance of conjugation in the algebra of complex numbers. We return to it in section 4.5 to get a geometric interpretation.

We use the conjugate to compute the inverse of a nonzero complex number z:

$$z^{-1} = \frac{1}{z} = \frac{\bar{z}}{\bar{z}z} = \frac{a - bi}{a^2 + b^2} = \frac{a}{a^2 + b^2} - \frac{b}{a^2 + b^2}i .$$

Exercise 3.24

Confirm that

$$(a + bi)\left(\frac{a}{a^2 + b^2} - \frac{b}{a^2 + b^2}i\right) = 1 .$$

Exercise 3.25

Calculate the division formula for complex numbers by noting that

$$\frac{a + bi}{c + di} = (a + bi)\,\frac{1}{c + di} .$$

Conjugation behaves very nicely regarding all the standard operations on complex numbers. For complex numbers z and w:

$$\overline{z+w} = \overline{z} + \overline{w} \qquad \overline{z \times w} = \overline{z} \times \overline{w} \qquad \overline{z^{-1}} = \overline{\left(\frac{1}{z}\right)} = \frac{1}{\overline{z}}$$

$$\overline{z-w} = \overline{z} - \overline{w} \qquad \overline{z^n} = \overline{z}^n \text{ for } n \text{ an integer} \qquad \overline{\left(\frac{z}{w}\right)} = \frac{\overline{z}}{\overline{w}} \text{ for } w \neq 0$$

The *absolute value* of a complex number z is

$$|z| = \sqrt{z\,\overline{z}}.$$

For $z = a + bi$, this is $\sqrt{a^2 + b^2}$.

Exercise 3.26

Prove

$$|z| = |\overline{z}|.$$

3.9.3   Units

A unit is a number with absolute value 1. The complex numbers have an infinite number of units, unlike the real numbers, which only have 1 and -1.

As complex numbers, 1, -1, i, and $-i$ are all units, but so are all $a + bi$ with $a^2 + b^2 = 1$. Thus,

$$\frac{\sqrt{2}}{2} \pm \frac{\sqrt{2}}{2}i \quad \text{and} \quad \frac{\sqrt{3}}{2} \pm \frac{1}{2}i$$

are units.

Exercise 3.27

Where have you seen numbers like those in the real and imaginary parts before?

Here's a hint: for any real number x, $\sin^2(x) + \cos^2(x) = 1$. That means if we look at complex numbers of the form $z = \cos(x) + \sin(x)i$, then $|z| = 1$. Numbers in this form are all units in **C**. Even better, these are the *only* units in **C**.

Seemingly out of nowhere, we have connected $\sqrt{-1}$, the real numbers extended by it, and trigonometry. These are key tools we need when we look at a qubit, the fundamental information object of quantum computing.

When we look at the geometry of complex numbers in section 4.5, I explain *Euler's formula*,

$$e^{xi} = \cos(x) + \sin(x)i \,.$$

From this comes *Euler's identity*

$$e^{\pi i} = -1 \quad \text{or} \quad e^{\pi i} - 1 = 0 \,,$$

where e is the base of the natural logarithms $= 2.171828\ldots.$.

Many people consider this the most beautiful equation in mathematics, connecting the integers (-1), an irrational number basic to calculus (e), another irrational central to trigonometry (π), and the complex numbers (i).

3.9.4 Polynomials and roots

Let $p(z)$ be a polynomial such that

$$p(z) = a_n z^n + a_{n-1} z^{n-1} + \cdots + a_2 z^2 + a_1 z + a_0$$

and at least one of the complex numbers $a_1, \ldots, a_n$ is not 0. Then there exists at least one complex number s such that $p(s) = 0$. s is a *root* of p, and $z - s$ divides $p(z)$ exactly.

We call the a_i the *coefficients* of p. Insisting that one of $a_1, \ldots, a_n$ is not 0 means p is not a constant polynomial. For example,

$$p(z) = 2 - 3i$$

is constant. There is no complex number s you can substitute for z that makes $p(s) = 0$. If $a_n \neq 0$, we call n the *degree* of the polynomial. A constant polynomial has degree 0.

Let's back up and see what this means. For $p(z) = z^2 - 1$, both $s = 1$ and $s = -1$ work. That is, $p(1) = p(-1) = 0$. In this case $p(z)$ has the real number coefficients $a_2 = 1$, $a_1 = 0$, and $a_0 = -1$. The roots are also real. The roots are related to the factorization of p via

$$p(z) = (z - (1))(z - (-1)) \,,$$

where I show the roots in parentheses. Written more simply,

$$p(z) = (z - 1)(z + 1) \,.$$

Consider another polynomial with real coefficients, $p(z) = z^2 + 1$. This is as simple as the previous one, and here $a_2 = 1$, $a_1 = 0$, and $a_0 = 1$. Stating $p(z) = 0$ means $z^2 + 1 = 0$ and so $z^2 = -1$. So any s that works must be a square root of -1! There is no such real number.

There are two and only two complex numbers that work: i and $-i$:

$$p(i) = p(-i) = 0 \qquad p(z) = (z - i)(z + i)$$

When $p(z)$ has real coefficients, *it is not automatically the case that it has real roots.* As we saw in section 3.1, when we considered that **N** is not closed under subtraction, **R** is not closed under finding real roots for nonconstant polynomials with real coefficients.

Just as **Z** fixes the subtraction closure problem for **N**, **C** fixes the root finding problem for nonconstant polynomials with coefficients in **R**. The statement at the beginning of this section says even more: **C** is closed under finding complex roots for nonconstant polynomials with complex coefficients.

This is a powerful and important property for a field to have. The phrase we use is that the complex numbers are *algebraically closed.* **Q** and **R** are not algebraically closed.

Consider the quadratic polynomial equation $ax^2 + bx + c = 0$ with a, b, and c real numbers and $a \neq 0$. We solve for x by the technique called *completing the square.*

First, note that

$$\left(x + \frac{b}{2a}\right)^2 = x^2 + \frac{b}{a}x + \left(\frac{b}{2a}\right)^2 = x^2 + \frac{b}{a}x + \frac{b^2}{4a^2}.$$

This may seem like an arbitrary equation, but it is a valuable relationship at the core of our algorithm. We now derive a formula for x, remembering that $a \neq 0$:

$$ax^2 + bx + c = 0 \Rightarrow x^2 + \frac{b}{a}x + \frac{c}{a} = 0$$

$$\Rightarrow \left(x^2 + \frac{b}{a}x + \frac{c}{a}\right) + \frac{b^2}{4a^2} = \frac{b^2}{4a^2}$$

$$\Rightarrow \left(x^2 + \frac{b}{a}x + \frac{b^2}{4a^2}\right) + \frac{c}{a} = \frac{b^2}{4a^2}$$

$$\Rightarrow x^2 + \frac{b}{a}x + \frac{b^2}{4a^2} = \frac{b^2}{4a^2} - \frac{c}{a}$$

$$\Rightarrow \left(x + \frac{b}{2a}\right)^2 = \frac{b^2}{4a^2} - \frac{c}{a}$$

$$\Rightarrow x + \frac{b}{2a} = \pm\sqrt{\frac{b^2}{4a^2} - \frac{c}{a}}$$

$$\Rightarrow x = -\frac{b}{2a} \pm \sqrt{\frac{b^2 - 4ac}{4a^2}}$$

$$\Rightarrow x = \frac{-b \pm \sqrt{b^2 - 4ac}}{2a}.$$

This is the *quadratic formula*, and now you know (or remember) how it is derived!

The significance of it, and why I went into such detail to calculate it, is that there are two possible values for x that you can plug into $ax^2 + bx + c$ to get 0:

$$\frac{-b + \sqrt{b^2 - 4ac}}{2a} \quad \text{and} \quad \frac{-b - \sqrt{b^2 - 4ac}}{2a}.$$

These are the roots of the polynomial.

When $b^2 - 4ac = 0$, we have one root $-\frac{b}{2a}$, but it is repeated twice. For example, $x^2 + 4x + 4$ has the repeated root 2.

When $b^2 - 4ac > 0$, we get two different real roots. The polynomial $x^2 + x - 6$ has the real roots 2 and -3.

When $b^2 - 4ac < 0$, we get two nonreal different but *conjugate* complex roots. Since

$$b^2 - 4ac < 0 \Rightarrow 4ac - b^2 > 0,$$

we have

$$\frac{-b + \sqrt{b^2 - 4ac}}{2a} = \frac{-b + \sqrt{(4ac - b^2)(-1)}}{2a}$$

$$= \frac{-b + \left(\sqrt{4ac - b^2}\right)i}{2a}$$

$$= \frac{-b}{2a} + \sqrt{\frac{4ac - b^2}{4a^2}}\, i$$

and

$$\frac{-b - \sqrt{b^2 - 4ac}}{2a} = \frac{-b - \sqrt{(4ac - b^2)(-1)}}{2a}$$

$$= \frac{-b - \left(\sqrt{4ac - b^2}\right)i}{2a}$$

$$= \frac{-b}{2a} - \sqrt{\frac{4ac - b^2}{4a^2}}\, i.$$

Since a real number is its own conjugate, this statement holds in all cases.

> If s is a complex root of the polynomial $ax^2 + bx + c$ with $a \neq 0$, b, and c **real numbers**, then the conjugate of s is also a root.

It also holds for polynomials of all degrees greater than 0 with real coefficients.

> If s is a complex root of the nth degree polynomial
>
> $$a_n x^n + a_{n-1} x^{n-1} + \cdots + a_1 x + a_0 \,,$$
>
> where all coefficients are **real**, $n > 0$, and $a_n \neq 0$, then the conjugate of s is also a root.

This statement is the *complex conjugate root theorem*, though you sometimes see the word "conjugate" omitted in the title.

3.10 Summary

There's more to numbers than you might have thought, despite using them daily. Starting with the simplest kind, the natural numbers **N**, we systematically added operations and properties to gain functionality. The idea of "closure" drove us to understand the value of extending to increasingly larger collections of numbers that could handle the problems we wanted to solve.

We briefly delved into abstract algebra to look at groups, rings, and fields and see their structure. Complex numbers are key to working with quantum computing, and we began to look at their algebraic properties. Though they involve the imaginary i, they are very real in describing the way the universe evidently works.

The following table brings together the number collections we have seen and some of their properties.

Number Collection	Section	Symbol	Closure	Structure
Natural numbers	3.1	N	addition, multiplication	semigroup
Whole numbers	3.2	Q	addition, multiplication	monoid
Integers (additive subgroup)	3.6.1	Z^+	addition, subtraction	group
Integers	3.3	Z	addition, subtraction, multiplication	ring
Rational numbers	3.4	Q	addition, subtraction, multiplication, division	field

Number Collection	Section	Symbol	Closure	Structure
A rational number field extension	3.6.3	$Q[\sqrt{2}]$	addition, subtraction, multiplication, division	field
Real numbers	3.5	R	addition, subtraction, multiplication, division, limits	field
Complex numbers	3.9	C	addition, subtraction, multiplication, division, limits, polynomial factorization, $i = \sqrt{-1}$	field
Modular integers	3.7	Z/nZ	addition, subtraction, multiplication	ring
Modular integers (multiplicative subgroup)	3.7	$(Z/nZ)^{\times}$	multiplication, division	group
Finite fields	3.7	F_p	addition, subtraction, multiplication, division	field

The following diagram shows the inclusion relationships among the collections of numbers. The expressions

$$A \subset B \quad \text{or} \quad \begin{matrix} B \\ \cup \\ A \end{matrix}$$

mean that A is included in B. For example, $\mathbf{Z}$ is included in $\mathbf{Q}$, which is included in $\mathbf{Q}[\sqrt{2}]$.

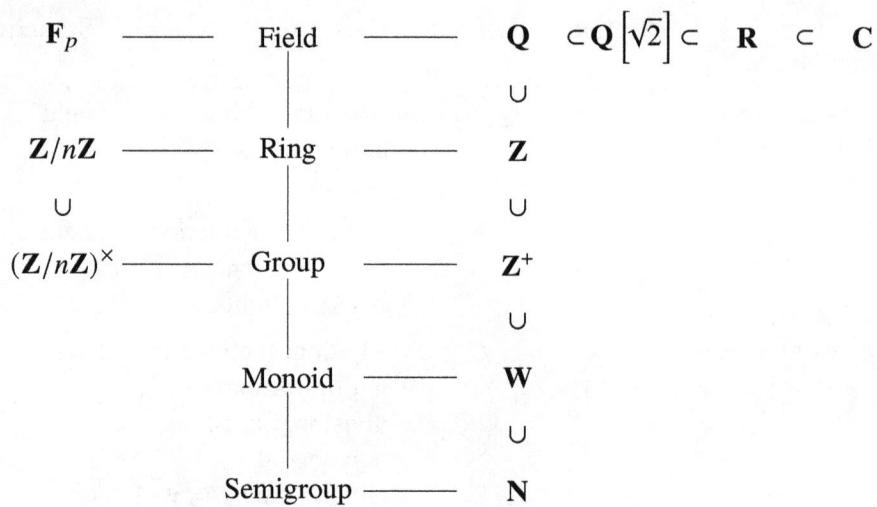

4

Planes and Circles and Spheres, Oh My

No employment can be managed without arithmetic, no mechanical invention without geometry.

– Benjamin Franklin

In the last chapter, we focused on the algebra of numbers and collections of objects that behave like numbers. We turn our attention to geometry and look at two and three dimensions. When we start working with qubits in Chapter 7, "One Qubit," we represent a single qubit as a sphere in three dimensions. Therefore, it's necessary to get comfortable with the geometric side of the mathematics before we tackle the quantum computing aspect.

Topics covered in this chapter

4.1 Functions

A function is one of the concepts in math that sounds pretty abstract but is straightforward once you get experience with it. Thought of in terms of numbers, a function takes a value and returns one and only one value.

For example, for any real number, we can square it. That process is a function from **R** to **R**. For any nonnegative real number, if we take the positive square root of it, we get another function. We would not have a function if we were to say we got both the positive and negative square roots.

We use the notation $f(x)$ for a function, meaning we start with some value x, do something to it indicated by the definition of f, and the result is $f(x)$. The f can be any letter or word, but we use f because the word "function" starts with it, and we are not being especially creative. It's common to see g and h and Greek letters such as γ, but we can use anything that starts with a letter.

We write a function definition like $f(x) = x^2$ or $g(x) = \sqrt{x}$ or $h(x) = 2x - 3$.

The set of values we can use for x is the *domain* of the function. The domain of $f(x) = x^2$ could be the integers, the real numbers, the complex numbers, or any other set that makes sense. When considering real numbers, the domain of $g(x) = \sqrt{x}$ is the set of nonnegative real numbers.

The *range* or *image* of a function is the set of values it produces. If the domain of $f(x) = x^2$ is **R**, the range is the set of all nonnegative real numbers. The same is true for the absolute value $|x|$. For $|x|$, I use notation instead of a function name such as $f(x)$ or $g(x)$.

Using the $f(x)$ notation is not mandatory when the context makes it clear we have a function. We can also use the arrow notation

$$x \mapsto 2^x$$

to show the input is x and the result is 2^x. We pronounce the arrow symbol "$\mapsto$" as "maps to."

When the range of a function is some subset of **R**, we say "*f* is real-valued." Similarly, we might say it is integer-valued or complex-valued.

Functions don't have to work on or produce numeric inputs and outputs. Consider the function *color(n)* on the integers in Figure 4.1 that produces the color white if *n* is even and black if *n* is odd. The domain is infinite, but the range has two elements.

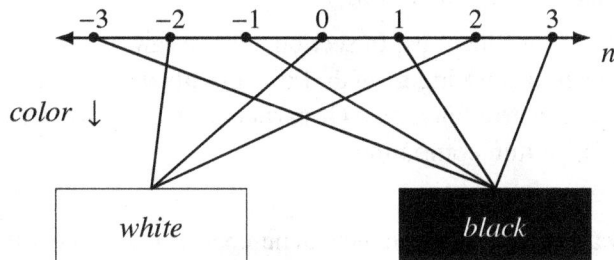

Figure 4.1: A function whose range is two colors

We can use another variation of the arrow notation to show the domain and range of a function. The notation

$$color : \mathbf{Z} \rightarrow \{white, black\}$$

indicates that the domain of *color* is the integers, and the range is the set $\{white, black\}$. A common range we will see later is $\{0, 1\}$.

We call a function that has only one value in its range *constant*. The function $zero(x) = 0$ is constant. So is the function $\cos^2(x) + \sin^2(x)$, though you need to know the trigonometric identity or calculus to realize that.

> Though we usually show function names such as *f* and *g* in italics, we display some names for special functions such as sin, cos, and log, in the regular font.

I use *x* and *n* as the domain variables in the above examples. Just like *f* is only one possibility for the function name, we can use any letter or word for the domain variable. *t* is another common choice, especially when we think of the domain as real numbers representing time. Don't use the same letter or word as the name of the function!

Exercise 4.1

What would be your personal function if we defined *height(t)* where *t* is your age in days?

We need not only define a function with only one formula. We can use different formulas for parts of the domain. For example,

$$f(x) = \begin{cases} x^2 & \text{when } x \geq 0 \\ -x^2 & \text{when } x < 0. \end{cases}$$

We call this a *piecewise function definition*.

There are many kinds of functions. In section 2.7, we saw exponential, logarithmic, and quadratic functions when discussing growth. Polynomials define functions, as do sine and cosine among the trigonometric functions. Of particular importance are the linear functions, which are essential to quantum computing.

We call a real-valued function f on the real numbers *linear* if the following conditions hold:

- if x and y are real numbers, then $f(x + y) = f(x) + f(y)$, and
- if a is a real number, then $f(ax) = af(x)$.

This implies $f(ax + by) = af(x) + bf(y)$ for real numbers a, b, x, and y.

The only linear functions that map real numbers to real numbers look like $f(x) = cx$, for c a fixed value. We call such a c a *constant*. For example, $f(x) = 7x$ or $f(x) = -x$. When we consider functions applied to more structured collections, the linear functions will be significantly less trivial.

What are the real-valued linear functions on the real numbers such that $|f(x)| = |x|$ for any x? Since $f(x) = cx$,

$$|f(x)| = |cx| = |c| \times |x| = |x|.$$

So, $|c| = 1$, and $c = 1$ or $c = -1$. When $c = 1$, we have the *identity* function: $id(x) = x$.

Can you reverse the effect of a function? If $f(x) = 3x - 1$, then if we apply

$$g(x) = \frac{1}{3}x + \frac{1}{3}$$

and get

$$g(f(x)) = \frac{1}{3}f(x) + \frac{1}{3}$$
$$= \frac{1}{3}(3x - 1) + \frac{1}{3} = x - \frac{1}{3} + \frac{1}{3}$$
$$= x = id(x).$$

g is the inverse of f because $g(f(x)) = x$. $id(x)$ is its own inverse.

Exercise 4.2

Does $f(x) = 5$ have an inverse?

Exercise 4.3

What conditions do you need to impose on the domain of $f(x) = x^2$ so that the positive $\sqrt{x}$ is the inverse?

If f and g are functions such that $g(f(x)) = x$ and $f(g(y)) = y$ for all x and y in the domains of f and g, respectively, then f and g are *invertible* and one is the inverse of the other.

4.2 The real plane

When we were building up the structure of the integers, we showed the traditional number line $\mathbf{R}^2$.

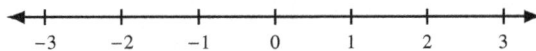

with the negative integers to the left of 0 and the positive ones to the right. Really, though, this was just part of the real number line:

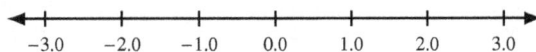

The line is one-dimensional in that we need only one value, or coordinate, to locate a point uniquely on the line. For a real number x, we represent the point on the line by (x). For example, the point (-2.6) is between the markings -3 and -2. We use or omit the parentheses when it is clear from the context whether we are referring to the point or the number that gives its relative position from 0.

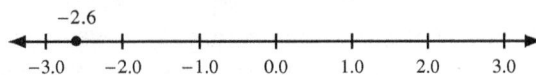

I drop the decimal points on the labels now that it is clear we have real numbers.

4.2.1 Moving to two dimensions

Suppose the number line sits in two dimensions so that we extend upwards and downwards:

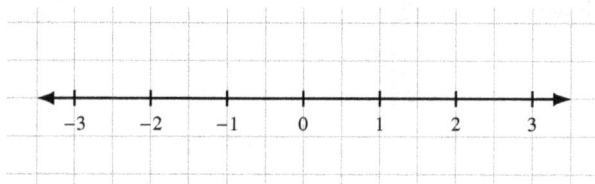

Since we need two coordinates for two dimensions, we position points with x- and y-coordinates from **R** and label the point (x, y). We call these *Cartesian coordinates* after the mathematician René Descartes. Another name for Cartesian coordinates is *rectangular coordinates*.

We position the point $(1, 3)$ on the upper-right part of the graph and $\left(-\frac{5}{2}, -1\right)$ on the lower left in Figure 4.2. We call the horizontal line the *x-axis* and the vertical line the *y-axis*.

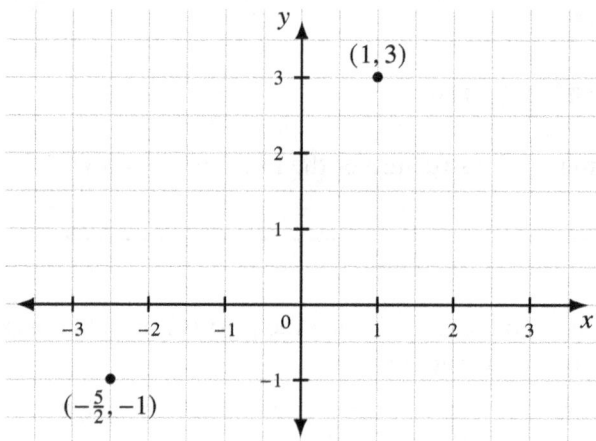

Figure 4.2: Plot with Cartesian coordinates

It may help you visualize this better if you think of the axes and points flat on a table in front of you. This is the graph of the *real plane*, denoted $\mathbf{R}^2$.

One last bit of information to help us navigate: the axes divide the plane into four areas, or *quadrants*. In the first quadrant **I**, in the upper right of Figure 4.3, x and y are positive.

If we move counterclockwise, the second quadrant **II** has negative x and positive y. The third (**III**) and fourth (**IV**) quadrants have $x < 0$ and $y < 0$, and $x > 0$ and $y < 0$, respectively.

4.2.2 Distance and length

Given two points in the real plane, how far apart are they?

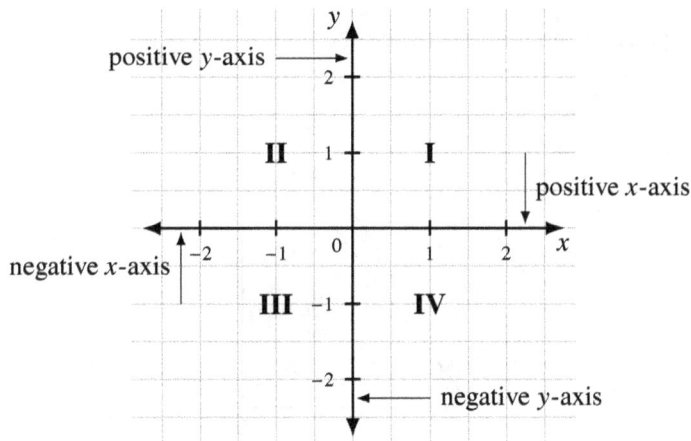

Figure 4.3: The four quadrants of the plane

What is the distance from $(1, 1)$ to $(4, 5)$ in Figure 4.4? This question is equivalent to asking for the length of the line segment between the two points.

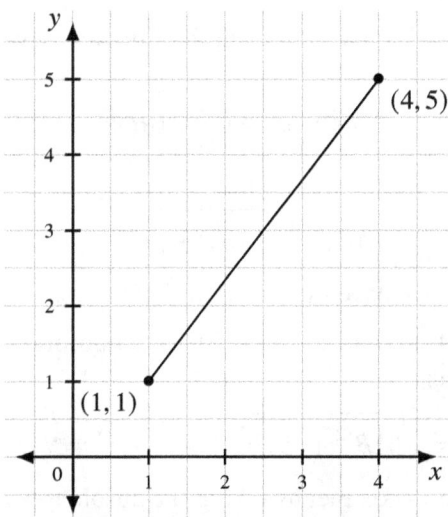

Figure 4.4: The distance between two points

Are we talking about miles, kilometers, feet, centimeters, or what? We typically refer to distance in some particular unit. In math, we often don't say which unless we are translating from a specific problem. We refer to generic ''units,'' though we might note, ''we measure x in meters.'' Unless necessary, we omit the kind of units, such as feet or meters.

The Pythagorean theorem states that in a *right triangle*, a triangle with one 90° angle, the square of the length of the hypotenuse is equal to the sum of the square of the length of one side and the square of the length of the other side.

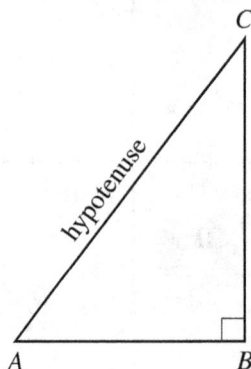

Figure 4.5: A triangle with corners A, B, and C

In Figure 4.5, we label the points on the corners of the triangle A, B, and C. One side of the triangle is the line segment AB, the other is BC, and the hypotenuse is AC. We show the $90°$ angle as the square near B.

If we use the notation $|AB|$ to mean the length of the line segment AB, the theorem tells us

$$|AC|^2 = |AB|^2 + |BC|^2$$

or

$$|AC| = \sqrt{|AB|^2 + |BC|^2}\,.$$

Expanding the example, we have the graph in Figure 4.6.

Let $A = (1,1)$, $B = (4,1)$, and $C = (4,5)$. By counting units on the axes, we have $|AB| = 3$ and $|BC| = 4$. Thus,

$$|AC| = \sqrt{|AB|^2 + |BC|^2} = \sqrt{3^2 + 4^2} = \sqrt{25} = 5\,.$$

"Counting units" along the x-axis means taking the absolute value of the difference of the x-coordinates. A similar statement holds for the y-axis.

It's rare for a triangle to have all its sides being natural numbers, but this is an example of a $3 : 4 : 5$ triangle where things work out nicely. If you multiply or divide each side by the same positive real number, the relationship still holds.

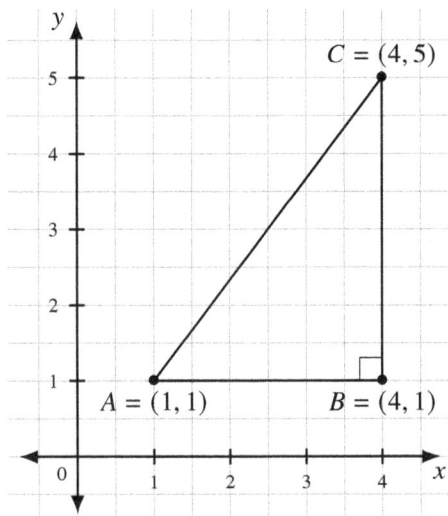

Figure 4.6: A triangle with corners A, B, and C and coordinates

Exercise 4.4

We call a group of three natural numbers $n : m : p$ a Pythagorean triple if $n^2 + m^2 = p^2$. Find two more such triples that are not simple multiples of $3 : 4 : 5$.

Given two points in the real plane with coordinates (a, b) and (c, d), the *distance* between the points is

$$\sqrt{(a - c)^2 + (b - d)^2}.$$

In particular, if the second point is the origin $(0, 0)$, the distance is

$$\sqrt{a^2 + b^2}.$$

4.2.3 Geometric figures in the real plane

Before looking at three dimensions and qubits, you must get comfortable finding your way around $\mathbf{R}^2$ with standard geometric figures such as lines and circles. Let's look at them and review plotting functions such as exponentials and logarithms.

Lines

Given two different points with coordinates (a, b) and (c, d), there is only one line you can draw between those points.

An essential notion of a line is that when you move from one point to another, the ratio of the change in distance between the y-coordinates and the change in distance between the x-coordinates is *constant*. This ratio is the *slope* of the line.

If $(1, 1)$ is a point on the line and the slope is 2, for every unit we move in the x direction, we change twice that much in the y direction. Move 1 unit in x (that is, to the right), and move 2 units in the y (up). Move -3 units in x (that is, to the left), and move -6 in the y (down).

For (x, y) to be on a line with slope m and given point (c, d), $x \neq c$, it must obey the equation

$$\frac{y - d}{x - c} = m.$$

How do we find m? If (a, b) is another given point on the line, $a \neq c$, it must also obey

$$\frac{b - d}{a - c} = m.$$

The slope of a vertical line is undefined.

Example

Find the equation of the line that passes between the points $(-1, -2)$ and $(2, 3)$. We begin by calculating the slope

$$m = \frac{-2 - 3}{-1 - 2} = \frac{-5}{-3} = \frac{5}{3}.$$

We have

$$\frac{y - -2}{x - -1} = \frac{y + 2}{x + 1} = \frac{5}{3}.$$

We rewrite this equation so we can compute y if we are given x:

$$y = \frac{5}{3}(x + 1) - 2 = \frac{5}{3}x - \frac{1}{3}.$$

This equation is in the *slope-intercept* form $y = mx + b$, which expresses y as a function of x. The slope m is the number in front of x, $\frac{5}{3}$. When $x = 0$, the line crosses the y-axis at $b = -\frac{1}{3}$, the *y-intercept*. You can see this in Figure 4.7.

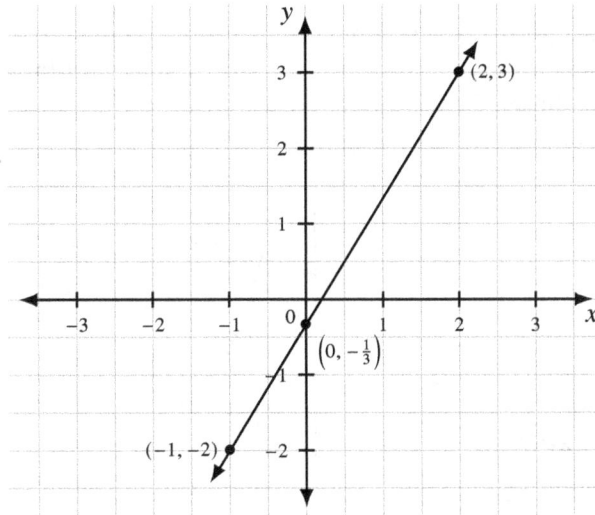

Figure 4.7: Graph of a line showing the y-intercept

Plotting functions

When we have a real-valued function on all or part of **R**, we can plot it as we saw for lines where $y = f(x)$. If you were to do this by hand, you would choose enough values of x, compute $f(x)$ for each x, plot each $(x, f(x))$, and then connect the points. The plot may not be a good rendition of the true graph.

Let's take $y = f(x) = \frac{1}{3}x^2$. We let x have integer values between -2 and 2. The smooth outer curve in Figure 4.8 is the correct plot, while the inner dashed one has straight lines connecting the few points we calculated.

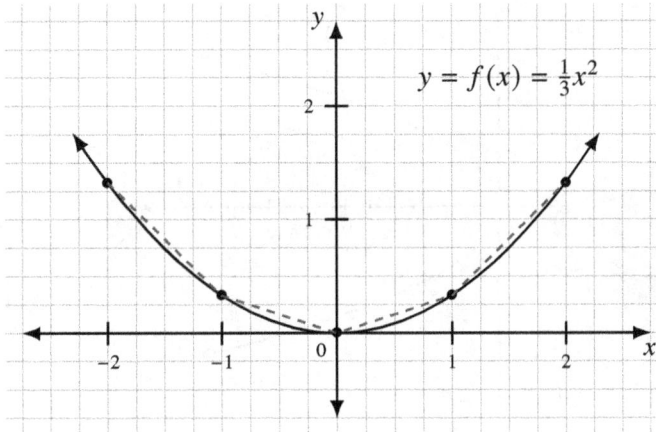

Figure 4.8: A plot with too few points

It's possible to make mistakes while plotting because you inadvertently include a value that is not in the domain. Let $y = f(x) = \left|\frac{1}{x}\right|$ for $x \neq 0$. If we plot for $x = -2, -1, 1,$ and 2 and are careless, we might see the dashed line plot in Figure 4.9. The function is not defined at 0, and the plot looks more like the two-part smooth solid curve.

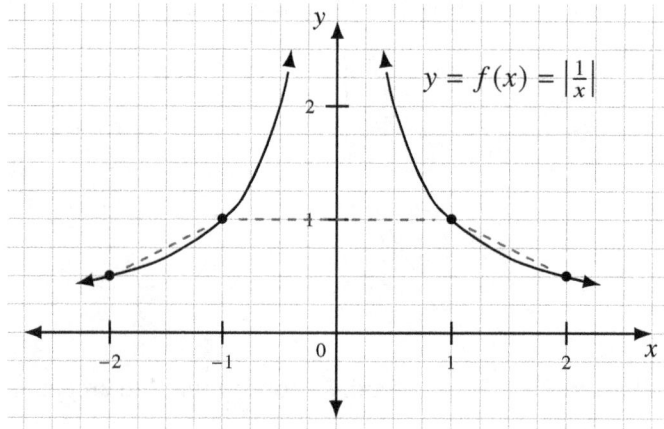

Figure 4.9: A plot of $y = f(x) = \left|\frac{1}{x}\right|$

We say $y = f(x) = \left|\frac{1}{x}\right|$ is not *continuous* at $x = 0$. We also say that $x = 0$ is a *discontinuity* of f. A discontinuity is a point where a function is not continuous.

Functions can be more sophisticated than mapping a number to a number. Instead, think of mapping a number to a point in the plane. If the input variable is t, we can take the formula for the point as $(g(t), h(t))$. We call this a *parameterized function*, and t is the *parameter*. This form includes the previous plotting cases because we can define $g(t)$ to be t.

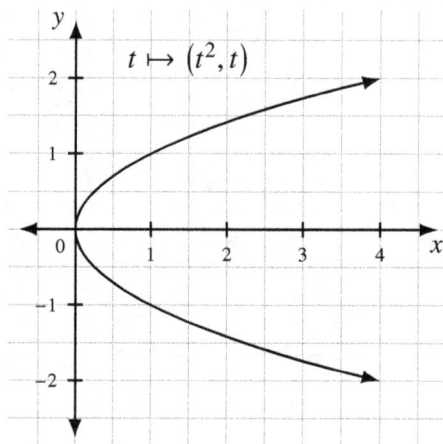

Figure 4.10: The plot of a parameterized parabolic function

We can directly plot the function $t \mapsto (t^2, t)$ from $\mathbf{R}$ to $\mathbf{R}^2$, shown as the parabola oriented horizontally in Figure 4.10.

Plotting parameterized functions can generate beautiful graphs such as spirals and multi-petal flowers. Figure 4.11 is the plot of

$$t \mapsto \left(\frac{t \cos(t)}{2\pi}, \frac{t \sin(t)}{2\pi} \right)$$

for $0 \le t \le 4\pi$.

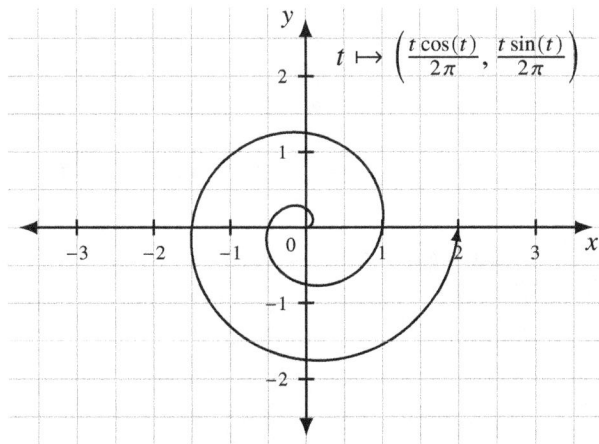

Figure 4.11: Parametric plot of a spiral

Figure 4.12 is the plot of

$$t \mapsto ((1 + \sin(9t)) \cos(t), (1 + \sin(9t)) \sin(t))$$

for $0 \le t \le 2\pi$. [31]

Circles

We define a circle by choosing one point as the center and then taking all points at a fixed positive distance, the *radius*, from that center. The *diameter* is twice the radius, and the *circumference* is the distance around the circle, equal to 2π times the radius.

Let $r > 0$ in $\mathbf{R}$ be the radius of the circle. If the coordinates of the center are (c, d) and a point (x, y) is distance r from the center, it satisfies the formula

$$\sqrt{(x - c)^2 + (y - d)^2} = r$$

or

$$(x - c)^2 + (y - d)^2 = r^2 .$$

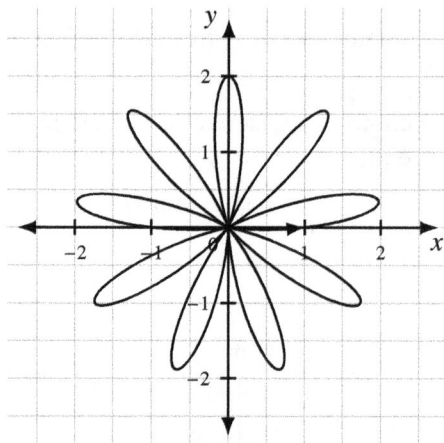

Figure 4.12: Parametric plot of a 9-petaled flower

Figure 4.13 is the plot of the circle of radius 2 centered at $(-1.5, 0.75)$. Its equation is $(x + 1.5)^2 + (y - 0.75)^2 = 2^2 = 4$.

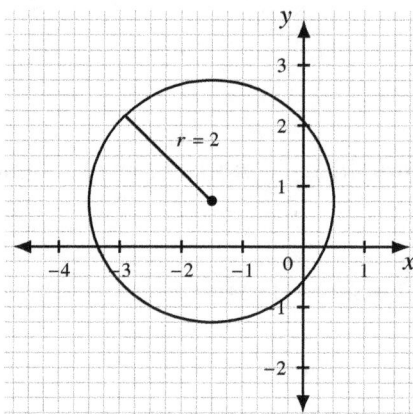

Figure 4.13: A circle with radius 2

Figure 4.14 is the plot of the *unit circle* of radius 1 centered at $(0, 0)$, the origin. Its equation is $x^2 + y^2 = 1$.

Exercise 4.5

How would you write y as a function of x in the equation of the unit circle? What are the domain and range of the function?

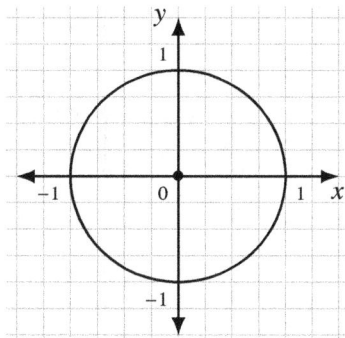

Figure 4.14: The unit circle centered at the origin

4.2.4 Exponentials and logarithms

An exponential function has the form

$$y = f(x) = c\,a^x$$

for constant real numbers $a > 0$, $a \neq 1$, and $c \neq 0$. Common choices for a are 2, 10, and e. For e, we define the function $\exp(x) = e^x$. For real x, $f(x)$ is positive or negative if c is. $f(0) = c$.

When c is positive and $0 < a < 1$, we have exponential decay. Figure 4.15 shows the plot when $a = \frac{1}{2}$. Radioactive decay follows this pattern.

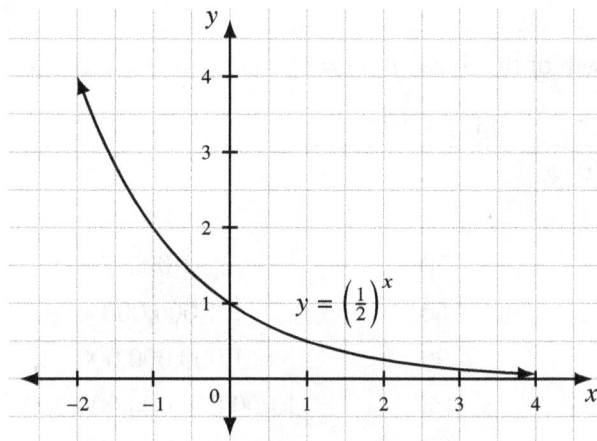

Figure 4.15: An example of exponential decay

If $a > 1$, we get exponential growth. Figure 4.16 compares $y = e^x$ and $y = 2^x$.

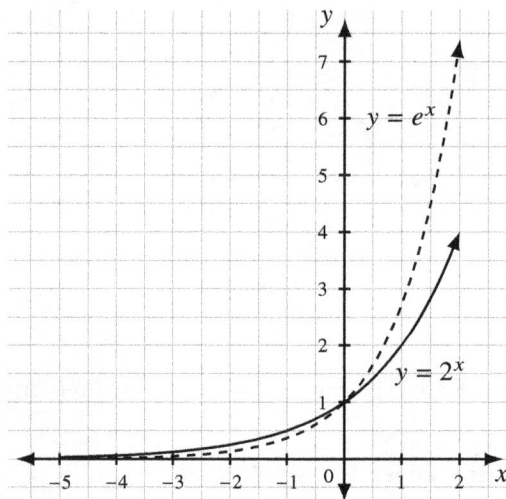

Figure 4.16: Two examples of exponential growth

Moore's Law, which was always more of an observation than a physically binding statement, said that roughly every two years, the computational power of a computer processor would double, and its size and energy requirements would be cut in half. While this no longer is the case, it was an example of exponential growth of power and decay of size and energy requirements. [154]

Compare the growth of the linear $f(x) = 10x$ exponential and $g(x) = 10^x$ functions:

x	$f(x) = 10x$	$g(x) = 10^x$
0	0	1
1	10	10
3	30	1,000
6	60	1,000,000
9	90	1,000,000,000
15	150	1,000,000,000,000,000

Generally, exponential growth is something to be controlled or avoided in computation unless it somehow involves your money.

If exponential functions can show fast growth, logarithmic ones do the opposite. A *logarithm* is an inverse function of an exponential one.

The real function $\log_2(x)$ for $c > 0$ returns the answer to the question, "To what power should I raise 2 to get x?"

$$\log_2(1) = 0 \quad \text{because} \quad 2^0 = 1$$
$$\log_2(2) = 1 \quad \text{because} \quad 2^1 = 2$$
$$\log_2(4) = 2 \quad \text{because} \quad 2^2 = 4$$
$$\log_2(64) = 6 \quad \text{because} \quad 2^6 = 64$$
$$\log_2(2048) = 11 \quad \text{because} \quad 2^{11} = 2048$$

If you work with computers long enough, you learn your powers of 2. $\log_2$ is the *binary logarithm*. The "inverse" behavior here shows $x = 2^{\log_2(x)}$ and $x = \log_2(2^x)$.

The natural logarithm is the inverse function to exponentiation by e. As a function name and shorthand for "$\log_e$" some authors use "ln" and others use "log." I use the latter. Figure 4.17 shows plots of the natural and binary logarithms.

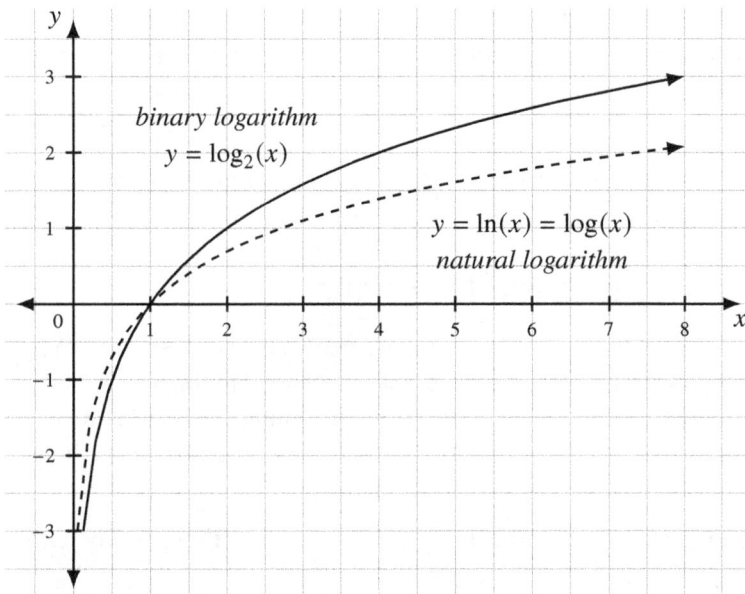

Figure 4.17: Plots of the natural and binary logarithms

For any positive base a, real number t, and positive real numbers x and y:

$$\log_a(xy) = \log_a(x) + \log_a(y)$$
$$\log_a\left(\frac{x}{y}\right) = \log_a(x) - \log_a(y)$$
$$\log_a(x^t) = t \log_a(x)$$

We can convert from one logarithmic base to another. For another base b,

$$\log_a(x) = \frac{\log_b(x)}{\log_b(a)}.$$

To derive this, if we set $t = \log_a(x)$, then $a^t = x$. Apply $\log_b$ to both sides and solve for t.

Exercise 4.6

Work out the details of deriving this formula. Show your work.

4.3 Trigonometry

When we discuss single qubits and what we can do with them in Chapter 7, "One Qubit," we will see that many of the operations we perform are rotations, and for these, we must know how to manipulate angles. The trigonometric functions like sine and cosine are foundational tools for working with angles, and this section reviews their properties and identities.

The Greek word *trígōnon* means "triangle," and *metron* means "measure."

4.3.1 The fundamental functions

Many people have heard that a circle has 360 degrees, also written 360°. Why 360? Looking around the web, you find stories about ancient Mesopotamians, Egyptians, and base 60 number systems. Whatever the reason, 360 is a convenient number because it is divisible by so many other numbers, such as 2, 3, 4, 5, 6, 8, 10, 12, 15, and so on. That is, it's easy to work with portions of 360° that are whole numbers.

Degrees don't have a natural meaning in mathematics, though. They are simply useful units of measurement. Instead, we use *radians*.

Since a circle of radius r has a circumference of $2\pi r$, if we go halfway around, we cover a distance of πr. One-quarter of the way covers $\frac{\pi}{2}r$.

When $r = 1$, we use fractions of 2π to determine how far around the circle we have gone, and we call this the *radian measure* of the corresponding angle. Halfway around is π radians. If we go around three times, we have 6π radians. Radians have real geometric meaning compared to degrees. When we move counterclockwise, the radian measure is positive and negative when we move clockwise.

With either degrees or radians, we begin measuring the angle from the positive x-axis.

Because we are dealing with a circle, an angle of $\frac{3\pi}{4}$ radians lands us on the same point as one of $-\frac{5\pi}{4}$ radians, as shown in Figure 4.18.

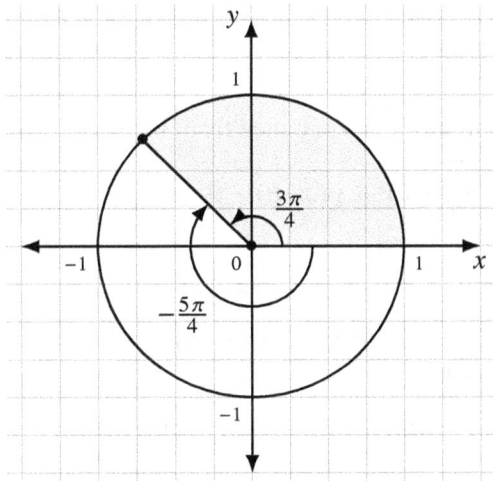

Figure 4.18: $\frac{3\pi}{4}$ radians is the same rotation as $-\frac{5\pi}{4}$ radians

We frequently use Greek letters as variable names when working with radians or degrees. The two most common are θ (theta) and φ (phi).

Using θ as the angle measurement, consider the plot where P is a point on the unit circle with $\theta = \frac{\pi}{3}$.

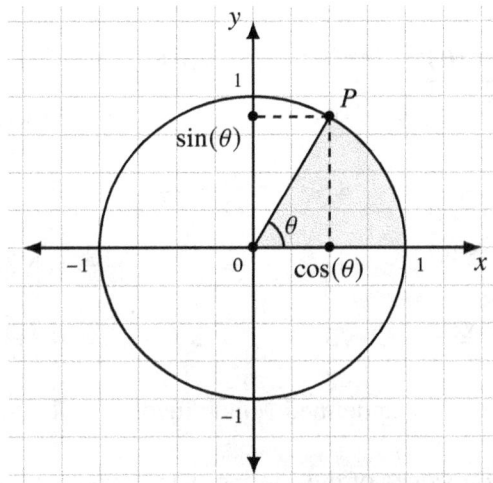

Figure 4.19: Definitions of the sine and cosine

We define the function $\cos(\theta)$, the *cosine* of θ, to be the x-coordinate of the point P. Similarly, the function $\sin(\theta)$, *sine* of θ, is the y coordinate of P. Though we draw P in the first quadrant, we extend the definition to all points on the unit circle in all quadrants and on the axes.

The cosine is just an x-coordinate, and the sine is just a y-coordinate. As functions, they have many elegant properties, but it all comes down to the geometry of a radius 1 circle around the origin.

Because P is on the unit circle, its distance from the origin $(0,0)$ is 1. Thus

$$1 = \sqrt{(\cos(\theta) - 0)^2 + (\sin(\theta) - 0)^2} = \sqrt{\cos^2(\theta) + \sin^2(\theta)}.$$

Squaring, we get

$$1 = \cos^2(\theta) + \sin^2(\theta).$$

This is the *fundamental identity of trigonometry*. It follows naturally from the definition of length and the Pythagorean theorem.

Instead of writing the longer $(\cos(\theta))^2$ in the above, I used the common shorthand $\cos^2(\theta)$.

If θ is negative, we consider $|\theta|$ but rotate clockwise from the positive x-axis. Look at the plot in Figure 4.19 to convince yourself that $\cos(-\theta) = \cos(\theta)$ and $\sin(-\theta) = -\sin(\theta)$. While this is not a rigorous mathematical proof, developing your geometric intuition is more important here.

We call a function f such as cos with the property $f(-x) = f(x)$ an *even* function. If $f(-x) = -f(x)$, then the function is *odd*. sin is an odd function.

θ	$\cos(\theta)$	$\sin(\theta)$	$\tan(\theta)$	$\sec(\theta)$	$\csc(\theta)$	$\cot(\theta)$
0	1	0	0	1	undefined	undefined
$\frac{\pi}{6}$	$\frac{\sqrt{3}}{2}$	$\frac{1}{2}$	$\frac{1}{\sqrt{3}} = \frac{\sqrt{3}}{3}$	$\frac{2}{\sqrt{3}} = \frac{2\sqrt{3}}{3}$	2	$\sqrt{3}$
$\frac{\pi}{4}$	$\frac{\sqrt{2}}{2}$	$\frac{\sqrt{2}}{2}$	1	$\frac{2}{\sqrt{2}} = \sqrt{2}$	$\frac{2}{\sqrt{2}} = \sqrt{2}$	1
$\frac{\pi}{3}$	$\frac{1}{2}$	$\frac{\sqrt{3}}{2}$	$\sqrt{3}$	2	$\frac{2}{\sqrt{3}} = \frac{2\sqrt{3}}{3}$	$\frac{1}{\sqrt{3}} = \frac{\sqrt{3}}{3}$
$\frac{\pi}{2}$	0	1	undefined	undefined	1	0

Figure 4.20: Common values of the trigonometric functions in the first quadrant

Another essential trigonometric function is the tangent, written $\tan(\theta)$ and defined by

$$\tan(\theta) = \frac{\sin(\theta)}{\cos(\theta)} \text{ for } \cos(\theta) \neq 0.$$

When does $\cos(\theta) = 0$? This happens whenever the x-coordinate is 0, so θ corresponds to a point on the y-axis. These values are

$$\theta = \frac{\pi}{2}, \frac{3\pi}{2}, -\frac{\pi}{2}, -\frac{3\pi}{2},$$

and integer multiples of each of these by 2π. These multiples correspond to going around the circle more than one time in either direction.

> The tangent is the slope of the line segment from the origin $(0, 0)$ to P.

The three remaining standard trigonometric functions are the secant, cosecant, and cotangent. These are defined, respectively, by

$$\sec(\theta) = \frac{1}{\cos(\theta)} = (\cos(\theta))^{-1} \text{ for } \cos(\theta) \neq 0$$

$$\csc(\theta) = \frac{1}{\sin(\theta)} = (\sin(\theta))^{-1} \text{ for } \sin(\theta) \neq 0$$

$$\cot(\theta) = \frac{\cos(\theta)}{\sin(\theta)} = (\tan(\theta))^{-1} \text{ for } \sin(\theta) \neq 0$$

These are connected to the fundamental identity by dividing by $\cos^2(\theta)$ or $\sin^2(\theta)$.

$$1 = \cos^2(\theta) + \sin^2(\theta)$$

$$\frac{1}{\cos^2(\theta)} = \frac{\cos^2(\theta)}{\cos^2(\theta)} + \frac{\sin^2(\theta)}{\cos^2(\theta)} \Rightarrow \sec^2(\theta) = 1 + \tan^2(\theta)$$

$$\frac{1}{\sin^2(\theta)} = \frac{\cos^2(\theta)}{\sin^2(\theta)} + \frac{\sin^2(\theta)}{\sin^2(\theta)} \Rightarrow \csc^2(\theta) = \cot^2(\theta) + 1$$

These identities hold when the denominators are not 0.

4.3.2   The inverse functions

Do the trigonometric functions have inverses? Yes, but we need to be very careful at stating the domains and ranges. We also have to decide what to call them. Three notations are common for the inverse tangent:

$$\tan^{-1}(x) \qquad \arctan(x) \qquad \text{atan}(x).$$

The first is consistent with calling f^{-1} the inverse of the function f but is confusing because of our shorthand with forms such as $\tan^2(x)$ meaning $\tan(x)^2$.

The third version is common in programming languages such as Python, Swift, Rust, C++, and Java. We use the middle version as it is traditional and relates to the arc that spans the angle.

The sine function (Figure 4.21) gives its name to the archetypal example of a wave, a *sinusoidal wave*.

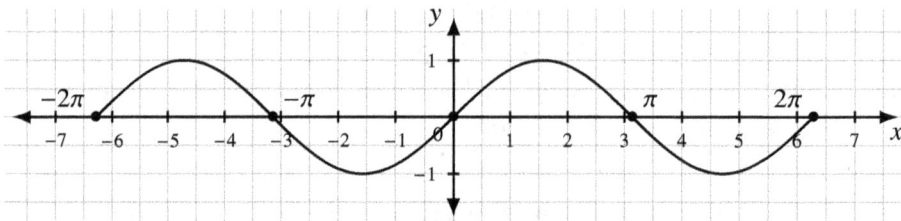

Figure 4.21: A plot of the sine function

In the portion of the graph I've shown in Figure 4.21, the plot crosses the x-axis five times. On this graph, $\sin(x) = 0$ when $x = -2\pi, -\pi, 0, \pi,$ and 2π. So what is arcsin(0)?

We must choose a range that ensures arcsin is single-valued and, therefore, a function.

arcsin(x) is a function with domain $-1 \le x \le 1$ and range $-\frac{\pi}{2} \le \text{arcsin}(x) \le \frac{\pi}{2}$.

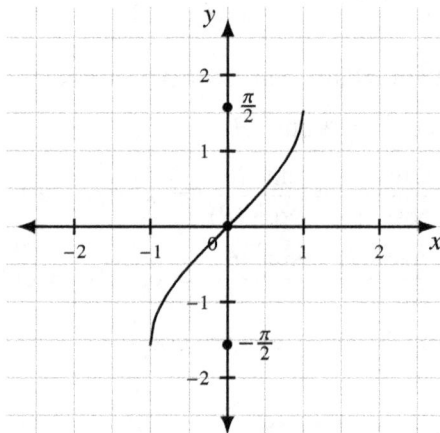

The inverse cosine arccos has a different range.

$\arccos(x)$ is a function with domain $-1 \leq x \leq 1$ and range $0 \leq \arccos(x) \leq \pi$.

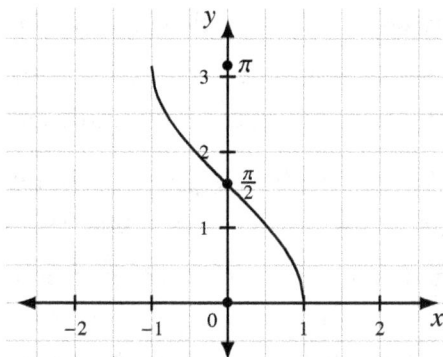

The inverse tangent arctan requires closer consideration because in the definition

$$\tan(x) = \frac{\sin(x)}{\cos(x)},$$

the denominator can be 0 when $\cos(x)$ is 0. The values of x we must look out for are $\frac{\pi}{2}$ and $-\frac{\pi}{2}$.

$\arctan(x)$ is a function with domain all of **R** and range $-\frac{\pi}{2} < \arctan(x) < \frac{\pi}{2}$.

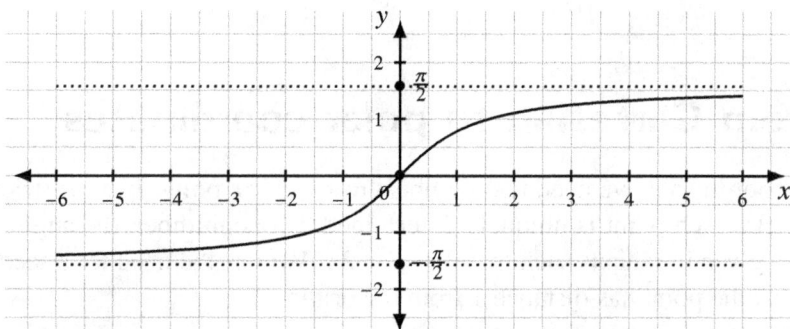

4.3.3 Additional identities

Several other trigonometric formulas are helpful. The sum and difference formulas express sin and cos when you have addition and subtraction of angles in the arguments:

$$\sin(\theta + \varphi) = \sin(\theta)\cos(\varphi) + \cos(\theta)\sin(\varphi)$$
$$\cos(\theta + \varphi) = \cos(\theta)\cos(\varphi) - \sin(\theta)\sin(\varphi)$$

$$\sin(\theta - \varphi) = \sin(\theta)\cos(\varphi) - \cos(\theta)\sin(\varphi)$$
$$\cos(\theta - \varphi) = \cos(\theta)\cos(\varphi) + \sin(\theta)\sin(\varphi)$$

The last two follow from the first two because cos is an even function, and sin is an odd function.

If we let $\theta = \varphi$ in the sum formulas, we get the double angle formulas:

$$\sin(2\theta) = 2\sin(\theta)\cos(\theta)$$
$$\cos(2\theta) = \cos^2(\theta) - \sin^2(\theta) = 2\cos^2(\theta) - 1 = 1 - 2\sin^2(\theta)$$

Exercise 4.7

Use the trigonometric identities to simplify

$$\frac{\sin(2x)}{\cos^2(x)}.$$

4.4 From Cartesian to polar coordinates

In Cartesian coordinates, we need two numbers to specify a point. If we restrict ourselves to the unit circle, each point is uniquely determined by one number, the angle φ from the positive x-axis given in radians such that $0 \leq \varphi < 2\pi$. We lost the need for a second number by insisting that the point has distance 1 from the origin.

More generally, let $P = (a, b))$ be a nonzero point (that is, a point that is not the origin) in $\mathbf{R}^2$. Let $r = \sqrt{a^2 + b^2}$ be the distance from P to the origin. The point

$$Q = \left(\frac{a}{r}, \frac{b}{r}\right)$$

is on the unit circle. There is a unique angle φ $0 \leq \varphi < 2\pi$ that corresponds to Q. With r, we can uniquely identify

$$P = (r\cos(\varphi), r\sin(\varphi)).$$

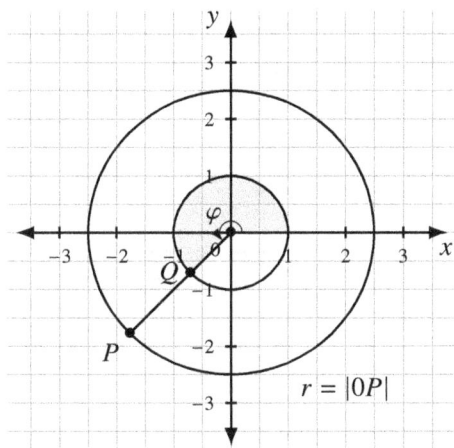

Figure 4.22: Polar and Cartesian coordinates

(r, φ) are called the *polar coordinates* of P. You may sometimes see the Greek letter ρ (rho) used instead of r.

Each nonzero point in $\mathbf{R}^2$ is uniquely determined by an angle φ given in radians such that $0 \leq \varphi < 2\pi$, and a positive real number r.

To uniquely identify P in the plot in Figure 4.22, $r = 2.5$ and $\varphi = \frac{5\pi}{4}$.

4.5 The complex "plane"

In section 3.9, we discussed the algebraic properties of $\mathbf{C}$, the complex numbers. We return to them again here to look at their geometry. For any point (a, b) in the real plane, consider the corresponding complex number $a + bi$.

In the graph of the complex numbers, the horizontal axis is the real part of the complex variable z, and the vertical axis is the imaginary part. These replace the x and y axes, respectively.

The plot in Figure 4.23 shows several complex values. That is not a *complex* plane despite appearances and some authors' terminology. A plane has two dimensions. We visualized $\mathbf{C}$, which is one-dimensional, in the two-dimensional *real* plane. We return to these issues about dimensions with respect to a field in section 5.2 when we look at vector spaces.

Historically, the complex plane has been called the *Argand plane* and the *Gauss plane*.

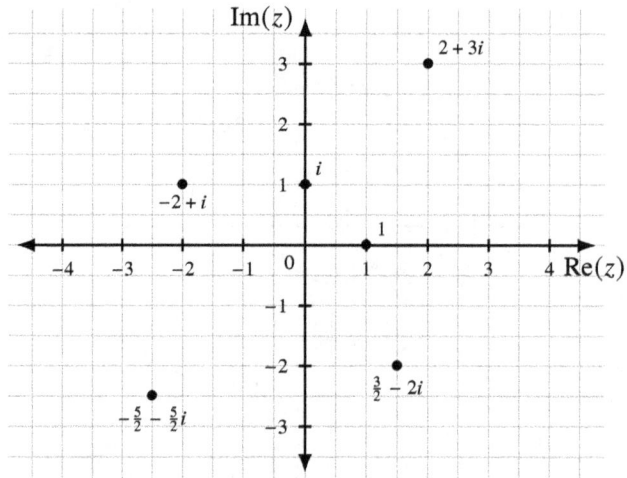

Figure 4.23: Values in the complex plane

4.5.1 Conjugation

Conjugation reflects a complex number across the horizontal $\text{Re}(z)$ axis. If the number has a 0 imaginary part, it is already on the $\text{Re}(z)$ axis, so nothing happens. Figure 4.24 shows several complex numbers and their conjugates.

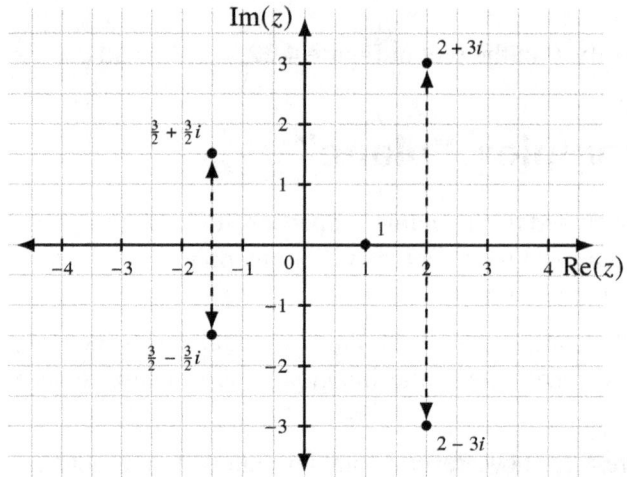

Figure 4.24: Conjugation of values in the complex plane

Exercise 4.8

What does conjugation do to 0? i?

4.5.2 Polar coordinates

As we saw for the Cartesian plane $\mathbf{R}^2$, we can use polar coordinates for a point. Therefore, we can also use them for any nonzero complex number.

Each nonzero point $a + bi$ in $\mathbf{C}$ is uniquely determined by an angle φ given in radians such that $0 \leq \varphi < 2\pi$, and a positive real number $r = |z|$. The arg function associates φ with z: $\arg(z) = \varphi$.

$$z = r\cos(\varphi) + r\sin(\varphi)\,i$$
$$= |z|\cos(\arg(z)) + |z|\sin(\arg(z))\,i$$

The angle φ is the *phase* of z, and $|z|$ is its *magnitude*.

The term "phase" for the angle φ of a complex number is used more in physics than in mathematics. I introduce it here because we need phase when describing a qubit's representation in section 7.1.

Any φ that is a nonzero integer multiple of 2π plus φ lands us on the same point, but we normalize our choice to be between 0 and 2π. Figure 4.25 shows the radius and phase of an example complex number.

Instead of using the (r, φ) notation or the longer $r\cos(\varphi) + r\sin(\varphi)i$ expression using polar coordinates, we adopt an exponential form incorporating both r and φ via Euler's formula.

4.5.3 Euler's formula

Leonhard Euler was a prolific eighteenth-century mathematician who made many contributions to multiple fields of science. He was the first to prove the connection between extending the exponential function to complex numbers and the $a + bi$ notation involving polar coordinates. That is, he showed

$$re^{\varphi i} = r\left(\cos(\varphi) + \sin(\varphi)\right) = r\cos(\varphi) + r\sin(\varphi)\,i\,.$$

We use this notation for the polar form of a complex number.

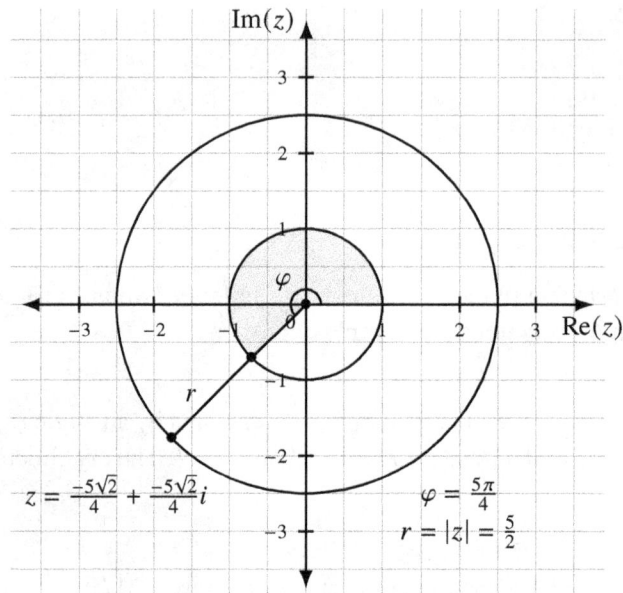

Figure 4.25: A complex number with its radius φ

When $r = 1$,

$$e^{\varphi i} = \cos(\varphi) + \sin(\varphi).$$

To learn more

The proof of Euler's formula is beyond the scope of this book, though we will see elements of it in section 12.3.1. The statement and its proof fall within the branch of mathematics called *complex analysis*, which you may think of as the extension of calculus from **R** to **C**. [4] [48] [160]

If z_1 and z_2 are nonzero complex numbers, then $|z_1 z_2| = |z_1| \times |z_2|$ and $\arg(z_1 z_2) = \arg(z_1) + \arg(z_2)$. Expressed in a longer form, if

$$z_1 = r_1 \cos(\varphi_1) + r_1 \sin(\varphi_1) i$$
$$z_2 = r_2 \cos(\varphi_2) + r_2 \sin(\varphi_2) i$$

then

$$z_1 z_2 = r_1 r_2 \cos(\varphi_1 + \varphi_2) + r_1 r_2 \sin(\varphi_1 + \varphi_2) i$$
$$= r_1 r_2 \left(\cos(\varphi_1 + \varphi_2) + \sin(\varphi_1 + \varphi_2) i \right)$$

and

$$\frac{z_1}{z_2} = \frac{r_1}{r_2} \cos(\varphi_1 - \varphi_2) + \frac{r_1}{r_2} \sin(\varphi_1 - \varphi_2) i$$

$$= \frac{r_1}{r_2} \Big(\cos(\varphi_1 - \varphi_2) + \sin(\varphi_1 - \varphi_2) \Big) i \, .$$

When we multiply complex numbers, we multiply the magnitudes and add the phases. When we divide complex numbers, we divide the magnitudes and subtract the phases.

By Euler's formula, if $z_1 = r_1 e^{\varphi_1 i}$ and $z_2 = r_2 e^{\varphi_2 i}$, then

$$z_1 z_2 = r_1 r_2 e^{(\varphi_1 + \varphi_2) i} \quad \text{and} \quad \frac{z_1}{z_2} = \frac{r_1}{r_2} e^{(\varphi_1 - \varphi_2) i} \, .$$

These forms are considerably simpler to use when multiplying or dividing complex numbers but much less so when adding or subtracting.

Multiplying a complex number by $e^{\varphi i}$ translates geometrically to rotating the complex number φ radians around 0. If φ is positive, the rotation is counterclockwise; for φ negative, it is clockwise.

If $z = r e^{\varphi i}$, its conjugate is $\overline{z} = r e^{-\varphi i}$.

Whether you think of a complex number as a real and imaginary part or as a phase and a magnitude, it holds two independent pieces of data represented as real numbers. This representation, with the algebraic and geometric properties, is why complex numbers appear in some unexpected places in physics and engineering.

Exercise 4.9

Let z_1 and z_2 be two nonzero numbers in **C**, and let c be a complex number with magnitude 1. Show that the angle between z_1 and z_2 is the same as the angle between cz_1 and cz_2.

4.6 Real three dimensions

When plotting in three dimensions, we need either three Cartesian coordinates (x_0, y_0, z_0) or a magnitude r and two angles φ and θ, as shown in Figure 4.26.

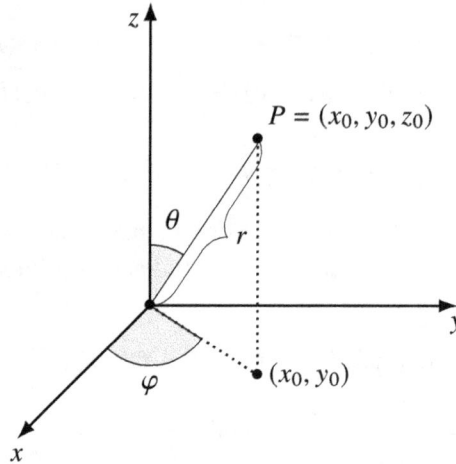

Figure 4.26: Polar coordinates in three dimensions

The magnitude is

$$r = |P| = \sqrt{x_0{}^2 + y_0{}^2 + z_0{}^2}\,.$$

φ is the angle from the positive x-axis to the dotted line from $(0,0)$ to the projection (x_0, y_0) of P into the xy-plane.

θ is the angle from the positive z-axis to the line segment $0P$.

That's a lot to absorb, but it builds up systematically from what we saw in $\mathbf{R}^2$. When $r = 1$, we get the *unit sphere* in $\mathbf{R}^3$. It's the set of all points (x_0, y_0, z_0) in $\mathbf{R}^3$ where $x_0^2 + y_0^2 + z_0^2 = 1$.

The *unit ball* is the set of all points where $x_0^2 + y_0^2 + z_0^2 \leq 1$.

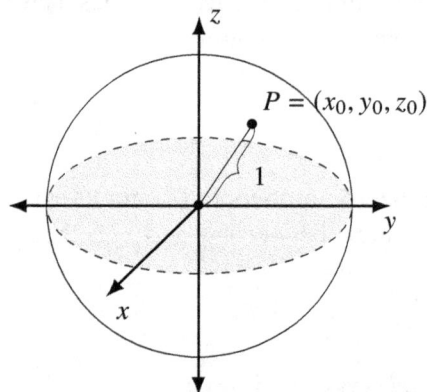

Figure 4.27: The unit sphere

We frequently return to the graphic in Figure 4.27 when considering the Bloch sphere representation of a qubit in section 7.5.

If we were in four real dimensions, we would need four coordinates (x, y, z, w) or, using subscripts, (x_1, x_2, x_3, x_4). The *unit hypersphere* is the set of all points such that $1 = x^2 + y^2 + z^2 + w^2$.

4.7 Summary

After handling algebra in Chapter 3, we tackled geometry here. The concept of ''function'' is core to most of mathematics and its application areas, such as physics. Functions allow us to connect one or more inputs with useful output. Plotting functions is an excellent way to visualize their behavior.

Two- and three-dimensional spaces are now familiar, and we learned and reviewed tools to allow us to use them effectively. Trigonometry demonstrates beautiful connections between algebra and geometry and falls out naturally from relationships such as the Pythagorean theorem.

The complex ''plane'' is like the real plane $\mathbf{R}^2$, but the algebra and geometry give more structure than points alone can provide. Euler's formula nicely ties together complex numbers and trigonometry in an easy-to-use notation that is the basis for how we define many quantum operations in Chapter 7, ''One Qubit,'' and Chapter 8, ''Two Qubits, Three.''

To learn more

Many readers were introduced to geometry in high school or its equivalent via theorems and proofs. If that part of the subject interests you, more advanced treatments explore axiomatic and geometric-algebraic approaches. [7] [51]

5

Dimensions

*... from a purely mathematical point of view it's just as easy
to think in 11 dimensions, as it is to think in three or four.*

– Stephen Hawking

We are familiar with many properties of objects, such as lines and circles in two dimensions, and cubes and spheres in three dimensions. If I ask you how long something is, you might take out a ruler or a tape measure. When you take a photo, you rotate your camera or phone in three dimensions without thinking too much about it.

Alas, there is math behind all these actions. The notion of something existing in one or more dimensions, indeed even the idea of what a dimension is, must be made more formal if we are to perform calculations. This is the concept of *vector spaces*. The study of what they are and what you can do with them is *linear algebra*.

Linear algebra is essential to pure and applied mathematics, physics, engineering, and the parts of computer science and software engineering that deal with graphics. It's also valuable in many parts of AI, such as machine learning. As we shall see throughout this book, linear algebra provides essential mathematical tools we need to express quantum information and operations.

Topics covered in this chapter

5.1 $\mathbf{R}^2$ and $\mathbf{C}^1$

In section 4.2, we looked at the real plane as a set of standard Cartesian coordinate pairs (x, y) with x and y in $\mathbf{R}$ representing points we can plot. We give these pairs an algebraic structure so that if u and v are in $\mathbf{R}^2$, then so is $u + v$. Also, if r is in $\mathbf{R}$, we say that r is a *scalar*. $r\,u$ and $r\,v$ are in $\mathbf{R}^2$ as well. We carry out the addition coordinate by coordinate. The multiplication by r, called *scalar multiplication*, is also done that way.

If $u = (u_1, u_2)$ and $v = (v_1, v_2)$,

$$u + v = (u_1 + v_1, u_2 + v_2) \quad \text{and} \quad ru = (ru_1, ru_2) \ .$$

Using the origin $O = (0,0)$ as the identity element, $\mathbf{R}^2$ is a commutative group under addition. With scalar multiplication by elements of the field $\mathbf{R}$, $\mathbf{R}^2$ is a two-dimensional *vector space* over $\mathbf{R}$.

Rather than considering them as pairs or points, we now call $\mathbf{u}$ and $\mathbf{v}$ vectors. I use **bold** to indicate a variable or a ''point'' is a vector. When we plot a vector, we draw it as an arrow from the origin $(0,0)$ to the point represented by the Cartesian coordinates. Figure 5.1 shows a plot of the vectors $\mathbf{u} = (3, 2)$, $\mathbf{v} = (1, -3)$, and their sum.

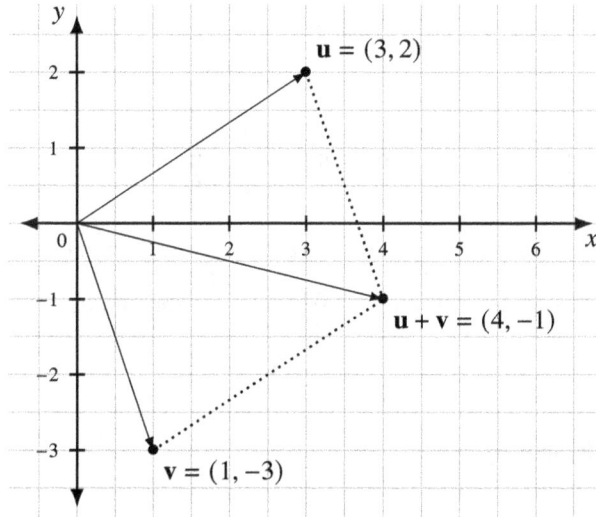

Figure 5.1: Two vectors and their sum

There are two special vectors: $\mathbf{e}_1$, associated with the Cartesian coordinates $(1, 0)$, and $\mathbf{e}_2$, associated with $(0, 1)$. We may write any vector with coordinates (a, b) as $a\,\mathbf{e}_1 + b\,\mathbf{e}_2$. If this sum equals $\mathbf{0} = (0, 0)$, then a and b must be zero, meaning $\mathbf{e}_1$ and $\mathbf{e}_2$ are *linearly independent*.

Because they have these properties, $\mathbf{e}_1$ and $\mathbf{e}_2$ are *basis vectors*, and these are the *standard basis vectors*, or the *standard basis*, for $\mathbf{R}^2$.

The central idea of Cartesian coordinates is that we are using $\mathbf{e}_1$ and $\mathbf{e}_2$. When we mention a point with coordinates (a, b), we mean the point corresponding to the vector $a\,\mathbf{e}_1 + b\,\mathbf{e}_2$. Assume we are using Cartesian coordinates and $\mathbf{e}_1$ and $\mathbf{e}_2$ unless stated otherwise.

Other pairs have this property as well. If

$$\mathbf{h}_1 = \frac{\sqrt{2}}{2}\mathbf{e}_1 + \frac{\sqrt{2}}{2}\mathbf{e}_2 \quad \text{and} \quad \mathbf{h}_2 = \frac{\sqrt{2}}{2}\mathbf{e}_1 - \frac{\sqrt{2}}{2}\mathbf{e}_2,$$

then

$$\mathbf{h}_1 + \mathbf{h}_2 = \sqrt{2}\,\mathbf{e}_1$$

$$\frac{1}{\sqrt{2}}\,(\mathbf{h}_1 + \mathbf{h}_2) = \mathbf{e}_1$$

and

$$\mathbf{h}_1 - \mathbf{h}_2 = \sqrt{2}\,\mathbf{e}_2$$

$$\frac{1}{\sqrt{2}}\,(\mathbf{h}_1 - \mathbf{h}_2) = \mathbf{e}_2\,.$$

Given the vector $3\mathbf{e}_1 + 0\mathbf{e}_2$, we have

$$3\mathbf{e}_1 + 0\mathbf{e}_2 = \frac{3}{\sqrt{2}}\,(\mathbf{h}_1 + \mathbf{h}_2) + \frac{0}{\sqrt{2}}\,(\mathbf{h}_1 - \mathbf{h}_2)$$

$$= \frac{3\sqrt{2}}{2}\,(\mathbf{h}_1 + \mathbf{h}_2) = \frac{3\sqrt{2}}{2}\mathbf{h}_1 + \frac{3\sqrt{2}}{2}\mathbf{h}_2\,.$$

So, the point with Cartesian coordinates $(3, 0)$ has the coordinates

$$\left(\frac{3\sqrt{2}}{2}, \frac{3\sqrt{2}}{2}\right)$$

when using the basis $\mathbf{h}_1$ and $\mathbf{h}_2$.

> Coordinates are relative to the basis you are using. Sometimes, a change of basis makes the algebra and geometry less complex and easier to understand.

For $\mathbf{u} = \mathbf{e}_1 + 2\mathbf{e}_2$, $\mathbf{v} = 2\mathbf{e}_1 - 3\mathbf{e}_2$, and $r = -1$, we have

$$\mathbf{u} + \mathbf{v} = 3\mathbf{e}_1 - \mathbf{e}_2$$

and

$$r\,\mathbf{u} = -\mathbf{e}_1 - 2\mathbf{e}_2\,.$$

Figure 5.2 shows the vectors and several arithmetic operations on them.

Observe that $\mathbf{u}$ and $r\,\mathbf{u}$ fall on the same line, which means they are not a basis: $\mathbf{0} = r\,\mathbf{v} - (r\,\mathbf{v})$. $\mathbf{u}$ and $r\,\mathbf{u}$ are *linearly dependent*.

The length of a vector $a\,\mathbf{e}_1 + b\,\mathbf{e}_2$ in $\mathbf{R}^2$ is $\sqrt{a^2 + b^2}$. We denote it $\|a\,\mathbf{e}_1 + b\,\mathbf{e}_2\|$. We use double vertical bars for the length instead of the single vertical bars for absolute value.

A vector of length 1 is a *unit vector*. $\mathbf{e}_1$ and $\mathbf{e}_2$ are unit basis vectors. So are $\mathbf{h}_1$ and $\mathbf{h}_2$.

For $\mathbf{R}^1$, $\mathbf{e}_1$, corresponding to (1) in its Cartesian coordinate, is the standard unit basis. For a vector $a\,\mathbf{e}_1$, its length is $\|a\,\mathbf{e}_1\| = |a|$. $|a|$ is the usual absolute value for real numbers.

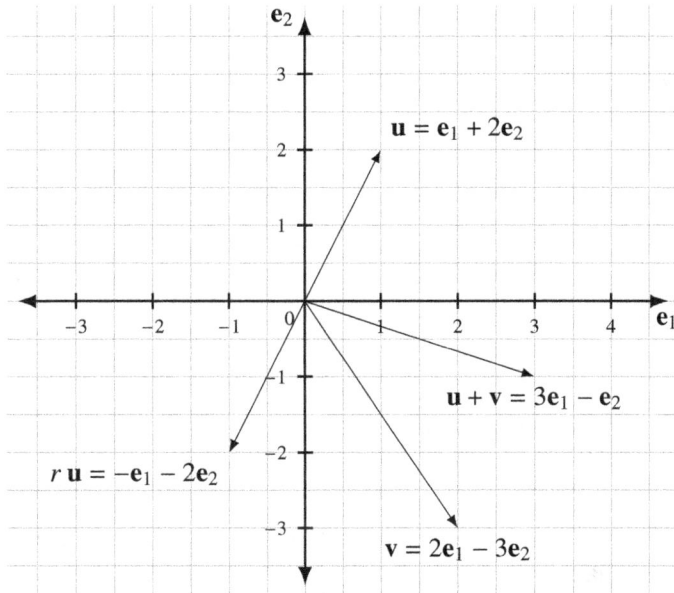

Figure 5.2: Arithmetic on two vectors

For $\mathbf{R}^3$, we use

$$\mathbf{e}_1 = (1, 0, 0) \qquad \mathbf{e}_2 = (0, 1, 0) \qquad \mathbf{e}_3 = (0, 0, 1)$$

in Cartesian coordinates. If $\mathbf{u} = u_1\mathbf{e}_1 + u_2\mathbf{e}_2 + u_3\mathbf{e}_3$ is in $\mathbf{R}^3$, then the length of $\mathbf{u}$ is

$$\|\mathbf{u}\| = \sqrt{u_1^2 + u_2^2 + u_3^2}\,.$$

As vectors spaces over $\mathbf{R}$, $\mathbf{R}^1$, $\mathbf{R}^2$, and $\mathbf{R}^3$ have dimensions 1, 2, and 3.

If you are driving at 100 kilometers per hour, that number is the *speed* at which you travel. If you include a direction, such as, ''I'm driving north at 100 kph,'' you are talking about *velocity*.

Velocity is a vector. If we represent north by $\mathbf{e}_2$ in $\mathbf{R}^2$, the above becomes $100\,\mathbf{e}_2$. Velocity does not say where you are, just how fast you are going in some direction.

Momentum is a vector equal to an object's mass times its velocity. At the quantum particle level, the *Heisenberg Uncertainty Principle* says that the more precisely we know a particle's position or momentum, the less precisely we can know the other.

$\mathbf{C}$ is a two-dimensional vector space over $\mathbf{R}$ with standard unit basis vectors $\mathbf{e}_1 = \mathbf{1} = (1,0)$ and $\mathbf{e}_2 = \boldsymbol{i} = (0,1)$. $\mathbf{C}^1$ is a one-dimensional vector space over $\mathbf{C}$ with standard unit basis vector $\mathbf{e}_1 = (1)$.

Since we are considering multiple fields with $\mathbf{R}$ contained in $\mathbf{C}$, let's fine-tune how we define a linear function beyond what we said in section 4.1.

A complex-valued function f on $\mathbf{C}$ is *linear* (more precisely, *complex linear*) if the following conditions hold for a, b, z, and w in $\mathbf{C}$:

$$f(z+w) = f(z) + f(w) \quad \text{and} \quad f(az) = af(z).$$

These imply $f(az + bw) = af(z) + bf(w)$.

We call a complex-valued function f on $\mathbf{C}$ *real linear* if the following conditions hold for a in $\mathbf{R}$ and z, and w in $\mathbf{C}$:

$$f(z+w) = f(z) + f(w) \quad \text{and} \quad f(az) = af(z).$$

Although the conditions look similar, not every real linear function is complex linear.

The definition of complex linear applies when considering $\mathbf{C} = \mathbf{C}^1$ as a one-dimensional vector space over itself. The definition of real linear applies when we consider it as a two-dimensional vector space over $\mathbf{R}$. We are primarily concerned with vector spaces over $\mathbf{C}$ for quantum computing.

If f is a function on $\mathbf{C}$ such that $|f(z)| = |z|$, then f preserves length. Such functions are *isometries*. If f is also linear, then it is a linear isometry.

The word stem *iso* comes from Greek and means "equal" or "identical." An "isometry" is a function where objects have an equal measure before and after the application. An isometry maps complex values on the unit circle to the unit circle.

Exercise 5.1

Any complex function $f(z) = e^{\varphi i}z$ for fixed $0 \le \varphi < 2\pi$ is a linear isometry. Prove that

$$f(z)\overline{f(z)} = 1.$$

What about conjugation? If $z = a + bi$, then

$$|z| = \sqrt{a^2 + b^2} = |\overline{z}|.$$

So, conjugation is an isometry, but is it linear? For

$$f(z) = \overline{z}$$

and a in $\mathbf{C}$,

$$f(az) = \overline{az} = \overline{a}\,\overline{z} = \overline{a}f(z)\,.$$

Conjugation is not complex linear, but it's close! It is real linear. We must consider conjugation frequently when we look at higher-dimensional complex vector spaces.

With this grounding in low-dimensional real vector spaces and the algebraic and geometric relationships between $\mathbf{R}^2$ and $\mathbf{C}$, we're ready to tackle generalizations of what we've been discussing and higher dimensions.

In quantum computing, vector spaces get very large. The mathematics for a 5-qubit quantum computer requires 32 complex dimensions! A 20-qubit system involves $2^{20} =$ 1,048,576 complex dimensions. The terminology and notation we develop simplify how we understand and manipulate such large vector spaces.

Until this point, I have distinguished between a point and a vector to which it corresponds. The coordinates of the point have been the coefficients when we write out the basis expression for the vector.

I'll now stop using language such as "the vector associated with the point" since we will primarily speak about vectors. I'll leave it to you to go back and forth between points and vectors as the content dictates.

When I give a list of coordinates such as $\mathbf{v} = (v_1, v_2, v_3, v_4)$ to describe a vector, remember these are all coefficients relative to some particular basis. By default, it is the standard basis, but the discussion will clarify if another basis is involved.

5.2 Vector spaces

The last section introduced several ideas about vector spaces using familiar notions from $\mathbf{R}^2$ and $\mathbf{C}$. It's time to generalize.

Let $\mathbf{F}$ be a field, for example, $\mathbf{Q}$, $\mathbf{R}$, or $\mathbf{C}$. Let V be a set of objects which we call vectors. We display vectors in bold such as $\mathbf{v}$.

We are interested in defining vector addition and a special kind of multiplication called scalar multiplication. If s is in $\mathbf{F}$, then we insist $s\mathbf{v}$ is in V for all $\mathbf{v}$ in V. The set V is closed under multiplication by scalars from the field $\mathbf{F}$. While V may have some kind of multiplication defined between its elements, we do not need to consider it here.

For any $\mathbf{v}_1$ and $\mathbf{v}_2$ in V, we also insist $\mathbf{v}_1 + \mathbf{v}_1$ is in V and that the addition is commutative. Thus, V is closed under addition. V must have an identity element $\mathbf{0}$ and additive inverses so that V is a commutative additive group.

V is almost a vector space over $\mathbf{F}$, but we insist on a few more conditions related to scalar multiplication. They concern the usual arithmetic properties we first saw with numbers. Let s_1 and s_2 be in $\mathbf{F}$. All the following must hold, with 1 the multiplicative identity of $\mathbf{F}$:

$$1\mathbf{v}_1 = \mathbf{v}_1 \qquad\qquad s_1\left(\mathbf{v}_1 + \mathbf{v}_2\right) = s_1\mathbf{v}_1 + s_1\mathbf{v}_2$$
$$\left(s_1 s_2\right)\mathbf{v}_1 = s_1\left(s_2\mathbf{v}_1\right) \qquad\qquad \left(s_1 + s_2\right)\mathbf{v}_1 = s_1\mathbf{v}_1 + s_2\mathbf{v}_1$$

We say V is a vector space over $\mathbf{F}$ when it meets all these requirements.

A vector space may have finite or infinite *dimensions*. The number is related to the size of a *basis*.

Let X be a possibly infinite subset of the vectors of V. Notationally, we refer to the elements of X as $\mathbf{x}_1$, $\mathbf{x}_2$, or $\mathbf{x}_n$, in general. If we can represent any vector $\mathbf{v}$ as a finite sum of elements $\mathbf{x}_j$ of X multiplied by scalars s_j from $\mathbf{F}$, then X *spans* V.

For example, a given $\mathbf{v}$ might be defined by

$$\mathbf{v} = s_3\mathbf{x}_3 + s_7\mathbf{x}_7 + s_{31}\mathbf{x}_{31}\ .$$

Another $\mathbf{u}$ in V might be

$$\mathbf{u} = s_1\mathbf{x}_1 + s_{70}\mathbf{x}_{70} + s_{397}\mathbf{x}_{397} + s_{7243}\mathbf{x}_{7243}\ .$$

$\mathbf{u}$ and $\mathbf{v}$ are linear combinations of elements of X.

X may contain more vectors than are strictly needed. With spanning, we only ensure that finite linear combinations of vectors from X give us all vectors in V.

The n vectors $\mathbf{x}_1, \ldots, \mathbf{x}_n$ in X are linearly independent if

$$s_1\mathbf{x}_1 + \cdots + s_n\mathbf{x}_n = \mathbf{0}$$

implies all the scalars $s_j = 0$ for $1 \le j \le n$.

Consider $\mathbf{R}^2$ and the vector collection X comprising $\mathbf{v}_1 = \mathbf{e}_1$, $\mathbf{x}_2 = \mathbf{e}_2$, and $\mathbf{x}_3 = (1, 1)$. X spans V, but we only need two of the three vectors to do so. In fact, $\mathbf{x}_3 = \mathbf{x}_1 + \mathbf{x}_2$.

If we rewrite the last equation as $\mathbf{x}_3 - \mathbf{x}_1 - \mathbf{x}_2 = \mathbf{0} = (0, 0)$, we have a linear combination of vectors of X with nonzero coefficients, yet their sum is $\mathbf{0}$. When this happens, the vectors are *linearly dependent*. If it cannot occur, the vectors in X are *linearly independent*.

Let X be a possibly infinite subset of the vectors of a vector space V over a field $\mathbf{F}$. If the vectors of X span V and are linearly independent, then X is a *basis* for V. If the number of vectors in X is finite, the size of X is the *dimension* of V.

Linear independence also implies there is a unique way to write a given vector as a linear combination of basis vectors. If

$$\mathbf{v} = a_1\mathbf{x}_1 + a_2\mathbf{x}_2 + \cdots + a_n\mathbf{x}_n$$
$$= b_1\mathbf{x}_1 + b_2\mathbf{x}_2 + \cdots + b_n\mathbf{x}_n$$

then $a_j = b_j$ for $1 \le j \le n$. Remember that when we say "unique," we mean "one and only one."

The standard basis, denoted E, is the set of vectors $\mathbf{e}_j$ that have 1 in the jth coordinate position and 0s elsewhere:

$$\mathbf{e}_1 = (1, 0, 0, \ldots, 0, 0, 0)$$
$$\mathbf{e}_2 = (0, 1, 0, \ldots, 0, 0, 0)$$
$$\vdots$$
$$\mathbf{e}_{n-1} = (0, 0, 0, \ldots, 0, 1, 0)$$
$$\mathbf{e}_n = \underbrace{(0, 0, 0, \ldots, 0, 0, 1)}_{n \text{ coordinates}}$$

For a given V, there can be different sets X that form bases. They are all finite or all infinite. The dimension is independent of your choice of basis. In some situations, it may make sense to change from one basis to another.

It's a little confusing to know when you use "basis" or "bases." *Basis* refers to an entire collection of vectors that span the vector space and are linearly independent. These are called *basis vectors*. If I have more than one basis, they are *bases*.

I usually pronounce "bases" in this context as "bay-seas" versus "base-is."

An alternative notation for vectors is to put a right-pointing arrow over the vector name. Authors do this in some texts, and instructors often use it when writing on blackboards or whiteboards:

$$\vec{v}$$

5.3 Linear maps

We've looked at linear functions several times to get a concrete idea of how they work. We must generalize this idea to vector spaces.

Let U and V be vector spaces over the same field $\mathbf{F}$. Let $\mathbf{u}_1$ and $\mathbf{u}_2$ be in U and s_1 and s_2 be scalars in $\mathbf{F}$.

The function $L : U \to V$ is a *linear map* if

$$L(\mathbf{u}_1 + \mathbf{u}_2) = L(\mathbf{u}_1) + L(\mathbf{u}_2) \quad \text{and} \quad L(s_1\mathbf{u}_1) = s_1 L(\mathbf{u}_1).$$

In particular, we have

$$L\left(s_1\mathbf{u}_1 + s_2\mathbf{u}_2\right) = s_1 L\left(\mathbf{u}_1\right) + s_2 L\left(\mathbf{u}_2\right).$$

When $U = V$, we also say L is a *linear transformation* of U or a *linear operator* on U.

All linear transformations on $\mathbf{R}^2$ look like

$$(x, y) \mapsto (ax + by, \, cx + dy),$$

using Cartesian coordinates, and with a, b, c, d, x, and y in $\mathbf{R}$. This is interesting because the linear transformations on $\mathbf{R}^1$ all look like the somewhat trivial $x \mapsto ax$.

Exercise 5.2

Show that the function

$$(x, y) \mapsto (ax + by, \, cx + dy)$$

for a, b, c, d, x, and y in $\mathbf{C}$ is a linear transformation of $\mathbf{C}^2$.

The linear transformations on $\mathbf{R}^3$ look like the messy

$$(x, y, z) \mapsto (ax + by + cz, \, dx + fy + gz, \, hx + jy + kz).$$

I skipped using e and i because they are special values. All numbers are real.

Look again at the forms for two- and three-dimensional linear transformations. Note

- If we think of x, y, and z as variables, they each appear with exponent 1 in each coordinate position.
- There are no constants such as 7 appearing in a term such as $ax + by + 7$ in any position.
- Any or all of the coefficients can be 0.

For $\mathbf{R}^2$ or $\mathbf{C}^2$, the map $(x, y) \mapsto (1x + 0y, 0x + 1y) = (x, y)$ is the identity I. It is its own inverse.

The map $(x, y) \mapsto (0x+0y, 0x+0y) = (0, 0)$ is the zero transformation. It is not invertible as it discards essential information. I think of it as the black hole of linear maps.

The map $(x, y) \mapsto (1x + 0y, 0x + 0y) = (x, 0)$ *projects* points onto the x-axis. It is also not invertible.

> **Exercise 5.3**
>
> What are the identity and zero transformations for $\mathbf{R}^3$ and $\mathbf{C}^3$?

In $\mathbf{R}^1$, the transformation $(x) \mapsto (ax)$ is invertible if and only if $a \neq 0$. For $\mathbf{R}^2$, $(x, y) \mapsto (ax + by, cx + dy)$ is invertible if and only if $ad - bc \neq 0$. These ideas of linearity and invertibility are less straightforward than you might initially think.

We get a special kind of linear map when the target is the field $\mathbf{F}$ itself, thought of as a one-dimensional vector space.

> Let $L : U \to \mathbf{F}$ be a linear map from a vector space U to its field of scalars. L is called a *linear form* or *linear functional*. All linear forms look like
> $$(u_1, u_2, \ldots, u_n) \mapsto a_1 u_1 + a_2 u_2 + \cdots + a_n u_n,$$
> with all a_j in $\mathbf{F}$, $1 \leq j \leq n$.

Once we get above one dimension, the structure of linear maps and transformations becomes more sophisticated.

5.3.1 Algebraic structure of linear transformations

Let V be a vector space over a field $\mathbf{F}$. If L and M are linear transformations on V, we can compose them by applying one after another
$$(L \circ M)(\mathbf{v}) = L(M(\mathbf{v}))$$
for $\mathbf{v}$ in V. It is very often the case that $L \circ M \neq M \circ L$: composition is not commutative in general. The order in which you apply linear transformations on a vector space of dimension 2 or greater makes a difference.

The identity transformation I maps a vector to itself: $I(\mathbf{v}) = \mathbf{v}$.

> The collection of invertible linear transformations on a vector space V over a field $\mathbf{F}$ form a noncommutative group under composition ''$\circ$'' with identity element I.

You can see that by understanding the concept of a group, we can compress a lot of information about linear transformations into a simple statement.

We can add and subtract linear transformations and take advantage of scalar multiplication in a vector space:

$$(L + M)(\mathbf{v}) = L(\mathbf{v}) + M(\mathbf{v})$$
$$-L(\mathbf{v}) = (-1)L(\mathbf{v}) = L(-\mathbf{v})$$
$$(L - M)(\mathbf{v}) = (L + -M)(\mathbf{v}) = L(v) + (-1)M(\mathbf{v}) = L(\mathbf{v}) + M(-\mathbf{v})$$

Because addition is commutative in V,

$$(L + M)(\mathbf{v}) = L(\mathbf{v}) + M(\mathbf{v}) = M(\mathbf{v}) + L(\mathbf{v}) = (M + L)\mathbf{v}.$$

The zero transformation maps every vector $\mathbf{v}$ to the zero vector $\mathbf{0}$.

> The collection of linear transformations on a vector space V over a field $\mathbf{F}$ form a commutative group under addition ''+'' with identity element the zero transformation.
>
> More than that, the collection of linear transformations on a vector space V over a field $\mathbf{F}$ form a noncommutative ring with the addition operation ''+'' and multiplication being the composition operation ''∘''.

5.3.2 Example linear transformations on $\mathbf{R}^2$

A linear transformation in one dimension is trivial, simply multiplication by a number. When we move to two dimensions, however, we start to see the richness and breadth of such transformations. In this section, we survey the kinds of linear transformations in the real plane.

Stretches and compressions

A stretch transformation moves points in some direction by a nonzero multiple. For example, it might double the y-coordinate. This category includes transformations that compress, or shrink, by a nonzero amount. An example is replacing the x-coordinate with one-third of its value. These two transformations are

$$(x, y) \mapsto (x, 2y) \quad \text{and} \quad (x, y) \mapsto (\tfrac{1}{3}x, y).$$

Figure 5.3 shows the effect of the two stretches on points on the unit circle.

A stretch can move in both x and y directions at the same time by either the same or different amounts: $(x, y) \mapsto (\pi x, \tfrac{5}{7}y)$, for example.

For nonzero a and b, the inverse of $(x, y) \mapsto (ax, by)$ is

$$(x, y) \mapsto \left(\frac{x}{a}, \frac{y}{b}\right).$$

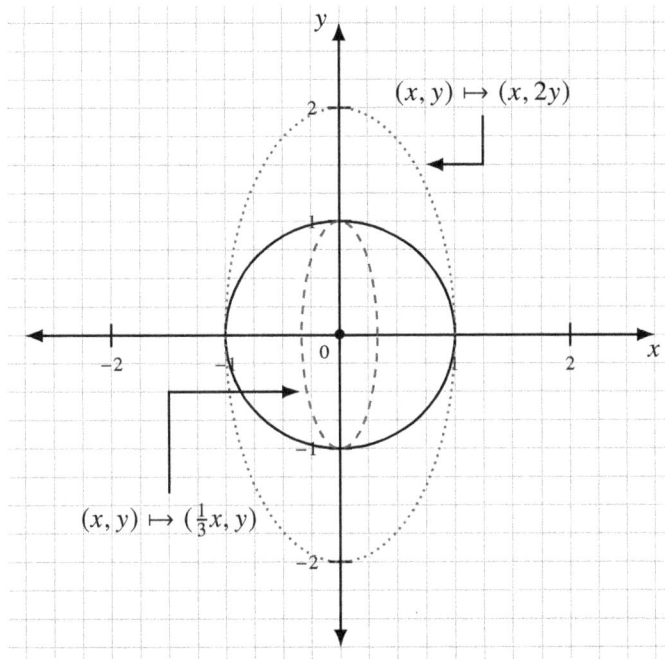

Figure 5.3: Stretch linear transformations

We cannot reverse the effect if either a or b is 0.

What if we want to stretch in other directions, such as the direction of the line $y = x$? You can accomplish this by a stretch in the x direction and then a $\frac{\pi}{4}$ rotation (that is, 45°).

Rotations

To rotate any point (x, y) by φ radians around the origin, apply the linear transformation

$$(x, y) \mapsto (x \cos(\varphi) - y \sin(\varphi), x \sin(\varphi) + y \cos(\varphi)).$$

But we knew this already! Why?

Think of (x, y) as the number $x + yi$ in **C**. From our discussion of Euler's formula, we know multiplying by $e^{\varphi i}$ rotates a complex number by φ radians around 0. Since $e^{\varphi i} = \cos(\varphi) + \sin(\varphi)i$,

$$\begin{aligned} e^{\varphi i} \times (x + yi) &= (\cos(\varphi) + \sin(\varphi)i) \times (x + yi) \\ &= x \cos(\varphi) + x \sin(\varphi)i + yi \cos(\varphi) + yi \sin(\varphi)i \\ &= (x \cos(\varphi) - y \sin(\varphi)) + (x \sin(\varphi) + y \cos(\varphi))i, \end{aligned}$$

which corresponds to the point $\left(x \cos(\varphi) - y \sin(\varphi), x \sin(\varphi) + y \cos(\varphi)\right)$ in $\mathbf{R}^2$.

If we want to rotate by $\frac{\pi}{6}$ radians = 30°, we first note that

$$\cos\left(\frac{\pi}{6}\right) = \frac{\sqrt{3}}{2} \quad \text{and} \quad \sin\left(\frac{\pi}{6}\right) = \frac{1}{2}.$$

The linear transformation is

$$(x, y) \longmapsto \left(\frac{\sqrt{3}}{2}x - \frac{1}{2}y, \frac{1}{2}x + \frac{\sqrt{3}}{2}y\right)$$

and is shown in Figure 5.4.

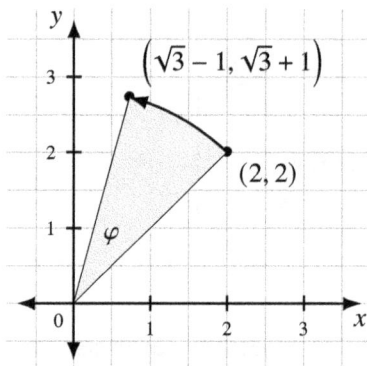

Figure 5.4: A rotation through $\varphi = \frac{\pi}{6}$ radians

When φ is positive or negative, the rotation is counterclockwise or clockwise. If $\varphi < 0$ or $\varphi \geq 2\pi$, we can replace it with one where $0 \leq \varphi < 2\pi$.

A rotation by φ is invertible: rotate by $-\varphi$ to get back to where you started.

Reflections

A reflection moves points from one side of a line to the other. If a point lies on the line, nothing happens. The reflected image is the same distance from the line as the original point. The line segment connecting the original and reflected image is perpendicular to the reflection line.

Let's reflect across the line $y = x$. The linear transformation is $(x, y) \longmapsto (y, x)$ and is shown in Figure 5.5.

The linear transformations $(x, y) \longmapsto (-x, y)$ and $(x, y) \longmapsto (x, -y)$ reflect across the y- and x-axes, respectively. The latter corresponds to complex conjugation as a real linear map.

Reflections are their own inverses.

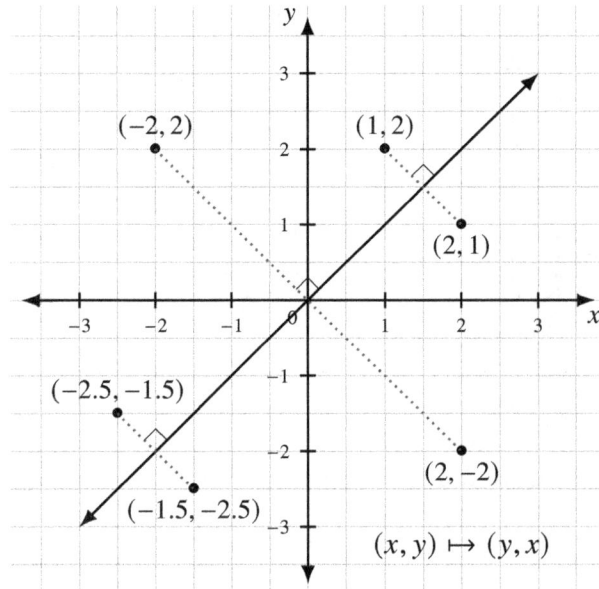

Figure 5.5: Reflections across the line $y = x$

Shears

Consider

$$f : (x, y) \mapsto (x, y + 3x) \quad \text{and} \quad g : (x, y) \mapsto (x + 3y, y).$$

They are linear transformations. The first is a *vertical shear*, and the second is a *horizontal shear*.

The first keeps the x-coordinate constant while shifting the y-coordinate by a multiple of the x-coordinate. When x is large, the shift is large, but the change is linear.

The second example leaves y constant but shifts x by an amount proportional to y. The graph in Figure 5.6 shows the effect of each transformation on the coordinates $(0,0)$, $(1,0)$, $(1,1)$, and $(0,1)$, the corners of the *unit square*. I've marked $(1,1)$ and where it goes under the two shear transformations.

The horizontal shear looks like you took a deck of playing cards and smoothly pushed the upper cards by varying amounts to create a slanted rhombus.

What is the inverse of f? By examination, we need to do nothing to the x-coordinate since f does not change it. For the second coordinate, $y - 3x$ undoes the shear. Vertical and horizontal shears are invertible linear transformations.

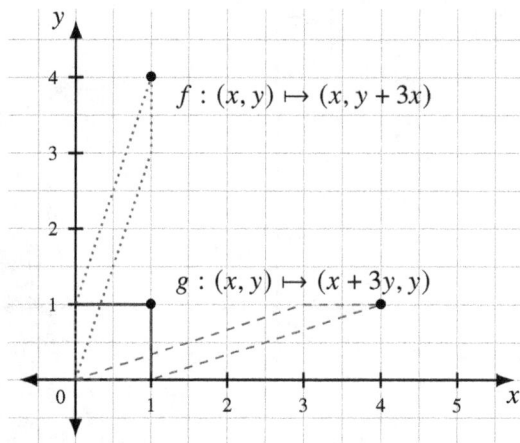

Figure 5.6: Horizontal and vertical shears

Projections

The previous linear transformations we considered in this section were all invertible. Here, we'll see some that are not.

Choose a line A and a point P. If P is on A, we are finished, as it is the value of the projection onto A. If not, draw the line B through P perpendicular to A. The intersection of B and A is the value of the projection.

Recall the reflection across the $y = x$ line? It is $(x, y) \mapsto (y, x)$. All we have to do for this reflection is swap the two coordinates. Essentially, a simple projection onto a line is a halfway reflection. Convince yourself that

$$(x, y) \mapsto \left(\frac{x + y}{2}, \frac{x + y}{2}\right)$$

is the projection onto the line $y = x$, and that its plot is shown in Figure 5.7. Anything along the line $y = -x$ ends up at the origin. This line is the *kernel* of the transformation.

As another example, the map $(x, y) \mapsto (0, y)$ is linear. It throws away the x-coordinate, replacing it with 0. It's not invertible because the point $(0, 3)$ is the image of an infinite number of points, including $(4, 3)$, $(-3636, 3)$, and $(e, 3)$. Anything of the form $(a, 3)$ maps to $(0, 3)$, for a a real number. If we apply this transformation, we have no idea which a we started with and so cannot reverse it. The map is a projection onto the y-axis.

Exercise 5.4

What is the kernel of $(x, y) \mapsto (0, y)$?

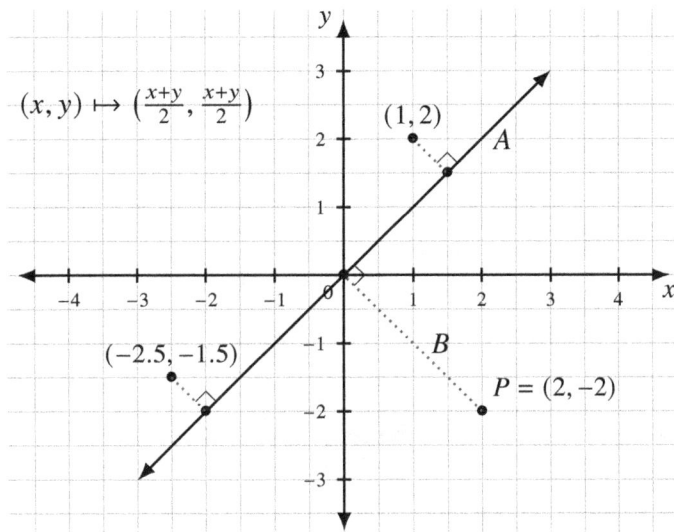

Figure 5.7: The projection onto the line $y = x$

Injections

A linear map f is *injective* if $f(x) = 0$ implies $x = 0$. Put another way, if $f(x) = f(y)$, then $x = y$. A linear transformation is injective if it is invertible.

Exercise 5.5

Show that

$$f(x) = 0 \Rightarrow x = 0 \quad \text{and} \quad f(x) = f(y) \Rightarrow x = y$$

are equivalent conditions for a linear map. (Recall that ''$\Rightarrow$'' means ''implies.'')

An *injection* is an injective linear map. Since we are not covering all of linear algebra, I'm using injections in a much less general way. I want you to imagine taking a vector space such as $\mathbf{R}^1$ and embedding it inside something bigger.

Indeed, we first showed this when we went from $\mathbf{R}^1$, the ''number line,'' to the real plane, $\mathbf{R}^2$, as shown in Figure 5.8.

If (t) is in $\mathbf{R}^1$, we can inject $\mathbf{R}^1$ into $\mathbf{R}^2$ by making the number line become the x-axis: $(t) \mapsto (t, 0)$.

We can inject $\mathbf{R}^1$ onto the line $y = x$ in $\mathbf{R}^2$ via $(t) \mapsto (t, t)$. The projection $(x, y) \mapsto (x)$ from the line $y = x$ undoes the injection.

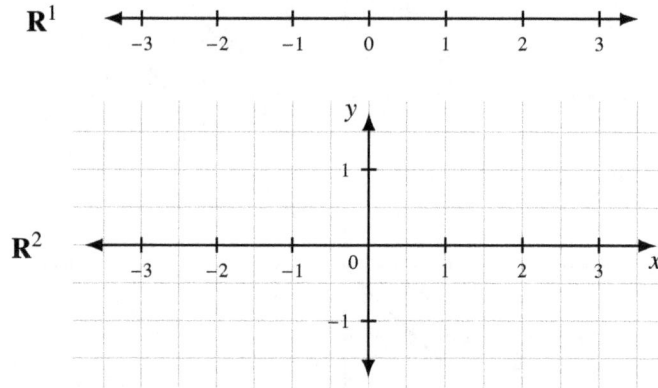

Figure 5.8: Moving from the real number line to the real plane

5.4   Matrices

If we write out the details of a linear transformation of a five-dimensional vector space over a field **F**, it looks like this:

$$(v_1, v_2, v_3, v_4, v_5) \mapsto (a_1v_1 + a_2v_2 + a_3v_3 + a_4v_4 + a_5v_5,$$
$$b_1v_1 + b_2v_2 + b_3v_3 + b_4v_4 + b_5v_5,$$
$$c_1v_1 + c_2v_2 + c_3v_3 + c_4v_4 + c_5v_5,$$
$$d_1v_1 + d_2v_2 + d_3v_3 + d_4v_4 + d_5v_5,$$
$$f_1v_1 + f_2v_2 + f_3v_3 + f_4v_4 + f_5v_5).$$

This notation is not practical, especially if we start looking at the formulas for compositions of linear maps. Hence, we introduce matrices.

We begin with notation and then move on to the algebra.

5.4.1   Notation and terminology

This array of values with entries in the field **F**

$$\begin{bmatrix} 2 & 5 & -1 & 0 \\ 1 & -9 & 2 & -4 \\ -3 & 0 & 0 & 6 \end{bmatrix}$$

is a 3-by-4 *matrix*: it has three rows, four columns, and $12 = 3 \times 4$ *entries*. The *dimension* of this matrix is 3-by-4.

When we need subscripts for the entries in a matrix, they look like this:

$$\begin{bmatrix} a_{1,1} & a_{1,2} & a_{1,3} \\ a_{2,1} & a_{2,2} & a_{2,3} \\ a_{3,1} & a_{3,2} & a_{3,3} \end{bmatrix}$$

for a 3-by-3 matrix. The first subscript is the *row index*, and the second is the *column index*.

In mathematics and physics, we use 1 as the first row or column index. In computer science and software coding, we use 0. Remember this if you translate from a formula to code or vice versa.

The general case for m rows and n columns is

$$\begin{bmatrix} a_{1,1} & a_{1,2} & \cdots & a_{1,n} \\ a_{2,1} & a_{2,2} & \cdots & a_{2,n} \\ \vdots & \vdots & \ddots & \vdots \\ a_{m,1} & a_{m,2} & \cdots & a_{m,n} \end{bmatrix}.$$

When the number of rows equals the number of columns, $m = n$, we have a square matrix. Most of the matrices we consider are square because these correspond to linear transformations on a vector space.

Matrix entries such as $a_{1,1}$, $a_{2,2}$, and $a_{3,3}$ lie on the diagonal of the matrix.

$$\begin{bmatrix} \boxed{a_{1,1}} & a_{1,2} & a_{1,3} \\ a_{2,1} & \boxed{a_{2,2}} & a_{2,3} \\ a_{3,1} & a_{3,2} & \boxed{a_{3,3}} \end{bmatrix}.$$

I put the diagonal entries in boxes for visual emphasis.

If all the off-diagonal entries are 0, we have a *diagonal matrix*. These are the most straightforward kinds of matrices with which to work.

A matrix with all 0 entries is a *zero matrix*, not surprisingly. A square matrix with 1s along the diagonal and 0s elsewhere is an *identity matrix*. We denote by I_n the n-by-n identity matrix. Here is I_4:

$$\begin{bmatrix} 1 & 0 & 0 & 0 \\ 0 & 1 & 0 & 0 \\ 0 & 0 & 1 & 0 \\ 0 & 0 & 0 & 1 \end{bmatrix}.$$

A matrix is *sparse* if almost all its entries are 0.

The *transpose* of a matrix is the new matrix we get by reflecting the elements across the diagonal. In the 2-by-2 case:

$$\begin{bmatrix} a & b \\ c & d \end{bmatrix} \xrightarrow{\text{transpose}} \begin{bmatrix} a & c \\ b & d \end{bmatrix}.$$

For a 2-by-3 matrix,

$$\begin{bmatrix} a & b & c \\ d & f & g \end{bmatrix} \xrightarrow{\text{transpose}} \begin{bmatrix} a & d \\ b & f \\ c & g \end{bmatrix}.$$

If A is a matrix, then we denote its transpose by A^T. For a 3-by-3 matrix, if

$$A = \begin{bmatrix} a_{1,1} & a_{1,2} & a_{1,3} \\ a_{2,1} & a_{2,2} & a_{2,3} \\ a_{3,1} & a_{3,2} & a_{3,3} \end{bmatrix} \quad \text{then} \quad A^\mathsf{T} = \begin{bmatrix} a_{1,1} & a_{2,1} & a_{3,1} \\ a_{1,2} & a_{2,2} & a_{3,2} \\ a_{1,3} & a_{2,3} & a_{3,3} \end{bmatrix}.$$

See how we interchanged the row and column subscript indices?

Taking the transpose does not change the diagonal entries. Taking the transpose of a square diagonal matrix does not change the matrix.

A matrix is *upper triangular* if all entries below the diagonal are zero. It is *lower triangular* if all entries above the diagonal are zero. The transpose of an upper triangular matrix is lower triangular, and vice versa.

An n-by-n square matrix A is *symmetric* if $A = A^\mathsf{T}$.

When the matrix has complex entries, that is, $\mathbf{F} = \mathbf{C}$, we call it a *complex matrix*. The conjugate of a complex matrix is the new matrix formed by taking the conjugate of each of the entries. For example:

$$A = \begin{bmatrix} 0 & 1+i & 3-2i \\ 7+i & -i & \frac{\sqrt{2}}{2} - \frac{\sqrt{2}}{2}i \end{bmatrix} \Rightarrow \overline{A} = \begin{bmatrix} 0 & 1-i & 3+2i \\ 7-i & i & \frac{\sqrt{2}}{2} + \frac{\sqrt{2}}{2}i \end{bmatrix}.$$

The *adjoint* of a complex matrix A is its conjugate transpose, denoted by $A^\dagger$. In either order, you take the complex conjugates of the entries and transpose the matrix.

Conjugation and taking adjoints have different notations between mathematics and physics and sometimes even between subfields of the subjects. As we saw in section 3.9.2, we use the ''line over'' notation for conjugation, while some people use an asterisk superscript such as z^*. This is further confusing since mathematicians use A^* for the adjoint. Physicists use a ''dagger'' $\dagger$ superscript for the same thing: $A^\dagger$. We use overlines and daggers.

An n-by-n square complex matrix A is *Hermitian* if $A = A^\dagger$. A Hermitian matrix is *self-adjoint*.

Hermitian matrices are named after the nineteenth-century mathematician Charles Hermite (Figure 5.9). Being Hermitian for a complex matrix is the extension of the concept of a real matrix being symmetric.

Figure 5.9: Charles Hermite, circa 1901

Exercise 5.6

Why are all the diagonal entries of a Hermitian matrix in **R**?

5.4.2 Matrices and linear maps

Before we get into the topic of this section, we must talk about how we write vectors. We can then use this notation to discuss the action of matrices and linear maps on those vectors.

Vector notation

So far, we have used the "bold text" notation such as $\mathbf{v}$ and $\mathbf{e}_1$, and the "I'm going to write this like the coordinates of a point, but you know it is really a vector" notation like $(2, 3)$ and $(v_1, v_2, \ldots, v_n)$.

While we continue to use these, we must add two additional forms to work with matrices.

For the vector $\mathbf{v} = (v_1, v_2, \ldots, v_n)$,

$$\begin{bmatrix} v_1 & v_2 & \cdots & v_n \end{bmatrix} \quad \text{and} \quad \begin{bmatrix} v_1 \\ v_2 \\ \vdots \\ v_n \end{bmatrix}$$

are the row and column vector forms of $\mathbf{v}$. It is no coincidence they look like 1-by-n and n-by-1 matrices. Whenever it is convenient, we think of them as such.

A vector in column form is a *column vector*. You can guess what a *row vector* is.

The coordinates are always relative to some basis X, which may be the standard basis E. If we need to indicate what basis we are using, we use its name as a subscript as in

$$(v_1, v_2, \ldots, v_n)_X \quad \text{or} \quad \begin{bmatrix} v_1 & v_2 & \cdots & v_n \end{bmatrix}_X \quad \text{or} \quad \begin{bmatrix} v_1 \\ v_2 \\ \vdots \\ v_n \end{bmatrix}_X .$$

There are yet two more vector notations we will use, Dirac's *bra-ket* forms. We define these in section 7.2 when we consider the mathematics of qubits.

Vector operations

The transpose of a row vector is a column vector and vice versa:

$$\begin{bmatrix} v_1 & v_2 & \cdots & v_n \end{bmatrix}^{\mathsf{T}} = \begin{bmatrix} v_1 \\ v_2 \\ \vdots \\ v_n \end{bmatrix} \quad \text{and} \quad \begin{bmatrix} v_1 \\ v_2 \\ \vdots \\ v_n \end{bmatrix}^{\mathsf{T}} = \begin{bmatrix} v_1 & v_2 & \cdots & v_n \end{bmatrix} .$$

The conjugate of a complex vector is the new vector we get by taking the complex conjugate of each entry:

$$\overline{\mathbf{v}} = (\overline{v_1}, \overline{v_2}, \ldots, \overline{v_n}) .$$

We have similar relationships with the adjoint as we do with the conjugation of row and column vectors:

$$\begin{bmatrix} v_1 & v_2 & \cdots & v_n \end{bmatrix}^\dagger = \begin{bmatrix} \overline{v_1} \\ \overline{v_2} \\ \vdots \\ \overline{v_n} \end{bmatrix} \quad \text{and} \quad \begin{bmatrix} v_1 \\ v_2 \\ \vdots \\ v_n \end{bmatrix}^\dagger = \begin{bmatrix} \overline{v_1} & \overline{v_2} & \cdots & \overline{v_n} \end{bmatrix} .$$

The *adjoint* of a complex vector $\mathbf{v}$ is its conjugate transpose, denoted $\mathbf{v}^\dagger$.

Applying the matrix of a linear transformation to a vector

When we apply a linear transformation to a vector, we get a different vector unless we use the identity transformation I. To do the arithmetic, we must use coordinates.

Here's how we apply a matrix to a column vector in the general 2-by-2 case:

$$\begin{bmatrix} a & b \\ c & d \end{bmatrix} \begin{bmatrix} x \\ y \end{bmatrix} = \begin{bmatrix} ax + by \\ cx + dy \end{bmatrix} .$$

We start with a vector and end up with another: $(x, y) \mapsto (ax+by, cx+dy)$. This is none other than the definition of a linear map from a two-dimensional vector space to a two-dimensional vector space.

To apply a linear transformation represented as a matrix to a vector, the number of columns in the matrix must equal the number of entries in the vector. The number of rows is the dimension of the target vector space.

We calculate row by row. To begin, we multiply the first matrix entry in the first row by the first vector entry. We then add this product to the second matrix entry in the first row multiplied by the second vector entry. We continue through the row, and the sum becomes the first coordinate of the result vector. We then move on to the second row and so forth.

$$
\begin{bmatrix}
a_{1,1} & a_{1,2} & \cdots & a_{1,n} \\
a_{2,1} & a_{2,2} & \cdots & a_{2,n} \\
\vdots & \vdots & \ddots & \vdots \\
a_{m,1} & a_{m,2} & \cdots & a_{m,n}
\end{bmatrix}
\begin{bmatrix}
v_1 \\ v_2 \\ \vdots \\ v_n
\end{bmatrix}
=
\begin{bmatrix}
a_{1,1}v_1 + a_{1,2}v_2 + \cdots + a_{1,n}v_n \\
a_{2,1}v_1 + a_{2,2}v_2 + \cdots + a_{2,n}v_n \\
\vdots \\
a_{m,1}v_1 + a_{m,2}v_2 + \cdots + a_{m,n}v_n
\end{bmatrix}
$$

We are mapping an n-dimensional vector to an m-dimensional one via an m-by-n matrix.

If A is a 1-by-n matrix or a row vector of length n, it defines a linear form to the field of scalars **F**. For a vector **v** in column form,

$$
\begin{bmatrix}
a_{1,1} & a_{1,2} & \cdots & a_{1,n}
\end{bmatrix}
\begin{bmatrix}
v_1 \\ v_2 \\ \vdots \\ v_n
\end{bmatrix}
= a_{1,1}v_1 + a_{1,2}v_2 + \cdots + a_{1,n}v_n .
$$

Coordinates for a vector are relative to a particular basis. If we use a different basis, the coordinates for the vector are different, but *it would still refer to the same vector*.

We also represent a matrix relative to a particular basis. If we change to a different basis, the matrix changes, but *both correspond to the same linear map*.

We use a specific (matrix, basis) pair when we make a linear transformation concrete for computation.

> The rank of a matrix A is the maximum number of linearly independent columns of A, thought of as vectors. Equivalently, the rank is the maximum number of linearly independent rows of A.
>
> The rank is a property of the linear map to which the matrix corresponds in the given basis and is independent of the basis we use.

If a symmetric matrix A has all entries in **R**, it is *positive definite* if for any nonzero real vector **v** of length n, $\mathbf{v}^\mathsf{T} A \mathbf{v} > 0$. If we only have $\mathbf{v}^\mathsf{T} A \mathbf{v} \geq 0$, then A is *positive semi-definite*.

An n-by-n Hermitian matrix is positive definite if for any nonzero complex vector **v** of length n, $\mathbf{v}^\dagger A \mathbf{v} > 0$. It is positive semi-definite if for any nonzero complex vector **v** of length n, $\mathbf{v}^\dagger A \mathbf{v} \geq 0$.

Example: Stretches and compressions

A stretch or compression in the direction of a basis vector is a diagonal matrix.

This map doubles the first coordinate in a stretch but compresses the second to one-quarter of its previous size:

$$(x, y) \mapsto (2x, 0.25y) \qquad \begin{bmatrix} 2 & 0 \\ 0 & 0.25 \end{bmatrix} \begin{bmatrix} x \\ y \end{bmatrix} = \begin{bmatrix} 2x \\ 0.25y \end{bmatrix}$$

You can see in Figure 5.10 how it affects the points on the unit circle.

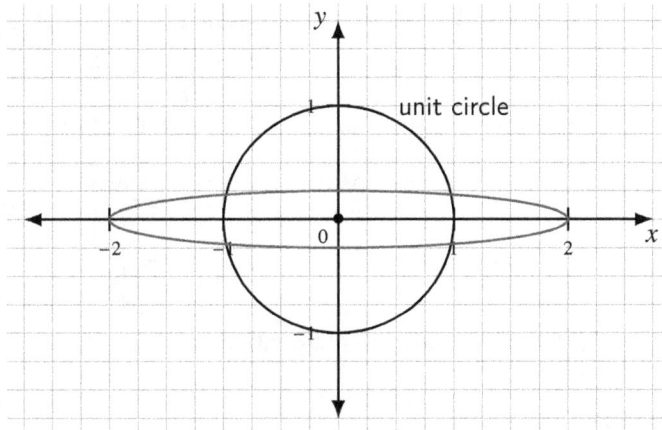

Figure 5.10: Two stretches and their effects on the unit circle

Example: Reflections

The "conjugation reflection" negates the second coordinate:

$$(x, y) \mapsto (x, -y) \qquad \begin{bmatrix} 1 & 0 \\ 0 & -1 \end{bmatrix} \begin{bmatrix} x \\ y \end{bmatrix} = \begin{bmatrix} x \\ -y \end{bmatrix}$$

In three dimensions, negating the y-coordinate reflects across the xz-plane:

$$C : (x, y, z) \mapsto (x, -y, z) \qquad \begin{bmatrix} 1 & 0 & 0 \\ 0 & -1 & 0 \\ 0 & 0 & 1 \end{bmatrix} \begin{bmatrix} x \\ y \\ z \end{bmatrix} = \begin{bmatrix} x \\ -y \\ z \end{bmatrix}$$

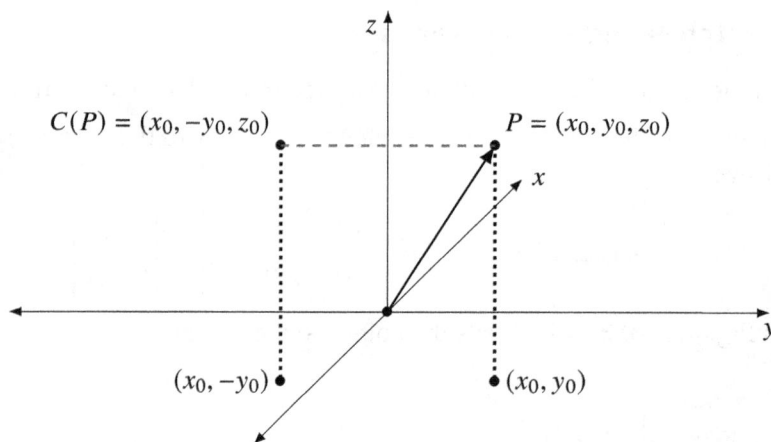

Figure 5.11: The reflection across the xz-plane in three dimensions

The reflection across the line $y = x$ swaps the two coordinates:

$$(x, y) \mapsto (y, x) \qquad \begin{bmatrix} 0 & 1 \\ 1 & 0 \end{bmatrix} \begin{bmatrix} x \\ y \end{bmatrix} = \begin{bmatrix} y \\ x \end{bmatrix}$$

The main diagonal is 0, and the off-diagonal elements do all the "work."

Example: Rotations

As we previously developed, the linear transformation

$$(x, y) \mapsto (x \cos(\theta) - y \sin(\theta), x \sin(\theta) + y \cos(\theta))$$

$$\begin{bmatrix} \cos(\theta) & -\sin(\theta) \\ \sin(\theta) & \cos(\theta) \end{bmatrix} \begin{bmatrix} x \\ y \end{bmatrix} = \begin{bmatrix} x \cos(\theta) - y \sin(\theta) \\ x \sin(\theta) + y \cos(\theta) \end{bmatrix}$$

rotates any point (x, y) by θ radians around the origin. This matrix has rank 2.

A $\frac{\pi}{2}$ radians = 90° rotation brings $(1, 0)$ to $(0, 1)$. This looks like it might be a reflection across the line $y = x$, but $(0, 1)$ itself is brought to $(-1, 0)$, not $(1, 0)$.

Exercise 5.8

What is the matrix for this linear transformation? What happens if you apply it four times?

In three dimensions,

$$(x, y, z) \mapsto (x \cos(\theta) - y \sin(\theta), x \sin(\theta) + y \cos(\theta), z)$$

$$\begin{bmatrix} \cos(\theta) & -\sin(\theta) & 0 \\ \sin(\theta) & \cos(\theta) & 0 \\ 0 & 0 & 1 \end{bmatrix} \begin{bmatrix} x \\ y \\ z \end{bmatrix} = \begin{bmatrix} x\cos(\theta) - y\sin(\theta) \\ x\sin(\theta) + y\cos(\theta) \\ z \end{bmatrix}$$

rotates any point (x, y, z) by θ radians around the z-axis. Similarly,

$$(x, y, z) \mapsto (x, y \cos(\theta) - z \sin(\theta), y \sin(\theta) + z \cos(\theta))$$

$$\begin{bmatrix} 1 & 0 & 0 \\ 0 & \cos(\theta) & -\sin(\theta) \\ 0 & \sin(\theta) & \cos(\theta) \end{bmatrix} \begin{bmatrix} x \\ y \\ z \end{bmatrix} = \begin{bmatrix} x \\ y\cos(\theta) - z\sin(\theta) \\ y\sin(\theta) + z\cos(\theta) \end{bmatrix}$$

rotates any point (x, y, z) by θ radians around the x-axis.

These are the matrix and trigonometry equations that allow video game software developers to move points and objects around with computer graphics.

Example: Shears

The vertical shear and horizontal shears

$$(x, y) \mapsto (x, y + 3x) \quad \text{and} \quad (x, y) \mapsto (x + 3y, y)$$

have the matrices

$$\begin{bmatrix} 1 & 0 \\ 3 & 1 \end{bmatrix} \quad \text{and} \quad \begin{bmatrix} 1 & 3 \\ 0 & 1 \end{bmatrix}.$$

At this point, you should be getting comfortable with the interplay of the matrix entries with the original coordinates.

Example: Projections

The transformation

$$(x, y, z) \mapsto (x, y) \qquad \begin{bmatrix} 1 & 0 & 0 \\ 0 & 1 & 0 \end{bmatrix} \begin{bmatrix} x \\ y \\ z \end{bmatrix} = \begin{bmatrix} x \\ y \end{bmatrix}$$

projects from 3 dimensions into 2. In terms of $\mathbf{R}^3$, it throws away the z-coordinate. The image is $\mathbf{R}^2$.

If you want to stay in $\mathbf{R}^3$, this version projects all points to the xy-plane, which is equivalent to $\mathbf{R}^2$.

$$(x, y, z) \mapsto (x, y, 0) \qquad \begin{bmatrix} 1 & 0 & 0 \\ 0 & 1 & 0 \\ 0 & 0 & 0 \end{bmatrix} \begin{bmatrix} x \\ y \\ z \end{bmatrix} = \begin{bmatrix} x \\ y \\ 0 \end{bmatrix}$$

The matrices for these projections have rank 2.

Exercise 5.9

What is the matrix

$$\begin{bmatrix} 1 & 0 & 0 \\ 0 & 1 & 0 \\ 0 & 0 & 0 \end{bmatrix}$$

multiplied by itself? What does this result mean geometrically?

The $\mathbf{R}^2$ projection onto the line $y = x$ is

$$(x, y) \mapsto \left(\frac{x + y}{2}, \frac{x + y}{2} \right) \qquad \begin{bmatrix} \frac{1}{2} & \frac{1}{2} \\ \frac{1}{2} & \frac{1}{2} \end{bmatrix} \begin{bmatrix} x \\ y \end{bmatrix} = \begin{bmatrix} \frac{x+y}{2} \\ \frac{x+y}{2} \end{bmatrix}$$

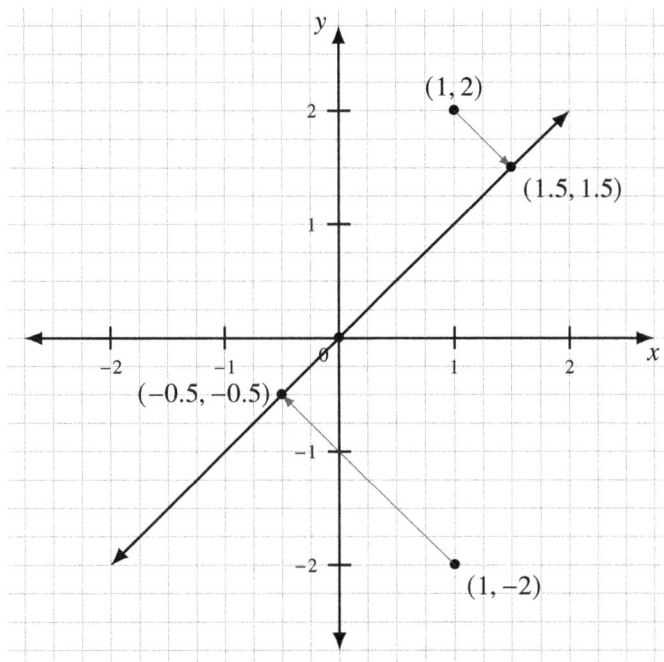

Figure 5.12: Reflection onto the line $y = x$

Exercise 5.10

What is the matrix

$$\begin{bmatrix} \frac{1}{2} & \frac{1}{2} \\ \frac{1}{2} & \frac{1}{2} \end{bmatrix}$$

multiplied by itself? What does this result mean geometrically? What is the rank of this matrix?

Example: Injections

Casually, an injection is when you map a vector space into another without sending multiple vectors to the same target vector. For these examples, I'm going to use it in a more limited sense of embedding a vector space inside another with a minimum number of changes.

$\mathbf{R}^1$ sits inside $\mathbf{R}^2$ in two different ways using the standard bases. The first way maps it to the x-axis:

$$(t) \mapsto (t, 0) \qquad \begin{bmatrix} 1 \\ 0 \end{bmatrix} \begin{bmatrix} t \end{bmatrix} = \begin{bmatrix} t \\ 0 \end{bmatrix}$$

and the second to the y-axis:

$$(t) \mapsto (0, t) \qquad \begin{bmatrix} 0 \\ 1 \end{bmatrix} \begin{bmatrix} t \end{bmatrix} = \begin{bmatrix} 0 \\ t \end{bmatrix}.$$

To inject $\mathbf{R}^2$ into $\mathbf{R}^3$ using the standard bases, you can send it to the xy-plane, the yz-plane, or the xz-plane. This last case is

$$(x, y) \mapsto (x, 0, y) \qquad \begin{bmatrix} 1 & 0 \\ 0 & 0 \\ 0 & 1 \end{bmatrix} \begin{bmatrix} x \\ y \end{bmatrix} = \begin{bmatrix} x \\ 0 \\ y \end{bmatrix}.$$

Exercise 5.11

What is the rank of this injection?

Example: Compositions

You compose transformations by applying them one after another. Let's look at the $\frac{\pi}{2}$ rotation and the reflection across the x-axis.

Per the above examples,

$$\begin{bmatrix} x \\ y \end{bmatrix} \xrightarrow{\text{rotate by } \frac{\pi}{2}} \begin{bmatrix} x\cos(\frac{\pi}{2}) - y\sin(\frac{\pi}{2}) \\ x\sin(\frac{\pi}{2}) + y\cos(\frac{\pi}{2}) \end{bmatrix} = \begin{bmatrix} -y \\ x \end{bmatrix} \xrightarrow{\text{reflect across } x\text{-axis}} \begin{bmatrix} -y \\ -x \end{bmatrix}$$

and

$$\begin{bmatrix} x \\ y \end{bmatrix} \xrightarrow{\text{reflect across } x\text{-axis}} \begin{bmatrix} x \\ -y \end{bmatrix} \xrightarrow{\text{rotate by } \frac{\pi}{2}} \begin{bmatrix} x\cos(\frac{\pi}{2}) - (-y)\sin(\frac{\pi}{2}) \\ x\sin(\frac{\pi}{2}) + (-y)\cos(\frac{\pi}{2}) \end{bmatrix} = \begin{bmatrix} y \\ x \end{bmatrix}.$$

In the first case, the point $(1, 0)$ is mapped to $(0, 1)$ and then $(0, -1)$. In the second, the same point is initially mapped to itself because it sits on the x-axis. Next, we rotate it to get $(0, 1)$. The composition formulas are not the same.

In general, the composition of linear transformations is not commutative.

Composition is done from right to left: $(f \circ g)(x) = f(g(x))$.

If you are trying to see how functions such as linear maps work, apply them to simple examples such as $(1,0)$ and $(0,1)$ or higher-dimensional analogs. That is, *see what the maps do to the standard basis vectors*.

We've now seen many of the common kinds of linear transformations. Composition gives us even more of them and some we have seen before.

5.5 Matrix algebra

So far, we have looked at matrices and their relationships to linear maps. We now investigate operations on one or more matrices. We'll first cover the general case of matrices which may have different numbers of rows and columns, and then move on to square matrices.

All matrices are over fields in this section, and when we manipulate multiple matrices, they all have entries in the same field. We can consider matrices over rings such as the integers, but we do not need to make this restriction for quantum computing.

5.5.1 Arithmetic of general matrices

Matrices of the same size, meaning they have the same number of rows and columns, can be added together entry by entry. For example,

$$\begin{bmatrix} 1 & 2 & 3 \\ 4 & 5 & 6 \end{bmatrix} + \begin{bmatrix} 1 & 3 & -\frac{4}{7} \\ -2 & \pi & 0 \end{bmatrix} = \begin{bmatrix} 2 & 5 & \frac{17}{7} \\ 2 & 5+\pi & 6 \end{bmatrix}.$$

The same is true for subtraction and negation:

$$\begin{bmatrix} 1 & 2 & 3 \\ 4 & 5 & 6 \end{bmatrix} - \begin{bmatrix} 1 & 3 & -\frac{4}{7} \\ -2 & \pi & 0 \end{bmatrix} = \begin{bmatrix} 0 & -1 & \frac{25}{7} \\ 6 & 5-\pi & 6 \end{bmatrix}$$

$$-\begin{bmatrix} 1 & 3 & -\frac{4}{7} \\ -2 & \pi & 6 \end{bmatrix} = \begin{bmatrix} -1 & -3 & \frac{4}{7} \\ 2 & -\pi & -6 \end{bmatrix}$$

We multiply by a scalar entry by entry:

$$5\begin{bmatrix} 1 & 3 & -\frac{4}{7} \\ -2 & \pi & 0 \end{bmatrix} = \begin{bmatrix} 5 & 15 & -\frac{20}{7} \\ -10 & 5\pi & 0 \end{bmatrix}.$$

Exercise 5.12

Verify that the set of *n*-by-*m* matrices over a field **F** for given integers *n* and *m* ≥ 1 is a vector space of dimension *n* × *m*, based on the definition in section 5.2. What is the "standard basis"?

The transpose of a sum or difference is the sum or difference of the transposes:

$$(A + B)^\mathsf{T} = A^\mathsf{T} + B^\mathsf{T}$$
$$(A - B)^\mathsf{T} = A^\mathsf{T} - B^\mathsf{T}$$
$$(-A)^\mathsf{T} = -\left(A^\mathsf{T}\right) = -A^\mathsf{T}$$

The same holds for *adjoints*, conjugate transposes, of complex matrices:

$$(A + B)^\dagger = A^\dagger + B^\dagger$$
$$(A - B)^\dagger = A^\dagger - B^\dagger$$
$$(-A)^\dagger = -\left(A^\dagger\right) = -A^\dagger$$

Now that we can add, subtract, and invert matrices, it's time to look at matrix multiplication. Its definition is more complicated and has an interesting requirement on some of the dimensions.

To multiply matrices *A* and *B*, the number of columns of *A* must equal the number of rows of *B*. Said another way, if *A* is an *n*-by-*m* matrix and *B* is an *m*-by-*p* matrix, then we can multiply them.

You may assume this condition is met when you see a matrix multiplication from this point on in this book.

Before we look at the general formula, here is how it works in a 2-by-2 case.

$$AB = \begin{bmatrix} a & b \\ c & d \end{bmatrix} \begin{bmatrix} u & v \\ w & x \end{bmatrix} = \begin{bmatrix} au + bw & av + bx \\ cu + dw & cv + dx \end{bmatrix} = C$$

Taking the first matrix *A* row by row, we successively sum up the products of the row entries with the corresponding column entries in the second matrix *B*. (Note to yourself: come back and visit here again once we have covered dot products in section 5.7.1.)

The 1, 1 entry of *C* is row number 1 of *A* lined up with column number 1 of *B*, and we multiply corresponding entries, then add them all up: *au* + *bw*.

The 1, 2 entry of C is row number 1 of A lined up with column number 2 of B, and we multiply corresponding entries, then add them all up: $av + bx$.

The 2, 1 entry of C is row number 2 of A lined up with column number 1 of B, and we multiply corresponding entries, then add them all up: $cu + dw$.

The 2, 2 entry of C is row number 2 of A lined up with column number 2 of B, and we multiply corresponding entries, then add them all up: $cv + dx$.

That was tedious, but you can see how the subscripts on the entries in the product correspond to the rows and columns from the original matrices.

We informally call this *subscript math*: you follow a procedure to keep the subscripts and the arithmetic straight.

In the general case, if

$$A = \begin{bmatrix} a_{1,1} & \cdots & a_{1,m} \\ \vdots & \vdots & \vdots \\ a_{n,1} & \cdots & a_{n,m} \end{bmatrix} \quad \text{and} \quad B = \begin{bmatrix} b_{1,1} & \cdots & b_{1,p} \\ \vdots & \vdots & \vdots \\ b_{m,1} & \cdots & b_{m,p} \end{bmatrix},$$

then

$$AB = \begin{bmatrix} a_{1,1}b_{1,1} + \cdots + a_{1,m}b_{m,1} & \cdots & a_{1,1}b_{1,p} + \cdots + a_{1,m}b_{m,p} \\ \vdots & \vdots & \vdots \\ a_{n,1}b_{1,1} + \cdots + a_{n,m}b_{m,1} & \cdots & a_{n,1}b_{1,p} + \cdots + a_{n,m}b_{m,p} \end{bmatrix}.$$

I remember this as "first row by the first column, first row by the second column, ..." and so on.

Exercise 5.13

What is the formula for the second entry in the second row of AB?

As linear maps, B takes us from a p-dimensional vector space to an m-dimensional one. A takes us from an m-dimensional vector space to an n-dimensional one. Applying B and then A brings us from p dimensions to n by way of m in the middle.

Transpositions operate on products by reversing the order: $AB^\mathsf{T} = B^\mathsf{T}A^\mathsf{T}$. Adjoints of complex matrices behave similarly: $AB^\dagger = B^\dagger A^\dagger$. Remember, the adjoint is the conjugate transpose.

5.5.2 Arithmetic of square matrices

Square matrices have additional properties, operations, and structure because of the possibility of computing their inverses.

Inverses

Let A be a square matrix. If there exists a square matrix B so that $AB = BA = I$, the identity matrix, then B is the inverse of A, denoted A^{-1}.

A and $B = A^{-1}$ necessarily have the same dimension. A^{-1} is the multiplicative inverse of A.

For a 2-by-2 matrix

$$A = \begin{bmatrix} a & b \\ c & d \end{bmatrix},$$

we multiply by

$$\begin{bmatrix} d & -b \\ -c & a \end{bmatrix}$$

to get

$$\begin{bmatrix} ad - bc & 0 \\ 0 & ad - bc \end{bmatrix}.$$

If $ad - bc \neq 0$, we can divide the second matrix by the scalar $ad - bc$ to get A^{-1}:

$$A^{-1} = \frac{1}{ad - bc} \begin{bmatrix} d & -b \\ -c & a \end{bmatrix} = \begin{bmatrix} \frac{d}{ad-bc} & -\frac{b}{ad-bc} \\ -\frac{c}{ad-bc} & \frac{a}{ad-bc} \end{bmatrix}.$$

Suppose A is a diagonal matrix and all the entries on the diagonal are nonzero. The inverse of A is diagonal, and the entries are the position-by-position inverses of A's diagonal. This is a mouthful, so it is easier to show you an example:

$$\begin{bmatrix} 3 & 0 & 0 \\ 0 & \pi^2 & 0 \\ 0 & 0 & -\frac{1}{4} \end{bmatrix}^{-1} = \begin{bmatrix} \frac{1}{3} & 0 & 0 \\ 0 & \frac{1}{\pi^2} & 0 \\ 0 & 0 & -4 \end{bmatrix}$$

Gaussian elimination

For higher-dimensional matrices, we can use the technique of *Gaussian elimination* to compute inverses and solve systems of linear equations.

Let's find the inverse of the matrix

$$\begin{bmatrix} 1 & 2 & -1 \\ 2 & 0 & 1 \\ 3 & 1 & 0 \end{bmatrix}.$$

We begin by positioning the identity matrix I_3 to the right of the above to get a 3-by-6 matrix. We draw a vertical line to divide the two halves.

$$\left[\begin{array}{ccc|ccc} 1 & 2 & -1 & 1 & 0 & 0 \\ 2 & 0 & 1 & 0 & 1 & 0 \\ 3 & 1 & 0 & 0 & 0 & 1 \end{array}\right].$$

The plan is to perform *elementary row operations* to transform the submatrix to the left of the vertical line into the identity matrix. The inverse will then be the submatrix to the right of the line. The matrix is not invertible if we cannot transform the left submatrix to I_3.

There are three allowable elementary row operations:

- multiply a row by a number that is not 0,
- interchange two different rows, and
- add a multiple of one row to a different row.

We perform these on the complete rows, which in this case have 6 entries each. Mathematical software such as MATLAB® and Mathematica® have built-in algorithms to determine which operations to do to which rows in which order. Here, we choose reasonable steps to convert the left-hand side to I_3.

Add −2 times the first row to the second row:

$$\left[\begin{array}{ccc|ccc} 1 & 2 & -1 & 1 & 0 & 0 \\ 2 & 0 & 1 & 0 & 1 & 0 \\ 3 & 1 & 0 & 0 & 0 & 1 \end{array}\right] \mapsto \left[\begin{array}{ccc|ccc} 1 & 2 & -1 & 1 & 0 & 0 \\ 0 & -4 & 3 & -2 & 1 & 0 \\ 3 & 1 & 0 & 0 & 0 & 1 \end{array}\right].$$

Add −3 times the first row to the third row:

$$\left[\begin{array}{ccc|ccc} 1 & 2 & -1 & 1 & 0 & 0 \\ 0 & -4 & 3 & -2 & 1 & 0 \\ 3 & 1 & 0 & 0 & 0 & 1 \end{array}\right] \mapsto \left[\begin{array}{ccc|ccc} 1 & 2 & -1 & 1 & 0 & 0 \\ 0 & -4 & 3 & -2 & 1 & 0 \\ 0 & -5 & 3 & -3 & 0 & 1 \end{array}\right].$$

The first column on the left is now the first column of I_3. Let's work on the second column.

Add -1 times the third row to the second row:

$$\left[\begin{array}{ccc|ccc} 1 & 2 & -1 & 1 & 0 & 0 \\ 0 & -4 & 3 & -2 & 1 & 0 \\ 0 & -5 & 3 & -3 & 0 & 1 \end{array}\right] \mapsto \left[\begin{array}{ccc|ccc} 1 & 2 & -1 & 1 & 0 & 0 \\ 0 & 1 & 0 & 1 & 1 & -1 \\ 0 & -5 & 3 & -3 & 0 & 1 \end{array}\right].$$

Add -2 times the second row to the first:

$$\left[\begin{array}{ccc|ccc} 1 & 2 & -1 & 1 & 0 & 0 \\ 0 & 1 & 0 & 1 & 1 & -1 \\ 0 & -5 & 3 & -3 & 0 & 1 \end{array}\right] \mapsto \left[\begin{array}{ccc|ccc} 1 & 0 & -1 & -1 & -2 & 2 \\ 0 & 1 & 0 & 1 & 1 & -1 \\ 0 & -5 & 3 & -3 & 0 & 1 \end{array}\right].$$

Add 5 times the second row to the third:

$$\left[\begin{array}{ccc|ccc} 1 & 0 & -1 & -1 & -2 & 2 \\ 0 & 1 & 0 & 1 & 1 & -1 \\ 0 & -5 & 3 & -3 & 0 & 1 \end{array}\right] \mapsto \left[\begin{array}{ccc|ccc} 1 & 0 & -1 & -1 & -2 & 2 \\ 0 & 1 & 0 & 1 & 1 & -1 \\ 0 & 0 & 3 & 2 & 5 & -4 \end{array}\right].$$

The second column on the left is complete. Multiply the third row by $\frac{1}{3}$:

$$\left[\begin{array}{ccc|ccc} 1 & 0 & -1 & -1 & -2 & 2 \\ 0 & 1 & 0 & 1 & 1 & -1 \\ 0 & 0 & 3 & 2 & 5 & -4 \end{array}\right] \mapsto \left[\begin{array}{ccc|ccc} 1 & 0 & -1 & -1 & -2 & 2 \\ 0 & 1 & 0 & 1 & 1 & -1 \\ 0 & 0 & 1 & \frac{2}{3} & \frac{5}{3} & -\frac{4}{3} \end{array}\right].$$

We complete the process by adding the third row to the first:

$$\left[\begin{array}{ccc|ccc} 1 & 0 & -1 & -1 & -2 & 2 \\ 0 & 1 & 0 & 1 & 1 & -1 \\ 0 & 0 & 1 & \frac{2}{3} & \frac{5}{3} & -\frac{4}{3} \end{array}\right] \mapsto \left[\begin{array}{ccc|ccc} 1 & 0 & 0 & -\frac{1}{3} & -\frac{1}{3} & \frac{2}{3} \\ 0 & 1 & 0 & 1 & 1 & -1 \\ 0 & 0 & 1 & \frac{2}{3} & \frac{5}{3} & -\frac{4}{3} \end{array}\right].$$

Through this process, we have computed

$$\left[\begin{array}{ccc} 1 & 2 & -1 \\ 2 & 0 & 1 \\ 3 & 1 & 0 \end{array}\right]^{-1} = \left[\begin{array}{ccc} -\frac{1}{3} & -\frac{1}{3} & \frac{2}{3} \\ 1 & 1 & -1 \\ \frac{2}{3} & \frac{5}{3} & -\frac{4}{3} \end{array}\right].$$

Exercise 5.14

(You knew this was coming …) Verify that the product of the matrix and the computed inverse is I_3.

If the matrix had not been invertible, we would have gotten all zeros in a row or column on the left at some point.

Carl Friedrich Gauss (Figure 5.13) was a prolific mathematician. His research included many areas of mathematics, including algebra and number theory, as well as physics and astronomy.

Figure 5.13: Carl Friedrich Gauss (1777–1855)

To learn more

The computational complexity of inversion of an n-by-n square matrix by Gaussian elimination is $O(n^3)$. Don Coppersmith and Shmuel Winograd developed an algorithm that brought this down to $O(n^{2.376})$ in 1987. [49] Subsequent optimizations have brought this complexity down only slightly.

5.6 The determinant and trace

Ah, the determinant, a function on square matrices that produces values in **F**. It's so elegant, so useful, tells us so much, and is such an annoying and error-prone thing to compute beyond the 2-by-2 case.

Let's look at its properties before we discuss its calculation. Let A be an n-by-n matrix. We denote its determinant by $\det(A)$:

- $\det(A) \neq 0$ if and only if A is invertible.
- For b a scalar in $\mathbf{F}$, $\det(bA) = b^n \det(A)$.
- If any row or column of A is all zeros, then $\det(A) = 0$. The determinant being zero does not imply a row or column is zero.
- If A is upper or lower triangular, the determinant is the product of the diagonal entries. If one of those diagonal entries is 0, the determinant is thus 0.
- In particular, $\det(I) = 1$ for I an identity matrix.
- The determinant behaves well when taking transposes and conjugates:

$$\det(A) = \det\left(A^{\mathsf{T}}\right) \qquad \det\left(\overline{A}\right) = \overline{\det(A)}$$

Exercise 5.15

Prove that the determinant of a matrix's adjoint is the conjugate of the matrix's determinant:

$$\det\left(A^{\dagger}\right) = \overline{\det(A)}\,.$$

Product rule for determinants

Let A and B be n-by-n square matrices. Then

$$\det(AB) = \det(A)\det(B) = \det(B)\det(A) = \det(BA)\,.$$

Exercise 5.16

Show that $\det\left(A^{-1}\right) = \frac{1}{\det(A)}$ for invertible A. Use the product rule for determinants.

For a 2-by-2 matrix,

$$\det\left(\begin{bmatrix} a & b \\ c & d \end{bmatrix}\right) = \begin{vmatrix} a & b \\ c & d \end{vmatrix} = ad - bc\,.$$

Note how we use vertical bars instead of brackets around the matrix entries to show we are taking the determinant.

Exercise 5.17

Given this formula, verify the determinant product rule for 2-by-2 matrices.

Exercise 5.18

What is the determinant of a rotation matrix in $\mathbf{R}^2$? Does it depend on the angle of rotation?

We used the elementary row operations when performing Gaussian elimination to find the inverse. They have these effects on the determinant d of a matrix A:

- if you multiply a row of A by a number $b \neq 0$, the new determinant is bd,
- if you interchange two different rows of A, the new determinant is $-d$, and
- if you add a multiple of one row to a different row, the determinant d does not change.

Exercise 5.19

Verify these in the 2-by-2 case using the formula for the determinant.

Exercise 5.20

For a fixed 2-by-2 matrix A, consider the matrix product BA.

- What matrix B multiplies the first row of A by 3?
- What matrix B interchanges the rows of A?
- What matrix B adds -2 times the first row of A to the second row of A?

Use the product rule to demonstrate the changes to the determinant for these three example row operations.

After 2-by-2, life gets more complicated, but we can again use Gaussian elimination and elementary row operations. Our goal is to transform the matrix into upper triangular form. We do this with row operations and keep track of the cumulative changes to the determinant in a variable m, which we initially set to 1.

Let's compute the determinant of this 3-by-3 matrix:

$$\begin{bmatrix} 3 & -1 & -2 \\ 5 & 5 & 5 \\ 4 & 2 & 1 \end{bmatrix} \qquad m = 1$$

Swap the first and second rows. Multiply m by -1.

$$\begin{bmatrix} 5 & 5 & 5 \\ 3 & -1 & -2 \\ 4 & 2 & 1 \end{bmatrix} \qquad m = -1$$

Multiply the first row and m by $\frac{1}{5}$.

$$\begin{bmatrix} 1 & 1 & 1 \\ 3 & -1 & -2 \\ 4 & 2 & 1 \end{bmatrix} \qquad m = -\frac{1}{5}$$

Multiply the first row by -3 and add it to the second row. m does not change.

$$\begin{bmatrix} 1 & 1 & 1 \\ 0 & -4 & -5 \\ 4 & 2 & 1 \end{bmatrix} \qquad m = -\frac{1}{5}$$

Multiply the first row by -4 and add it to the third row. m does not change.

$$\begin{bmatrix} 1 & 1 & 1 \\ 0 & -4 & -5 \\ 0 & -2 & -3 \end{bmatrix} \qquad m = -\frac{1}{5}$$

Multiply the second row by $-\frac{1}{2}$ and add it to the third row. m does not change.

$$\begin{bmatrix} 1 & 1 & 1 \\ 0 & -4 & -5 \\ 0 & 0 & -\frac{1}{2} \end{bmatrix} \qquad m = -\frac{1}{5}$$

The determinant of this diagonal matrix is the product of the diagonal elements: 2. We get the determinant of the original matrix by dividing by m:

$$\begin{vmatrix} 3 & -1 & -2 \\ 5 & 5 & 5 \\ 4 & 2 & 1 \end{vmatrix} = -10.$$

There are other ways to compute a determinant by taking determinants of submatrices, multiplying them by other matrix entries, and remembering when to add or subtract them. Here is one such formula in the 3-by-3 case:

$$\begin{vmatrix} a_{1,1} & a_{1,2} & a_{1,3} \\ a_{2,1} & a_{2,2} & a_{2,3} \\ a_{3,1} & a_{3,2} & a_{3,3} \end{vmatrix} = a_{1,1} \begin{vmatrix} a_{2,2} & a_{2,3} \\ a_{3,2} & a_{3,3} \end{vmatrix} - a_{1,2} \begin{vmatrix} a_{2,1} & a_{2,3} \\ a_{3,1} & a_{3,3} \end{vmatrix} + a_{1,3} \begin{vmatrix} a_{2,1} & a_{2,2} \\ a_{3,1} & a_{3,2} \end{vmatrix}.$$

If you work this out, you get

$$-a_{1,1}\,a_{2,3}\,a_{3,2} + a_{1,1}\,a_{2,2}\,a_{3,3} + a_{1,2}\,a_{2,3}\,a_{3,1}$$
$$-a_{1,2}\,a_{2,1}\,a_{3,3} - a_{1,3}\,a_{2,2}\,a_{3,1} + a_{1,3}\,a_{2,1}\,a_{3,2}.$$

This process is an example of a *cofactor expansion* to compute a determinant.

Exercise 5.21

Examine the sum and show that the determinant does not change if we replace the matrix with its transpose.

Exercise 5.22

Show by cofactor expansion that

$$\begin{vmatrix} 3 & -1 & -2 \\ 5 & 5 & 5 \\ 4 & 2 & 1 \end{vmatrix} = -10.$$

If

$$A = \begin{bmatrix} a_{1,1} & a_{1,2} & \cdots & a_{1,m} \\ a_{2,1} & a_{2,2} & \cdots & a_{2,m} \\ a_{3,1} & a_{3,2} & \cdots & a_{3,m} \\ \vdots & \vdots & \ddots & \vdots \\ a_{n,1} & a_{n,2} & \cdots & a_{n,m} \end{bmatrix},$$

define $A_{i,j}$ as the submatrix of A gotten by removing the ith row and the jth column. For example,

$$A_{2,1} = \begin{bmatrix} a_{1,1} & a_{1,2} & \cdots & a_{1,m} \\ a_{2,1} & a_{2,2} & a_{2,m} \\ a_{3,1} & a_{3,2} & \cdots & a_{3,m} \\ \vdots & & \ddots & \vdots \\ a_{n,1} & a_{n,2} & \cdots & a_{n,m} \end{bmatrix} = \begin{bmatrix} a_{1,2} & \cdots & a_{1,m} \\ a_{3,2} & \cdots & a_{3,m} \\ \vdots & \ddots & \vdots \\ a_{n,2} & \cdots & a_{n,m} \end{bmatrix}.$$

The cofactor $c_{i,j} = (-1)^{i+j}\det(A_{i,j})$. For any fixed row index i,

$$\det(A) = c_{i,1}a_{i,1} + c_{i,2}a_{i,2} + \cdots + c_{i,n}a_{i,n}.$$

Alternatively, for fixed column index j,

$$\det(A) = c_{1,j}a_{1,j} + c_{2,j}a_{2,j} + \cdots + c_{n,j}a_{n,j}.$$

The 3-by-3 calculation we saw previously has $j = 1$.

To use the cofactor expansion method effectively, find a row or column with a maximum number of zeros and use the first or second form to compute the determinant.

Does the determinant have a geometric interpretation? Consider the matrix

$$A = \begin{bmatrix} 2 & 0 \\ 2 & 3 \end{bmatrix} = \begin{bmatrix} 1 & 0 \\ 1 & 1 \end{bmatrix}\begin{bmatrix} 2 & 0 \\ 0 & 3 \end{bmatrix}.$$

This linear transformation on $\mathbf{R}^2$ first stretches by 2 in the x direction and 3 in the y direction, followed by a vertical shear. (Remember, multiplication corresponds to composition and we do it from right to left.) It has this effect on the unit square shown in Figure 5.14.

The area of a parallelogram is its height times its width, which is $3 \times 2 = 6$ in this case.

Using the formula for the 2-by-2 determinant, $\det(A) = (2 \times 3) - (0 \times 2) = 6$. Had we multiplied by a reflection matrix across the x-axis, we would have gotten the mirror image parallelogram with the same area, but the determinant would have been -6.

For a 2-by-2 matrix A operating on $\mathbf{R}^2$, the area of the parallelogram formed by applying A to the unit square is $|\det(A)|$.

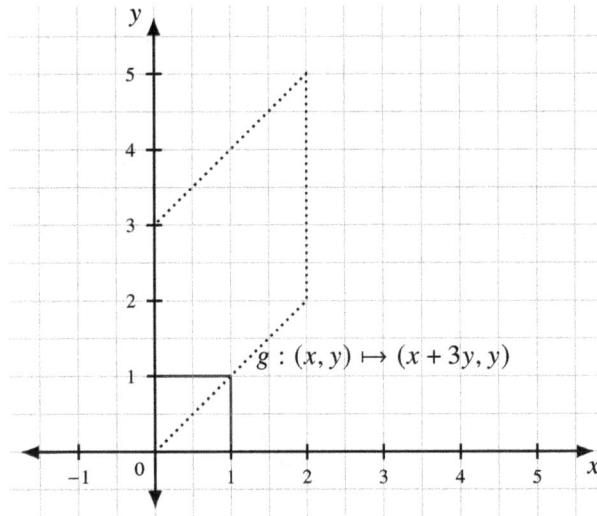

Figure 5.14: Linear transformation that stretches and shears

Exercise 5.23

Draw the effect on the unit square by multiplying by the product of the matrices

$$\begin{bmatrix} 1 & 0 \\ 0 & -1 \end{bmatrix} \begin{bmatrix} 2 & 0 \\ 2 & 3 \end{bmatrix}$$

and compute its determinant.

In $\mathbf{R}^3$, the unit cube is formed by completing the cube starting with the standard basis $\mathbf{e}_1 = (1,0,0)$, $\mathbf{e}_2 = (0,1,0)$, and $\mathbf{e}_3 = (0,0,1)$ to get the other corners at $(0,0,0)$, $(0,1,1)$, $(1,0,1)$, $(1,1,0)$, and $(1,1,1)$.

For a 3-by-3 matrix A operating on $\mathbf{R}^3$, the volume of the parallelepiped formed by applying A to the unit cube is $|\det(A)|$.

You get the idea.

In the general case of the n-dimensional real vector space $\mathbf{R}^n$, the points

$$(x_1, x_2, \ldots, x_n)$$

with each coordinate having a value of either 0 or 1 gives us the 2^n corners of the unit *hypercube*. The multidimensional volume of the unit hypercube is 1.

For an *n*-by-*n>* matrix *A* operating on $\mathbf{R}^n$, the multidimensional volume of the *hyperparallelepiped* formed by applying *A* to the unit hypercube is $|\det(A)|$. (I'm not the first to use "hyperparallelepiped," but I wish I had been.)

If the area or volume is 0, the image of the linear transformation collapses to something that is less than *n*-dimensional. Hence, it is not invertible. Think of collapsing the points in the cube in Figure 5.15 to its square base via a projection such as $(x, y, z) \mapsto (x, y, 0)$. We cannot recover what the original *z* value was.

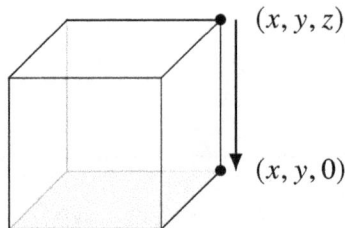

Figure 5.15: Collapsing a cube onto its base square

While all matrices with given dimensions over a field are a vector space, subsets of these matrices can have additional algebraic structure.

For a given *n* in **N**, the collection of all *n*-by-*n* **invertible** square matrices with entries in **F** forms a group under matrix multiplication called the *general linear group* of degree *n* over **F**. We denote it by $\mathbf{GL}(n, \mathbf{F})$.

The collection of all *n*-by-*n* square matrices with entries in **F** and **determinant 1** forms a group under multiplication called the *special linear group* of degree *n* over **F**. We denote it $\mathbf{SL}(n, \mathbf{F})$, and it is a subgroup of the general linear group $\mathbf{GL}(n, \mathbf{F})$.

Whereas the determinant of a square matrix can be hard to compute, calculating the *trace* is easy: add the diagonal elements. Its value is in **F**.

If

$$A = \begin{bmatrix} a_{1,1} & \cdots & a_{1,n} \\ \vdots & \vdots & \vdots \\ a_{n,1} & \cdots & a_{n,n} \end{bmatrix},$$

then the trace of A is

$$\text{tr}(A) = a_{1,1} + a_{2,2} + \cdots + a_{n,n} .$$

The trace is a linear map from the vector space of all n-by-n matrices over **F** to **F**. This follows from the entry-by-entry definitions of addition and scalar multiplication.

For A, B, and C square matrices and d in **F**,

$$\text{tr}(A + B) = \text{tr}(A) + \text{tr}(B)$$
$$\text{tr}(dA) = d \, \text{tr}(A)$$
$$\text{tr}(-A) = -\text{tr}(A)$$
$$\text{tr}(AB) = \text{tr}(BA)$$
$$\text{tr}(ABC) = \text{tr}(CAB) = \text{tr}(BCA)$$

Exercise 5.24

Show how $\text{tr}(AB) = \text{tr}(BA)$ implies $\text{tr}(ABC) = \text{tr}(CAB) = \text{tr}(BCA)$.

While it is true that $\text{tr}(AB) = \text{tr}(BA)$, it is **not** generally true that $\text{tr}(AB) = \text{tr}(A)\text{tr}(B)$. This is an easy mistake to make. The determinant behaves well under multiplication, and the trace behaves well under addition.

Transposing a square matrix does not change the main diagonal, so

$$\text{tr}(A) = \text{tr}\left(A^{\mathsf{T}}\right).$$

For a complex square matrix,

$$\text{tr}\left(\overline{A}\right) = \text{tr}\left(A^{\dagger}\right) = \overline{\text{tr}(A)} .$$

Exercise 5.25

Why is the trace of a Hermitian matrix real?

The trace does not have a simple geometric interpretation like the determinant, but it enters the picture when we consider changing from one basis of a vector space to another. While I present it here for square matrices, we define the trace for all matrices: just sum the entries on the main diagonal.

5.7 Length and preserving it

Length is a natural notion in the real world, but it needs to be defined precisely in vector spaces. Using complex numbers complicates things because we need to use conjugation. Length is related to *magnitude*, which measures how big something is. Understanding length and norms is key to the mathematics of quantum algorithms, as we shall see in Chapter 10, ''From Circuits to Algorithms.''

5.7.1 Dot products

Let V be a finite-dimensional vector space over $\mathbf{R}$, and let $\mathbf{v} = (v_1, v_2, \ldots, v_n)$ and $\mathbf{w} = (w_1, w_2, \ldots, w_n)$ be two vectors in V.

The *dot product* ''·'' of $\mathbf{v}$ and $\mathbf{w}$ is the sum of the products of the corresponding entries in $\mathbf{v}$ and $\mathbf{w}$:

$$\mathbf{v} \cdot \mathbf{w} = v_1 w_1 + v_2 w_2 + \cdots + v_n w_n .$$

If we think of $\mathbf{v}$ and $\mathbf{w}$ as row vectors and so as 1-by-n matrices, then

$$\mathbf{v} \cdot \mathbf{w} = \mathbf{v} \mathbf{w}^{\mathsf{T}} .$$

The dot product of the basis vectors $\mathbf{e}_1 = (1, 0)$ and $\mathbf{e}_2 = (0, 1)$ is 0. When this happens for real vectors, we say they are *orthogonal*.

Another such real orthogonal basis pair is

$$\mathbf{h}_1 = \left(\frac{\sqrt{2}}{2}, \frac{\sqrt{2}}{2} \right) \quad \text{and} \quad \mathbf{h}_2 = \left(\frac{\sqrt{2}}{2}, -\frac{\sqrt{2}}{2} \right),$$

as shown in Figure 5.16, because

$$\frac{\sqrt{2}}{2} \frac{\sqrt{2}}{2} + \frac{\sqrt{2}}{2} \left(-\frac{\sqrt{2}}{2} \right) = \frac{2}{4} - \frac{2}{4} = 0.$$

5.7.2 Inner products

Continuing with V over $\mathbf{F} = \mathbf{R}$ or $\mathbf{F} = \mathbf{C}$, let $\mathbf{u}$, $\mathbf{v}$, and $\mathbf{w}$ be in V. We define an *inner product* $\langle \mathbf{v}, \mathbf{w} \rangle$ on two vectors to be an $\mathbf{F}$-valued function such that:

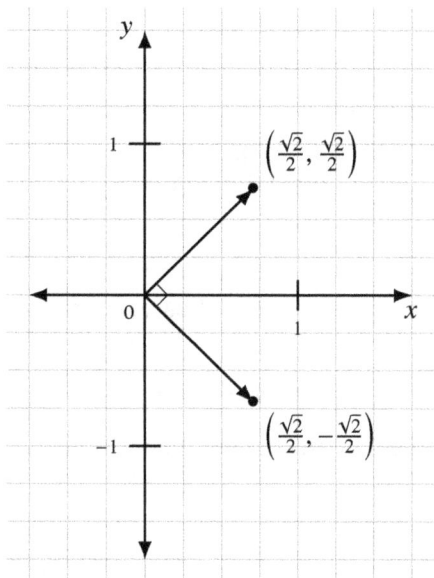

Figure 5.16: An orthogonal pair of vectors

- $\langle \mathbf{v}, \mathbf{v} \rangle$ is real and ≥ 0
- $\langle \mathbf{v}, \mathbf{v} \rangle = 0$ if and only if $\mathbf{v}$ is zero
- $\langle \mathbf{u}, \mathbf{v} + \mathbf{w} \rangle = \langle \mathbf{u}, \mathbf{v} \rangle + \langle \mathbf{u}, \mathbf{w} \rangle$
- $\langle \mathbf{v}, a\mathbf{w} \rangle = a\langle \mathbf{v}, \mathbf{w} \rangle$ for a in $\mathbf{F}$

with the conjugation rule

$$\langle \mathbf{v}, \mathbf{w} \rangle = \overline{\langle \mathbf{w}, \mathbf{v} \rangle}\,.$$

At this point, some mathematicians might say, "Wait, your complex inner product is linear in the second position instead of the first!". I learned that these should be the third and fourth conditions defining an inner product:

- $\langle \mathbf{u} + \mathbf{v}, \mathbf{w} \rangle = \langle \mathbf{u}, \mathbf{w} \rangle + \langle \mathbf{v}, \mathbf{w} \rangle$
- $\langle a\mathbf{v}, \mathbf{w} \rangle = a\langle \mathbf{v}, \mathbf{w} \rangle$ for a in $\mathbf{F}$

Alas, physicists use the first forms, making conventions such as Dirac's bra-ket notation work out more easily. So we'll adopt the physicists' version of this, though it pains me.

It's helpful if you look at this again, thinking about a real vector space and conjugation being the identity function there. The dot product for a vector space over $\mathbf{R}$ is an example of a real inner product. Experiment with the conditions above for the left-hand side of the inner product.

The inner product with the **0** vector on either side is 0.

Exercise 5.26

Why is

$$\langle a\mathbf{v}, \mathbf{w} \rangle = \overline{a}\langle \mathbf{v}, \mathbf{w} \rangle$$

for a in $\mathbf{F}$?

Whereas $\langle \mathbf{v}, \mathbf{w} \rangle = \mathbf{v} \cdot \mathbf{w}$ sufficed in the real case, it does not in the complex one. The correct generalization is

$$\langle \mathbf{v}, \mathbf{w} \rangle = \overline{\mathbf{v}} \cdot \mathbf{w}.$$

Unless otherwise specified, these are the default inner products we use for real and complex vector spaces.

Exercise 5.27

Let V be a real or complex vector space and a a real or complex scalar, respectively. If $|a| = 1$, show that

$$\langle a\mathbf{v}, a\mathbf{w} \rangle = \langle \mathbf{v}, \mathbf{w} \rangle.$$

The properties of the complex inner product imply that if A is a square complex matrix, then

$$\langle A\mathbf{v}, \mathbf{w} \rangle = \langle \mathbf{v}, A^{\dagger}\mathbf{w} \rangle.$$

That is, you can move the application of a linear transformation from one side of an inner product to the other by taking its conjugate transpose.

If we think of $\mathbf{v}$ and $\mathbf{w}$ as complex row vectors and so 1-by-n matrices, then

$$\langle \mathbf{v}, \mathbf{w} \rangle = \overline{\mathbf{v}} \mathbf{w}^{\mathsf{T}}.$$

A vector space with an inner product is called … wait for it … an *inner product space*.

If A is a Hermitian matrix, then $\langle A\mathbf{v}, \mathbf{w} \rangle = \langle \mathbf{v}, A\mathbf{w} \rangle$ for all vectors $\mathbf{v}$ and $\mathbf{w}$ in V.

Exercise 5.28

If V is a vector space over $\mathbf{F}$ and $\mathbf{F} = \mathbf{R}$, is the inner product

$$\langle , \rangle : V \oplus V \to \mathbf{F}$$

a bilinear map? What if $\mathbf{F} = \mathbf{C}$? Don't forget about conjugation.

5.7.3 Euclidean norm

Let $\mathbf{v} = (v_1, v_2, \ldots, v_n)$ be a vector in V. The *Euclidean norm* of $\mathbf{v}$, also called the *length* of $\mathbf{v}$, is

$$\|\mathbf{v}\| = \sqrt{\langle \mathbf{v}, \mathbf{v} \rangle} \,.$$

A vector with length 1 is a *unit vector*. Two unit vectors are *orthonormal* if they are orthogonal, meaning their inner product is 0. A set of unit vectors such as a basis is orthonormal if the vectors are pairwise orthogonal.

The standard basis vectors in any vector space $\mathbf{R}^n$ or $\mathbf{C}^n$ for n and m integers ≥ 1 are orthonormal.

Basis vectors don't need to be orthonormal, but it is very helpful in calculations. This is because of the possible cancellation in inner products and the vector lengths not skewing the contributions of the sizes of the coordinates.

For example, if $\mathbf{v}$ is a unit vector then $\|a\,\mathbf{v}\| = |a| \times \|\mathbf{v}\| = |a|$.

A matrix whose columns are orthonormal with respect to each other or whose rows are orthonormal to each other is an *orthogonal matrix*.

Exercise 5.29

Why is the transpose of an orthogonal matrix A also the inverse of A?

A real or complex finite dimensional vector space with the default inner product and Euclidean norm is an example of a *Hilbert space*, named after the mathematician David Hilbert, shown in Figure 5.17. Hilbert spaces may have infinite dimensions and use other norms. It's very common in quantum mechanics and quantum computing to talk about Hilbert spaces, but you only need to remember the particular examples we discuss here.

We can now give another interpretation of the dot product and Euclidean norm in a vector space V over $\mathbf{R}$. Let $\mathbf{v}$ and $\mathbf{w}$ be in V. The dot product of these vectors is equal to the product of their lengths times the cosine of the angle θ between them:

$$\mathbf{v} \cdot \mathbf{w} = \|\mathbf{v}\|\,\|\mathbf{w}\| \cos(\theta) \,.$$

As an example, let $\mathbf{v} = (4, 0)$ and $\mathbf{w} = (2, 3)$ in $\mathbf{R}^2$:

$$\mathbf{v} \cdot \mathbf{w} = 4 \times 2 + 0 \times 3 = 8 \qquad \|\mathbf{v}\| = \sqrt{4^2 + 0^2} = 4 \qquad \|\mathbf{w}\| = \sqrt{2^2 + 3^2} = \sqrt{13}$$

and so $8 = 4\sqrt{13} \cos(\theta)$. Solving for $\cos(\theta)$, we find it equals $\frac{2}{\sqrt{13}} \approx 0.5547$. Here, "$\approx$" means "approximately equal to."

Figure 5.17: David Hilbert in 1912

Applying the *inverse cosine* function arccos via a calculator or software, we find that $\theta \approx 0.9827$. Figure 5.18 shows the vectors and the angle.

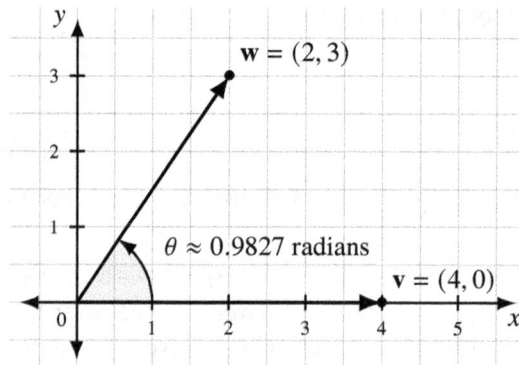

Figure 5.18: The angle related to the dot product of two vectors

When $\cos(\theta) = 0$, the two vectors are at a right angle to each other and so are orthogonal. From the formula, this implies the dot product is zero.

5.7.4 Reflections again

In two dimensions, if $\mathbf{v} = (v_1, v_2)$ is a nonzero vector, then $\mathbf{w} = (-v_2, v_1)$ is orthogonal to $\mathbf{v}$ because $\mathbf{v} \cdot \mathbf{w} = 0$. The vectors have the same length. If we set

$$\mathbf{v}' = \left(\frac{v_1}{\|\mathbf{v}\|}, \frac{v_2}{\|\mathbf{v}\|} \right) \quad \text{and} \quad \mathbf{w}' = \left(-\frac{v_2}{\|\mathbf{v}\|}, \frac{v_1}{\|\mathbf{v}\|} \right),$$

then $\mathbf{v}'$ and $\mathbf{w}'$ are orthonormal because they have length 1 and are orthogonal.

The notation $\mathbf{v}'$ is pronounced "v prime." It's a common way of showing that we have modified a named object such as the vector $\mathbf{v}$ somehow.

If $\mathbf{v} = (3, 4)$ then $\mathbf{w} = (-4, 3)$. Therefore,

$$\mathbf{v}' = \left(\frac{3}{5}, \frac{4}{5}\right) \quad \text{and} \quad \mathbf{w}' = \left(-\frac{4}{5}, \frac{3}{5}\right),$$

with their plot in Figure 5.19.

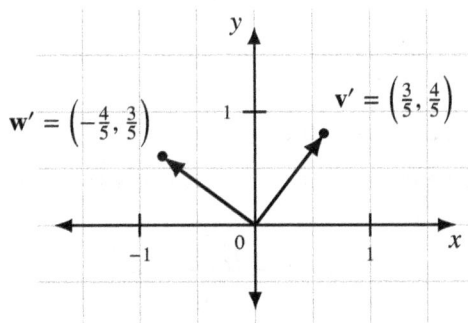

Figure 5.19: Two orthonormal vectors in $\mathbf{R}^2$ that are not the standard basis

Given a line L through the origin in $\mathbf{R}^2$, let $\mathbf{v}$ be a unit vector on the line. For example, if L is the x-axis, we can take $\mathbf{v} = (1, 0)$ or $(-1, 0)$. Let $\mathbf{w}$ be a unit vector orthogonal to $\mathbf{v}$.

The transformation

$$\mathbf{x} \mapsto \mathbf{x} - 2(\mathbf{x} \cdot \mathbf{w})\mathbf{w}$$

is a reflection across the line L.

Let's see an example of such a reflection. If L is the x-axis, we can take $\mathbf{v} = (1, 0)$ and $\mathbf{w} = (0, 1)$. Then

$$(x, y) \mapsto (x, y) - 2((x, y) \cdot (0, 1)) (0, 1)$$
$$= (x, y) - (0, 2y) = (x, -y),$$

which we know is the correct reflection.

Similarly, let L be the line $y = x$. Take

$$\mathbf{v} = \left(\frac{\sqrt{2}}{2}, \frac{\sqrt{2}}{2}\right) \quad \text{and} \quad \mathbf{w} = \left(-\frac{\sqrt{2}}{2}, \frac{\sqrt{2}}{2}\right).$$

So,

$$(x, y) \mapsto (x, y) - 2\left((x, y) \cdot \left(-\frac{\sqrt{2}}{2}, \frac{\sqrt{2}}{2}\right)\right)\left(-\frac{\sqrt{2}}{2}, \frac{\sqrt{2}}{2}\right)$$

$$= (x, y) - 2\left(-x\frac{\sqrt{2}}{2} + y\frac{\sqrt{2}}{2}\right)\left(-\frac{\sqrt{2}}{2}, \frac{\sqrt{2}}{2}\right)$$

$$= (x, y) - 2\left(\frac{1}{2}x - \frac{1}{2}y, -\frac{1}{2}x + \frac{1}{2}y\right)$$

$$= (x, y) - (x - y, -x + y)$$

$$= (y, x).$$

We saw this when we first looked at reflections.

This transformation has a matrix. Let $\mathbf{x} = (x_1, x_2)$, $\mathbf{v} = (v_1, v_2)$, and $\mathbf{w} = (-v_2, v_1)$. We write out

$$\mathbf{x} \mapsto \mathbf{x} - 2(\mathbf{x} \cdot \mathbf{w}) \, \mathbf{w}$$

as

$$(x_1, x_2) \mapsto (x_1, x_2) - 2((x_1, x_2) \cdot (-v_2, v_1)) (-v_2, v_1)$$

$$= (x_1, x_2) - 2(-x_1 v_2 + x_2 v_1)(-v_2, v_1)$$

$$= (x_1, x_2) + (2x_1 v_2 - 2x_2 v_1)(-v_2, v_1)$$

$$= (x_1, x_2) + \left(-2x_1 v_2^2 + 2x_2 v_1 v_2, \; 2x_1 v_1 v_2 - 2x_2 v_1^2\right)$$

$$= \left(x_1 - 2x_1 v_2^2 + 2x_2 v_1 v_2, \; x_2 + 2x_1 v_1 v_2 - 2x_2 v_1^2\right)$$

$$= \left(x_1\left(1 - 2v_2^2\right) + x_2\left(2v_1 v_2\right), \; x_1\left(2v_1 v_2\right) + x_2\left(1 - 2v_1^2\right)\right)$$

$$= \begin{bmatrix} 1 - 2v_2^2 & 2v_1 v_2 \\ 2v_1 v_2 & 1 - 2v_1^2 \end{bmatrix} \begin{bmatrix} x_1 \\ x_2 \end{bmatrix}.$$

Exercise 5.30

Since **v** is a unit vector, $v_1^2 + v_2^2 = 1$. What is the determinant of the reflection transformation matrix

$$A = \begin{bmatrix} 1 - 2v_2^2 & 2v_1v_2 \\ 2v_1v_2 & 1 - 2v_1^2 \end{bmatrix} ?$$

Show that $A\,A = A^2 = I_2$, that is, that A is its own inverse. Simplify the expressions as much as possible.

Since **v** is a unit vector, there is an angle θ such that $v_1 = \cos(\theta)$ and $v_2 = \sin(\theta)$. θ is the angle that **v** makes with the positive x-axis. We can rewrite the transformation matrix using the trigonometric forms:

$$A = \begin{bmatrix} 1 - 2v_2^2 & 2v_1v_2 \\ 2v_1v_2 & 1 - 2v_1^2 \end{bmatrix} = \begin{bmatrix} 1 - 2\sin^2(\theta) & 2\cos(\theta)\sin(\theta) \\ 2\cos(\theta)\sin(\theta) & 1 - 2\cos^2(\theta) \end{bmatrix}.$$

Recalling the trigonometric double angle formulas, and computing

$$1 - 2\cos^2(\theta) = 1 - 2(1 - \sin^2(\theta)) = -\cos(2\theta),$$

the last matrix for A reduces, perhaps surprisingly, to

$$\begin{bmatrix} 1 - 2\sin^2(\theta) & 2\cos(\theta)\sin(\theta) \\ 2\cos(\theta)\sin(\theta) & 1 - 2\cos^2(\theta) \end{bmatrix} = \begin{bmatrix} \cos(2\theta) & \sin(2\theta) \\ \sin(2\theta) & -\cos(2\theta) \end{bmatrix}.$$

Let L be a line through the origin in $\mathbf{R}^2$. Let θ be the angle the line makes with the positive x-axis. The transformation matrix for the reflection across the line is

$$\begin{bmatrix} \cos(2\theta) & \sin(2\theta) \\ \sin(2\theta) & -\cos(2\theta) \end{bmatrix}.$$

Let's compose this with another reflection for an angle φ:

$$\begin{bmatrix} \cos(2\theta) & \sin(2\theta) \\ \sin(2\theta) & -\cos(2\theta) \end{bmatrix} \begin{bmatrix} \cos(2\varphi) & \sin(2\varphi) \\ \sin(2\varphi) & -\cos(2\varphi) \end{bmatrix}.$$

This equals

$$\begin{bmatrix} \cos(2\theta)\cos(2\varphi) + \sin(2\theta)\sin(2\varphi) & \cos(2\theta)\sin(2\varphi) - \sin(2\theta)\cos(2\varphi) \\ \sin(2\theta)\cos(2\varphi) + \sin(2\theta)\sin(2\varphi) & \sin(2\theta)\sin(2\varphi) + \cos(2\theta)\cos(2\varphi) \end{bmatrix}$$

or

$$\begin{bmatrix} \cos(2\theta - 2\varphi) & -\sin(2\theta - 2\varphi) \\ \sin(2\theta - 2\varphi) & \cos(2\theta - 2\varphi) \end{bmatrix}$$

because of the trigonometric sum and difference formulas.

Drum roll, please ...

This is a rotation matrix for an angle of $2\theta - 2\varphi$!

> The composition of two reflection transformations in $\mathbf{R}^2$ is a rotation.

5.7.5   Projections again

Let $\mathbf{v}$ and $\mathbf{w}$ be vectors in a real or complex inner product space V, and suppose $\mathbf{v} \neq \mathbf{w}$. We define the linear map

$$\text{proj}_{\mathbf{v}} : V \to V$$

by

$$\text{proj}_{\mathbf{v}}(\mathbf{w}) = \frac{\langle \mathbf{v}, \mathbf{w} \rangle}{\langle \mathbf{v}, \mathbf{v} \rangle} \mathbf{v}.$$

This map is the *orthogonal projection of* $\mathbf{w}$ *onto* $\mathbf{v}$.

If $\mathbf{v}$ and $\mathbf{w}$ are orthogonal, the result is $\mathbf{0}$. If $\mathbf{w}$ is a multiple of $\mathbf{v}$, $\mathbf{w} = a\mathbf{v}$, so

$$\text{proj}_{\mathbf{v}}(\mathbf{w}) = \text{proj}_{\mathbf{v}}(a\mathbf{v}) = \frac{\langle \mathbf{v}, a\mathbf{v} \rangle}{\langle \mathbf{v}, \mathbf{v} \rangle} \mathbf{v} = a\frac{\langle \mathbf{v}, \mathbf{v} \rangle}{\langle \mathbf{v}, \mathbf{v} \rangle} \mathbf{v} = a\mathbf{v} = \mathbf{w}.$$

If $\mathbf{v}$ is a unit vector, the definition of $\text{proj}_{\mathbf{v}}$ simplifies to

$$\text{proj}_{\mathbf{v}}(\mathbf{w}) = \langle \mathbf{v}, \mathbf{w} \rangle \mathbf{v}.$$

Exercise 5.31

What is the projection of $(2, 3)$ onto $(4, 0)$?

Exercise 5.32

What is the projection of $(2, 1, 0)$ onto $(1, 1, 0)$?

5.7.6 The Gram-Schmidt orthonormalization process

Let

$$X = \{\mathbf{x}_1, \mathbf{x}_2, \dots, \mathbf{x}_n\}$$

be a set of linearly independent vectors spanning a subspace of a real or complex vector space V. The subspace need not be all of V, though it could be. For example, $(1, 1, 0)$ and $(1, -2, 0)$ span a 2-dimensional subspace of $\mathbf{R}^3$.

Starting with X, we use the *Gram-Schmidt process* to find a new orthonormal basis

$$Y = \{\mathbf{y}_1, \mathbf{y}_2, \dots, \mathbf{y}_n\}$$

that spans the same subspace.

We begin by setting $\mathbf{y}_1$ to $\mathbf{x}_1$:

$$\mathbf{y}_1 = \mathbf{x}_1.$$

We will normalize the $\mathbf{y}_j$ once we have computed them all.

To compute $\mathbf{y}_2$, recall the orthogonal projection from section 5.7.5 for $\mathbf{y}_1$:

$$\text{proj}_{\mathbf{y}_1}(\mathbf{w}) = \frac{\langle \mathbf{y}_1, \mathbf{w} \rangle}{\langle \mathbf{y}_1, \mathbf{y}_1 \rangle} \mathbf{y}_1.$$

We define

$$\mathbf{y}_2 = \mathbf{x}_2 - \text{proj}_{\mathbf{y}_1}(\mathbf{x}_2).$$

Then,

$$\langle \mathbf{y}_1, \mathbf{y}_2 \rangle = \left\langle \mathbf{y}_1, \mathbf{x}_2 - \text{proj}_{\mathbf{y}_1}(\mathbf{x}_2) \right\rangle$$

$$= \left\langle \mathbf{y}_1, \mathbf{x}_2 - \frac{\langle \mathbf{y}_1, \mathbf{x}_2 \rangle}{\langle \mathbf{y}_1, \mathbf{y}_1 \rangle} \mathbf{y}_1 \right\rangle$$

$$= \langle \mathbf{y}_1, \mathbf{x}_2 \rangle - \left\langle \mathbf{y}_1, \frac{\langle \mathbf{y}_1, \mathbf{x}_2 \rangle}{\langle \mathbf{y}_1, \mathbf{y}_1 \rangle} \mathbf{y}_1 \right\rangle$$

$$= \langle \mathbf{y}_1, \mathbf{x}_2 \rangle - \frac{\langle \mathbf{y}_1, \mathbf{x}_2 \rangle}{\langle \mathbf{y}_1, \mathbf{y}_1 \rangle} \langle \mathbf{y}_1, \mathbf{y}_1 \rangle$$

$$= \langle \mathbf{y}_1, \mathbf{x}_2 \rangle - \frac{\langle \mathbf{y}_1, \mathbf{y}_1 \rangle}{\langle \mathbf{y}_1, \mathbf{y}_1 \rangle} \langle \mathbf{y}_1, \mathbf{x}_2 \rangle$$

$$= \langle \mathbf{y}_1, \mathbf{x}_2 \rangle - \langle \mathbf{y}_1, \mathbf{x}_2 \rangle$$

$$= 0 \,.$$

Thus, $\mathbf{y}_1$ and $\mathbf{y}_2$ are orthogonal.

Next, define

$$\mathbf{y}_3 = \mathbf{x}_3 - \text{proj}_{\mathbf{y}_1}(\mathbf{x}_3) - \text{proj}_{\mathbf{y}_2}(\mathbf{x}_3) \,.$$

Continue in this way until we finally define

$$\mathbf{y}_n = \mathbf{x}_n - \text{proj}_{\mathbf{y}_1}(\mathbf{x}_n) - \text{proj}_{\mathbf{y}_2}(\mathbf{x}_n) - \cdots - \text{proj}_{\mathbf{y}_{n-1}}(\mathbf{x}_n) \,.$$

The vectors $\mathbf{y}_j$ are pairwise orthogonal. Normalize each by redefining

$$\mathbf{y}_j = \frac{\mathbf{y}_j}{\|\mathbf{y}_j\|}$$

for $0 \leq j \leq n$.

By construction, Y is an orthonormal basis spanning the same subspace as X.

Exercise 5.33

Verify that $\mathbf{y}_3$ is orthogonal to each of $\mathbf{y}_1$ and $\mathbf{y}_2$.

Exercise 5.34

Perform the Gram-Schmidt orthonormalization process on the vectors $(2, 0)$ and $(3, 3)$ in $\mathbf{R}^2$.

5.8 Unitary transformations

What are the characteristics of linear transformations that preserve length? If $L : V \to V$ and it is always true that $\|L\mathbf{v}\| = \|\mathbf{v}\|$, what can we say about the matrix of L?

A complex square matrix U is *unitary* if its adjoint $U^\dagger$ is its inverse U^{-1}. Hence, $UU^\dagger = U^\dagger U = I$. The columns of U are orthonormal, as are the rows, which follows from the definition of the complex inner product.

For a unitary matrix U, $|\det(U)| = 1$ because

$$
\begin{aligned}
1 &= \det(I) & &= \det(UU^\dagger) \\
&= \det(U)\det(U^\dagger) & &= \det(U)\det\left(\overline{U}^{\mathsf T}\right) \\
&= \det(U)\det\left(\overline{U}\right) & &= \det(U)\,\overline{\det(U)} \\
&= |\det(U)|^2 .
\end{aligned}
$$

To prove that unitary matrices preserve length, we must do more transposition and conjugation math:

$$\|U\mathbf{v}\|^2 = \langle U\mathbf{v}, U\mathbf{v}\rangle = \left\langle \mathbf{v}, U^\dagger U\mathbf{v}\right\rangle = \langle \mathbf{v}, \mathbf{v}\rangle = \|\mathbf{v}\|^2 .$$

Since the lengths are nonnegative, $\|U\mathbf{v}\| = \|\mathbf{v}\|$. Conversely, if this holds, we must have $UU^\dagger = I$.

Rotations and reflections are unitary. An orthogonal matrix is unitary.

> The matrices corresponding to gates/operations on qubits are all unitary.

Identity matrices are unitary, as are the three Pauli matrices:

$$
\sigma_x = \begin{bmatrix} 0 & 1 \\ 1 & 0 \end{bmatrix} \qquad
\sigma_y = \begin{bmatrix} 0 & -i \\ i & 0 \end{bmatrix} \qquad
\sigma_z = \begin{bmatrix} 1 & 0 \\ 0 & -1 \end{bmatrix}
$$

The Greek letter σ is "sigma."

The Pauli matrices have great importance in quantum mechanics and satisfy several useful identities.

$$
\begin{aligned}
\det(\sigma_x) &= \det(\sigma_y) = \det(\sigma_z) = -1 \\
\mathrm{tr}(\sigma_x) &= \mathrm{tr}(\sigma_y) = \mathrm{tr}(\sigma_z) = 0 \\
\sigma_x^2 &= \sigma_y^2 = \sigma_z^2 = -i\sigma_x\sigma_y\sigma_z = I_2 \\
\sigma_x\sigma_y &= i\sigma_z = -\sigma_y\sigma_x \\
\sigma_y\sigma_z &= i\sigma_x = -\sigma_z\sigma_y \\
\sigma_z\sigma_x &= i\sigma_y = -\sigma_x\sigma_z
\end{aligned}
$$

This is a Hadamard matrix, also unitary:

$$
\begin{bmatrix}
\frac{1}{2} & \frac{1}{2} & \frac{1}{2} & \frac{1}{2} \\
\frac{1}{2} & -\frac{1}{2} & \frac{1}{2} & -\frac{1}{2} \\
\frac{1}{2} & \frac{1}{2} & -\frac{1}{2} & -\frac{1}{2} \\
\frac{1}{2} & -\frac{1}{2} & -\frac{1}{2} & \frac{1}{2}
\end{bmatrix}
= \frac{1}{2}
\begin{bmatrix}
1 & 1 & 1 & 1 \\
1 & -1 & 1 & -1 \\
1 & 1 & -1 & -1 \\
1 & -1 & -1 & 1
\end{bmatrix}.
$$

Computationally, being unitary is a good property for a matrix because computing inverses can be challenging, but adjoints are straightforward.

The product $U_1 U_2$ of two unitary matrices U_1 and U_2 is unitary:

$$
(U_1 U_2)(U_1 U_2)^\dagger = (U_1 U_2)\left(U_2^\dagger U_1^\dagger\right) = U_1 \left(U_2 U_2^\dagger\right) U_1^\dagger = U_1 U_1^\dagger = I.
$$

For a given integer n in **N**, the collection of all n-by-n unitary matrices with entries in **F** form a group under multiplication called the *unitary group* of degree n over **F**. We denote it by $\mathbf{U}(n, \mathbf{F})$. It is a subgroup of $\mathbf{GL}(n, \mathbf{F})$, the general linear group of degree n over **F**.

For a given integer n in **N**, the collection of all n-by-n unitary matrices with entries in **F** and **determinant 1** form a group under multiplication called the *special unitary group* of degree n over **F**. We denote it $\mathbf{SU}(n, \mathbf{F})$.

$\mathbf{SU}(n, \mathbf{F})$ is a subgroup of $\mathbf{U}(n, \mathbf{F})$. It is also a subgroup of $\mathbf{SL}(n, \mathbf{F})$, the special linear group of degree n over **F**.

Unitary and Hermitian matrices, linear operators, and transformations are the most important kinds for quantum computing. We will use the terms *unitary operator* and *Hermitian operator* when the discussion is not focused on a particular basis.

Exercise 5.35

Let **F** be **R** or **C**, and let c be a scalar in **F** with absolute value 1. Show that if U is in $\mathbf{U}(n, \mathbf{F})$, so is cU. Show that there exists a scalar c so that cU is in $\mathbf{SU}(n, \mathbf{F})$.

Exercise 5.36

Let P be an n-by-n square matrix, all of whose entries are either 0 or 1. Further, assume that each row and each column of P contains exactly one 1. P is an example of a *permutation matrix*.

- If A is an n-by-n matrix, how does PA differ from A with respect to the order of its rows?
- How does AP differ from A with respect to the order of its columns?
- Show that P is unitary.

To learn more

We can treat linear algebra abstractly [101] [149] [210], or we can approach it as a tool for applied mathematics [209] [203] or engineering [161]. Sometimes, authors present it simply as manipulations of matrices and vectors. Depending on your background, you may find one text or another more comfortable.

5.9 Change of basis

Given an n-dimensional vector space V, we can choose different bases for V. Let's call two of them

$$X = \{\mathbf{x}_1, \mathbf{x}_2, \ldots, \mathbf{x}_n\} \quad \text{and} \quad Y = \{\mathbf{y}_1, \mathbf{y}_2, \ldots, \mathbf{y}_n\} \ .$$

If $\mathbf{v}$ is a vector in V, it has one set of coordinates corresponding to X and another set for Y. How do we change from one set of coordinates for $\mathbf{v}$ to the other?

Let's look at an example demonstrating how the choice of basis can make things easier.

Suppose we have city blocks laid out in a rectilinear pattern as in Figure 5.20. We use the basis vectors $\mathbf{x}_1 = (1, 0)$ and $\mathbf{x}_2 = (0, 2)$ to position ourselves. I've given the coordinates using the standard basis.

I can give you directions by saying, "Go north along $\mathbf{x}_2$ for 1 block, turn right, and go east along $\mathbf{x}_1$ for 2 blocks." That puts you where the star is in the picture. In terms of the X basis, the position is $2\mathbf{x}_1 + \mathbf{x}_2$.

$\mathbf{x}_1$ and $\mathbf{x}_2$ are not the same lengths so the "units" work well with the width and height of the city blocks. Basis vectors need not have length one, of course.

Things don't work out well if our city grid is at an angle instead of a north-south, east-west orientation. Indeed, cities are laid out based on their history, their growth, and their

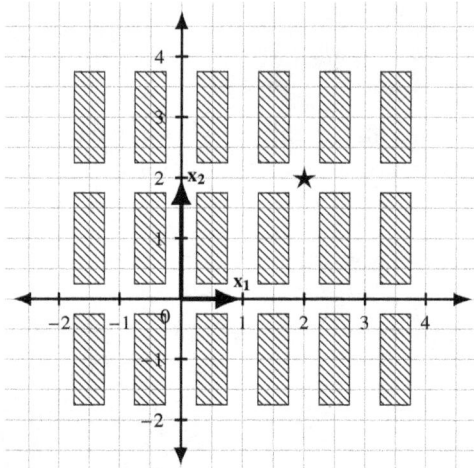

Figure 5.20: City blocks laid out according to the standard basis grid

geographic settings. x_1 and x_2 no longer work if we want to walk along one basis vector and then the other. We would walk through buildings if we followed those paths, as in Figure 5.21.

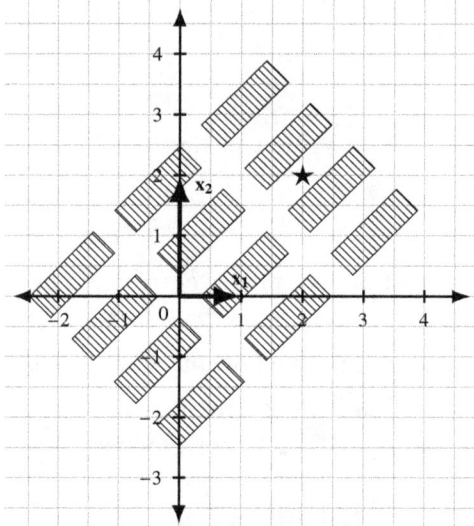

Figure 5.21: City blocks rotated from the standard grid

We need to change to another basis more suitable for what we are trying to accomplish. We must find one that makes computation and moving around easier.

We select new basis vectors y_1 and y_2, which align better with our road layout. Our city and the locations in it now use a new coordinate system, as shown in Figure 5.22.

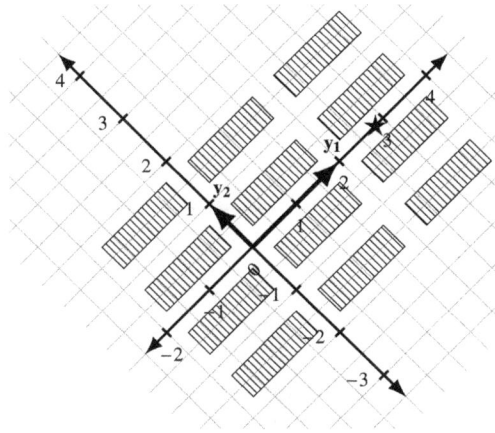

Figure 5.22: City blocks laid out according to a new basis

To get to the star, we now say, "Walk $\sqrt{2}$ blocks along $\mathbf{y}_1$." For those who don't navigate using square roots, that's about 1.4 blocks.

Exercise 5.37

Calculate why the distance you walk is $\sqrt{2}$ blocks.

Getting back to bases and moving between them, consider

$$X = E = \{\mathbf{x}_1 = \mathbf{e}_1 = (1,0), \mathbf{x}_2 = \mathbf{e}_2 = (0,1)\}$$

and

$$Y = \{\mathbf{y}_1 = (2,-1)_E, \mathbf{y}_2 = (3,2)_E\} \ .$$

Coordinates are relative to the standard basis in these initial definitions and are shown in Figure 5.23.

We define

$$U_{Y,E} = \begin{bmatrix} 2 & 3 \\ -1 & 2 \end{bmatrix},$$

where the columns are coordinates of each basis vector in Y relative to E.

If we first let $\mathbf{v}_Y = (1,0)$ be the vector $\mathbf{y}_1$ *written relative to the basis* Y, then

$$U_{Y,E}\,\mathbf{v}_Y = \begin{bmatrix} 2 & 3 \\ -1 & 2 \end{bmatrix} \begin{bmatrix} 1 \\ 0 \end{bmatrix}_Y = \begin{bmatrix} 2 \\ -1 \end{bmatrix}_E = \text{the coordinates of } \mathbf{y_1} \text{ relative to } E.$$

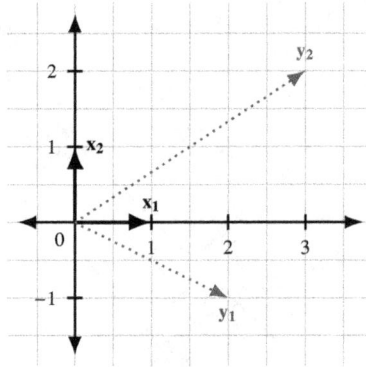

Figure 5.23: New basis vectors with standard basis coordinates

Now, let $\mathbf{v}_Y = (0, 1)$ the vector $\mathbf{y}_2$ *written relative to the basis Y,*

$$U_{Y,E}\,\mathbf{v}_Y = \begin{bmatrix} 2 & 3 \\ -1 & 2 \end{bmatrix}\begin{bmatrix} 0 \\ 1 \end{bmatrix}_Y = \begin{bmatrix} 3 \\ 2 \end{bmatrix}_E = \text{the coordinates of } \mathbf{y}_2 \text{ relative to } E.$$

> The matrix $U_{Y,E}$ transforms the coordinates of a vector $\mathbf{v}$ written relative to the basis Y to the coordinates for $\mathbf{v}$ written relative to the standard basis E. The columns of $U_{Y,E}$ are the basis vectors Y written in coordinates relative to E.

What if we want to go from coordinates relative to E to coordinates relative to X? This is easy: use the inverse of $U_{Y,E}$:

$$U_{E,Y} = U_{Y,E}^{-1}.$$

In our example,

$$U_{Y,E} = \begin{bmatrix} 2 & 3 \\ -1 & 2 \end{bmatrix} \quad \text{and} \quad U_{E,Y} = U_{Y,E}^{-1} = \begin{bmatrix} \frac{2}{7} & -\frac{3}{7} \\ \frac{1}{7} & \frac{2}{7} \end{bmatrix}.$$

Exercise 5.38

Verify the product of $U_{E,Y}$ and the coordinate vector of $\mathbf{y}_1$ written relative to E is equal to $(1, 0)_X$. What should it be for $\mathbf{y}_2$?

It is not always the case that we are moving between E and another basis. Even when neither X nor Y is E, we can still use the standard basis.

Here is a fundamental thing to remember about changing bases: if you want to go from a representation under basis X to one under Y, go through the standard basis E as an intermediate step.

To go from arbitrary bases X and Y, compute $U_{X,E}$ and $U_{Y,E}$. By composition,

$$U_{X,Y} = U_{E,Y}\, U_{X,E} = U_{Y,E}^{-1}\, U_{X,E}\,.$$

Suppose $L : V \to V$ is a linear transformation. L has a matrix A_X relative to basis X and another, different matrix A_Y relative to another basis Y. They both implement the same linear transformation.

What is the relationship between A_X and A_Y?

This topic can be confusing because it is easy to get yourself working with the wrong matrix or its inverse. If you start with the basic idea of what you are trying to represent, the rest takes care of itself.

Suppose we have a vector $\mathbf{v}_X$ with coordinates relative to X. Also, assume we know A_Y, but don't know A_X. How can we apply L and discover A_X?

We first convert $\mathbf{v}_X$ to its representation $\mathbf{v}_Y$ relative to Y using

$$\mathbf{v}_Y = U_{X,Y}\mathbf{v}_X\,.$$

We now apply L by multiplying by A_Y on the left:

$$A_Y\mathbf{v}_Y = A_Y U_{X,Y}\mathbf{v}_X\,.$$

Are we finished? We started with a vector using the X basis, but our result after applying L via A_Y uses the Y basis. We must convert the answer back to the X basis. We now know A_X:

$$A_X\mathbf{v}_X = \left(U_{X,Y}^{-1}A_Y U_{X,Y}\right)\mathbf{v}_X = \left(U_{Y,X}A_Y U_{X,Y}\right)\mathbf{v}_X$$

$$A_X = U_{X,Y}^{-1}A_Y U_{X,Y}$$

We say that the matrices A and B are *similar* if there exists an invertible matrix U such that

$$B = U^{-1}AU\,.$$

We have found a way to convert between similar matrices representing the same linear transformation L relative to different bases. Given a matrix A for L relative to some basis, can we find a diagonal matrix B to which it is similar? If so, we can learn a lot about L and its behavior.

Exercise 5.39

Show that $\det(A_X) = \det(A_Y)$ and hence is an intrinsic property of L independent of the choice of basis.

Exercise 5.40

Prove the two equalities:

$$U_{X,Y} A_X = A_Y U_{X,Y} \quad \text{and} \quad U_{Y,X} A_Y = A_X U_{Y,X}.$$

5.10   Eigenvectors and eigenvalues

Let's review some of the features of diagonal matrices. Recall that a diagonal matrix has 0s everywhere except maybe on the main diagonal. A simple example for $\mathbf{R}^3$ is

$$A = \begin{bmatrix} 3 & 0 & 0 \\ 0 & 1 & 0 \\ 0 & 0 & -2 \end{bmatrix}.$$

Its effect on the standard basis vectors $\mathbf{e}_1$, $\mathbf{e}_2$, and $\mathbf{e}_3$ is to stretch by a factor of 3 along the first, leave the second alone, reflect across the xy-plane, and then stretch by a factor of 2 along the third.

A general diagonal matrix looks like

$$D = \begin{bmatrix} d_1 & 0 & \cdots & 0 & 0 \\ 0 & d_2 & \cdots & 0 & 0 \\ \vdots & \vdots & \ddots & \vdots & \vdots \\ 0 & 0 & \cdots & d_{n-1} & 0 \\ 0 & 0 & \cdots & 0 & d_n \end{bmatrix}.$$

Of course, we might be dealing with a small matrix and not have quite so many zeros. Some of the d_j might be zero.

For a diagonal matrix D as above,

- $\det(D) = d_1 d_2 \ldots d_n$.
- $\text{tr}(D) = d_1 + d_2 + \cdots + d_n$.

- $D^{\mathsf{T}} = D$.
- D is invertible if and only if none of the d_j are 0.
- If D is invertible,

$$D^{-1} = \begin{bmatrix} \dfrac{1}{d_1} & 0 & \cdots & 0 & 0 \\ 0 & \dfrac{1}{d_2} & \cdots & 0 & 0 \\ \vdots & \vdots & \ddots & \vdots & \vdots \\ 0 & 0 & \cdots & \dfrac{1}{d_{n-1}} & 0 \\ 0 & 0 & \cdots & 0 & \dfrac{1}{d_n} \end{bmatrix} \quad \text{and} \quad \det\left(D^{-1}\right) = \frac{1}{\det(D)}\,.$$

- If $\{\mathbf{b}_1, \mathbf{b}_2, \ldots, \mathbf{b}_n\}$ is the basis we are using, then

$$D\,\mathbf{b}_1 = d_1\mathbf{b}_1 \qquad D\,\mathbf{b}_2 = d_2\mathbf{b}_2 \qquad \ldots \qquad D\,\mathbf{b}_n = d_n\mathbf{b}_n\,.$$

Focusing on this last effect on the basis vectors, given a general and not necessarily diagonal square matrix A, is there a vector $\mathbf{v}$ and a scalar λ such that $A\mathbf{v} = \lambda\mathbf{v}$? That is, does the linear transformation represented by A have the effect of stretching in the direction of $\mathbf{v}$ by λ?

Two things to note: first, it is traditional to use the Greek letter lambda = λ in this context. Second, I'm abusing terminology a little here. If λ is real and negative, we are technically stretching by $|\lambda|$ and doing a reflection.

> Let A be a square matrix with entries in $\mathbf{F}$. If there exists a nonzero vector $\mathbf{v}$ and a scalar λ such that $A\mathbf{v} = \lambda\mathbf{v}$, then $\mathbf{v}$ is an *eigenvector* of A, and λ is the corresponding *eigenvalue*. ''Eigen'' comes from German and means ''own'' or ''inherent.''
>
> We also call eigenvectors *characteristic vectors*, and we similarly call eigenvalues *characteristic values*, though the more German versions are in general use.

How can we find eigenvectors and their eigenvalues? We use the determinant.

If $A\mathbf{v} = \lambda\mathbf{v}$, then $A\mathbf{v} - \lambda\mathbf{v} = \mathbf{0}$, where $\mathbf{0}$ is the zero vector of length n. Matrix-wise, this is

$$(A - \lambda I_n)\,\mathbf{v} = \mathbf{0}\,,$$

where I_n is the n-by-n identity matrix. If the matrix $A - \lambda I_n$ is invertible, we can multiply both sides of the equation by the inverse and conclude that $\mathbf{v} = 0$, a contradiction. So $A - \lambda I_n$ is not invertible and has determinant 0:

$$\det(A - \lambda I_n) = 0\,.$$

This expression is a polynomial in the single variable λ. Its roots are the eigenvalues of A! An eigenvalue may show up more than once. In that case, we say the eigenvalue has *multiplicity* greater than 1.

Exercise 5.41

If $A = I_n$, what is the multiplicity of the eigenvalue 1?

Exercise 5.42

If A is a 2-by-2 square matrix, show that

$$\det(A - \lambda I_2) = \lambda^2 - \text{tr}(A)\lambda + \det(A).$$

Also show that

$$A^2 - \text{tr}(A)A + \det(A)I_2 = \text{the 2-by-2 zero matrix.}$$

Let's tease this apart in the real and complex 2-by-2 cases. We begin with the case that is only slightly more than trivial: the diagonal matrix

$$\begin{bmatrix} 1 & 0 \\ 0 & -1 \end{bmatrix}.$$

By inspection, 1 is the eigenvalue for eigenvector $\mathbf{e}_1$ and -1 is the eigenvalue for $\mathbf{e}_2$.

We do the computation via determinants:

$$\det\left(\begin{bmatrix} 1 & 0 \\ 0 & -1 \end{bmatrix} - \lambda \begin{bmatrix} 1 & 0 \\ 0 & 1 \end{bmatrix}\right) = \det\left(\begin{bmatrix} 1 - \lambda & 0 \\ 0 & -1 - \lambda \end{bmatrix}\right)$$

$$= \lambda^2 - 1 = (\lambda + 1)(\lambda - 1) = 0.$$

This confirms the eigenvalues are $\lambda_1 = 1$ and $\lambda_2 = -1$.

The eigenvalues of a diagonal matrix are the diagonal entries. The corresponding eigenvectors are the standard basis vectors.

Let's consider a more complicated example and also compute the eigenvectors. Let

$$A = \begin{bmatrix} 3 & 3 \\ 2 & 4 \end{bmatrix}.$$

Then

$$\det\left(\begin{bmatrix} 3 & 3 \\ 2 & 4 \end{bmatrix} - \lambda \begin{bmatrix} 1 & 0 \\ 0 & 1 \end{bmatrix}\right) = \begin{vmatrix} 3 - \lambda & 3 \\ 2 & 4 - \lambda \end{vmatrix}$$

$$= \lambda^2 - 7\lambda + 6$$
$$= (\lambda - 6)(\lambda - 1)$$
$$= 0.$$

The eigenvalues are $\lambda_1 = 6$ and $\lambda + 2 = 1$. To find the eigenvectors for each, solve

$$\begin{bmatrix} 3 - \lambda & 3 \\ 2 & 4 - \lambda \end{bmatrix} \begin{bmatrix} x \\ y \end{bmatrix} = \begin{bmatrix} 0 \\ 0 \end{bmatrix}$$

for $\lambda = \lambda_1 = 6$ and $\lambda = \lambda_2 = 1$, in turn.

For $\lambda = 6$, this is

$$-3x + 3y = 0$$
$$2x - 2y = 0$$

Either case tells us $y = x$, so we can choose any point along that line to represent the vector. We let $\mathbf{v}_1 = (1, 1)$.

For $\lambda = 1$, this is

$$2x + 3y = 0$$
$$2x + 3y = 0$$

We have $y = -\frac{2}{3}x$. Choose $\mathbf{v}_2 = \left(1, -\frac{2}{3}\right)$.

Let's verify these:

$$A\mathbf{v}_1 = \begin{bmatrix} 3 & 3 \\ 2 & 4 \end{bmatrix} \begin{bmatrix} 1 \\ 1 \end{bmatrix} = \begin{bmatrix} 6 \\ 6 \end{bmatrix} = 6\mathbf{v}_1$$

and

$$A\mathbf{v}_2 = \begin{bmatrix} 3 & 3 \\ 2 & 4 \end{bmatrix} \begin{bmatrix} 1 \\ -\frac{2}{3} \end{bmatrix} = \begin{bmatrix} 3 - 3\frac{2}{3} \\ 2 - 4\frac{2}{3} \end{bmatrix} = \begin{bmatrix} 1 \\ -\frac{2}{3} \end{bmatrix} = 1\mathbf{v}_2.$$

Neither $\mathbf{v}_1$ nor $\mathbf{v}_2$ is a unit vector. We could have chosen $\mathbf{v}_1 = \left(\frac{\sqrt{2}}{2}, \frac{\sqrt{2}}{2}\right)$ on the line $y = x$ as a unit eigenvector.

Exercise 5.43

What are two choices for $\mathbf{v}_2$ on the line $y = -\frac{2}{3}x$ that would have made $\mathbf{v}_2$ a unit eigenvector?

These eigenvectors $\mathbf{v}_1$ and $\mathbf{v}_2$ are not orthogonal as their dot product is $\frac{1}{3}$, which is nonzero.

For comparison, I've drawn a dotted line vector in Figure 5.24 that is perpendicular to $\mathbf{v}_1$.

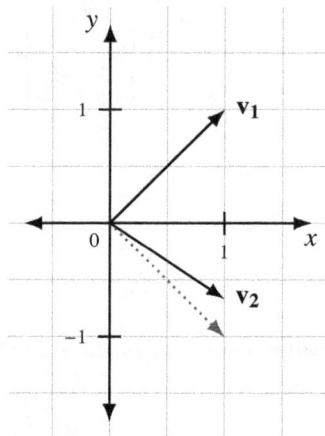

Figure 5.24: Nonorthogonal eigenvectors

The final example has

$$A = \begin{bmatrix} 1 & 1 \\ -1 & 1 \end{bmatrix},$$

and so

$$\det\left(\begin{bmatrix} 1 & 1 \\ -1 & 1 \end{bmatrix} - \lambda \begin{bmatrix} 1 & 0 \\ 0 & 1 \end{bmatrix}\right) = \begin{vmatrix} 1 - \lambda & 1 \\ -1 & 1 - \lambda \end{vmatrix} = \lambda^2 - 2\lambda + 2 = 0.$$

Notice I left out the factorization step. By the quadratic formula, the factorization is

$$(\lambda + (-1 - i))\,(\lambda + (-1 + i)) = (\lambda - (1 + i))\,(\lambda - (1 - i)).$$

The eigenvalues are $\lambda_1 = 1 + i$ and $\lambda_2 = 1 - i$. Whoops.

This simple-looking real matrix A does not have real eigenvalues, only complex ones. Thus, it does not have eigenvectors in $\mathbf{R}^2$.

If, instead of working in $\mathbf{R}^2$, we were in $\mathbf{C}^2$, we could proceed and find eigenvectors using the method in the previous example.

Exercise 5.44

What are the eigenvectors for

$$A = \begin{bmatrix} 1 & 1 \\ -1 & 1 \end{bmatrix}$$

on $\mathbf{C}^2$ that correspond to λ_1 and λ_2?

In these 2-by-2 cases, it is easy to take determinants and factor the polynomials. It gets more challenging as the dimension gets higher. People have developed algorithms and software to compute or estimate eigenvalues and eigenvectors. These are called *eigensolvers*.

Let A be a complex n-by-n matrix on $\mathbf{C}^n$. The polynomial $\det(A - \lambda I_n)$ in the single variable λ can be completely factored over $\mathbf{C}$. Therefore, A has n eigenvalues and n corresponding eigenvectors. Some eigenvalues may appear more than once.

The determinant of A, $\det(A)$, is the product of the n eigenvalues. The trace of A, $\operatorname{tr}(A)$, is their sum.

All is not lost for real matrices. The mathematician Augustin-Louis Cauchy proved that if a real square matrix A is symmetric, it has real eigenvalues. We can change to an orthonormal basis where the new matrix of the linear transformation represented by A (in the old basis) is a diagonal matrix. The diagonal entries are none other than the eigenvalues with the orthonormal basis as eigenvalues.

Let's look at some additional facts related to diagonal matrices.

A matrix A is diagonalizable if there exists an invertible matrix V such that

$$D = V^{-1}AV$$

and D is a diagonal matrix. There is a change of basis so that we can represent the transformation corresponding to A relative to the original basis by D relative to the new basis.

If we can compute all the eigenvalues of a complex matrix, can we diagonalize it? Not quite.

A complex matrix A is diagonalizable if all its eigenvalues are different. Diagonalizing a complex matrix with repeated eigenvalues may be possible, but this is not true in general.

If A is Hermitian, all its eigenvalues are positive if and only if it is positive definite. For each positive semi-definite matrix A, there is exactly one positive semi-definite matrix B such that $A = B^2$. We call B the square root of A, and we write it as $A^{\frac{1}{2}}$.

Spectral theorem

Let A be a complex n-by-n Hermitian matrix. All the eigenvalues of A are real, the eigenvectors corresponding to different eigenvalues are orthogonal, and we can always find a basis of $\mathbf{C}^n$ consisting of eigenvectors of A. Since we can always normalize eigenvectors, we can make this basis orthonormal. [137, Section 14.6]

In section 12.3, we show that there is a unitary change of basis for a Hermitian transformation so that it can be represented by a real diagonal matrix.

Since unitary matrices are so important for quantum computing, I note they have a crucial property regarding being transformed into a diagonal matrix.

Let U be a complex unitary matrix. There exists a **unitary** matrix V and a unitary diagonal matrix D so that $U = V^\dagger D V$.

Since $V^\dagger = V^{-1}$ because it is unitary, this means that $VUV^\dagger = D$: there is a unitary change of basis for a unitary transformation so that it can be represented by a unitary diagonal matrix.

Exercise 5.45

Are the diagonal elements in D necessarily the eigenvalues of the complex unitary matrix U?

5.11 Direct sums

Our treatment of vector spaces has alternated between the fairly concrete examples of $\mathbf{R}^2$ and $\mathbf{R}^3$ and the more abstract definition presented in section 5.2. I continue going back and forth with the fundamental idea of the *direct sum* of two vector spaces over the same field $\mathbf{F}$.

In a vague and neither concrete nor abstract sense, a direct sum is when you push two vector spaces together. It's one of the ways you can construct a new vector space from existing ones.

Let V and W be two vector spaces of dimensions n and m over $\mathbf{F}$. If we write $\mathbf{v} = (v_1, v_2, \ldots, v_n)$ and $\mathbf{w} = (w_1, w_2, \ldots, w_m)$, then

$$\mathbf{v} \oplus \mathbf{w} = (v_1, v_2, \ldots, v_n, w_1, w_2, \ldots, w_m)$$

in the direct sum vector space $V \oplus W$. It has dimension $n + m$.

All the requirements regarding addition and scalar multiplication follow directly from this definition because we perform those operations coordinate by coordinate. We've simply added more coordinates.

Exercise 5.46

Suppose $\mathbf{v}$, V, $\mathbf{w}$, and W are as above. Let U be a vector space over $\mathbf{F}$, and let

$$L_V : U \to V \quad \text{and} \quad L_W : U \to W$$

be linear maps. Show that $L : U \to V \oplus W$ defined for $\mathbf{u}$ in U by

$$L(\mathbf{u}) = L_V(\mathbf{u}) \oplus L_W(\mathbf{u})$$

is a linear map.

Exercise 5.47

Suppose $\mathbf{v}$, V, $\mathbf{w}$, and W are as above. Let U be a vector space over $\mathbf{F}$, and let

$$L_V : V \to U \quad \text{and} \quad L_W : W \to U$$

be linear maps. Show that $L_V \oplus L_W : V \oplus W \to U$ defined by

$$(L_V \oplus L_W)(\mathbf{v} \oplus \mathbf{w}) = L_V(\mathbf{v}) + L_W(\mathbf{w})$$

is a linear map.

There are four special linear maps for $V \oplus W$. Two are injections, and two are projections:

- $\text{inj}_V : V \to V \oplus W$ maps

$$(v_1, v_2, \ldots, v_n) \mapsto \left(v_1, v_2, \ldots, v_n, \underbrace{0, \ldots, 0}_{m \text{ times}} \right)$$

- $\text{inj}_W : W \to V \oplus W$ maps

$$(w_1, w_2, \ldots, w_m) \mapsto \left(\underbrace{0, \ldots, 0}_{n \text{ times}}, w_1, w_2, \ldots, w_m \right)$$

- $\text{proj}_V : V \oplus W \to V$

$$(v_1, v_2, \ldots, v_n, w_1, w_2, \ldots, w_m) \mapsto (v_1, v_2, \ldots, v_n)$$

- $\text{proj}_W : V \oplus W \to W$

$$(v_1, v_2, \ldots, v_n, w_1, w_2, \ldots, w_m) \mapsto (w_1, w_2, \ldots, w_m)$$

The composition $\text{proj}_V \circ \text{inj}_V$ is the identity transformation on V, as is $\text{proj}_W \circ \text{inj}_W$ on W.

The matrix equation for inj_V is

$$\begin{bmatrix} 1 & 0 & \cdots & 0 \\ 0 & 1 & \cdots & 0 \\ \vdots & \vdots & & \vdots \\ 0 & 0 & \cdots & 1 \\ 0 & 0 & \cdots & 0 \\ \vdots & \vdots & & \vdots \\ 0 & 0 & \cdots & 0 \end{bmatrix} \begin{bmatrix} v_1 \\ v_2 \\ \vdots \\ v_n \end{bmatrix} = \begin{bmatrix} v_1 & v_2 & \cdots & v_n & 0 & \cdots & 0 \end{bmatrix}.$$

Exercise 5.48

What are the matrix equations for the other three maps?

Starting with $\mathbf{R}^1$, you can create $\mathbf{R}^2 = \mathbf{R}^1 \oplus \mathbf{R}^1$ and
$$\mathbf{R}^3 = \mathbf{R}^1 \oplus \mathbf{R}^1 \oplus \mathbf{R}^1 = \mathbf{R}^2 \oplus \mathbf{R}^1 = \mathbf{R}^1 \oplus \mathbf{R}^2 .$$

Exercise 5.49

How many combinations are there that make $\mathbf{R}^4$? $\mathbf{R}^{10}$?

We can construct $\mathbf{C}^2$ from $\mathbf{C}^1$ in the same way, and combine two $\mathbf{C}^2$ to create $\mathbf{C}^4$. Everything works smoothly because of the way we have concatenated the coordinates.

There's another technique to build a new vector space from two existing ones. It's the *tensor product* and is essential mathematics for using multiple qubits in quantum computing. Unfortunately, it's a little messier. We cover it in section 8.1, immediately before we need it to explain entangling qubits.

5.12 Homomorphisms

When functions operate on collections with algebraic structure, we usually require additional properties to be preserved. We can now redefine linear maps and transformations of vector spaces in terms of these functions, called *homomorphisms*.

5.12.1 Group homomorphisms

Suppose $(\mathbf{G}, \star)$ and $(\mathbf{H}, \bullet)$ are groups, which we first explored in section 3.6.1. The function $f : \mathbf{G} \to \mathbf{H}$ is a *group homomorphism* if for any two elements a and b in $\mathbf{G}$,

$$f(a \star b) = f(a) \bullet f(b).$$

This means that f is not just a function, but it preserves the operations of the groups.

We have the following properties for group homomorphisms:

- $f(id_\mathbf{G}) = f(id_\mathbf{G} \star id_\mathbf{G}) = f(id_\mathbf{G}) \bullet f(id_\mathbf{G})$, which means $f(id_\mathbf{G}) = id_\mathbf{H}$.
- $id_\mathbf{H} = f(id_\mathbf{G}) = f(a \star a^{-1}) = f(a) \bullet f(a^{-1})$, which means $f(a^{-1}) = f(a)^{-1}$.

The set of all elements a in $\mathbf{G}$ such that $f(a) = id_\mathbf{H}$ is called the *kernel of f*. It is a subgroup of $\mathbf{G}$.

If $f(a) = f(b)$ implies that $a = b$, then f is a *monomorphism*. We also then say that f is *one-to-one*, f is *injective*, or that f *embeds* $\mathbf{G}$ in $\mathbf{H}$. f is injective if its kernel contains the single element $id_\mathbf{G}$.

Exercise 5.50

Re-express the monomorphism condition in terms of $f(a \star b^{-1})$.

The *image of* f is the set of all elements in **H** that look like $f(a)$ for some a in **G**. The image of f is a subgroup of **H**.

If for every h in **H**, there is some a in **G** so that $f(a) = h$, then f is *surjective* and is called an *epimorphism*. **H** is the image of f, and f *covers* **H**.

A group homomorphism that is both injective and surjective is an *isomorphism*. **G** and **H** are "the same" ("isomorphic") subject to mapping elements from the first group to the second.

Finally, if **G** = **H** and f is an isomorphism, we call f an *automorphism*.

Examples

The standard embeddings $\mathbf{Z} \to \mathbf{Q}$, $\mathbf{Q} \to \mathbf{R}$, and $\mathbf{R} \to \mathbf{C}$ are all additive group monomorphisms.

Let n be a positive integer > 1. The set of numbers $\{0, 1, 2, \ldots, n - 1\}$ is a group under addition denoted $\mathbf{Z}/n\mathbf{Z}$. These are the integers mod n that we saw in section 3.7. The function

$$g : \mathbf{Z} \to \mathbf{Z}/n\mathbf{Z}$$

that maps an integer j to j mod n is an epimorphism but not a monomorphism.

Exercise 5.51

What is the kernel of g?

Consider the set of elements $\{2^n\}$ in **Q** for all integers n, with the multiplication operation "$\times$". We define the function

$$h : (\mathbf{Z}, +) \to (\{2^n\}, \times)$$

by $n \mapsto 2^n$.

Exercise 5.52

Is h a homomorphism? Monomorphism? Epimorphism? Isomorphism?

5.12.2 Ring and field homomorphisms

Suppose $(\mathbf{S}_1, +, \times)$ and $(\mathbf{S}_2, +, \times)$ are two rings. The function $f : \mathbf{S}_1 \to \mathbf{S}_2$ is a *ring homomorphism* if

- f is a group homomorphism for "+" (and so $f\left(0_{S_1}\right) = 0_{S_2}$),
- for any two elements a and b in $\mathbf{S}_1$, $f(a \times b) = f(a) \times f(b)$, and
- $f\left(1_{S_1}\right) = 1_{S_2}$.

Exercise 5.53

Show that for any three elements a, b, and c in $\mathbf{S}_1$,

$$f(a \times (b + c)) = f(a) \times (f(b) + f(c)) .$$

Exercise 5.54

Define monomorphisms, epimorphisms, and isomorphisms for rings.

The standard embeddings $\mathbf{Z} \to \mathbf{Q}, \mathbf{Q} \to \mathbf{R}$, and $\mathbf{R} \to \mathbf{C}$ are all ring monomorphisms.

I now drop the subscripts on terms such as 0_{S_2} because the additive and multiplicative identity elements will be apparent from the context.

A field homomorphism is simply a ring homomorphism.

Suppose $(\mathbf{F}_1, +, \times)$ and $(\mathbf{F}_2, +, \times)$ are two fields, and f is a homomorphism from the first to the second. Let's examine the kernel of f, the set of elements in $\mathbf{F}_1$ that map to 0 in $\mathbf{F}_2$.

We know that 0 is in the kernel, so suppose we have a nonzero a in $\mathbf{F}_1$ with $f(a) = 0$. Since $\mathbf{F}_1$ is a field, there exists an a^{-1} with $a \times a^{-1} = 1$.

$$1 = f(1) = f(a \times a^{-1}) = f(a) \times f(a^{-1}) = 0 \times f(a^{-1}) = 0 .$$

Since $1 \neq 0$, this is a contradiction, and no such nonzero a exists.

The kernel of every field homomorphism contains only 0. Every field homomorphism is a monomorphism.

5.12.3 Vector space homomorphisms

A vector space homomorphism is an additive group homomorphism that preserves scalar multiplication by elements in the underlying field. In addition to rules such as

$$f(\mathbf{v} + \mathbf{w}) = f(\mathbf{v}) + f(\mathbf{w}) ,$$

we also insist that $f(a\mathbf{v}) = af(\mathbf{v})$ for a scalar a.

For the remainder of this section, let U, V, and W be vector spaces over the same field $\mathbf{F}$.

A linear map $f : U \rightarrow V$, as we defined it in section 5.3, is a vector space homomorphism.

A vector space homomorphism from U to itself that preserves scalar multiplication is a linear transformation.

The kernel of a vector space linear map f is a vector space, which we call *null space* of f. We call the dimension of the null space of f the *nullity*. For $f : U \rightarrow V$, then the *rank* of f is the dimension of U minus the nullity of f.

Exercise 5.55

If
$$f : U \oplus V \rightarrow W$$
is a homomorphism, show that $\mathbf{u} \mapsto f(\mathbf{u} \oplus \mathbf{0})$ is a homomorphism from U to W.

We have the notions of monomorphism and epimorphism for a vector space linear map $f : V \rightarrow W$:

- f is a monomorphism (is "one-to-one") if $f(\mathbf{v}_1) = f(\mathbf{v}_2)$ implies $\mathbf{v}_1 = \mathbf{v}_2$. One vector in the range is the image of only one vector in the domain.
- f is an epimorphism (is "onto") if for any $\mathbf{w}$ in W, there is some $\mathbf{v}$ in V such that $f(\mathbf{v}) = \mathbf{w}$. Any vector in W is the image of a vector from V. In this way, "f covers" W.

If f is a monomorphism and an epimorphism, then it is an isomorphism. Necessarily, V and W have the same dimension. If f is represented by a matrix A in some basis, then the inverse function f^{-1}, which is a linear map, has matrix A^{-1}.

To learn more

Homomorphisms are not just especially nice functions, they are core to mathematics. You can't do group theory without them, and groups are fundamental in the hierarchy of mathematical structures. [73] [131]

5.13 Systems of linear equations

The two equations

$$2x + 3y = 5$$
$$x - 2y = 2$$

together are an example of a system of linear equations. On the left of the equal signs are linear expressions, and on the right are constants. In $\mathbf{R}^2$, these represent two lines. In general, two lines in $\mathbf{R}^2$ may be the same, be parallel and so never intersect, or intersect at a single point.

If we use subscripted variables, the same relationship might be expressed by

$$2x_1 + 3x_2 = 5$$
$$x_1 - 2x_2 = 2$$

We can further rewrite this in matrix and vector form as

$$\begin{bmatrix} 2 & 3 \\ 1 & -2 \end{bmatrix} \begin{bmatrix} x_1 \\ x_2 \end{bmatrix} = \begin{bmatrix} 5 \\ 2 \end{bmatrix}.$$

If we let

$$A = \begin{bmatrix} 2 & 3 \\ 1 & -2 \end{bmatrix} \qquad \mathbf{x} = \begin{bmatrix} x_1 \\ x_2 \end{bmatrix} \qquad \mathbf{b} = \begin{bmatrix} 5 \\ 2 \end{bmatrix}$$

then our system is simply $A\mathbf{x} = \mathbf{b}$. This is a standard form for writing such systems of any dimension, and we call it a linear equation.

Our goal may be to solve for all of $\mathbf{x}$, learn only some of the x_j, or understand some function f applied to $\mathbf{x}$. If A is invertible, then

$$A\mathbf{x} = \mathbf{b} \implies A^{-1}A\mathbf{x} = A^{-1}\mathbf{b} \implies \mathbf{x} = A^{-1}\mathbf{b}.$$

In this case, there is one possible value for $\mathbf{x}$. If A is not invertible, then there might be no solution or a vector space's worth of solutions.

Exercise 5.56

Solve for x_1 and x_2 in

$$2x_1 + 3x_2 = 5$$
$$x_1 - 2x_2 = 2$$

and graph the result.

Exercise 5.57

Find a system of two equations in two variables that has no solution. Find a system whose solution is a line. Find a system whose solution is $\mathbf{R}^2$.

Suppose we have a linear equation $A\mathbf{x} = \mathbf{b}$ with A an invertible square matrix. Assume $\mathbf{b}$ is not quite an exact quantity, perhaps because we got it from approximation or reading scientific instruments. If $\mathbf{b}_0$ is the "right answer," then $\mathbf{b} = \mathbf{b}_0 + \epsilon$ for some little (we hope) error vector ϵ. So,

$$A\mathbf{x} = \mathbf{b} = \mathbf{b}_0 + \epsilon$$

and

$$\mathbf{x} = A^{-1}\mathbf{b} = A^{-1}(\mathbf{b}_0 + \epsilon) = A^{-1}\mathbf{b}_0 + A^{-1}\epsilon.$$

$\mathbf{x}$ differs from the "correct" value $A^{-1}\mathbf{b}_0$ by $A^{-1}\epsilon$.

If $\mathbf{b} \neq \mathbf{0}$, we can look at how large the error ϵ is compared to $\mathbf{b}$ by examining the ratio $\dfrac{\|\epsilon\|}{\|\mathbf{b}\|}$. Similarly, if we look at

$$\frac{\left\|A^{-1}\epsilon\right\|}{\left\|A^{-1}\mathbf{b}\right\|},$$

we can see the relative error in the solution.

How much does a nonzero error in $\mathbf{b}$ translate to the error in the solution? We take yet another quotient,

$$\frac{\dfrac{\left\|A^{-1}\epsilon\right\|}{\left\|A^{-1}\mathbf{b}\right\|}}{\dfrac{\|\epsilon\|}{\|\mathbf{b}\|}}.$$

Do small errors get magnified, or are they kept in check when we look at the solution?

We want to know this as a property of A, so we define

$$\kappa(A) = \text{maximum of } \frac{\dfrac{\left\|A^{-1}\epsilon\right\|}{\left\|A^{-1}\mathbf{b}\right\|}}{\dfrac{\|\epsilon\|}{\|\mathbf{b}\|}} \text{ over all nonzero } \epsilon \text{ and nonzero } \mathbf{b}.$$

We call $\kappa(A)$ the *condition number* of A (κ is the Greek letter "kappa").

The condition number is ≥ 1. The closer the value is to 1, the better-behaved A is in the presence of errors.

Exercise 5.58

By rearranging the fractions,

$$\frac{\dfrac{\left\|A^{-1}\epsilon\right\|}{\left\|A^{-1}\mathbf{b}\right\|}}{\dfrac{\|\epsilon\|}{\|\mathbf{b}\|}} = \frac{\left\|A^{-1}\epsilon\right\|}{\left\|A^{-1}\mathbf{b}\right\|}\frac{\|\mathbf{b}\|}{\|\epsilon\|} = \frac{\left\|A^{-1}\epsilon\right\|}{\|\epsilon\|}\frac{\|\mathbf{b}\|}{\left\|A^{-1}\mathbf{b}\right\|}.$$

Show that if A is a unitary matrix, the condition number $\kappa(A) = 1$. Hint: if A is unitary, then so is A^{-1}.

When the condition number is very large, we have an "ill-posed" or "ill-conditioned" problem. Small errors in the input can translate to large errors in the answer. Algorithmically, it may translate to very bad performance or wildly inaccurate results. A different algorithm or additional information about the problem may be necessary for more stable computation.

5.14   Summary

Linear algebra is the area of mathematics where we gain the language and tools necessary for understanding and working with spaces of arbitrary dimension. General quantum mechanics in physics uses infinite dimensional spaces. Our needs are simpler, and we focused on vectors, linear transformations, and matrices in finite dimensions.

The fundamental quantum unit of information is the qubit, and its states can be represented in a two-dimensional complex vector space. We now have almost all the tools necessary to jump from the purely mathematical description to one that takes in the evidence from models of the physical world of the very small. One preliminary topic remains, and we tackle that in the next chapter: probability.

6

What Do You Mean "Probably"?

*Any one who considers arithmetical methods of producing
random digits is, of course, in a state of sin.*

– John von Neumann [224]

Here's the key to what we cover in this chapter: in any given situation, the sum of the probabilities of all the possible things that could happen always adds up to 1.

In this short chapter, I cover the basics of practical probability theory to get us started on quantum computing and its applications.

Topics covered in this chapter

6.1   Being discrete

Sometimes, it seems like probability is the study of flipping coins or rolling dice, given the number of books that explain it in those ways. It's tough to break away from these convenient examples. An advantage shared by both is that they make it easy to explain discrete events and independence. A set of events is *discrete* if there are only a finite number of them or if we can put them in one-to-one correspondence with **Z**.

For the sake of mixing it up, suppose we have a cookie machine. It's a big box with a button on top. Every time you press the button, a cookie pops out of a slot on the bottom. There are four kinds of cookies: **chocolate**, **sugar**, **oatmeal**, and **coconut**.

Assume, for the moment, there is no limit to the number of cookies our machine can distribute. You get a million cookies if you hit the button a million times. Also, assume you get a random cookie each time. What does this mean, ''random''?

Without a rigorous definition, random means that the odds of getting any of the cookies are the same as any other. That is, roughly one-fourth of the time, I would get **chocolate**, one-fourth of the time I would get **sugar**, one-fourth of the time I would get **oatmeal**, and one-fourth of the time I would get **coconut**.

The *probability* of getting a **sugar** cookie, say, is $0.25 = \frac{1}{4}$, and the sum of the probabilities for all the cookies is 1.0. Since there are four individual and separate possible outcomes, we say this is a *discrete* situation. We write this as

$$P\,(\textbf{chocolate}) = P\,(\textbf{sugar}) = P\,(\textbf{oatmeal}) = P\,(\textbf{coconut}) = \frac{1}{4} = 0.25\,,$$

with

$$P\,(\textbf{chocolate}) + P\,(\textbf{sugar}) + P\,(\textbf{oatmeal}) + P\,(\textbf{coconut}) = 1.0\,.$$

We use $P(x)$ to denote the probability of x happening, where $0 \le P(x) \le 1$. By definition, if the probability is 1, it always happens; if it is 0, it never happens. If the probability is neither 0 nor 1, then it is neither impossible nor certain, respectively.

Exercise 6.1

What is the probability of my *not* getting a **coconut** cookie with one push of the button?

Now, let's change this situation. The last time the cookie service person came, they accidentally loaded the **coconut** slot inside the machine with **chocolate** cookies. This mistake changes the odds:

$$P(\textbf{chocolate}) = 0.5 = \frac{1}{2}$$

$$P(\textbf{sugar}) = P(\textbf{oatmeal}) = 0.25 = \frac{1}{4}$$

$$P(\textbf{coconut}) = 0$$

The sum of the probabilities is still 1, as it must be, but the chance of getting a **chocolate** cookie is now twice as large as it was. The probability of getting a **coconut** cookie is 0, which is another way of saying it is impossible.

Had the service person simply forgotten to fill the **coconut** slot, we would have

$$P(\textbf{chocolate}) = P(\textbf{sugar}) = P(\textbf{oatmeal}) = 0.\overline{3} = \frac{1}{3}$$

$$P(\textbf{coconut}) = 0$$

Since we are only talking about probabilities, it is quite possible for me to get three **chocolate** cookies in a row after I hit the button three times. We do not have enough data points for the observed results to be consistently close to the probabilities. It is only when I press the button many, many times that I will start seeing the ratio of the number of times I saw the desired event to the total number of events approaching the probability.

If I press the button 100 times, I might see the following numbers:

Kind of cookie	Number of times seen	Ratio of seen/100
chocolate	22	0.22
sugar	26	0.26
oatmeal	25	0.25
coconut	27	0.27

Assuming everything is as balanced as I think, I'll eventually be approaching the mathematical probabilities.

If I instead saw

Kind of cookie	Number of times seen	Ratio of seen/100
chocolate	0	0.0
sugar	48	0.48
oatmeal	52	0.52
coconut	0	0.0

I would rightfully suspect something was wrong. I would wonder if there were roughly the same number of **sugar** and **oatmeal** cookies in the machine but no **chocolate** or **coconut** cookies. When experimentation varies significantly from prediction, examining your assumptions, hardware, and software makes sense.

Let's look at what happens when we get one cookie followed by another. What is the probability of getting an **oatmeal** cookie and then a **sugar** cookie? It is

$$P(\textbf{oatmeal and then sugar}) = P(\textbf{oatmeal}) \times P(\textbf{sugar})$$

$$= 0.25 \times 0.25 = 0.0625 = \frac{1}{16}.$$

Observe that there are 4 choices for the first cookie, and then 4 choices for the second, which means 16 possibilities for both. These look like

chocolate + chocolate	chocolate + sugar	chocolate + oatmeal	chocolate + coconut
sugar + chocolate	sugar + sugar	sugar + oatmeal	sugar + coconut
oatmeal + chocolate	oatmeal + sugar	oatmeal + oatmeal	oatmeal + oatmeal
coconut + chocolate	coconut + sugar	coconut + oatmeal	coconut + coconut

Getting **oatmeal** and then **sugar** is one of the 16 choices.

What about ending up with one **oatmeal** and one **sugar** cookie? Here, it doesn't matter which order the machine gives them to me. Two of the 16 possibilities yield this combination, so

$$P(\textbf{oatmeal and sugar}) = \frac{2}{16} = \frac{1}{8} = 0.125$$

or

$$P(\textbf{oatmeal and then sugar}) = P(\textbf{sugar and then oatmeal}).$$

Exercise 6.2

What is the probability of my getting a **chocolate** cookie on the first push of the button and then *not* getting a **chocolate** cookie on the second?

6.2 More formally

In the last section, there were initially four different possible outcomes: the four kinds of cookies that could pop out of our machine. In this situation, our *sample space* is the collection

$$\{\textbf{chocolate, sugar, oatmeal, coconut}\}.$$

We also say that these four are the values of a *random variable*. Random variables usually have names such as X and Y.

A *probability distribution* assigns a probability to each possible outcome, which are the values of the random variable. The probability distribution for the balanced case is

chocolate $\rightarrow$ 0.25   **sugar** $\rightarrow$ 0.25

oatmeal $\rightarrow$ 0.25   **coconut** $\rightarrow$ 0.25

When the probabilities are all equal, as in this case, we have a *uniform distribution*.

If our sample space is finite or, at most, *countably infinite*, we say it is *discrete*. A set is countably infinite if it can be put in one-to-one correspondence with **Z**.

The sample space is *continuous* if it can be put in correspondence with some portion of **R** or a higher dimensional space. As you boil water, the sample space of its temperatures varies continuously from its starting point to the boiling point. Just because your thermometer only reads out decimals, it does not mean the temperature itself does not change smoothly within its range.

This raises an important distinction. Though the sample space of temperatures is continuous, the sample space of temperatures *as read out on a digital thermometer* is discrete. The thermometer represents it by the displayed numbers to one or two decimal places. The discrete sample space is an approximation of the continuous one.

When we use numeric methods on computers for working in such situations, we are more likely to use continuous techniques. These involve calculus, which I have not made a prerequisite for this book, and so we will not cover them. We do not need the techniques for our quantum computing discussion.

Our discrete sample spaces will usually be the basis vectors in complex vector spaces of dimension 2^n, where n is the number of qubits.

6.3 Wrong again?

Suppose you have a faulty calculator that does not always compute the correct result.

If the probability of getting the wrong answer is p, the probability of getting the correct answer is $1 - p$. We call this the *complementary* probability. We assume $0 < p < 1$. Assuming there is no connection between the attempts, the probability of getting the wrong answer two times in a row is p^2, and the probability of getting the correct answer two times in a row is $(1 - p)^2$.

Exercise 6.3

Compute p^2 and $(1-p)^2$ for $p = 0$, $p = 0.5$, and $p = 1.0$.

To make this analysis useful, we want the probability of failure p to be nonzero.

For n independent attempts, the probability of getting the wrong answer is p^n. Let's suppose $p = 0.6$. We get the wrong answer 60% of the time in many attempts. We get the correct answer 40% of the time.

After 10 attempts, the probability of getting the wrong answer every time is $0.6^{10} \approx 0.006$.

On the other hand, suppose I want to have a very low probability of having always gotten the wrong answer. It's traditional to use the Greek letter ϵ (pronounced "epsilon") for small numbers such as error rates. For example, I might want the chance of never getting the correct answer to be less than $\epsilon = 10^{-6} = 0.000001$.

For this, we solve

$$p^n < \epsilon$$

for n. Having a variable in the exponent tells you, "Use a logarithm!" Doing so,

$$n \log(p) < \log(\epsilon).$$

Here is a subtle point: since $0 < p < 1$, $\log(p) < 0$. In general, if $a < b$ and $c < 0$, then $ac > bc$. I now divide both sides by $\log(p)$, but I must flip "<"; to ">":

$$n > \frac{\log(\epsilon)}{\log(p)}.$$

In our example, $p = 0.6$ and $\epsilon = 10^{-6}$. A quick Python computation yields $n > 27$:

```
import math
math.log(10**-6) / math.log(0.6)
```

```
27.04545331166308
```

Exercise 6.4

Does it matter which logarithm you use? Do you get a different answer if you use $\log_2$, $\log_{10}$, or $\ln = \log_e$?

6.4   Probability and error detection

Let's return to our repetition code for error detection from section 2.1. The specific example we look at is sending information represented in bits via a *binary symmetric channel*. The probability that I will get an error by flipping a **0** to a **1** or a **1** to a **0** is p. The probability that no error occurs is $1 - p$, as above.

For a binary symmetric channel, we have two representations for information, the bits **0** and **1**, and hence "binary." The probability of something wrong happening to a **0** or **1** is the same, and that's the symmetry.

The process for sending the information to someone whom I will call Alicia is:

1. Create a message to be sent.
2. Transform that message by encoding it to contain extra information, allowing Alicia the possibility to repair the message if it is damaged en route.
3. Send the message to Alicia. "Noise" in the transmission may introduce errors in the encoded message.
4. Decode the message, using the extra information to try to fix any transmission errors.
5. Give the message to Alicia.

Figure 6.1 shows this process from start to finish.

Figure 6.1: The process of sending information on a noisy channel

For this simple example, I send a single bit and encode it by making three copies. I encode **0** as **000** and **1** as **111**.

The number of **1**s in an encoded message (with or without errors) is called its *weight*. The decoding scheme in this example is

$$\text{decoded received message} = \begin{cases} \mathbf{0} & \text{if } weight(\text{received message}) \leq 1 \\ \mathbf{1} & \text{otherwise.} \end{cases}$$

There are eight possible bit triplets Alicia can receive:

$$\mathbf{000} \quad \mathbf{001} \quad \mathbf{010} \quad \mathbf{100} \quad \mathbf{111} \quad \mathbf{101} \quad \mathbf{110} \quad \mathbf{101} \, .$$

If there are more **0**s than **1**s, Alicia decodes or "fixes" the message by making the result **0**. Similarly, if there are more **1**s than **0**s, Alicia decodes the message by making the result **1**.

The result is the original if at most one error occurred. This is why we made an odd number of copies.

Alicia correctly decodes the first four triplets as **0** if that's what I sent. They each have zero or one error. The last four triplets are the cases where two or three errors occurred.

Exercise 6.5

What's the similar observation if I had sent **1**?

Assume I sent **0**. There is one possible received message, **000**, where no error popped up, and that has probability $(1 - p)^3$.

There are three results with only one error: **001, 010**, and **100**. The total probability of seeing one of these is

$$(1 - p)(1 - p)p + (1 - p)p(1 - p) + p(1 - p)(1 - p) = 3p(1 - p)^2 .$$

In total, the probability that I receive the correct message or can fix it is

$$(1 - p)^3 + 3p(1 - p)^2 = (1 - p)^2 \left(1 - p + 3p\right) = (1 - p)^2(1 + 2p) .$$

If $p = 1.0$, this probability is 0, as you would expect. We can't fix anything. If $p = 0.0$, there are no errors, and the probability of ending up with the correct message is 1.0. Figure 6.2 shows a graph of the probability of a single-bit error occurring versus the probability of our ability to fix it.

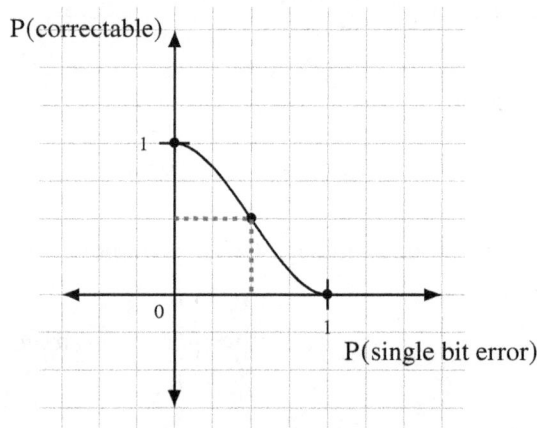

Figure 6.2: The probability of fixing an error versus the probability of it occurring

If there is an equal chance of error or no error, $p = 0.5$, and the probability we can repair the message is also 0.5. If the chance of error is one in ten, $p = 0.1$, the probability that it was correct or we can fix it is 0.972.

Exercise 6.6

What is the maximum value of p I can have so that my chance of getting the right message or being able to correct it is 0.9999?

6.5 Randomness

Many programming languages have functions that return pseudo-random numbers. The prefix "pseudo" is there because they are not genuinely random numbers but, nevertheless, they do well on statistical measurements of how well-distributed the results are.

Given four possible events, E_0, E_1, E_2, and E_3, with associated probabilities p_0, p_1, p_2, and p_3, how might we use random numbers to simulate these events happening with

$$p_0 = 0.15 \qquad p_1 = 0.37 \qquad p_2 = 0.26 \qquad p_3 = 0.22$$

The probabilities add up to 1.0, as expected.

In Python, the `random()` function returns a random real number r such that $0.0 \leq r < 1.0$. We determine that one of the E_0, E_1, E_2, and E_3, events occurred based on the value of r computed.

If you are not using Python, use whatever similar function is available in your programming language and environment.

The general scheme is to run the following steps in order:

1. If $r < p_0$, we have observed E_0, and we **stop**.
2. If not, but $r < p_0 + p_1$, we have observed E_1, and we **stop**.
3. If not, but $r < p_0 + p_1 + p_2$, we have observed E_2, and we **stop**.
4. If not, we have observed E_3, and we **stop**.

The code in Figure 6.3 simulates this sampling a given number of times.

On a run for 100 samples, we see the events distributed in this way:

```
sample_n_times([0.15, 0.37, 0.26, 0.22], 100)


Results for 100 simulated samples

Event  Actual Probability  Simulated Probability
  0            0.15                 0.11
  1            0.37                 0.33
  2            0.26                 0.37
  3            0.22                 0.19
```

```python
import random

def sample_n_times(probabilities, n):
    # set seed for repeatability
    random.seed(n)

    probability_sums = []
    number_of_probabilities = len(probabilities)
    sum = 0.0
    for probability in probabilities:
        sum += probability
        probability_sums.append(sum)

    # ensure final value is 1.0 to avoid round-off error
    probability_sums[number_of_probabilities - 1] = 1.0
    counts = [0 for probabilities in probabilities]

    for _ in range(n):
        r = random.random()
        for j in range(number_of_probabilities):
            if r < probability_sums[j]:
                counts[j] = counts[j] + 1
                break

    pad_width = len(str(len(probabilities)))
    print(f"\nResults for {n} simulated samples")
    print("\nEvent  Actual Probability  Simulated Probability")
    for j in range(number_of_probabilities):
        print(f"  {j:{pad_width}}{(13-pad_width)*' '}"
              f"{probabilities[j]}{14*' '}"
              f"{round(float(counts[j])/n, 4)}")
```

Figure 6.3: Sample Python code demonstrating sampling

The values are close but not very close. It's probability, after all.

Significantly increasing the number of samples to 1 million produces values much closer to the expected probabilities:

```python
sample_n_times([0.15, 0.37, 0.26, 0.22], 1000000)
```

```
Results for 1000000 simulated samples

Event  Actual Probability  Simulated Probability
  0           0.15                 0.1497
```

1	0.37	0.3704
2	0.26	0.2595
3	0.22	0.2205

Interestingly, one potential use of quantum technology is to generate truly random numbers. Using a quantum device to simulate quantum computing in an otherwise classical algorithm would be odd!

To learn more

When I talk about Python in this book, I always mean version 3. The tutorial and reference material on the official website is excellent. [214] There are many good books that teach you how to code in this important, modern programming language for systems, science, and data analysis. [143] [191]

I also recommend my book, *Dancing with Python*. [211]

6.6 Expectation

Let's look at the numeric finite discrete distribution of the random variable X with the probabilities given in this table:

Value	2	5	9	13	14
Probability	0.14	0.22	0.37	0.06	0.21

If the process producing these values continues over time, what value would we "expect" to see?

If they all have the same probability of occurring, the *expected value* or *expectation*, $E(X)$ is their average:

$$E(X) = \frac{2+5+9+13+14}{5} = 8.6 .$$

Note that the answer does not need to be, and often isn't, one of the values in the distribution.

Since each value of X has a given probability, the expected value is instead the weighted average

$$E(X) = 2 \times 0.14 + 5 \times 0.22 + 9 \times 0.37 + 13 \times 0.06 + 14 \times 0.21 = 8.43 .$$

If someone simply gives you a list of values for a random variable, you can assume a uniform distribution, and the expected value is the usual average or *mean*. We sometimes use the notation $\mu(X)$ instead of $E(X)$. μ is the lowercase Greek letter "mu."

If X is a random variable with values $\{x_1, x_2, \ldots, x_n\}$ and corresponding probabilities p_k, such that $p_1 + p_2 + \cdots + p_n = 1$, then

$$E(X) = \mu(X) = p_1 x_1 + p_2 x_2 + \cdots + p_n x_n.$$

For a uniform distribution, each $p_k = \frac{1}{n}$, so

$$E(X) = \mu(X) = \frac{x_1 + x_2 + \cdots + x_n}{n}.$$

How much do the values in X differ from the expected value $E(X)$? For a uniform distribution, the average of the amounts each x_k varies from $E(X)$ is

$$\frac{|x_1 - E(X)| + |x_2 - E(X)| + \cdots + |x_n - E(X)|}{n}.$$

However, absolute values can make calculations difficult and unwieldy, particularly those in calculus, so we define the variance using squares. This is not that strange, since one way of defining $|x|$ is $\sqrt{x^2}$, where we always take the positive real square root.

We now define the variance Var:

$$\mathrm{Var}(X) = \frac{(x_1 - E(X))^2 + (x_2 - E(X))^2 + \cdots + (x_n - E(X))^2}{n}$$
$$= E((X - E(X))^2).$$

The notation $(X - E(X))^2$ refers to the new set of values $(x_k - E(X))^2$ for each x_k in X.

$$(X - E(X))^2 = \left\{ (x_1 - E(X))^2, (x_2 - E(X))^2, \ldots, (x_n - E(X))^2 \right\}.$$

For a distribution where each x_k has probability p_k, and all the p_k add up to 1, the formula for the variance is

$$\mathrm{Var}(X) = p_1 (x_1 - E(X))^2 + p_2 (x_2 - E(X))^2 + \cdots + p_n (x_n - E(X))^2$$
$$= E((X - E(X))^2).$$

We often use the notation σ^2 instead of $\mathrm{Var}(X)$. The standard deviation σ of X is the square root of the variance $\sqrt{\mathrm{Var}(X)}$.

For a coin flip,

$$X = \left\{ x_1 = 0 = \text{tails}, x_2 = 1 = \text{heads} \right\},$$

with $p_1 = p_2 = 0.5$. Then,

$$E(X) = \frac{0 + 1}{2} = \frac{1}{2}$$

and

$$\text{Var}(X) = \sigma^2 = \frac{\left(0 - \frac{1}{2}\right)^2 + \left(1 - \frac{1}{2}\right)^2}{2} = \frac{1}{4},$$

with the standard deviation

$$\sigma = \sqrt{\frac{1}{4}} = \frac{1}{2}.$$

When flipping the coin multiple times, I use the notation X_j to mean "the result of the jth coin flip." So X_1 is the result of the first coin flip, and X_{652} is the 652nd. These have the values of 1 for heads and 0 for tails.

When I flip the coin 20 times, the number of heads is $X_1 + \cdots + X_{20}$. More generally, for n flips, the number of heads is $X_1 + X_2 + \cdots + X_n$, and the number of tails is n minus this number. The possible values taken on by the X_j are identical and have the same distributions.

I'm doing the same thing many times, with the same probabilities, and there are no connections between the X_j. The answer I get for any X_j is independent of what happens for any other.

We return to expectation in the context of measuring qubits in section 7.3.4.

6.7   Hellinger distance

This section examines how we can measure the similarity between two comparable collections using the concept of *Hellinger distance*. The idea is that if the two collections are "close to each other distance-wise," they are similar.

Consider the game of pool, played with a cue and solid and striped balls on a table. Suppose I have a large box and place one hundred yellow pool balls, one hundred red pool balls, one hundred blue pool balls, and one hundred purple pool balls in the box. I mix the balls thoroughly, so if I reach in and take out a ball, I have the same probability of getting one color as any other. That is, I have a uniform distribution of the balls.

I reach into the box and remove one hundred balls. I record the colors and the count of each:

	yellow	red	blue	purple
Me	19	27	25	29

I put the balls back in the box, stir them up well, and then you remove one hundred balls. Oddly, you pull out balls with the same counts:

	yellow	red	blue	purple
You	19	27	25	29

We want to measure the difference between my collection and your collection. If we call this difference the *distance*, in this case, the collections have distance 0: they are the same.

The distance between two vectors $\mathbf{v} = (v_1, \ldots, v_n)$ and $\mathbf{w} = (w_1, \ldots, w_n)$ is

$$\|\mathbf{v} - \mathbf{w}\| = \sqrt{(v_1 - w_1)^2 + \cdots + (v_n - w_n)^2}.$$

If we use $\mathbf{v} = \mathbf{w} = (19, 27, 25, 29)$ for the counts of the balls in our collections, we see that

$$\|\mathbf{v} - \mathbf{w}\| = 0.$$

We now create a new distance measurement and normalize it so that its values lie between 0 and 1, inclusively. To fix ideas, suppose we repeat the ball collection process and get these new counts:

	yellow	red	blue	purple
Me	50	0	50	0
You	0	50	0	50

We begin by replacing each count by itself divided by the total number of balls in the collection. The new vectors and the distance between them are:

$$\mathbf{v} = \left(\frac{1}{2}, 0, \frac{1}{2}, 0\right) \qquad \mathbf{w} = \left(0, \frac{1}{2}, 0, \frac{1}{2}\right)$$

$$\|\mathbf{v} - \mathbf{w}\| = \sqrt{\left(\frac{1}{2}\right)^2 + \left(\frac{1}{2}\right)^2 + \left(\frac{1}{2}\right)^2 + \left(\frac{1}{2}\right)^2} = 1$$

This result is promising because the two collections are maximally different.

The lengths of $\mathbf{v}$ and $\mathbf{w}$ are equal:

$$\sqrt{\left(\frac{1}{2}\right)^2 + 0^2 + \left(\frac{1}{2}\right)^2 + 0^2} = \sqrt{0^2 + \left(\frac{1}{2}\right)^2 + 0^2 + \left(\frac{1}{2}\right)^2} = \sqrt{\frac{1}{2}} = \frac{\sqrt{2}}{2}.$$

We turn $\mathbf{v}$ and $\mathbf{w}$ into unit vectors by dividing them by their lengths:

$$\mathbf{v} = \left(\frac{\sqrt{2}}{2}, 0, \frac{\sqrt{2}}{2}, 0\right) \qquad \mathbf{w} = \left(0, \frac{\sqrt{2}}{2}, 0, \frac{\sqrt{2}}{2}\right)$$

$$\|\mathbf{v} - \mathbf{w}\| = \sqrt{\left(\frac{\sqrt{2}}{2}\right)^2 + \left(\frac{\sqrt{2}}{2}\right)^2 + \left(\frac{\sqrt{2}}{2}\right)^2 + \left(\frac{\sqrt{2}}{2}\right)^2} = \sqrt{2}$$

Finally, we normalize our new distance by dividing by $\sqrt{2}$ so that the maximum value is 1.

Let V and W be two collections, each having the same total number t of n types of items. Let $\mathbf{v} = (v_1, \ldots, v_n)$ and $\mathbf{w} = (w_1, \ldots, w_n)$ be vectors of nonnegative integers, where each v_j and w_j is the count of item type j in V and W, respectively.

We define and calculate the Hellinger distance between V and W by

$$H(V,W) = \frac{\sqrt{2}}{2} \sqrt{\left(\sqrt{\frac{v_1}{t}} - \sqrt{\frac{w_1}{t}}\right)^2 + \cdots + \left(\sqrt{\frac{v_n}{t}} - \sqrt{\frac{w_n}{t}}\right)^2}$$

$$= \frac{\sqrt{2}}{2\sqrt{t}} \sqrt{\left(\sqrt{v_1} - \sqrt{w_1}\right)^2 + \cdots + \left(\sqrt{v_n} - \sqrt{w_n}\right)^2}$$

When $V = W$, $H(V,W) = 0$. [163]

Exercise 6.7

Suppose that every time a $v_j > 0$, the corresponding $w_j = 0$, and every time a $w_j > 0$, the corresponding $v_j = 1$. Show that $H(V,W) = 1$.

Hint: what is the sum of all the counts for V and W together?

We can recast this in terms of distributions. Let P and Q be two distributions on the same n random variables. Then,

$$P = (p_1, p_2, \ldots, p_n)$$
$$Q = (q_1, q_2, \ldots, q_n)$$

$$H(P,Q) = \frac{\sqrt{2}}{2} \sqrt{\left(\sqrt{p_1} - \sqrt{q_1}\right)^2 + \left(\sqrt{p_1} - \sqrt{q_1}\right)^2 + \cdots + \left(\sqrt{p_n} - \sqrt{q_n}\right)^2}$$

If P is an expected distribution, such as a uniform distribution, but we actually see Q when we take samples, we sometimes say that $H(P,Q)$ is the *Hellinger error* and that $1 - H(P,Q)$ is the *Hellinger fidelity*.

We return to Hellinger distance in section 11.6.2 when we look at the Greenberger-Horne-Zeilinger performance benchmark for quantum computers.

6.8   Markov and Chebyshev go to the casino

In this section, we work through the probability math of estimating π as we previously explored in section 1.5. We dropped coins into a square and looked at how many of them had their centers on or inside a circle.

There are two important inequalities involving expected values, variances, and error terms. Let X be a finite random variable with a known distribution so that

$$E(X) = p_1 x_1 + p_2 x_2 + \cdots + p_n x_n$$

and each $x_k \geq 0$.

Markov's Inequality

For a real number $a > 0$,

$$P(X > a) \leq \frac{E(X)}{a}.$$

In Markov's Inequality, the expression $P(X > a)$ means "look at all the x_k in X, and for all those where $x_k > a$, add up the p_k to get $P(X > a)$."

Exercise 6.8

Show that Markov's Inequality holds for the distribution at the beginning of section 6.6 for $a = 3$. Repeat the calculation for $a = 10$.

Chebyshev's Inequality

For any finite random variable X with a known distribution and a real number $\epsilon > 0$,

$$P(|X - E(X)| \geq \epsilon) \leq \frac{\text{Var}(X)}{\epsilon^2} = \frac{\sigma^2}{\epsilon^2}.$$

Equivalently,

$$P(|X - E(X)| < \epsilon) = 1 - P(|X - E(X)| \geq \epsilon)$$

$$\geq 1 - \frac{\text{Var}(X)}{\epsilon^2} = 1 - \frac{\sigma^2}{\epsilon^2}.$$

In Chebyshev's Inequality, the expression $P(|X - E(X)| \geq \epsilon)$ means "look at all the x_k in X and for those whose distance from the expected value $E(X)$ is greater than or equal to

---

Figure 6.4: Andrey Markov, circa 1875

ϵ, add up the $P(|X - E(X)| \geq \epsilon)$." Think of ϵ as an error term related to the probability of being away from the expected value.

Figure 6.5: Pafnuty Chebyshev, circa 1890

From Chebyshev's Inequality, we get a result that is useful when we take samples X_j, such as coin flips or the Monte Carlo samples described in section 1.5.

Weak Law of Large Numbers

Let the set of X_j for $1 \leq j \leq n$ be independent, identical random variables with identical distributions. Let $\mu = E(X_j)$, which is the same for all j. Then,

$$P\left(\left|\frac{X_1 + \cdots + X_n}{n} - \mu\right| \geq \epsilon\right) \leq \frac{\text{Var}(X)}{n\epsilon^2} = \frac{\sigma^2}{n\epsilon^2}.$$

As n gets larger, the expression on the right gets closer to 0 because ϵ and σ^2 do not change.

Informally, the Weak Law says that we can get as close as we want to the mean by increasing the sample size.

What does this tell us about the probability of getting fewer than 7 heads when I do ten coin flips? Remember that, in this case, $\mu = \frac{1}{2}$ and $\sigma^2 = \frac{1}{4}$. Let's use $\epsilon = \frac{1}{5}$:

P(we get fewer than 7 heads) $= P(X_1 + \cdots + X_{10} < 7)$

$$= P\left(\frac{X_1 + \cdots + X_{10}}{10} < \frac{7}{10}\right)$$

$$= P\left(\frac{X_1 + \cdots + X_{10}}{10} - \frac{5}{10} < \frac{2}{10}\right)$$

$$= P\left(\left|\frac{X_1 + \cdots + X_{10}}{10} - \frac{1}{2}\right| < \frac{1}{5}\right)$$

$$= 1 - P\left(\left|\frac{X_1 + \cdots + X_{10}}{10} - \frac{1}{2}\right| \geq \frac{1}{5}\right)$$

$$\geq \frac{\sigma^2}{n\epsilon^2} = \frac{\left(\frac{1}{2}\right)^2}{10\left(\frac{1}{5}\right)^2} = \frac{25}{10 \times 4} = \frac{25}{40} = 0.625.$$

The probability of getting fewer than 7 heads in 10 flips is greater than or equal to 0.625.

Exercise 6.9

Repeat the calculation for fewer than 70 heads in 100 flips and fewer than 700 heads in 1,000 flips.

In section 1.5, we started using a Monte Carlo method to estimate the value of π by randomly placing coins in a 2-by-2 square inscribed in a unit circle. It's easier to use the language of points instead of coins, where the point is the coin's center.

The plot in Figure 6.6 uses 200 random points and yields 3.14 as the approximation.

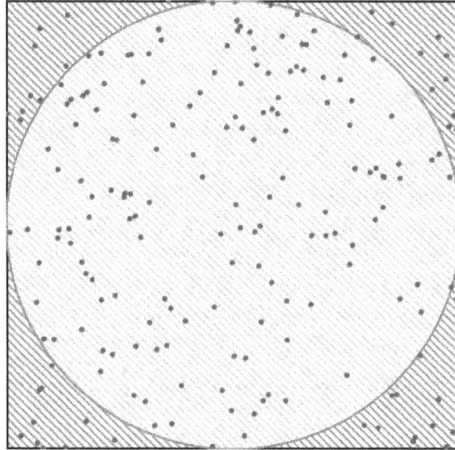

Figure 6.6: 200 points dropped in the square

Let's analyze this as we did for the coin flips. In this case,

$$X = \{x_1 = 0 = \text{\textbf{point does not land in circle,}}$$

$$x_2 = 1 = \text{\textbf{point lands on or inside circle}}\}.$$

So X_1 is dropping the first random point into the square, and $X_{1000000}$ is dropping the 1 millionth. The value is 1 for either of these if the point is in the circle. We have

$$P(X_k = 1) = \frac{\pi}{4} \approx 0.78539816339$$

because the area of the circle is π and the area of the square is 4.

The expected value μ is this probability. For the variance,

$$\text{Var}(X) = \sigma^2 = \frac{\left(0 - \frac{\pi}{4}\right)^2 + \left(1 - \frac{\pi}{4}\right)^2}{2} = \frac{\pi^2}{16} - \frac{\pi}{4} + \frac{1}{2} \approx 0.3314521116706366.$$

We put these values into the Weak Law of Large Numbers:

$$P\left(\left|4\frac{X_1 + \cdots + X_n}{n} - \pi\right| \geq 4\epsilon\right) = P\left(\left|\frac{X_1 + \cdots + X_n}{n} - \frac{\pi}{4}\right| \geq \epsilon\right) \leq \frac{\frac{\pi^2}{16} - \frac{\pi}{4} + \frac{1}{2}}{n\epsilon^2}.$$

Suppose we want the probability of the difference between π and 4 times the approximation to be greater than $0.01 = \frac{1}{100}$. First,

$$P\left(\left|4\frac{X_1 + \cdots + X_n}{n} - \pi\right| \geq \frac{1}{100}\right) = P\left(\left|\frac{X_1 + \cdots + X_n}{n} - \frac{\pi}{4}\right| \geq \frac{1}{400}\right).$$

So $\epsilon = \frac{1}{400}$ and

$$\frac{\frac{\pi^2}{16} - \frac{\pi}{4} + \frac{1}{2}}{n\epsilon^2} = \frac{\frac{\pi^2}{16} - \frac{\pi}{4} + \frac{1}{2}}{n\left(\frac{1}{400}\right)^2} \approx \frac{53032.338}{n}.$$

In Python, this calculation is

```
from math import pi
x = (pi**2 / 16.0 - pi / 4.0 + 0.5) / (1/400)**2
print(f"{x:,.3f}")     # print x to 3 decimal places with commas
```

```
53,032.338
```

If we want the probability of the error being this small to be less than 5% = 0.05, we solve for n in

$$\frac{53032.337}{n} = 0.05$$

and get $n \approx 106,064.676$. That is, we want the probability of the estimate being off by, at most, $0.01 = 10^{-2}$ (in the second decimal place) to be less than or equal to 5%, we need the number of points to be at least 106,065.

If we repeat the calculation and want the probability of the estimate being off by at most $0.0001 = 1/10000$, we need $n \geq 530,323,379$. To put it another way, we need n this large to get the estimate this close with probability 99.9999%:

```
print(f"{(x/0.0001):,.3f}")
```

```
530,323,378.673
```

Finally, if we want the probability of the estimate to π being off by, at most, $0.00001 = 10^{-5}$ (in the fifth decimal place) to be less than $0.0001 = 1/10000$, we need $n \geq 5,303,233,787$:

```
print(f"{(x/0.00001):,.3f}")
```

```
5,303,233,786.730
```

As you can see, we need many points to estimate π accurately to even a small number of digits. In the last case, we needed well more than five billion, three hundred million points.

6.9 Summary

In this chapter, we covered the elements of probability necessary for our treatment of quantum computing and its applications. When we work with qubits and circuits in the following chapters, we will use discrete sample spaces, although they can get quite large. In these cases, the sizes of the sample spaces will be powers of 2.

Our goal in a quantum algorithm is to adjust the probability distribution so that the element in the sample space with the highest probability is the best solution to some problem. Indeed, the manipulation of *probability amplitudes* leads us to find what we hope is the best answer. My treatment of algorithms in Chapter 9, "Wiring Up the Circuits," and Chapter 10, "From Circuits to Algorithms," does not go deeply into probability calculations, but it does so sufficiently to give you an idea of how probability interacts with interference, complexity, and the number of times we must run a calculation to be confident we have seen the correct answer.

To learn more

Hundreds of books cover probability and statistics. These are for the applied beginner all the way to the theoretician, with many solid and complete treatments. [15]

Probability has applications in many areas of science and engineering, including AI/machine learning and cryptography. [112] [50]

II

Quantum Computing

7

One Qubit

Anyone who is not shocked by quantum theory has not understood it.

– Niels Bohr [10]

A *quantum bit*, or *qubit*, is the fundamental information unit of quantum computing. In this chapter, I give a mathematical definition of a qubit based on the foundational material in the first part of this book. Together, we examine the operations you can perform on a single qubit from mathematical and computational perspectives.

Despite a single qubit living in a seemingly strange two-dimensional complex Hilbert space, we can visualize it, its superposition, and its behavior by projecting it onto the surface of a sphere in $\mathbf{R}^3$.

All vector spaces considered in this chapter are over $\mathbf{C}$, the field of complex numbers introduced in section 3.9. All bases are orthonormal unless otherwise specified.

Topics covered in this chapter

7.1 Introducing quantum bits

If you have seen descriptions of qubits elsewhere, you may have read something like ''a qubit implements a two-state quantum mechanical system and is the quantum analog of a classical bit.'' As we saw in section 2.1, a bit also has two states, 0 and 1.

Those other discussions usually include one or more of the following: light switches, spinning electrons, polarized light, and rotating coins or donuts. These approaches have merit and are the basis for teasing apart the difference between the quantum and classical situations. The electron and polarized light examples do depict quantum systems.

Otherwise, analogies tend to be imperfect and eventually may lead you into corners where their behavior and your understanding are not consistent with the actual situation. For this reason, we developed the essential mathematics and insight to reason accurately what happens in quantum computing.

Let's begin by thinking about a classical bit and a quantum bit.

On the left in Figure 7.1, we have the classical situation where a bit can only take on the values **0** and **1**, and only one of those *states* at any given time. You can look at the bit at any time and, assuming nothing has happened to change the state, the bit stays in that state.

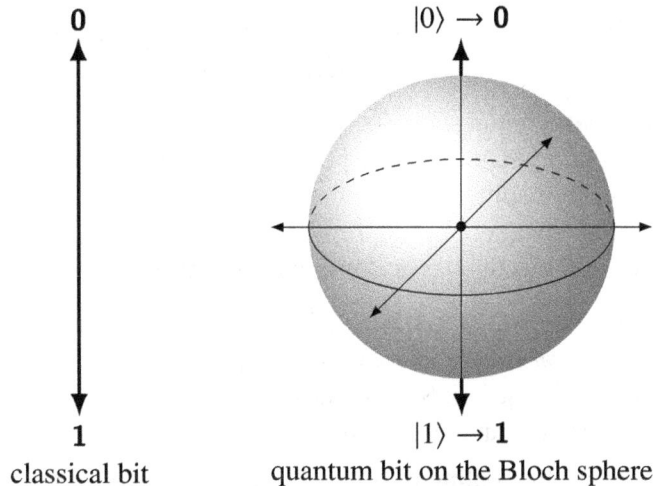

0

$|0\rangle \rightarrow$ **0**

1

$|1\rangle \rightarrow$ **1**

classical bit

quantum bit on the Bloch sphere

Figure 7.1: The classical versus quantum bit

We change the notation slightly for the sphere and the quantum situation on the right in Figure 7.1. The qubit always becomes the state $|0\rangle$ (pronounced "ket 0") or $|1\rangle$ (pronounced "ket 1") when we read information from it by a process we call *measurement*. However, it is possible to move it into *superposition* at one of the infinite number of other states on the sphere and change from one to another while we are computing.

Measurement says, "Ok, I'm going to peek at the qubit now," and the result is always a $|0\rangle$ or $|1\rangle$ once you do so. We can then read that out as a bit value of **0** or **1**. Some people refer to measurement as *readout*.

Yes, this is weird. This is quantum mechanics, which has amazed, confounded, surprised, and delighted people since the 1920s. Quantum computing is based on and takes advantage of this behavior.

Continuing with the right side, we represent all the states the qubit could be in as points on the unit sphere. $|0\rangle$ is at the north pole, and $|1\rangle$ is at the south. Points on the sphere "equal" quantum states. In the next section, I define more precisely what we mean when we write $|0\rangle$ and $|1\rangle$.

I need to state and then clarify something about superposition. Mathematically, the qubit is always in superposition because its state can be at the poles $|0\rangle$ or $|1\rangle$ or any point on the sphere in between. However, by slight abuse of terminology, people typically mean the state is in superposition when it is *not* $|0\rangle$ or $|1\rangle$. If the state is not one of the poles, we have a nontrivial superposition. "Move into superposition" usually means we move the state to a point on the equator.

A quantum algorithm uses several qubits, which together constitute a *quantum register*. From the viewpoint of a single qubit, its activity looks like:

1. I, the qubit, am in the initial state $|0\rangle$.
2. I may get moved into a standard superposition. Don't peek!
3. Steps in the algorithm apply zero or more reversible operations to me.
4. I get measured and always become $|0\rangle$ or $|1\rangle$.
5. When these get read out for classical use, we convert them to **0** or **1**.

It's what happens in steps 2 and 3 that make quantum computing interesting. For the unit sphere, called the *Bloch sphere* in quantum computing, step 2 means I get moved to a designated point/state on the equator. Step 3 translates to getting moved to other points/states. This movement results from what the algorithm is doing.

The final two steps are like telling the qubit, "Look, you can't stay somewhere in superposition forever. You must decide whether you will be **0** or **1**. This is not optional." Where it is in superposition, the state it is in on the sphere, determines the relative probabilities of the qubit, ultimately yielding a classical bit value of **0** or **1**.

If the state lies on the equator, then with perfect randomness, it will end up being **0** half the time and **1** half the time.

Though the Bloch sphere is a convenient and visual representation, the linear algebraic description of a qubit is more fundamental, in my opinion. We go back and forth between them when one or the other makes it easier to understand some aspect of quantum computing.

A *qubit*—a *quantum bit*—is the fundamental unit of quantum information. At any given time, it is in a superposition state represented by a linear combination of the orthonormal vectors $|0\rangle$ and $|1\rangle$ in $\mathbf{C}^2$:

$$a|0\rangle + b|1\rangle \text{ where } |a|^2 + |b|^2 = 1 .$$

Through *measurement*, a qubit is forced to collapse irreversibly through projection to either $|0\rangle$ or $|1\rangle$ with probability $|a|^2$ or $|b|^2$, respectively. We call a and b *probability amplitudes*.

If necessary, we can convert ("read out") $|0\rangle$ and $|1\rangle$ to classical bit values of **0** and **1**.

The word "collapse" comes from the physical interpretation of a quantum system where measurement causes a superposition to move to one of two choices. We examine what collapses when we look at the quantum description of the polarization of photons in section 11.9.3.

One qubit by itself is not very interesting, despite all the mathematical formalism. An algorithm needs to compute a result, which should translate to something meaningful. A single qubit eventually produces one classical **0** or **1** when measured and read; we need many qubits to represent useful information.

Quantum algorithms are fascinating because of how multiple qubits interact when they are in their pre-measured states when we can use the full power of linear algebra in $\mathbf{C}^2$. *Entanglement* is when two or more qubits are so tightly correlated that we cannot learn something about one without learning about the other(s).

7.2 Bras and kets

It's now time to formalize our understanding of $|0\rangle$ and $|1\rangle$ and relate them to the discussion of linear algebra in Chapter 5, ''Dimensions.''

When we previously looked at vector notation in section 5.4.2, we saw several forms, such as

$$\mathbf{v} = (v_1, v_2, \dots, v_n)$$
$$= \begin{bmatrix} v_1 & v_2 & \cdots & v_n \end{bmatrix} \text{ as a row vector}$$
$$= \begin{bmatrix} v_1 \\ v_2 \\ \vdots \\ v_n \end{bmatrix} \text{ as a column vector.}$$

We now add two more invented by Paul Dirac, an English theoretical physicist, for use in quantum mechanics. They simplify many of the expressions we use in quantum computing.

Given a vector $\mathbf{v} = (v_1, v_2, \dots, v_n)$, we denote by $\langle v|$, pronounced ''bra-v,'' the row vector

$$\langle v| = \begin{bmatrix} \overline{v_1} & \overline{v_2} & \cdots & \overline{v_n} \end{bmatrix}$$

where we take the complex conjugate of each entry.

For $\mathbf{w} = (w_1, w_2, \dots, w_n)$, $|w\rangle$, pronounced ''ket-w,'' is the column vector

$$|w\rangle = \begin{bmatrix} w_1 \\ w_2 \\ \vdots \\ w_m \end{bmatrix}$$

without the conjugations.

To avoid notational overload, I continue to put vector names in a bold font such as **v** when I use them in isolation but will drop the bold in the bra or ket forms. The forms make it clear that a vector is involved.

When $n = m$, the bra-ket $\langle v|w \rangle = \langle v| \, |w \rangle = (\langle v|)(|w \rangle)$ is the usual *inner product* from section 5.7.2.

$$\langle v|w \rangle = \langle \mathbf{v}, \mathbf{w} \rangle = \overline{v_1}w_1 + \overline{v_2}w_2 + \cdots \overline{v_n}w_n \,.$$

The length of **v** is $\|\mathbf{v}\| = \sqrt{\langle v|v \rangle}$.

$|v\rangle\langle w|$ is the *outer product*

$$|v\rangle\langle w| = \begin{bmatrix} v_1\overline{w_1} & v_1\overline{w_2} & \cdots & v_1\overline{w_m} \\ v_2\overline{w_1} & v_2\overline{w_2} & \cdots & v_2\overline{w_m} \\ \vdots & \vdots & \ddots & \vdots \\ v_n\overline{w_1} & v_n\overline{w_2} & \cdots & v_n\overline{w_m} \end{bmatrix} .$$

To learn more

As mathematicians and physicists work with concepts, they need a concise way of conveying what they mean. Good notation can make a statement or a proof much clearer and more insightful to the reader. Over time, the symbols and expressions that prove to be most useful win out while the others fade away into the archives. In the case of Dirac's bra-ket notation, it has become ubiquitous across quantum mechanics and now quantum computing. [68, Section 1.6] [124, Section 6.2]

Example

If $\mathbf{v} = (3, -i)$ and $\mathbf{w} = (2 + i, 4)$, then

$$\langle v| = \begin{bmatrix} 3 & i \end{bmatrix} \quad \text{and} \quad |w\rangle = \begin{bmatrix} 2 + i \\ 4 \end{bmatrix}$$

and

$$\langle v|w \rangle = 3(2 + i) + 4i = 6 + 7i$$

$$|v\rangle\langle w| = \begin{bmatrix} 3(2 - i) & 3 \times 4 \\ i(2 - i) & i \times 4 \end{bmatrix} = \begin{bmatrix} 6 - 3i & 12 \\ 1 + 2i & 4i \end{bmatrix}$$

As you will see, we also use symbols within bras or kets to label them, even though we may not list the coordinates. Typical examples are $|0\rangle$, $|1\rangle$, $|+\rangle$, $|-\rangle$, $|i\rangle$, $|-i\rangle$, $|\varphi\rangle$, and $|\psi\rangle$.

Just as we use n for a generic number in $\mathbf{N}$ or z for a number in $\mathbf{C}$, $|\psi\rangle$ is a general-purpose labeled ket. We pronounce the Greek letter ψ as "psi."

> $|0\rangle$ is $(1, 0) = \mathbf{e}_1$ and $|1\rangle$ is $(0, 1) = \mathbf{e}_2$ relative to the standard orthonormal basis for $\mathbf{C}^2$. Remember, vectors exist independently of their representation relative to a given basis. We frequently call $|0\rangle$ and $|1\rangle$ the *computational basis*.

If we use another orthonormal basis, then $|0\rangle$ and $|1\rangle$ would still be the same vectors but with different coordinates.

In the same way, relative to the standard basis, $|+\rangle = \left(\frac{\sqrt{2}}{2}, \frac{\sqrt{2}}{2}\right)$ and $|-\rangle = \left(\frac{\sqrt{2}}{2}, -\frac{\sqrt{2}}{2}\right)$. Like $|0\rangle$ and $|1\rangle$, these are an orthonormal basis for $\mathbf{C}^2$.

To remember which is $|0\rangle$ and which is $|1\rangle$, look at the second coordinate in the standard basis. For $|+\rangle$ and $|-\rangle$, look at the sign of the second coordinate.

Though we use the notation $|0\rangle$ and $|1\rangle$, **they are not equal to the numbers 0 and 1!** I show a connection later when we discuss measuring the state of a qubit, but keep them separate in your mind. The reason I highlight this is that, as a basis, we can write any vector in $\mathbf{C}^2$ as a linear combination

$$a|0\rangle + b|1\rangle \text{ for } a \text{ and } b \text{ in } \mathbf{C}.$$

You might be tempted to say such a vector is "0 and 1 at the same time!". Don't say that. It's just a linear combination. It's also a cliché that one should not use unless one knows what it means.

Just as we saw that a 1-by-n matrix or a row vector defines a linear form, so does a bra on the left combined with a ket on the right. For a vector $\mathbf{a} = (a_1, a_2, \ldots, a_n)$,

$$\langle a| = \begin{bmatrix} \overline{a_1} & \overline{a_2} & \cdots & \overline{a_n} \end{bmatrix},$$

and this corresponds to the linear form

$$\langle a|v\rangle = \langle \mathbf{a}, \mathbf{v}\rangle = \overline{a_1}v_1 + \overline{a_2}v_2 + \cdots + \overline{a_n}v_n$$

for all $\mathbf{v}$ in a complex n-dimensional vector space.

Exercise 7.1

What are the coordinates for $|0\rangle$ in the basis

$$(\frac{\sqrt{3}}{2}, \frac{1}{2}) \text{ and } (-\frac{1}{2}, \frac{\sqrt{3}}{2}) ?$$

What are the coordinates for $|1\rangle$? This diagram may help:

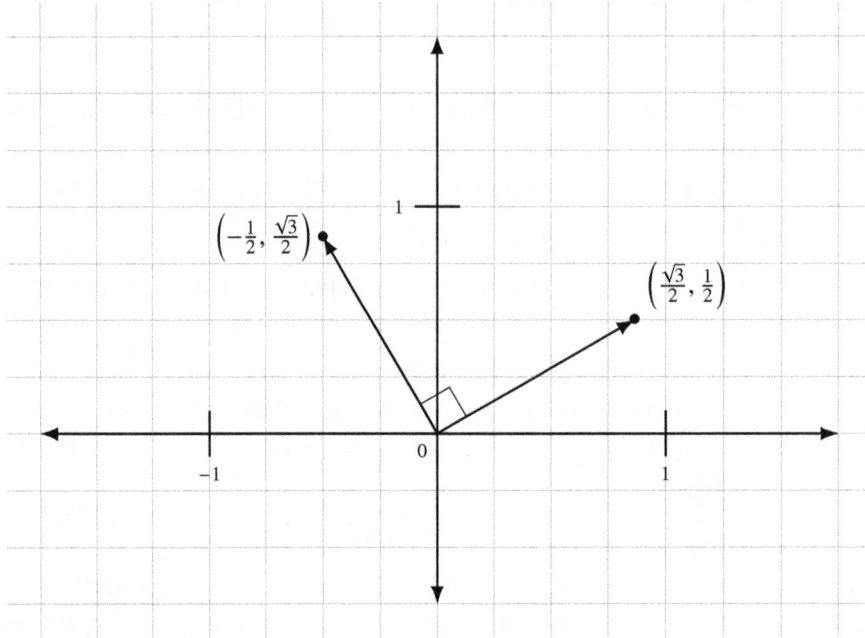

If L is a linear transformation on a complex vector space, we write $L|w\rangle$ for "L applied to $|w\rangle$." If A is a matrix for L, we use the form $A|w\rangle$ for "A multiplied by $|w\rangle$." Both A and the explicit column representation of $|w\rangle$ use the same basis.

For a bra $\langle v|$, what does $\langle v|L$ mean? If A is again a matrix for L, then $\langle v|L$ is $\langle v|A$, and we do the matrix multiplication between the row vector and the matrix.

These all have the nice property that we can slide L and A from the bra to the ket and back:

$$\langle v|L \times |w\rangle = (\langle v|L)|w\rangle) = \langle v|(L|w\rangle) = \langle v| \times L|w\rangle$$
$$\langle v|A \times |w\rangle = (\langle v|A)|w\rangle) = \langle v|(A|w\rangle) = \langle v| \times A|w\rangle$$

Let's get rid of unneeded parentheses and "$\times$" symbols: write $\langle v|L|w\rangle$ for the first case and $\langle v|A|w\rangle$ for the matrix version in the second.

Let V be an n-dimensional vector space and let $\{|e_1\rangle, \ldots, |e_n\rangle\}$ and $\{\langle e_1|, \ldots, \langle e_n|\}$ be the standard basis $\{\mathbf{e}_1, \ldots, \mathbf{e}_n\}$ in ket and bra forms. If A is an n-by-n square matrix, the (i, j)-th entry of A is $A_{i,j} = \langle e_i|A|e_j\rangle$.

$|e_i\rangle\langle e_j|$ is an n-by-n square matrix with a 1 in the (i, j)-th position and 0 elsewhere. The sum of the n^2 matrices $|e_i\rangle A_{i,j}\langle e_j|$ is A.

Exercise 7.2

Let A be the 2-by-2 complex matrix

$$\begin{bmatrix} a & b \\ c & d \end{bmatrix}.$$

Compute each $|e_i\rangle A_{i,j}\langle e_j|$ and show that their sum is A.

Exercise 7.3

Let $\mathbf{v}$ and $\mathbf{w}$ be vectors as above, and A and B be n-by-n matrices. Show that

$$|A\mathbf{v}\rangle\langle B\mathbf{w}| = A\,|\mathbf{v}\rangle\langle\mathbf{w}|\,\overline{B}^{\mathsf{T}} = A\,|\mathbf{v}\rangle\langle\mathbf{w}|\,B^{\dagger}.$$

Show that if $\mathbf{v} = \mathbf{w}$ and $A = B$, then $|A\mathbf{v}\rangle\langle A\mathbf{v}| = |\mathbf{v}\rangle\langle\mathbf{v}|\,A^{\dagger}$. For clarity, I show the vectors in bold in the bras and kets.

We define matrices

$$P(i) = |e_i\rangle\langle e_i|$$
$$P(i, j) = P(i) + P(j) \text{ for } i \neq j$$
$$P(i, j, k) = P(i) + P(j) + P(k) \text{ for } i \neq j, i \neq k, \text{ and } j \neq k$$

We can consider P having up to n arguments, with no argument equal to any other. They are each diagonal matrices and trivially Hermitian. (Though I use P here, this is not for probability as we used it in Chapter 6, "What Do You Mean "Probably"?.")

Exercise 7.4

Show that

$$P(i)P(j) = \begin{cases} 1 & \text{if } i = j \\ 0 & \text{otherwise.} \end{cases}$$

> A matrix A is a *projector* or a *projection matrix* if $A^2 = A$. The rank of the projector is the dimension of its image vector space. $P(i)$ has rank 1, $P(i, j)$ has rank 2, and so on. $P(1, \ldots, n) = I_n$, the n-by-n identity matrix.

Why did I bother introducing this new bra-ket notation? First, it's what scientists and practitioners in quantum mechanics and quantum computing use, and you must know their language. Second, while it now only seems like a modest improvement over the vector and linear transformation notation we developed in Chapter 5, "Dimensions," it dramatically simplifies expressions involving multiple qubits. It provides, I hope, greater clarity and faster understanding for you.

7.3 The complex math and physics of a single qubit

Let's revisit our definition of a qubit from section 7.1. This time, we break it into two pieces: a mathematical and a physical/quantum mechanical part.

> **Mathematics**
>
> A *qubit*—a *quantum bit*—is the fundamental unit of quantum information. At any given time, it is in a superposition state represented by a linear combination of vectors $|0\rangle$ and $|1\rangle$ in $\mathbf{C}^2$:
>
> $$a|0\rangle + b|1\rangle \quad \text{where} \quad |a|^2 + |b|^2 = 1 .$$

> **Physics**
>
> Through *measurement*, a qubit is forced to collapse irreversibly to either $|0\rangle$ or $|1\rangle$. The probability of its doing either is $|a|^2$ and $|b|^2$, respectively. a and b are called *probability amplitudes*.
>
> When we measure, do we get a bit **0** or **1**, or a qubit $|0\rangle$ or $|1\rangle$? Technically, it is the former, but by abuse of notation, we often show it as the latter. You can only get **0** when you measure $|0\rangle$, and you can only get **1** when you measure $|1\rangle$.

The mathematical portion is the linear algebra of a two-dimensional complex vector space. As a vector, the qubit state has length 1. Linear transformations must preserve this length and are isometries. Their matrices are unitary. Being unitary, they are invertible: moving a qubit from one state to another is always reversible.

When we built circuits that manipulated bits in section 2.4, only one of the core gates, **not**, was reversible. When we make quantum circuits using qubits in Chapter 9, "Wiring Up the Circuits," all the gates are reversible, but the measurement operation is not. Mathematically, we can think of a quantum circuit as applying unitary matrices to vectors representing qubit states.

Mathematics is elegant and beautiful in its own right but is often only a tool for other fields. We frequently use it to build models that allow us to reason how things may work in the so-called "real world." These models are not the real world but are our best efforts to formalize the relationships that seem to make things behave the way they do.

Linear algebra by itself does not say the probability amplitudes affect whether we get $|0\rangle$ or $|1\rangle$ when a qubit is measured. We employ linear algebra, complex numbers, and probability to represent much of quantum computing. We must use our understanding of the physical system to interpret what the mathematics mean. Mathematical formalism can only get us so far in developing our structure: physics must give us additional relationships that bring us further.

In particular, measurement is a physical action. It causes us to drop from a superposition state involving $|0\rangle$ and $|1\rangle$ to one or the other. Mathematics describes the probability of getting either, but does not force one value or another.

7.3.1 Quantum state representation

If $|\psi\rangle = a|0\rangle + b|1\rangle$ is a quantum state, we know that $\||\psi\|| = \langle\psi|\psi\rangle^2 = |a|^2 + |b|^2 = 1$.

The values $|a|^2$ and $|b|^2$ are nonnegative numbers in **R** that are the probabilities that $|\psi\rangle$ will go to $|0\rangle$ or $|1\rangle$, respectively, when measured.

Consider the following example in which, for illustrative purposes, I have made some simplifications and taken some labeling liberties. Suppose a and b can only be real.

Let $a = \frac{1}{2}$ and $b = \frac{\sqrt{3}}{2}$. Then $|a|^2 = \left|\frac{1}{2}\right|^2 = \frac{1}{4} = 0.25$ and $|b|^2 = \left|\frac{\sqrt{3}}{2}\right|^2 = \frac{3}{4} = 0.75$. The state of the qubit has a 25% chance of collapsing to $|0\rangle$ when measured and a 75% chance of collapsing to $|1\rangle$. You can see this in Figure 7.2.

If c is in **C** with $|c| = 1$, then

$$c|\psi\rangle = |c\psi\rangle = ca|0\rangle + cb|1\rangle,$$

with

$$|ca|^2 = |c|^2|a|^2 = |a|^2 \quad \text{and} \quad |cb|^2 = |c|^2|b|^2 = |b|^2.$$

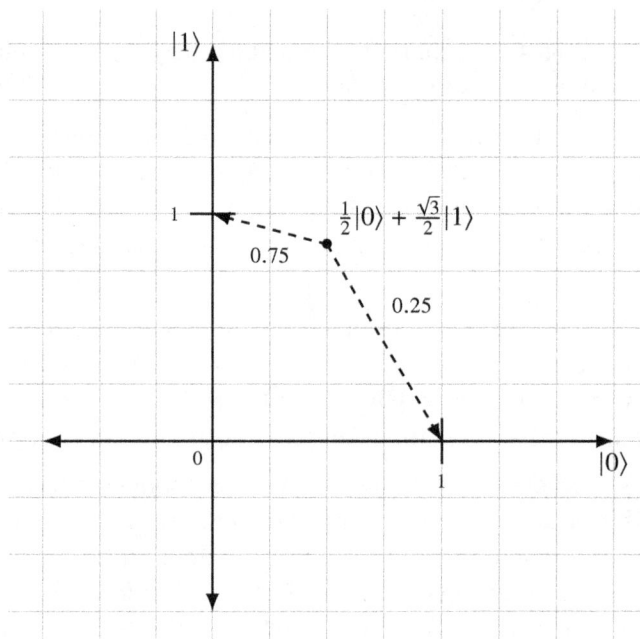

Figure 7.2: Probabilities of collapsing to 0 or 1

Multiplying a quantum state by a complex number of absolute value 1 does not change the probability of obtaining $|0\rangle$ or $|1\rangle$ upon measurement. We say there is no *observable* difference in doing this multiplication. As we know from section 4.5, all complex numbers with absolute value 1 are on the unit circle and look like $e^{\varphi i} = \cos(\varphi) + \sin(\varphi)i$.

> We identify two quantum states if they only differ by a multiple of a complex unit. Recall that a unit has absolute value equal to 1. Such numbers look like $e^{\varphi i}$ for $0 \le \varphi < 2\pi$.
>
> When we perform some action and then say "$|\psi\rangle$ is not changed," we mean that it is fine if the result is $e^{\varphi i}|\psi\rangle$. This point is easy to miss because you might expect $|\psi\rangle$ to be literally unchanged.

Let's re-express a and b in polar form:

$$a = r_1 e^{\varphi_1 i}$$
$$b = r_2 e^{\varphi_2 i}$$
$$|\psi\rangle = a|0\rangle + b|1\rangle = r_1 e^{\varphi_1 i}|0\rangle + r_2 e^{\varphi_2 i}|1\rangle$$

with r_1, r_2, φ_1, and φ_2 in **R**. r_1 and r_2 are ≥ 0, and $0 \le \varphi_1, \varphi_2 < 2\pi$.

If either a or b is 0, the other is 1, and we have the basis kets. Assume $a \neq 0$ and so $r_1 \neq 0$. Then

$$r_1 e^{\varphi_1 i}|0\rangle + r_2 e^{\varphi_2 i}|1\rangle = e^{\varphi_1 i}\left(r_1|0\rangle + r_2 e^{(\varphi_2 - \varphi_1)i}|1\rangle\right),$$

with $e^{\varphi_1 i}$ in **C** with absolute value equal to 1.

There's a whole lot of subscripting and superscripting going on there! The net is this: from the perspective of measurement and observable results,

$$a|0\rangle + b|1\rangle = r_1 e^{\varphi_1 i}|0\rangle + r_2 e^{\varphi_2 i}|1\rangle$$

is effectively the same as

$$r_1|0\rangle + r_2 e^{(\varphi_2 - \varphi_1)i}|1\rangle,$$

and the coefficient a of $|0\rangle$ is real.

We are left with two degrees of freedom for the state of a qubit:

- One related to the magnitudes, since r_1 and r_2 are dependent via $r_1^2 + r_2^2 = 1$
- The *relative phase* $\varphi = \varphi_1 - \varphi_2$

The relative phase is significant and is important when we see *interference* in section 9.6, a technique used in quantum algorithms.

We can represent the state of a single qubit $|\psi\rangle$ by

$$|\psi\rangle = r_1|0\rangle + r_2 e^{\varphi i}|1\rangle$$

with r_1 and r_2 in **R**, $r_1^2 + r_2^2 = 1$, and $0 \leq \varphi < 2\pi$. Moreover, we can find θ with

$$r_1 = \cos\left(\frac{\theta}{2}\right) \quad \text{and} \quad r_2 = \sin\left(\frac{\theta}{2}\right)$$

so that

$$|\psi\rangle = \cos\left(\frac{\theta}{2}\right)|0\rangle + \sin\left(\frac{\theta}{2}\right)e^{\varphi i}|1\rangle.$$

When two quantum states $|\psi\rangle_1$ and $|\psi\rangle_2$ differ only by a complex unit multiple u,

$$|\psi\rangle_2 = u|\psi\rangle_1,$$

we cannot tell the difference between them when we measure. That is, u is not observable. u is called a *global phase*. The expression "up to a global phase" means that we consider two quantum states equivalent if one differs from the other only by multiplication by a complex unit.

7.3.2 Unitary matrices mapping to standard form

If $|\psi\rangle = \cos\left(\frac{\theta}{2}\right)|0\rangle + \sin\left(\frac{\theta}{2}\right)e^{\varphi i}|1\rangle$ is an arbitrary quantum state where we have made the first probability amplitude real, then what does a 2-by-2 unitary matrix U look like that maps $|0\rangle$ to $|\psi\rangle$:

$$U|0\rangle = U\begin{bmatrix}1\\0\end{bmatrix} = |\psi\rangle = \cos\left(\frac{\theta}{2}\right)|0\rangle + \sin\left(\frac{\theta}{2}\right)e^{\varphi i}|1\rangle \ ?$$

By inspection,

$$U = \begin{bmatrix} \cos\left(\frac{\theta}{2}\right) & a \\ \sin\left(\frac{\theta}{2}\right)e^{\varphi i} & b \end{bmatrix}$$

for some complex numbers a and b. Since U is unitary, $I_2 = UU^{-1} = UU^\dagger$, where

$$U^\dagger = \overline{U^T} = \begin{bmatrix} \cos\left(\frac{\theta}{2}\right) & \sin\left(\frac{\theta}{2}\right)e^{\varphi i} \\ \overline{a} & \overline{b} \end{bmatrix} = \begin{bmatrix} \cos\left(\frac{\theta}{2}\right) & \sin\left(\frac{\theta}{2}\right)e^{-\varphi i} \\ \overline{a} & \overline{b} \end{bmatrix}.$$

Using the explicit form of the inverse of a 2-by-2 matrix,

$$U^{-1} = \frac{1}{\det(U)}\begin{bmatrix} b & -a \\ -\sin\left(\frac{\theta}{2}\right)e^{\varphi i} & \cos\left(\frac{\theta}{2}\right) \end{bmatrix}.$$

Since U is unitary, $|\det(U)| = 1$ and $\det(U)$ is a complex unit. Choose a real number δ so that $\det(U) = e^{\delta i}$. ("δ" is the lowercase Greek letter "delta.")

$U^{-1} = U^\dagger$ means

$$U^{-1} = \frac{1}{\det(U)}\begin{bmatrix} b & -a \\ -\sin\left(\frac{\theta}{2}\right)e^{\varphi i} & \cos\left(\frac{\theta}{2}\right) \end{bmatrix}$$

$$= e^{-\delta i}\begin{bmatrix} b & -a \\ -\sin\left(\frac{\theta}{2}\right)e^{\varphi i} & \cos\left(\frac{\theta}{2}\right) \end{bmatrix}$$

$$= \begin{bmatrix} \cos\left(\frac{\theta}{2}\right) & \sin\left(\frac{\theta}{2}\right)e^{-\varphi i} \\ \overline{a} & \overline{b} \end{bmatrix} = U^\dagger.$$

Thus,

$$e^{-\delta i}b = \cos\left(\frac{\theta}{2}\right) \quad \text{and} \quad -e^{-\delta i}a = \sin\left(\frac{\theta}{2}\right)e^{-\varphi i}$$

and

$$b = \cos\left(\frac{\theta}{2}\right) e^{\delta i} \quad \text{and} \quad a = -\sin\left(\frac{\theta}{2}\right) e^{-\varphi i} e^{\delta i}.$$

This makes

$$U = \begin{bmatrix} \cos\left(\frac{\theta}{2}\right) & -\sin\left(\frac{\theta}{2}\right) e^{\delta i - \varphi i} \\ \sin\left(\frac{\theta}{2}\right) e^{\varphi i} & \cos\left(\frac{\theta}{2}\right) e^{\delta i} \end{bmatrix}.$$

Though we do not use it further in this book, an alternative form defines $\lambda = \delta - \varphi$. We can then parameterize U by three numbers: θ, φ, and λ, with

$$U(\theta, \varphi, \lambda) = \begin{bmatrix} \cos\left(\frac{\theta}{2}\right) & -\sin\left(\frac{\theta}{2}\right) e^{\lambda i} \\ \sin\left(\frac{\theta}{2}\right) e^{\varphi i} & \cos\left(\frac{\theta}{2}\right) e^{\lambda i + \varphi i} \end{bmatrix}.$$

You may wonder why we have three angles here, though we only need two for the Bloch sphere. These are *Euler angles*, one of the classical methods of describing how some object is rotationally oriented in space relative to some fixed set of axes. [66] Similar to these are the angles we use when we state an airplane's roll, pitch, and yaw while in the air.

Qiskit uses Euler angles to define its **U** gate. [184]

7.3.3   The density matrix

For $|\psi\rangle = a|0\rangle + b|1\rangle$, we define the *density matrix* ρ of $|\psi\rangle$ as

$$\rho = |\psi\rangle\langle\psi| = \begin{bmatrix} a\bar{a} & a\bar{b} \\ b\bar{a} & b\bar{b} \end{bmatrix} = \begin{bmatrix} |a|^2 & a\bar{b} \\ b\bar{a} & |b|^2 \end{bmatrix}.$$

We commonly use the Greek letter ρ (''rho'') as the symbol representing the density matrix. Note that $\text{tr}(\rho) = \text{tr}(|\psi\rangle\langle\psi|) = 1$ and that ρ is Hermitian.

Exercise 7.5

What is $\det(\rho) = \det(|\psi\rangle\langle\psi|)$?

For $|\psi\rangle$ expressed by $r_1|0\rangle + r_2 e^{\varphi i}|1\rangle$, with r_1 and r_2 in **R** and nonnegative, the density matrix is

$$\rho = |\psi\rangle\langle\psi| = \begin{bmatrix} r_1^2 & r_1 r_2 e^{-\varphi i} \\ r_1 r_2 e^{\varphi i} & r_2^2 \end{bmatrix}.$$

From this, we can compute:

$$r_1 = \sqrt{\rho_{1,1}} \qquad r_2 = \sqrt{\rho_{2,2}} \qquad e^{\varphi i} = \frac{\rho_{2,1}}{r_1 r_2}$$

Up to a global phase, we have not lost anything from going from the ket to the density matrix.

Exercise 7.6

What can you tell about the original ket if you are given its density matrix

$$\rho = \begin{bmatrix} d_{1,1} & d_{1,2} \\ d_{2,1} & d_{2,2} \end{bmatrix} ?$$

If we use two angles with $|\psi\rangle = r_1 e^{\varphi_1 i}|0\rangle + r_2 e^{\varphi_2 i}|1\rangle$, r_1 and r_2 in $\mathbf{R}$ and nonnegative, the density matrix is

$$\rho = |\psi\rangle\langle\psi| = \begin{bmatrix} r_1^2 & r_1 r_2 e^{i(\varphi_1 - \varphi_2)} \\ r_1 r_2 e^{-i(\varphi_1 - \varphi_2)} & r_2^2 \end{bmatrix}.$$

If you set $\varphi = -(\varphi_1 - \varphi_2)$, this reduces to the previous case where we had already made the probability amplitude of $|0\rangle$ real.

Exercise 7.7

Show that two 1-qubit quantum states that differ only by a global phase have the same density matrix. Put another way, the density matrix is independent of any global phase.

7.3.4 Observables and expectation

The matrices $M_0 = |0\rangle\langle0|$ and $M_1 = |1\rangle\langle1|$ are projectors and Hermitian matrices. If $|\psi\rangle = a|0\rangle + b|1\rangle$,

$$\langle\psi|M_0|\psi\rangle = \left\langle\psi\left| \left(|0\rangle\langle0|\right)\right|\psi\right\rangle$$
$$= \langle\psi|0\rangle\langle0|\psi\rangle$$
$$= \begin{bmatrix} \bar{a} & \bar{b} \end{bmatrix} \begin{bmatrix} 1 \\ 0 \end{bmatrix} \begin{bmatrix} 1 & 0 \end{bmatrix} \begin{bmatrix} a \\ b \end{bmatrix}$$

$$= \begin{bmatrix} \bar{a} & \bar{b} \end{bmatrix} \begin{bmatrix} 1 & 0 \\ 0 & 0 \end{bmatrix} \begin{bmatrix} a \\ b \end{bmatrix}$$

$$= \begin{bmatrix} \bar{a} & \bar{b} \end{bmatrix} \begin{bmatrix} a \\ 0 \end{bmatrix} = |a|^2 .$$

Similarly, $\langle \psi | M_1 | \psi \rangle = |b|^2$.

$\langle \psi | M_0 | \psi \rangle = |a|^2$ is the probability of measuring $|0\rangle$, and $\langle \psi | M_1 | \psi \rangle = |b|^2$ is the probability of measuring $|1\rangle$.

The eigenvalues of M_0 are 0 and 1, corresponding to eigenvectors $|1\rangle$ and $|0\rangle$, respectively. M_1 has the same eigenvalues, with the eigenvectors reversed. M_0 and M_1 are both examples of *observables*: Hermitian matrices whose eigenvectors form a basis for the quantum state space.

Exercise 7.8

What is the relationship between the coefficients of the basis elements formed by the eigenvectors and the probabilities of seeing those basis elements when we measure?

Now let's turn this around and suppose A is an observable. A is a Hermitian matrix with eigenvectors $|v_1\rangle$ and $|v_2\rangle$ corresponding to eigenvalues λ_1 and λ_2. We use $|v_1\rangle$ as the label for the eigenvector corresponding to λ_1.

By definition,

$$A|v_1\rangle = \lambda_1 |v_1\rangle \quad \text{and} \quad A|v_2\rangle = \lambda_2 |v_2\rangle .$$

As stated at the end of section 5.10, we may assume that the eigenvectors $|v_1\rangle$ and $|v_2\rangle$ form an orthonormal basis of $\mathbf{C}^2$.

If $|\psi\rangle = a|v_1\rangle + b|v_2\rangle$ with $\langle \psi | \psi \rangle = 1$, by the properties of the inner product,

$$a = \langle v_1 | \psi \rangle \quad \text{and} \quad b = \langle v_2 | \psi \rangle$$

and thus

$$|\psi\rangle = \langle v_1 | \psi \rangle |v_1\rangle + \langle v_2 | \psi \rangle |v_2\rangle .$$

This basis is related to A. When we *measure* the observable A, the probability of getting $|v_1\rangle$ is $|\langle v_1 | \psi \rangle|^2$, and the probability of getting $|v_2\rangle$ is $|\langle v_2 | \psi \rangle|^2$.

Now that we have a set of values and corresponding probabilities for when we might get them, it is reasonable to talk about expectation as we first discussed in section 6.6.

The expected value, or expectation, $\langle A \rangle$ of A given the state $|\psi\rangle$ is

$$\langle A \rangle = |\langle v_1|\psi\rangle|^2 \lambda_1 + |\langle v_2|\psi\rangle|^2 \lambda_2 .$$

Remember that $|\langle v_1|\psi\rangle|^2 + |\langle v_2|\psi\rangle|^2 = 1$.

Exercise 7.9

Why does $|\langle v_1|\psi\rangle|^2 = \langle\psi|v_1\rangle\langle v_1|\psi\rangle$? Hint: recall that for complex vectors $\mathbf{v}$ and $\mathbf{w}$,

$$\langle \mathbf{v}, \mathbf{w} \rangle = \overline{\langle \mathbf{w}, \mathbf{v} \rangle} .$$

We can simplify this:

$$
\begin{aligned}
\langle A \rangle \ &= |\langle v_1|\psi\rangle|^2 \lambda_1 + |\langle v_2|\psi\rangle|^2 \lambda_2 \\
&= \langle\psi|v_1\rangle\langle v_1|\psi\rangle\lambda_1 + \langle\psi|v_2\rangle\langle v_2|\psi\rangle\lambda_2 \quad \text{because } |\langle v_1|\psi\rangle|^2 = \langle\psi|v_1\rangle\langle v_1|\psi\rangle \\
&= \langle\psi|A|v_1\rangle\langle v_1|\psi\rangle + \langle\psi|A|v_2\rangle\langle v_2|\psi\rangle \quad \text{because } A|v_1\rangle = \lambda_1|v_1\rangle \\
&= \langle\psi| \quad A\big(|v_1\rangle\langle v_1| + |v_2\rangle\langle v_2|\big) \quad |\psi\rangle \\
&= \langle\psi|A|\psi\rangle .
\end{aligned}
$$

I think this calculation shows the elegance of the bra-ket notation.

Exercise 7.10

What are $\langle M_0 \rangle$ and $\langle M_0 \rangle$ for $|\psi\rangle = a|v_1\rangle + b|v_2\rangle$?

7.4 A nonlinear projection

In Chapter 5, "Dimensions," we saw linear projections, such as mapping any point in the real plane to the line $y = x$. Now, we look at a special kind of projection that is nonlinear. We map almost every point on the unit circle onto a line. We will use this in the next section when we discuss the Bloch sphere.

Figure 7.3 shows a unit circle and the line $y = -1$ that sits right below it.

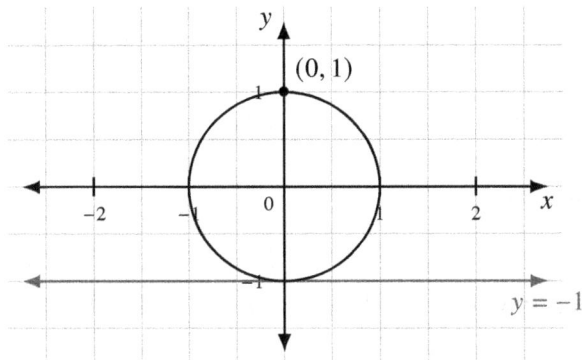

Figure 7.3: The unit circle in $\mathbf{R}^2$ resting on the line $y = -1$

We can map every point on the circle except $(0, 1)$, the north pole, to a point on the line $y = -1$. We simply draw a line from $(0, 1)$ through the point on the circle. The result is where that line intersects $y = -1$, as shown in Figure 7.4. The south pole maps to itself. We want different points on the circle to map to different points on the line.

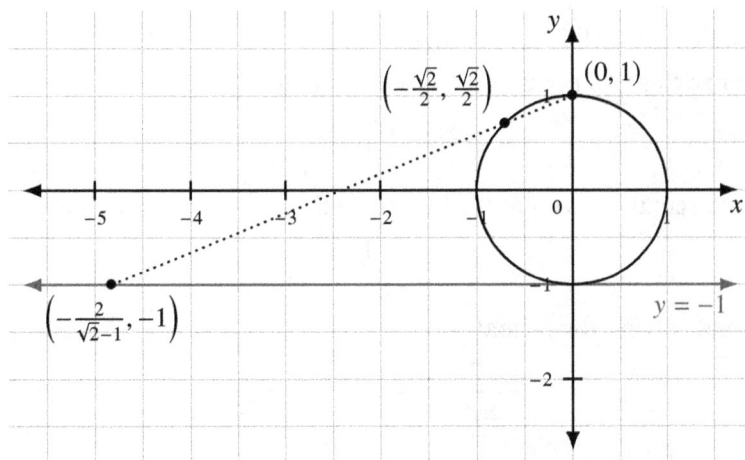

Figure 7.4: Projecting a point on the unit circle onto the line $y = -1$

The point where it intersects the line is

$$\left(-\frac{2}{\sqrt{2}-1}, -1\right) .$$

We compute this using the slope-intercept form.

We know two points on the line: the north pole $(0, 1)$ and the point on the circle $(-\frac{\sqrt{2}}{2}, \frac{\sqrt{2}}{2})$.

The slope m is the difference in y values divided by the difference in x values:

$$m = \frac{1 - \frac{\sqrt{2}}{2}}{0 - -\frac{\sqrt{2}}{2}} = \frac{1 - \frac{\sqrt{2}}{2}}{\frac{\sqrt{2}}{2}} = \frac{2 - \sqrt{2}}{\sqrt{2}} = \frac{2\sqrt{2} - 2}{2} = \sqrt{2} - 1.$$

When $x = 0$, $y = 1$. The equation of the line is

$$y = \left(\sqrt{2} - 1\right)x + 1.$$

To see where it intersects the line $y = -1$, we just set $y = -1$ in the equation and solve:

$$-1 = \left(\sqrt{2} - 1\right)x + 1$$

and so

$$-2 = \left(\sqrt{2} - 1\right)x$$

and so

$$-\frac{2}{\sqrt{2} - 1} = x.$$

By construction, the y-coordinate is always -1.

Let's generalize this to a point (x_0, y_0) on the circle. The slope is

$$m = \frac{y_0 - 1}{x_0 - 0} = \frac{y_0 - 1}{x_0}.$$

The line must intersect the y-axis at $(0, 1)$, and so the equation of the line is

$$y = \frac{y_0 - 1}{x_0}x + 1.$$

Setting $y = -1$ and solving for x yields

$$-\frac{2}{\frac{y_0-1}{x_0}} = -\frac{2x_0}{y_0 - 1} = x.$$

The image of the projection is

$$\left(-\frac{2x_0}{y_0 - 1}, -1\right).$$

Exercise 7.11

Does this generalized method give us the same answer we calculated earlier for

$$(x_0, y_0) = \left(-\frac{\sqrt{2}}{2}, \frac{\sqrt{2}}{2}\right)?$$

This general formula works for every point on the circle except for $y_0 = 1$, the north pole.

Exercise 7.12

What point on the circle maps to $(0, -1)$?

Is this projection f invertible?

$$f : \text{unit circle} - \{(0, 1)\} \rightarrow \mathbf{R}$$

where the image is the x-coordinate on the line $y = -1$. What is the inverse function f^{-1} with $f^{-1} \circ f = $ the identity function? If we knew this, we could map the real line to the unit circle with the removed point $(0, 1)$.

To construct f^{-1}, we begin with an a in $\mathbf{R}$. We want $f^{-1}(a)$ to be a point on the unit circle (x_0, y_0). What's the most defining aspect of a point on the unit circle? It's the relationship

$$x_0^2 + y_0^2 = 1 \,.$$

Given a, consider the point $(a, -1)$ on the line $y = -1$. We draw the line from this point to the north pole $(0, 1)$ and ask: where does this line intersect the unit circle?

The slope m is $-\frac{2}{a}$, and the complete equation of the line is

$$y = -\frac{2}{a}x + 1 \,.$$

We will return to this quotient for m later in the discussion.

Exercise 7.13

Verify that the slope is $-\frac{2}{a}$.

Continuing with the equation above, we square both sides:

$$y^2 = \frac{4}{a^2}x^2 - \frac{4}{a}x + 1 \,.$$

Substituting in x_0 and y_0:

$$y_0^2 = \frac{4}{a^2}x_0^2 - \frac{4}{a}x_0 + 1 \,.$$

But $x_0^2 + y_0^2 = 1$! Thus,

$$1 - x_0^2 = \frac{4}{a^2}x_0^2 - \frac{4}{a}x_0 + 1 \,.$$

Negating and moving the terms on the left side to the right and then simplifying yields

$$0 = \left(\frac{4}{a^2} + 1\right)x_0^2 - \frac{4}{a}x_0 = x_0\left(\left(\frac{4}{a^2} + 1\right)x_0 - \frac{4}{a}\right).$$

We can rule out $x_0 = 0$ because that would give us the north pole. Therefore,

$$0 = \left(\frac{4}{a^2} + 1\right)x_0 - \frac{4}{a} = \frac{4 + a^2}{a^2}x_0 - \frac{4}{a}$$

or

$$0 = \left(4 + a^2\right)x_0 - 4a$$

or

$$\frac{4a}{4 + a^2} = x_0.$$

If $a = 2$, then $x_0 = 1$ and $y_0 = 0$. So, $f^{-1}(2) = (1, 0)$. What if $a = -4$? Then

$$x_0 = \frac{-16}{4 + 16} = -\frac{4}{5}.$$

Given the equation of the unit circle from section 4.2.3,

$$\left(-\frac{4}{5}\right)^2 + y_0^2 = 1$$

and

$$y_0^2 = 1 - \frac{16}{25} = \frac{9}{25},$$

and we inconclusively conclude $y_0 = \pm\frac{3}{5}$. Which is it?

By inspection of the graph in Figure 7.5, when $|a| \geq 2$, then $y_0 \geq 0$. Similarly, $|a| < 2$ implies $y_0 < 0$. Since $a = -4$, we conclusively conclude $y_0 = \frac{3}{5}$.

Exercise 7.14

It's unacceptable to say, ''I looked at the graph and proved this result.'' Show algebraically that $|a| \geq 2$ means $y_0 \geq 0$, and $|x| < 2$ means $y_0 < 0$.

Although I said, ''The slope m of the line is $-\frac{2}{a}$,'' **I never said anything about a being nonzero.**

The case $a = 0$ is special because it corresponds to the point directly under the north and south poles on $y = -1$. The line through the north pole is vertical, and so has slope ∞. Here, $f^{-1}(0) = (0, -1)$.

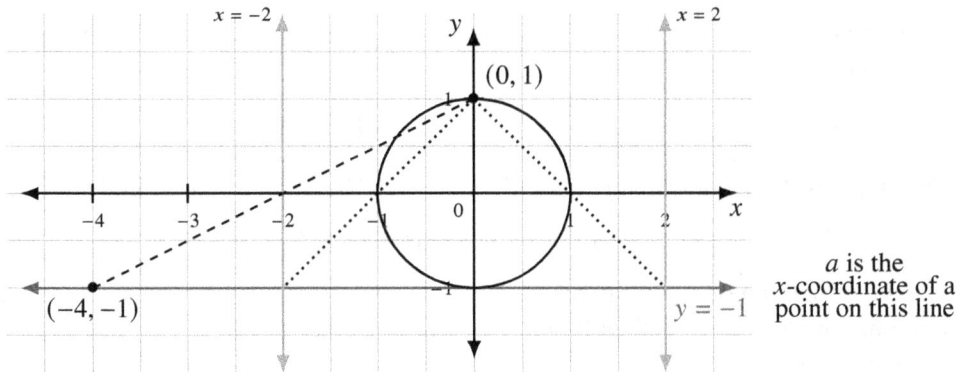

Figure 7.5: Projections for different values of a

We can now fully describe f and f^{-1}.

If f is the projection of a point (x_0, y_0), $y + 0 \neq 1$, on the unit circle onto the line $y = -1$, then its image is $(a, -1)$, where

$$a = -\frac{2x_0}{y_0 - 1}.$$

We define the inverse function $f^{-1}(a)$ for an a in **R** by

$$f^{-1}(a) = (0, -1) \quad \text{when} \quad a = 0$$

and $f^{-1}(a) = (x, y)$, with

$$x = \begin{cases} \dfrac{4a}{4 + a^2} + \sqrt{1 - \left(\dfrac{4a}{4 + a^2}\right)^2} & \text{when } |a| \geq 2 \\[3ex] \dfrac{4a}{4 + a^2} - \sqrt{1 - \left(\dfrac{4a}{4 + a^2}\right)^2} & \text{otherwise} \end{cases}$$

and

$$y = -\frac{2}{a}x + 1.$$

Our intermediate computations disallowed the case $a = 0$, though we handle it in the above.

Though we used trigonometry in the above analysis, we did not use angles. To conclude this section, let's quickly recast what we worked out but give the point on the unit circle by its angle $0 \leq \theta < 2\pi$ rather than Cartesian coordinates.

We need to exclude $\theta = \frac{\pi}{2}$ because this is the north pole. To keep our functions straight, we call this one g:

$$g : \left(0 \le \theta \le \frac{\pi}{2}\right) \text{ or } \left(\frac{\pi}{2} \le \theta < 2\pi\right) \to \mathbf{R},$$

where the image is the x-coordinate on the line $y = -1$. The definition is straightforward:

$$g(\theta) = f(\cos(\theta), \sin(\theta)).$$

If g is the projection of a point given by an angle θ such that $0 \le \theta < 2\pi$, $\theta \ne \frac{\pi}{2}$, on the unit circle onto the line $y = -1$, then its image is $(a, -1)$ where

$$a = -\frac{2\cos(\theta)}{\sin(\theta) - 1}.$$

What about g^{-1}? In this example, we want to go from -4 to the value of θ. The graph of the situation is shown in Figure 7.6.

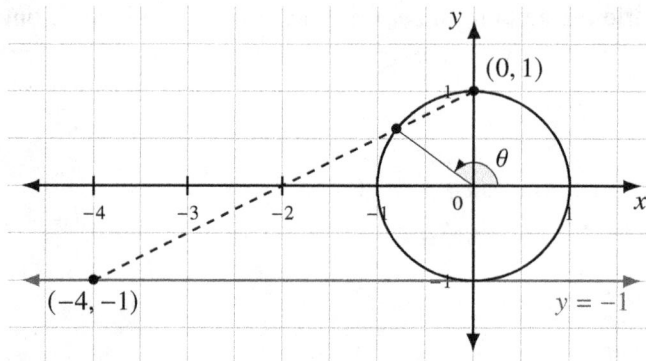

Figure 7.6: Inverting the projection from the unit circle

Let

$$\theta = \arccos(x_0) = \arccos\left(\frac{4a}{4 + a^2}\right).$$

By the definition of the inverse cosine, this has a value between 0 and π, inclusive. This alone does not tell us if the point is on the upper or lower half of the unit circle.

Let a be in $\mathbf{R}$ and

$$\theta = \arccos\left(\frac{4a}{4+a^2}\right).$$

We define the inverse function $g^{-1}(a)$ by

$$g^{-1}(a) = \begin{cases} \theta & \text{when } |a| \geq 1 \\ 2\pi - \theta & \text{otherwise.} \end{cases}$$

In this projection, we take an object that lives in two dimensions but is determined by one variable θ and map it to the one-dimensional line $\mathbf{R}^1$. Here, dimensions map to the idea of "degrees of freedom" as we express through the linear independence of a basis. Though the unit circle lives in $\mathbf{R}^3$, the relationship $x_0^2 + y_0^2 = 1$ means

$$x_0 = \pm\sqrt{1 - y_0^2},$$

and so x_0 is not independent of y_0. Under what circumstances can we take an object in a higher-dimensional space and map it to an object in a lower dimensional one?

In three real dimensions, the equivalent process of mapping a sphere onto a plane is a *stereographic projection*.

7.5   The Bloch sphere

We describe the state of a qubit by a vector

$$a|0\rangle + b|1\rangle = r_1 e^{\varphi_1 i}|0\rangle + r_2 e^{\varphi_2 i}|1\rangle$$

in $\mathbf{C}^2$ with r_1 and r_1 nonnegative numbers in $\mathbf{R}$.

The magnitudes r_1 and r_1 are related by $r_1^2 + r_2^2 = 1$. This is a mathematical condition.

We saw in section 7.3 that it's the relative phase of $\varphi_2 - \varphi_1$ that is significant and not the individual phases φ_1 and φ_2. This is a physical condition and means we can take a to be real.

We also saw that we could represent a quantum state as

$$|\psi\rangle = \cos\left(\frac{\theta}{2}\right)|0\rangle + \sin\left(\frac{\theta}{2}\right)e^{\varphi i}|1\rangle.$$

We do this via a nonlinear projection and a change of coordinates and get a point on the surface of the *Bloch sphere*, shown in Figure 7.7.

The two angles have the ranges $0 \leq \theta \leq \pi$ and $0 \leq \varphi < 2\pi$. θ is measured from the positive z-axis and φ from the positive x-axis in the xy-plane.

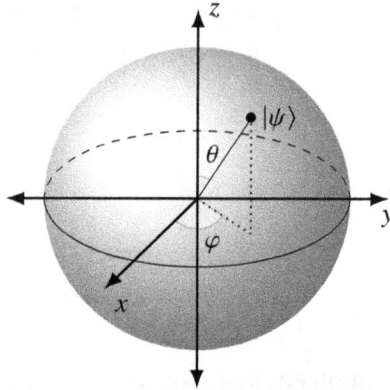

Figure 7.7: The Bloch sphere

The nonlinear projection is from the three-dimensional surface of qubit states of the hypersphere in $\mathbf{C}^2$, considered as $\mathbf{R}^4$, to the two-dimensional surface of the Bloch sphere. The key property that allows us to do this is that we can ignore the global phase.

We start by asking, "What are all the vectors in $\mathbf{C}^2$ of length 1?" to get the hypersphere. We then state, "We're going to say that any two points on the hypersphere are the 'same' if they are different only by a complex number multiple of magnitude 1." With these properties and equivalences, along with some algebra and geometry, we get the points on the Bloch sphere as the possible quantum states of a qubit.

It's easy to get confused here when we see $|\psi\rangle$. Is this on the Bloch sphere, or is it in $\mathbf{C}^2$? We do not distinguish these cases by notation, so I will clarify them by context.

Given a point/state on the Bloch sphere given by θ and φ, we can go back to $|\psi\rangle = a|0\rangle + b|1\rangle$ in $\mathbf{C}^2$ by

$$a = \cos\left(\frac{\theta}{2}\right) \quad \text{and} \quad b = e^{\varphi i}\sin\left(\frac{\theta}{2}\right).$$

Note that a is real.

On the other hand, if

$$a|0\rangle + b|1\rangle = r_1 e^{\varphi_1 i}|0\rangle + r_2 e^{\varphi_2 i}|1\rangle ,$$

what are θ and φ? Note that r_1 and r_1 are nonnegative.

If $a = 0$, then $b = 1$, and we have $|1\rangle$. We map this to $\theta = \pi$ and $\varphi = 0$. If $a = 1$, then $b = 0$, and we have $|0\rangle$, which goes to $\theta = 0$ and $\varphi = 0$.

Assume neither a nor b is 0, so r_1 and r_1 are positive real numbers. We rewrite

$$r_1 e^{\varphi_1 i}|0\rangle + r_2 e^{\varphi_2 i}|1\rangle = \left(e^{\varphi_1 i}\right)\left(r_1|0\rangle + r_2 e^{i(\varphi_2 - \varphi_2)}|1\rangle\right)$$

and can discard the $e^{\varphi_1 i}$ as it is not physically observable. We are left with

$$r_1|0\rangle + r_2 e^{i(\varphi_2 - \varphi_1)}|1\rangle.$$

We let $\varphi = \varphi_2 - \varphi_1$, adjusted to be an equivalent angle between 0 and 2π by adding 2π if the difference is negative.

Since $r_1^2 + r_2^2 = 1$, the point (r_1, r_2) is on the unit circle *in the first quadrant*. We can identify an angle $\theta_0 = \arccos(r_1)$ with $0 < \theta_0 < \frac{\pi}{2}$ so that

$$r_1 = \cos(\theta_0) \quad \text{and} \quad r_2 = \sin(\theta_0).$$

Let $\theta = 2\theta_0$.

Let's go back to $|0\rangle$ and examine the choices we made above for θ and φ:

$$|0\rangle = r_1 e^{\varphi_1 i}|0\rangle + r_2 e^{\varphi_2 i} = 1 e^{\varphi_1 i}|0\rangle + 0 e^{\varphi_2 i}|1\rangle.$$

By pulling out and discarding $e^{\varphi_1 i}$ as we have done several times, we are considering

$$1|0\rangle + 0 e^{(\varphi_2 - \varphi_1)i}|1\rangle.$$

Our choice of θ_0 is $\arccos(1) = 0$, and thus $\theta = 2\theta_0$ is also 0, and we are at the sphere's north pole. The rotation φ around the z-axis is meaningless, so we choose it to be 0.

We cannot choose φ_2 uniquely because of the multiplication by 0 in front of $e^{\varphi_2 i}$. We might as well choose $\varphi_2 = \varphi_1$ and $\varphi = 0$.

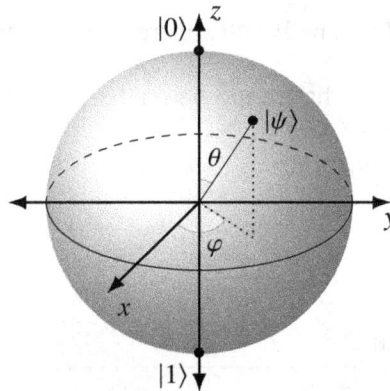

Figure 7.8: The Bloch sphere with $|0\rangle$ and $|1\rangle$

We have worked out the mappings to and from the Bloch sphere for qubit states in $\mathbf{C}^2$. $|0\rangle$ maps to the north pole, and $|1\rangle$ maps to the south pole, as shown in Figure 7.8.

Exercise 7.15

Are our choices $\theta = \pi$ and $\varphi = 0$ for $|1\rangle$ also reasonable?

Exercise 7.16

What about $|+\rangle = (\frac{\sqrt{2}}{2}, \frac{\sqrt{2}}{2})$ and $|-\rangle = (\frac{\sqrt{2}}{2}, -\frac{\sqrt{2}}{2})$?

Show that $|+\rangle$ maps to $\theta = \frac{\pi}{2}$ and $\varphi = 0$ on the Bloch sphere. Then, show that $|-\rangle$ maps to $\theta = \frac{\pi}{2}$ and $\varphi = \pi$. What are these points using Cartesian coordinates in $\mathbf{R}^3$?

The kets $|0\rangle$ and $|1\rangle$ lie on the z-axis, and $|+\rangle$ and $|-\rangle$ lie on the x-axis, as in Figure 7.9.

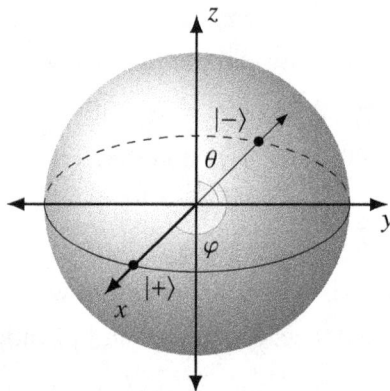

Figure 7.9: The Bloch sphere with $|+\rangle$ and $|-\rangle$

What is the orthonormal basis that would lie on the y-axis? Let's call them $|\mathbf{A}\rangle$ and $|\mathbf{B}\rangle$ for now and label them in Figure 7.10.

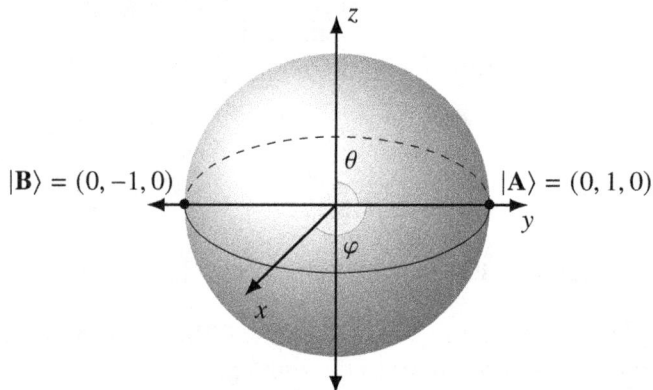

Figure 7.10: The Bloch sphere with mystery kets on the y-axis

The two points in which we are interested have Cartesian coordinates $(0, 1, 0)$ and $(0, -1, 0)$. For each of them, we can take $\theta = \frac{\pi}{2}$. For $|\mathbf{A}\rangle$, we use $\varphi = \frac{\pi}{2}$, and for $|\mathbf{B}\rangle$, $\varphi = \frac{3\pi}{2}$.

We use these to go back to $|\psi\rangle = a|0\rangle + b|1\rangle$ in $\mathbf{C}^2$. We set

$$a = \cos\left(\frac{\theta}{2}\right) \quad \text{and} \quad b = e^{\varphi i} \sin\left(\frac{\theta}{2}\right)$$

to get

$$a = \frac{\sqrt{2}}{2} \quad \text{and} \quad b = e^{\frac{\pi}{2}i} \frac{\sqrt{2}}{2} = \frac{\sqrt{2}}{2}i \,.$$

So,

$$|\mathbf{A}\rangle = \frac{\sqrt{2}}{2}\left(|0\rangle + i|1\rangle\right) \quad \text{and} \quad |\mathbf{B}\rangle = \frac{\sqrt{2}}{2}\left(|0\rangle - i|1\rangle\right).$$

With this, we officially rename these kets as

$$|i\rangle = \frac{\sqrt{2}}{2}\left(|0\rangle + i|1\rangle\right) \quad \text{and} \quad |-i\rangle = \frac{\sqrt{2}}{2}\left(|0\rangle - i|1\rangle\right).$$

Exercise 7.17

Verify that $|i\rangle$ and $|-i\rangle$ are orthonormal.

We can now fully label the Bloch sphere in Figure 7.11.

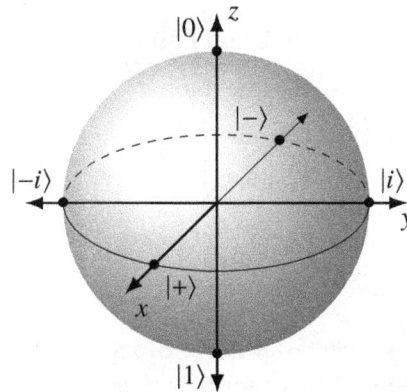

Figure 7.11: The complete Bloch sphere

From the evidence we've seen in three cases, an orthonormal basis in $\mathbf{C}^2$ maps to two opposite points on the Bloch sphere. Start thinking about why this is the case.

Every quantum state on the equator has an equal probability of producing $|0\rangle$ or $|1\rangle$ when measured. That is, if a state is on the equator, then in terms of its coordinates a and b in $a|0\rangle + b|1\rangle$ in $\mathbf{C}^2$, $|a|^2 = |b|^2 = \frac{1}{2} = 0.5$.

Naturally, the state $|0\rangle$ has probability 1.0 of yielding itself when measured and probability 0.0 of producing $|1\rangle$. These probabilities are reversed for $|1\rangle$.

For a latitude on the Bloch sphere that is not the equator, as in Figure 7.12, the probabilities of collapsing to $|0\rangle$ or $|1\rangle$ are different but still add up to 1.0. The likelihood of yielding $|0\rangle$ is the same for every point on that latitude. Ditto for $|1\rangle$.

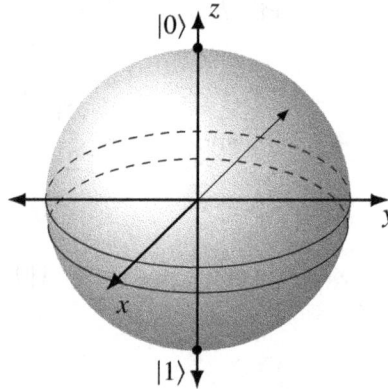

Figure 7.12: The Bloch sphere with a latitude below the equator

We have now seen three pairs of basis elements, and they go by different names:

Basis	Common name	Bloch sphere axis name
$\{|0\rangle, |1\rangle\}$	Computational	Z
$\{|+\rangle, |-\rangle\}$	Hadamard	X
$\{|i\rangle, |-i\rangle\} = \{|\circlearrowright\rangle, |\circlearrowleft\rangle\}$	Circular	Y

The Y basis is the same as the circular basis. In this case, we also have the alternative notation $|i\rangle = |\circlearrowright\rangle$ and $|-i\rangle = |\circlearrowleft\rangle$.

The eponymous sphere is named after Felix Bloch, the scientist shown in Figure 7.13, who won the 1962 Nobel Prize in Physics for his nuclear magnetic resonance (NMR) work. [18]

7.6 Professor Hadamard, meet Professor Pauli

Other than mapping the state of a qubit to a Bloch sphere and looking at it differently, what can you do with a qubit? This section looks at the operations, also called gates, which you can apply to a single qubit. Later, we expand our exploration to gates with multiple qubits

Figure 7.13: Felix Bloch (1905–1983) in 1961

as inputs and outputs. In Chapter 9, "Wiring Up the Circuits," we build circuits with these gates to implement algorithms.

Here, for example, is a circuit with one qubit initialized to $|0\rangle$ that performs one operation, **X**, and then measures the qubit. The result of the measurement is $|m_0\rangle$.

$$q_0: |0\rangle \boxed{\textbf{X}} \boxed{\measuredangle} \ |m_0\rangle = |1\rangle$$

Quantum gates are always reversible, but some other operations are not. Quantum gates correspond to unitary transformations. Measurement is irreversible, and so is the $|0\rangle$ **RESET** operation described in section 7.6.14.

When I include the measurement operation in a circuit in the next chapter and beyond, it looks like this:

$$\boxed{\measuredangle}$$

Measurement returns a $|0\rangle$ or $|1\rangle$. Mathematically, we do not worry about how it happens other than the probability.

Since a qubit state is a two-dimensional complex ket or vector, all quantum gates have 2-by-2 matrices with complex entries relative to some basis. This makes them small and very easy to manipulate. They are unitary matrices.

If A is a complex square matrix, then it is *unitary* if its adjoint $A^\dagger$ is also its inverse A^{-1}. Hence $AA^\dagger = A^\dagger A = I$. The columns of A are orthonormal, as are the rows.

$|\det(A)| = 1$. This equality says the **absolute value of the determinant** is 1, not that the determinant is 1. Since it is a unit in **C**, the determinant is $e^{\varphi i}$ for $0 \leq \varphi < 2\pi$.

The remainder of this section is a catalog of the most useful and commonly used 1-qubit quantum gates. As you will see, there is often more than one way to accomplish the same qubit state change. Why you would want to do so is the topic of Chapter 9, "Wiring Up the Circuits."

7.6.1 The quantum ID gate

The **ID** gate does nothing, but we typically employ it when constructing or drawing circuits to show something happening to every qubit at every step. We can represent it by multiplication by I_2, the 2-by-2 identity matrix. I_2 is both unitary and Hermitian.

When I include the **ID** gate in a circuit, it looks like this:

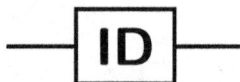

$$-\boxed{\text{ID}}-$$

We also put the **ID** gate in a circuit to indicate a place to pause or delay. Its presence allows, for example, researchers to calculate measurements of the decoherence of a qubit.

7.6.2 The quantum X gate

The **X** gate has the matrix

$$\sigma_x = \begin{bmatrix} 0 & 1 \\ 1 & 0 \end{bmatrix}$$

and this is the Pauli **X** matrix, named after Wolfgang Pauli, who won the Nobel Prize in Physics in 1945 (Figure 7.14). σ_x is both unitary and Hermitian. I often use the same name (in this case, **X**) for both the gate and its matrix in the standard basis kets. When we are not considering the matrix with respect to a specific basic, we refer to the **X** operator.

We also consider I_2 a Pauli matrix and refer to it as σ_0.

It has the property that

$$\sigma_x|0\rangle = |1\rangle \quad \text{and} \quad \sigma_x|1\rangle = |0\rangle .$$

Figure 7.14: The physicist Wolfgang Pauli, 1900–1958

It "flips" between $|0\rangle$ and $|1\rangle$. The classic **not** gate is

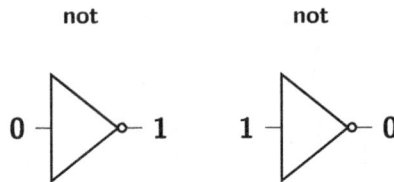

The **not** gate is a "bit flip," and, by analogy, we also say **X** is a bit flip.

For $|\psi\rangle = a|0\rangle + b|1\rangle$ in $\mathbf{C}^2$,

$$\mathbf{X}|\psi\rangle = b|0\rangle + a|1\rangle.$$

X reverses the probabilities of measuring $|0\rangle$ and $|1\rangle$.

In terms of the Bloch sphere, the **X** gate rotates by π around the x-axis. So, the poles are flipped, and points in the lower hemisphere move to the upper, and vice versa.

Since $\mathbf{X} \circ \mathbf{X} = \mathbf{ID}$, the **X** gate is its own inverse. This is reasonable because, in the classical case, it is also true that **not** $\circ$ **not** is the identity operation.

When we considered rotations, we saw that the matrix for $\mathbf{R}^3$ that does a rotation around the x-axis by θ radians works like

$$\begin{bmatrix} 1 & 0 & 0 \\ 0 & \cos(\theta) & -\sin(\theta) \\ 0 & \sin(\theta) & \cos(\theta) \end{bmatrix} \begin{bmatrix} x \\ y \\ z \end{bmatrix} = \begin{bmatrix} x \\ y\cos(\theta) - z\sin(\theta) \\ y\sin(\theta) + z\cos(\theta) \end{bmatrix}.$$

Plugging in $\theta = \pi$, the rotation matrix is

$$\begin{bmatrix} 1 & 0 & 0 \\ 0 & -1 & 0 \\ 0 & 0 & -1 \end{bmatrix}.$$

In $\mathbf{R}^3$ standard coordinates, $|0\rangle = (0,0,1)$ and $|1\rangle = (0,0,-1)$. Applying the rotation matrix, we get:

$$\begin{bmatrix} 1 & 0 & 0 \\ 0 & -1 & 0 \\ 0 & 0 & -1 \end{bmatrix} \begin{bmatrix} 0 \\ 0 \\ 1 \end{bmatrix} = \begin{bmatrix} 0 \\ 0 \\ -1 \end{bmatrix} \quad \text{and} \quad \begin{bmatrix} 1 & 0 & 0 \\ 0 & -1 & 0 \\ 0 & 0 & -1 \end{bmatrix} \begin{bmatrix} 0 \\ 0 \\ -1 \end{bmatrix} = \begin{bmatrix} 0 \\ 0 \\ 1 \end{bmatrix}.$$

You can see this flipped $|0\rangle$ and $|1\rangle$. What about $|+\rangle$ and $|-\rangle$?

$$\begin{bmatrix} 1 & 0 & 0 \\ 0 & -1 & 0 \\ 0 & 0 & -1 \end{bmatrix} \begin{bmatrix} 1 \\ 0 \\ 0 \end{bmatrix} = \begin{bmatrix} 1 \\ 0 \\ 0 \end{bmatrix} \quad \text{and} \quad \begin{bmatrix} 1 & 0 & 0 \\ 0 & -1 & 0 \\ 0 & 0 & -1 \end{bmatrix} \begin{bmatrix} -1 \\ 0 \\ 0 \end{bmatrix} = \begin{bmatrix} -1 \\ 0 \\ 0 \end{bmatrix}.$$

As you would expect from looking at the geometry of the Bloch sphere, it leaves these alone.

Exercise 7.18

What does the **X** gate do to $|i\rangle$ and $|-i\rangle$?

Exercise 7.19

What are the eigenvectors and eigenvalues of σ_x in $\mathbf{C}^2$ relative to the standard basis?

When I include the **X** gate in a circuit, it looks like this:

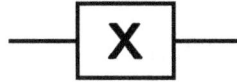

You may also see it shown in some literature and software tools as a circle surrounding a plus sign:

The horizontal line, called a *wire*, represents the qubit and its state. The input state enters on the left, the **X** unitary transformation is applied, and the new quantum state result comes out on the right side.

7.6.3   The quantum Z gate

The **Z** gate has the matrix

$$\sigma_z = \begin{bmatrix} 1 & 0 \\ 0 & -1 \end{bmatrix} = \begin{bmatrix} 1 & 0 \\ 0 & e^{\pi i} \end{bmatrix}$$

and this is the Pauli **Z** matrix. It rotates qubit states by π around the z-axis on the Bloch sphere. σ_z is both unitary and Hermitian.

The **Z** gate swaps $|+\rangle$ and $|-\rangle$ as well as $|i\rangle$ and $|-i\rangle$. It leaves $|0\rangle$ and $|1\rangle$ alone on the Bloch sphere.

Since **Z** ∘ **Z** = **ID**, the **Z** gate is its own inverse. If you rotate by π and then rotate by π again, you end up back where you started.

For $|\psi\rangle = a|0\rangle + b|1\rangle$ in $\mathbf{C}^2$,

$$\mathbf{Z}|\psi\rangle = \mathbf{Z}\left(a|0\rangle + b|1\rangle\right) = a|0\rangle - b|1\rangle.$$

The probabilities of measuring $|0\rangle$ and $|1\rangle$ do not change after applying **Z**.

In $\mathbf{C}^2$, σ_z has eigenvalues +1 and −1 for eigenvectors $|0\rangle$ and $|1\rangle$, respectively. Per section 7.3.4, **Z** or σ_z is the observable for the standard computational basis $|0\rangle$ and $|1\rangle$.

Remember that $|1\rangle$ and $-|1\rangle = e^{\pi i}|1\rangle$ in $\mathbf{C}^2$ map to the same point we are also calling $|1\rangle$ on the Bloch sphere because they differ only by multiplication by a unit, $-1 = e^{\pi i}$. If we express

$$|\psi\rangle = r_1 e^{\theta_1 i}|0\rangle + r_2 e^{\theta_2 i}|1\rangle,$$

then

$$
\begin{aligned}
\sigma_z|\psi\rangle &= r_1 e^{\theta_1 i}|0\rangle - r_2 e^{\theta_2 i}|1\rangle \\
&= r_1 e^{\theta_1 i}|0\rangle + e^{\pi i} r_2 e^{\theta_2 i}|1\rangle \\
&= r_1 e^{\theta_1 i}|0\rangle + r_2 e^{(\pi+\theta_2)i}|1\rangle \\
&= e^{\theta_1 i}\left(r_1|0\rangle + r_2 e^{(\pi+\theta_2-\theta_1)i}|1\rangle \right).
\end{aligned}
$$

We change the relative phase of $|\psi\rangle$ to π plus that relative phase, adjusted to be between 0 and 2π. This is a *phase flip*, and we call $\mathbf{Z}$ a phase flip gate. Since it reverses the sign of the second amplitude, it is also called a *sign flip* gate.

When I include the $\mathbf{Z}$ gate in a circuit, it looks like this:

$$-\boxed{\mathbf{Z}}-$$

Exercise 7.20

Show by calculation that $\mathbf{X} \circ \mathbf{Z} = -\mathbf{Z} \circ \mathbf{X}$.

7.6.4 The quantum Y gate

The **Y** gate has the matrix

$$
\sigma_y = \begin{bmatrix} 0 & -i \\ i & 0 \end{bmatrix} = i \begin{bmatrix} 0 & -1 \\ 1 & 0 \end{bmatrix}
$$

and this is the Pauli **Y** matrix. It rotates qubit states by π around the y-axis on the Bloch sphere. σ_y is both unitary and Hermitian.

It swaps $|0\rangle$ and $|1\rangle$ and so is a bit flip. It also interchanges $|+\rangle$ and $|-\rangle$ but leaves $|i\rangle$ and $|-i\rangle$ alone.

Since $\mathbf{Y} \circ \mathbf{Y} = \mathbf{ID}$, the **Y** gate is its own inverse.

For $|\psi\rangle = a|0\rangle + b|1\rangle$ in $\mathbf{C}^2$,

$$\begin{aligned}
\mathbf{Y}|\psi\rangle &= \mathbf{Y}\left(a|0\rangle + b|1\rangle\right) \\
&= -bi|0\rangle + ai|1\rangle \\
&= -i\left(b|0\rangle - a|1\rangle\right) \\
&= e^{\frac{3\pi}{2}i}\left(b|0\rangle - a|1\rangle\right).
\end{aligned}$$

From this, we can see that $\mathbf{Y}$ simultaneously does a bit flip and a phase flip. In $\mathbf{C}^2$, σ_y has eigenvalues $+1$ and -1 for eigenvectors $|i\rangle$ and $|-i\rangle$, respectively.

If $|\psi\rangle = a|0\rangle + b|1\rangle$ in $\mathbf{C}^2$, then a bit flip interchanges the coefficients of $|0\rangle$ and $|1\rangle$. A phase flip changes the sign of the coefficient of $|1\rangle$. A simultaneous bit and phase flip does both:

$$a|0\rangle + b|1\rangle \mapsto b|0\rangle - a|1\rangle.$$

When I include the $\mathbf{Y}$ gate in a circuit, it looks like this:

Exercise 7.21

What is the 3-by-3 rotation matrix for the $\mathbf{Y}$ gate?

Exercise 7.22

Show by calculation that $\mathbf{X} \circ \mathbf{Y} = -\mathbf{Y} \circ \mathbf{X}$ and $\mathbf{Z} \circ \mathbf{Y} = -\mathbf{Y} \circ \mathbf{Z}$.

7.6.5 The quantum H gate

The $\mathbf{H}$ gate, or $\mathbf{H}^{\otimes 1}$ or Hadamard gate, has the matrix

$$\mathbf{H} = \begin{bmatrix} \frac{\sqrt{2}}{2} & \frac{\sqrt{2}}{2} \\ \frac{\sqrt{2}}{2} & -\frac{\sqrt{2}}{2} \end{bmatrix} = \frac{\sqrt{2}}{2}\begin{bmatrix} 1 & 1 \\ 1 & -1 \end{bmatrix}$$

operating on $\mathbf{C}^2$.

By matrix multiplication,

$$\mathbf{H}|0\rangle = \frac{\sqrt{2}}{2}(|0\rangle + |1\rangle) = |+\rangle \quad \text{and} \quad \mathbf{H}|1\rangle = \frac{\sqrt{2}}{2}(|0\rangle - |1\rangle) = |-\rangle.$$

By linearity,

$$\mathbf{H}|+\rangle = \mathbf{H}\left(\frac{\sqrt{2}}{2}(|0\rangle + |1\rangle)\right) = \frac{\sqrt{2}}{2}(\mathbf{H}|0\rangle + \mathbf{H}|1\rangle)$$

$$= \frac{\sqrt{2}}{2}\left(\frac{\sqrt{2}}{2}(|0\rangle + |1\rangle) + \frac{\sqrt{2}}{2}(|0\rangle - |1\rangle)\right) = \frac{1}{2}(|0\rangle + |1\rangle + |0\rangle - |1\rangle) = |0\rangle.$$

Exercise 7.23

Show that $\mathbf{H}|-\rangle = |1\rangle$.

The Hadamard gate, named after Jacques Hadamard (Figure 7.15), is one of the most frequently used gates in quantum computing. **H** is often the first gate applied in a circuit. When you read "put the qubit in superposition," it usually means "take the qubit initialized in the $|0\rangle$ state and apply **H** to it."

Figure 7.15: The mathematician Jacques Hadamard, 1865–1963

The Hadamard matrix is the change of basis matrix from $\{|0\rangle, |1\rangle\}$ to $\{|+\rangle, |-\rangle\}$. Since $\mathbf{H} \circ \mathbf{H} = \mathbf{ID}$, the **H** gate is its own inverse.

A change of basis from the computational basis $\{|0\rangle, |1\rangle\}$ to the Hadamard basis $\{|+\rangle, |-\rangle\}$ changes a bit flip **X** to a phase flip **Z**.

When I include the **H** gate in a circuit, it looks like this:

$$\boxed{\text{H}}$$

Consider $|b\rangle$, where b is 0 or 1. The expression $(-1)^b$ is 1 when $b = 0$ and -1 when $b = 1$.

For our **H** gate, we look at

$$\text{H}|0\rangle = \frac{\sqrt{2}}{2}(|0\rangle + |1\rangle) \quad \text{and} \quad \text{H}|1\rangle = \frac{\sqrt{2}}{2}(|0\rangle - |1\rangle)$$

and notice that

$$\text{H}|b\rangle = \frac{\sqrt{2}}{2}\left(|0\rangle + (-1)^b|1\rangle\right).$$

When $b = 0$, we have $|0\rangle$ going to $\frac{\sqrt{2}}{2}(|0\rangle + |1\rangle)$. For $b = 1$, we end up with $\frac{\sqrt{2}}{2}(|0\rangle - |1\rangle)$.

Exercise 7.24

Using matrix calculations, show that $\text{X} = \text{H} \circ \text{Z} \circ \text{H}$.

Exercise 7.25

What is $\text{H} \circ \text{X} \circ \text{H}$?

Exercise 7.26

What is the 3-by-3 matrix for the **H** gate on the Bloch sphere? It is the product of two 3-by-3 rotation matrices. What are they?

7.6.6   The quantum R_φ^z gates

We can generalize the phase-changing behavior of the **Z** gate by noting

$$\sigma_z = \begin{bmatrix} 1 & 0 \\ 0 & -1 \end{bmatrix} = \begin{bmatrix} 1 & 0 \\ 0 & e^{\pi i} \end{bmatrix} = \begin{bmatrix} 1 & 0 \\ 0 & e^{\varphi i} \end{bmatrix} \text{ where } \varphi = \pi.$$

This last form is the template for the collection of gates given the name $\mathbf{R}_\varphi^z$:

$$\mathbf{R}_\varphi^z = \begin{bmatrix} 1 & 0 \\ 0 & e^{\varphi i} \end{bmatrix} = \begin{bmatrix} 1 & 0 \\ 0 & \cos(\varphi) + \sin(\varphi)i \end{bmatrix}$$

$$\mathbf{R}_\varphi^z |0\rangle = |0\rangle$$

$$\mathbf{R}_\varphi^z |1\rangle = e^{\varphi i} |1\rangle = (\cos(\varphi) + \sin(\varphi)i)\,|1\rangle$$

$|1\rangle$ is an eigenvector of $\mathbf{R}_\varphi^z$ with eigenvalue $e^{\varphi i}$.

This collection is infinite as φ can take on any radian value greater than or equal to 0 and less than 2π. These gates change the phase of a qubit state by φ. This is a parameterized z-rotation gate, with φ being the parameter.

Exercise 7.27

What is the 3-by-3 rotation matrix for $\mathbf{R}_\varphi^z$? For **Z**?

The inverse of $\mathbf{R}_\varphi^z$ is $\mathbf{R}_{2\pi-\varphi}^z$. $\mathbf{R}_0^z = \mathbf{ID}$. $\mathbf{R}_\pi^z = \mathbf{Z}$.

When I include the $\mathbf{R}_\varphi^z$ gate in a circuit for a particular value of φ, it looks like this:

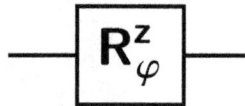

Since

$$\begin{bmatrix} 1 & 0 \\ 0 & e^{\varphi i} \end{bmatrix} = e^{\frac{\varphi i}{2}} \begin{bmatrix} e^{-\frac{\varphi i}{2}} & 0 \\ 0 & e^{\frac{\varphi i}{2}} \end{bmatrix},$$

an alternative form of the matrix for $\mathbf{R}_\varphi^z$ up to a global phase change is

$$\mathbf{R}_\varphi^z = \begin{bmatrix} e^{-\frac{\varphi i}{2}} & 0 \\ 0 & e^{\frac{\varphi i}{2}} \end{bmatrix} = \cos\left(\frac{\varphi}{2}\right) I_2 - \sin\left(\frac{\varphi}{2}\right) i\sigma_z .$$

$e^{\frac{\varphi i}{2}}$ is a complex unit, and multiplication by it is not observable when we measure.

7.6.7 The quantum S gate

The **S** gate is a shorthand for $\mathbf{R}_{\frac{\pi}{2}}^z$. After applying, we adjust the phase to be greater than or equal to 0 and less than 2π:

$$\mathbf{S} = \mathbf{R}_{\frac{\pi}{2}}^z = \begin{bmatrix} 1 & 0 \\ 0 & e^{\frac{\pi i}{2}} \end{bmatrix} = \begin{bmatrix} 1 & 0 \\ 0 & i \end{bmatrix}$$

$$\mathbf{S}|0\rangle = \mathbf{R}_{\frac{\pi}{2}}^z|0\rangle = |0\rangle$$

$$\mathbf{S}|1\rangle = \mathbf{R}_{\frac{\pi}{2}}^z|1\rangle = e^{\frac{\pi i}{2}}|1\rangle = i|1\rangle$$

$|1\rangle$ is an eigenvector of **S** with eigenvalue i.

Exercise 7.28

What is the 3-by-3 rotation matrix for the **S** gate?

When I include the **S** gate in a circuit, it looks like this:

Traditionally and confusingly, the **S** gate is also known as the $\frac{\pi}{4}$ gate. This is because we can express the matrix in this way:

$$\begin{bmatrix} 1 & 0 \\ 0 & e^{\frac{\pi i}{2}} \end{bmatrix} = e^{\frac{\pi i}{4}} \begin{bmatrix} e^{-\frac{\pi i}{4}} & 0 \\ 0 & e^{\frac{\pi i}{4}} \end{bmatrix} .$$

The unit factor $e^{\frac{\pi i}{4}}$ in front does not have an observable effect on the quantum state of the result of applying **S**. Some authors call **S** "the phase gate," but I won't.

7.6.8 The quantum $\mathbf{S}^\dagger$ gate

The $\mathbf{S}^\dagger$ (pronounced "S dagger") gate is a shorthand for $\mathbf{R}^z_{\frac{3\pi}{2}} = \mathbf{R}^z_{-\frac{\pi}{2}}$. After applying, we adjust the phase to be greater than or equal to 0 and less than 2π:

$$\mathbf{S}^\dagger = \mathbf{R}^z_{\frac{3\pi}{2}} = \begin{bmatrix} 1 & 0 \\ 0 & e^{\frac{3\pi i}{2}} \end{bmatrix} = \begin{bmatrix} 1 & 0 \\ 0 & -i \end{bmatrix}$$

$$\mathbf{S}^\dagger|0\rangle = \mathbf{R}^z_{\frac{3\pi}{2}}|0\rangle = |0\rangle$$

$$\mathbf{S}^\dagger|1\rangle = \mathbf{R}^z_{\frac{3\pi}{2}}|1\rangle = e^{\frac{3\pi i}{2}}|1\rangle = -i|1\rangle$$

$|1\rangle$ is an eigenvector of $\mathbf{S}^\dagger$ with eigenvalue $-i$.

The gate gets its name because the matrix for $\mathbf{S}^\dagger$ is the adjoint of the $\mathbf{S}$ matrix:

$$\begin{bmatrix} 1 & 0 \\ 0 & i \end{bmatrix}^\dagger = \begin{bmatrix} 1 & 0 \\ 0 & -i \end{bmatrix}.$$

Exercise 7.29

What is the 3-by-3 rotation matrix for the $\mathbf{S}^\dagger$?

When I include the $\mathbf{S}^\dagger$ gate in a circuit, it looks like this:

7.6.9 The quantum T gate

The **T** gate is a shorthand for $\mathbf{R}^z_{\frac{\pi}{4}}$. After applying, we adjust the phase to be greater than or equal to 0 and less than 2π:

$$\mathbf{T} = \mathbf{R}^z_{\frac{\pi}{4}} = \begin{bmatrix} 1 & 0 \\ 0 & e^{\frac{\pi i}{4}} \end{bmatrix} = \begin{bmatrix} 1 & 0 \\ 0 & \cos\left(\frac{\pi}{4}\right) + \sin\left(\frac{\pi}{4}\right)i \end{bmatrix} = \begin{bmatrix} 1 & 0 \\ 0 & \frac{\sqrt{2}}{2} + \frac{\sqrt{2}}{2}i \end{bmatrix}$$

$$\mathbf{T}|0\rangle = \mathbf{R}^z_{\frac{\pi}{4}}|0\rangle = |0\rangle$$

$$\mathbf{T}|1\rangle = \mathbf{R}^z_{\frac{\pi}{4}}|1\rangle = e^{\frac{\pi i}{4}}|1\rangle = \left(\cos\left(\frac{\pi}{4}\right) + \sin\left(\frac{\pi}{4}\right)i\right)|1\rangle = \left(\frac{\sqrt{2}}{2} + \frac{\sqrt{2}}{2}i\right)|1\rangle$$

$|1\rangle$ is an eigenvector of **T** with eigenvalue $\frac{\sqrt{2}}{2} + \frac{\sqrt{2}}{2}i$.

Exercise 7.30

What is the 3-by-3 rotation matrix for the **T** gate?

We can get the **S** by applying the **T** twice: $\textbf{S} = \textbf{T} \circ \textbf{T}$.

When I include the **T** gate in a circuit, it looks like this:

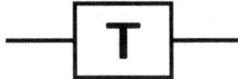

The **T** gate is also known as the $\frac{\pi}{8}$ gate. We can write its matrix as

$$\begin{bmatrix} 1 & 0 \\ 0 & e^{\frac{\pi i}{4}} \end{bmatrix} = e^{\frac{\pi i}{8}} \begin{bmatrix} e^{-\frac{\pi i}{8}} & 0 \\ 0 & e^{\frac{\pi i}{8}} \end{bmatrix}.$$

The unit factor $e^{\frac{\pi i}{8}}$ in front does not have an observable effect on the quantum state of the result of applying **T**.

7.6.10   The quantum $\textbf{T}^\dagger$ gate

The $\textbf{T}^\dagger$ gate (pronounced "T dagger") is a shorthand for $\textbf{R}^z_{\frac{7\pi}{4}} = \textbf{R}^z_{-\frac{\pi}{4}}$. After applying, we adjust the phase to be greater than or equal to 0 and less than 2π:

$$\textbf{T}^\dagger = \textbf{R}^z_{\frac{7\pi}{4}} = \begin{bmatrix} 1 & 0 \\ 0 & e^{\frac{7\pi i}{2}} \end{bmatrix} = \begin{bmatrix} 1 & 0 \\ 0 & \cos\left(\frac{7\pi}{4}\right) + \sin\left(\frac{7\pi}{4}\right)i \end{bmatrix} = \begin{bmatrix} 1 & 0 \\ 0 & \frac{\sqrt{2}}{2} - \frac{\sqrt{2}}{2}i \end{bmatrix}$$

$$\textbf{T}^\dagger|0\rangle = \textbf{R}^z_{\frac{7\pi}{2}}|0\rangle = |0\rangle$$

$$\textbf{T}^\dagger|1\rangle = \textbf{R}^z_{\frac{7\pi}{2}}|1\rangle = \left(\cos\left(\frac{7\pi}{4}\right) + \sin\left(\frac{7\pi}{4}\right)i\right)|1\rangle = \left(\frac{\sqrt{2}}{2} - \frac{\sqrt{2}}{2}i\right)|1\rangle$$

$|1\rangle$ is an eigenvector of $\textbf{T}^\dagger$ with eigenvalue $\frac{\sqrt{2}}{2} - \frac{\sqrt{2}}{2}i$.

It gets its name because the matrix for $\textbf{T}^\dagger$ is the adjoint of the **T** matrix:

$$\begin{bmatrix} 1 & 0 \\ 0 & \frac{\sqrt{2}}{2} + \frac{\sqrt{2}}{2}i \end{bmatrix}^\dagger = \begin{bmatrix} 1 & 0 \\ 0 & \frac{\sqrt{2}}{2} - \frac{\sqrt{2}}{2}i \end{bmatrix}.$$

Exercise 7.31

What is the 3-by-3 rotation matrix for the $\mathbf{T}^\dagger$ gate?

We can get the $\mathbf{S}^\dagger$ by applying the $\mathbf{T}^\dagger$ twice: $\mathbf{S}^\dagger = \mathbf{T}^\dagger \circ \mathbf{T}^\dagger$.

When I include the $\mathbf{T}^\dagger$ gate in a circuit, it looks like this:

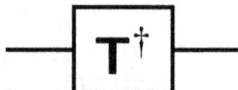

$$\boxed{\mathbf{T}^\dagger}$$

7.6.11   The quantum $\mathbf{Ph}_\varphi$ global phase gate

Our next 1-qubit parameterized gate is the global phase gate $\mathbf{Ph}_\varphi$:

$$\mathbf{Ph}_\varphi = \begin{bmatrix} e^{\varphi i} & 0 \\ 0 & e^{\varphi i} \end{bmatrix} = e^{\varphi i} \begin{bmatrix} 1 & 0 \\ 0 & 1 \end{bmatrix} = e^{\varphi i} I_2$$

$$\mathbf{Ph}_\varphi |0\rangle = e^{\varphi i} |0\rangle$$

$$\mathbf{Ph}_\varphi |1\rangle = e^{\varphi i} |1\rangle$$

$\mathbf{Ph}_\varphi$ has no observable effect on the qubit when it is measured.

Exercise 7.32

What gate do you get when $\varphi = 0$?

Exercise 7.33

How does this differ from the $\mathbf{R}^z_\varphi$ gate?

When I include the $\mathbf{Ph}_\varphi$ gate in a circuit, it looks like this:

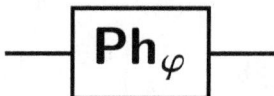

$$\boxed{\mathbf{Ph}_\varphi}$$

7.6.12 The quantum R_φ^x and R_φ^y gates

Just as $\mathbf{R}_\varphi^z$ is an arbitrary rotation around the z-axis, we can define gates that rotate around the x- and y-axes:

$$\mathbf{R}_\varphi^x = \begin{bmatrix} \cos\left(\frac{\varphi}{2}\right) & -\sin\left(\frac{\varphi}{2}\right)i \\ -\sin\left(\frac{\varphi}{2}\right)i & \cos\left(\frac{\varphi}{2}\right) \end{bmatrix} = \cos\left(\frac{\varphi}{2}\right)I_2 - \cos\left(\frac{\varphi}{2}\right)i\sigma_x$$

and

$$\mathbf{R}_\varphi^y = \begin{bmatrix} \cos\left(\frac{\varphi}{2}\right) & -\sin\left(\frac{\varphi}{2}\right) \\ \sin\left(\frac{\varphi}{2}\right) & \cos\left(\frac{\varphi}{2}\right) \end{bmatrix} = \cos\left(\frac{\varphi}{2}\right)I_2 - \cos\left(\frac{\varphi}{2}\right)i\sigma_y .$$

These are parameterized x- and y-rotation gates, with φ being the parameter.

When I include these gates in circuits, they look like this:

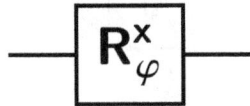

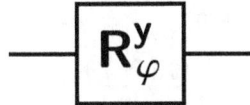

Exercise 7.34

Show that $\mathbf{H} = \mathbf{X} \circ \mathbf{R}_{\frac{\pi}{2}}^y$.

7.6.13 The quantum $\sqrt{\text{NOT}}$ gate

Another gate used in the quantum computing literature is the "square root of **NOT**" gate. It has the matrix

$$\frac{1}{2}\begin{bmatrix} 1+i & 1-i \\ 1-i & 1+i \end{bmatrix} = \begin{bmatrix} \frac{1}{2}+\frac{1}{2}i & \frac{1}{2}-\frac{1}{2}i \\ \frac{1}{2}-\frac{1}{2}i & \frac{1}{2}+\frac{1}{2}i \end{bmatrix} .$$

Squaring this, $\sqrt{\text{NOT}} \circ \sqrt{\text{NOT}}$, we get

$$\frac{1}{2}\begin{bmatrix} 1+i & 1-i \\ 1-i & 1+i \end{bmatrix} \times \frac{1}{2}\begin{bmatrix} 1+i & 1-i \\ 1-i & 1+i \end{bmatrix} = \begin{bmatrix} 0 & 1 \\ 1 & 0 \end{bmatrix} = \textbf{X}.$$

The **X** gate is the quantum version of **not**, and that's how this gate gets its name.

Exercise 7.35

Show that $\sqrt{\text{NOT}}$ is unitary. What is its determinant? What does it do to $|0\rangle$ and $|1\rangle$?

When I include this gate in a circuit, it looks like this:

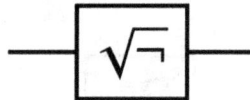

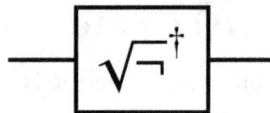

$$-\boxed{\sqrt{\neg}}-$$

The adjoint of this gate has the matrix

$$\frac{1}{2}\begin{bmatrix} 1-i & 1+i \\ 1+i & 1-i \end{bmatrix} = \begin{bmatrix} \frac{1}{2}-\frac{1}{2}i & \frac{1}{2}+\frac{1}{2}i \\ \frac{1}{2}+\frac{1}{2}i & \frac{1}{2}-\frac{1}{2}i \end{bmatrix}.$$

Exercise 7.36

What is the square of the adjoint of the "square root of **NOT**" gate?

When I include this gate in a circuit, it looks like this:

$$-\boxed{\sqrt{\neg}^{\dagger}}-$$

Exercise 7.37

What are the matrices for the $\sqrt{\textbf{Y}}$ and $\sqrt{\textbf{Z}}$ gates?

7.6.14 The quantum $|0\rangle$ RESET operation

Though it is not a reversible unitary operation, and hence, not a gate, some quantum computing software environments allow you to reset a qubit in the middle of a circuit to $|0\rangle$. This operation, denoted $|0\rangle$ **RESET**, is convenient if you use a qubit as a temporary scratchpad for multiple values within an algorithm.

This operation may make your code nonportable across different quantum computing architectures and software development kits.

When I include this operation in a circuit, it looks like this:

7.7 Gates and unitary matrices

The collection of all 2-by-2 unitary matrices (section 5.8) with entries in **C** form a group under multiplication called the *unitary group* of degree 2. We denote it by $\mathbf{U}(2, \mathbf{C})$. It is a subgroup of $\mathbf{GL}(2, \mathbf{C})$, the general linear group of degree 2 over **C**.

Every 1-qubit gate corresponds to such a unitary matrix. We can create all 2-by-2 unitary matrices from the identity and Pauli matrices.

We can write any $\mathbf{U}(2, \mathbf{C})$ as a product of a complex unit times a linear combination of unitary matrices

$$U = e^{\theta i}\left(c_{I_2}I_2 + c_{\sigma_x}\sigma_x + c_{\sigma_y}\sigma_y + c_{\sigma_z}\sigma_z\right)$$

with

$$I_2 = \sigma_0 = \begin{bmatrix} 1 & 0 \\ 0 & 1 \end{bmatrix} \quad \sigma_x = \begin{bmatrix} 0 & 1 \\ 1 & 0 \end{bmatrix} \quad \sigma_y = \begin{bmatrix} 0 & -i \\ i & 0 \end{bmatrix} \quad \sigma_z = \begin{bmatrix} 1 & 0 \\ 0 & -1 \end{bmatrix},$$

where we have the following definitions, properties, and identities:

- $0 \le \theta < 2\pi$
- c_{I_2} is in **R**
- $c_{\sigma_x}, c_{\sigma_y}$, and c_{σ_z} are in **C**
- $|c_{I_2}|^2 + |c_{\sigma_x}|^2 + |c_{\sigma_y}|^2 + |c_{\sigma_z}|^2 = 1$

and

$$\text{Re}\left(c_{I_2}\overline{c_{\sigma_x}}\right) + \text{Im}\left(c_{\sigma_y}\overline{c_{\sigma_z}}\right) = 0$$

$$\text{Re}\left(c_{I_2}\overline{c_{\sigma_y}}\right) + \text{Im}\left(c_{\sigma_x}\overline{c_{\sigma_z}}\right) = 0$$

$$\text{Re}\left(c_{I_2}\overline{c_{\sigma_z}}\right) + \text{Im}\left(c_{\sigma_x}\overline{c_{\sigma_y}}\right) = 0$$

The complex unit only affects the global phase of the qubit state and so is not observable. We do not see its effect when we measure because it does not affect the probability of seeing one thing or another. [64]

Exercise 7.38

What does this mean in terms of the **ID**, **X**, **Y**, and **Z** gates?

In section 12.3, we will see an important connection between Hermitian and unitary matrices. For now, we can state properties of 2-by-2 Hermitian matrices that are less restrictive than the properties for unitary matrices stated above.

We can write a complex 2-by-2 Hermitian matrix H as a real linear combination of the Pauli matrices

$$H = c_{I_2}I_2 + c_{\sigma_x}\sigma_x + c_{\sigma_y}\sigma_y + c_{\sigma_z}\sigma_z$$

with $I_2 = \sigma_0$, the 2-by-2 identity matrix; σ_x, σ_y, and σ_z the Pauli matrices; and c_{I_2}, c_{σ_x}, c_{σ_y}, and c_{σ_z} scalars in $\mathbf{R}$.

Exercise 7.39

Let

$$H = \begin{bmatrix} a & c \\ \overline{c} & b \end{bmatrix}$$

be a 2-by-2 Hermitian matrix, with a and b in $\mathbf{R}$ and c in $\mathbf{C}$. Show that

$$H = \frac{a}{2}\left(I_2 + \sigma_z\right) + \frac{b}{2}\left(I_2 - \sigma_z\right) + \text{Re}(c)\sigma_x - \text{Im}(c)\sigma_y.$$

This demonstrates that I_2, σ_x, σ_y, and σ_z are a basis of the *real* vector space of 2-by-2 *complex* Hermitian matrices.

7.8 Summary

The quantum states of a qubit are the unit vectors in $\mathbf{C}^2$, where we identify two states as equivalent if they differ only by a multiple of a complex unit. To better visualize actions on a qubit, we introduced the Bloch sphere in $\mathbf{R}^3$ and showed where special orthonormal bases map onto the sphere.

Any new idea seems to deserve its own notation, and we did not disappoint when we introduced Dirac's bra-ket representation of vectors. This significantly simplifies calculation when working with multiple qubits.

Given the ket form of qubit states, we introduced the standard 1-qubit gate operations. In the classical case in section 2.4, we could only perform one operation on a single bit, **not**. In the quantum case, there are many (in fact, an infinite number) of single-qubit operations.

We next look at how to work with two or more qubits and the quantum gates that operate on them. We also introduce entanglement, an essential notion from quantum mechanics.

8

Two Qubits, Three

Not only is the Universe stranger than we think, it is stranger than we can think.

– Werner Heisenberg [106]

In the previous chapter, we defined qubits and saw what we could do with just one of them. Things now start to get exponential with every additional qubit added because entanglement allows the size of the working state space to double.

This chapter is about how multiple qubits can behave together and then building a collection of tools to manipulate those qubits. These include the concept of entanglement, a requirement for quantum computing. We also examine important 2-qubit gates such as **CNOT** and **SWAP**. This will lead us into Chapter 9, ''Wiring Up the Circuits,'' and Chapter 10, ''From Circuits to Algorithms,'' where we look at algorithms and build circuits that use this machinery.

I explain the uncertain fate of Schrödinger's cat before we conclude this chapter.

All vector spaces considered in this chapter are over **C**, the field of complex numbers introduced in section 3.9. All bases are orthonormal unless otherwise specified.

Topics covered in this chapter

8.1 Tensor products

In this section, I introduce the linear algebra construction of a *tensor product*. If the direct sum seems to concatenate two vector spaces, then the tensor product interleaves them. In the first case, if we start with dimensions n and m, we end up with a new vector space of $n + m$ dimensions. For the tensor product, we get nm dimensions.

We can quickly get vector spaces with high dimensions through this multiplicative effect. We must use our algebraic intuition and tools more than our geometric ones.

The initial construction is straight linear algebra, but we specialize it later to quantum computing and working with multiple qubits.

Vector spaces

Let V and W be two finite-dimensional vector spaces over $\mathbf{F}$. We define a new vector space $V \otimes W$, pronounced "V tensor W" or "the tensor product of V and W," as the vector space generated by addition and scalar multiplication of all formal objects $\mathbf{v} \otimes \mathbf{w}$ for each $\mathbf{v}$ in V and $\mathbf{w}$ in W.

> Note I say "generated by." Not all vectors in $V \otimes W$ look like $\mathbf{v} \otimes \mathbf{w}$ for some $\mathbf{v}$ in V and $\mathbf{w}$ in W. For example, a vector might have the form $2\mathbf{v}_1 \otimes \mathbf{w}_3 + 9\mathbf{v}_4\mathbf{w}_7$.

If a is a scalar in $\mathbf{F}$, then

$$a(\mathbf{v} \otimes \mathbf{w}) = (a\mathbf{v}) \otimes \mathbf{w} = \mathbf{v} \otimes (a\mathbf{w}).$$

For $\mathbf{v}$ in V and $\mathbf{w}_1$ and $\mathbf{w}_2$ in W,

$$\mathbf{v} \otimes (\mathbf{w}_1 + \mathbf{w}_2) = \mathbf{v} \otimes \mathbf{w}_1 + \mathbf{v} \otimes \mathbf{w}_2.$$

For $\mathbf{v}_1$ and $\mathbf{v}_2$ in V and $\mathbf{w}$ in W,

$$(\mathbf{v}_1 + \mathbf{v}_2) \otimes \mathbf{w} = \mathbf{v}_1 \otimes \mathbf{w} + \mathbf{v}_2 \otimes \mathbf{w} \,.$$

If $f : V \oplus W \to U$ is a bilinear map, then $f^{\otimes} : V \otimes W \to U$ is a linear map defined by

$$f^{\otimes}(\mathbf{v} \otimes \mathbf{w}) = f(\mathbf{v}, \mathbf{w}) \,.$$

If $\{\mathbf{v}_1, \ldots, \mathbf{v}_n\}$ and $\{\mathbf{w}_1, \ldots, \mathbf{w}_m\}$ are bases for V and W, then

$$\mathbf{v}_1 \otimes \mathbf{w}_1, \mathbf{v}_1 \otimes \mathbf{w}_2, \ldots, \mathbf{v}_1 \otimes \mathbf{w}_m,$$

$$\vdots$$

$$\mathbf{v}_n \otimes \mathbf{w}_1, \mathbf{v}_n \otimes \mathbf{w}_2, \ldots, \mathbf{v}_n \otimes \mathbf{w}_m$$

are basis vectors of $V \otimes W$. There are $n \times m$ of them, and this is the dimension of $V \otimes W$.

For two additional vectors spaces X and Y over $\mathbf{F}$, if

$$f : V \to X \quad \text{and} \quad g : W \to Y$$

are linear maps, then so is

$$f \otimes g : V \otimes W \to X \otimes Y \,,$$

where we define

$$(f \otimes g)(\mathbf{v} \otimes \mathbf{w}) = f(\mathbf{v}) \otimes g(\mathbf{w}) \,.$$

Exercise 8.1

Confirm $f \otimes g$ is a linear map.

If f and g are both monomorphisms, so is $f \otimes g$. If they are both epimorphisms, so is $f \otimes g$.

Matrices

If we have

$$A = \begin{bmatrix} a_{1,1} & a_{1,2} \\ a_{2,1} & a_{2,2} \end{bmatrix} \quad \text{and} \quad B = \begin{bmatrix} b_{1,1} & b_{1,2} \\ b_{2,1} & b_{2,2} \end{bmatrix},$$

then the regular matrix product is

$$AB = \begin{bmatrix} a_{1,1}b_{1,1} + a_{1,2}b_{2,1} & a_{1,1}b_{1,2} + a_{1,2}b_{2,2} \\ a_{2,1}b_{1,1} + a_{2,2}b_{2,1} & a_{2,1}b_{1,2} + a_{2,2}b_{2,2} \end{bmatrix}.$$

The matrix *tensor* "$\otimes$", also called the *Kronecker product*, for 2-by-2 matrices is

$$A \otimes B = \begin{bmatrix} a_{1,1}B & a_{1,2}B \\ a_{2,1}B & a_{2,2}B \end{bmatrix}$$

$$= \begin{bmatrix} a_{1,1}\begin{bmatrix} b_{1,1} & b_{1,2} \\ b_{2,1} & b_{2,2} \end{bmatrix} & a_{1,2}\begin{bmatrix} b_{1,1} & b_{1,2} \\ b_{2,1} & b_{2,2} \end{bmatrix} \\ a_{2,1}\begin{bmatrix} b_{1,1} & b_{1,2} \\ b_{2,1} & b_{2,2} \end{bmatrix} & a_{2,2}\begin{bmatrix} b_{1,1} & b_{1,2} \\ b_{2,1} & b_{2,2} \end{bmatrix} \end{bmatrix}$$

$$= \begin{bmatrix} a_{1,1}b_{1,1} & a_{1,1}b_{1,2} & a_{1,2}b_{1,1} & a_{1,2}b_{1,2} \\ a_{1,1}b_{2,1} & a_{1,1}b_{2,2} & a_{1,2}b_{2,1} & a_{1,2}b_{2,2} \\ a_{2,1}b_{1,1} & a_{2,1}b_{1,2} & a_{2,2}b_{1,1} & a_{2,2}b_{1,2} \\ a_{2,1}b_{2,1} & a_{2,1}b_{2,2} & a_{2,2}b_{2,1} & a_{2,2}b_{2,2} \end{bmatrix},$$

and this is with respect to the $e_1 \otimes e_1$, $e_1 \otimes e_2$, $e_2 \otimes e_1$, and $e_2 \otimes e_2$ basis.

I'm abusing the notation in the second line of the expansion of $A \otimes B$ to show we get a block of elements in the new matrix by multiplying an entry of the first by every entry in the second. The same kind of construction rules applies to larger matrices.

Tensor products combine nicely with traditional products. For two additional matrices C and D,

$$(A \otimes B)(C \otimes D) = AC \otimes BD.$$

Exercise 8.2

For matrices A and B, show that $(A \otimes B)^\mathsf{T} = A^\mathsf{T} \otimes B^\mathsf{T}$. If A and B are invertible matrices, show that $(A \otimes B)^{-1} = A^{-1} \otimes B^{-1}$.

Exercise 8.3

For complex matrices A and B, show that

$$\overline{A \otimes B} = \overline{A} \otimes \overline{B} \quad \text{and} \quad (A \otimes B)^\dagger = A^\dagger \otimes B^\dagger.$$

If A and B are Hermitian matrices, show that $A \otimes B$ is Hermitian. If A and B are unitary matrices, show that $A \otimes B$ is unitary.

Exercise 8.4

For the two unitary matrices

$$\mathbf{H} = \begin{bmatrix} \frac{\sqrt{2}}{2} & \frac{\sqrt{2}}{2} \\ \frac{\sqrt{2}}{2} & -\frac{\sqrt{2}}{2} \end{bmatrix} \quad \text{and} \quad \sigma_y = \begin{bmatrix} 0 & -i \\ i & 0 \end{bmatrix},$$

which are the Hadamard and Pauli σ_y matrices, respectively, show that

$$\mathbf{H} \otimes \sigma_y = \begin{bmatrix} 0 & -\frac{\sqrt{2}}{2}i & 0 & -\frac{\sqrt{2}}{2}i \\ \frac{\sqrt{2}}{2}i & 0 & \frac{\sqrt{2}}{2}i & 0 \\ 0 & -\frac{\sqrt{2}}{2}i & 0 & \frac{\sqrt{2}}{2}i \\ \frac{\sqrt{2}}{2}i & 0 & -\frac{\sqrt{2}}{2}i & 0 \end{bmatrix}$$

and it is unitary.

Vectors

We do something similar with vectors. If $\mathbf{v} = (v_1, v_2, v_3)$ in V and $\mathbf{w} = (w_1, w_2)$ in W, then

$$\mathbf{v} \otimes \mathbf{w} = (v_1\mathbf{w}, v_2\mathbf{w}, v_3\mathbf{w}) = (v_1w_1, v_1w_2, \quad v_2w_1, v_2w_2, \quad v_3w_1, v_3w_2) \ .$$

I've again taken liberties in the second term to show we get three entries by multiplying the second vector by an entry in the first.

If V and W have Euclidean norms, then

$$
\begin{aligned}
\|\mathbf{v} \otimes \mathbf{w}\|^2 &= \|(v_1w_1, v_1w_2, \quad v_2w_1, v_2w_2, \quad v_3w_1, v_3w_2)\|^2 \\
&= |v_1w_1|^2 + |v_1w_2|^2 + |v_2w_1|^2 + |v_2w_2|^2 + |v_3w_1|^2 + |v_3w_2|^2 \\
&= |v_1|^2|w_1|^2 + |v_1|^2|w_2|^2 + |v_2|^2|w_1|^2 + |v_2|^2|w_2|^2 + |v_3|^2|w_1|^2 + |v_3|^2|w_2|^2 \\
&= |v_1|^2 \left(|w_1|^2 + |w_2|^2\right) + |v_2|^2 \left(|w_1|^2 + |w_2|^2\right) + |v_3|^2 \left(|w_1|^2 + |w_2|^2\right) \\
&= \left(|v_1|^2 + |v_2|^2 + |v_3|^2\right) \left(|w_1|^2 + |w_2|^2\right) \\
&= \|\mathbf{v}\|^2 \|\mathbf{w}\|^2 \ .
\end{aligned}
$$

This is generally true for finite-dimensional vector spaces V and W with Euclidean norms.

For $\mathbf{R}^2 \otimes \mathbf{R}^2$ or $\mathbf{C}^2 \otimes \mathbf{C}^2$,

$$\mathbf{e}_1 \otimes \mathbf{e}_1 = (1,0) \otimes (1,0) = (1,0,0,0) \qquad \mathbf{e}_1 \otimes \mathbf{e}_2 = (1,0) \otimes (0,1) = (0,1,0,0)$$
$$\mathbf{e}_2 \otimes \mathbf{e}_1 = (0,1) \otimes (1,0) = (0,0,1,0) \qquad \mathbf{e}_2 \otimes \mathbf{e}_2 = (0,1) \otimes (0,1) = (0,0,0,1)$$

A tensor product example with ice cream

We now take a brief culinary diversion to compare direct sums and tensor products. Let V be the 3-dimensional vector space with the basis **chocolate ice cream**, **vanilla ice cream**, and **mint chocolate chip ice cream**. For the 4-dimensional vector space W, the basis is **chocolate fudge sauce**, **caramel sauce**, **mango sauce**, and **raspberry sauce**.

Vectors in $V \oplus W$ are linear combinations of the 7 $(= 3 + 4)$ foods:

chocolate ice cream
vanilla ice cream
mint chocolate chip ice cream
chocolate fudge sauce
caramel sauce
mango sauce
raspberry sauce

Vectors in $V \otimes W$ are linear combinations of the 12 $(= 3 \times 4)$ food combinations:

chocolate ice cream $\otimes$ **chocolate fudge sauce**
chocolate ice cream $\otimes$ **caramel sauce**
chocolate ice cream $\otimes$ **mango sauce**
chocolate ice cream $\otimes$ **raspberry sauce**

vanilla ice cream $\otimes$ **chocolate fudge sauce**
vanilla ice cream $\otimes$ **caramel sauce**
vanilla ice cream $\otimes$ **mango sauce**
vanilla ice cream $\otimes$ **raspberry sauce**

mint chocolate chip ice cream $\otimes$ **chocolate fudge sauce**
mint chocolate chip ice cream $\otimes$ **caramel sauce**
mint chocolate chip ice cream $\otimes$ **mango sauce**
mint chocolate chip ice cream $\otimes$ **raspberry sauce**

We get every possible pairing with the tensor product. Now, back to the math.

A complex example

Consider $\mathbf{C}^2$ with standard basis $\mathbf{e}_1$ and $\mathbf{e}_2$. Both $\mathbf{C}^2 \oplus \mathbf{C}^2$ and $\mathbf{C}^2 \otimes \mathbf{C}^2$ have four dimensions. These are *isomorphic*: we have an invertible linear map from all of the first vector space to all of the second. What is it?

Since $\mathbf{C}^2 \oplus \mathbf{C}^2 = \mathbf{C}^4$, it has the standard basis $\mathbf{f}_1 = (1, 0, 0, 0)$, $\mathbf{f}_2 = (0, 1, 0, 0)$, $\mathbf{f}_3 = (0, 0, 1, 0)$, and $\mathbf{f}_4 = (0, 0, 0, 1)$. (I'm using "$\mathbf{f}$" instead of "$\mathbf{e}$" in this second case to avoid confusion.)

We map $\mathbf{C}^2 \oplus \mathbf{C}^2 = \mathbf{C}^4 \to \mathbf{C}^2 \otimes \mathbf{C}^2$ by

$$\mathbf{f}_1 \mapsto \mathbf{e}_1 \otimes \mathbf{e}_1 \qquad\qquad \mathbf{f}_2 \mapsto \mathbf{e}_1 \otimes \mathbf{e}_2$$
$$\mathbf{f}_3 \mapsto \mathbf{e}_2 \otimes \mathbf{e}_1 \qquad\qquad \mathbf{f}_4 \mapsto \mathbf{e}_2 \otimes \mathbf{e}_2$$

This is not the only isomorphism, but it is natural given our calculation of the coordinates of the vectors such as $\mathbf{e}_1 \otimes \mathbf{e}_2$.

Another interesting basis for $\mathbf{C}^2 \otimes \mathbf{C}^2$ is

$$\frac{\sqrt{2}}{2}\left(\mathbf{e}_1 \otimes \mathbf{e}_1 + \mathbf{e}_2 \otimes \mathbf{e}_2\right) \qquad\qquad \frac{\sqrt{2}}{2}\left(\mathbf{e}_1 \otimes \mathbf{e}_1 - \mathbf{e}_2 \otimes \mathbf{e}_2\right)$$
$$\frac{\sqrt{2}}{2}\left(\mathbf{e}_1 \otimes \mathbf{e}_2 + \mathbf{e}_2 \otimes \mathbf{e}_1\right) \qquad\qquad \frac{\sqrt{2}}{2}\left(\mathbf{e}_1 \otimes \mathbf{e}_2 - \mathbf{e}_2 \otimes \mathbf{e}_1\right)$$

Continuing on, $\mathbf{C}^2 \oplus \mathbf{C}^2 \oplus \mathbf{C}^2 = \mathbf{C}^6$, but $\mathbf{C}^2 \otimes \mathbf{C}^2 \otimes \mathbf{C}^2$ has 8 dimensions. If we tensor ten copies of $\mathbf{C}^2$ together, we get $2^{10} = 1,024$ dimensions.

> The process of tensoring with more copies of $\mathbf{C}^2$ is exponential in the number of dimensions.

To learn more

> Tensor products are not always included in introductory linear algebra texts, so you may not have seen them before, even if you have studied the subject. More complete mathematical treatments cover tensor products of vectors and matrices but may also generalize them using category theory. [101] [131] [145]

In the next section, we use the tensor product as the underpinning of qubit entanglement and show what they look like and how they behave with bra-ket notation.

8.2 Entanglement

We've now seen many gate operations we can apply to a single qubit to change its state. In section 2.5, we worked through how to use classical logic gates to build a circuit for addition.

While we can apply **not** to a single bit, all the other operations require at least two bits for input. In the same way, we need to work with multiple qubits to produce interesting and useful results.

8.2.1 Moving from one to two qubits

We represent the states of a single qubit by vectors of length 1 in $\mathbf{C}^2$. We consider any two states equivalent if they differ only by multiplication by a complex unit. This is what we mean when we say that the states are ''equal up to a global phase.''

Each qubit starts by having its own associated copy of $\mathbf{C}^2$. When we have a quantum system with two qubits, we do not consider their collective states in a single $\mathbf{C}^2$ instance. Instead, we use the tensor product of the two copies of $\mathbf{C}^2$ and the tensor products of the quantum state vectors. This construction gives us a four-dimensional complex vector space where this ''4'' is 2×2 rather than the arithmetically equal $2 + 2$.

The tensor product of two unitary matrices is unitary, leading naturally to quantum gates on multiple qubits.

The tensor product is the machinery that allows us to build quantum systems from two or more smaller systems. The notation for working with these tensor products starts as fairly bulky, but significant simplifications demonstrate the advantages of bras and kets.

Let q_1 and q_2 be two qubits and let $\{|0\rangle_1, |1\rangle_1\}$ and $\{|0\rangle_2, |1\rangle_2\}$ be the standard orthonormal basis kets for each of their $\mathbf{C}^2$ state spaces. Let

$$|\psi\rangle_1 = a_1|0\rangle_1 + b_1|1\rangle_1 \quad \text{with} \quad |a_1|^2 + |b_1|^2 = 1$$

and

$$|\psi\rangle_2 = a_2|0\rangle_2 + b_2|1\rangle_2 \quad \text{with} \quad |a_2|^2 + |b_2|^2 = 1.$$

The four kets

$$|0\rangle_1 \otimes |0\rangle_2, \ |0\rangle_1 \otimes |1\rangle_2, \ |1\rangle_1 \otimes |0\rangle_2, \text{ and } |1\rangle_1 \otimes |1\rangle_2$$

are a basis for the combined state space $\mathbf{C}^2 \otimes \mathbf{C}^2$ for q_1 and q_2.

From the standard properties of tensor products,

$$|\psi\rangle_1 \otimes |\psi\rangle_2 = a_1 a_2 |0\rangle_1 \otimes |0\rangle_2 + a_1 b_2 |0\rangle_1 \otimes |1\rangle_2 +$$
$$b_1 a_2 |1\rangle_1 \otimes |0\rangle_2 + b_1 b_2 |1\rangle_1 \otimes |1\rangle_2 .$$

First simplification: we can assume there is a tensor product between basis kets from the original but different qubit state spaces. We omit the "$\otimes$" symbols on the right-hand side:

$$|\psi\rangle_1 \otimes |\psi\rangle_2 = a_1 a_2 |0\rangle_1 |0\rangle_2 + a_1 b_2 |0\rangle_1 |1\rangle_2 +$$
$$b_1 a_2 |1\rangle_1 |0\rangle_2 + b_1 b_2 |1\rangle_1 |1\rangle_2 .$$

Second simplification: we do not tensor kets in the same state space, so we can drop the subscripts on the basis kets. We use the order in which they are listed to determine from where they came:

$$|\psi\rangle_1 \otimes |\psi\rangle_2 = a_1 a_2 |0\rangle |0\rangle + a_1 b_2 |0\rangle |1\rangle +$$
$$b_1 a_2 |1\rangle |0\rangle + b_1 b_2 |1\rangle |1\rangle .$$

Third simplification: we can merge adjacent basis kets inside a single ket. This is new notation for us but shows the conciseness of what Dirac conceived:

$$|\psi\rangle_1 \otimes |\psi\rangle_2 = a_1 a_2 |00\rangle + a_1 b_2 |01\rangle +$$
$$b_1 a_2 |10\rangle + b_1 b_2 |11\rangle .$$

When we use general coordinates, the expression looks like

$$a_{00} |00\rangle + a_{01} |01\rangle + a_{10} |10\rangle + a_{11} |11\rangle .$$

Since we're going to be looking at and applying matrices, it's handy to determine the column vector forms for the 2-qubit basis kets in $\mathbf{C}^2 \otimes \mathbf{C}^2$:

$$|00\rangle = \begin{bmatrix} 1 \\ 0 \\ 0 \\ 0 \end{bmatrix} \quad |01\rangle = \begin{bmatrix} 0 \\ 1 \\ 0 \\ 0 \end{bmatrix} \quad |10\rangle = \begin{bmatrix} 0 \\ 0 \\ 1 \\ 0 \end{bmatrix} \quad |11\rangle = \begin{bmatrix} 0 \\ 0 \\ 0 \\ 1 \end{bmatrix} .$$

We compute these from

$$|0\rangle = \begin{bmatrix} 1 \\ 0 \end{bmatrix} \quad \text{and} \quad |1\rangle = \begin{bmatrix} 0 \\ 1 \end{bmatrix}$$

and observe that, for example,

$$|01\rangle = |0\rangle \otimes |1\rangle = \begin{bmatrix} 1 \\ 0 \end{bmatrix} \otimes \begin{bmatrix} 0 \\ 1 \end{bmatrix} = \begin{bmatrix} 1\begin{bmatrix}0\\1\end{bmatrix} \\ 0\begin{bmatrix}0\\1\end{bmatrix} \end{bmatrix} = \begin{bmatrix} 1\times 0 \\ 1\times 1 \\ 0\times 0 \\ 0\times 1 \end{bmatrix} = \begin{bmatrix} 0 \\ 1 \\ 0 \\ 0 \end{bmatrix}.$$

Exercise 8.5

Verify that the stated column vector forms of $|00\rangle$, $|10\rangle$, and $|11\rangle$ are correct.

Note that $\langle 01|01\rangle = 1$ but $\langle 01|11\rangle = 0$. This is generally true: when both sides are equal for these four vectors, their $\langle|\rangle$ is 1. When they are unequal, they are 0. This is a restatement of saying they are an orthonormal basis.

We will see a fourth form when we look at the general case.

Look at the coefficients in $a_1a_2|00\rangle + a_1b_2|01\rangle + b_1a_2|10\rangle + b_1b_2|11\rangle$. Is it still true that the sum of the squares of the absolute values of the coefficients equals 1? Why would we expect this to be the case?

When we measure the 2-qubit system, each of their states will drop to $|0\rangle$ or $|1\rangle$. There are four possible outcomes: $|00\rangle$, $|01\rangle$, $|10\rangle$, and $|11\rangle$. The sum of the probabilities of each case occurring must add up to 1. By extension from the 1-qubit case, we would expect that in

$$|\psi\rangle_1 \otimes |\psi\rangle_2 = a_1a_2|00\rangle + a_1b_2|01\rangle + b_1a_2|10\rangle + b_1b_2|11\rangle,$$

we would have the coefficients be probability amplitudes. The probability of getting $|01\rangle$, for example, is $|a_1b_2|^2$. The sum is therefore

$$|a_1a_2|^2 + |a_1b_2|^2 + |b_1a_2|^2 + |b_1b_2|^2 = 1.$$

Does the math support this? It does:

$$\begin{aligned}
|a_1a_2|^2 + |a_1b_2|^2 + |b_1a_2|^2 + |b_1b_2|^2 &= |a_1|^2|a_2|^2 + |a_1|^2|b_2|^2 + |b_1|^2|a_2|^2 + |b_1|^2|b_2|^2 \\
&= |a_1|^2\left(|a_2|^2 + |b_2|^2\right) + |b_1|^2\left(|a_2|^2 + |b_2|^2\right) \\
&= |a_1|^2(1) + |b_1|^2(1) \\
&= |a_1|^2 + |b_1|^2 \\
&= 1.
\end{aligned}$$

This is pretty spectacular, in my view. The mathematical model we have been building is aligning with the physical interpretation.

Measurement causes the state of each qubit to become, or collapse to, $|0\rangle$ or $|1\rangle$. Do they operate independently, or can there be combined qubit states that express a greater linkage than might seem obvious?

At any given time, two qubits are in superposition states represented by a linear combination of vectors $|00\rangle$, $|01\rangle$, $|10\rangle$, and $|11\rangle$ in $\mathbf{C}^2 \otimes \mathbf{C}^2$:

$$a_{00}|00\rangle + a_{01}|01\rangle + a_{10}|10\rangle + a_{11}|11\rangle\,,$$

where

$$|a_{00}|^2 + |a_{01}|^2 + |a_{10}|^2 + |a_{11}|^2 = 1\,.$$

Through *measurement*, the qubits are forced to collapse irreversibly through projection to $|00\rangle$, $|01\rangle$, $|10\rangle$, or $|11\rangle$. The probability of their doing so is $|a_{00}|^2$, $|a_{01}|^2$, $|a_{10}|^2$, or $|a_{11}|^2$, respectively. We call a_{00}, a_{01}, a_{10}, and a_{11} *probability amplitudes*.

If necessary, we can convert ("read out") $|00\rangle$, $|01\rangle$, $|10\rangle$, and $|11\rangle$ to classical bit string values of **00**, **01**, **10**, and **11**.

If our qubits q_1 and q_2 are in the combined state

$$0\,|00\rangle + \frac{\sqrt{2}}{2}|01\rangle + \frac{\sqrt{2}}{2}|10\rangle + 0\,|11\rangle = \frac{\sqrt{2}}{2}|01\rangle + \frac{\sqrt{2}}{2}|10\rangle\,,$$

then, when we measure, we expect to get $|10\rangle$ half the time and $|01\rangle$ the other half of the time, given a large number of measurements. We never get $|00\rangle$ or $|11\rangle$.

I now give you q_1, and I keep q_2. I'm very excited to have my qubit, so I immediately measure it. I get a $|1\rangle$! What do you get?

For q_2, two possible states that could collapse to $|1\rangle$: $|01\rangle$ and $|11\rangle$. But the probability of getting the second is 0! So when measured, you must get $|0\rangle$.

Before measurement, the qubits were in a state of *entanglement*. They were so tightly correlated that when the measurement value of one became known, it uniquely determined the second. You cannot do this with bits. With superposition, entanglement is one of the key differentiators between quantum and classical computing.

The entangled state we just used is known as a *Bell state*, and there are four of them:

$$|\Phi^+\rangle = \frac{\sqrt{2}}{2}|00\rangle + \frac{\sqrt{2}}{2}|11\rangle \qquad\qquad |\Psi^+\rangle = \frac{\sqrt{2}}{2}|01\rangle + \frac{\sqrt{2}}{2}|10\rangle$$

$$|\Phi^-\rangle = \frac{\sqrt{2}}{2}|00\rangle - \frac{\sqrt{2}}{2}|11\rangle \qquad\qquad |\Psi^-\rangle = \frac{\sqrt{2}}{2}|01\rangle - \frac{\sqrt{2}}{2}|10\rangle$$

We used $|\Psi^+\rangle$ in the example above.

Φ is the Greek capital letter "Phi," and Ψ is the Greek capital letter "Psi." φ and ψ are their lowercase counterparts. The names of the Bell states using Φ and Ψ are standard in the literature.

Exercise 8.6

Show that

$$|00\rangle = \frac{\sqrt{2}}{2}\left(|\Phi^+\rangle + |\Phi^-\rangle\right) \qquad\qquad |11\rangle = \frac{\sqrt{2}}{2}\left(|\Phi^+\rangle - |\Phi^-\rangle\right)$$

$$|01\rangle = \frac{\sqrt{2}}{2}\left(|\Psi^+\rangle + |\Psi^-\rangle\right) \qquad\qquad |10\rangle = \frac{\sqrt{2}}{2}\left(|\Psi^+\rangle - |\Psi^-\rangle\right)$$

Together, the four states $|\Phi^+\rangle$, $|\Phi^-\rangle$, $|\Psi^+\rangle$, and $|\Psi^-\rangle$ are an orthonormal basis for $\mathbf{C}^2$. They are named after physicist John Stewart Bell.

Let $|\Psi\rangle$ be a 2-qubit quantum state in $\mathbf{C}^2 \otimes \mathbf{C}^2$. $|\Psi\rangle$ is *entangled* if and only if we **cannot** write it as the tensor products of two 1-qubit kets:

$$|\psi\rangle_1 \otimes |\psi\rangle_2 = (a_1|0\rangle_1 + b_1|1\rangle_1) \otimes (a_2|0\rangle_2 + b_2|1\rangle_2) ,$$

where

$$|\psi\rangle_1 = a_1|0\rangle_1 + b_1|1\rangle_1 \quad \text{and} \quad |\psi\rangle_2 = a_2|0\rangle_2 + b_2|1\rangle_2 .$$

Suppose $|\Psi^+\rangle$ is not entangled. Then there exist a_1, b_1, a_2, and b_2 in $\mathbf{C}$, as above, with

$$|\Psi^+\rangle = 0|00\rangle + \frac{\sqrt{2}}{2}|01\rangle + \frac{\sqrt{2}}{2}|10\rangle + 0|11\rangle$$

$$= a_1a_2|00\rangle + a_1b_2|01\rangle + b_1a_2|10\rangle + b_1b_2|11\rangle .$$

This gives us four relationships:

$$a_1a_2 = 0 \qquad a_1b_2 = \tfrac{\sqrt{2}}{2} \qquad b_1a_2 = \tfrac{\sqrt{2}}{2} \qquad b_1b_2 = 0$$

From the first, either a_1 or a_2 is 0. Assume $a_1 = 0$. But then $0 = a_1b_2 = \frac{\sqrt{2}}{2}$. This is a contradiction. So $a_2 = 0$ must be 0. Again, though, $0 = b_1a_2 = \frac{\sqrt{2}}{2}$, and we have another impossibility. Therefore, we cannot write $|\Psi^+\rangle$ as the tensor product of two 1-qubit kets, and it is an entangled state.

If a 2-qubit quantum state is not entangled, we can separate it into the tensor product of two 1-qubit states. For this reason, we say that if a quantum state is not entangled, it is *separable*.

Exercise 8.7

Is

$$\frac{\sqrt{2}}{2}|00\rangle + \frac{\sqrt{2}}{2}|01\rangle$$

an entangled state?

There is something I want to highlight that may be confusing at first. Given two vectors in $\mathbf{C}^2$ of the forms $a_1\mathbf{e}_1 + b_1\mathbf{e}_2$ and $a_2\mathbf{e}_1 + b_2\mathbf{e}_2$, we must use the **sums** of all such tensor products

$$(a_1\mathbf{e}_1 + b_1\mathbf{e}_2) \otimes (a_2\mathbf{e}_1 + b_2\mathbf{e}_2) = a_1a_2\mathbf{e}_1 \otimes \mathbf{e}_1 + a_1b_2\mathbf{e}_1 \otimes \mathbf{e}_2 +$$
$$b_1a_2\mathbf{e}_2 \otimes \mathbf{e}_1 + b_1b_2\mathbf{e}_2 \otimes \mathbf{e}_2$$

with all possible complex number coordinates a_1, b_1, a_2, and b_2 to generate the entire $\mathbf{C}^2 \otimes \mathbf{C}^2$ vector space.

When we consider the 2-qubit quantum states in $\mathbf{C}^2 \otimes \mathbf{C}^2$, they look like

$$a_{00}|00\rangle + a_{01}|01\rangle + a_{10}|10\rangle + a_{11}|11\rangle$$

and we insist that the sum of the squares of the probability amplitudes a_{jk} is 1. The set of 2-qubit quantum states is not all of $\mathbf{C}^2 \otimes \mathbf{C}^2$, though we call $\mathbf{C}^2 \otimes \mathbf{C}^2$ the *state space*.

Exercise 8.8

There is an infinite number of entangled states and an infinite number of separable states in $\mathbf{C}^2$. Given that, in what sense are there more entangled states than separable ones?

8.2.2   The general case

Every time we add a qubit to a quantum system to create a new one, the state space doubles in dimension. We multiply the dimension of the original system's state space by 2 when we do the tensor product. A 3-qubit quantum system has a state space of dimension 8. An n-qubit system's state space has 2^n dimensions.

Let n in $\mathbf{N}$ be greater than 1 and Q be an n-qubit quantum system. The state space associated with Q has 2^n dimensions. We write it as $(\mathbf{C}^2)^{\otimes n}$, which means $\mathbf{C}^2$ tensored with itself n times.

It includes the elementary tensor products of the 1-qubit states for each of the n qubits:

$$(a_1|0\rangle_1 + b_1|1\rangle_1) \otimes \cdots \otimes (a_n|0\rangle_n + b_n|1\rangle_n) .$$

We can use more concise notation and write this as

$$\bigotimes_{i=j}^{n} \left(a_j|0\rangle_j + b_j|1\rangle_j \right) .$$

For each expression on the right-hand side, we sequentially substitute in values for j from 1 to n. We then take the tensor product of the n sums.

A quantum state in $(\mathbf{C}^2)^{\otimes n}$ is *separable* if it can be written as such an elementary state and is *entangled* otherwise.

How do we express a general quantum state in $(\mathbf{C}^2)^{\otimes n}$? First, it's much easier to use bit string ket notation such as $|11010111\rangle$ than

$$|1\rangle \otimes |1\rangle \otimes |0\rangle \otimes |1\rangle \otimes |0\rangle \otimes |1\rangle \otimes |1\rangle \otimes |1\rangle .$$

Second, knowing we have 8 qubits, we could also write this as $|215\rangle_8$, where the number inside the ket is a whole number *in base 10*. The subscript indicates how many qubits there are. In the 2-qubit case:

$$|00\rangle = |0\rangle_2 \qquad |01\rangle = |1\rangle_2 \qquad |10\rangle = |2\rangle_2 \qquad |11\rangle = |3\rangle_2$$

The sets of n-qubit kets for $(\mathbf{C}^2)^{\otimes n}$ composed of only 0s and 1s are called *computational bases*. For example,

$$|000\rangle \quad |001\rangle \quad |010\rangle \quad |011\rangle \quad |100\rangle \quad |101\rangle \quad |110\rangle \quad |111\rangle$$

is the computational basis for $\mathbf{C}^2 \otimes \mathbf{C}^2 \otimes \mathbf{C}^2$.

These are the same as

$$|0\rangle_3 \quad |1\rangle_3 \quad |2\rangle_3 \quad |3\rangle_3 \quad |4\rangle_3 \quad |5\rangle_3 \quad |6\rangle_3 \quad |7\rangle_3$$

When we use this decimal ket notation, we number the probability amplitudes/coefficients using the value inside the ket symbol. For a general quantum state with n qubits,

$$|\psi\rangle = a_0|0\rangle_n + a_1|1\rangle_n + a_2|2\rangle_n + \cdots + a_{2^n-1}|2^n - 1\rangle_n$$

and we have

$$|a_0|^2 + |a_1|^2 + |a_2|^2 + \cdots + |a_{2^n-1}|^2 = 1 .$$

However we write the quantum state, the sum of the squares of the absolute values of the probability amplitudes is 1.

If we want to write a ket such as

$$\left| \underbrace{00000000000 \ldots 00000000000}_{n} \right\rangle,$$

we shorthand it to $|0\rangle^{\otimes n}$. Some authors use $|\mathbf{0}\rangle$ when the n is understood.

For a given n, let $|\varphi\rangle$ and $|\psi\rangle$ be two computational basis kets. Then

$$\langle \varphi | \psi \rangle = \begin{cases} 1 & \text{if } |\varphi\rangle = |\psi\rangle \\ 0 & \text{otherwise.} \end{cases}$$

If $|\varphi\rangle$ has a 1 in the jth position and 0 elsewhere in its full vector expansion, and $|\psi\rangle$ has a 1 in the kth position and 0 elsewhere, then $|\varphi\rangle\langle\psi|$ is the n-by-n square matrix that has 0s everywhere except for the (j, k) position, where it is 1. For example,

$$|0\rangle\langle 0| = \begin{bmatrix} 1 & 0 \\ 0 & 0 \end{bmatrix} \quad \text{and} \quad |1\rangle\langle 0| = \begin{bmatrix} 0 & 0 \\ 1 & 0 \end{bmatrix}.$$

Note that $|0\rangle\langle 0| + |1\rangle\langle 1| = I_2$, the 2-by-2 identity matrix.

8.2.3 The density matrix again

If $|\psi\rangle$ is a multi-qubit quantum state, we define its *density matrix* ρ in the same way as the 1-qubit case in section 7.3.3:

$$\rho = |\psi\rangle\langle\psi| \,.$$

That is, if

$$|\psi\rangle = a_0|0\rangle_n + a_1|1\rangle_n + a_2|2\rangle_n + \cdots + a_{2^n-1}|2^n - 1\rangle_n \,,$$

then

$$\rho = |\psi\rangle\langle\psi| = \begin{bmatrix} a_0 & a_1 & a_2 & \cdots & a_{2^n-1} \end{bmatrix} \otimes \begin{bmatrix} \overline{a_0} \\ \overline{a_1} \\ \overline{a_2} \\ \vdots \\ \overline{a_{2^n-1}} \end{bmatrix}$$

$$= \begin{bmatrix} a_0\overline{a_0} & a_1\overline{a_0} & a_2\overline{a_0} & \cdots & a_{2^n-1}\overline{a_0} \\ a_0\overline{a_1} & a_1\overline{a_1} & a_2\overline{a_1} & \cdots & a_{2^n-1}\overline{a_1} \\ a_0\overline{a_2} & a_1\overline{a_2} & a_2\overline{a_2} & \cdots & a_{2^n-1}\overline{a_2} \\ \vdots & \vdots & \vdots & \ddots & \vdots \\ a_0\overline{a_{2^n-1}} & a_1\overline{a_{2^n-1}} & a_2\overline{a_{2^n-1}} & \cdots & a_{2^n-1}\overline{a_{2^n-1}} \end{bmatrix},$$

and this matrix is equal to

$$\begin{bmatrix} |a_0|^2 & a_1\overline{a_0} & a_2\overline{a_0} & \cdots & a_{2^n-1}\overline{a_0} \\ a_0\overline{a_1} & |a_1|^2 & a_2\overline{a_1} & \cdots & a_{2^n-1}\overline{a_1} \\ a_0\overline{a_2} & a_1\overline{a_2} & |a_2|^2 & \cdots & a_{2^n-1}\overline{a_2} \\ \vdots & \vdots & \vdots & \ddots & \vdots \\ a_0\overline{a_{2^n-1}} & a_1\overline{a_{2^n-1}} & a_2\overline{a_{2^n-1}} & \cdots & |a_{2^n-1}|^2 \end{bmatrix}.$$

The diagonal elements are real, $\text{tr}(\rho) = 1$, and ρ is Hermitian and positive semi-definite. ρ has a unique positive semi-definite square root matrix $\rho^{\frac{1}{2}}$.

Let U be a unitary 2^n-by-2^n matrix. What is the relationship between the density matrices of $|\psi\rangle$ and $|U\psi\rangle$? From Exercise 7.3, we have

$$|U\psi\rangle\langle U\psi| = U\,|\psi\rangle\langle\psi|\,U^\dagger = U\rho U^\dagger = U\rho U^{-1}.$$

8.3 Multi-qubit gates

A quantum gate operation on one qubit has a 2-by-2 unitary square matrix relative to some basis, as we saw in section 5.9. For two qubits, the matrix is 4-by-4. For ten, it is 2^{10}-by-2^{10}, which is 1,024-by-1,024. We now look at how to work with common lower-dimensional gates, allowing you to extrapolate to larger ones.

We can tensor any two 1-qubit gates to create a 2-qubit gate. For example,

$$(\mathbf{X} \otimes \mathbf{Z})|11\rangle = (\mathbf{X} \otimes \mathbf{Z})(|1\rangle \otimes |1\rangle) = (\mathbf{X}|1\rangle) \otimes (\mathbf{Z}|1\rangle) = |0\rangle \otimes (-|1\rangle) = -|01\rangle.$$

Let's examine what we get when we tensor together multiple 1-qubit Hadamard $\mathbf{H}$ gates.

8.3.1 The quantum $H^{\otimes n}$ gate

We start by looking at what applying a Hadamard H to each qubit in a 2-qubit system means. The H gate has the matrix

$$H = \begin{bmatrix} \frac{\sqrt{2}}{2} & \frac{\sqrt{2}}{2} \\ \frac{\sqrt{2}}{2} & -\frac{\sqrt{2}}{2} \end{bmatrix} = \frac{\sqrt{2}}{2} \begin{bmatrix} 1 & 1 \\ 1 & -1 \end{bmatrix}$$

operating on $\mathbf{C}^2$. Starting with the two qubit states

$$|\psi\rangle_1 = a_1|0\rangle_1 + b_1|1\rangle_1 \quad \text{and} \quad |\psi\rangle_2 = a_2|0\rangle_2 + b_2|1\rangle_2,$$

applying H to each qubit means to compute

$$(H|\psi\rangle_1) \otimes (H|\psi\rangle_2),$$

which is the same as

$$(H \otimes H)(|\psi\rangle_1 \otimes |\psi\rangle_2) = H^{\otimes 2}(a_1 a_2|00\rangle + a_1 b_2|01\rangle + b_1 a_2|10\rangle + b_1 b_2|11\rangle)$$

for some 4-by-4 unitary matrix $H^{\otimes 2}$. Given the definition of H and the technique of creating a matrix tensor product in section 8.1, we can compute

$$H^{\otimes 2} = \begin{bmatrix} \frac{1}{2} & \frac{1}{2} & \frac{1}{2} & \frac{1}{2} \\ \frac{1}{2} & -\frac{1}{2} & \frac{1}{2} & -\frac{1}{2} \\ \frac{1}{2} & \frac{1}{2} & -\frac{1}{2} & -\frac{1}{2} \\ \frac{1}{2} & -\frac{1}{2} & -\frac{1}{2} & \frac{1}{2} \end{bmatrix} = \frac{1}{2} \begin{bmatrix} 1 & 1 & 1 & 1 \\ 1 & -1 & 1 & -1 \\ 1 & 1 & -1 & -1 \\ 1 & -1 & -1 & 1 \end{bmatrix} = \frac{\sqrt{2}}{2} \begin{bmatrix} H & H \\ H & -H \end{bmatrix}.$$

This matrix puts both qubits that are each initially initialized to $|0\rangle$ into superposition in a 2-qubit system. Note the recursive definition of $H^{\otimes 2}$ in terms of matrix blocks of H matrices.

Though we could draw $H^{\otimes 2}$ as having two inputs and two outputs, we instead show it by applying H to each qubit in a circuit:

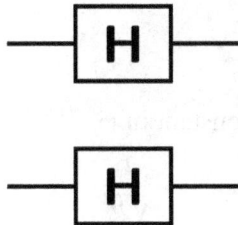

For a 3-qubit system, the corresponding $\mathbf{H}^{\otimes 3}$ matrix is

$$\frac{\sqrt{2}}{4} \begin{bmatrix} 1 & 1 & 1 & 1 & 1 & 1 & 1 & 1 \\ 1 & -1 & 1 & -1 & 1 & -1 & 1 & -1 \\ 1 & 1 & -1 & -1 & 1 & 1 & -1 & -1 \\ 1 & -1 & -1 & 1 & 1 & -1 & -1 & 1 \\ 1 & 1 & 1 & 1 & -1 & -1 & -1 & -1 \\ 1 & -1 & 1 & -1 & -1 & 1 & -1 & 1 \\ 1 & 1 & -1 & -1 & -1 & -1 & 1 & 1 \\ 1 & -1 & -1 & 1 & -1 & 1 & 1 & -1 \end{bmatrix} = \frac{\sqrt{2}}{2} \begin{bmatrix} \mathbf{H}^{\otimes 2} & \mathbf{H}^{\otimes 2} \\ \mathbf{H}^{\otimes 2} & -\mathbf{H}^{\otimes 2} \end{bmatrix} .$$

Recall from section 7.6.5 that $\mathbf{H}|0\rangle = |+\rangle$. That is,

$$\mathbf{H}|0\rangle = \frac{\sqrt{2}}{2} (|0\rangle + |1\rangle) .$$

From this, it follows that

$$\mathbf{H}^{\otimes 2}|00\rangle = (\mathbf{H} \otimes \mathbf{H}) (|0\rangle \otimes |0\rangle)$$

$$= \left(\frac{\sqrt{2}}{2} (|0\rangle + |1\rangle) \right) \otimes \left(\frac{\sqrt{2}}{2} (|0\rangle + |1\rangle) \right)$$

$$= \frac{1}{2} (|00\rangle + |01\rangle + |10\rangle + |11\rangle) .$$

Also,

$$\mathbf{H}^{\otimes 3}|000\rangle = \frac{\sqrt{2}}{4} (|000\rangle + |001\rangle + |010\rangle + |011\rangle + |100\rangle + |101\rangle + |110\rangle + |111\rangle) .$$

The pattern continues. Applying the Hadamard gates to each qubit initialized to $|0\rangle$ creates a *balanced superposition* with equal amplitudes involving all the ket basis vectors. The number out front, $\frac{\sqrt{2}}{4}$ in the last case, is there to ensure that the square of the absolute value of the ket is 1. It is the *normalization constant*.

Exercise 8.9

Show that the normalization constant in $\mathbf{H}^{\otimes n}|0\rangle^{\otimes n}$ is

$$\frac{1}{\sqrt{2^n}}$$

where n is the number of qubits.

If you have three classical bits, you can represent all of the following but *only one at a time:*

000   001   010   011   100   101   110   111

In contrast, the 3-qubit state $\mathbf{H}^{\otimes 3}|0\rangle_3$ contains each of the corresponding ket basis forms *at the same time.*

Here, the decimal notation for a basis ket is remarkably concise. We can rewrite the last equality as

$$\mathbf{H}^{\otimes 3}|0\rangle_3 = \frac{\sqrt{2}}{4}\left(|0\rangle_3 + |1\rangle_3 + |2\rangle_3 + |3\rangle_3 + |4\rangle_3 + |5\rangle_3 + |6\rangle_3 + |7\rangle_3\right).$$

We can define the Hadamard gate matrices $\mathbf{H}^{\otimes n}$ recursively by

$$\mathbf{H}^{\otimes n} = \frac{\sqrt{2}}{2}\begin{bmatrix} \mathbf{H}^{\otimes n-1} & \mathbf{H}^{\otimes n-1} \\ \mathbf{H}^{\otimes n-1} & -\mathbf{H}^{\otimes n-1} \end{bmatrix},$$

where $\mathbf{H}^{\otimes 1} = \mathbf{H}$.

Since we are now using multiple qubits, it is a good time to introduce summation notation with the Greek capital letter Sigma, Σ, to simplify formulas and equations. For example,

$$\sum_{j=1}^{4} j = 1 + 2 + 3 + 4 = 10.$$

This expression means we start with $j = 1$ and, in turn, consider $j = 2$, $j = 3$, and $j = 4$. We set the initial value of the sum to 0 and then add each evaluation of the formula to the right of Σ with the current value of j. 1 is the *lower bound* for j, and 4 is the *upper bound*.

Here is another example:

$$\sum_{j=0}^{2} \cos(j\pi) = \cos(0\pi) + \cos(1\pi) + \cos(2\pi) = 1.$$

The upper bound may involve a variable, and we can use a summation variable other than j:

$$\sum_{m=0}^{n-1} 2^m = 2^0 + 2^1 + \cdots + 2^{n-1} = 2^n - 1.$$

The lower bound need not be constant, either.

The general form for an n-qubit quantum register state using decimal ket notation is

$$|\psi\rangle = \sum_{j=0}^{2^n-1} a_j |j\rangle_n, \text{ where } 1 = \sum_{j=0}^{2^n-1} |a_j|^2.$$

With this, we can express the formula for the balanced superposition of n qubits:

$$\mathbf{H}^{\otimes n}|0\rangle_n = \frac{1}{\sqrt{2^n}} \sum_{j=0}^{2^n-1} |j\rangle_n.$$

We can drop the subscript n on the kets if we know we are working with a specific number of qubits:

$$\mathbf{H}^{\otimes n}|0\rangle = \frac{1}{\sqrt{2^n}} \sum_{j=0}^{2^n-1} |j\rangle.$$

Exercise 8.10

Fully write out

$$\mathbf{H}^{\otimes 4}|0\rangle = \frac{1}{\sqrt{2^4}} \sum_{j=0}^{2^4-1} |j\rangle.$$

Expand the kets using binary notation.

We have a similar notation for products:

$$\prod_{j=1}^{4} j = 1 \times 2 \times 3 \times 4.$$

For example, if we factor a positive integer N into a set of primes $\{p_1, p_2, \ldots, p_n\}$ and each prime p_j occurs m_j times, then

$$N = \prod_{j=1}^{n} p_j^{m_j}.$$

Let's now consider 2-qubit gates that are not such tensor products of 1-qubit gates.

8.3.2 The quantum SWAP gate

In section 7.6.2, we demonstrated that the **X** gate is a bit flip: given $|\psi\rangle = a|0\rangle + b|1\rangle$, $\mathbf{X}|\psi\rangle = b|0\rangle + a|1\rangle$. We have interchanged the two probability amplitudes.

Now that we are considering two qubits, is there a gate that switches their quantum states? What does this even mean?

Given the quantum states

$$|\psi\rangle_1 = a_1|0\rangle_1 + b_1|1\rangle_1 \quad \text{and} \quad |\psi\rangle_2 = a_2|0\rangle_2 + b_2|1\rangle_2,$$

we can tensor them in either order:

$$|\psi\rangle_1 \otimes |\psi\rangle_2 = a_1a_2|00\rangle + \boldsymbol{a_1b_2}|01\rangle + \boldsymbol{b_1a_2}|10\rangle + b_1b_2|11\rangle$$

$$|\psi\rangle_2 \otimes |\psi\rangle_1 = a_2a_1|00\rangle + a_2b_1|01\rangle + b_2a_1|10\rangle + b_2b_1|11\rangle$$
$$= a_1a_2|00\rangle + \boldsymbol{b_1a_2}|01\rangle + \boldsymbol{a_1b_2}|10\rangle + b_1b_2|11\rangle.$$

The first and the fourth amplitudes are the same, but we switched the second and third when we reversed the tensor order.

The matrix

$$M = \begin{bmatrix} 1 & 0 & 0 & 0 \\ 0 & 0 & 1 & 0 \\ 0 & 1 & 0 & 0 \\ 0 & 0 & 0 & 1 \end{bmatrix}$$

is an example of a 4-by-4 *permutation matrix*. To create a matrix that swaps the second and third amplitude of a 2-qubit quantum state (or entries in a column vector), begin with I_4 and interchange the second and third columns. This is M.

For a general vector $|v\rangle$,

$$M|v\rangle = M \begin{bmatrix} v_1 \\ v_2 \\ v_3 \\ v_4 \end{bmatrix} = \begin{bmatrix} v_1 \\ v_3 \\ v_2 \\ v_4 \end{bmatrix}.$$

Therefore, $M(|\psi\rangle_1 \otimes |\psi\rangle_2) = |\psi\rangle_2 \otimes |\psi\rangle_1$.

When used this way, we call the quantum gate with the matrix M in the standard ket basis the **SWAP** gate.

When I include the **SWAP** gate in a circuit, it spans two wires:

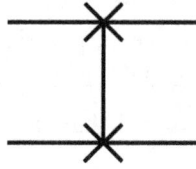

Remember the ×s!

8.3.3 The quantum CNOT / CX gate

The **CNOT** gate, also called the **CX** gate, is one of the most significant gates in quantum computing. We use it to create entangled qubits. It's not the only gate that can do it, but it's simple and very commonly used.

The "**C**" in **CNOT** is for "controlled." Unlike the 1-qubit **X** gate, which unconditionally flips $|0\rangle$ to $|1\rangle$ and vice versa, **CNOT** has two qubit inputs and two outputs. Remember that quantum gates must be reversible. For this reason, we must have the same number of inputs as outputs. We call the qubits q_1 and q_2 and their states $|\psi\rangle_1$ and $|\psi\rangle_2$, respectively.

This is the way **CNOT** works: it takes two inputs, $|\psi\rangle_1$ and $|\psi\rangle_2$:

- If $|\psi\rangle_1$ is $|1\rangle$, then the state of q_1 remains $|\psi\rangle_1$, but $|\psi\rangle_2$ becomes $\mathbf{X}|\psi\rangle_2$.
- If $|\psi\rangle_1$ is $|0\rangle$, the states of q_1 and q_2 are unchanged.
- Otherwise, we use linearity on $|\psi\rangle_1 = a_1|0\rangle + b_1|1\rangle$ to compute the new state for $|\psi\rangle_2$.

The **CNOT** gate is a conditional bit flip.

In the classical case, we create a controlled **not** from an **xor** with this circuit:

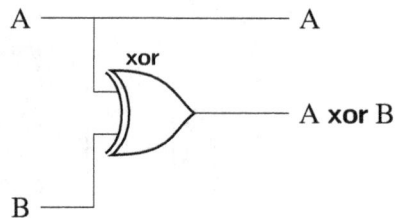

The matrix for **CNOT** is

$$\begin{bmatrix} 1 & 0 & 0 & 0 \\ 0 & 1 & 0 & 0 \\ 0 & 0 & 0 & 1 \\ 0 & 0 & 1 & 0 \end{bmatrix}.$$

It is a permutation matrix that swaps the third and fourth amplitudes of $|\psi\rangle_1 \otimes |\psi\rangle_2$. The upper-left 2-by-2 submatrix is I_2, and the lower-right 2-by-2 submatrix is the **X** matrix. It is more evident if we rewrite the matrix in block form as

$$\left[\begin{array}{cc|cc} 1 & 0 & 0 & 0 \\ 0 & 1 & 0 & 0 \\ \hline 0 & 0 & 0 & 1 \\ 0 & 0 & 1 & 0 \end{array}\right].$$

When I include the **CNOT** gate in a circuit, it spans two wires. The top line is the control qubit:

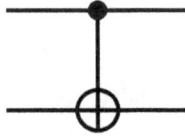

CNOT operates on the standard $\mathbf{C}^2 \otimes \mathbf{C}^2$ basis as

$$\mathbf{CNOT}\,|00\rangle = |00\rangle \qquad \mathbf{CNOT}\,|01\rangle = |01\rangle$$
$$\mathbf{CNOT}\,|10\rangle = |11\rangle \qquad \mathbf{CNOT}\,|11\rangle = |10\rangle$$

By linearity,

$$\mathbf{CNOT}\,(a_{00}|00\rangle + a_{01}|01\rangle + a_{10}|10\rangle + a_{11}|11\rangle)$$
$$= a_{00}\,\mathbf{CNOT}|00\rangle + a_{01}\,\mathbf{CNOT}|01\rangle + a_{10}\,\mathbf{CNOT}|10\rangle + a_{11}\,\mathbf{CNOT}|11\rangle$$
$$= a_{00}|00\rangle + a_{01}|01\rangle + a_{10}|11\rangle + a_{11}|10\rangle$$
$$= a_{00}|00\rangle + a_{01}|01\rangle + a_{11}|10\rangle + a_{10}|11\rangle.$$

We use **CNOT** to create the entangled Bell states. We save the construction until section 9.3.3 when we have more circuit machinery in hand.

Reverse CNOT with Hadamard gates

Applying the change-of-basis Hadamard **H** gates before and after **CNOT** illustrates an interesting property of **CNOT**. The matrix form of $\mathbf{H}^{\otimes 2} \circ \mathbf{CNOT} \circ \mathbf{H}^{\otimes 2}$ is

$$M = \underbrace{\begin{bmatrix} \frac{1}{2} & \frac{1}{2} & \frac{1}{2} & \frac{1}{2} \\ \frac{1}{2} & -\frac{1}{2} & \frac{1}{2} & -\frac{1}{2} \\ \frac{1}{2} & \frac{1}{2} & -\frac{1}{2} & -\frac{1}{2} \\ \frac{1}{2} & -\frac{1}{2} & -\frac{1}{2} & \frac{1}{2} \end{bmatrix}}_{\mathbf{H}^{\otimes 2}} \underbrace{\begin{bmatrix} 1 & 0 & 0 & 0 \\ 0 & 1 & 0 & 0 \\ 0 & 0 & 0 & 1 \\ 0 & 0 & 1 & 0 \end{bmatrix}}_{\mathbf{CNOT}} \underbrace{\begin{bmatrix} \frac{1}{2} & \frac{1}{2} & \frac{1}{2} & \frac{1}{2} \\ \frac{1}{2} & -\frac{1}{2} & \frac{1}{2} & -\frac{1}{2} \\ \frac{1}{2} & \frac{1}{2} & -\frac{1}{2} & -\frac{1}{2} \\ \frac{1}{2} & -\frac{1}{2} & -\frac{1}{2} & \frac{1}{2} \end{bmatrix}}_{\mathbf{H}^{\otimes 2}}$$

$$= \begin{bmatrix} 1 & 0 & 0 & 0 \\ 0 & 0 & 0 & 1 \\ 0 & 0 & 1 & 0 \\ 0 & 1 & 0 & 0 \end{bmatrix}.$$

What can we tell about this? By inspection, we can see it is a permutation operation that swaps the second and fourth coefficients of the standard ket expression in $\mathbf{C}^2 \otimes \mathbf{C}^2$.

The effect of M on the standard basis kets is

$$M \left|00\right\rangle = \left|00\right\rangle \qquad M \left|01\right\rangle = \left|11\right\rangle \qquad M \left|10\right\rangle = \left|10\right\rangle \qquad M \left|11\right\rangle = \left|01\right\rangle.$$

Examine what happens by looking at the second qubit. If it is $\left|1\right\rangle$, then the first qubit flips. If it is $\left|0\right\rangle$, then the first qubit remains the same.

This is the opposite behavior of **CNOT**, yet it is constructed from it with Hadamard operations before and after. With **CNOT**, it appeared that the state of the second qubit was controlled by the first. In this construction, it is the opposite. By changing the basis to and from $\left|+\right\rangle$ and $\left|-\right\rangle$, we have evidence that **CNOT** is doing more than we perhaps expected.

If we wanted the control qubit to be the second one in this way, we would draw it with the ''•'' on the bottom. We sometimes call this a **reverse CNOT**:

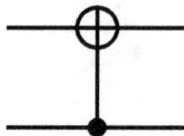

Reverse CNOT with SWAP gates

We can also create a **reverse CNOT** by performing a **SWAP**, a **CNOT**, and another **SWAP**. We interchange the control and target qubit states, do a regular **CNOT**, and then switch the qubit states again.

To verify this, let's look at the matrices:

$$\text{SWAP} \circ \text{CNOT} \circ \text{SWAP} = \underbrace{\begin{bmatrix} 1 & 0 & 0 & 0 \\ 0 & 0 & 1 & 0 \\ 0 & 1 & 0 & 0 \\ 0 & 0 & 0 & 1 \end{bmatrix}}_{\text{SWAP}} \underbrace{\begin{bmatrix} 1 & 0 & 0 & 0 \\ 0 & 1 & 0 & 0 \\ 0 & 0 & 0 & 1 \\ 0 & 0 & 1 & 0 \end{bmatrix}}_{\text{CNOT}} \underbrace{\begin{bmatrix} 1 & 0 & 0 & 0 \\ 0 & 0 & 1 & 0 \\ 0 & 1 & 0 & 0 \\ 0 & 0 & 0 & 1 \end{bmatrix}}_{\text{SWAP}}$$

$$= \begin{bmatrix} 1 & 0 & 0 & 0 \\ 0 & 0 & 0 & 1 \\ 0 & 0 & 1 & 0 \\ 0 & 1 & 0 & 0 \end{bmatrix}.$$

This is the same matrix we computed for **reverse CNOT** using $H^{\otimes 2}$ gates.

Using the two **SWAP** gates is a general method for creating a "reverse controlled" gate.

CNOT on nonadjacent qubits

What does the **CNOT** matrix look like for qubits not next to each other?

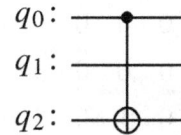

This configuration is as if we have an **ID** gate on q_0, and the control wire jumps over it to q_2:

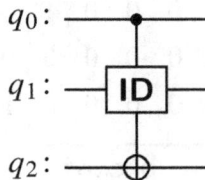

While we know how to compute the tensor product of matrices of 1- and 2-qubit gates, it is not apparent how we handle this gate with a qubit between two others. The behavior we want is equivalent to

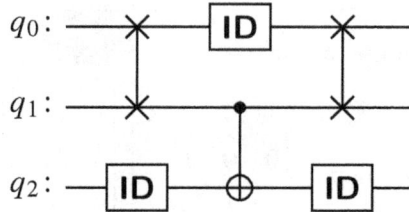

Written as a composition, this is the same as

$$(\textbf{SWAP}_{0,1} \otimes \textbf{ID}) \circ (\textbf{ID} \otimes \textbf{CNOT}_{1,2}) \circ (\textbf{SWAP}_{0,1} \otimes \textbf{ID}),$$

where the subscripts indicate on which qubits the **SWAP** and **CNOT** gates operate.

We can now express this as matrix products of matrix tensor products:

$$\left(
\underbrace{\begin{bmatrix} 1 & 0 & 0 & 0 \\ 0 & 0 & 1 & 0 \\ 0 & 1 & 0 & 0 \\ 0 & 0 & 0 & 1 \end{bmatrix}}_{\text{SWAP}} \otimes \underbrace{\begin{bmatrix} 1 & 0 \\ 0 & 1 \end{bmatrix}}_{\text{ID}}
\right)\left(
\underbrace{\begin{bmatrix} 1 & 0 \\ 0 & 1 \end{bmatrix}}_{\text{ID}} \otimes \underbrace{\begin{bmatrix} 1 & 0 & 0 & 0 \\ 0 & 1 & 0 & 0 \\ 0 & 0 & 0 & 1 \\ 0 & 0 & 1 & 0 \end{bmatrix}}_{\text{CNOT}}
\right)\left(
\underbrace{\begin{bmatrix} 1 & 0 & 0 & 0 \\ 0 & 0 & 1 & 0 \\ 0 & 1 & 0 & 0 \\ 0 & 0 & 0 & 1 \end{bmatrix}}_{\text{SWAP}} \otimes \underbrace{\begin{bmatrix} 1 & 0 \\ 0 & 1 \end{bmatrix}}_{\text{ID}}
\right)$$

which is

$$\underbrace{\begin{bmatrix}
1 & 0 & 0 & 0 & 0 & 0 & 0 & 0 \\
0 & 1 & 0 & 0 & 0 & 0 & 0 & 0 \\
0 & 0 & 0 & 0 & 1 & 0 & 0 & 0 \\
0 & 0 & 0 & 0 & 0 & 1 & 0 & 0 \\
0 & 0 & 1 & 0 & 0 & 0 & 0 & 0 \\
0 & 0 & 0 & 1 & 0 & 0 & 0 & 0 \\
0 & 0 & 0 & 0 & 0 & 0 & 1 & 0 \\
0 & 0 & 0 & 0 & 0 & 0 & 0 & 1
\end{bmatrix}}_{\text{SWAP}\otimes\text{ID}}
\underbrace{\begin{bmatrix}
1 & 0 & 0 & 0 & 0 & 0 & 0 & 0 \\
0 & 1 & 0 & 0 & 0 & 0 & 0 & 0 \\
0 & 0 & 0 & 1 & 0 & 0 & 0 & 0 \\
0 & 0 & 1 & 0 & 0 & 0 & 0 & 0 \\
0 & 0 & 0 & 0 & 1 & 0 & 0 & 0 \\
0 & 0 & 0 & 0 & 0 & 0 & 1 & 0 \\
0 & 0 & 0 & 0 & 0 & 0 & 0 & 1 \\
0 & 0 & 0 & 0 & 0 & 0 & 1 & 0
\end{bmatrix}}_{\text{ID}\otimes\text{CNOT}}
\underbrace{\begin{bmatrix}
1 & 0 & 0 & 0 & 0 & 0 & 0 & 0 \\
0 & 1 & 0 & 0 & 0 & 0 & 0 & 0 \\
0 & 0 & 0 & 0 & 1 & 0 & 0 & 0 \\
0 & 0 & 0 & 0 & 0 & 1 & 0 & 0 \\
0 & 0 & 1 & 0 & 0 & 0 & 0 & 0 \\
0 & 0 & 0 & 1 & 0 & 0 & 0 & 0 \\
0 & 0 & 0 & 0 & 0 & 0 & 1 & 0 \\
0 & 0 & 0 & 0 & 0 & 0 & 0 & 1
\end{bmatrix}}_{\text{SWAP}\otimes\text{ID}}$$

and this is equal to

$$C = \begin{bmatrix} 1 & 0 & 0 & 0 & 0 & 0 & 0 & 0 \\ 0 & 1 & 0 & 0 & 0 & 0 & 0 & 0 \\ 0 & 0 & 1 & 0 & 0 & 0 & 0 & 0 \\ 0 & 0 & 0 & 1 & 0 & 0 & 0 & 0 \\ 0 & 0 & 0 & 0 & 0 & 1 & 0 & 0 \\ 0 & 0 & 0 & 0 & 1 & 0 & 0 & 0 \\ 0 & 0 & 0 & 0 & 0 & 0 & 0 & 1 \\ 0 & 0 & 0 & 0 & 0 & 0 & 1 & 0 \end{bmatrix}.$$

Let's see what this does to the 3-qubit basis kets. To be concise, I use the transpose of row vectors for the kets:

$$C|000\rangle = C\begin{bmatrix}1\,0\,0\,0\,0\,0\,0\,0\end{bmatrix}^{\mathsf{T}} = \begin{bmatrix}1\,0\,0\,0\,0\,0\,0\,0\end{bmatrix}^{\mathsf{T}} = |000\rangle$$
$$C|001\rangle = C\begin{bmatrix}0\,1\,0\,0\,0\,0\,0\,0\end{bmatrix}^{\mathsf{T}} = \begin{bmatrix}0\,1\,0\,0\,0\,0\,0\,0\end{bmatrix}^{\mathsf{T}} = |001\rangle$$
$$C|010\rangle = C\begin{bmatrix}0\,0\,1\,0\,0\,0\,0\,0\end{bmatrix}^{\mathsf{T}} = \begin{bmatrix}0\,0\,1\,0\,0\,0\,0\,0\end{bmatrix}^{\mathsf{T}} = |010\rangle$$
$$C|011\rangle = C\begin{bmatrix}0\,0\,0\,1\,0\,0\,0\,0\end{bmatrix}^{\mathsf{T}} = \begin{bmatrix}0\,0\,0\,1\,0\,0\,0\,0\end{bmatrix}^{\mathsf{T}} = |011\rangle$$
$$C|100\rangle = C\begin{bmatrix}0\,0\,0\,0\,1\,0\,0\,0\end{bmatrix}^{\mathsf{T}} = \begin{bmatrix}0\,0\,0\,0\,0\,1\,0\,0\end{bmatrix}^{\mathsf{T}} = |101\rangle$$
$$C|101\rangle = C\begin{bmatrix}0\,0\,0\,0\,0\,1\,0\,0\end{bmatrix}^{\mathsf{T}} = \begin{bmatrix}0\,0\,0\,0\,1\,0\,0\,0\end{bmatrix}^{\mathsf{T}} = |100\rangle$$
$$C|110\rangle = C\begin{bmatrix}0\,0\,0\,0\,0\,0\,1\,0\end{bmatrix}^{\mathsf{T}} = \begin{bmatrix}0\,0\,0\,0\,0\,0\,0\,1\end{bmatrix}^{\mathsf{T}} = |111\rangle$$
$$C|111\rangle = C\begin{bmatrix}0\,0\,0\,0\,0\,0\,0\,1\end{bmatrix}^{\mathsf{T}} = \begin{bmatrix}0\,0\,0\,0\,0\,0\,1\,0\end{bmatrix}^{\mathsf{T}} = |110\rangle$$

First, note that the state of the middle qubits is not changed. Second, the state of the first qubit controls whether the third qubit's state flips. So, C is the correct matrix for **CNOT** between q_0 and q_2.

Exercise 8.11

What is the matrix in this example if we replace the **CNOT** with a **reverse CNOT**?

Exercise 8.12

Compute the matrix for

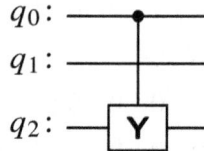

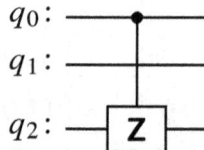

q_0: ●
q_1:
q_2: Y

Exercise 8.13

Compute the matrix for

q_0: ●
q_1:
q_2: Z

In an actual quantum computer, we may be able to connect two qubits directly and perform a **CNOT** with no **SWAP** gates. If we cannot connect them, we must insert **SWAP** gates before we can do a controlled operation. The 3-qubit connectivity map on the left side of Figure 8.1 does not require a **SWAP** for a **CNOT** between q_0 and q_2, but the right side does:

Figure 8.1: Fully versus partially connected qubits

Adding extra gates can reduce performance, so reducing the number of them can be a critical optimization from the quantum circuit you write to the final circuit executed on hardware. The qubit connectivity influences how we can create the most efficient circuits for specific hardware.

8.3.4 Controlling other 1-qubit gates

We can also create controlled 2-qubit gates for other 1-qubit gates. In block matrix form,

$$\mathbf{CY} = \left[\begin{array}{cc|cc} 1 & 0 & 0 & 0 \\ 0 & 1 & 0 & 0 \\ \hline 0 & 0 & 0 & -i \\ 0 & 0 & i & 0 \end{array}\right] \quad \text{and} \quad \mathbf{CH} = \left[\begin{array}{cc|cc} 1 & 0 & 0 & 0 \\ 0 & 1 & 0 & 0 \\ \hline 0 & 0 & \frac{\sqrt{2}}{2} & \frac{\sqrt{2}}{2} \\ 0 & 0 & \frac{\sqrt{2}}{2} & -\frac{\sqrt{2}}{2} \end{array}\right]$$

are the matrices in the standard basis for the **CY** and **CH** gates.

Exercise 8.14

What is the matrix for the controlled-$\sqrt{\mathbf{NOT}}$ gate, where $\sqrt{\mathbf{NOT}}$ is defined in section 7.6.13?

Exercise 8.15

On some types of quantum computers, it is easier to implement a **CZ** gate than a **CX** = **CNOT** gate. We know from section 7.6.5 that $\mathbf{Z} = \mathbf{H} \circ \mathbf{X} \circ \mathbf{H}$.

Draw a circuit involving **CZ** that implements **CX**.

In general, if

$$\mathbf{U} = \begin{bmatrix} a & b \\ c & d \end{bmatrix}$$

is a unitary matrix, then the matrix for the controlled-**U** (**CU**) gate

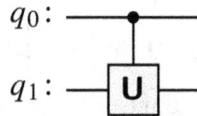

is

$$
CU = \left[\begin{array}{cc|cc}
1 & 0 & 0 & 0 \\
0 & 1 & 0 & 0 \\
\hline
0 & 0 & a & b \\
0 & 0 & c & d
\end{array}\right].
$$

We can reverse the states of the control and target qubits by putting a **SWAP** gate before and after the **CU** gate. The new matrix is

$$
\text{reverse } CU = \underbrace{\begin{bmatrix}
1 & 0 & 0 & 0 \\
0 & 0 & 1 & 0 \\
0 & 1 & 0 & 0 \\
0 & 0 & 0 & 1
\end{bmatrix}}_{\text{SWAP}}
\underbrace{\begin{bmatrix}
1 & 0 & 0 & 0 \\
0 & 1 & 0 & 0 \\
0 & 0 & a & b \\
0 & 0 & c & d
\end{bmatrix}}_{\text{CU}}
\underbrace{\begin{bmatrix}
1 & 0 & 0 & 0 \\
0 & 0 & 1 & 0 \\
0 & 1 & 0 & 0 \\
0 & 0 & 0 & 1
\end{bmatrix}}_{\text{SWAP}}
$$

$$
= \begin{bmatrix}
1 & 0 & 0 & 0 \\
0 & a & 0 & b \\
0 & 0 & 1 & 0 \\
0 & c & 0 & d
\end{bmatrix}.
$$

If **U** has a diagonal matrix, the **CU** and **reverse CU** gates have diagonal matrices.

In particular, suppose **U** is the R_φ^z gate from section 7.6.6. The matrices for the CR_φ^z and reverse CR_φ^z gates are the same:

$$
CR_\varphi^z = \text{reverse } CR_\varphi^z = \begin{bmatrix}
1 & 0 & 0 & 0 \\
0 & 1 & 0 & 0 \\
0 & 0 & 1 & 0 \\
0 & 0 & 0 & e^{\varphi i}
\end{bmatrix} = \begin{bmatrix}
1 & 0 & 0 & 0 \\
0 & 1 & 0 & 0 \\
0 & 0 & 1 & 0 \\
0 & 0 & 0 & \cos(\varphi) + \sin(\varphi)i
\end{bmatrix}.
$$

This means that each qubit can act as a control for the other, and each can be a target of the other.

CR_φ^z is a parameterized gate, with φ being the parameter. We often specify a particular radian value for φ, such as $CR_{\frac{\pi}{8}}^z$.

When I include the CR_φ^z gate in a circuit, it has what should now be a familiar form:

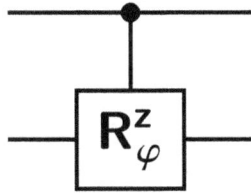

For the special case of the **CZ** gate, we show it with two controls to emphasize the symmetry:

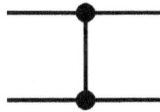

Exercise 8.16

What are the definitions of and matrices for the **CR**$^x_\varphi$ and **CR**$^y_\varphi$ gates?

Exercise 8.17

What are the matrices for the controlled and reverse controlled global phase gate **Ph**$_\varphi$ from section 7.6.11?

8.3.5 The quantum ZZ and R$^{zz}_\varphi$ gates

We conclude our discussion of 2-qubit gates in this chapter with several additional gates you may see in the quantum computing literature, particularly for quantum machine learning. [3]

The unparameterized **ZZ** gate is the tensor product $Z \otimes Z$ of two standard **Z** gates. It has the matrix

$$
\begin{bmatrix} 1 & 0 \\ 0 & -1 \end{bmatrix} \otimes \begin{bmatrix} 1 & 0 \\ 0 & -1 \end{bmatrix} = \begin{bmatrix} 1\begin{bmatrix} 1 & 0 \\ 0 & -1 \end{bmatrix} & 0\begin{bmatrix} 1 & 0 \\ 0 & -1 \end{bmatrix} \\ 0\begin{bmatrix} 1 & 0 \\ 0 & -1 \end{bmatrix} & -1\begin{bmatrix} 1 & 0 \\ 0 & -1 \end{bmatrix} \end{bmatrix} = \begin{bmatrix} 1 & 0 & 0 & 0 \\ 0 & -1 & 0 & 0 \\ 0 & 0 & -1 & 0 \\ 0 & 0 & 0 & 1 \end{bmatrix}.
$$

The parameterized version of the **ZZ** gate is the $\mathbf{R}_{\varphi}^{zz}$ gate with the matrix

$$
\begin{bmatrix}
e^{-\frac{i\varphi}{2}} & 0 & 0 & 0 \\
0 & e^{\frac{i\varphi}{2}} & 0 & 0 \\
0 & 0 & e^{\frac{i\varphi}{2}} & 0 \\
0 & 0 & 0 & e^{-\frac{i\varphi}{2}}
\end{bmatrix}.
$$

When $\varphi = \frac{\pi}{2}$, the matrix is

$$
\frac{\sqrt{2}}{2}
\begin{bmatrix}
1-i & 0 & 0 & 0 \\
0 & 1+i & 0 & 0 \\
0 & 0 & 1+i & 0 \\
0 & 0 & 0 & 1-i
\end{bmatrix}.
$$

The entry in the upper left of the matrix is

$$
e^{-\frac{i\pi/2}{2}} = e^{-\frac{i\pi}{4}} = \cos\left(-\frac{\pi}{4}\right) + i\sin\left(-\frac{\pi}{4}\right) = \frac{\sqrt{2}}{2}(1-i).
$$

Although I described this for two adjacent qubits, we can consider qubits with greater separation and tensor products with identity matrices. We will see this in section 12.8.1.

Exercise 8.18

Verify that $\mathbf{R}_0^{zz} = \mathbf{ID}$, $\mathbf{R}_{\pi}^{zz} = -\mathbf{Z} \otimes \mathbf{Z}$ and $\mathbf{R}_{2\pi}^{zz} = -\mathbf{ID} \otimes \mathbf{ID}$.

Exercise 8.19

What are the matrices for the **XX**, $\mathbf{R}_{\varphi}^{xx}$, **YY**, and $\mathbf{R}_{\varphi}^{yy}$ gates?

8.3.6   The quantum Toffoli CCNOT gate

The quantum Toffoli **CCNOT** gate is a double control gate operating on three qubits. If the states of the first two qubits are $|1\rangle$, the gate applies **X** to the third. For any other combination of $|0\rangle$ and $|1\rangle$ as states of the first two qubits, the state of the third qubit does not change. For general states for the first two qubits, we use linearity to determine the effect on the third qubit. In all cases, it is **ID** for the first two qubits.

Its matrix is an 8-by-8 permutation matrix that swaps the last two coefficients, like **CNOT**:

$$
\begin{bmatrix}
1 & 0 & 0 & 0 & 0 & 0 & 0 & 0 \\
0 & 1 & 0 & 0 & 0 & 0 & 0 & 0 \\
0 & 0 & 1 & 0 & 0 & 0 & 0 & 0 \\
0 & 0 & 0 & 1 & 0 & 0 & 0 & 0 \\
0 & 0 & 0 & 0 & 1 & 0 & 0 & 0 \\
0 & 0 & 0 & 0 & 0 & 1 & 0 & 0 \\
0 & 0 & 0 & 0 & 0 & 0 & 0 & 1 \\
0 & 0 & 0 & 0 & 0 & 0 & 1 & 0
\end{bmatrix} .
$$

The **CCNOT** gate spans three wires in a circuit. The top two lines are the control qubits:

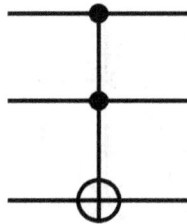

The Toffoli gate is also known as the **CCX** gate. It is an example of a *multi-controlled gate*.

8.3.7 The quantum Fredkin CSWAP gate

The quantum Fredkin **CSWAP** gate is a control gate operating on three qubits. If the state of the first qubit is $|1\rangle$, the states of the second and third qubits are swapped, as in **SWAP**. If it is $|0\rangle$, nothing changes. For general states $a|0\rangle + b|1\rangle$ for the first qubit, we use linearity to determine the effects on the second and third qubits.

Its matrix is an 8-by-8 permutation matrix:

$$\begin{bmatrix} 1 & 0 & 0 & 0 & 0 & 0 & 0 & 0 \\ 0 & 1 & 0 & 0 & 0 & 0 & 0 & 0 \\ 0 & 0 & 1 & 0 & 0 & 0 & 0 & 0 \\ 0 & 0 & 0 & 1 & 0 & 0 & 0 & 0 \\ 0 & 0 & 0 & 0 & 1 & 0 & 0 & 0 \\ 0 & 0 & 0 & 0 & 0 & 0 & 1 & 0 \\ 0 & 0 & 0 & 0 & 0 & 1 & 0 & 0 \\ 0 & 0 & 0 & 0 & 0 & 0 & 0 & 1 \end{bmatrix}.$$

Like the **CCNOT**, the **CSWAP** gate spans three wires. The top line is the control qubit:

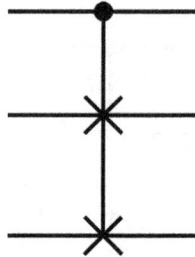

8.4   The cat

In 1935, physicist Erwin Schrödinger (Figure 8.2) proposed a thought experiment that would spawn close to a century of profound scientific and philosophical thought and many bad jokes. Our explanation of the fate of Schrödinger's cat uses several qubits and **CNOT** gates.

Thought experiments are common among mathematicians and scientists. The basic premise is that the idea is not something you would really *do* but something you want to think through to understand the implications and consequences.

Schrödinger's experiment was his attempt to show how the *Copenhagen interpretation* promoted by Niels Bohr (Figure 8.3) and Werner Heisenberg in the late 1920s could lead to a ridiculous conclusion for large objects. [79] This interpretation is one of the popular ideas for how and why quantum mechanics works, and it includes the ideas of probabilities, indeterminism, and irreversible measurement. There are other interpretations, such as the *Many-worlds* and *hidden variables* theories. [97]

By ''large'' here, I mean ''large as a cat.''

Figure 8.2: Erwin Schrödinger in 1933

Exercise 8.20

Research and read about the role the city of Copenhagen in Denmark played in the development of quantum mechanics.

The setup

In a large steel box containing more than enough air for a cat to breathe for several hours, we place a small amount of radioactive material with a 0.5 probability of having a single atom decay and emitting one particle per hour.

We also add a Geiger counter that can detect that single emission, plus a connected hammer that can smash open a closed vial of cyanide poison. If the Geiger counter detects anything, the hammer swings, and the cyanide releases into the air.

We now place the confused-looking but otherwise charming cat into the box and seal the top.

Feel free to replace the cat with something else that would not survive in the presence of cyanide.

The wait

While we let time go by, we wonder about the cat's state. Is he doing well, or has he cast off his mortal coil? Has the radioactive emission occurred and triggered the hammer?

Until we look, we don't know. As far as our knowledge goes, the cat is in a superposition of being dead and alive. Our opening the top and observing what has happened in the box causes

---

Figure 8.3: Niels Bohr in 1922

the superposition to collapse to $|\textbf{dead}\rangle = |0\rangle$ or $|\textbf{alive}\rangle = |1\rangle$. This behavior is according to the Copenhagen interpretation.

In the *Many-worlds* interpretation, two realities are created when the opportunity for a choice is made. In one world, the cat is dead. In the other, it is not.

Let's express this situation in the language of a quantum circuit.

A circuit

Consider this simple circuit with two **CNOT** gates:

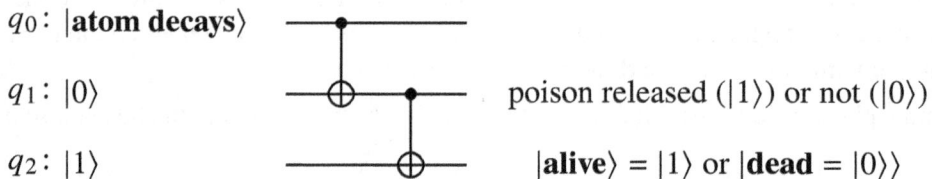

For q_0, an input state of $|0\rangle$ means no atom decays when the circuit runs, while $|1\rangle$ means the atom emitted a particle.

q_1 is set to an initial state of $|0\rangle$ but is flipped to $|1\rangle$ if an atom decays. The $|1\rangle$ causes the hammer to break the vial and the cyanide to enter the air.

For q_2, the cat starts in $|\textbf{alive}\rangle = |1\rangle$. The final state of the cat only switches to $|\textbf{dead}\rangle = |0\rangle$ if the poison is released.

8.5   Summary

This chapter introduced the standard 2-qubit and 3-qubit gate operations to complement the classical forms from section 2.4. The **CNOT / X** and **CZ** gates allow us to entangle qubits. Entanglement, along with superposition and interference, is essential in quantum computing.

Our cat-in-the-box was translated into quantum terms and got its own circuit.

Now that we have a collection of gates, it's time to put them into circuits and implement algorithms. We begin doing that in the next chapter. In section 9.3, we will see how we can create any quantum gate by combining others, at least to a very close approximation. This extends our discussion of logic gate universality in section 2.4.

9

Wiring Up the Circuits

The world is all gates, all opportunities, strings of tension
waiting to be struck.

– Ralph Waldo Emerson

Now that we understand qubits and the operations we can apply to one or more of them, it's time to string together the actions to do something useful. In this chapter, we build out circuits and discuss their properties. From there, we survey basic algorithms, such as those that involve oracles and searches. Through this, you'll better understand the core programming idioms in quantum computing.

Nontrivial quantum algorithms take advantage of qubit entanglement, the graceful way qubits work together and interact until we get a result. I think of this scripted interplay among qubits as an elegant dance, and that's how this book got its title.

Topics covered in this chapter

9.1 So many gates

In practice, a hardware quantum computer implements a core set of primitive gates, and we construct the others using circuits of the primitives. These core operations may be among the ones we saw in the last chapter, or they may be much stranger looking: you can consider any 2-by-2 unitary matrix a 1-qubit gate.

The primitive gates depend on the technology used to create the physical quantum computer. We construct more advanced gates from these primitive gates. For example, the *Qiskit* and *Cirq* open-source quantum computing frameworks provide a large selection of gates you can use. [41] [179]

At the hardware level, experimental physicists and engineers work to optimize the core gates. Above that, other physicists and computer scientists try to create the best-performing higher-level gates.

In the classical case, machine code is extremely low-level and directly instructs the processor. Above that is assembly code, which abstracts the machine code a bit and makes certain common operations easier. The C programming language is above assembly code but still gives you fine control over memory usage. Above there, you get high-level languages such as Python, C++, Go, and Swift. At this level, you need to know very little, if anything, about the hardware on which you are running.

In this chapter, I stick to the most commonly available quantum gates as we build out the circuits.

9.2 From gates to circuits

A *quantum register* is a collection of qubits we use for computation. We number the qubits in the register with labels such as $q_0, q_1, \ldots, q_{n-1}$ or $q_1, q_2, \ldots, q_n$. The quantum system initializes all qubits in a register to state $|0\rangle$.

A *quantum circuit* is a sequence of gates applied to one or more qubits in a quantum register.

In some algorithms, we group qubits into one or more labeled registers to better delineate their roles. It's common to have an *upper register* and a *lower register*, for example.

Let's look at some simple example circuits to see how we put them together and what we call their components.

9.2.1 Constructing a circuit

The simplest circuit is

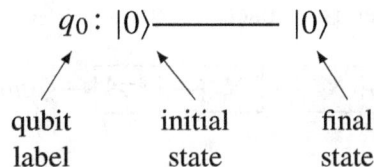

$$q_0: |0\rangle \longrightarrow |0\rangle$$

qubit   initial   final
label   state   state

We give qubit q_0 the initial state $|0\rangle$, but then nothing else happens. The register contains one qubit.

Slightly more interesting is

$$q_0: |0\rangle \longrightarrow \boxed{\nearrow} \longrightarrow |m_0\rangle = |0\rangle$$

We initialize qubit q_0 to $|0\rangle$ and do an immediate measurement. $|m_0\rangle$ holds its measurement state, which, of course, must be $|0\rangle$. When I show a measurement result such as $|m_0\rangle$, it can only have the value $|0\rangle$ or $|1\rangle$. We interpret these states as **0** or **1** if the context requires it.

Each horizontal application of gates for a qubit is called a *wire* or a *line*. Another "do nothing" circuit invokes the **ID** gate and then a measurement:

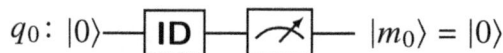

$$q_0: |0\rangle \!-\!\boxed{\textbf{ID}}\!-\!\boxed{\nearrow}\!-\ |m_0\rangle = |0\rangle$$

The result is the same. The wire has depth 1: we count the gates but do not include the final measurement. The depth of a circuit is the maximum of the depths of its wires. We often omit the **ID** gate in circuits that have multiple wires. You'll see the bare wire where the gate would have been.

To exercise a gate that changes state, we use **X** to flip from $|0\rangle$ to $|1\rangle$:

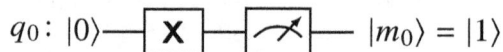

$$q_0: |0\rangle \!-\!\boxed{\textbf{X}}\!-\!\boxed{\nearrow}\!-\ |m_0\rangle = |1\rangle$$

The circuit has width 1 because it involves 1 qubit in a nontrivial way.

The next circuit operates on a 3-qubit quantum register, but it also only has width 1.

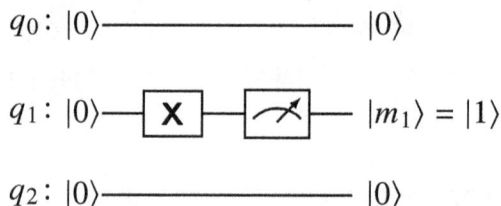

$$q_0: |0\rangle \!-\!\!-\!\!-\!\!-\!\!-\!\!-\!\!-\!\!-\!\!-\ |0\rangle$$

$$q_1: |0\rangle \!-\!\boxed{\textbf{X}}\!-\!\boxed{\nearrow}\!-\ |m_1\rangle = |1\rangle$$

$$q_2: |0\rangle \!-\!\!-\!\!-\!\!-\!\!-\!\!-\!\!-\!\!-\!\!-\ |0\rangle$$

Two consecutive **X** gates return us back to $|0\rangle$:

$$q_0: |0\rangle \!-\!\boxed{\textbf{X}}\!-\!\boxed{\textbf{X}}\!-\!\boxed{\nearrow}\!-\ |m_0\rangle = |0\rangle$$

This is a circuit of depth 2.

> Software development frameworks for classical computing have been available since at least the 1990s. These provide the tools and libraries you need to create applications. As an industry, we have learned the best practices for giving coders what they need for efficient software creation.

When you use a quantum software development framework such as Qiskit or Cirq, it may optimize your circuit. One technique is to remove unneeded gates.

The Hadamard **H** gate puts the qubit into a nontrivial superposition. Upon measurement, it collapses to either $|0\rangle$ or $|1\rangle$ with equal probability.

$$q_0: |0\rangle \quad \boxed{H} \quad \boxed{\nearrow} \quad |m_0\rangle = |0\rangle \text{ or } |1\rangle$$

A sequence of two consecutive **H** gates with no measurement in between is the same as an **ID** gate. You can optimize a circuit by removing the successive **H** gates, since **H** is its own inverse. The results of the gates on the two wires in the following circuit are equivalent:

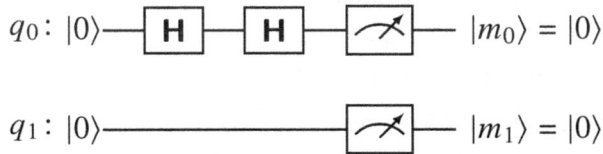

$$q_0: |0\rangle \quad \boxed{H} \quad \boxed{H} \quad \boxed{\nearrow} \quad |m_0\rangle = |0\rangle$$

$$q_1: |0\rangle \quad \boxed{\nearrow} \quad |m_1\rangle = |0\rangle$$

The first has depth 2, but is depth 0 after optimization.

In the following circuit, the first wire has depth 2, and the second has depth 3. The circuit depth is 3, the maximum of the wire depths. The register contains two qubits.

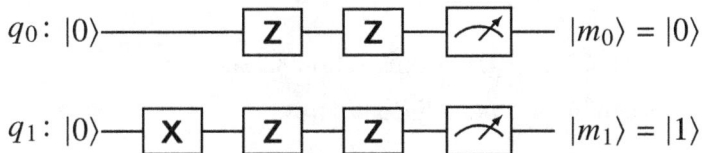

$$q_0: |0\rangle \quad \boxed{Z} \quad \boxed{Z} \quad \boxed{\nearrow} \quad |m_0\rangle = |0\rangle$$

$$q_1: |0\rangle \quad \boxed{X} \quad \boxed{Z} \quad \boxed{Z} \quad \boxed{\nearrow} \quad |m_1\rangle = |1\rangle$$

Exercise 9.1

After removing unneeded gates from the previous circuit, what is the circuit depth?

Next up, consider

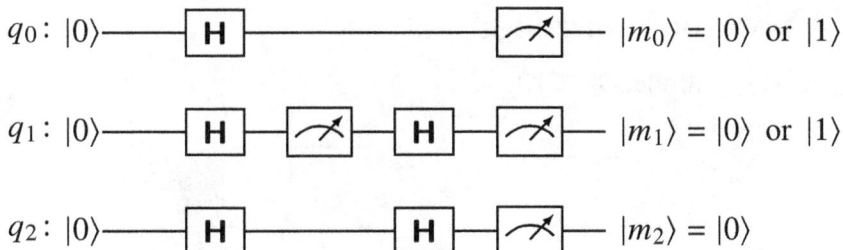

$$q_0: |0\rangle \quad \boxed{H} \quad \boxed{\nearrow} \quad |m_0\rangle = |0\rangle \text{ or } |1\rangle$$

$$q_1: |0\rangle \quad \boxed{H} \quad \boxed{\nearrow} \quad \boxed{H} \quad \boxed{\nearrow} \quad |m_1\rangle = |0\rangle \text{ or } |1\rangle$$

$$q_2: |0\rangle \quad \boxed{H} \quad \boxed{H} \quad \boxed{\nearrow} \quad |m_2\rangle = |0\rangle$$

This last circuit is a prime example of quantum randomness. In the first wire, we put q_0 into superposition. When measured, it is either $|0\rangle$ or $|1\rangle$ with equal probability.

In the second wire, we do an **H** followed by measurement. The state is then 50–50 randomly $|0\rangle$ or $|1\rangle$. We do another **H** followed by measurement. Again, the state is 50–50 $|0\rangle$ or $|1\rangle$.

If we omit the measurement in the middle, the qubit stays in superposition, and the two **H** gates cancel each other. We always get $|0\rangle$.

The real-life situation we typically use to illustrate this involves flipping a coin, which can land heads up or down. If it starts heads up and you flip it, it lands randomly heads up or down. If you flip it again, it still lands heads up or down with equal probabilities if it is a fair coin. This classical behavior happens whether or not you peek at the coin between flips.

Quantum theory instead says *if you do not peek,* the coin lands after the second flip in the same state it started. Weird but true.

Two-qubit gates such as **CNOT** affect more than one qubit. This circuit inverts the standard **CNOT** behavior so that the second qubit is the control:

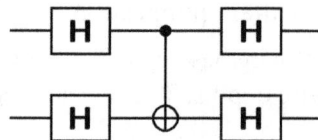

It implements a **reverse CNOT** gate from section 8.3.3.

Multi-qubit gates can involve nonadjacent wires.

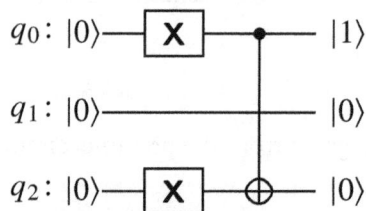

9.2.2   A note on controlled gates

A **CNOT** gate is a controlled-**X** (**CX**).

Its matrix is

$$
\left[
\begin{array}{cc|cc}
1 & 0 & 0 & 0 \\
0 & 1 & 0 & 0 \\
\hline
0 & 0 & 0 & 1 \\
0 & 0 & 1 & 0
\end{array}
\right].
$$

The identity matrix is in the upper left, and the **X** matrix is in the lower right. In basis kets and the computational basis, we have

$$
\mathbf{CNOT}|00\rangle =
\begin{bmatrix}
1 & 0 & 0 & 0 \\
0 & 1 & 0 & 0 \\
0 & 0 & 0 & 1 \\
0 & 0 & 1 & 0
\end{bmatrix}
\begin{bmatrix}
1 \\ 0 \\ 0 \\ 0
\end{bmatrix}
=
\begin{bmatrix}
1 \\ 0 \\ 0 \\ 0
\end{bmatrix}
= |00\rangle
$$

and

$$
\mathbf{CNOT}|10\rangle =
\begin{bmatrix}
1 & 0 & 0 & 0 \\
0 & 1 & 0 & 0 \\
0 & 0 & 0 & 1 \\
0 & 0 & 1 & 0
\end{bmatrix}
\begin{bmatrix}
0 \\ 0 \\ 1 \\ 0
\end{bmatrix}
=
\begin{bmatrix}
0 \\ 0 \\ 0 \\ 1
\end{bmatrix}
= |11\rangle .
$$

The results are what we expect. In these two cases, the second qubit state flips from $|0\rangle$ and $|1\rangle$ only if the first qubit is $|1\rangle$.

But what if I were to tell you that

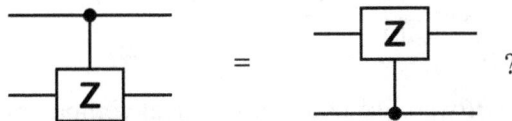

That doesn't seem right. I thought nothing happened to the control qubit! On the left, the top qubit state should "stay the same," and ditto for the bottom qubit on the right. But if these two circuits are equivalent, something odd is going on.

For the version on the left, we have

$$
\begin{aligned}
|0\rangle \otimes |0\rangle &\mapsto |0\rangle \otimes |0\rangle \\
|0\rangle \otimes |1\rangle &\mapsto |0\rangle \otimes |1\rangle \\
|1\rangle \otimes |0\rangle &\mapsto |1\rangle \otimes |0\rangle \\
|1\rangle \otimes |1\rangle &\mapsto |1\rangle \otimes (-|1\rangle) .
\end{aligned}
$$

On the right,

$$\begin{aligned}
|0\rangle \otimes |0\rangle &\mapsto |0\rangle \otimes |0\rangle \\
|0\rangle \otimes |1\rangle &\mapsto |0\rangle \otimes |1\rangle \\
|1\rangle \otimes |0\rangle &\mapsto |1\rangle \otimes |0\rangle \\
|1\rangle \otimes |1\rangle &\mapsto (-|1\rangle) \otimes |1\rangle .
\end{aligned}$$

Look at the last lines. If the controlled gates operate in the same way, then

$$|1\rangle \otimes (-|1\rangle) = (-|1\rangle) \otimes |1\rangle = (-1)\,(|1\rangle \otimes |1\rangle) .$$

This equality follows from the bilinearity of the tensor product: we can move the scalar -1 from one side of the tensor to the other or out in front. Hence, the two controlled gates are equivalent.

9.3 Building blocks and universality

In section 2.4, we discussed classical gates, and I illustrated how to create an **or** gate from **nand** gates. **nand** is universal because we can make all the other classical logic gates from it. For example,

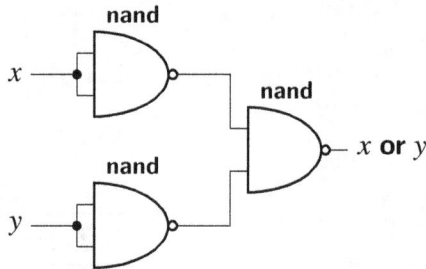

We could construct any software we code for classical computers from millions of **nand** gates, but it would be horribly inefficient. There are higher-level gates and circuits in modern processors that are tremendously faster.

The basic **CNOT** acts like a **xor** on the standard kets.

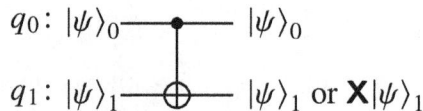

This maps the basis kets in this way:

$$|00\rangle \mapsto |00\rangle \qquad |10\rangle \mapsto |11\rangle$$
$$|01\rangle \mapsto |01\rangle \qquad |11\rangle \mapsto |10\rangle$$

The **xor** result is the final qubit state of q_1. More than simply a logic operation, this implements addition mod 2. That is, this standard gate does a basic arithmetic operation "$\oplus$". For example, $|1\rangle \oplus |1\rangle = |0\rangle$ and $|1\rangle \oplus |0\rangle = |1\rangle$.

If we do not want to modify one of the input qubits, we can put the value of the **xor** in a third output, or *ancilla*, qubit.

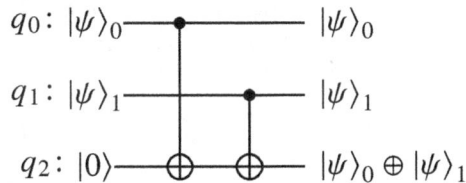

$$
\begin{array}{ll}
q_0: |\psi\rangle_0 & |\psi\rangle_0 \\
q_1: |\psi\rangle_1 & |\psi\rangle_1 \\
q_2: |0\rangle & |\psi\rangle_0 \oplus |\psi\rangle_1
\end{array}
$$

Exercise 9.2

Suppose we have three input qubits, q_0, q_1, and q_2, in states $|\psi\rangle_0$, $|\psi\rangle_1$, and $|\psi\rangle_2$, respectively. We want to put $|\psi\rangle_0 \oplus |\psi\rangle_1$ in ancilla qubit q_3 and put $|\psi\rangle_0 \oplus |\psi\rangle_2$ in ancilla qubit q_4. Draw the circuit that does this.

9.3.1   The Toffoli gate

The quantum Toffoli **CCNOT** gate operates on three qubits. If the first two qubits are $|1\rangle$, it flips the third. If they are some other combination of $|0\rangle$ and $|1\rangle$, the gate does nothing. For general quantum states, we use linearity to determine the effect on the third qubit. For example,

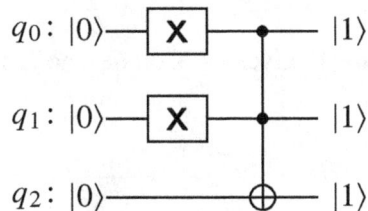

$$
\begin{array}{lll}
q_0: |0\rangle & \boxed{X} & |1\rangle \\
q_1: |0\rangle & \boxed{X} & |1\rangle \\
q_2: |0\rangle & & |1\rangle
\end{array}
$$

In this example, we move q_0 and q_1 into the $|1\rangle$ state. The Toffoli gate then flips the state of q_2 from $|0\rangle$ to $|1\rangle$.

Consider this particular use of the gate:

$$q_0: |\psi\rangle_0 \quad\quad\quad\bullet\quad\quad |\psi\rangle_0$$
$$q_1: |\psi\rangle_1 \quad\quad\quad\bullet\quad\quad |\psi\rangle_1$$
$$q_2: |0\rangle \quad \boxed{\mathbf{X}}\quad \oplus\quad |\psi\rangle_2$$

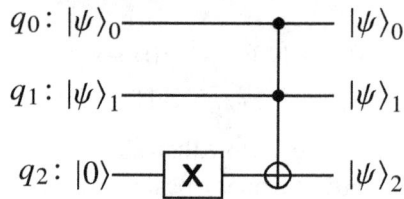

What is the value of $|\psi\rangle_2$ as $|\psi\rangle_0$ and $|\psi\rangle_1$ take on values of $|0\rangle$ and $|1\rangle$?

Compare the ket table on the left with the truth table for **nand** on the right in Figure 9.1. Substituting $|1\rangle$ for **True** and $|0\rangle$ for **False**, they are identical.

$|\psi\rangle_0$	$|\psi\rangle_1$	$|\psi\rangle_2$	p	q	p **nand** q
$|1\rangle$	$|1\rangle$	$|0\rangle$	True	True	False
$|1\rangle$	$|0\rangle$	$|1\rangle$	True	False	True
$|0\rangle$	$|1\rangle$	$|1\rangle$	False	True	True
$|0\rangle$	$|0\rangle$	$|1\rangle$	False	False	True

Figure 9.1: Simulating a nand gate with a Toffoli gate

If you set the state of the first qubit to $|1\rangle$, the Toffoli gate reduces to **CNOT** on q_1 add q_2.

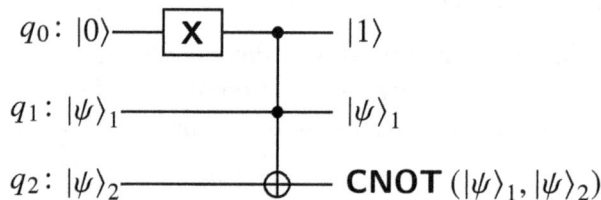

$$q_0: |0\rangle \quad \boxed{\mathbf{X}}\quad \bullet \quad |1\rangle$$
$$q_1: |\psi\rangle_1 \quad\quad\quad \bullet \quad |\psi\rangle_1$$
$$q_2: |\psi\rangle_2 \quad\quad\quad \oplus \quad \mathbf{CNOT}\,(|\psi\rangle_1, |\psi\rangle_2)$$

Setting the first two states to $|1\rangle$ gives us **X** on q_2, though this is a complicated way of producing that gate:

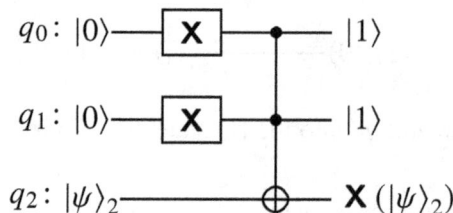

$$q_0: |0\rangle \quad \boxed{\mathbf{X}}\quad \bullet \quad |1\rangle$$
$$q_1: |0\rangle \quad \boxed{\mathbf{X}}\quad \bullet \quad |1\rangle$$
$$q_2: |\psi\rangle_2 \quad\quad\quad \oplus \quad \mathbf{X}\,(|\psi\rangle_2)$$

The basic Toffoli gate has the same effect as **and** on the basis kets $|0\rangle$ and $|1\rangle$ when you set the third qubit's initial state to $|0\rangle$.

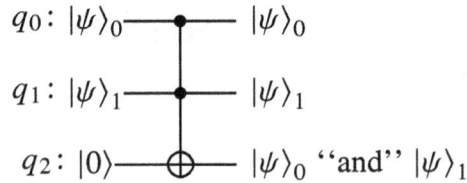

$$q_0: |\psi\rangle_0 \quad\bullet\quad |\psi\rangle_0$$
$$q_1: |\psi\rangle_1 \quad\bullet\quad |\psi\rangle_1$$
$$q_2: |0\rangle \quad\oplus\quad |\psi\rangle_0 \text{ ``and'' } |\psi\rangle_1$$

The initial values are the states for q_0 and q_1.

9.3.2 Making nand reversible

The **nand** boolean logic gate is universal, but it is not reversible. The gate has two inputs but only one output. We can create a reversible gate by using another bit and an **xor** gate.

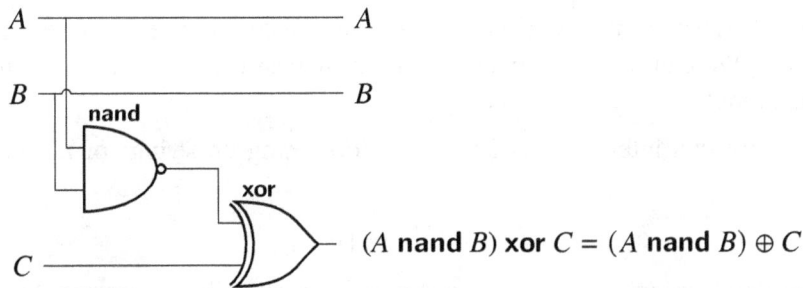

$(A \text{ nand } B) \text{ xor } C = (A \text{ nand } B) \oplus C$

When $C = 0$, we get the result of the **nand** gate. Recall that "$\oplus$" is an alternate notation for **xor**, and we can think of it as bit addition mode 2.

To go backward, we already know A and B, but how do we get C? Any bit value **xor**ed with itself is **0**. So

$$(A \text{ nand } B) \text{ xor } (A \text{ nand } B) \text{ xor } C = 0 \text{ xor } C = C.$$

Exercise 9.3

Show that the circuit is its own inverse.

This method also works to create reversible versions of the **and, or, xor, nor,** and **xnor** gates. Note that **not** is already reversible.

Exercise 9.4

By a similar construction, the method works for logic operations with more than two inputs. How would you extend this method to make a logic operation with three inputs and one output reversible? Draw the circuit.

Exercise 9.5

How would you extend this method to make a logic operation with three inputs and two outputs reversible? Draw the circuit.

Since **nand** is universal, we can construct any logic operation with n inputs and one output from it. From the above, we can build a reversible version of the logic operation from reversible gates.

In section 9.3.1, we saw that we could use the Toffoli gate to create the quantum equivalent of a **nand** gate. We can create a quantum circuit, necessarily reversible, from any logic operation on n input bits.

In general, we can interpret any function f operating on strings of n bits as a logic operation:

$$f : \{0, 1\}^n \to \{0, 1\}$$

With the considerations in this section, we can make it reversible by **xor**ing it with another input bit. We can also construct a quantum circuit that implements the reversible operation. We will see this again when we discuss oracles.

Starting in section 9.5, we shall see that specific algorithms that take advantage of quantum properties can be significantly faster than classical alternatives. In the years to come, we will eventually employ classical and quantum computers in a complementary but integrated fashion, taking advantage of their best and most powerful features.

9.3.3 Building more complicated circuits

What are the computed states in the following circuit? The circuit has three 2-qubit gates: a **CNOT**, a **reverse CNOT**, and a final **CNOT**.

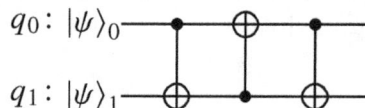

It has this effect on the standard basis kets:

$$|00\rangle \mapsto |00\rangle \qquad |10\rangle \mapsto |01\rangle$$
$$|01\rangle \mapsto |10\rangle \qquad |11\rangle \mapsto |11\rangle$$

Let's examine the states after each gate for the beginning state $|01\rangle$. After the first **CNOT**, the state is still $|01\rangle$. The **reverse CNOT** changes the state to $|11\rangle$. The final **CNOT** moves it to $|10\rangle$. It appears to swap the states of the two qubits.

If we do not have the **SWAP** gate available when coding for a particular quantum computer, we can implement it this way as a reusable circuit. We can take it further and use only Hadamard **H** and **CNOT** gates.

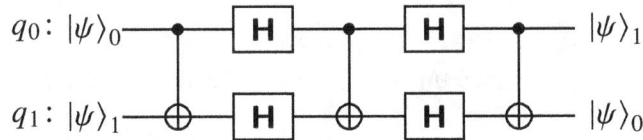

I hope you are getting the sense that some gates are especially valuable as building blocks for other gates. It appears that with some ingenuity, we can do almost anything.

Exercise 9.6

Show that this circuit

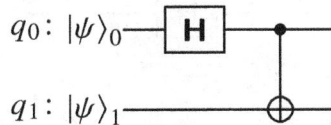

creates the four Bell states

$$|\Phi^+\rangle = \tfrac{\sqrt{2}}{2}|00\rangle + \tfrac{\sqrt{2}}{2}|11\rangle \qquad |\Psi^+\rangle = \tfrac{\sqrt{2}}{2}|01\rangle + \tfrac{\sqrt{2}}{2}|10\rangle$$

$$|\Phi^-\rangle = \tfrac{\sqrt{2}}{2}|00\rangle - \tfrac{\sqrt{2}}{2}|11\rangle \qquad |\Psi^-\rangle = \tfrac{\sqrt{2}}{2}|01\rangle - \tfrac{\sqrt{2}}{2}|10\rangle$$

from the standard basis kets $|00\rangle$, $|01\rangle$, $|10\rangle$, and $|11\rangle$.

Exercise 9.7

What do you get if you apply the same circuit again to each of the four Bell states? Use linearity. This is an example of measurement relative to a basis other than $|00\rangle$, $|01\rangle$, $|10\rangle$, and $|11\rangle$.

Among all the gates we have discussed, several are more fundamental than others, especially **H** and **CNOT**. Just as **nand** was universal for classical logic gates, is there a finite set of quantum gates from which we can create all the others?

No. We cannot get all the quantum gates from a finite set because of the infinite number of $\mathbf{R}_\varphi^z$ gates as φ varies between 0 and 2π.

If we start with the 1-qubit gates built from all the 2-by-2 complex unitary matrices and throw in the **CNOT** gate, we get a universal, albeit infinite, set. We can even construct all n-qubit gates from blocks of these.

It's beyond the scope of this book, but it is possible to numerically closely approximate the effect of any quantum gate using combinations of only **CNOT**, **H**, and **T**. [162, Section 4.5]

Exercise 9.8

The circuit

$$q_0 : |0\rangle - \boxed{H} - \bullet$$
$$q_1 : |0\rangle - \oplus - \bullet$$
$$q_2 : |0\rangle - \oplus$$

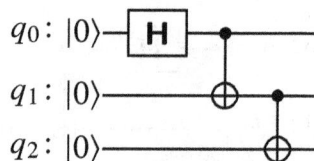

creates the entangled Greenberger-Horne-Zeilinger (GHZ) state. What is this state in terms of kets? Show your calculations.

9.3.4 Copying a qubit

In classical computing, we often make copies of information. For example, we might have a database and extract information from it for processing. The original data remains in the database, and we just work with a copy. Can we do that with quantum computing?

Let's try to put together a circuit that makes a copy of a qubit's state. We're looking for something like

$q_0: |\psi\rangle_0$ —[**CLONE**]— $|\psi\rangle_0$

$q_1: |0\rangle$ —[ ]— $|\psi\rangle_0$

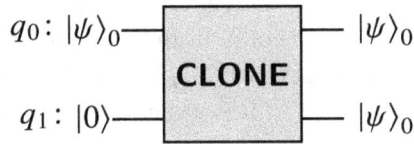

The initial state of q_1 doesn't matter since it is a placeholder we want to replace with the state of q_0. We are not looking for a gate that clones one particular qubit state but one that makes a copy of **any** arbitrary state.

If the **CLONE** gate exists, let C be its unitary matrix in the standard ket basis in $\mathbf{C}^2 \otimes \mathbf{C}^2$. As usual, we take

$$|\psi\rangle_0 = a|0\rangle + b|1\rangle.$$

The result after cloning is $|\psi\rangle_0 \otimes |\psi\rangle_0$. That is,

$$C\left(|\psi\rangle_0 \otimes |0\rangle\right) = |\psi\rangle_0 \otimes |\psi\rangle_0.$$

Are these really equal? On the left,

$$
\begin{aligned}
C\left(|\psi\rangle_0 \otimes |0\rangle\right) &= C\left((a|0\rangle + b|1\rangle) \otimes |0\rangle\right) \\
&= C\left(a|0\rangle \otimes |0\rangle + b|1\rangle \otimes |0\rangle\right) \\
&= aC\left(|0\rangle \otimes |0\rangle\right) + bC\left(|1\rangle \otimes |0\rangle\right) \\
&= a|00\rangle + b|11\rangle.
\end{aligned}
$$

Exercise 9.9

Explain the equality

$$aC\left(|0\rangle \otimes |0\rangle\right) + bC\left(|1\rangle \otimes |0\rangle\right) = a|00\rangle + b|11\rangle.$$

On the right,

$$
\begin{aligned}
|\psi\rangle_0 \otimes |\psi\rangle_0 &= (a|0\rangle + b|1\rangle) \otimes (a|0\rangle + b|1\rangle) \\
&= a^2|00\rangle + ab|01\rangle + ab|10\rangle + b^2|11\rangle.
\end{aligned}
$$

For arbitrary a and b in $\mathbf{C}$ with $|a|^2 + |b|^2 = 1$,

$$a|00\rangle + b|11\rangle \neq a^2|00\rangle + ab|01\rangle + ab|10\rangle + b^2|11\rangle.$$

There is no **CLONE** gate that can duplicate the quantum state of a qubit. This is the *No-Cloning Theorem* and has ramifications for the design of algorithms, how we might do quantum error correction, and the ultimate creation of quantum memory.

Did this result surprise you? In the classical case, we can clone a bit value, but this is not possible for a qubit state. It falls out naturally from the theory, but is quite a restriction. The result was first formulated by James Park in 1970 [170] and proved independently in 1982 by Wootters and Zurek [238] and Dieks [67]. It is a central concept within the field of Quantum Information Theory.

9.3.5 Teleportation

If I can't copy a qubit's state and give it to you, is there any way for you to get it even if mine is destroyed? The answer is yes, and we call the process *quantum teleportation*. The technique was first published in 1993 by Charles Bennett et al. [12]

Though the name sounds like something out of science fiction, it doesn't involve demate-rialization, rematerialization, or faster-than-light travel.

The technique involves three qubits: M, which is my qubit; Y, which is your qubit; and Q, which is the qubit whose state I want to transfer from me to you. We use entanglement as the connection and transference mechanism, but we also require two classical bits of information transmitted via traditional means.

The qubit Q is in some arbitrary quantum state $|\psi\rangle_Q = a|0\rangle + b|1\rangle$. When we are done, you will know this state, but I will no longer have access to it.

We begin by entangling M and Y. There are infinite ways of doing this, but the usual choice is to use one of the four Bell states. I'll use

$$|\Phi^+\rangle = \frac{\sqrt{2}}{2}|00\rangle + \frac{\sqrt{2}}{2}|11\rangle,$$

but you can use any of them with appropriate changes to the algorithm and math below.

To keep track of which qubit belongs to whom, I modify the notation slightly so that

$$|\Phi^+\rangle_{MY} = \frac{\sqrt{2}}{2}|00\rangle_{MY} + \frac{\sqrt{2}}{2}|11\rangle_{MY}.$$

The first qubit is mine, and the second is yours.

Suppose we did this entanglement while we were physically close, but now you can get on a plane and go as far away as you wish. You might even take a trip to a space station orbiting the planet. The qubits are entangled and will stay that way in this scenario.

Next, I put Q into the mix to get

$$|\psi\rangle_Q \otimes |\Phi^+\rangle_{MY} = \left(a|0\rangle_Q + b|1\rangle_Q\right) \otimes \left(\frac{\sqrt{2}}{2}|00\rangle_{MY} + \frac{\sqrt{2}}{2}|11\rangle_{MY}\right).$$

Consider the identities I first introduced in Exercise 9.6:

$$|00\rangle = \tfrac{\sqrt{2}}{2}\left(|\Phi^+\rangle + |\Phi^-\rangle\right) \qquad |11\rangle = \tfrac{\sqrt{2}}{2}\left(|\Phi^+\rangle - |\Phi^-\rangle\right)$$

$$|01\rangle = \tfrac{\sqrt{2}}{2}\left(|\Psi^+\rangle + |\Psi^-\rangle\right) \qquad |10\rangle = \tfrac{\sqrt{2}}{2}\left(|\Psi^+\rangle - |\Psi^-\rangle\right).$$

Using linearity, we rewrite the above in the following way:

$$\left(a|0\rangle_Q + b|1\rangle_Q\right) \otimes \left(\frac{\sqrt{2}}{2}|00\rangle_{MY} + \frac{\sqrt{2}}{2}|11\rangle_{MY}\right)$$

$$= \frac{\sqrt{2}}{2}\left(a|000\rangle_{QMY} + a|011\rangle_{QMY} + b|100\rangle_{QMY} + b|111\rangle_{QMY}\right)$$

$$= \frac{\sqrt{2}}{2}\left(a|00\rangle_{QM} \otimes |0\rangle_Y + a|01\rangle_{QM} \otimes |1\rangle_Y + b|10\rangle_{QM} \otimes |0\rangle_Y + b|11\rangle_{QM} \otimes |1\rangle_Y\right)$$

$$= \frac{\sqrt{2}}{2}\left(a\frac{\sqrt{2}}{2}\left(|\Phi^+\rangle_{QM} + |\Phi^-\rangle_{QM}\right) \otimes |0\rangle_Y + a\frac{\sqrt{2}}{2}\left(|\Psi^+\rangle_{QM} + |\Psi^-\rangle_{QM}\right) \otimes |1\rangle_Y\right.$$
$$\left. + b\frac{\sqrt{2}}{2}\left(|\Psi^+\rangle_{QM} - |\Psi^-\rangle_{QM}\right) \otimes |0\rangle_Y + b\frac{\sqrt{2}}{2}\left(|\Phi^+\rangle_{QM} - |\Phi^-\rangle_{QM}\right) \otimes |1\rangle_Y\right)$$

$$= \frac{1}{2}\left(a\left(|\Phi^+\rangle_{QM} + |\Phi^-\rangle_{QM}\right) \otimes |0\rangle_Y + a\left(|\Psi^+\rangle_{QM} + |\Psi^-\rangle_{QM}\right) \otimes |1\rangle_Y\right.$$
$$\left. + b\left(|\Psi^+\rangle_{QM} - |\Psi^-\rangle_{QM}\right) \otimes |0\rangle_Y + b\left(|\Phi^+\rangle_{QM} - |\Phi^-\rangle_{QM}\right) \otimes |1\rangle_Y\right)$$

$$= \frac{1}{2}\left(\left(|\Phi^+\rangle_{QM} + |\Phi^-\rangle_{QM}\right) \otimes a|0\rangle_Y + \left(|\Psi^+\rangle_{QM} + |\Psi^-\rangle_{QM}\right) \otimes a|1\rangle_Y\right.$$
$$\left. + \left(|\Psi^+\rangle_{QM} - |\Psi^-\rangle_{QM}\right) \otimes b|0\rangle_Y + \left(|\Phi^+\rangle_{QM} - |\Phi^-\rangle_{QM}\right) \otimes b|1\rangle_Y\right)$$

$$= \frac{1}{2}\left(|\Phi^+\rangle_{QM} \otimes a|0\rangle_Y + |\Phi^-\rangle_{QM} \otimes a|0\rangle_Y + |\Psi^+\rangle_{QM} \otimes a|1\rangle_Y + |\Psi^-\rangle_{QM} \otimes a|1\rangle_Y\right.$$
$$\left. + |\Psi^+\rangle_{QM} \otimes b|0\rangle_Y - |\Psi^-\rangle_{QM} \otimes b|0\rangle_Y + |\Phi^+\rangle_{QM} \otimes b|1\rangle_Y - |\Phi^-\rangle_{QM} \otimes b|1\rangle_Y\right)$$

$$= \frac{1}{2}\left(|\Phi^+\rangle_{QM} \otimes (a|0\rangle_Y + b|1\rangle_Y) + |\Phi^-\rangle_{QM} \otimes (a|0\rangle_Y - b|1\rangle_Y)\right.$$
$$\left. + |\Psi^+\rangle_{QM} \otimes (b|0\rangle_Y + a|1\rangle_Y) + |\Psi^-\rangle_{QM} \otimes (-b|0\rangle_Y + a|1\rangle_Y)\right)$$

Note the coefficients and signs in the last expression.

That was a lot of ket manipulation! Note what happened: the a and the b, which started in the state of Q, which I own, are now on Y, which you own. Other than entangling qubits, we did not do any measurement; we just rewrote the ket and tensor formulas.

Now, I measure. I don't do it relative to the $|00\rangle$, $|01\rangle$, $|10\rangle$, and $|11\rangle$ basis, I do it relative to $|\Phi^+\rangle$, $|\Phi^-\rangle$, $|\Psi^+\rangle$, and $|\Psi^-\rangle$. After measurement, I have exactly one of the expressions

$$|\Phi^+\rangle_{QM} \otimes (a|0\rangle_Y + b|1\rangle_Y) \qquad\qquad |\Phi^-\rangle_{QM} \otimes (a|0\rangle_Y - b|1\rangle_Y)$$

$$|\Psi^+\rangle_{QM} \otimes (b|0\rangle_Y + a|1\rangle_Y) \qquad\qquad |\Psi^-\rangle_{QM} \otimes (-b|0\rangle_Y + a|1\rangle_Y)$$

The probability of getting one of them is 0.25, **and I know which one I have** by looking at Q and M! My measurement did not affect Y other than breaking the entanglement. The original quantum state of Q was destroyed.

Now, I call you up, text you, email you, or send you a letter through the post and tell you which of the four basis vectors I observed. This information is represented by a number using two bits, and I send it using a classical communication channel.

Exercise 9.10

You can get these bits by reversing the circuit shown in Exercise 8.6: apply a **CNOT** gate to QM and then an **H** gate to Q. Which 2-bit strings correspond to each of $|\Phi^+\rangle_{QM}$, $|\Phi^-\rangle_{QM}$, $|\Psi^+\rangle_{QM}$, and $|\Psi^-\rangle_{QM}$?

If I saw $|\Phi^+\rangle_{QM}$, the quantum state of Q was successfully teleported to Y, and you have nothing else to do.

If I saw $|\Phi^-\rangle_{QM}$, the quantum state of Y has the sign of b wrong. You apply a **Z** gate to do the phase flip, and Y now has the original state of Q.

If I saw $|\Psi^+\rangle_{QM}$, the quantum state of Y has a and b reversed. You apply an **X** gate to do the bit flip, and Y now has the original state of Q.

If I saw $|\Psi^-\rangle_{QM}$, the quantum state of Y has a and b reversed with the wrong signs. You apply an **X** gate and then a **Z** gate.

Exercise 9.11

Do the math and the post-measurement analysis using $|\Psi^-\rangle_{QM}$ instead of $|\Phi^+\rangle_{QM}$.

Exercise 9.12

Create the quantum circuit for teleportation, as I have described it here.

Rather than using "me" and "you" and M and Y, it's common to see "Alice" and "Bob" and "A" and "B" in the literature.

9.4 Arithmetic

In section 2.5, we looked at the rudimentary ideas of doing binary addition via logic gates. We'll revisit that but see how to do it using quantum gates. Like most such algorithms, researchers have published many papers on optimizing the circuits using methods such as the Quantum Fourier Transform, which we cover in section 10.1.

Addition

I keep to a straightforward approach to help bridge the gap between classical and quantum versions. The gates we use are simple, and we replace bits with qubits. Instead of **0** and **1**, we use $|0\rangle$ and $|1\rangle$, respectively. We call the data input qubits $|x\rangle$ and $|y\rangle$, and each is in the state $|0\rangle$ or $|1\rangle$ at any given time. We are essentially mimicking what we would do in the classical case.

If we do not worry about carry-in and carry-out qubits, our circuit looks like

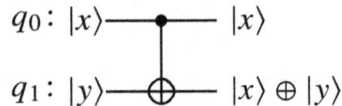

$$q_0: |x\rangle \quad\bullet\quad |x\rangle$$
$$q_1: |y\rangle \quad\oplus\quad |x\rangle \oplus |y\rangle$$

where "$\oplus$" is addition modulo 2. We implement this as a **CNOT** gate acting as an **xor**. We use q_1 to store this computed output, replacing the original $|y\rangle$ input.

To include a carry-out state $|c_{out}\rangle$, we employ a Toffoli **CCNOT** gate and use a third qubit, q_2, to hold the value.

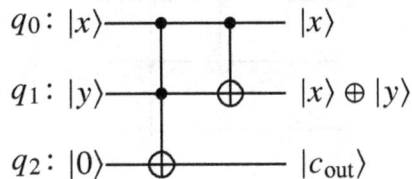

$$q_0: |x\rangle \quad\bullet\quad |x\rangle$$
$$q_1: |y\rangle \quad\bullet\ \oplus\quad |x\rangle \oplus |y\rangle$$
$$q_2: |0\rangle \quad\oplus\quad |c_{out}\rangle$$

Exercise 9.13

Why do we place the Toffoli **CCNOT** gate before the **CNOT** gate? Are they interchangeable?

The only thing remaining to consider is a carry-in state $|c_{in}\rangle$. We put this in a new qubit and rearrange the circuit slightly.

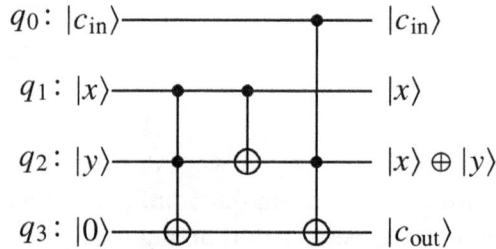

$$q_0: |c_{in}\rangle \quad\quad\quad\quad\quad\quad |c_{in}\rangle$$
$$q_1: |x\rangle \quad\quad\quad\quad\quad\quad |x\rangle$$
$$q_2: |y\rangle \quad\quad\quad\quad\quad |x\rangle \oplus |y\rangle$$
$$q_3: |0\rangle \quad\quad\quad\quad\quad\quad |c_{out}\rangle$$

Note how the first two qubits on which the final Toffoli gate operates are nonadjacent.

Our inputs are in qubits 0, 1, and 2, and the outputs are in qubits 2 and 3. We call this a **CARRY** gate. Rather than spell out all the individual operations, we can write it as its own gate:

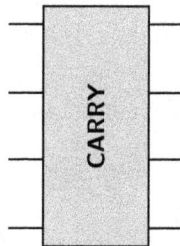

Since this is a quantum gate, it is reversible. We call the gate we get by running **CARRY** backward the **CARRY**$^{-1}$ gate:

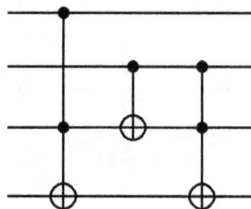

In general-purpose gates, we do not always specify whether any particular qubit should be $|0\rangle$ or $|1\rangle$.

We now define **SUM**: it takes the inputs from the first two qubits and adds the result to what was in the third qubit. It does not worry about any carry qubits.

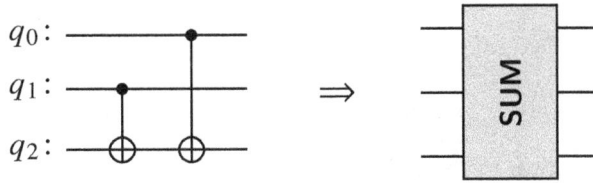

With this background, we can combine the pieces to create a circuit that adds two binary numbers of three bits each. We represent the first number as $x = x_2x_1x_0$ and the second as $y = y_2y_1y_0$. Because of carries, the result can have four bits. We might have $x = 011_2$ and $y = 101_2$, for example. It's important to pay attention to the bit/qubit ordering in algorithms as it is easy to use them in the reverse and, therefore, incorrect direction.

x_0 and y_0 are the *least* significant bits, and x_2 and y_2 are the *most* significant bits. By analogy, in the decimal real number 247, 2 is the most significant digit, and 7 is the least.

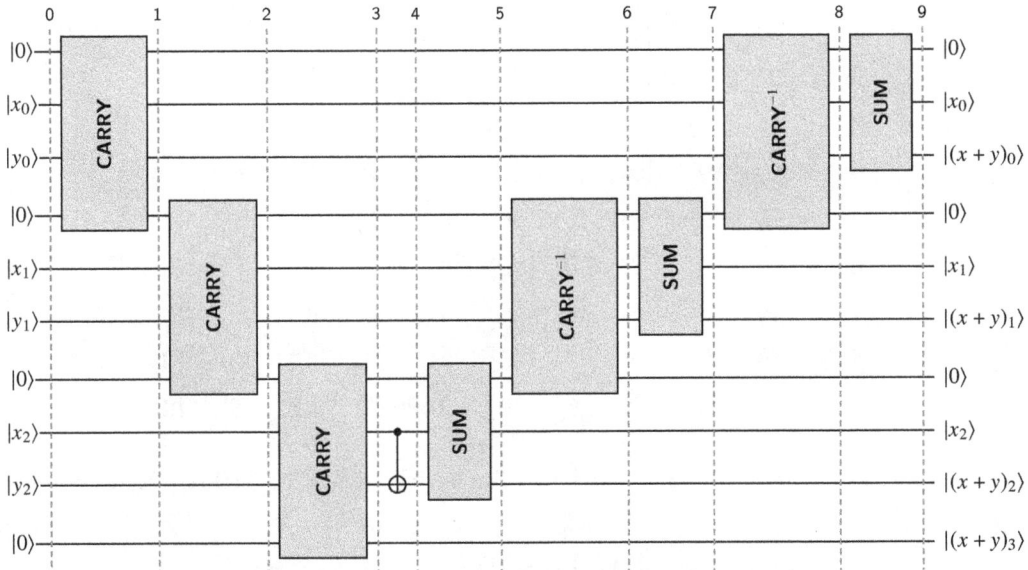

Figure 9.2: The 3-qubit adder circuit

In the circuit in Figure 9.2, I've labeled the steps with vertical lines with numbers. From the least significant qubit to the most, the sum will be in qubits 2, 5, 8, and 9.

When we give $|0\rangle$ inputs to **CARRY, CARRY^{-1}**, and **SUM**, they produce $|0\rangle$ outputs. The circuit above successfully adds $|000\rangle$ to $|000\rangle$ to produce $|000\rangle$. Let's try $1 + 1$. In this case, $x = y = |001\rangle$. We start with the least significant bits as the uppermost inputs and work downwards. We have

$$q_0 = |0\rangle \quad q_1 = |1\rangle \quad q_2 = |1\rangle \quad q_3 = |0\rangle \quad q_4 = |0\rangle$$

$$q_5 = |0\rangle \quad q_6 = |0\rangle \quad q_7 = |0\rangle \quad q_8 = |0\rangle \quad q_9 = |0\rangle$$

Let's trace the evolution of the qubit states as we move from left to right in the circuit. The top line in the following table labels the steps, and the first column labels the qubits. The bulk of the table gives the quantum state values of the qubits before a step with the given number.

We expect to see $|1\rangle$ in qubits 1 and 5 and $|0\rangle$ elsewhere.

					Step					
Qubit	**0**	**1**	**2**	**3**	**4**	**5**	**6**	**7**	**8**	**9**
0	$|0\rangle$	$|0\rangle$	$|0\rangle$	$|0\rangle$	$|0\rangle$	$|0\rangle$	$|0\rangle$	$|0\rangle$	$|0\rangle$	$|0\rangle$
1	$|1\rangle$	$|1\rangle$	$|1\rangle$	$|1\rangle$	$|1\rangle$	$|1\rangle$	$|1\rangle$	$|1\rangle$	$|1\rangle$	$|1\rangle$
2	$|1\rangle$	$|0\rangle$	$|0\rangle$	$|0\rangle$	$|0\rangle$	$|0\rangle$	$|0\rangle$	$|0\rangle$	$|1\rangle$	$\mathbf{|0\rangle}$
3	$|0\rangle$	$|1\rangle$	$|1\rangle$	$|1\rangle$	$|1\rangle$	$|1\rangle$	$|1\rangle$	$|1\rangle$	$|0\rangle$	$|0\rangle$
4	$|0\rangle$	$|0\rangle$	$|0\rangle$	$|0\rangle$	$|0\rangle$	$|0\rangle$	$|0\rangle$	$|0\rangle$	$|0\rangle$	$|0\rangle$
5	$|0\rangle$	$|0\rangle$	$|0\rangle$	$|0\rangle$	$|0\rangle$	$|0\rangle$	$|0\rangle$	$|1\rangle$	$|1\rangle$	$\mathbf{|1\rangle}$
6	$|0\rangle$	$|0\rangle$	$|0\rangle$	$|0\rangle$	$|0\rangle$	$|0\rangle$	$|0\rangle$	$|0\rangle$	$|0\rangle$	$|0\rangle$
7	$|0\rangle$	$|0\rangle$	$|0\rangle$	$|0\rangle$	$|0\rangle$	$|0\rangle$	$|0\rangle$	$|0\rangle$	$|0\rangle$	$|0\rangle$
8	$|0\rangle$	$|0\rangle$	$|0\rangle$	$|0\rangle$	$|0\rangle$	$|0\rangle$	$|0\rangle$	$|0\rangle$	$|0\rangle$	$\mathbf{|0\rangle}$
9	$|0\rangle$	$|0\rangle$	$|0\rangle$	$|0\rangle$	$|0\rangle$	$|0\rangle$	$|0\rangle$	$|0\rangle$	$|0\rangle$	$\mathbf{|0\rangle}$

Success! Let's add $x = 111_2$ and $y = 101_2$. The answer should be 1100_2. The qubit inputs are

$$q_0 = |0\rangle \quad q_1 = |1\rangle \quad q_2 = |1\rangle \quad q_3 = |0\rangle \quad q_4 = |1\rangle$$

$$q_5 = |0\rangle \quad q_6 = |0\rangle \quad q_7 = |1\rangle \quad q_8 = |1\rangle \quad q_9 = |0\rangle$$

When we run it through the circuit, we expect to see the output

$$q_0 = |0\rangle \quad q_1 = |1\rangle \quad q_2 = |0\rangle \quad q_3 = |0\rangle \quad q_4 = |1\rangle$$

$$q_5 = |0\rangle \quad q_6 = |0\rangle \quad q_7 = |1\rangle \quad q_8 = |1\rangle \quad q_9 = |1\rangle$$

The evolution is

Qubit	Step 0	1	2	3	4	5	6	7	8	9
0	$|0\rangle$	$|0\rangle$	$|0\rangle$	$|0\rangle$	$|0\rangle$	$|0\rangle$	$|0\rangle$	$|0\rangle$	$|0\rangle$	$|0\rangle$
1	$|1\rangle$	$|1\rangle$	$|1\rangle$	$|1\rangle$	$|1\rangle$	$|1\rangle$	$|1\rangle$	$|1\rangle$	$|1\rangle$	$|1\rangle$
2	$|1\rangle$	$|0\rangle$	$|0\rangle$	$|0\rangle$	$|0\rangle$	$|0\rangle$	$|0\rangle$	$|0\rangle$	$|1\rangle$	$\mathbf{|0\rangle}$
3	$|0\rangle$	$|1\rangle$	$|1\rangle$	$|1\rangle$	$|1\rangle$	$|1\rangle$	$|1\rangle$	$|1\rangle$	$|0\rangle$	$|0\rangle$
4	$|1\rangle$	$|1\rangle$	$|1\rangle$	$|1\rangle$	$|1\rangle$	$|1\rangle$	$|1\rangle$	$|1\rangle$	$|1\rangle$	$|1\rangle$
5	$|0\rangle$	$|0\rangle$	$|1\rangle$	$|1\rangle$	$|1\rangle$	$|1\rangle$	$|0\rangle$	$|0\rangle$	$|0\rangle$	$\mathbf{|0\rangle}$
6	$|0\rangle$	$|0\rangle$	$|1\rangle$	$|1\rangle$	$|1\rangle$	$|1\rangle$	$|0\rangle$	$|0\rangle$	$|0\rangle$	$|0\rangle$
7	$|1\rangle$	$|1\rangle$	$|1\rangle$	$|1\rangle$	$|1\rangle$	$|1\rangle$	$|1\rangle$	$|1\rangle$	$|1\rangle$	$|1\rangle$
8	$|1\rangle$	$|1\rangle$	$|1\rangle$	$|1\rangle$	$|1\rangle$	$|1\rangle$	$|1\rangle$	$|1\rangle$	$|1\rangle$	$\mathbf{|1\rangle}$
9	$|0\rangle$	$|0\rangle$	$|0\rangle$	$|1\rangle$	$|1\rangle$	$|1\rangle$	$|1\rangle$	$|1\rangle$	$|1\rangle$	$\mathbf{|1\rangle}$

and we again get the correct answer.

As implemented in the circuit, this algorithm is slightly more complicated than it might seem it needs to be. When we are finished, we want to reset the carry qubits 0, 3, and 6 back to their initial values. No reversible gate operation sets the state of a qubit absolutely to $|0\rangle$ or $|1\rangle$. Therefore, to get back to an initial value, we must reverse the steps that got us there. Setting them to their known initial values allows us to reuse the qubits later if we wish.

> If we allow ourselves to use irreversible operations, we can employ the $|0\rangle$ **RESET** operation described in section 7.6.14. If we want $|1\rangle$, we follow the reset with an **X** gate.

To use this circuit to add two numbers, each represented by 3 qubits, we needed 10 qubits. Generally, to add n numbers, we need $3(n + 1) + 1$ qubits if we do addition this way. The number of qubits we need is $O(n)$ to add two n bit/qubit numbers.

> To add these two n bit/qubit numbers, we need n **CARRY** gates, n **SUM** gates, $n - 1$ **CARRY**$^{-1}$ gates, and one **CNOT** gate. Since the number of included gates is fixed, this tells us we need $O(n)$ gates.

CARRY, **CARRY**$^{-1}$, and **SUM** are examples of *circuit subroutines*, reusable portions of a circuit that we might call several times.

> ### Exercise 9.14
>
> Counting all the steps in the **CARRY**, **CARRY**$^{-1}$, and **SUM** circuit subroutines, what is the depth of the 3-qubit adder circuit? What is the depth of an n qubit adder circuit?

As I mentioned at the beginning of the section, researchers have developed much more efficient quantum algorithms for arithmetic operations. However, if you can perform such arithmetic on a classical processor, it will be much faster than quantum alternatives today. You would typically do arithmetic on a quantum computing system only if it were part of a larger quantum algorithm.

> ### Exercise 9.15
>
> What do you get when you run a reversible addition circuit backward? A subtraction circuit! Examine the full adder circuit and determine where you would place the bits-s/qubits of x and y in the input to the reverse circuit to compute $x - y$. Is this a complete subtraction circuit, or are there restrictions on x and y?

Multiplication

It's possible to translate other classical algorithms for arithmetic into quantum versions similarly. Rather than add $x = 111_2$ and $y = 101_2$, let's multiply them by the method you learned for integer multiplication.

$$
\begin{array}{rcccccc}
 & & & & 1 & 1 & 1 \\
 & & \times & & 1 & 0 & 1 \\
\hline
 & & & & 1 & 1 & 1 \\
+ & & & 0 & 0 & 0 & \\
+ & & 1 & 1 & 1 & & \\
\hline
 & 1 & 0 & 0 & 0 & 1 & 1 \\
\end{array}
$$

For each of the three qubits, we produce three partial sums, which we then add. We do the qubit-wise multiplication with Toffoli gates.

More generally, we need $O(n)$ gates to produce n partial sums. We then do $n - 1$ additions.

Multiplication of two n-bit/qubit numbers requires $O(n^2)$ gates.

Exercise 9.16

Write a reversible circuit to create the three partial sums for multiplying two 3-qubit numbers.

Exponentiation

Next up is exponentiation. Given an integer x, say you want to compute x^9. You can do 8 multiplications by

$$xxxxxxxx$$

or you can note that

$$x^9 = x((x^2)^2)^2.$$

This expression requires only 4 multiplications:

1. Set $a_1 = xx$.
2. Set $a_2 = a_1 a_1$.
3. Set $a_3 = a_2 a_2$.
4. Set $a_4 = a_3 x$.

Then $x^9 = a_4$. We call this technique *repeated squaring*. Note that $9 = 1001_2$.

For

$$x^{15} = x\left(x^7\right)^2 = x\left(xx^6\right)^2 = x\left(x\left(x^3\right)^2\right)^2 = x\left(x\,(xxx)^2\right)^2,$$

we need 7 multiplications and $15 = 1111_2$. For

$$x^{32} = \left(\left(\left((xx)^2\right)^2\right)^2\right)^2$$

we need 5 multiplications and $32 = 100000_2$.

In general, if we need n bits to represent the exponent b, we can compute x^b with no more than $2n$ multiplications. Exponentiation is $O(n)$ in the number of multiplications.

If the binary representation of b is $b_{n-1}b_{n-2}\cdots b_1b_0$ with b_0 the least significant bit, then

$$x^b = x^{b_{n-1}2^{n-1}} \times x^{b_{n-2}2^{n-2}} \times \cdots \times x^{b_1 2^1} \times x^{b_0 2^0}.$$

For example, for $b = 13 = 1101_2$,

$$x^{13} = x^{1\times 2^3} \times x^{1\times 2^2} \times x^{0\times 2^1} \times x^{1\times 2^0}.$$

Raising an n bit/qubit number to an n bit/qubit exponent is

$$O(n) \times O(n) \times O(n) = O\left(n^3\right)$$

in the number of gates.

Modular arithmetic can be done either by subtraction or division with quotient and remainder. For example,

$$17 \bmod 11 \equiv (17 - 11) \bmod 11 \equiv 6 \bmod 11.$$

Alternatively, $17 \div 11 = 1$ with *remainder* 6. The 1 is the *quotient*.

The Python `divmod` function takes two numbers and returns the (quotient, remainder) pair.

To learn more

The ways you learned to do arithmetic are not always the most efficient methods to do it on a computer. [53, Chapter 9] Those techniques form a good starting place to think about how you might implement and modify them for a quantum computing system, but you must consider how the quantum programming model differs from the classical one. [95] [172, Section 2.4] You can then investigate how to write and optimize new algorithms using quantum gates and circuits. [89] [90]

9.5   Welcome to Delphi

In ancient Greece, the Oracle of Delphi was a high priestess at the Temple of Apollo who issued prophecies under the right conditions and during warm weather.

In computer science, an oracle is a function that we supply with data, and it responds with a **1** for yes and a **0** for no. Our oracles cannot answer random questions; we build them to respond to specific queries. For an algorithm using an oracle, two things are significant:

- The implementation of the oracle must be as fast and efficient as possible.
- We want to call the oracle as few times as possible to minimize the algorithm's complexity.

An oracle is a *black box*, meaning we understand its behavior but not how it does what it does. We use it without seeing inside it.

Since we can represent all classical data by bits, we express the inputs to the oracle function as strings of zeros and ones. If we call the function f, which is traditional, we can express it as

$$f : \{0, 1\}^n \rightarrow \{0, 1\}$$

It might help you to think of **1** as **True** and **0** as **False**. We can also consider f as a logic operation implemented via a classical logic circuit, as we saw in section 9.3.2.

In section 2.1, we introduced the 7-bit ASCII character set. Let's define an example f by

$$f(\mathbf{x}) = f(x_0 x_1 x_2 x_3 x_4 x_5 x_6) = \begin{cases} 1 & \text{if } x_0 x_1 x_2 x_3 x_4 x_5 x_6 = \mathbf{1000010} = \text{'B'} \\ 0 & \text{otherwise} \end{cases}$$

where each x_j is either **0** or **1**. $f(\mathbf{1101010}) = \mathbf{0}$, but $f(\mathbf{1000010}) = \mathbf{1}$.

Though the test above is a simple equality, I don't state how we implement it: it is a black box. For example, suppose

$$f(\mathbf{x}) = \begin{cases} 1 & \text{if } \mathbf{x} = 1 \\ 0 & \text{otherwise} \end{cases}$$

and I pass it the mathematical expression $\sin^2(z) + \cos^2(z)$ encoded as zeros and ones. The oracle would have to understand trigonometry to answer correctly.

For quantum computing, we would call the oracle with a ket, as in this example:

$$f(|\psi\rangle) = \begin{cases} |1\rangle & \text{if } |\psi\rangle = |1000010\rangle = |66\rangle_7 \\ |0\rangle & \text{otherwise .} \end{cases}$$

We are primarily interested in the action of the oracle on the standard basis kets.

Here's another oracle:

$$f(|x_0 x_1 x_2 x_3 x_4 x_5 x_6 x_7\rangle) = \begin{cases} |1\rangle & \text{if } (x_0 x_1 x_2 x_3) \times (x_4 x_5 x_6 x_7) = 1111_2 \\ |0\rangle & \text{otherwise .} \end{cases}$$

This returns $|1\rangle$ if the product of the two binary numbers encoded in the two halves of the input is 1111_2 (= 15 decimal). The oracle doesn't need to know how to factor; it needs to know how to multiply and test for equality.

In practice, for quantum computing, we must encapsulate the function of the oracle within a unitary matrix and gate $\mathbf{U}_f$. (The $\mathbf{U}$ in $\mathbf{U}_f$ stands for "unitary.") One way to do it is to adjust the sign of a ket that meets the oracle's criteria for success. Here are the steps:

1. Encode the data we are searching through as standard basis kets $|x\rangle$. For example, if we have 100 data items, use 7 qubits (because $2^7 = 128$) and assign each data element to a basis ket $|x\rangle_7$.
2. Let our oracle f produce $f(|y\rangle) = 1$ for one special encoded piece of data $|y\rangle$, 0 otherwise.
3. Find a unitary (hence reversible) matrix $\mathbf{U}_f$ such that

$$\mathbf{U}_f|x\rangle = \begin{cases} -|y\rangle & \text{if } |x\rangle = |y\rangle \text{ (which means } f(|y\rangle) = 1) \\ |x\rangle & \text{otherwise}. \end{cases}$$

The last definition means $\mathbf{U}_f$ inverts the sign of the ket input that satisfies the condition of the oracle and leaves the rest alone.

I think most mathematical/quantum expressions of how oracles and their corresponding unitary matrices work look very complicated. I don't think the last is an exception. Let's translate this via a simple example.

We have two qubits, and we want the oracle to return $|1\rangle$ if we give it $|01\rangle$, $|0\rangle$ otherwise. For $|\psi\rangle$ being one of the standard basis kets $|00\rangle$, $|01\rangle$, $|10\rangle$, or $|11\rangle$,

$$f(|\psi\rangle) = \begin{cases} |1\rangle & \text{if } |\psi\rangle = |01\rangle \\ |0\rangle & \text{if } |\psi\rangle = |00\rangle, |10\rangle, \text{ or } |11\rangle. \end{cases}$$

$\mathbf{U}_f = \mathbf{U}_{|01\rangle}$ should behave as

$$\mathbf{U}_f|\psi\rangle = \mathbf{U}_{|01\rangle}|\psi\rangle = \begin{cases} -|\psi\rangle = -|01\rangle & \text{if } |\psi\rangle = |01\rangle \\ |\psi\rangle & \text{if } |\psi\rangle = |00\rangle, |10\rangle, \text{ or } |11\rangle. \end{cases}$$

In standard vector notation, recall we have

$$|00\rangle = \begin{bmatrix} 1 \\ 0 \\ 0 \\ 0 \end{bmatrix} \quad |01\rangle = \begin{bmatrix} 0 \\ 1 \\ 0 \\ 0 \end{bmatrix} \quad |10\rangle = \begin{bmatrix} 0 \\ 0 \\ 1 \\ 0 \end{bmatrix} \quad |11\rangle = \begin{bmatrix} 0 \\ 0 \\ 0 \\ 1 \end{bmatrix}.$$

Then, the matrix

$$\mathbf{U}_f = \begin{bmatrix} 1 & 0 & 0 & 0 \\ 0 & -1 & 0 & 0 \\ 0 & 0 & 1 & 0 \\ 0 & 0 & 0 & 1 \end{bmatrix}$$

does what we need.

Exercise 9.17

What's the determinant of this matrix? Is the matrix unitary?

Depending on the algorithm and how we use the oracle, we might create a different $\mathbf{U}_f$, but it must still reflect what f tells us. While we think of $\mathbf{U}_f$ as a matrix, we implement it as a circuit. The trick is to construct it to be highly computationally efficient.

9.6 Amplitude amplification and interference

Suppose we have three qubits, and one of their quantum state standard basis kets $\{|000\rangle, \ldots, |111\rangle\}$ corresponds to a solution to some problem. We want to devise an algorithm to pick the correct ket and find the answer. I'm purposely not telling you the problem or how the kets map to the data and solution. Just assume we want to identify one of them that the algorithm can determine as best.

The first question is how to see that this best ket stands out from the others. The general form for a 3-qubit quantum register state is

$$\sum_{j=0}^{7} a_j |j\rangle_3 = a_0|000\rangle + a_1|001\rangle + a_2|010\rangle + a_3|011\rangle +$$

$$a_4|100\rangle + a_5|101\rangle + a_6|110\rangle + a_7|111\rangle$$

with

$$1 = \sum_{j=0}^{7} |a_j|^2 .$$

If we initialize each qubit to $|0\rangle$ and then apply $\mathbf{H}^{\otimes 3}$, we get a balanced superposition:

$$|\varphi\rangle = \mathbf{H}^{\otimes 3}|000\rangle = \sum_{j=0}^{7} a_j|j\rangle = \sum_{j=0}^{7} \frac{1}{\sqrt{8}}|j\rangle = \frac{1}{\sqrt{8}} \sum_{j=0}^{7} |j\rangle .$$

All the coefficients are equal, and the square of each absolute value is $\frac{1}{8}$. If we measure the qubits now, we have an equal chance of getting any of the eight basis kets.

At the qubit level, we have done a change of basis from the computational basis $\{|0\rangle, |1\rangle\}$ to $\{|+\rangle, |-\rangle\}$ via **H**.

We manipulate the qubit states through *amplitude amplification* so that the basis ket representing the best solution has the coefficient a_j with the largest probability $|a_j|^2$. We want to make $|a_j|^2$ as large as possible, ideally equal to 1.0. That basis ket will have the highest chance of being observed when we measure.

Ultimately, this is the goal of every quantum algorithm: have the results of the final qubit measurements correspond with high probability to the best solution.

In practice, we often create a reusable circuit subroutine that we call several times. Each time, it gets us closer to what we hope is the ideal result by increasing its corresponding probability. We also decrease the probabilities of the "bad" options.

9.6.1   Flipping the sign

Let me show how this might evolve. In the graph in Figure 9.3, the vertical axis shows the probability amplitudes. That is, we map the coefficients a_j on this. Typically, these are general values in **C**, but for simplicity, we assume they are in **R** in this example.

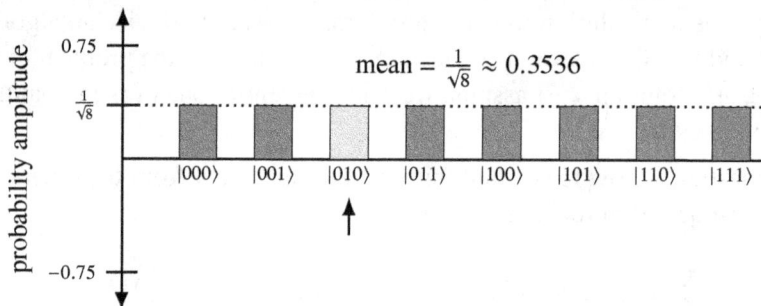

Figure 9.3: 3 qubits in balanced superposition

I've highlighted one ket, $|010\rangle$, that I want to modify over several interactions to increase its probability. I've chosen it at random to show the process. The dotted line marks the average of the probability amplitudes.

In the previous section, we saw how to negate the sign for a given ket in a balanced superposition. Let's do that now for $|010\rangle$. Create an 8-by-8 matrix $U_{|010\rangle}$, which is the identity matrix, except for the $(3, 3)$ entry, which we change to -1. After applying this, the situation changes to Figure 9.4.

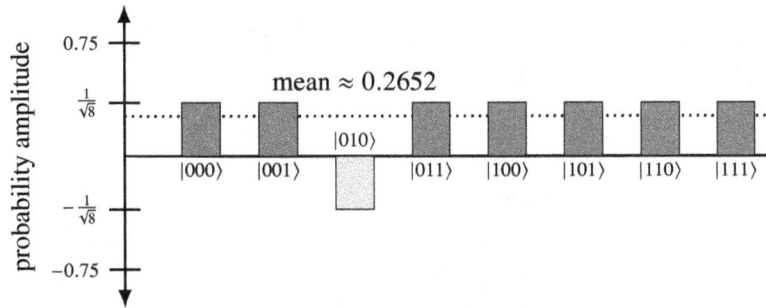

Figure 9.4: Negating the amplitude for $|010\rangle$

Note how the average amplitude has dropped. The sum of the squares of the absolute values of the amplitudes is still 1. Each basis ket has the same probability of being the result when measured.

Exercise 9.18

What is the new average amplitude?

In this 3-qubit example, we had one particular basis ket whose sign we wanted to flip, the third. In general, the oracle completely determines which basis ket we sign-flip.

Now for the clever trick.

9.6.2 Inversion about the mean

Let $S = \{s_j\}$ be a finite collection of numbers in **R**, and let m be the mean (average) of the numbers. Create a new collection T containing the numbers $\{t_j = 2m - s_j\}$. T has the following properties:

- The average of the numbers in T is still m.
- $s_j = 2m - t_j$, so the mapping from S to T is reversible.
- If $s_j = m$, then $t_j = s_j = m$.
- $t_j - m = m - s_j$, and so $|t_j - m| = |s_j - m|$.
- If $s_j < m$, then $t_j > m$, and if $s_j > m$, then $t_j < m$.

We call this process *inversion about the mean*.

Exercise 9.19

Prove each of these statements.

Let's see what this does when our collection is $S = \{1, -2, 3, 4\}$. The average, or mean, is $\frac{3}{2}$, so $T = \{2, 5, 0, -1\}$, as shown in Figure 9.5.

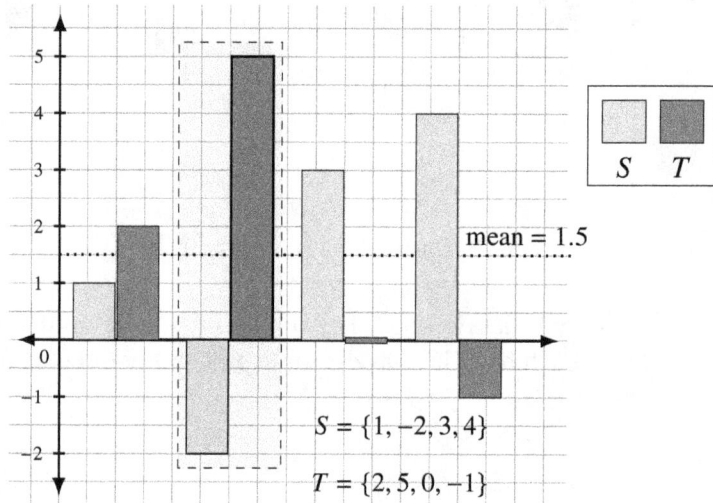

Figure 9.5: First example of inversion about the mean

Note in the rectangle with the dashed lines how much higher above the mean is the result 5 in T for the single negative value -2 in S.

For a second example, let

$$S = \{-1.5, 1.5, 1.5, 1.5\}.$$

The absolute values of the data are the same, but the first number is negative and the others are positive. The mean $m = 0.75$ and $T = \{3, 0, 0, 0\}$. After this transformation, the lone negative value stands out significantly once inverted about the mean in the dashed box in Figure 9.6.

Recall from section 7.2 that the *outer product* is

$$|v\rangle\langle w| = \begin{bmatrix} v_1\overline{w_1} & v_1\overline{w_2} & \cdots & v_1\overline{w_m} \\ v_2\overline{w_1} & v_2\overline{w_2} & \cdots & v_2\overline{w_m} \\ \vdots & \vdots & \ddots & \vdots \\ v_n\overline{w_1} & v_n\overline{w_2} & \cdots & v_n\overline{w_m} \end{bmatrix}.$$

Consider

$$\mathbf{U}_\varphi = 2|\varphi\rangle\langle\varphi| - I_8$$

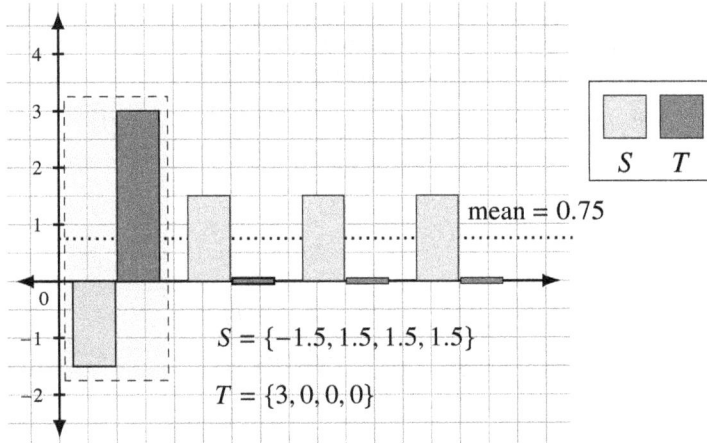

Figure 9.6: Second example of inversion about the mean

for

$$|\varphi\rangle = \sum_{j=0}^{7} \frac{1}{\sqrt{8}} |j\rangle$$

where I_8 is the 8-by-8 identity matrix. The form should look familiar to you from what we discussed above for S and T. This unitary matrix performs an inversion about the mean, where, by "mean," we are talking about the balanced superposition ket $|\varphi\rangle = \mathbf{H}^{\otimes 3}|000\rangle$.

Exercise 9.20

What is the matrix for $\mathbf{U}_\varphi$? Show it is a unitary matrix.

We can take our amplitudes in the 3-qubit example and invert about the mean. Figure 9.7 shows the result.

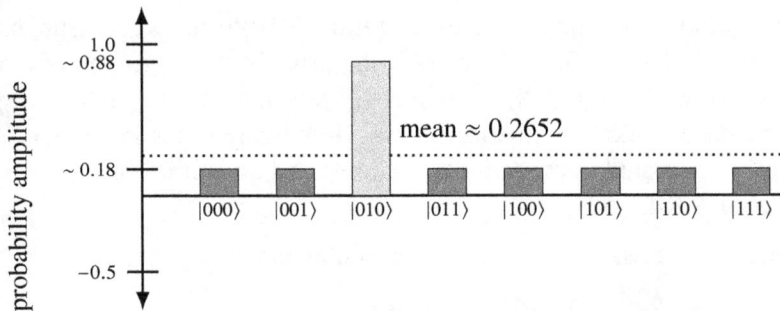

Figure 9.7: Inversion about mean after applying oracle once

After negating the amplitude of $|010\rangle$ and inverting about the mean once, the probability of getting $|010\rangle$ when we measure is approximately $|0.88|^2 \approx 0.77$. Can we do better? Figure 9.8 shows what we get when we again negate the amplitude of $|010\rangle$ and invert about the mean.

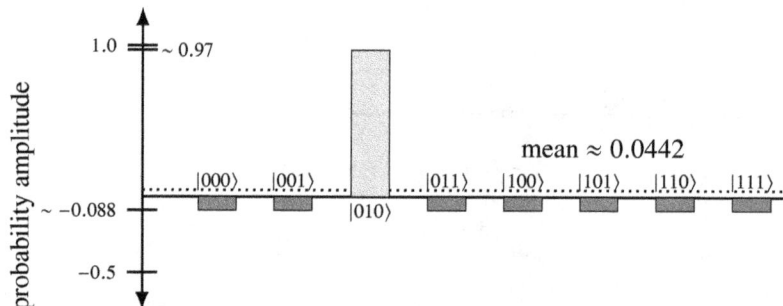

Figure 9.8: Inversion about mean after applying oracle twice

The probability of seeing $|010\rangle$ when we measure is approximately $|0.97|^2 \approx 0.94$! It seems like the more we negate and invert, the larger the probability of getting the "right" answer. Let's see if the trend continues in Figure 9.9.

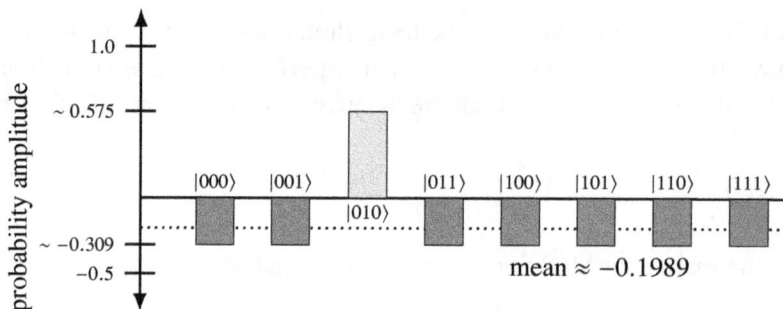

Figure 9.9: Inversion about mean after applying oracle three times

Well, this is unfortunate. The probability of getting $|010\rangle$ when we measure has decreased to approximately $|0.575|^2 \approx 0.33$. Moreover, the probability of getting one of the seven "wrong" kets is now about $|0.309|^2 \approx 0.095$. By repeating the negate/invert process too many times, we have made the situation worse. How many times is enough to maximize the probability? Is it related to the number of qubits and quantum states? We return to this question in section 9.6.4.

In general, for n qubits, we perform this inversion about the mean by

$$\mathbf{U}_\varphi = 2|\varphi\rangle\langle\varphi| - I_{2^n} ,$$

where

$$|\varphi\rangle = \mathbf{H}^{\otimes n}|0\rangle^{\otimes n} = \sum_{j=0}^{2^n-1} \frac{1}{\sqrt{2^n}}|j\rangle = \frac{1}{\sqrt{2^n}}\sum_{j=0}^{2^n-1}|j\rangle$$

and I_{2^n} is the 2^n-by-2^n identity matrix. Using linearity, we can re-express it using gate notation as

$$\begin{aligned}
\mathbf{U}_\varphi &= 2|\varphi\rangle\langle\varphi| - I_{2^n} \\
&= 2\mathbf{H}^{\otimes n}\left(|0\rangle^{\otimes n}\langle 0|^{\otimes n}\right)\mathbf{H}^{\otimes n} - \mathbf{ID}^{\otimes n} \\
&= 2\mathbf{H}^{\otimes n}\left(|0\rangle^{\otimes n}\langle 0|^{\otimes n}\right)\mathbf{H}^{\otimes n} - \mathbf{H}^{\otimes n}\mathbf{ID}^{\otimes n}\mathbf{H}^{\otimes n} \\
&= \mathbf{H}^{\otimes n}\left(2|0\rangle^{\otimes n}\langle 0|^{\otimes n} - \mathbf{ID}^{\otimes n}\right)\mathbf{H}^{\otimes n}.
\end{aligned}$$

This gate is the *Grover diffusion operator*. [99] [23]

The full circuit for 3 qubits is shown in Figure 9.10.

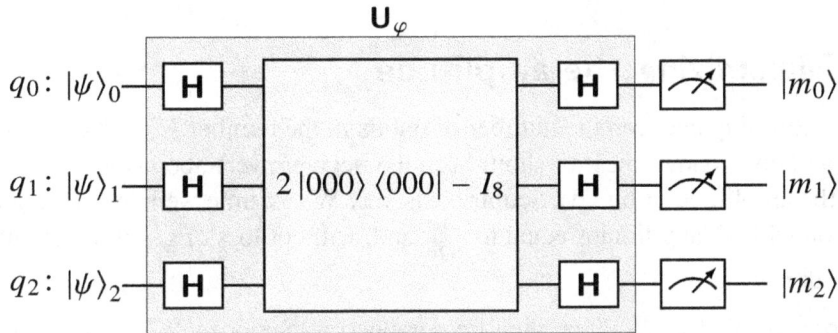

Figure 9.10: The 3-qubit circuit for inversion about the mean

We employ this operator as a reusable circuit subroutine. The inputs vary based on where in the full circuit it is used.

9.6.3 Interference

Inversion about the mean is an example of using *interference* to find the best answer. We perform some action to manipulate the probability amplitudes to make the ''good'' result more likely to be seen when we measure while simultaneously making the ''bad'' ones highly unlikely. We boost the good choice via *constructive interference* and reduce the bad ones by *destructive interference*.

Mathematically and computationally, think of interference as doing something that affects the complex probability amplitudes in a quantum state. When the effect is positive in that it increases the chance of getting the correct answer corresponding to a basis ket when we measure, we say the interference is *constructive*. If the effect decreases our chance of getting a wrong answer, the interference in *destructive*. Since the sum of the squares of the absolute values of the amplitudes must be 1, we often perform constructive and destructive interference at the same time.

The concept of interference comes from physics. For example, if you drop a pebble (**A**) in a pond, you see waves moving out in a circular pattern from where the pebble hit the water. If you drop a second pebble (**B**) 25cm from the first, its waves move out but collide with those from **A**.

Suppose the collision point is where a wave from **A** has a crest above the pond's surface. If the crest of the wave from **B** is also above the surface of the pond, the resultant combined wave will be higher than either original wave. This is constructive interference. If the crest of the wave from **B** is below the pond's surface, the new wave will have a lower crest than **A**'s wave. This is destructive interference.

See Figure 11.26 for an example of how two sinusoidal waves interact when they overlap.

9.6.4 Maximizing the amplitude

Is there a relationship between the number of qubits n, the number $N = 2^n$ of their standard basis kets, and how many times we should run the negate/invert-about-the-mean process to maximize the amplitude of one particular basis ket? We assume we begin with a balanced superposition with all amplitudes equal to $\frac{1}{\sqrt{2^n}}$ and, without loss of generality, that basis ket we care about is $|0\rangle^{\otimes n}$.

Let's look at this from a linear algebra perspective. Suppose N is an integer ≥ 4, and consider the vector of length N

$$\begin{bmatrix} \frac{1}{\sqrt{N}} & \frac{1}{\sqrt{N}} & \cdots & \frac{1}{\sqrt{N}} \end{bmatrix}.$$

We are not restricting N to be a power of 2. Negate the first entry to get

$$\begin{bmatrix} -\frac{1}{\sqrt{N}} & \frac{1}{\sqrt{N}} & \cdots & \frac{1}{\sqrt{N}} \end{bmatrix}.$$

The mean m of the elements in this vector is

$$m = \frac{-\frac{1}{\sqrt{N}} + (N-1)\frac{1}{\sqrt{N}}}{N} = \frac{(N-2)\frac{1}{\sqrt{N}}}{N} = \frac{N-2}{N}\frac{1}{\sqrt{N}}.$$

We invert the vector around m to get

$$\left[2m - -\tfrac{1}{\sqrt{N}} \quad 2m - \tfrac{1}{\sqrt{N}} \quad \ldots \quad 2m - \tfrac{1}{\sqrt{N}} \right]$$

$$= \left[2\tfrac{N-2}{N}\tfrac{1}{\sqrt{N}} - -\tfrac{1}{\sqrt{N}} \quad 2\tfrac{N-2}{N}\tfrac{1}{\sqrt{N}} - \tfrac{1}{\sqrt{N}} \quad \ldots \quad 2\tfrac{N-2}{N}\tfrac{1}{\sqrt{N}} - \tfrac{1}{\sqrt{N}} \right]$$

$$= \left[\left(2\tfrac{N-2}{N} + 1\right)\tfrac{1}{\sqrt{N}} \quad \left(2\tfrac{N-2}{N} - 1\right)\tfrac{1}{\sqrt{N}} \quad \ldots \quad \left(2\tfrac{N-2}{N} - 1\right)\tfrac{1}{\sqrt{N}} \right]$$

$$= \left[\tfrac{3N-4}{N}\tfrac{1}{\sqrt{N}} \quad \tfrac{N-4}{N}\tfrac{1}{\sqrt{N}} \quad \ldots \quad \tfrac{N-4}{N}\tfrac{1}{\sqrt{N}} \right] .$$

When $N = 4$, the original vector is

$$\left[\tfrac{1}{\sqrt{4}} \quad \tfrac{1}{\sqrt{4}} \quad \tfrac{1}{\sqrt{4}} \quad \tfrac{1}{\sqrt{4}} \right]$$

and when we negate the first entry, we have

$$\left[-\tfrac{1}{\sqrt{4}} \quad \tfrac{1}{\sqrt{4}} \quad \tfrac{1}{\sqrt{4}} \quad \tfrac{1}{\sqrt{4}} \right] .$$

Using our formula, the inversion about the mean is

$$\left[\tfrac{3\times4-4}{4}\tfrac{1}{\sqrt{4}} \quad \tfrac{4-4}{4}\tfrac{1}{\sqrt{4}} \quad \tfrac{4-4}{4}\tfrac{1}{\sqrt{4}} \quad \tfrac{4-4}{4}\tfrac{1}{\sqrt{4}} \right] = \left[\left(\tfrac{3\times4-4}{4}\right)\tfrac{1}{\sqrt{4}} \quad 0 \quad 0 \quad 0 \right]$$

$$= \left[1 \quad 0 \quad 0 \quad 0 \right] .$$

In one negate/invert-about-the-mean iteration, we have maximized the first entry.

Beyond this point, the general formula gets messy, so let's do some calculations with Python. For increasing integer values of N, we want to know how many iterations are necessary to maximize the first entry.

We begin by importing the Python libraries we need for the computations and plotting.

```
import math
import matplotlib.pyplot as plt
import numpy as np
```

Next, we define `invert_about_mean` to invert the **R** entries in a vector of floats (actually a Python list) about the average of the entries.

```
# Invert a vector of floats around the mean of
# the elements

def invert_about_mean(vector: list[float]) -> list[float]:
    mean = float(sum(vector)) / len(vector)
    return [2 * mean - s for s in vector]
```

We now define `compute_maximum_amplitude`. It takes a positive integer N and returns a Python tuple of integers: the maximum first entry value we see when we repeat the negate/invert-about-the-mean process and the number of iterations required to reach that maximum. We initialize the vector with the N entries equal to $\frac{1}{\sqrt{N}}$, a "balanced superposition," though we are not dealing with quantum states here. When N is an integer power of 2, this analysis holds for amplitude amplification.

```
# Compute the maximum obtained amplitude and iteration
# number when it is obtained via amplitude amplification

def compute_maximum_amplitude(N: int) -> tuple[int]:
    vector = [1.0 / math.sqrt(N)] * N
    max_amplitude = 0.0
    max_amplitude_iteration = 0
    iteration = 1

    while True:
        # Negate the first amplitude
        vector[0] = -vector[0]

        # Invert about the mean
        vector = invert_about_mean(vector)

        if vector[0] > max_amplitude:
            max_amplitude = vector[0]
            max_amplitude_iteration = iteration
            iteration += 1
        else:
            return max_amplitude, max_amplitude_iteration
```

For example, we can compute these values for $2^{10} = 1024$:

```
compute_maximum_amplitude(2**10)
```

```
(0.9997305860802842, 25)
```

With these definitions, we can draw the plot in Figure 9.11 with **matplotlib** to see if there is a relationship between N and the number of iterations we need to maximize the first entry..

```
# Define lists of floats for plotting

Ns: list[float] = []
```

```
required_iterations: list[float] = []

for N in range(4, 256):
    max_amplitude, max_amplitude_iteration = \
        compute_maximum_amplitude(N)
    Ns.append(N)
    required_iterations.append(max_amplitude_iteration)

plt.figure(figsize=(6, 3))
plt.plot(Ns, required_iterations,
    color=(0.636, 0.098, 0.122),
    label="Required iterations")
plt.xlabel("N")
plt.ylabel("Iterations")
plt.legend(loc="lower right")
```

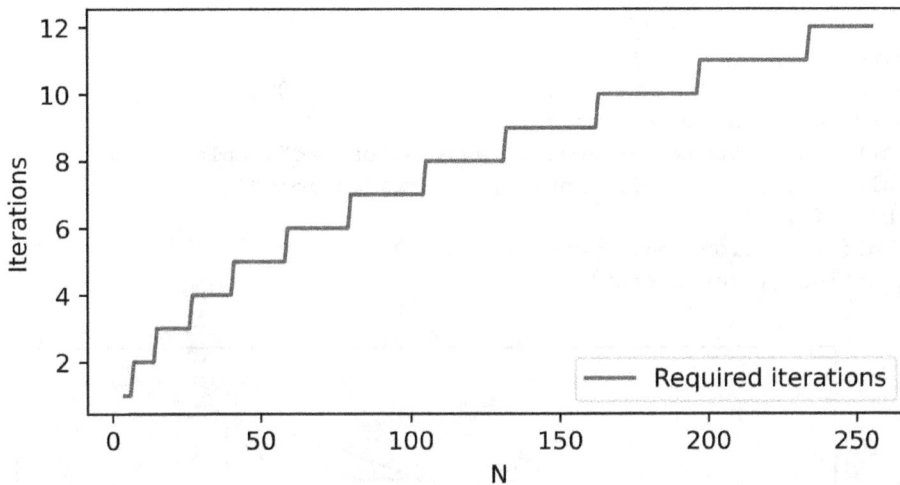

Figure 9.11: Required iterations to maximize the first entry

This looks very much like the plot of $y = \sqrt{x}$ in Figure 9.12.

In fact, our plot of the iterations to maximize the first entry is very similar to a square root plot with a constant multiple of $\frac{\pi}{4}$, as you can see in Figure 9.13.

```
pi4_approximations: list[float] = [ ]

for N in range(4, 256):
    pi4_approximations.append((math.pi / 4 * math.sqrt(N)))
```

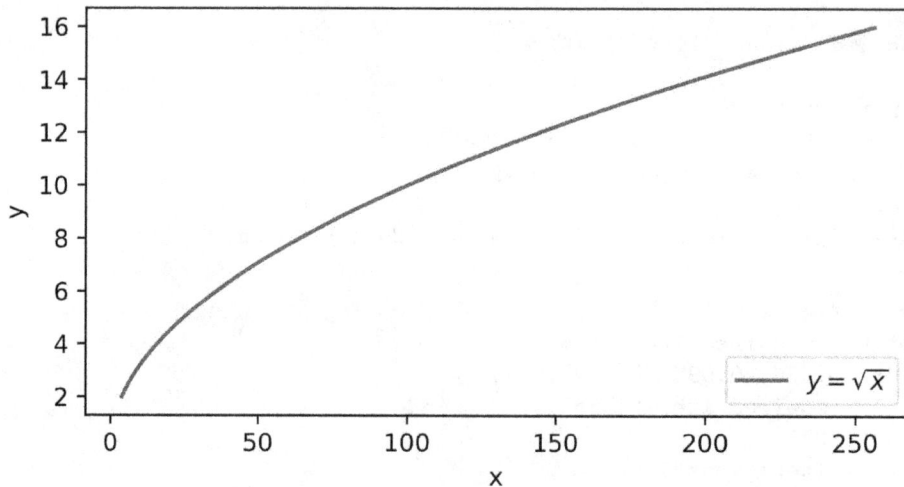

Figure 9.12: Plot of $y = \sqrt{x}$

```
plt.figure(figsize=(6, 3))
plt.plot(Ns, required_iterations, color=(0.636, 0.098, 0.122),
    label="Required iterations")
plt.plot(Ns, pi4_approximations, linestyle="dashed", color=(0.0, 0.263, 0.808),
    label="$\\frac{\\pi}{4}\\sqrt{N}$ approximations")
plt.xlabel("N")
plt.ylabel("Iterations and approximations")
plt.legend(loc="lower right")
```

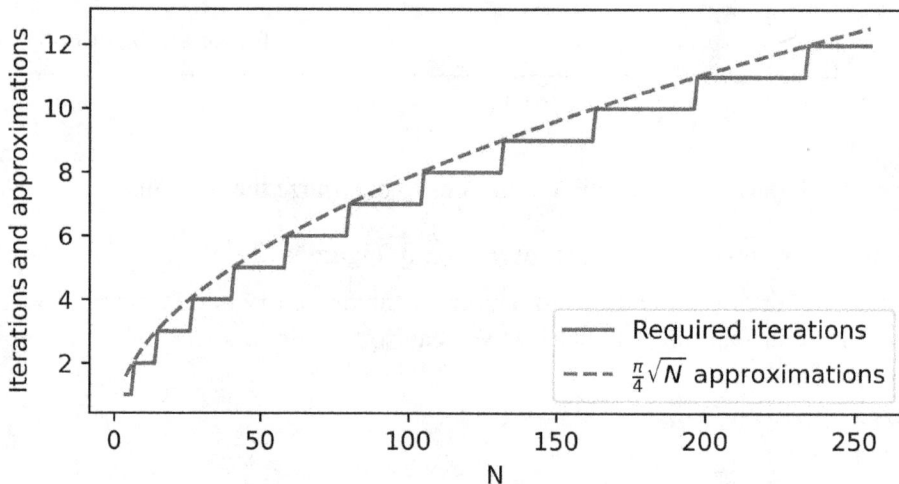

Figure 9.13: Required iterations to maximize the first entry with $\frac{\pi}{4}\sqrt{N}$ approximations

When we are working with N a power of two, the calculation of the approximate number of iterations is simpler than the general case:

$$\frac{\pi}{4}\sqrt{2^n} = \begin{cases} \pi 2^{\frac{n}{2}-2} = \pi 2^{\frac{n-4}{2}} & \text{if } n \text{ is even} \\ \pi\sqrt{2}\,2^{\frac{n-1}{2}-2} = \pi\sqrt{2}\,2^{\frac{n-5}{2}} & \text{if } n \text{ is odd} \end{cases}$$

To learn more

While we now have empirical evidence that the approximation closely matches the number of iterations necessary to maximize the first entry, this is not a proof. In particular, we have not shown why it is a good approximation and where the constant $\frac{\pi}{4}$ comes from. More advanced texts contain this analysis. [137, Chapter 13] [162, Section 6.1.4]

9.7 Searching with Grover

We just saw how if we have one standard basis ket in mind, we flip the probability amplitude and then amplify the amplitude for that ket. When we repeat the process enough times, we are likely to measure the right ket with high probability.

In the last section, I showed that we could pick out the known ket $|010\rangle$ from among all the kets. So I found what I knew was there, and even knew where it was beforehand. We can use these techniques more generally. In this section, we put everything together to describe the famous quantum search algorithm discovered by Lov Kumar Grover, a computer scientist. The algorithm is based on amplitude amplification.

9.7.1 Grover's search algorithm

Instead of using the magic gate matrix $\mathbf{U}_{|010\rangle}$, which flips the sign of the amplitude of the given ket, we instead employ $\mathbf{U}_f$, which is related to the oracle f.

I have an oracle that I can call, but I cannot see into it. I create $\mathbf{U}_f$, and then by repeating the pair $\mathbf{U}_f$ and $\mathbf{U}_\varphi$ enough times, I can find the special element for which f returns 1. How many times is enough?

In section 2.8.2, we saw that in the worst case, we have to look through every item in an unstructured collection of size N to see if something we want to locate is present. If we add random access and pre-sort, we can locate it in $O(\log(N))$ time via a binary search. Using Grover's search algorithm on unstructured data can significantly decrease the time required.

To make it concrete, suppose you say, "I'm thinking of a number between 1 and 100," and then you give me an oracle f that can identify the number. I can find the number you are thinking of in approximately $10 = \sqrt{100}$ iterations of $\mathbf{U}_f\mathbf{U}_\varphi$. Classically, it can require 99 calls to the oracle.

Exercise 9.21

Why 99 and not 100?

We go from $O(N)$ to $O\left(\sqrt{N}\right)$ for $N = 100$, a quadratic improvement. It doesn't look like much of a gain for small numbers, but going from $10,000 = 10^4$ to $100 = 10^2$ is significant.

As we saw in section 9.6.4, we can be even more precise: it takes approximately $\frac{\pi}{4}\sqrt{N} \approx 0.7854\sqrt{N}$ iterations to maximize the probability of getting the object for which you are searching.

Figure 9.14 shows the circuit for performing the search.

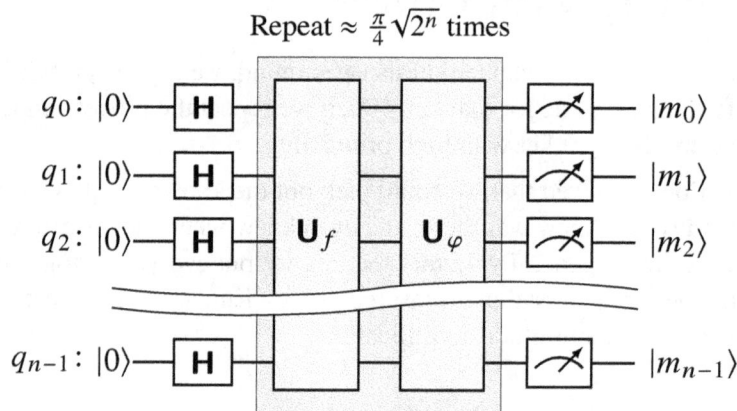

Figure 9.14: The Grover search circuit

Here are the steps for using the Grover search algorithm:

1. Identify the data you want to search. Let N be the number of items.
2. Find the smallest positive n in $\mathbf{Z}$ such that $N \leq 2^n$. You need n qubits for the search algorithm.
3. Figure out a way to map uniquely from the data items to search to basis kets such as $|j\rangle_n$ for $j < N$. Presumably, we can go from the data object to the basis ket and back again. See section 13.2.
4. Use an oracle f and gate/matrix $\mathbf{U}_f$ that flips the sign of the object for which you are searching.
5. Run the $\mathbf{U}_f \mathbf{U}_\varphi$ circuit $\frac{\pi}{4}\sqrt{N}$ times, rounding down.

6. Measure and read off the ket corresponding to the item sought in the data. Map this back to the item within the data collection.
7. If the answer is not correct, repeat the above. The chance of error is $O\left(\frac{1}{N}\right)$.

In our examples, we create and then use the oracle. In practice, someone else will give us the oracle and its operation is opaque to us.

Suppose I work for a company and there is an employee database. A database administrator writes an oracle that answers true or false to the question, "Is this the employee identification number for Robert Sutor?". I don't know how the oracle is implemented, but I can use it.

Some implementations of the oracle require $n + 1$ qubits.

The oracles we have discussed return **1** for one and only one input, but some oracles return **1** for several possibilities. Grover's search algorithm can still be used and finds one of the items even faster: if there are t possible matches, the number of iterations is $O\left(\sqrt{\frac{N}{t}}\right)$. More precisely, it is approximately

$$\frac{\pi}{4}\sqrt{\frac{N}{t}}.$$

9.7.2 Using the oracle

Just as different circuits do the same thing more or less efficiently, there are other ways of coding the Grover search circuit.

We now analyze the search circuit in Figure 9.15. Though the oracle identifies one basis ket uniquely, I'm not going to tell you which one it is ahead of time.

You wouldn't go to all this trouble to find one object out of four. Nevertheless, it shows many of the characteristic aspects of larger examples.

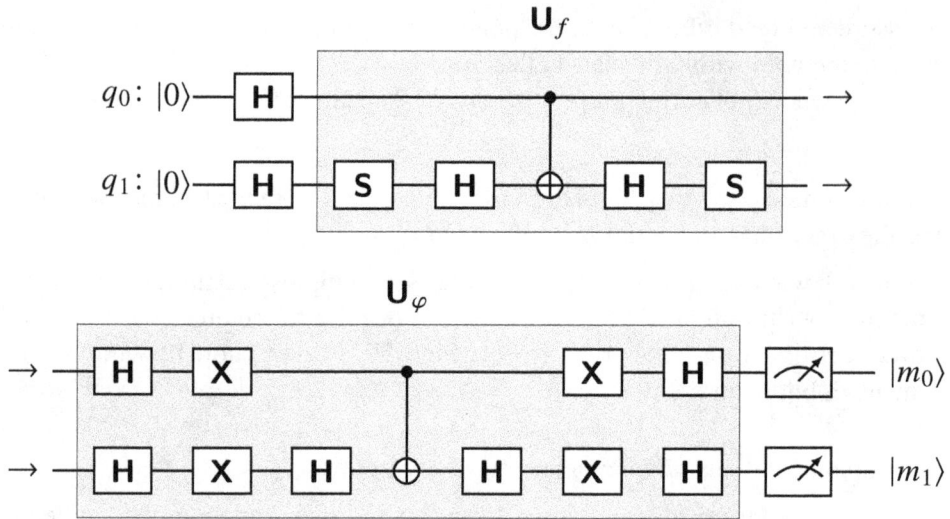

Figure 9.15: A Grover search circuit with depth 13 and width 2

Circuit section 1: Balanced superposition

After initializing the two qubits to $|0\rangle$ in Figure 9.15, we place the entire quantum register in a balanced superposition.

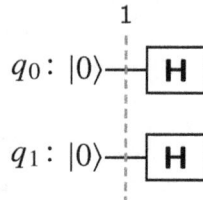

The vertical dashed line allows me to describe the steps in the circuit sections and does not affect the computation. The gate steps are within each section, numbered from 1 going left to right. Each step's operations are to the right of the dashed line labeled with the step's number.

The state of the register after step 1 and section 1 is

Step	State
1	$\frac{1}{2}(|00\rangle + |01\rangle + |10\rangle + |11\rangle)$

Circuit section 2: U_f

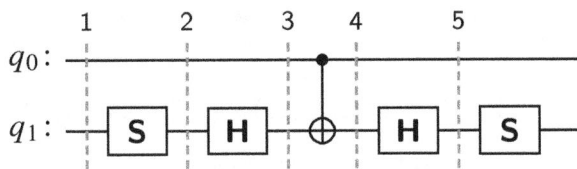

The states of the quantum register after each step are

Step	State
1	$\frac{1}{2}(\|00\rangle + i\|01\rangle + \|10\rangle + i\|11\rangle)$
2	$\frac{\sqrt{2}}{4}((1+i)\|00\rangle + (1-i)\|01\rangle + (1+i)\|10\rangle + (1-i)\|11\rangle)$
3	$\frac{\sqrt{2}}{4}((1+i)\|00\rangle + (1-i)\|01\rangle + (1-i)\|10\rangle + (1+i)\|11\rangle)$
4	$\frac{1}{2}(\|00\rangle + i\|01\rangle + \|10\rangle - i\|11\rangle)$
5	$\frac{1}{2}(\|00\rangle - \|01\rangle + \|10\rangle + \|11\rangle)$

Circuit section 3: U_φ

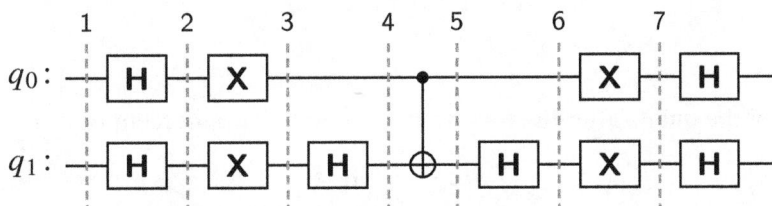

The states of the quantum register after each step are

Step	State
1	$\frac{1}{2}(|00\rangle + |01\rangle - |10\rangle + |11\rangle)$
2	$\frac{1}{2}(|00\rangle - |01\rangle + |10\rangle + |11\rangle)$
3	$\frac{\sqrt{2}}{2}(|01\rangle + |10\rangle)$
4	$\frac{\sqrt{2}}{2}(|01\rangle + |11\rangle)$
5	$\frac{1}{2}(|00\rangle - |01\rangle + |10\rangle - |11\rangle)$
6	$\frac{1}{2}(-|00\rangle + |01\rangle - |10\rangle + |11\rangle)$
7	$-|01\rangle$

Circuit section 4: Measurement

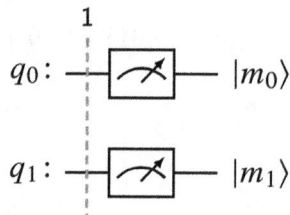

The state of the qubits after the final step and before measurement is

Step	State
1	$-|01\rangle$

With 100% probability, $|01\rangle$ is the answer.

9.7.3 Understanding the oracle

We know that the circuit section

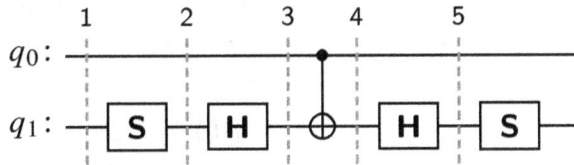

implements the oracle and the sign flip for $|01\rangle$ in the balanced superposition. How and why does it work?

Let's work from the inside out and examine what

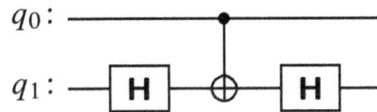

does to the standard basis kets.

When the state of q_0 is $|0\rangle$, the **CNOT** does nothing, and q_1 remains the same. The two **H** gates cancel each other. So $|00\rangle$ and $|01\rangle$ are untouched.

When the state of q_0 is $|1\rangle$, the **CNOT** flips between $|0\rangle$ and $|1\rangle$. The first **H** gate takes

$$|0\rangle \mapsto \frac{\sqrt{2}}{2}|0\rangle + \frac{\sqrt{2}}{2}|1\rangle = |+\rangle \quad \text{and} \quad |1\rangle \mapsto \frac{\sqrt{2}}{2}|0\rangle - \frac{\sqrt{2}}{2}|1\rangle = |-\rangle .$$

The **CNOT** interchanges $|0\rangle$ and $|1\rangle$, yielding

$$\frac{\sqrt{2}}{2}|0\rangle + \frac{\sqrt{2}}{2}|1\rangle = |+\rangle \quad \text{and} \quad -\frac{\sqrt{2}}{2}|0\rangle + \frac{\sqrt{2}}{2}|1\rangle = -|-\rangle .$$

The final **H** undoes the superposition, and we get

$$|0\rangle \quad \text{and} \quad -|1\rangle .$$

All together, we have

$$|00\rangle \mapsto |00\rangle \qquad\qquad |10\rangle \mapsto |10\rangle$$
$$|01\rangle \mapsto |01\rangle \qquad\qquad |11\rangle \mapsto -|11\rangle$$

> This is a good idiom to remember to flip the sign of $|11\rangle$ only. Had we wanted our oracle to identify $|11\rangle$, this would have been the $\mathbf{U}_f$ *subcircuit* we would use for $|11\rangle$.

We haven't figured out $|01\rangle$ yet, but we have another $\mathbf{U}_f$ in hand!

The **S** gate leaves $|0\rangle$ alone but takes $|1\rangle$ to $i|1\rangle$. Applied a second time, it gives us the state $ii|1\rangle = -|1\rangle$. Two applications are the same as the **Z** gate. Applying the **S** gate on the second qubit produces

$$|00\rangle \mapsto |00\rangle \qquad\qquad |10\rangle \mapsto |10\rangle$$
$$|01\rangle \mapsto i|01\rangle \qquad\qquad |11\rangle \mapsto i|11\rangle$$

We now apply the $|11\rangle$ sign flip

$$|00\rangle \mapsto |00\rangle \qquad\qquad |10\rangle \mapsto |10\rangle$$
$$|01\rangle \mapsto i|01\rangle \qquad\qquad |11\rangle \mapsto -i|11\rangle$$

and **S** one more time

$$|00\rangle \mapsto |00\rangle \qquad\qquad |10\rangle \mapsto |10\rangle$$
$$|01\rangle \mapsto ii|01\rangle \qquad\qquad |11\rangle \mapsto -ii|11\rangle$$

which is

$$|00\rangle \mapsto |00\rangle \qquad\qquad |10\rangle \mapsto |10\rangle$$
$$|01\rangle \mapsto -|01\rangle \qquad\qquad |11\rangle \mapsto |11\rangle$$

and it does what we want! Complex numbers are your friend.

Exercise 9.22

Construct the subcircuit for flipping the sign of $|10\rangle$.

Exercise 9.23

Construct the subcircuit for flipping the sign of $|00\rangle$

You construct circuits for algorithms by learning or devising idioms, implementing them into subcircuits, and then reusing them to complete your task. You should look for symmetry and ask yourself why it is present and what function it performs.

We can extend Grover's search algorithm in various ways. Suppose we have N items, and instead of trying to find one distinguished item among them, our oracle will somehow identify K of them. We do not know what K is *a priori*. Given Grover, we would expect to be able to find K in something like $O\left(\sqrt{\frac{N}{K}}\right)$ queries to the oracle, and this is almost true up to an ϵ that shows up in both how closely we approximate K and within the $O()$ expression.

To learn more

The original 1998 proof of Grover's search algorithm involved the Quantum Fourier Transform (QFT), which we work through in section 10.1. [24] A more recent proof in 2019 dispenses with the need for the QFT. [1] Both techniques involve amplitude amplification.

9.7.4   The data problem

A quantum computer is not a big data machine. There is no way to quickly input large amounts of data before the loading operations exhaust the physical qubit coherence times.

In Grover's search algorithm, we do not have to pre-load all the data as long as the oracle can correctly identify the object we need.

How do we construct the oracle? If the data is complicated, we might need a very sophisticated oracle circuit subroutine. The subroutine likely involves many steps, and, again, our coherence time might limit what we can compute. Suppose the oracle involved the multiplication of numbers with a few dozen digits. In that case, we could require hundreds of qubits and circuit steps unless we can do this arithmetic on a classical processor.

Grover's search algorithm works best as a circuit subroutine for information already represented within the states of the qubits or implicitly usable. The algorithm could be ideal if another quantum algorithm requires a fast search of data to which it has direct access or a very fast oracle.

9.8   The Deutsch-Jozsa algorithm

I will now walk you through another early quantum algorithm that employs oracles. It shows us another form in which we express oracles in quantum circuits.

Let's begin with an example. Suppose I buy two standard decks of 52 playing cards. In a separate room where you cannot see me, I create a single deck of 52 cards where one of the following is true:

1. All the cards are red, or all the cards are black.
2. Half the cards (26) are black, and half are red.

We call the first option "constant" and the second "balanced."

I now go to you and give you the problem of finding out which of the two possibilities is the case for the deck I am holding. You do so by looking at and then discarding cards at the top of the deck.

In the best case, the first card is one color, and the second is the other. Therefore, the deck is balanced. In the worst case, you must examine $27 = 1 + 52/2$ cards. The first 26 cards might be black, say. If the next is black, then all are black. If it is red, the deck is balanced.

If we have an oracle, we ask, "Is the card at the top of the deck black?". It returns **1** if it is, **0** if it is red. As I stated, we must consult the oracle 27 times in the worst case to get the correct answer.

When we first saw the definition of an oracle, we expressed it as a function f operating on strings of n bits

$$f : \{0, 1\}^n \rightarrow \{0, 1\} \ .$$

When translating this to quantum computing, we consider standard basis kets instead of bit strings.

Examples

- $f : \{0, 1\}^2 \mapsto 0$ is a constant oracle.
- $f : \{0, 1\}^2 \mapsto 1$ is a constant oracle.
- $f = \textsf{xor} : \{0, 1\}^2 \rightarrow \{0, 1\}$ is a balanced oracle.
- $f : \{0, 1\}^3 \rightarrow \{0, 1\}$ where $f(b_2 b_1 b_0) \mapsto b_0$ is a balanced oracle. This oracle answers the question, "Is $b_2 b_1 b_0$ an odd number?".

Our new problem is this: for all possible bit strings of length n or standard basis kets for n qubits, the oracle f either always returns **0** or always returns **1**, and so it is constant, or it is balanced. How many calls to the oracle do we need to determine whether it is constant or balanced?

There are 2^n bit strings of length n, and the brute force classical approach could require our looking (that is, calling the oracle) at one more than half of them, which is $2^{n-1} + 1$.

The quantum solution to this, with all the improvements to the original, is called the *Deutsch-Jozsa algorithm*. It was discovered by physicist David Deutsch (Figure 9.16) and mathematician Richard Jozsa, and was based on earlier work by Deutsch. It requires one call to the oracle. [63]

9.8.1 More Hadamard math

When we first saw the single qubit Hadamard gate in section 7.6.5, I remarked there was a nice relationship between the 0s and 1s and exponents

$$\mathsf{H}|u\rangle = \frac{\sqrt{2}}{2} \left(|0\rangle + (-1)^u |1\rangle\right)$$

Figure 9.16: David Deutsch in 2017 after receiving the Dirac Medal

when u is one of 0, 1. With summation notation, we can make this even more concise:

$$\mathsf{H}|u\rangle = \frac{\sqrt{2}}{2}\left((-1)^{u\times 0}|0\rangle + (-1)^{u\times 1}|1\rangle\right) = \frac{\sqrt{2}}{2}\sum_{v \text{ in } \{0,1\}}(-1)^{uv}|v\rangle .$$

Note how we use the powers of -1 to change the signs of kets. For a physicist, this is a *phase change*. For a regular person, this is a *change of sign*.

The cleverness continues as we look at more qubits. [231] [230]

For bit strings u of length 2, that is, of the form $\{0,1\}^2$, we have the corresponding standard basis kets $|00\rangle$, $|01\rangle$, $|10\rangle$, and $|11\rangle$. In this case, when we say $|u\rangle$ for u in $\{0,1\}^2$, we mean these basis kets. I use subscripts to label the individual bits. Therefore

$$|u\rangle = |u_1 u_2\rangle \quad \text{and} \quad |v\rangle = |v_1 v_2\rangle$$

where u_1, u_2, v_1, and v_2 are each 0 or 1. Using this convention,

$$(\mathsf{H} \otimes \mathsf{H})\,|u\rangle = \mathsf{H}|u_1\rangle \otimes \mathsf{H}|u_2\rangle$$

$$= \left(\frac{\sqrt{2}}{2}\sum_{v_1 \text{ in } \{0,1\}}(-1)^{u_1 v_1}|v_1\rangle\right) \otimes \left(\frac{\sqrt{2}}{2}\sum_{v_2 \text{ in } \{0,1\}}(-1)^{u_2 y_2}|v_2\rangle\right)$$

$$= \frac{1}{2}\sum_{v \text{ in } \{0,1\}^2}(-1)^{u_1 v_1 + u_2 v_2}|v\rangle .$$

Exercise 9.24

Confirm

$$(\mathbf{H} \otimes \mathbf{H})\,|00\rangle = \frac{1}{2}(|00\rangle + |01\rangle + |10\rangle + |11\rangle)\,.$$

The exponent $u_1 v_1 + u_2 v_2$ for -1 looks like a dot product. We rewrite the last line above to conclude

$$(\mathbf{H} \otimes \mathbf{H})\,|u\rangle = \frac{1}{2} \sum_{v \text{ in } \{0,1\}^2} (-1)^{u \cdot v}|v\rangle\,.$$

The final generalization is to n qubits. After calculations such as the above, the formula becomes

$$\mathbf{H}^{\otimes n}|u\rangle = \frac{1}{\sqrt{2^n}} \sum_{v \text{ in } \{0,1\}^n} (-1)^{u \cdot v}|v\rangle$$

for u a bit string of length n. This shows how Hadamard gates transform standard kets in a particularly nice way. We can simplify this even more by computing the dot product mod 2. It makes no difference as an exponent for -1.

Exercise 9.25

Using this formula, fully write out the ket expressions for $\mathbf{H}^{\otimes 3}|000\rangle$, $\mathbf{H}^{\otimes 3}|001\rangle$, and $\mathbf{H}^{\otimes 3}|110\rangle$.

Let's compute a special case that we need in the Deutsch-Jozsa algorithm. For u, we take a bit string of n **0**s with a single **1** tacked on at the end. So $|u\rangle = |0\rangle^{\otimes n} \otimes |1\rangle$. In this case, $u \cdot v = v_{n+1}$ because $u_j = 0$ for $1 \leq j \leq n$ and $u_{n+1} = 1$.

$$\mathbf{H}^{\otimes n+1}|0\cdots01\rangle = \frac{1}{\sqrt{2^{n+1}}} \sum_{v \text{ in } \{0,1\}^{n+1}} (-1)^{v_{n+1}}|v\rangle$$

That last bit of v is controlling the sign. Let's isolate that by rewriting $|v\rangle = |x\rangle \otimes |y\rangle$ where y is now the last bit. The formula becomes

$$\mathbf{H}^{\otimes n+1}|0\cdots01\rangle = \frac{1}{\sqrt{2^{n+1}}} \sum_{x \text{ in } \{0,1\}^n} \sum_{y \text{ in } \{0,1\}} (-1)^{y}|x\rangle \otimes |y\rangle$$

$$= \frac{1}{\sqrt{2^{n+1}}} \sum_{x \text{ in } \{0,1\}^n} \Big(|x\rangle \otimes |0\rangle - |x\rangle \otimes |1\rangle\Big)$$

$$= \frac{1}{\sqrt{2^{n+1}}} \sum_{x \text{ in } \{0,1\}^n} |x\rangle \otimes \Big(|0\rangle - |1\rangle\Big)$$

$$= \frac{1}{\sqrt{2^n}} \sum_{x \text{ in } \{0,1\}^n} |x\rangle \otimes \left(\frac{\sqrt{2}}{2}|0\rangle - \frac{\sqrt{2}}{2}|1\rangle\right)$$

$$= \left(\frac{1}{\sqrt{2^n}} \sum_{x \text{ in } \{0,1\}^n} |x\rangle\right) \otimes \left(\frac{\sqrt{2}}{2}|0\rangle - \frac{\sqrt{2}}{2}|1\rangle\right)$$

$$= \mathbf{H}^{\otimes n}|0\rangle^{\otimes n} \otimes \mathbf{H}|1\rangle$$

I worked through the computation so you could see common arithmetic methods for working with Hadamard gates.

Exercise 9.26

How do we get from the third line to the fourth?

Exercise 9.27

Why do we have the equality

$$\frac{1}{\sqrt{2^n}} \sum_{x \text{ in } \{0,1\}^n} |x\rangle = \mathbf{H}^{\otimes n}|0\rangle^{\otimes n}$$

between lines (5) and (6) in the equation?

9.8.2 Another oracle circuit

The oracle for Grover search in section 9.7.1 was incorporated into the circuit and modified only the input states. Here, we'll look at another way of constructing a circuit with an oracle.

There are $n + 1$ wires in the circuit in Figure 9.17. n of those represent the bit strings, and we initialize those to $|0\rangle$. The extra wire at the bottom of the diagram is for a "work" or "scratchpad" qubit. It's not part of the input data, but we need it to do our computation. More formally, we call it an *ancilla qubit*.

Aside from giving us an extra place to put information, we can also initialize an ancilla qubit to a known state. Algorithmically, we then know the state of the ancilla, but we likely don't precisely know the states of the others. In our circuit, q_n starts in state $|0\rangle$, but we use an **X** gate to flip it to $|1\rangle$.

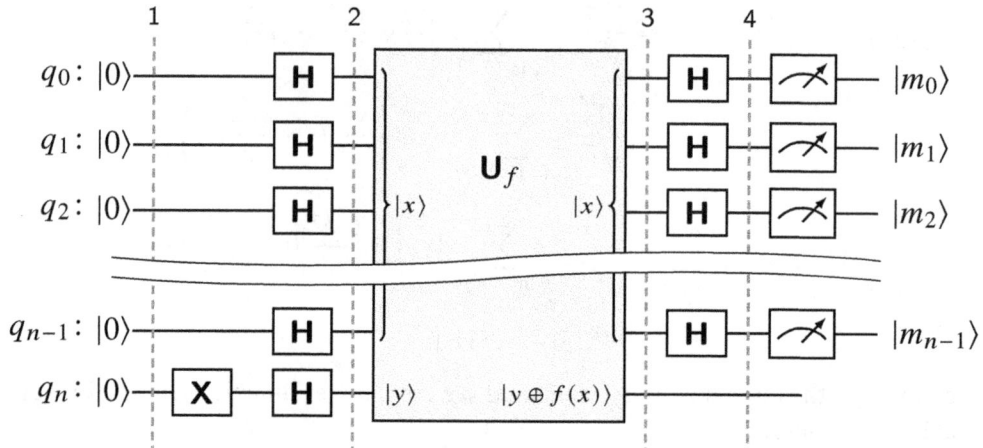

Figure 9.17: The Deutsch-Jozsa circuit

Is there a quantum gate that turns an arbitrary state directly into either $|0\rangle$ or $|1\rangle$? If there were, such a gate would not be reversible and so not unitary. We can initialize an ancilla qubit to a precise value as we did here. If we are willing to sacrifice the portability of our code, we can also use the $|0\rangle$ **RESET** operation I describe in section 7.6.14.

Circuit section 1: Superposition

This part of the circuit implements the superposition from section 9.8.1:

$$\mathbf{H}^{\otimes n+1}|0\cdots01\rangle = \left(\frac{1}{\sqrt{2^n}}\sum_{x \text{ in } \{0,1\}^n}|x\rangle\right)\otimes\left(\frac{\sqrt{2}}{2}|0\rangle - \frac{\sqrt{2}}{2}|1\rangle\right)$$

$$= \mathbf{H}^{\otimes n}|0\rangle^{\otimes n}\otimes\mathbf{H}|1\rangle .$$

Circuit section 2: $\mathbf{U}_f$

In the inputs to $\mathbf{U}_f$, we label the collective states for the n "data" qubits q_0 through q_{n-1} as $|x\rangle$. We label the state for the ancilla qubit q_n as $|y\rangle$. All together, the input to $\mathbf{U}_f$ is $|x\rangle\otimes|y\rangle$.

The output is $|x\rangle\otimes|y\oplus f(x)\rangle$. Remember, $f(x)$ always returns $\mathbf{0}$ or $\mathbf{1}$, and "$\oplus$" is addition mod 2. We discussed transformations of this kind in section 9.3.2.

Applying $\mathbf{U}_f$ to

$$\left(\frac{1}{\sqrt{2^n}}\sum_{x \text{ in } \{0,1\}^n}|x\rangle\right)\otimes\left(\frac{\sqrt{2}}{2}|0\rangle - \frac{\sqrt{2}}{2}|1\rangle\right)$$

yields

$$\left(\frac{1}{\sqrt{2^n}} \sum_{x \text{ in } \{0,1\}^n} |x\rangle\right) \otimes \left(\frac{\sqrt{2}}{2}|0 \oplus f(x)\rangle - \frac{\sqrt{2}}{2}|1 \oplus f(x)\rangle\right)$$

by linearity, which is

$$\left(\frac{1}{\sqrt{2^n}} \sum_{x \text{ in } \{0,1\}^n} |x\rangle\right) \otimes \left(\frac{\sqrt{2}}{2}|f(x)\rangle - \frac{\sqrt{2}}{2}|1 \oplus f(x)\rangle\right).$$

If $f(x) = \mathbf{0}$, then the right-hand side is

$$\frac{\sqrt{2}}{2}|f(x)\rangle - \frac{\sqrt{2}}{2}|1 \oplus f(x)\rangle = \frac{\sqrt{2}}{2}|0\rangle - \frac{\sqrt{2}}{2}|1\rangle.$$

When $f(x) = \mathbf{1}$, the only other possibility, we have

$$\frac{\sqrt{2}}{2}|1\rangle - \frac{\sqrt{2}}{2}|0\rangle.$$

Note how the signs reverse. We can combine both these equations into

$$\frac{\sqrt{2}}{2}|f(x)\rangle - \frac{\sqrt{2}}{2}|1 \oplus f(x)\rangle = (-1)^{f(x)}\frac{\sqrt{2}}{2}(|0\rangle - |1\rangle).$$

The full result of $\mathbf{U}_f$ is

$$\left(\frac{1}{\sqrt{2^n}} \sum_{x \text{ in } \{0,1\}^n} |x\rangle\right) \otimes \left(\frac{\sqrt{2}}{2}|0 \oplus f(x)\rangle - \frac{\sqrt{2}}{2}|1 \oplus f(x)\rangle\right)$$

$$= \left(\frac{1}{\sqrt{2^n}} \sum_{x \text{ in } \{0,1\}^n} |x\rangle\right) \otimes \left((-1)^{f(x)}\frac{\sqrt{2}}{2}(|0\rangle - |1\rangle)\right)$$

$$= \left(\frac{1}{\sqrt{2^n}} \sum_{x \text{ in } \{0,1\}^n} (-1)^{f(x)}|x\rangle\right) \otimes \left(\frac{\sqrt{2}}{2}(|0\rangle - |1\rangle)\right)$$

The expression to the right of "$\otimes$" is constant, and we no longer need it. Remember that this is the state of the ancilla qubit q_n. I've indicated that we can discard it by not measuring it in the circuit diagram.

The output of the $\mathbf{U}_f$ gate for the n data qubits q_0 to q_{n-1} is

$$\frac{1}{\sqrt{2^n}} \sum_{x \text{ in } \{0,1\}^n} (-1)^{f(x)}|x\rangle.$$

We have encoded the effect of the oracle into the phase of each $|x\rangle$. We've done this by multiplying $|x\rangle$ by a value of absolute value 1, namely $(-1)^{f(x)}$. We call this technique *phase kickback*.

Circuit section 3: Final H gates

We apply the $\mathbf{H}^{\otimes n}$ gate to the above expression using the formula

$$\mathbf{H}^{\otimes n}|u\rangle = \frac{1}{\sqrt{2^n}} \sum_{v \text{ in } \{0,1\}^n} (-1)^{u \cdot v}|v\rangle$$

from section 9.8.1. This produces

$$\frac{1}{2^n} \sum_{x \text{ in } \{0,1\}^n} (-1)^{f(x)} \left(\sum_{v \text{ in } \{0,1\}^n} (-1)^{x \cdot v}|v\rangle \right)$$

By rearranging terms, we can move the inner sum to the outside:

$$\frac{1}{2^n} \sum_{v \text{ in } \{0,1\}^n} \left(\sum_{x \text{ in } \{0,1\}^n} (-1)^{f(x)}(-1)^{x \cdot v} \right)|v\rangle .$$

Before we turn to measurement, let me say that I know this section is very intensive with all the arithmetic with the Σ summations. We compress a lot of information about the kets and their amplitudes into formulas and then manipulate and simplify them. **Working through each until you are comfortable with what is happening in each is worth your time.**

Circuit section 4: Measurement

Given

$$\frac{1}{2^n} \sum_{v \text{ in } \{0,1\}^n} \left(\sum_{x \text{ in } \{0,1\}^n} (-1)^{f(x)}(-1)^{x \cdot v} \right)|v\rangle ,$$

if f is constant, then all the $f(x)$ are the same and equal to $f(0)$. We can rewrite the above as

$$\frac{1}{2^n}(-1)^{f(0)} \sum_{v \text{ in } \{0,1\}^n} \left(\sum_{x \text{ in } \{0,1\}^n} (-1)^{x \cdot v} \right)|v\rangle .$$

The inner sum

$$\sum_{x \text{ in } \{0,1\}^n} (-1)^{x \cdot v}$$

is a special form. It is equal to 2^n if v is the zero-bit string and is 0 otherwise.

If v is the zero-bit string, then

$$\sum_{x \text{ in } \{0,1\}^n} (-1)^{x \cdot v} = \sum_{x \text{ in } \{0,1\}^n} (-1)^0 = \sum_{x \text{ in } \{0,1\}^n} 1 = 2^n .$$

I leave to the reader the proof for when v is nonzero. Begin with the case that one bit in v is **1**, and the rest are **0**. Without loss of generality, you may assume the nonzero bit is the left-most. Prove the assertion in this case. Next, do the same if the two left-most bits are **1** and the rest are **0**. Complete the proof by induction: show that if the statement is true for $n - 1$, then you can prove it is true for n.

Exercise 9.28

Confirm this for $n = 2$.

Using this equality, we have

$$\frac{1}{2^n}(-1)^{f(0)} \sum_{v \text{ in } \{0,1\}^n} \left(\sum_{x \text{ in } \{0,1\}^n} (-1)^{x \cdot v} \right) |v\rangle = \frac{1}{2^n}(-1)^{f(0)} 2^n |0\rangle^{\otimes n}$$

$$= (-1)^{f(0)} |0\rangle^{\otimes n} .$$

The amplitude $(-1)^{f(0)}$ has absolute value 1, and does not affect the measurement.

If f is constant, the result upon measurement is $|0\rangle^{\otimes n}$ with 100% probability.

We can glean more by looking at

$$\frac{1}{2^n} \sum_{v \text{ in } \{0,1\}^n} \left(\sum_{x \text{ in } \{0,1\}^n} (-1)^{f(x)}(-1)^{x \cdot v} \right) |v\rangle .$$

When $|v\rangle = |0\rangle^{\otimes n}$, this expression reduces to

$$\frac{1}{2^n} \left(\sum_{x \text{ in } \{0,1\}^n} (-1)^{f(x)} \right) |0\rangle^{\otimes n} .$$

This expression is the amplitude for $|0\rangle^{\otimes n}$. It equals ± 1 when f is constant and 0 when f is balanced. The first case is constructive interference, and the second is destructive interference.

> When we run the Deutsch-Jozsa algorithm, if we get $|0\rangle^{\otimes n}$ after measurement, then the oracle is constant. Otherwise, it is balanced. We get $|0\rangle^{\otimes n}$ if and only if the oracle is constant.

9.9 The Bernstein-Vazirani algorithm

Suppose I were to say to you:

> *I'm thinking of a number from 0 to 15 inclusive.*
> *Ask me questions to guess which one it is.*

How would you go about guessing the number? How many questions would you need?

This is a search problem, but it has some structure. The numbers in the collection we are searching are consecutive and ordered. There is no reason to consider an $O(n)$ sequence of questions such as

> "Is it 0?" No.
> "Is it 1?" No.
> "Is it 2?" No.
> $\vdots$
> "Is it 13?" Yes.

Grover could help with an $O(\sqrt{n})$ approach, but we can do better with $O(\log_2(n))$ classically:

> "Is it greater than 7?" Yes.
> "Is it greater than 11?" Yes.
> "Is it greater than 13?" No.
> "Is it greater than 12?" Yes.
> "The answer is 13."

In this example, I acted as the oracle, responding "Yes" = **1** or "No" = **0** to your questions. You called the oracle four times, or $O(\log_2(16))$.

With the Bernstein-Vazirani algorithm, you need to call the oracle once. [14]

9.9.1 The problem

Instead of thinking of numbers between 0 and 15, let's consider bit strings **0000, 0001, 0010, ..., 1110, 1111**. The number I asked you to guess was a "secret string," s, which was 13 = **1101**.

My oracle function $f : \{0,1\}^4 \rightarrow \{0,1\}$ returns the dot product mod 2 of the secret string s and the bit string you pass as input. For example,

$$f(\mathbf{1000}) = s \cdot \mathbf{1000} = \mathbf{1101} \cdot \mathbf{1000} = 1$$
$$f(\mathbf{0100}) = s \cdot \mathbf{0100} = \mathbf{1101} \cdot \mathbf{0100} = 1$$
$$f(\mathbf{0010}) = s \cdot \mathbf{0010} = \mathbf{1101} \cdot \mathbf{0010} = 0$$
$$f(\mathbf{0001}) = s \cdot \mathbf{0001} = \mathbf{1101} \cdot \mathbf{0001} = 1$$

and this sequence of four calls to the oracle determines the secret string uniquely. The algorithm in this example is $O(\log_2(16))$.

Our problem is to construct a circuit that determines s.

Exercise 9.29

How is the algorithm on numbers with questions such as "Is it greater than x?" equivalent to the algorithm on bit strings using the dot product mod 2?

9.9.2 The circuit

We begin by generalizing our bit strings from length 4 to length n. The secret string s is $s_{n-1} \cdots s_1 s_0$ with each $s_j = \mathbf{0}$ or $\mathbf{1}$, $0 \leq j \leq n-1$. The oracle $f : \{0,1\}^n \rightarrow \{0,1\}$ computes the dot product mod 2 of s and its input bit string.

By $\mathbf{0}^n$, we denote the string of length n containing only $\mathbf{0}$s:

$$\mathbf{0}^n = \underbrace{\mathbf{000 \ldots 00}}_{n} .$$

For example, if $n = 2$, then

$$\{0,1\}^2 = \{\mathbf{00}, \mathbf{01}, \mathbf{10}, \mathbf{11}\}$$

and $\mathbf{0}^2 = \mathbf{00}$.

The circuit for the algorithm uses a direct implementation of $\mathbf{U}_f$, which maps $|x\rangle$ to $(-1)^{f(x)}|x\rangle$ as in Figure 9.18, or a variation of Deutsch-Jozsa with the secret string oracle as in Figure 9.19.

In either case, before measurement, we have the same quantum state expression

$$\frac{1}{2^n} \sum_{v \text{ in } \{0,1\}^n} \left(\sum_{x \text{ in } \{0,1\}^n} (-1)^{f(x)} (-1)^{x \cdot v} \right) |v\rangle = \frac{1}{2^n} \sum_{v \text{ in } \{0,1\}^n} \left(\sum_{x \text{ in } \{0,1\}^n} (-1)^{f(x) + x \cdot v} \right) |v\rangle .$$

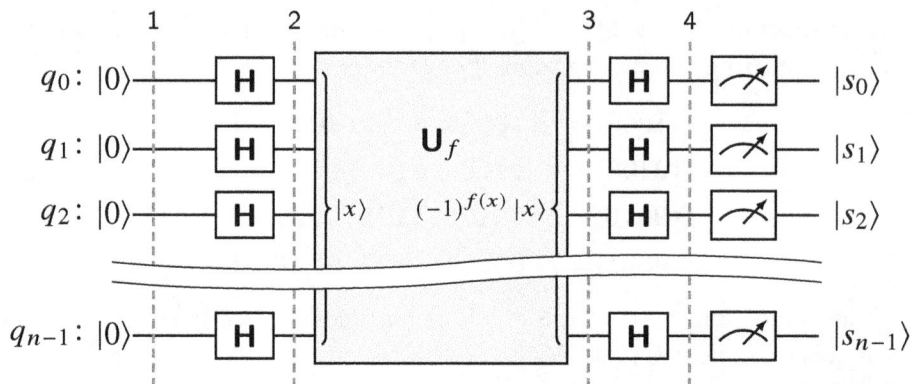

Figure 9.18: The Bernstein-Vazirani circuit

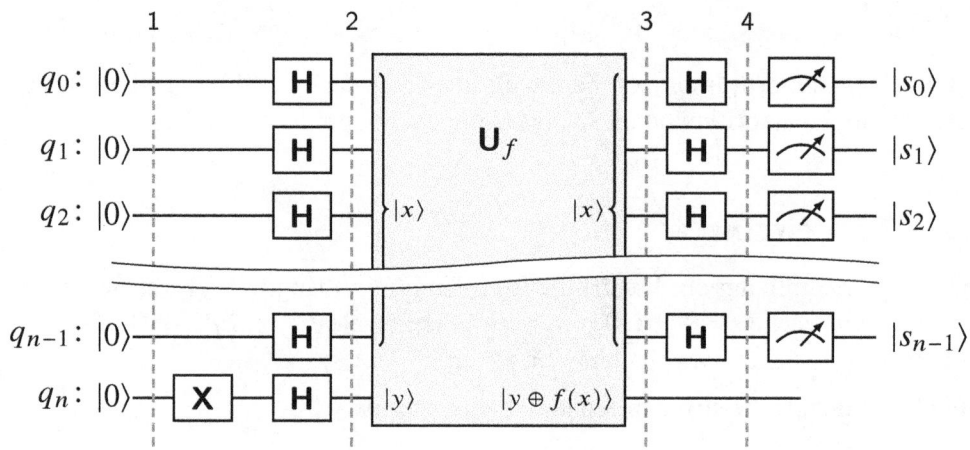

Figure 9.19: The Bernstein-Vazirani circuit as a variation of Deutsch-Jozsa

If we fix one value of $|v\rangle$, the inner sum is

$$\frac{1}{2^n} \sum_{x \text{ in } \{0,1\}^n} (-1)^{f(x)+x\cdot v} = \frac{1}{2^n} \sum_{x \text{ in } \{0,1\}^n} (-1)^{x\cdot s+x\cdot v}$$

$$= \frac{1}{2^n} \sum_{x \text{ in } \{0,1\}^n} (-1)^{x\cdot(s+v)}$$

$$= \frac{1}{2^n} \sum_{x \text{ in } \{0,1\}^n} (-1)^{x\cdot(s\oplus v)}$$

$$= \begin{cases} 1 & \text{if } s \oplus v = \mathbf{0}^n \\ 0 & \text{otherwise.} \end{cases}$$

Here, "$\oplus$" is bit-by-bit addition mod 2. When does $s \oplus v = \mathbf{0}^n$? This is true only if $s = v$. When we measure the sum over all $|v\rangle$, the only ket with nonzero amplitude is $|s\rangle$. Thus, the circuit finds our secret string with one call to the oracle.

9.10 Simon's algorithm

We'll cover one more algorithm using an oracle before leaving this chapter: *Simon's algorithm*. It may seem like an odd use of an oracle, but the techniques are further used in section 10.6 when we develop function period finding before tackling Shor's factoring algorithm.

We do not study Simon's algorithm for its wide applicability. Rather, it demonstrates how a quantum algorithm can demonstrate an exponential improvement over the classical approach. So while this particular algorithm may not have much use, it gives people confidence that future quantum computing algorithms will perform significantly better than anything we can do today on problems of societal or commercial importance.

9.10.1 The problem

Our problem is finding how a function's values on the whole numbers $\mathbf{W}$ repeat themselves.

A function

$$f : \{\mathbf{0}, \mathbf{1}\}^n \rightarrow \{\mathbf{0}, \mathbf{1}\}^n$$

takes binary strings of length n to other such binary strings. For any two x and y in $\{\mathbf{0}, \mathbf{1}\}^n$, when does $f(x) = f(y)$?

In general, we don't know, but let's add the requirement that $f(x) = f(y)$ if and only if $x \oplus y = \mathbf{0}^n$ for all x and y, or there exists some nonzero bit string r in $\{\mathbf{0}, \mathbf{1}\}^n$ such that $f(x) = f(y)$ if and only if $x \oplus y = r$ for all x and y.

What does it mean if $x \oplus y = \mathbf{0}^n$? For single bits b_1 and b_2, $b_1 \oplus b_2 = \mathbf{0}$ if and only if b_1 and b_2 are both $\mathbf{0}$ or both $\mathbf{1}$. That is, they are equal. So $x \oplus y = \mathbf{0}^n$ means that x and y are the same in each of the n bit positions, so $x = y$. It's then obvious that $f(x) = f(y)$.

For this case where $x \oplus y = \mathbf{0}^n$, the condition on f says $f(x) = f(y)$ only if $x = y$. f is *one-to-one*, meaning each element in its domain maps to a unique element in its range.

Exercise 9.30

If we further label the one-to-one function f as

$$f : A = \{0, 1\}^n \rightarrow B = \{0, 1\}^n \, ,$$

show that for every binary n-string z in B, there is a binary n-string x in A such that $f(x) = z$.

The other possibility is that there is a nonzero bit string r of length n so that $x \oplus y = r$ **for every** x and y if $f(x) = f(y)$. Moreover, if $x \oplus y = r$, then $f(x) = f(y)$.

What is r?

Exercise 9.31

Let $f : \{0, 1\}^3 \rightarrow \{0, 1\}^3$ be defined by

$000 \mapsto 101$	$001 \mapsto 010$	$010 \mapsto 000$	$011 \mapsto 110$
$100 \mapsto 000$	$101 \mapsto 110$	$110 \mapsto 101$	$111 \mapsto 010$

What is r?

In section 2.8.1, I introduced the "big O" notation. The number of interesting operations used to solve a problem on n objects is $O(f(n))$ if there is a positive number c in **R** and an m in **Z** such that

$$\text{number of operations } \leq cf(n)$$

once $n \geq m$, for some function f.

The problem is **at most as hard** as $c\, f(n)$. How do we say it is at least as hard as something else?

The number of interesting operations used to solve a problem on n objects is $\Omega(f(n))$ if there is a positive number c in **R** and an integer m such that

$$\text{number of operations } \geq cf(n)$$

once $n \geq m$, for some function f. ("Ω" is the Greek capital letter Omega.)

The problem is **at least as hard** as $c f(n)$.

If we were to proceed classically by brute force, we would have to call f many times to ensure we find the correct r. How many? Well, there are 2^n possible r values to consider. Even with refinements and optimizations, the problem is $\Omega(\sqrt{2^n})$, which is exponentially hard.

With Simon's quantum algorithm, we can find r with $O(n)$ calls to the oracle f.

Exercise 9.32

Continuing as before, for

$$f : A = \{0, 1\}^n \to B = \{0, 1\}^n \, ,$$

with r nonzero, show that f is *two-to-one*. That is, if $f(x) = z$ with z in B, then there is one and only one other $y \neq x$ such that we also have $f(y) = z$. Both x and y are in A. Hint: begin by thinking about $x \oplus y$.

9.10.2 The circuit

From this point on, our task is to find r, and we will assume $r \neq \mathbf{0}^n$. Since r has n bits, we need at least n qubits to represent this answer. For example, if we work with integers with 2048 bits, we need at least 2048 qubits.

In Figure 9.20, I show the circuit for Simon's algorithm.

This looks familiar. We apply **H** gates to several qubits, do something amazing and mysterious with $\mathbf{U}_f$, apply more **H** gates, and then interpret what is output.

We need and use the n qubits at the top because $f : \{0, 1\}^n \to \{0, 1\}^n$. We also use n ancilla qubits at the bottom. All told, we need $2n$ qubits, and we may need to iterate the algorithm multiple times, as we work through it.

In the Deutsch-Jozsa circuit in Figure 9.17,

$$\mathbf{U}_f : |x\rangle \otimes |y\rangle \mapsto |x\rangle \otimes |y \oplus f(x)\rangle$$

where $|x\rangle$ is the quantum state of the top n qubits, but $|y\rangle$ is the state of a single ancilla qubit. The same expression holds here as well, except that $|x\rangle$, $|y\rangle$, and $|y \oplus f(x)\rangle$ each encompass a quantum state of n qubits.

By computations similar to what we worked through in section 9.8.2 for the Deutsch-Jozsa algorithm, the states of the qubits change in the following way in the circuit.

As we begin circuit section 1, the initial state of the qubits is

$$|0\rangle^{\otimes n} \otimes |0\rangle^{\otimes n} \, .$$

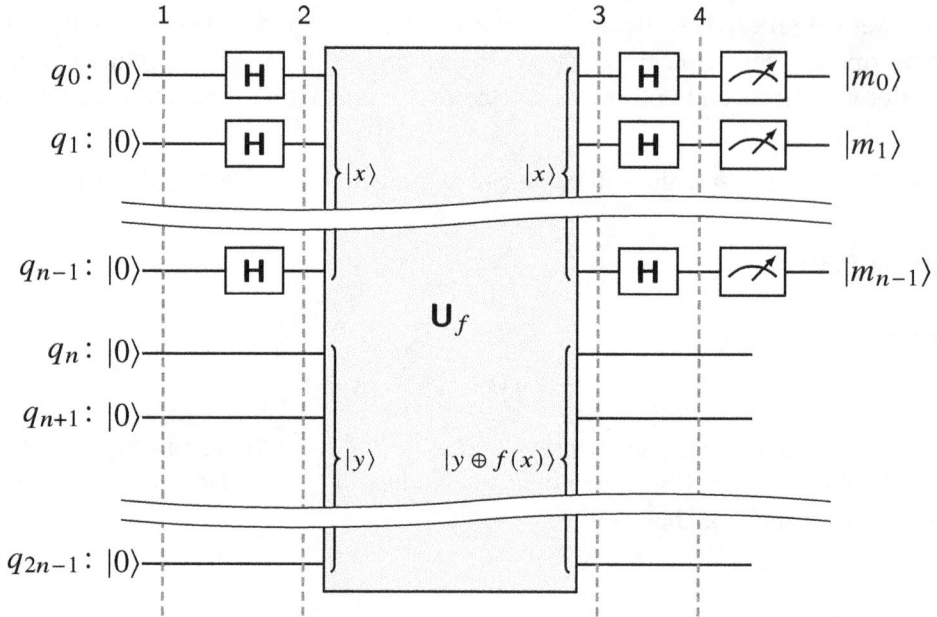

Figure 9.20: The Simon's algorithm circuit

We then apply the **H** gates to the first n qubits to get

$$\left(\frac{1}{\sqrt{2^n}} \sum_{x \text{ in } \{0,1\}^n} |x\rangle \right) \otimes |0\rangle^{\otimes n}.$$

We have a balanced superposition of the first n qubits, but we are still in the initial state for the last n qubits.

Next, apply $\mathbf{U}_f$ in circuit section 2. Since

$$|x\rangle \otimes |y\rangle = |x\rangle \otimes |y \oplus f(x)\rangle$$

under this transformation, we now have

$$|x\rangle \otimes |y \oplus f(x)\rangle = |x\rangle \otimes |\mathbf{0}^n \oplus f(x)\rangle = |x\rangle \otimes |f(x)\rangle.$$

We conclude the circuit by applying **H** gates again to the first n qubits in circuit section 3. Given the identities for the Hadamard transformation on multiple qubits from section 9.8.1, we end up with

$$\frac{1}{2^n} \sum_{x \text{ in } \{0,1\}^n} \sum_{u \text{ in } \{0,1\}^n} (-1)^{x \cdot u} |u\rangle \otimes |f(x)\rangle$$

which is the same as

$$\sum_{u \text{ in } \{0,1\}^n} |u\rangle \otimes \left(\frac{1}{2^n} \sum_{x \text{ in } \{0,1\}^n} (-1)^{x \cdot u} |f(x)\rangle \right).$$

As before, "·" is a dot product where we do the addition modulo 2.

9.10.3 Analysis of the circuit results

The above represents a quantum state, so the sum of the squares of the absolute values of the coefficients of the $|u\rangle \otimes |f(x)\rangle$ is 1:

$$\sum_{u \text{ in } \{0,1\}^n} \sum_{x \text{ in } \{0,1\}^n} \left| \frac{1}{2^n} (-1)^{x \cdot u} \right|^2 = 1.$$

In the expression

$$\sum_{u \text{ in } \{0,1\}^n} |u\rangle \otimes \left(\frac{1}{2^n} \sum_{x \text{ in } \{0,1\}^n} (-1)^{x \cdot u} |f(x)\rangle \right),$$

the probability of observing a particular $|u\rangle$ is the square of the magnitude of the coefficient. That is, we will see $|u\rangle$ with probability

$$\left\| \frac{1}{2^n} \sum_{x \text{ in } \{0,1\}^n} (-1)^{x \cdot u} |f(x)\rangle \right\|^2.$$

The case $r = 1$

In the case of $r = 0$, f is one-to-one. Because there are a finite number of values, when we iterate over all the x values, we are also iterating over all the $f(x)$, just in a different order. Taking the sum of the squares of the coefficients for all the $|x\rangle$ yields the same value as the sum of the squares of the coefficients when we use the $|f(x)\rangle$.

Put another way, two vectors that differ only by a permutation of their coefficients have the same length.

For each $|f(x)\rangle$, we square each

$$\frac{(-1)^{x \cdot u}}{2^n}$$

to get

$$\frac{1}{2^{2n}}$$

and then add up all 2^n of the $|f(x)\rangle$. Hence

$$\left\| \frac{1}{2^n} \sum_{x \text{ in } \{0,1\}^n} (-1)^{x \cdot u} |f(x)\rangle \right\|^2 = 2^n \frac{1}{2^{2n}} = \frac{1}{2^n}.$$

With this, we conclude that when $r = 0$, the probability of seeing any of the 2^n values of $|u\rangle$ when we measure is 2^{-n}. If we run the circuit many times and see this uniform distribution of the $|u\rangle$, we might suspect $r = 0$.

Though it is trivial in this case, note that because $r = 0$, this uniform distribution of kets we observe is equal to all $|u\rangle$ such that $u \cdot r = 0$.

The case $r \neq 0$

We now explicitly assume that $r \neq 0$ and therefore f is two-to-one. While x can take on any of the 2^n values in $\{\mathbf{0}, \mathbf{1}\}^n$, $f(x)$ will only land on half of them. I call this subset $\{\mathbf{0}, \mathbf{1}\}_f^n$. It is the range of f.

For a particular z in $\{\mathbf{0}, \mathbf{1}\}_f^n$, there are exactly two binary n-strings that map to it: some x_z and its companion $x_z \oplus r$.

The probability of observing a particular $|u\rangle$ when we measure is still

$$\left\| \frac{1}{2^n} \sum_{x \text{ in } \{0,1\}^n} (-1)^{x \cdot u} |f(x)\rangle \right\|^2,$$

but we can rewrite this as

$$\left\| \frac{1}{2^n} \sum_{z \text{ in } \{0,1\}_f^n} \left((-1)^{x_z \cdot u} + (-1)^{(x_z \oplus r) \cdot u} \right) |z\rangle \right\|^2.$$

Via some arithmetic on the exponents, this is further equal to

$$\left\| \frac{1}{2^n} \sum_{z \text{ in } \{0,1\}_f^n} (-1)^{x_z \cdot u} \left(1 + (-1)^{r \cdot u} \right) |z\rangle \right\|^2 = \begin{cases} 0 & \text{if } r \cdot u = 1 \\ \dfrac{1}{2^{n-1}} & \text{if } r \cdot u = 0. \end{cases}$$

Exercise 9.33

Show that $(x_z \oplus r) \cdot u = (x_z \cdot u) \oplus (r \cdot u)$.

Less trivially than in the case $r = 0$, the uniform distribution of kets we observe here is on all $|u\rangle$ such that $u \cdot r = 0$.

But what is r?

Randomness is involved in this quantum algorithm. When we run the circuit several times, we should see various values when we measure $|u\rangle$. Suppose we execute it $n - 2$ more times and get $n - 1$ binary strings $u_1, \ldots, u_{n-1}$. Now, assume the u_k are different and linearly independent vectors. This is a big assumption, but let's go with it for a while.

This means that

$$u_1 \cdot r = u_2 \cdot r = \cdots = u_{n-1} \cdot r = 0$$

or

$$(u_{1,1} r_1 + u_{1,2} r_2 + \cdots + u_{1,n} r_n) \bmod 2 = 0$$
$$(u_{2,1} r_1 + u_{2,2} r_2 + \cdots + u_{2,n} r_n) \bmod 2 = 0$$
$$\vdots$$
$$(u_{n-1,1} r_1 + u_{n-1,2} r_2 + \cdots + u_{n-1,n} r_n) \bmod 2 = 0$$

Since the u_k are linearly independent, we can uniquely solve for $(r_1, \ldots, r_n) = r$ via a binary form of Gaussian elimination.

We test to see if $f(\mathbf{0}^n) = f(\mathbf{0}^n \oplus r) = f(r)$. If this is true, we are assured that r is our answer. If not, we must have $r = \mathbf{0}^n$.

Exercise 9.34

Why must $r = \mathbf{0}^n$ in this last case?

The only remaining question is whether we can find the n linearly independent u_k. Obviously, they exist among the 2^n binary n-strings, but if we must search all those strings, our algorithm will be exponential.

Via the analysis in [150, Appendix G], the chance of success of finding a linearly independent set of n binary n-strings within a collection of $n + k$ nonzero binary n-strings produced by our circuit is

$$1 - \frac{1}{2^{k+1}}.$$

We can find such a set and hence determine r, with a chance of failure less than one in a billion by choosing $k = 30$. We only need to run the circuit $n + 30$ times to have such a small probability of not correctly determining r.

Exercise 9.35

What parts of the overall algorithm involve quantum processing, and what parts involve classical?

The expression $f(x) = f(x \oplus r)$ looks a lot like $f(x) = f(x + r)$, which seems to imply that f starts repeating itself after r values. This would make f a periodic function, and r would be its period.

We are familiar with periodic functions on the real numbers from trigonometry. Both the sine and the cosine are such because $\cos(x) = \cos(x + r)$ and $\sin(x) = \sin(x + r)$ with $r = 2\pi$. Figure 9.21 shows the sine function and how it repeats.

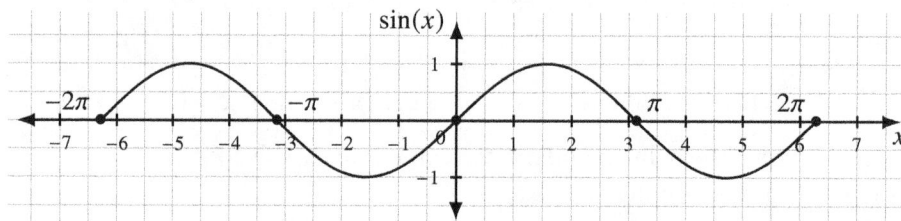

Figure 9.21: The sine function showing how it repeats itself with period 2π

Simon's algorithm inspired Peter Shor when he developed a more general quantum period finding routine as part of his famous integer factorization algorithm. We cover the former in section 10.6 and the latter in section 10.7.

9.11 Summary

This chapter examined how to link gates together for multiple qubits to create circuits. Circuits implement algorithms, and these are the building blocks for solutions. After all, we're not only interested in the theory of how one might do quantum computing; we want to accomplish real work.

We looked at some well-known basic algorithms for quantum computing, including Simon's, Bernstein-Vazirani, Deutsch-Jozsa, amplitude amplification, and Grover's search.

Quantum computing will show its advantage when it can perform calculations that are intractable today. To be valuable, quadratic or exponential speed increases over classical methods will be required.

The next chapter considers integer factorization and Shor's factoring algorithm. We define the Quantum Fourier Transform, phase estimation, and function period finding.

10

From Circuits to Algorithms

I am among those who think that science has great beauty.

– Marie Curie

In the last chapter, we became comfortable putting together gates to create circuits for simple algorithms. We're now ready to look at more advanced quantum algorithms and consider how and when to use them.

Our target in this chapter is Peter Shor's 1995 algorithm for factoring large integers, which is almost exponentially faster than classical methods. To get there, we need more tools, such as the Quantum Fourier Transform, phase kickback, eigenvalue and phase estimation, and function order and period finding. These are essential techniques in their own right but are necessary in combination for quantum factoring.

We also return to the idea of complexity that we first saw for classical algorithms in section 2.8. This allows us to understand what "almost exponentially faster" means.

This chapter contains more mathematics and equations for quantum computing than we have encountered previously. I recommend you take the time to understand the linear algebra and complex number computations throughout. While they may appear daunting initially, the techniques are used frequently in quantum computing algorithms.

Topics covered in this chapter

10.1 Quantum Fourier Transform

The Quantum Fourier Transform (QFT) is widely used in quantum computing. We need it in this chapter to estimate eigenvalues via the function order and period finding algorithm in section 10.5. We then use that in Shor's factoring algorithm in section 10.7. If that weren't enough, the Hadamard **H** is the 1-qubit QFT, and we've seen many examples of its use.

Other applications of the QFT include quantum Monte Carlo, [76] and the Harrow-Hassidim-Loyd (HHL) algorithm for solving systems of linear equations under restrictive conditions. [104] [62]

Most treatments of the QFT start by comparing it to the classical Discrete Fourier Transform and then the Fast Fourier Transform. If you don't know either of these, don't worry. I'm presenting the QFT in detail for its own sake in quantum computing. Should you know about or read up about the classical analogs, the similarities should be apparent. [168]

The QFT algorithm depends heavily on understanding complex roots of 1: solutions to equations such as $z^n - 1 = 0$. We begin our discussion there with the necessary mathematics to manipulate these *roots of unity*.

10.1.1   Roots of unity

We are all familiar with square roots. For example, $\sqrt{4}$ is equal to either 2 or -2. We can also write $\sqrt{2} = 2^{\frac{1}{2}}$ and say there are two "2nd-roots of 2." Similarly, 5 is a cube root, or "3rd root," of 125. We generally talk about an "N^{th}-root" for some natural number N. When considering the complex numbers, we have a rich collection of such "N^{th}-roots" for 1.

> Let N be a natural number. An Nth *root of unity* is a complex number ω such that $\omega^N = 1$. "ω" is the lowercase Greek letter "omega." There are N N^{th} roots of unity, and 1 is always one of those.
>
> Suppose ω is an Nth root of unity, and we can write every other N^{th} root of unity as ω^k for some k in **N**. We then say ω is a *primitive* N^{th} root of unity. If N is prime number, **every** N^{th} root of unity is primitive except for the number 1.

For $N = 1$, there is only one first root of unity, and that is 1 itself. When $N = 2$, there are two second roots of unity: 1 and -1. The latter is primitive.

With $N = 3$, we can start to see a pattern. For this, remember Euler's formula

$$e^{\varphi i} = \cos(\varphi) + \sin(\varphi)i$$

and $\left|e^{\varphi i}\right| = 1$. If $\varphi = 2\pi$, we go around the unit circle and back to 1. If $\varphi = \frac{2\pi}{3}$, we go only one-third of the way. Rotating another $\varphi = \frac{2\pi}{3}$ radians, we get to two-thirds around. The third roots of unity are

$$\omega_0 = e^{\frac{0 \times 2\pi}{3}i} = 1$$

$$\omega_1 = e^{\frac{1 \times 2\pi}{3}i} = \cos\left(\frac{2\pi}{3}\right) + \sin\left(\frac{2\pi}{3}\right)i = -\frac{1}{2} + \frac{\sqrt{3}}{2}i$$

$$\omega_2 = e^{\frac{2 \times 2\pi}{3}i} = \cos\left(\frac{4\pi}{3}\right) + \sin\left(\frac{4\pi}{3}\right)i = -\frac{1}{2} - \frac{\sqrt{3}}{2}i$$

and ω_1 and ω_2 are both primitive third roots of unity because 3 is a prime number. We show these in Figure 10.1.

Since ω_1 and ω_2 are primitive, we can get the other third roots of unity by raising ω_1 and ω_2 to powers:

$$\omega_1^2 = \omega_2 \qquad \omega_1^3 = 1 \qquad \omega_2^2 = \omega_1 \qquad \omega_2^3 = 1$$

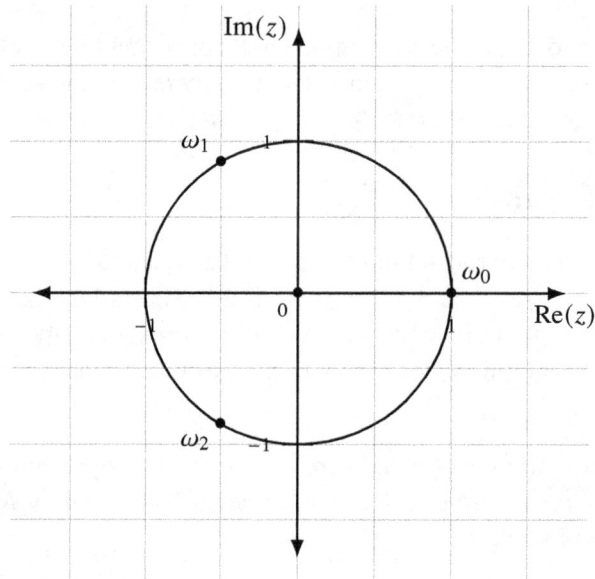

Figure 10.1: Graph of third roots of unity

For $N = 4$, we can do something similar, although the situation is much simple, as you see in Figure 10.2.

$$\omega_0 = e^{\frac{0 \times 2\pi}{4}i} = 1$$

$$\omega_1 = e^{\frac{1 \times 2\pi}{4}i} = \cos\left(\frac{\pi}{2}\right) + \sin\left(\frac{\pi}{2}\right)i = i$$

$$\omega_2 = e^{\frac{2 \times 2\pi}{4}i} = \cos(\pi) + \sin(\pi)i = -1$$

$$\omega_3 = e^{\frac{3 \times 2\pi}{4}i} = \cos\left(\frac{3\pi}{2}\right) + \sin\left(\frac{3\pi}{2}\right)i = -i$$

Note something else here: for the first time, we see overlaps in the collection of roots of unity for different N. This happens when the greatest common divisor of the various N is greater than 1.

Exercise 10.1

What are the primitive fourth roots of unity?

For $N = 5$ and above, we continue in this way.

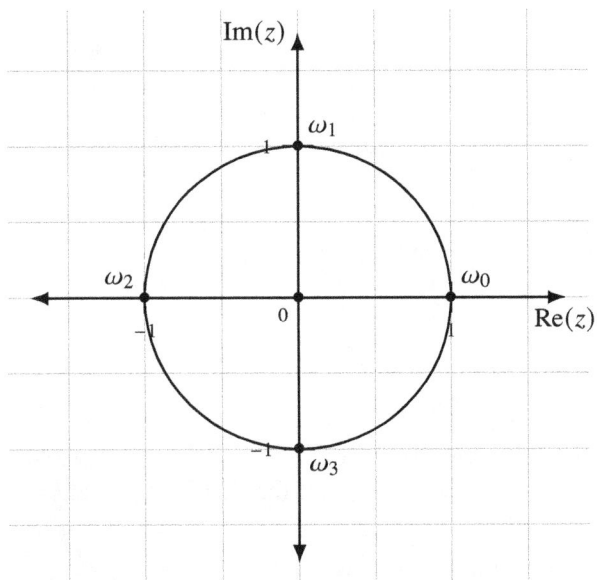

Figure 10.2: Graph of fourth roots of unity

The expression

$$\omega = e^{\frac{2\pi i}{N}}$$

is a primitive N^{th} root of unity.

When there is a fraction in the exponent of such expressions, pulling the i into the numerator is common, as I have done here.

For some particular N, let ω be an Nth root of unity. What is ω^{-1}? This one is easy because

$$1 = \omega\,\overline{\omega} = \omega\,\omega^{-1}.$$

Complex conjugation to the rescue again!

If

$$\omega_k = e^{\frac{2\pi k i}{N}}$$

is a root of unity, then so is

$$\overline{\omega_k} = \omega_k^{-1} = e^{-\frac{2\pi k i}{N}}.$$

Exercise 10.2

Show that if ω_k is a primitive N^{th} root of unity, so is its conjugate. Start by assuming that the conjugate is not primitive, and see if that leads to a contradiction.

We can factor the polynomial $x^N - 1$ as

$$x^N - 1 = (x - 1)(x^{N-1} + x^{N-2} + \cdots + x + 1).$$

Every N^{th} root of unity satisfies $x^N - 1 = 0$. The first factor $x - 1$ is 0 only for $x = 1$. Therefore, every other N^{th} root of unity $\omega \neq 1$ satisfies

$$0 = \omega^{N-1} + \omega^{N-2} + \cdots + \omega + 1.$$

We can re-express this as

$$0 = \sum_{k=0}^{N-1} \omega^k \text{ with } \omega \neq 1.$$

Taking it a step further, let

$$\omega = e^{\frac{2\pi i}{N}}.$$

Then,

$$0 = \sum_{k=0}^{N-1} e^{\frac{2\pi k i}{N}} = \sum_{k=0}^{N-1} e^{-\frac{2\pi k i}{N}}$$

with the second equality holding because we are using the conjugate of ω instead of ω as the Nth root of unity. Thought of another way, we are adding together the same set of roots of unity, just in a different order. In these equivalent versions, this is called the *summation formula*.

For j and k in **Z**, we define the *Kronecker delta function* $\delta_{j,k}$ by

$$\delta_{j,k} = \begin{cases} 0 & \text{if } j \neq k \\ 1 & \text{if } j = k. \end{cases}$$

The delta function is named after mathematician Leopold Kronecker (Figure 10.3).

Figure 10.3: Leopold Kronecker in 1865

For $0 \leq j < N$, the *extended summation formula* is

$$\sum_{k=0}^{N-1} e^{\frac{2\pi j k i}{N}} = \sum_{k=0}^{N-1} e^{-\frac{2\pi j k i}{N}} = N\delta_{j,0} = \begin{cases} 0 & \text{if } \delta_{j,0} = 0 \\ N & \text{if } \delta_{j,0} = 1. \end{cases}$$

To see this, let

$$\omega_1 = e^{\frac{2\pi i}{N}}.$$

This is a primitive N^{th} root of unity, and for any $0 < j < N$,

$$\omega_2 = \omega_1^j = e^{\frac{2\pi j i}{N}}$$

is another N^{th} root of unity $\neq 1$. From the summation formula, we have

$$0 = \sum_{k=0}^{N-1} \omega_2^k = \sum_{k=0}^{N-1} e^{\frac{2\pi j k i}{N}}.$$

When $j = 0$, we simply add 1 to itself N times.

Exercise 10.3

For n in $\mathbf{N}$, describe the n-by-n square matrix where the entry in row j and column k is $\delta_{j,k}$.

Exercise 10.4

For a given N, let $\{\omega_0, \omega_1, \ldots, \omega_{N-2}, \omega_{N-1}\}$ be the Nth roots of unity. What is their product

$$\omega_0 \, \omega_1 \cdots \omega_{N-2} \, \omega_{N-2} \, ?$$

To start thinking about this, look at

$$(x - \omega_0)\,(x - \omega_1) \cdots (x - \omega_{N-2})\,(x - \omega_{N-1})\;.$$

To learn more

Roots of unity are an essential concept and tool in several parts of mathematics, especially algebra [131] [73] and algebraic number theory [115] [151].

10.1.2   The formula

As we saw in section 8.2.2, we can write a general quantum state $|\varphi\rangle$ on n qubits as

$$|\varphi\rangle = \sum_{j=0}^{2^n-1} a_j |j\rangle_n = \sum_{j=0}^{N-1} a_j |j\rangle_n$$

for $N = 2^n$ and using the ket subscripting notation from section 8.2.2. There are N amplitudes a_j corresponding to the N standard decimal notation basis kets $|j\rangle_n$. For a fixed $|\varphi\rangle$, we get a complex-valued function

$$a : \{0, 1, 2, \ldots, N-1\} \to a_j\,,$$

where $a(j) = a_j$. We also know that

$$1 = \sum_{j=0}^{N-1} |a_j|^2\,.$$

Definition

The *Quantum Fourier Transform (QFT)* of $|\varphi\rangle$ is

$$\mathbf{QFT}_n : |\varphi\rangle = \sum_{j=0}^{N-1} a_j |j\rangle_n \mapsto \sum_{j=0}^{N-1} b_j |j\rangle_n ,$$

where

$$b_j = \frac{1}{\sqrt{N}} \sum_{k=0}^{N-1} a_k e^{\frac{2\pi jki}{N}} .$$

We can simplify this by letting

$$\omega = e^{\frac{2\pi i}{N}} ,$$

which is a primitive N^{th} root of unity:

$$b_j = \frac{1}{\sqrt{N}} \sum_{k=0}^{N-1} a_k \omega^{jk} .$$

For $N = 2^n$ and

$$|\varphi\rangle = \sum_{j=0}^{N-1} a_j |j\rangle_n ,$$

its QFT is

$$\mathbf{QFT}_n \Big(|\varphi\rangle \Big) = \frac{1}{\sqrt{N}} \sum_{j=0}^{N-1} \sum_{k=0}^{N-1} a_k \omega^{jk} |j\rangle_n$$

for

$$\omega = e^{\frac{2\pi i}{N}} ,$$

a primitive N^{th} root of unity.

Exercise 10.5

Show that $\mathbf{QFT}_n$ is a linear transformation.

Exercise 10.6

Show that

$$\mathbf{QFT}_n\left(|0\rangle^{\otimes n}\right) = \frac{1}{\sqrt{N}} \sum_{j=0}^{N-1} |j\rangle_n.$$

When we have one qubit, $N = 2$ and $\omega = -1$. So

$$b_j = \frac{1}{\sqrt{2}}\left(a_0(-1)^{-0j} + a_1(-1)^{1j}\right) = \frac{\sqrt{2}}{2}\left(a_0 + a_1(-1)^j\right).$$

For $|\psi\rangle = |0\rangle$, $a_0 = 1$ and $a_1 = 0$. So, $b_0 = b_1 = \frac{\sqrt{2}}{2}$. For $|\psi\rangle = |1\rangle$, $a_0 = 0$ and $a_1 = 1$. So, $b_0 = \frac{\sqrt{2}}{2}$ and $b_1 = -\frac{\sqrt{2}}{2}$.

All together,

$$\mathbf{QFT}_1|0\rangle = \frac{\sqrt{2}}{2}\left(|0\rangle + |1\rangle\right) = |+\rangle$$

$$\mathbf{QFT}_1|1\rangle = \frac{\sqrt{2}}{2}\left(|0\rangle - |1\rangle\right) = |-\rangle$$

This is none other than **H**!

So $\mathbf{QFT}_1 = \mathbf{H}$. Is $\mathbf{QFT}_n = \mathbf{H}^{\otimes n}$? No, and we can see this by looking at its matrix.

QFT matrix

From its definition, you can see that $\mathbf{QFT}_n$ has the matrix

$$\mathbf{QFT}_n = \frac{1}{\sqrt{N}}\begin{bmatrix} 1 & 1 & 1 & 1 & \cdots & 1 \\ 1 & \omega & \omega^2 & \omega^3 & \cdots & \omega^{N-1} \\ 1 & \omega^2 & \omega^4 & \omega^6 & \cdots & \omega^{2(N-1)} \\ 1 & \omega^3 & \omega^6 & \omega^9 & \cdots & \omega^{3(N-1)} \\ \vdots & \vdots & \vdots & \vdots & \ddots & \vdots \\ 1 & \omega^{N-1} & \omega^{2(N-1)} & \omega^{3(N-1)} & \cdots & \omega^{(N-1)(N-1)} \end{bmatrix}.$$

Since ω is an Nth root of unity, we can simplify several exponents. For example:

$$\omega^{(N-1)(N-1)} = \omega^{N^2-2N+1} = \omega$$

$$\text{because } \omega^{N^2} = (\omega^N)^N = 1^N = 1$$

$$\omega^{kN} = \omega^N = 1 \text{ for } k \text{ in } \mathbf{Z}$$

$$\omega^{2(N-1)} = \omega^{2N-2} = \omega^{N+N-2} = \omega^{N-2}$$

$$\omega^{-1} = \omega^{N-1}$$

Applying rules such as these, we get

$$\mathbf{QFT}_n = \frac{1}{\sqrt{N}}
\begin{bmatrix}
1 & 1 & 1 & 1 & \cdots & 1 \\
1 & \omega & \omega^2 & \omega^3 & \cdots & \omega^{N-1} \\
1 & \omega^2 & \omega^4 & \omega^6 & \cdots & \omega^{N-2} \\
1 & \omega^3 & \omega^6 & \omega^9 & \cdots & \omega^{N-3} \\
\vdots & \vdots & \vdots & \vdots & \ddots & \vdots \\
1 & \omega^{N-1} & \omega^{N-2} & \omega^{N-3} & \cdots & \omega
\end{bmatrix}.$$

Exercise 10.7

Verify that the above is, in fact, the matrix of $\mathbf{QFT}_n$ and that $\mathbf{QFT}_n$ is unitary. For the latter, what is $\mathbf{QFT}_n \times \mathbf{QFT}_n{}^\dagger$?

For $n = 1$, this is

$$\mathbf{QFT}_1 = \frac{\sqrt{2}}{2}
\begin{bmatrix}
1 & 1 \\
1 & (-1)^1
\end{bmatrix}
= \frac{\sqrt{2}}{2}
\begin{bmatrix}
1 & 1 \\
1 & -1
\end{bmatrix}
= \mathbf{H},$$

as previously noted. But when $n = 2$, $N = 4$ and $\omega = i$,

$$\mathbf{QFT}_2 = \frac{1}{2}
\begin{bmatrix}
1 & 1 & 1 & 1 \\
1 & i & -1 & -i \\
1 & -1 & 1 & -1 \\
1 & -i & -1 & i
\end{bmatrix}
\quad \text{and} \quad
\mathbf{H}^{\otimes 2} = \frac{1}{2}
\begin{bmatrix}
1 & 1 & 1 & 1 \\
1 & -1 & 1 & -1 \\
1 & 1 & -1 & -1 \\
1 & -1 & -1 & 1
\end{bmatrix}.$$

So $\mathbf{QFT}_n \neq \mathbf{H}^{\otimes n}$, in general.

Recursive matrix

The higher Hadamard matrices $\mathbf{H}^{\otimes n}$ are defined recursively in terms of the lower ones by

$$\mathbf{H}^{\otimes n+1} = \frac{\sqrt{2}}{2} \begin{bmatrix} \mathbf{H}^{\otimes n} & \mathbf{H}^{\otimes n} \\ \mathbf{H}^{\otimes n} & -\mathbf{H}^{\otimes n} \end{bmatrix}.$$

Is there a similar decomposition for $\mathbf{QFT}_n$?

Yes, but there are other matrix factors. Namely,

$$\mathbf{QFT}_{n+1} = \begin{bmatrix} I_N & \Omega_N \\ I_N & -\Omega_N \end{bmatrix} \begin{bmatrix} \mathbf{QFT}_n & 0 \\ 0 & \mathbf{QFT}_n \end{bmatrix} P_{2^{n+1}},$$

where:

- $N = 2^n$,
- I_N is the n-by-n identity matrix,
- ω is the primitive N^{th} root of unity $e^{\frac{2\pi i}{N}}$,
- Ω_N is the diagonal matrix

$$\Omega_N = \begin{bmatrix} 1 & 0 & 0 & 0 & \cdots & 0 \\ 0 & \omega & 0 & 0 & \cdots & 0 \\ 0 & 0 & \omega^2 & 0 & \cdots & 0 \\ \vdots & \vdots & \vdots & \vdots & \ddots & \vdots \\ 0 & 0 & 0 & 0 & \cdots & \omega^{N-1} \end{bmatrix}, \text{ and}$$

- $P_{2^{n+1}}$ is a *shuffle transform* defined by setting its i, j entry via the formula

$$(P_{2^{n+1}})_{j,k} = \begin{cases} 1 & \text{if } 2(j-1) = k - 1 \\ 1 & \text{if } 2(j - 1 - 2^n) + 1 = k - 1 \\ 0 & \text{otherwise.} \end{cases}$$

Remember that the matrix's first row and column index is 1.

We do not derive this here, but it moves the vector entries with odd-numbered indices to the front, followed by the even ones. For example,

$$P_{2^2} \begin{bmatrix} v_1 \\ v_2 \\ v_3 \\ v_4 \end{bmatrix} = \begin{bmatrix} v_1 \\ v_3 \\ v_2 \\ v_4 \end{bmatrix},$$

where

$$P_{2^2} = \begin{bmatrix} 1 & 0 & 0 & 0 \\ 0 & 0 & 1 & 0 \\ 0 & 1 & 0 & 0 \\ 0 & 0 & 0 & 1 \end{bmatrix}.$$

Given this recursive decomposition, we can break down a QFT into smaller and smaller gates.

Exercise 10.8

Compute P_{2^3}.

10.1.3   The circuit

Recall from section 7.6.7 that an $\mathbf{R}^z_{\frac{\pi}{2}} = \mathbf{S}$ gate is a rotation given by the matrix

$$\begin{bmatrix} 1 & 0 \\ 0 & e^{\frac{\pi i}{2}} \end{bmatrix} = \begin{bmatrix} 1 & 0 \\ 0 & e^{\frac{2\pi i}{2^2}} \end{bmatrix}.$$

$e^{\frac{\pi}{2}} = i$ is a fourth root of unity.

Consider the following circuit:

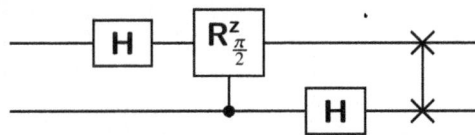

Re-expressed in matrices, it is

$$\left(\underbrace{\begin{bmatrix} \frac{\sqrt{2}}{2} & \frac{\sqrt{2}}{2} \\ \frac{\sqrt{2}}{2} & -\frac{\sqrt{2}}{2} \end{bmatrix}}_{H} \otimes \underbrace{\begin{bmatrix} 1 & 0 \\ 0 & 1 \end{bmatrix}}_{ID} \right) \underbrace{\begin{bmatrix} 1 & 0 & 0 & 0 \\ 0 & 1 & 0 & 0 \\ 0 & 0 & 1 & 0 \\ 0 & 0 & 0 & e^{\frac{\pi i}{2}} \end{bmatrix}}_{\text{reverse } CR^z_{\frac{\pi}{2}}} \left(\underbrace{\begin{bmatrix} 1 & 0 \\ 0 & 1 \end{bmatrix}}_{ID} \otimes \underbrace{\begin{bmatrix} \frac{\sqrt{2}}{2} & \frac{\sqrt{2}}{2} \\ \frac{\sqrt{2}}{2} & -\frac{\sqrt{2}}{2} \end{bmatrix}}_{H} \right) \underbrace{\begin{bmatrix} 1 & 0 & 0 & 0 \\ 0 & 0 & 1 & 0 \\ 0 & 1 & 0 & 0 \\ 0 & 0 & 0 & 1 \end{bmatrix}}_{\text{SWAP}}$$

We know from section 8.3.4 that the matrix for the **reverse** $\mathbf{CR}^{\mathbf{z}}_{\varphi}$ gate is the same as that for the $\mathbf{CR}^{\mathbf{z}}_{\varphi}$.

Expanding the tensor products, we get

$$
\begin{bmatrix} \frac{\sqrt{2}}{2} & 0 & \frac{\sqrt{2}}{2} & 0 \\ 0 & \frac{\sqrt{2}}{2} & 0 & \frac{\sqrt{2}}{2} \\ \frac{\sqrt{2}}{2} & 0 & -\frac{\sqrt{2}}{2} & 0 \\ 0 & \frac{\sqrt{2}}{2} & 0 & -\frac{\sqrt{2}}{2} \end{bmatrix}
\begin{bmatrix} 1 & 0 & 0 & 0 \\ 0 & 1 & 0 & 0 \\ 0 & 0 & 1 & 0 \\ 0 & 0 & 0 & \end{bmatrix}
\begin{bmatrix} \frac{\sqrt{2}}{2} & \frac{\sqrt{2}}{2} & 0 & 0 \\ \frac{\sqrt{2}}{2} & -\frac{\sqrt{2}}{2} & 0 & 0 \\ 0 & 0 & \frac{\sqrt{2}}{2} & \frac{\sqrt{2}}{2} \\ 0 & 0 & \frac{\sqrt{2}}{2} & -\frac{\sqrt{2}}{2} \end{bmatrix}
\begin{bmatrix} 1 & 0 & 0 & 0 \\ 0 & 0 & 1 & 0 \\ 0 & 1 & 0 & 0 \\ 0 & 0 & 0 & 1 \end{bmatrix}.
$$

Multiplying the first two matrices and multiplying the last two matrices yields

$$
\begin{bmatrix} \frac{\sqrt{2}}{2} & 0 & \frac{\sqrt{2}}{2} & 0 \\ 0 & \frac{\sqrt{2}}{2} & 0 & \frac{\sqrt{2}}{2}e^{\frac{\pi i}{2}} \\ \frac{\sqrt{2}}{2} & 0 & -\frac{\sqrt{2}}{2} & 0 \\ 0 & \frac{\sqrt{2}}{2} & 0 & -\frac{\sqrt{2}}{2}e^{\frac{\pi i}{2}} \end{bmatrix}
\begin{bmatrix} \frac{\sqrt{2}}{2} & 0 & \frac{\sqrt{2}}{2} & 0 \\ \frac{\sqrt{2}}{2} & 0 & -\frac{\sqrt{2}}{2} & 0 \\ 0 & \frac{\sqrt{2}}{2} & 0 & \frac{\sqrt{2}}{2} \\ 0 & \frac{\sqrt{2}}{2} & 0 & -\frac{\sqrt{2}}{2} \end{bmatrix}.
$$

The final matrix product is

$$
\begin{bmatrix} \frac{1}{2} & \frac{1}{2} & \frac{1}{2} & \frac{1}{2} \\ \frac{1}{2} & \frac{1}{2}e^{\frac{\pi i}{2}} & -\frac{1}{2} & -\frac{1}{2}e^{\frac{\pi i}{2}} \\ \frac{1}{2} & -\frac{1}{2} & \frac{1}{2} & -\frac{1}{2} \\ \frac{1}{2} & -\frac{1}{2}e^{\frac{\pi i}{2}} & -\frac{1}{2} & \frac{1}{2}e^{\frac{\pi i}{2}} \end{bmatrix}
= \frac{1}{2}
\begin{bmatrix} 1 & 1 & 1 & 1 \\ 1 & i & -1 & -i \\ 1 & -1 & 1 & -1 \\ 1 & -i & -1 & i \end{bmatrix}
= \mathbf{QFT}_2 .
$$

The given circuit generates $\mathbf{QFT}_2$.

We need to add another controlled rotation gate for the $\mathbf{QFT}_3$ circuit, shown in Figure 10.4.

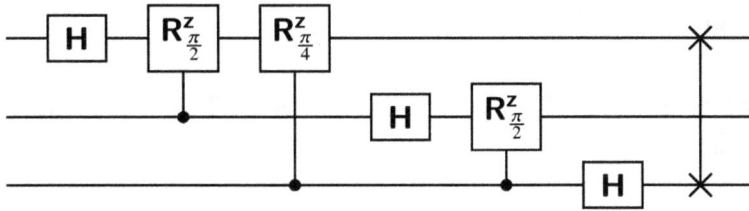

Figure 10.4: The QFT circuit for three qubits

Exercise 10.9

Use the matrices for the gates in Figure 10.4 to confirm that it computes the **QFT**$_3$ matrix.

We define

$$\mathbf{ROT}_k = \mathbf{R}^z_{\frac{\pi}{2^{k-1}}} \, .$$

So $\mathbf{R}^z_{\frac{\pi}{2}} = \mathbf{ROT}_2$ and $\mathbf{R}^z_{\frac{\pi}{4}} = \mathbf{ROT}_3$.

Rewriting the **QFT**$_3$ circuit in terms of **ROT**$_k$ gives

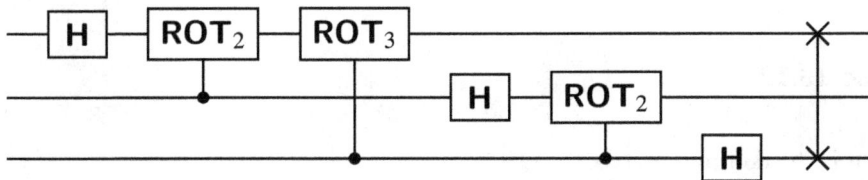

The pattern becomes clear when we extend this to four qubits and **QFT**$_4$.

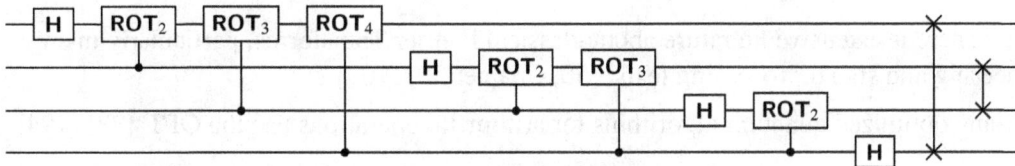

Exercise 10.10

Using many instances of ''…'', can you sketch the circuit for **QFT**$_n$?

Exercise 10.11

The circuit depth of **QFT**$_3$ is 7 and the depth of **QFT**$_4$ is 12. What is the circuit depth of **QFT**$_n$?

10.1.4   The inverse Quantum Fourier Transform

In some circuits, we need the *inverse Quantum Fourier Transform*, **QFT**$_n^{-1}$. We get this by running **QFT**$_n$ *backward*. This is possible because all gates ultimately correspond to unitary operators, which are invertible and reversible.

For $N = 2^n$ and

$$|\varphi\rangle = \sum_{j=0}^{N-1} a_j |j\rangle_n,$$

its inverse QFT is

$$\mathbf{QFT}_n^{-1}\big(|\varphi\rangle\big) = \frac{1}{\sqrt{N}} \sum_{j=0}^{N-1}\sum_{k=0}^{N-1} a_k \overline{\omega}^{jk} |j\rangle_n = \frac{1}{\sqrt{N}} \sum_{j=0}^{N-1}\sum_{k=0}^{N-1} a_k e^{-\frac{2\pi i j k}{N}} |j\rangle_n$$

for $\omega = e^{\frac{2\pi i}{N}}$, a primitive N^{th} root of unity.

Exercise 10.12

What is the defining matrix for **QFT**$_n^{-1}$?

To learn more

There is extensive literature about classical Fourier Transforms, particularly in engineering and signal processing texts. [50, Chapter 30] [103]

Many optimized quantum algorithms for arithmetic operations use the QFT. [72] [194]

10.2   Factoring

It is hard to do a web search and find ''practical'' applications of factoring integers. Many results say things such as ''factoring integers is a tool for factoring polynomials'' and

---

''factoring integers is useful for solving some differential equations.'' These examples are fine, but it seems like math to do more math.

One area where factoring comes into play is cryptography. Some cryptographic protocols assume you cannot easily factor some large numbers because those factors are related to encryption and decryption methods.

In this section, we examine several classical methods for factoring. Although they involve some sophisticated mathematics, they are currently insufficient for breaking arbitrary large integers into their prime components. This discussion sets us up for the final section of this chapter, which focuses on the breakthrough quantum factoring algorithm named after its discoverer, mathematician Peter Shor, Figure 10.5. Given a *sufficiently large, powerful, and fault-tolerant, error-corrected quantum computer*, Shor's algorithm can factor large integers almost exponentially faster than classical methods.

Figure 10.5: Peter Shor after receiving the 2017 Dirac Medal

10.2.1   The factoring problem

Most people don't worry about factoring integers once they graduate from high school or are no longer teenagers. In this book, we first encountered factoring when we discussed integers. In

$$-60 = (-1)\, 2^2\, 3\, 5$$

the -1 is a unit, and 2, 3, and 5 are examples of prime numbers. They are irreducible because their only factors are 1 and themselves.

At the time of this writing, the largest confirmed prime number is $2^{82,589,933} - 1$ and has 24,862,048 digits. [169] Determining whether a number is prime or factoring that number are different but related problems. The part of mathematics that studies these topics is called number theory.

While it can be hard to factor large integers, it is not simply the size that makes it difficult. The number

$$10^{25000000} = 2^{25000000} \, 5^{25000000}$$

is bigger than the above prime but is trivially factorable.

When we factor an N in $\mathbf{Z}$ greater than 1, we express it as a product

$$N = p_1 \, p_2 \, \cdots \, p_{n-1} \, p_n \,,$$

for some integer $n \geq 1$ with all the p_j prime numbers. We sort the primes from smallest to largest, which means $p_j \leq p_k$ if $j < k$. Some primes may be repeated more than once. If, for example, 11 appears in the factorization five times, then we say 11 has *multiplicity* 5. The notation we use to show that a p_j is a factor of N is $p_j \mid N$. Read this as "p_j divides N."

If $n = 1$, N itself is prime. While our goal is to find all the p_j factors, we want to start by finding one p_j and then continue by factoring the smaller integer $N \div p_j$. As we explore factoring, we focus on that first prime factor and then reuse our methods, basic or advanced, to do what's left.

10.2.2 Big integers

On a 64-bit classical processor, the largest natural number you can represent is

$$2^{64} - 1 = 18,446,744,073,709,551,615 \,.$$

For positive and negative integers, one bit is reserved for the sign, so the largest number we can represent is

$$2^{63} - 1 = 9,223,372,036,854,775,807 \,.$$

These may look big, but from a factoring perspective, they are small. We know all the primes that go well above these values.

What would you do if you wanted to factor 18,446,744,073,709,551,617, which is $(2^{64} - 1) + 2$? The processor cannot hold the number directly in its hardware.

We fix this by creating "bignum" or "big integer" objects in software. These can be as large as computer memory permits. We split the big integer across multiple hardware integers and then write software routines for negation, addition, subtraction, multiplication, division, and (related) quotients and remainders. The division operation is the trickiest to code correctly, although it is well-known how to do it. [126]

Scientific applications often support big integers. These include Maple, Mathematica, MATLAB®, and cryptographic software. Python, Erlang, Haskell, Julia, Ruby, and many variants of Lisp and Scheme are programming languages that provide built-in big integers. Other languages provide the functionality via library extensions.

The GNU Multiple Precision Arithmetic Library implements highly optimized low-level routines for arbitrary precision integers and other number types. It is distributed under the dual GNU LGPL v3 and GNU GPL v2 licenses. [85]

10.2.3 Classical factoring: basic methods

We categorize classical factoring techniques into basic arithmetic attempts to reduce a number N into prime factors and more advanced versions that require sophisticated mathematics. We go into detail on the former and survey the latter.

Trial division

If $N = 1$ or $N = -1$, we are done. If N is negative, we note the unit is -1, and we can assume N is positive.

There is one and only one even prime number, and that is 2. If N is even, meaning that the last digit is one of 0, 2, 4, 6, or 8, then $p_1 = 2$. Continue with $N = N \div 2$. If this N is even, then $p_2 = 2$, and reset $N = N \div 2$. Keep going until N is not even. If N ever becomes 1 in the factoring processes, we are finished.

At this point, N is odd, and we may have some initial p_j factors equal to 2. To see if 3 is a factor, we use a trick you may have learned while young.

Write N as a sequence of digits

$$d_t d_{t-1} \ldots d_2 d_1 d_0 ,$$

where each d_j is one of 0, 1, 2, 3, 4, 5, 6, 7, 8, or 9. For example, if $N = 475$ then $d_2 = 4$, $d_1 = 7$, and $d_0 = 5$.

Then, N is divisible by 3 if and only if

$$d_t + d_{t-1} + \cdots + d_2 + d_1 + d_0$$

is divisible by 3. Repeat this process on the sum if necessary.

To prove this, let N be as above. Then,

$$N = d_t 10^t + d_{t-1} 10^{t-1} + \cdots + d_2 10^2 + d_1 10^1 d_0 10^0 .$$

If $N \equiv 0 \bmod 3$, then N is divisible by 3.

By modular arithmetic, which we discussed in section 3.7,

$$N \bmod 3 \equiv \left(\sum_{j=0}^{t} d_j 10^j \right) \bmod 3$$

$$\equiv \sum_{j=0}^{t} \left(d_j 10^j \bmod 3 \right) \equiv \sum_{j=0}^{t} \left(d_j \bmod 3 \right) \left(10^j \bmod 3 \right)$$

$$\equiv \sum_{j=0}^{t} \left(d_j \bmod 3 \right) \equiv \left(\sum_{j=0}^{t} d_j \right) \bmod 3 \,,$$

because every $10^j \equiv 1 \bmod 3$.

There are no special tricks for 4 because we already factored out any 2s. $5 \mid N$ if the last digit is 0 or 5. Because 6 is 2×3, there is nothing to do.

For the prime 7, we can do trial division: divide N by 7, and if there is no remainder, 7 is a factor. There is nothing to do for 8, 9, or 10. For the prime 11, it is trial division again.

I have described one mode of attack: start with a list of sorted primes and see if N is divisible by each in turn. You don't need to look at all primes $< N$ or even $\le N \div 2$; you need to look at those $\le \sqrt{N}$.

Exercise 10.13

If the prime $p \mid N$, $p \neq N$, and $p \ge \sqrt{N}$, why is there another prime $q \le \sqrt{N}$, where $q \mid N$?

This technique is not a practical method of finding factors once N gets large because division is computationally expensive, and you must do many of them. It's not difficult to find the *integer square root* of N, denoted $\lfloor \sqrt{N} \rfloor$, which is the largest integer s such that $s^2 \le N$. If $s^2 = N$, then N is a square.

Sieve of Eratosthenes

How would we create a list of primes to use in trial division? A classical way (I really mean "classical" – it's from ancient Greece) is the *Sieve of Eratosthenes*. Let's see how this works to find all primes less than or equal to 30. We "sift" through the numbers and eliminate the composite values.

We begin by creating a list of all numbers in **N** less than or equal to 30. We shade all the boxes and selectively remove the shading for the nonprimes. We "mark" a box by removing its shading. When we are finished, only the primes are in shaded boxes. Since 1 is not a prime, we mark it.

1	2	3	4	5	6	7	8	9	10

11	12	13	14	15	16	17	18	19	20

21	22	23	24	25	26	27	28	29	30

The first number that is not marked is 2. It must be prime. Mark each of $2 + 2 = 4$, $2 + 2 + 2 = 6$, $2 + 2 + 2 + 2 = 8$, and so on. The numbers we are marking are all multiples of 2 and, therefore, are not prime. We get:

1	2	3	4	5	6	7	8	9	10

11	12	13	14	15	16	17	18	19	20

21	22	23	24	25	26	27	28	29	30

After 2, the next number that is not marked is 3. It must be prime. We mark $3 + 3 = 6$, $3 + 3 + 3 = 9$, etc.

Exercise 10.14

Why would it be fine to start marking at 3^2, and then $3^2 + 3$ instead of $3 + 3$ and then $3 + 3 + 3$?

It is efficient to add 3 to the last number we marked. We can use multiplication, but that's more computation than we need:

1	2	3	4	5	6	7	8	9	10

11	12	13	14	15	16	17	18	19	20

21	22	23	24	25	26	27	28	29	30

After continuing in this manner, we end up with

$$1 \quad 2 \quad 3 \quad 4 \quad 5 \quad 6 \quad 7 \quad 8 \quad 9 \quad 10$$

$$11 \quad 12 \quad 13 \quad 14 \quad 15 \quad 16 \quad 17 \quad 18 \quad 19 \quad 20$$

$$21 \quad 22 \quad 23 \quad 24 \quad 25 \quad 26 \quad 27 \quad 28 \quad 29 \quad 30$$

The integers that remain are prime. This is not a terrible way to create a list of a few hundred or thousand primes, but you would not want to do this to find primes with millions of digits.

Here is a simple Python implementation of the sieve:

```python
def list_of_primes(n):
    # Return a list of primes <= n using the
    # Sieve of Eratosthenes

    # Prepare the list of numbers containing [0,1,...,n]
    numbers = list(range(n + 1))

    # Mark the first two numbers by setting them to 0
    numbers[0] = numbers[1] = 0

    # The first prime is 2
    p = 2

    # Cycle through the numbers, marking nonprimes
    while p < n:
        if p:
            index = p + p
            while index <= n:
                numbers[index] = 0
                index += p
        p += 1

    # Return the primes left in the list
    return [i for i in numbers if i != 0]
```

The output for the example above and a larger set of primes is:

```python
list_of_primes(30)

[2, 3, 5, 7, 11, 13, 17, 19, 23, 29]
```

```
list_of_primes(300)
```

```
[2, 3, 5, 7, 11, 13, 17, 19, 23, 29, 31,
37, 41, 43, 47, 53, 59, 61, 67, 71, 73,
79, 83, 89, 97, 101, 103, 107, 109, 113,
127, 131, 137, 139, 149, 151, 157, 163,
167, 173, 179, 181, 191, 193, 197, 199,
211, 223, 227, 229, 233, 239, 241, 251,
257, 263, 269, 271, 277, 281, 283, 293]
```

For a given number N, there are number theoretic algorithms such as the Miller-Rabin test to see if N is prime, or at least prime with high probability.

Finding powers

A further factoring technique is testing whether N is a power of another integer. We can determine whether N is an mth power using an efficient algorithm called Newton's method. The most efficient method for this test runs in $O(\log(N))$ time. [13] Which m do we need to try?

If $2^m > N$, then any other positive integer raised to the mth power is also too big. Therefore, we need $2^m \leq N$. By taking base 2 logarithms and noting that both sides are greater than one, we need to look at all m in $\mathbf{Z}$ such that

$$m \leq \log_2(N).$$

For $N = 1 + 10^{50}$, for example, a maximum of $m = 167$ suffices.

Fermat's method

Another basic factoring method is due to mathematician Pierre de Fermat (Figure 10.6).

We can assume that N is odd and greater than 1. Therefore, there is a positive k in $\mathbf{Z}$ with $N = 2k + 1$. Then,

$$(k + 1)^2 - k^2 = k^2 + 2k + 1 - k^2 = 2k + 1 = N.$$

For example,

$$75 = 2 \times 37 + 1 = 38^2 - 37^2.$$

In this way, we can represent 75 as a difference of squares. Also, note that

$$75 = 100 - 25 = 10^2 - 5^2,$$

so the representation is not unique.

Figure 10.6: Pierre de Fermat, 1601–1665

Thus, we can always represent odd N as the difference of two squares $N = u^2 - v^2$. Then,

$$N = u^2 - v^2 = (u + v)(u - v) \text{ where } u \neq \pm v.$$

If we can find choices of u and v so that neither $u+v$ nor $u-v$ is 1, we have a factorization.

Another way of saying the above is

$$u^2 \equiv v^2 \bmod N, \text{ where } u \neq \pm v.$$

Since N is odd, $N - 1$ and $N + 1$ are both even, and

$$N = \left(\frac{N+1}{2}\right)^2 - \left(\frac{N-1}{2}\right)^2,$$

one possible pair of choices is $u = \frac{N+1}{2}$ and $v = \frac{N-1}{2}$.

Suppose $N = 87$. Setting

$$u = \frac{87 + 1}{2} = 44 \quad \text{and} \quad v = \frac{87 - 1}{2} = 43$$

yields $u + v = 87$ and $u - v = 1$. This choice of u and v does not help us. These particular choices for finding a pair never work because

$$u - v = \frac{N+1}{2} - \frac{N-1}{2} = \frac{N+1-N+1}{2} = 1.$$

In any case, since 87 is prime, we cannot find a good pair that works. Is there a better alternative or approach?

Start by computing the integer square root s of N. If $s^2 = N$, we have found a factor. Otherwise, set $u = s + 1$ and consider $u^2 - N$. If this is a square, then it is v^2. If it is not, increment u by 1 and try again. Since $N = (u + v)(u - v)$, we can stop when $u + v \geq s$.

(In fact, we can stop a little sooner, but this shows there is a point after which we need not continue.)

Let's try $N = 143$. Then, $s = 11$ and, since $s^2 \neq 143$, set $u = s + 1 = 12$. $u^2 - N = 144 - 143 = 1$, so set $v = 1$. v is a perfect square, so

$$N = (u + v)(u - v) = 13 \times 11.$$

This works well when $u + v$ and $u - v$ are both close to $\sqrt{N}$. When they are not, we need to do many iterations and computations.

Exercise 10.15

Use Fermat's method to factor 3,493,157. Use it again to factor 13,205,947.

10.2.4 Classical factoring: advanced methods

In Fermat's method, we tried to find u and v such that

$$u^2 \equiv v^2 \bmod N \text{ where } u \neq \pm v.$$

We call this a *congruence* of squares modulo N. If we had such a congruence, we could create the factorization

$$(u + v)(u - v) \equiv 0 \bmod N.$$

This does not say $(u + v)(u - v) = N$ but, rather, that there is a nonzero integer c such that $(u + v)(u - v) = cN$.

Given this, let $g = \gcd(u + v, N)$. Then, g and N/g is a possible factorization of N. If either of these is 1, we have failed and have to find new candidates for u and v.

The key question is: how efficiently can we find u and v that are likely to work?

In Fermat's method, we work outwards from the integer square root of N, hoping to find a factor near it. Let's briefly look at more advanced number theoretic approaches. The details are beyond the scope of this book but are well described elsewhere. [112] [128] [53]

Let B be in $\mathbf{Z}$ and ≥ 2. We call a positive integer *B-smooth* if all its prime factors are $\leq B$. B is an upper bound on the size of the primes.

Exercise 10.16

What's the smallest integer B so that 12 is *B*-smooth? What about 7,623?

> A *factor base* is a set P of prime numbers. Typically, given a bound B as above, P is the set of all primes $\le B$.

The following is *Dixon's method*, named after its discoverer, mathematician John D. Dixon. For a given N to factor, choose B and hence P. Let n be the number of primes in P. We want to find $n + 1$ distinct positive integers f_j such that $j^2 \bmod N$ is B-smooth. Said another way,

$$f_j^2 \bmod N = \prod_{k=1}^{n} p_k^{e_{j,k}}$$

for nonnegative integer exponents $e_{j,k}$.

How do we find these f_j? We choose them randomly between $1 +$ the integer square root of N and N. Suppose $N = 17$. Then, the integer square root of N is 4. In Python, the code

```
import random
random.seed(1.5)
[random.randint(5, 17) for _ in range(10)]
```

```
[13, 9, 7, 14, 12, 13, 8, 7, 10, 17]
```

returns ten random integers greater than or equal to 5 and less than 17. I used `seed` so that `randint` returns the same sequence of random numbers each time.

Now that we have our collection of f_j, look at the product

$$\prod_{j=1}^{n+1} f_j^2 \equiv \prod_{k=1}^{n} p_k^{e_{j,1}+\cdots+e_{j,n}} \bmod N .$$

By using linear algebraic methods on the matrix

$$\begin{bmatrix} e_{1,1} & e_{1,2} & \cdots & e_{1,n} \\ e_{2,1} & e_{2,2} & \cdots & e_{2,n} \\ \vdots & \vdots & \ddots & \vdots \\ e_{n,1} & e_{n,2} & \cdots & e_{n,n} \end{bmatrix},$$

we can find replacement values for the exponents so that the congruence still holds and $e_{j,1} + \cdots + e_{j,n}$ is **even**. This means that the right-hand side of

$$\prod_{j=1}^{n+1} f_j^2 \equiv \prod_{k=1}^{n} p_k^{e_{j,1}+\cdots+e_{j,n}} \bmod N$$

is a square, as is the left. This equation has the form

$$u^2 \equiv v^2 \bmod N, \text{ where } u \neq \pm v,$$

and we can proceed to test if we have a factor. If we don't, we can look for different f_j, or increase B and keep trying.

Full treatments of the algorithm put bounds on the value of B. Can we find better congruences of squares, faster? The f_j we use are smooth numbers. Can we sift through all the possibilities better so that we need not consider as many bad candidates?

To learn more

Beyond Dixon's algorithm, there are more powerful and complicated number theoretic algorithms that generalize the sieving techniques to find smooth numbers much faster. The *quadratic sieve* and the *general number field sieve* are examples, with the latter being the most efficient factoring algorithm for very large integers. [29] [112, Chapter 3]

10.3 How hard can that be, again?

In section 2.8, we first saw and used the O() notation for sorting and searching. Bubble sort runs in $O(n^2)$ time, and merge sort is $O(n \log(n))$. A brute force search is $O(n)$, but adding sorting and random access allows a binary search to be $O(\log(n))$.

We now look at complexity again to understand why Shor's factoring algorithm is a big improvement on known classical methods.

10.3.1 Time is not always on your side

All algorithms are of polynomial time because we can bound them, in this case, by $O(n^2)$. More precisely, there is a hierarchy of time complexities. For the examples above,

Algorithm	Complexity	Name
Bubble sort	$O(n^2)$	quadratic time
Merge sort	$O(n \log(n))$	quasilinear time
Brute force search	$O(n)$	linear time
Binary search	$O(\log(n))$	logarithmic time

Polynomial time is higher than all of these, but we can say each runs in at least polynomial time.

We are concerned with this because there is a special distinction between polynomial and exponential time. The latter describes exponential growth and can cause problems to become quickly intractable. All these descriptions apply to large n. Even though an exponential running time sounds terrible, the algorithm may still be feasible when n is small.

Something running in exponential time has its execution time proportional to $2^{f(n)}$. Here, $f(n)$ is a polynomial in n, such as $n^2 - n + 1$. Double exponential time is even worse: the time is proportional to $2^{2^{f(n)}}$.

Subexponential is an improvement over exponential. It means for every $b > 1$ in $\mathbf{R}$, the running time is less than b^n. [119]

For example, an algorithm that runs in

$$ O\left(2^{n^{0.25}}\right) $$

time is subexponential.

There are many subtleties concerning classical and quantum complexity, and a complete discussion involves traditional and quantum Turing machines. As we only need to understand where quantum computing can be better than classical computing, I won't delve into a full and formal description of complexity theory here.

Fermat's method of factoring integers is of exponential time. The general number field sieve is subexponential. There is no known polynomial time classical algorithm for factoring.

10.3.2 Complexity classes

When you learned to add and multiply, you learned *deterministic* algorithms for each. Given the same input numbers, you executed a series of steps that always led to the same answer. No randomness was involved. When you encounter random numbers as you continue through this book, chances are you are looking at a nondeterministic algorithm.

A nondeterministic algorithm may involve probability and choices that could produce different answers. Even if the answers are the same, the choices made inside the algorithm may cause it to run quite quickly or excruciatingly slowly. More formally, a poor choice can cause an exponential runtime, while a good one can enable polynomial time execution.

The complexity class P refers to the collection of problems that can be solved in polynomial time using a deterministic algorithm.

The class NP is the collection of problems whose solutions can be checked in polynomial time. We do not know if P = NP, but you could become wealthy via industry prizes if you could prove it or its contrary. Checking a solution by asking a question such as "Is $p \times q$ equal to N?" is an example of a *decision problem*.

Consider integer factorization: we do not know if there is a classical way of factoring a composite integer in polynomial time. Once done, we can easily multiply the factors to see if the solution is correct. We do not know if classical factorization is in P, but we know it is in NP.

If **P** ≠ **NP**, we can represent the set of problems as shown in Figure 10.7. Not all NP problems are equally difficult. They are defined by their ability to check solutions in polynomial time.

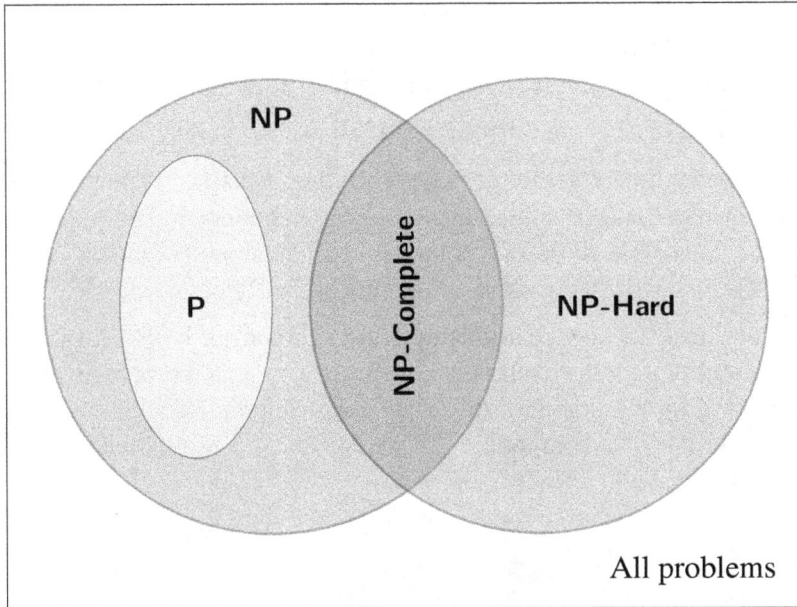

Figure 10.7: The relationships among several complexity classes

I've shown two new terms: NP-Hard and NP-Complete. The first is easier to explain: the problems in NP-Hard are at least as hard as the most difficult ones in NP.

For NP-Complete, first let *A* and *B* be any two problems. We say that we can "reduce *A* to *B* in polynomial time" if, by a series of manipulations, we can express *A* as an instance of *B*. [234]

We now define a problem *B* to be NP-Complete if it is NP-Hard and we can transform and reduce any problem *A* in NP to *B* by a polynomial time algorithm.

As an analogy, suppose one problem (*A*) is "travel to the Empire State Building in New York City." For problem *B*, we express it as "drive to any location in New York City." *B* is hard because of the need to get to any location and the difficulty of driving to it. *A* can be reduced to *B* because we need to get to one location somehow.

A problem is in NP-Hard if we can reduce any NP problem to it. As you can see from Figure 10.7, the class of NP-Hard problems intersects NP but is larger. The intersection is the NP-Complete class, the hardest problems in NP to which all others can be reduced. An NP-Hard problem that is not in NP cannot be solved or verified in polynomial time.

There are many, many (many, many, ...) complexity classes that you may find interesting enough to learn more about beyond what we have discussed. BPP is the class of decision problems that can execute in polynomial time but with a caveat. BPP stands for "bounded-error probabilistic polynomial time." Since probability is involved, an algorithm that solves this problem may not always return the correct answer. The "bounded" part of the name is made concrete by insisting the correct answer is gotten at least two-thirds of the time.

The class P is in BPP, but we do not know if all problems in NP are in BPP.

The above classifications refer to problems solved on a classical computer. For quantum computers, we consider the BQP class, those solvable in bounded-error polynomial time on a quantum computer. BQP is short for "bounded-error quantum polynomial time." Loosely speaking, BQP corresponds to quantum computers as BPP does to classical computers.

However, there is a stronger relationship. Any problem in BPP is also in BQP. This follows from our ability to perform classical operations on a quantum computer, although it might be extremely slow. We examined this in section 9.3 and section 9.3.1 when we saw that **nand** is universal for classical computing, and we can create a **nand** on a quantum computer via a quantum Toffoli gate.

> **To learn more**
>
> A strong grounding in classical algorithms and complexity theory is necessary for you to become proficient in quantum algorithms. [50] [199] I particularly recommend the book *Algorithms* by Dasgupta, Papadimitrious, and Vazirani, as it goes deeper into NP-Complete problems and provides a brief introduction introduction to quantum algorithms. [61] I recommend you further investigate BPP and BQP. [229]

10.4 Phase kickback

In section 9.8.2, we saw an example of phase kickback while working with oracles. In this section, we look at the concept again in the context of controlled z-rotation gates. We need this within Shor's factoring algorithm to estimate eigenvalues.

Consider the circuit in Figure 10.8.

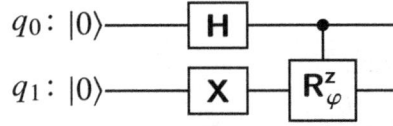

Figure 10.8: A circuit with a Hadamard and controlled z-rotation gate

As we saw in section 7.6.6, $|1\rangle$ is an eigenvector of $\mathbf{R}_\varphi^z$ with eigenvalue $e^{\varphi i}$:

$$\mathbf{R}_\varphi^z = \begin{bmatrix} 1 & 0 \\ 0 & e^{\varphi i} \end{bmatrix} = \begin{bmatrix} 1 & 0 \\ 0 & \cos(\varphi) + \sin(\varphi)i \end{bmatrix}$$

$$\mathbf{R}_\varphi^z|0\rangle = |0\rangle$$

$$\mathbf{R}_\varphi^z|1\rangle = e^{\varphi i}|1\rangle = (\cos(\varphi) + \sin(\varphi)i)\,|1\rangle$$

The initial quantum state in Figure 10.8 is $|00\rangle = |0\rangle \otimes |0\rangle$ We apply $\mathbf{H} \otimes \mathbf{X}$, yielding

$$(\mathbf{H} \otimes \mathbf{X})\,(|0\rangle \otimes |0\rangle) = (\mathbf{H}|0\rangle) \otimes (\mathbf{X}|0\rangle)$$

$$= \left(\frac{\sqrt{2}}{2}|0\rangle + \frac{\sqrt{2}}{2}|1\rangle \right) \otimes |1\rangle$$

$$= \frac{\sqrt{2}}{2}|01\rangle + \frac{\sqrt{2}}{2}|11\rangle$$

$$= \frac{\sqrt{2}}{2}\,(|01\rangle + |11\rangle)\,.$$

We apply the $\mathbf{CR}_\varphi^z$:

$$\mathbf{CR}_\varphi^z \left(\frac{\sqrt{2}}{2}|01\rangle + \frac{\sqrt{2}}{2}|11\rangle \right) = \frac{\sqrt{2}}{2}\,\mathbf{CR}_\varphi^z\,(|01\rangle + |11\rangle)$$

$$= \frac{\sqrt{2}}{2}\,\left(|01\rangle + e^{\varphi i}|11\rangle\right)$$

$$= \frac{\sqrt{2}}{2}\,\left(|0\rangle + e^{\varphi i}|1\rangle\right) \otimes |1\rangle$$

We began with q_0 as the control qubit. The phase from the $\mathbf{R}_\varphi^z$ gate conditionally applied to q_1 ends up causing the phase $e^{\varphi i}$ to appear in the state of q_0. The state of q_1 was not changed from $|1\rangle$. This is the phase kickback!

We can generalize this technique. Let $\mathbf{U}$ be a 1-qubit quantum operator with eigenvalue $|\psi\rangle$. Then,

$$\mathbf{U}|\psi\rangle = e^{\varphi i}|\psi\rangle$$

for some φ.

Figure 10.9 is our new circuit.

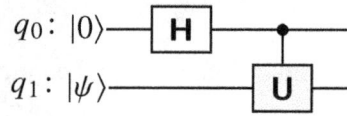

Figure 10.9: The general circuit for phase kickback

We apply the Hadamard gate on q_0 and then **CU** on both qubits:

$$\mathbf{CU}\left(\frac{\sqrt{2}}{2}|0\rangle|\psi\rangle + \frac{\sqrt{2}}{2}|1\rangle|\psi\rangle\right) = \frac{\sqrt{2}}{2}\,\mathbf{CU}\left(|0\rangle|\psi\rangle + |1\rangle|\psi\rangle\right)$$

$$= \frac{\sqrt{2}}{2}\left(|0\rangle|\psi\rangle + e^{\varphi i}|1\rangle|\psi\rangle\right)$$

$$= \frac{\sqrt{2}}{2}\left(|0\rangle + e^{\varphi i}|1\rangle\right) \otimes |\psi\rangle$$

Once again, we have kicked back the phase onto the control qubit, leaving the target qubit unchanged.

Can we estimate φ from this? Let's add another Hadamard gate, and look at the resulting quantum state. The circuit is in

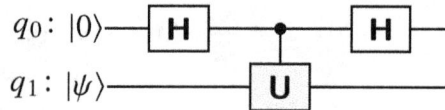

Figure 10.10: Trying to estimate φ with phase kickback

Our new state is

$$(\mathbf{H} \otimes \mathbf{ID})\left(\frac{\sqrt{2}}{2}\left(|0\rangle + e^{\varphi i}|1\rangle\right) \otimes |\psi\rangle\right)$$

$$= \frac{\sqrt{2}}{2}\left(\frac{\sqrt{2}}{2}|0\rangle + \frac{\sqrt{2}}{2}|1\rangle + e^{\varphi i}\frac{\sqrt{2}}{2}|0\rangle - e^{\varphi i}\frac{\sqrt{2}}{2}|0\rangle\right) \otimes |\psi\rangle$$

$$= \left(\frac{(1 + e^{\varphi i})}{2}|0\rangle + \frac{(1 - e^{\varphi i})}{2}|1\rangle\right) \otimes |\psi\rangle$$

$$= e^{\frac{\varphi}{2}i} \left(\frac{e^{-\frac{\varphi}{2}i} + e^{\frac{\varphi}{2}i}}{2}|0\rangle + \frac{e^{-\frac{\varphi}{2}i} - e^{\frac{\varphi}{2}i}}{2}|1\rangle \right) \otimes |\psi\rangle$$

$$= e^{\frac{\varphi}{2}i} \left(\cos\left(\frac{\varphi}{2}\right)|0\rangle - \sin\left(\frac{\varphi}{2}\right)i|1\rangle \right) \otimes |\psi\rangle .$$

$e^{\frac{\varphi}{2}i}$ is a complex unit and only affects the global phase.

Exercise 10.17

Using the basic trigonometric identities from section 4.3, show that

$$\cos\left(\frac{\varphi}{2}\right) = \frac{e^{-\frac{\varphi}{2}i} + e^{\frac{\varphi}{2}i}}{2} \quad \text{and} \quad -\sin\left(\frac{\varphi}{2}\right)i = \frac{e^{-\frac{\varphi}{2}i} - e^{\frac{\varphi}{2}i}}{2} .$$

Suppose we run this circuit m times and get $|0\rangle$ k times and $|1\rangle$ $m - k$ times when we measure q_0. We then have approximations

$$\frac{k}{m} \approx \left|\cos\left(\frac{\varphi}{2}\right)\right|^2 \quad \text{and} \quad \frac{m-k}{m} \approx \left|-\sin\left(\frac{\varphi}{2}\right)i\right|^2 = \left|\sin\left(\frac{\varphi}{2}\right)\right|^2 .$$

Unfortunately, we cannot distinguish the signs of the cosine and sine expressions. Also, we may have to use a very large m to get a good approximation because of quantum randomness.

In the next section, we see another way of estimating the phase. We still use phase kickback, but employ the inverse QFT to get as close as we wish to the actual phase value.

10.5   Eigenvalue and phase estimation

The next tool we need for Shor's factoring algorithm is a way to estimate the eigenvalues of a special unitary operation we construct.

Let U be an n-by-n square matrix with complex entries. From section 5.10, the solutions λ of the equation

$$\det(U - \lambda I_N) = 0$$

are the *eigenvalues* $\{\lambda_1, \ldots, \lambda_N\}$ of U. Some of the λ_j may be equal. If a particular eigenvalue λ_j shows up k times among the N values, we say λ_j has *multiplicity k*.

Each eigenvalue λ_j corresponds to an *eigenvector* $\mathbf{v}_j$ so that

$$U\mathbf{v}_j = \lambda_j \mathbf{v}_j .$$

We can take each $\mathbf{v}_j$ to be a unit vector. When U is unitary, each λ_j is a complex unit.

We have so far represented an eigenvalue λ of a unitary matrix as $e^{\varphi i}$ with $0 \leq \varphi < 2\pi$. We now, instead, think of the eigenvalue as $e^{2\pi\varphi i}$ with $0 \leq \varphi < 1$.

This change allows us to consider the binary representation of φ as a number greater than or equal to 0 and less than 1, as shown in section 3.5.3. An approximation to φ to m bits looks like

$$\varphi \approx (0.b_1 b_2 \ldots b_{m-1} b_m)_2$$
$$= b_1 2^{-1} + b_2 2^{-2} + \cdots + b_{m-1} 2^{-(m-1)} + b_m 2^{-m}$$
$$= \sum_{j=1}^{m} b_j 2^{-j},$$

where each b_j is 0 or 1. Increasing m may improve the approximation if φ does not have a finite binary expansion. We can write the approximation to the eigenvalue as

$$e^{2\pi\varphi i} \approx e^{2\pi(0.b_1 b_2 \ldots b_{m-1} b_m)_2 \, i}.$$

We are ready to pose the question whose solution we outline in this section:

Let **U** be a quantum transformation/gate on n qubits
with corresponding 2^n-by-2^n square matrix U.
If $|\psi\rangle$ is an eigenvector of **U** (and of U, by abuse of notation) [233],
can we closely estimate φ, where $e^{2\pi\varphi i}$ is the eigenvalue
corresponding to $|\psi\rangle$ and $0 \leq \varphi < 1$?

Some authors call the eigenvector $|\psi\rangle$ an *eigenket* of **U**.

Suppose **U**, $|\psi\rangle$, and $e^{2\pi\varphi}$ are as above. By applying **U** multiple times,

$$\mathbf{U}^1|\psi\rangle = \mathbf{U}|\psi\rangle = e^{2\pi\varphi i}|\psi\rangle$$
$$\mathbf{U}^2|\psi\rangle = \mathbf{U}\left(e^{2\pi\varphi i}|\psi\rangle\right) = e^{2\pi\varphi i}\mathbf{U}\left(|\psi\rangle\right)$$
$$= e^{2\pi\varphi i}e^{2\pi\varphi i}|\psi\rangle = e^{(2+2)\pi\varphi i}|\psi\rangle$$
$$\mathbf{U}^3|\psi\rangle = \mathbf{U}\left(e^{(2+2)\pi\varphi i}|\psi\rangle\right) = e^{(2+2+2)\pi\varphi i}|\psi\rangle$$
$$\vdots$$
$$\mathbf{U}^k|\psi\rangle = e^{2k\pi\varphi i}|\psi\rangle.$$

If $k = 2^j$, then

$$\mathbf{U}^{2^j}|\psi\rangle = e^{2^{j+1}\pi\varphi i}|\psi\rangle.$$

We use this in the circuit for phase estimation with a controlled-$\mathbf{U}^k$ gate:

---

[436]

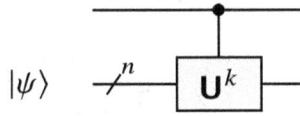

The

$$\not\!\!\!/^{n}$$

indicates that $|\psi\rangle$ is on an n-qubit quantum register, and $\mathbf{U}^k$ has n quantum state inputs and outputs. $\mathbf{U}^k$ executes only if the above wire's input is $|1\rangle$.

Let m be the number of bits we need to get as close as necessary to the original phase. We use m qubits on the upper portion of the circuit, the "upper register."

When $m = 1$, our phase estimation circuit is

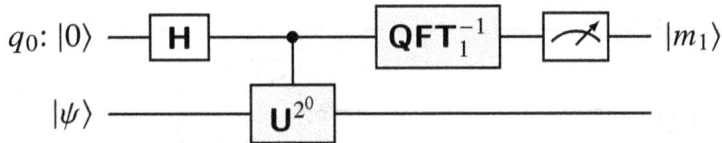

We modify the quantum state in the upper register (which is q_0, in this case) by the phase kickback we describe in section 10.4. We then take the inverse QFT, for reasons we describe below.

Before the inverse QFT, the state is

$$\frac{\sqrt{2}}{2}\left(|0\rangle + e^{2\pi\varphi i}|1\rangle\right) \otimes |\psi\rangle.$$

Since $m = 1$,

$$\mathbf{QFT}_1^{-1} = \mathbf{H}^{-1} = \mathbf{H},$$

and so the final state before measurement is

$$\left(\frac{\left(1 + e^{2\pi\varphi i}\right)}{2}|0\rangle + \frac{\left(1 - e^{2\pi\varphi i}\right)}{2}|1\rangle\right) \otimes |\psi\rangle.$$

To begin to show the general structure of the result of phase estimation, we rewrite the state of q_0:

$$\left(\frac{\left(1 + e^{2\pi\varphi i}\right)}{2}|0\rangle + \frac{\left(1 - e^{2\pi\varphi i}\right)}{2}|1\rangle\right) = \frac{1}{2}\left(\left(1 + e^{2\pi\varphi i}\right)|0\rangle + \left(1 - e^{2\pi\varphi i}\right)|1\rangle\right)$$

$$= \left(\sum_{j=0}^{2^1-1} \underbrace{\left(\frac{1}{2^1} \sum_{k=0}^{2^1-1} e^{-\frac{2\pi ki}{2^1}\left(j-2^1\varphi\right)} \right)}_{\text{probability amplitude}} |j\rangle_1 \right)$$

$$= \left(\sum_{j=0}^{2^m-1} \underbrace{\left(\frac{1}{2^m} \sum_{k=0}^{2^m-1} e^{-\frac{2\pi ki}{2^m}\left(j-2^m\varphi\right)} \right)}_{\text{probability amplitude}} |j\rangle_m \right) \text{ for } m=1.$$

When $m = 2$, our phase estimation circuit is

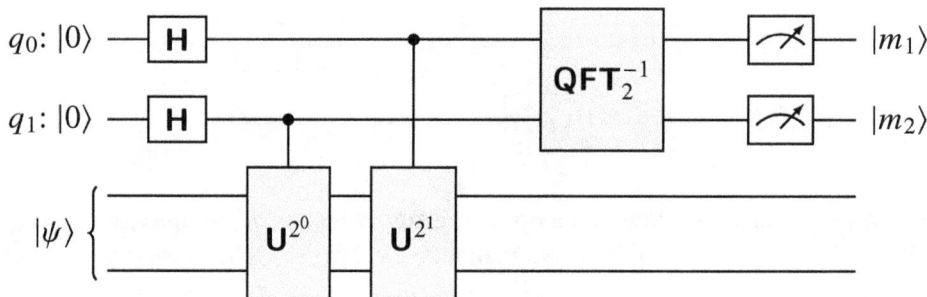

The state of the upper register before applying $\mathbf{QFT}_2^{-1}$ is

$$\frac{1}{2} \left(|0\rangle + e^{2\pi 2^1 \varphi i}|1\rangle \right) \otimes \left(|0\rangle + e^{2\pi 2^0 \varphi i}|1\rangle \right)$$

$$= \frac{1}{2} \left(|00\rangle + e^{2\pi 2^0 \varphi i}|01\rangle + e^{2\pi 2^1 \varphi i}|10\rangle + e^{2\pi \boxed{3}\varphi i}|11\rangle \right)$$

$$= \frac{1}{2} \left(|00\rangle + e^{2\pi 2^0 \varphi i}|01\rangle + e^{2\pi 2^1 \varphi i}|10\rangle + e^{2\pi \boxed{\left(2^2-1\right)}\varphi i}|11\rangle \right)$$

$$= \frac{1}{2} \sum_{j=0}^{2^2-1} e^{2\pi j \varphi i}|j\rangle_2.$$

I've highlighted two terms in the exponents to show the pattern.

In this 2-qubit case,

$$\mathbf{QFT}_2 = \frac{1}{\sqrt{4}} \begin{bmatrix} 1 & 1 & 1 & 1 \\ 1 & \omega & \omega^2 & \omega^3 \\ 1 & \omega^2 & \omega^4 & \omega^6 \\ 1 & \omega^3 & \omega^6 & \omega^9 \end{bmatrix} = \frac{1}{2} \begin{bmatrix} 1 & 1 & 1 & 1 \\ 1 & i & -1 & -i \\ 1 & -1 & 1 & -1 \\ 1 & -i & -1 & i \end{bmatrix}$$

because

$$\omega = e^{\frac{2\pi i}{2^2}} = i$$

is a primitive fourth root of unity. Since this matrix is unitary, its inverse is its conjugate transpose

$$\mathbf{QFT}_2^{-1} = \frac{1}{2} \begin{bmatrix} 1 & 1 & 1 & 1 \\ 1 & -i & -1 & i \\ 1 & -1 & 1 & -1 \\ 1 & i & -1 & -i \end{bmatrix}.$$

For $N = 2^2$ and given the quantum state

$$\sum_{j=0}^{2^2-1} a_j |j\rangle_2,$$

its inverse QFT is

$$\mathbf{QFT}_2^{-1}\left(\sum_{j=0}^{2^2-1} a_j|j\rangle_2\right) = \frac{1}{\sqrt{2^2}} \sum_{j=0}^{2^2-1}\sum_{k=0}^{2^2-1} a_k e^{-\frac{2\pi ijk}{2^2}} |j\rangle_2.$$

In our circuit, $a_k = \frac{1}{2}e^{2\pi\varphi ki}$. Putting all this together, the final upper register before measurement is

$$\frac{1}{2^2}\sum_{j=0}^{2^2-1}\sum_{k=0}^{2^2-1} e^{2\pi\varphi ki} e^{-\frac{2\pi jki}{2^2}} |j\rangle_2 = \frac{1}{2^2}\sum_{j=0}^{2^2-1}\sum_{k=0}^{2^2-1} e^{2\pi\varphi ki - \frac{2\pi jki}{2^2}} |j\rangle_2$$

$$= \frac{1}{2^2}\sum_{j=0}^{2^2-1}\sum_{k=0}^{2^2-1} e^{-\frac{2\pi ki}{2^2}\left(j-2^2\varphi\right)} |j\rangle_2$$

$$= \sum_{j=0}^{2^2-1} \underbrace{\left(\frac{1}{2^2} \sum_{k=0}^{2^2-1} e^{-\frac{2\pi ki}{2^2}(j-2^2\varphi)} \right)}_{\text{probability amplitude}} |j\rangle_2$$

$$= \left(\sum_{j=0}^{2^m-1} \underbrace{\left(\frac{1}{2^m} \sum_{k=0}^{2^m-1} e^{-\frac{2\pi ki}{2^m}(j-2^m\varphi)} \right)}_{\text{probability amplitude}} |j\rangle_m \right) \quad \text{for } m = 2.$$

Obvious, right? (I'm joking.)

Let me state why we have some of the elements in these messy expressions:

- φ is the phase we want to estimate.
- The $|j\rangle_2$ are the standard basis kets.
- The sums involving the $|j\rangle_2$ are from superpositions.
- The exponential forms involving e are roots of unity or other complex numbers with absolute value 1.

While the expressions look complicated, because they are, each part is there because of some gate action to construct a final quantum state that will allow us to estimate φ.

In general, we keep adding gates on the bottom up to $\mathbf{U}^{2^{m-1}}$, as shown in Figure 10.11.

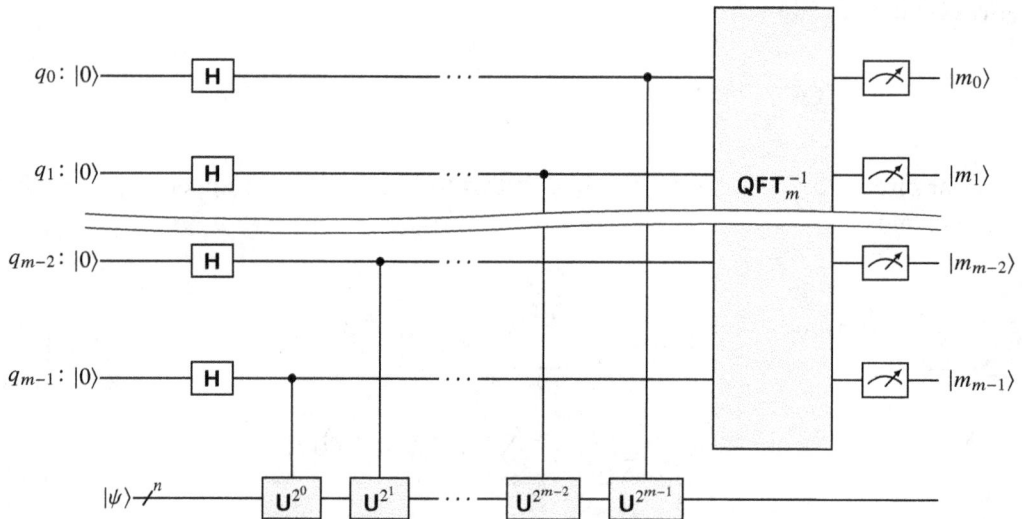

Figure 10.11: The phase estimation circuit for n qubits

The general form of the final upper register for m qubits instead of 2 is

$$\sum_{j=0}^{2^m-1} \underbrace{\left(\frac{1}{2^m} \sum_{k=0}^{2^m-1} e^{-\frac{2\pi ki}{2^m}(j-2^m\varphi)} \right)}_{\text{probability amplitude}} |j\rangle_m \,.$$

Exercise 10.18

What is the probability amplitude of $|j\rangle$ if j ever exactly equals $2^m\varphi$?

Including the upper register and the lower register (which is $|\psi\rangle$), the full pre-measurement state at the end of the circuit is

$$\left(\sum_{j=0}^{2^m-1} \underbrace{\left(\frac{1}{2^m} \sum_{k=0}^{2^m-1} e^{-\frac{2\pi ki}{2^m}(j-2^m\varphi)} \right)}_{\text{probability amplitude}} |j\rangle_m \right) \otimes |\psi\rangle \,.$$

Let's get an estimate for φ. We do so by finding a good rational number approximation for it.

Even though we do not know φ, there exists a closest c in $\mathbf{Z}$ that is within $\frac{1}{2}$ of $2^m\varphi$. To be concrete,

$$c = \left\lfloor 2^m\varphi + \frac{1}{2} \right\rfloor \,.$$

We want to find c so that $\frac{c}{2^m}$ is a good approximation of φ. For example, if $m = 10$ and $\varphi = \frac{1}{2}$, then $c = 2^9 = 512$ works exactly. If $\varphi = \frac{1}{3}$,

$$c = \left\lfloor 2^{10}\frac{1}{3} + \frac{1}{2} \right\rfloor = 341 \,.$$

There is also a real number d that we define as

$$d = \varphi - \frac{c}{2^m} \Rightarrow 2^m\varphi = c + 2^m d \text{ with } 0 \le |2^m d| < \frac{1}{2} \,.$$

$|d|$ measures how far away φ is from its rational approximation $\frac{c}{2^m}$.

We want the measured state of the upper register to be $|c\rangle$. By increasing m, the number of qubits in the upper register, we can get a more accurate approximation.

This is the crux of what the algorithm does: find $|c\rangle$ as the measured standard basis ket in the upper register as a good approximation to $2^m\varphi$.

Given these definitions of c and d, we rewrite the upper register quantum state as

$$\sum_{j=0}^{2^m-1} \left(\frac{1}{2^m} \sum_{k=0}^{2^m-1} e^{-\frac{2\pi ki}{2^m}(j-2^m\varphi)} \right) |j\rangle_m = \sum_{j=0}^{2^m-1} \left(\frac{1}{2^m} \sum_{k=0}^{2^m-1} e^{-\frac{2\pi ki}{2^m}(j-c)} e^{2\pi dki} \right) |j\rangle_m.$$

The probability of getting $|c\rangle$ is the square of the absolute value of the probability amplitude when $j = c$. That is,

$$\mathrm{P}(|c\rangle) = \left| \frac{1}{2^m} \sum_{k=0}^{2^m-1} e^{-\frac{2\pi ki}{2^m}(c-c)} e^{2\pi dki} \right|^2 = \left| \frac{1}{2^m} \sum_{k=0}^{2^m-1} e^{2\pi dki} \right|^2.$$

If $d = 0$, the expression on the right is

$$\left| \frac{1}{2^m} \sum_{k=0}^{2^m-1} e^{2\pi dki} \right|^2 = \left| \frac{1}{2^m} \sum_{k=0}^{2^m-1} 1 \right|^2 = \frac{1}{2^m} 2^m = 1$$

and the measured result of the upper register is $|c\rangle$ with probability 1. This happens when $\varphi = \frac{c}{2^m}$ is a rational number.

This is why we used the inverse QFT. When $d = 0$ and φ is exactly $\frac{c}{2^m}$, the section of the phase estimation circuit before the inverse QFT produces a QFT expression. Applying the inverse QFT then gives us $|c\rangle$ with probability 1.

Exercise 10.19

Suppose $\mathbf{U} = \mathbf{S}$ from section 7.6.7. Compute the phase estimates with $m = 1$ and $m = 2$ qubits.

All is not lost if $d \neq 0$. In that case, the circuit returns the correct answer with probability $\frac{4}{\pi^2} \approx 0.405$. [45, Section 5] [150, Section 3.7] We must run the circuit multiple times to get the correct answer. If you run the circuit 28 or more times, the probability of never getting the correct answer is less than 10^{-6}, as we saw in section 6.3.

Exercise 10.20

Suppose $\mathbf{U} = \mathbf{R}^{\mathbf{z}}_{\frac{\pi}{6}}$ from section 7.6.6. Compute the phase estimates with $m = 1$ and $m = 2$ qubits.

10.6 Order and period finding

The next tool we need for Shor's algorithm is an algorithm to find out when certain types of functions start repeating themselves.

Consider the function $k \mapsto a^k$ on whole numbers k for a fixed a in **N** greater than 1. For example, if $a = 3$, the first 12 values are

$$3^0 = 1 \qquad 3^1 = 3 \qquad 3^2 = 9 \qquad 3^3 = 27$$
$$3^4 = 81 \qquad 3^5 = 243 \qquad 3^6 = 729 \qquad 3^7 = 2187$$
$$3^8 = 6561 \qquad 3^9 = 19683 \qquad 3^{10} = 59049 \qquad 3^{11} = 177147$$

or in Python:

```
[3**n for n in range(12)]
```

```
[1, 3, 9, 27, 81, 243, 729, 2187, 6561, 19683, 59049, 177147]
```

As we look at larger exponents k, the values of 3^k will get larger and larger.

If we instead use modular arithmetic, as we saw in section 3.7, 3^k cannot get arbitrarily large. For example, modulo $M = 13$, the values we get for the function $k \mapsto a^k \bmod 13$ are

```
[3**n % 13 for n in range(12)]
```

```
[1, 3, 9, 1, 3, 9, 1, 3, 9, 1, 3, 9]
```

Here, % is the Python "remainder operator," and it implements modular integer arithmetic.

Working modulo $M = 16$ yields

```
[3**n % 16 for n in range(12)]
```

```
[1, 3, 9, 11, 1, 3, 9, 11, 1, 3, 9, 11]
```

Finally, for modulo $M = 22$, we get

```
[3**n % 22 for n in range(12)]
```

```
[1, 3, 9, 5, 15, 1, 3, 9, 5, 15, 1, 3]
```

In each case, the sequence starts repeating. That is, the sequences, and hence the functions, are *periodic*. Recall from section 3.4.1 that two integers are coprime if their greatest common divisor is 1. If we define $f_a(x) = a^x \bmod M$ for a coprime to M, then the smallest positive integer r such that $f_a(x) = f_a(x+r)$ for all x is called the *period* of f_a.

Exercise 10.21

What happens when we work modulo $M = 23, 24,$ and 25?

For $M = 13$ in the first example, the period $r = 3$. For $M = 16$, $r = 4$. In the final example with $M = 22$, the period $r = 5$.

Given such an a as above, we can look at all $a^1, a^2, a^3, \ldots \bmod M$ and ask: what is the smallest r in $\mathbf{N}$, if it exists, such that $a^r \equiv 1 \bmod M$? If there is such an r, it is called the *order* of $a \bmod M$. Then, $a^{x+r} \equiv a^x \bmod M$ by multiplication by a^x. Thus, r is also the period of f_a. For this reason, the "period-finding problem" is equivalent to the "order-finding problem."

In the rest of this section, we develop a hybrid quantum-classical algorithm to find the order of such an a, with a few conditions. This algorithm is significant because one of its applications is integer factorization.

With such an r in hand, and assuming it is even,

$$a^r \equiv 1 \bmod M \implies a^r - 1 \equiv 0 \bmod M \implies \left(a^{\frac{r}{2}} + 1\right)\left(a^{\frac{r}{2}} - 1\right) \equiv 0 \bmod M.$$

Given a good a, a good even r, and Euclid's algorithm, we might be able to find a factorization of M.

Let

$$\ell_{\text{bits}} = \lceil \log_2(M) \rceil$$

be the number of bits we need to represent M. (Recall that $\lceil x \rceil$, the *ceiling* of x, is the smallest integer $\geq x$.) For example, if $M = 7 = 111_2$, then $\ell_{\text{bits}} = 3$.

Set

$$\ell_\epsilon = 2\ell_{\text{bits}} + 1 + \left\lceil \log_2\left(2 + \frac{1}{2\epsilon}\right)\right\rceil$$

for some very small ϵ in $\mathbf{R}$.

We use phase estimation with continued fractions (section 3.5.4) to compute the order r of a modulo M. For $0 \le j \le r - 1$, we find approximations of the phases $\varphi_j = \frac{j}{r}$ accurate to $2\ell_{\text{bits}} + 1$ bits with probability $\ge \frac{1-\epsilon}{r}$. The smaller our ϵ is, the larger our ℓ_ϵ is.

Exercise 10.22

What are ℓ_{bits} and ℓ_ϵ for $M = 20$ and $\epsilon = 0.001$?

I've chosen to use ℓ to remind us that ℓ_{bits} and ℓ_ϵ are lengths of quantum registers.

To learn more

In what follows, I generally follow the approach in Nielsen and Chuang, although there are many variations in the literature, such as in Watrous, whose ideas I reflect here. [162, Section 5.3.1] [231]

10.6.1 Modular exponentiation

Since we are finding periods of functions or orders of numbers modulo M, we must be able to compute $a^x \bmod M$ in a quantum way.

For a binary string y of length ℓ_{bits}, that is, y is in $\{0, 1\}^{\ell_{\text{bits}}}$, define

$$U|y\rangle = \begin{cases} |ay \bmod M\rangle & \text{if } 0 \le y < M \\ |y\rangle & \text{if } M \le y < 2^{\ell_{\text{bits}}}. \end{cases}$$

Remember that a is coprime to M, which means they share no nontrivial factors. This is the same as saying $\gcd(a, M) = 1$, so there exists b and c in $\mathbf{Z}$ so that $ab + Mc = 1$. Looking at this modulo M,

$$1 = ab + Mc \equiv ab \bmod M.$$

Thus, a is invertible modulo M with $a^{-1} = b$.

When I write an expression such as $|i \bmod M\rangle$, it is shorthand for $|i \bmod M\rangle_{\ell_{\text{bits}}}$.

The $|y\rangle$ are the computational basis vectors in a $2^{\ell_{\text{bits}}}$-dimensional vector space over $\mathbf{C}$. U is a $2^{\ell_{\text{bits}}}$-by-$2^{\ell_{\text{bits}}}$ square matrix. The lower right $(2^{\ell_{\text{bits}}} - M)$-by-$(2^{\ell_{\text{bits}}} - M)$ submatrix is the identity matrix. The upper-left M-by-M submatrix is a permutation matrix because a is invertible modulo M. All other matrix entries are zero. Hence, all of U is a permutation matrix consisting of 0s and 1s, and so is unitary.

If we apply U multiple times, we get multiplication and, hence, exponentiation by repeated squaring:

$$U^2|y\rangle = UU|y\rangle = U|ay \bmod M\rangle = \left|a^2y \bmod M\right\rangle.$$

For example,

$$
\begin{aligned}
U^{15}|y\rangle &= U(U^7)^2|y\rangle = U(UU^6)^2|y\rangle \\
&= U(U(U^3)^2)^2|y\rangle = U(U(UUU)^2)^2|y\rangle \\
&= \left|a^{15}y \bmod M\right\rangle.
\end{aligned}
$$

As we saw at the end of section 9.4, for any nonnegative integer z with binary representation $z_k z_{k-1} \cdots z_1 z_0$, with z_0 the least significant bit,

$$a^z = a^{z_{k-1}2^{k-1}} \times a^{z_{k-2}2^{k-2}} \times \cdots \times a^{z_1 2^1} \times a^{z_0 2^0}.$$

We can define

$$
\begin{aligned}
|z\rangle|y\rangle &\mapsto |z\rangle U^{z_{k-1}2^{k-1}} \times U^{z_{k-2}2^{k-2}} \times \cdots \times U^{z_1 2^1} \times U^{z_0 2^0} \\
&= |z\rangle\left|a^{z_{k-1}2^{k-1}} \times a^{z_{k-2}2^{k-2}} \times \cdots \times a^{z_1 2^1} \times a^{z_0 2^0} \times y \bmod M\right\rangle \\
&= |z\rangle|a^z y \bmod M\rangle.
\end{aligned}
$$

In practice, we allow k to be as large as ℓ_ϵ.

With these observations and calculations, we know how to do quantum modular exponentiation. Like many such quantum circuit subroutines, we may need additional qubits for the computations outside the main circuit description. As in section 9.4, we can do modular exponentiation in $O\left(\ell_{\text{bits}}^3\right)$ gates using algorithms similar to the simple classical versions.

We have one last thing to observe about U before we move on to the circuit for order finding and its analysis. With r the order of a modulo M, the kets

$$\left|w_j\right\rangle = \frac{1}{\sqrt{r}} \sum_{k=0}^{r-1} e^{-\frac{2\pi kji}{r}} \left|a^k \bmod M\right\rangle$$

are eigenvectors of U for $0 \le j \le r$. To test this, we apply U to each of these expressions:

$$
\begin{aligned}
U\left|w_j\right\rangle &= U\left(\frac{1}{\sqrt{r}} \sum_{k=0}^{r-1} e^{-\frac{2\pi kji}{r}} \left|a^k \bmod M\right\rangle\right) \\
&= \frac{1}{\sqrt{r}} \sum_{k=0}^{r-1} e^{-\frac{2\pi kji}{r}} \left|a^{k+1} \bmod M\right\rangle
\end{aligned}
$$

$$= \frac{1}{\sqrt{r}} \sum_{k=0}^{r-1} e^{-\frac{2\pi(k+1-1)ji}{r}} \left| a^{k+1} \bmod M \right\rangle$$

$$= \frac{1}{\sqrt{r}} \sum_{k=0}^{r-1} e^{-\frac{2\pi(k+1)ji}{r}} e^{-\frac{2\pi(-1)ji}{r}} \left| a^{k+1} \bmod M \right\rangle$$

$$= e^{\frac{2\pi ij}{r}} \frac{1}{\sqrt{r}} \sum_{k=0}^{r-1} e^{-\frac{2\pi(k+1)ji}{r}} \left| a^{k+1} \bmod M \right\rangle$$

$$= e^{\frac{2\pi ji}{r}} \left| w_j \right\rangle .$$

Even though we use r explicitly in the above equations, remember that we do not know what it is yet! We have shown only that the eigenvalues corresponding to the eigenvectors $\left| w_j \right\rangle$ are

$$e^{\frac{2\pi ji}{r}}$$

as j goes from 0 to $r-1$. We use phase estimation to get at those eigenvalues and, hence, r.

Exercise 10.23

Remembering that r is the order of a modulo M, show that

$$\sum_{k=0}^{r-1} e^{-\frac{2\pi kji}{r}} \left| a^k \bmod M \right\rangle = \sum_{k=0}^{r-1} e^{-\frac{2\pi(k+1)ji}{r}} \left| a^{k+1} \bmod M \right\rangle .$$

10.6.2 The circuit

To set up our circuit, we need two quantum registers. Since we use phase estimation, the first register needs enough qubits to get us the accuracy we need. This is ℓ_ϵ. The number of qubits in the second register is ℓ_{bits}.

The circuit for the quantum portion of the order-finding algorithm is in Figure 10.12. The part of the circuit labeled $\mathbf{U_{PE}}$ is the core of the setup for the phase estimation. Referring back to the general phase estimation circuit in Figure 10.11, $\mathbf{U_{PE}}$ needs to prepare an eigenvector in the second register and handle the controlled $\mathbf{U}^{2^j}$ gates.

Unfortunately, there is nothing that allows us to create

$$\left| w_j \right\rangle = \frac{1}{\sqrt{r}} \sum_{k=0}^{r-1} e^{-\frac{2\pi kji}{r}} \left| a^k \bmod M \right\rangle$$

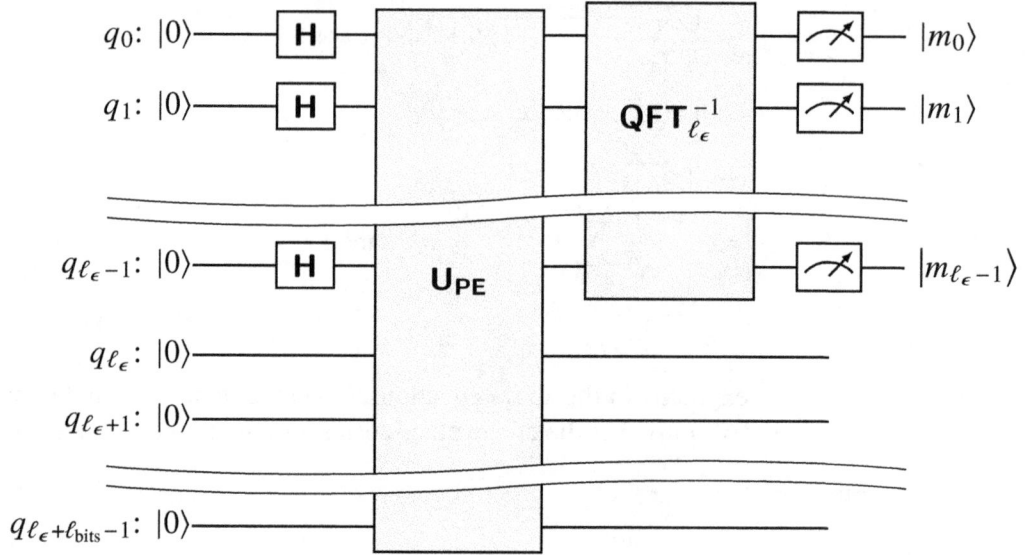

Figure 10.12: The order-finding circuit

directly. The phases φ_j we wish to estimate are $\frac{j}{r}$.

When in a quandary in a quantum algorithm, create a superposition! Consider

$$\frac{1}{\sqrt{r}} \sum_{j=0}^{r-1} |w_j\rangle .$$

The $\frac{1}{\sqrt{r}}$ out front is the common probability amplitude of all the kets. Squaring this and multiplying by r gives us the required value of 1. Expanding the expression,

$$\frac{1}{\sqrt{r}} \sum_{j=0}^{r-1} |w_j\rangle = \frac{1}{\sqrt{r}} \sum_{j=0}^{r-1} \frac{1}{\sqrt{r}} \sum_{k=0}^{r-1} e^{-\frac{2\pi k j i}{r}} |a^k \bmod M\rangle$$

$$= \frac{1}{\sqrt{r}} \sum_{k=0}^{r-1} \frac{1}{\sqrt{r}} \sum_{j=0}^{r-1} e^{-\frac{2\pi k j i}{r}} |a^k \bmod M\rangle$$

$$= \frac{1}{\sqrt{r}} \sum_{k=0}^{r-1} \frac{1}{\sqrt{r}} \left[\sum_{j=0}^{r-1} e^{-\frac{2\pi k j i}{r}} \right] |a^k \bmod M\rangle$$

$$= \frac{1}{\sqrt{r}} \sum_{k=0}^{r-1} \frac{1}{\sqrt{r}} r \delta_{k,0} |a^k \bmod M\rangle$$

$$= |a^0 \bmod M\rangle$$
$$= |1\rangle_{\ell_{\text{bits}}},$$

where the equality involving $\delta_{k,0}$ follows from the extended summation formula for roots of unity in section 10.1.1.

The value $|1\rangle_{\ell_{\text{bits}}}$ is **not** $|11\cdots11\rangle_{\ell_{\text{bits}}}$ but is instead the ket $|00\cdots01\rangle_{\ell_{\text{bits}}}$, assuming the right-most bit is the least significant.

So while we cannot prepare an individual eigenvector $|w_j\rangle$, it is simple to prepare $|1\rangle_{\ell_{\text{bits}}}$, as in this circuit:

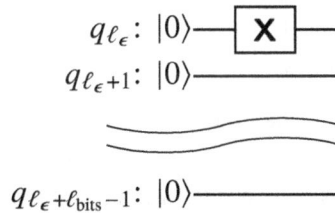

$$q\ell_\epsilon: |0\rangle - \boxed{\mathbf{X}} -$$
$$q\ell_{\epsilon+1}: |0\rangle -$$
$$q\ell_\epsilon+\ell_{\text{bits}}-1: |0\rangle -$$

This is the first part of $\mathbf{U_{PE}}$ for the lower quantum register. $\mathbf{U_{PE}}$ is the sequence of controlled-$\mathbf{U}^{2^j}$ gates from Figure 10.11.

Unlike the phase estimation algorithm, we use a superposition of eigenvectors instead of a single one as the input to the lower quantum register. We're not finished because what comes out of our circuit after applying the inverse QFT requires more work to get to r. In the next section, we use continued fractions to bring us closer to the factorization.

10.6.3 The continued fraction part

We chose ℓ_ϵ so that for $0 \le j \le r-1$, we can find approximations φ_j to the phases $\frac{j}{r}$ of U's eigenvalues accurate to $2\ell_{\text{bits}} + 1$ bits, with probability $\ge \frac{1-\epsilon}{r}$. j satisfies $0 \le j < r$, where each j is as probable as another. This is another way of saying that the j we get are uniformly distributed.

The output of the phase estimation algorithm after measurement is

$$\varphi_j = \frac{c_j}{2^\epsilon} \approx \frac{j}{r}.$$

We've done a lot of quantum work, and we have in hand a rational number $\frac{c_j}{2^\epsilon}$ approximation to $\frac{j}{r}$. We want to get to $\frac{j}{r}$ and then r.

If $\gcd(c_j, 2^\epsilon) \ne 1$, we try again because the fraction is not in reduced form. If c_j and 2^ϵ are coprime, we test if

$$a^{2^\epsilon} \equiv 1 \bmod M.$$

If this succeeds, we take $r = 2^\epsilon$, and we are finished. c_j and 2^ϵ will be coprime if and only if c_j is odd, and there are many such candidates less than 2^ϵ.

We might just get a bad result with $\frac{c_j}{2^\epsilon}$ being, essentially, garbage. In this case, we can try again or decrease ϵ, thereby increasing ℓ_ϵ.

We now employ the following result about approximations and continued fractions.

> Let $\frac{a}{b}$ be a rational number in reduced form. Every reduced rational number $\frac{c}{d}$ that satisfies
> $$\left| \frac{a}{b} - \frac{c}{d} \right| < \frac{1}{2d^2}$$
> is a convergent of $\frac{a}{b}$. [122, Theorem 19]
>
> (We discussed continued fractions and convergents in section 3.5.4.)

This statement is quite powerful: given two rational numbers, if the second is sufficiently close to the first, then the second is a convergent of the first. Reworking this for our situation gives the following result.

> By our choice of ℓ_{bits} and ℓ_ϵ, every reduced rational number $\varphi_j = \frac{c_j}{2^\epsilon}$ that satisfies
> $$\left| \varphi_j - \frac{j}{r} \right| = \left| \frac{c_j}{2^\epsilon} - \frac{j}{r} \right| < \frac{1}{2r^2}$$
> is a convergent of $\frac{j}{r}$.

If $\frac{c_j}{2^\epsilon}$ is a good approximation to $\frac{j}{r}$ then it is accurate to $2\ell_{\text{bits}} + 1$ bits with probability $\geq \frac{1-\epsilon}{r}$. What does it mean for some x to be accurate to some y for some number of bits b? Simply that

$$|x - y| \leq \frac{1}{2^b} = 2^{-b}.$$

Therefore,

$$\left| \varphi_j - \frac{j}{r} \right| = \left| \frac{c_j}{2^\epsilon} - \frac{j}{r} \right| \leq \frac{1}{2^{2\ell_{\text{bits}}+1}} = \frac{1}{2 \times \left(2^{\ell_{\text{bits}}} \right)^2} \leq \frac{1}{2M^2} < \frac{1}{2r^2}$$

by our definition of ℓ_{bits} and noting that $r \leq M$.

We now start computing the convergents for the known reduced fraction $\frac{c_j}{2^\epsilon}$. Among these will be $\frac{j}{r}$ in reduced form. We test the denominators of the convergents as candidates for r. When we find one that works, we are done.

The complexity of the overall algorithm is dominated by the quantum modular exponentiation, and so is $O\left(\ell_{\text{bits}}^3\right)$.

10.7 Shor's factoring algorithm

We now have the tools we need for Shor's factoring algorithm to factor integers in polynomial time on a sufficiently large quantum computer. The is a near-exponential improvement over the best known classical methods we described in section 10.2.

The complete algorithm has both classical and quantum components. Work is done on both kinds of machines to get to the answer. The quantum portion drops us down to polynomial complexity in the number of gates using phase estimation, order finding, modular exponentiation, and the QFT.

Let odd M in **Z** be greater than 3 for which you have already tried the basic tricks from section 10.2.3 to check that it is not a multiple of 3, 5, 7, and so on. So that you don't waste your time, you should also try trial division using a small list of primes, although this is not necessary. It is necessary, however, to make sure that M is not a power of a prime number, and you can use Newton's method to test this.

So M is an odd positive number in **Z** that is not a power of a prime. It has a reasonable chance of being composite.

The following is the general approach to Shor's factoring algorithm given M as above:

1. Choose a random number a such that $1 < a < M$. Keep track of these values, since we might need to repeat this step.
2. Check if $\gcd(a, M) = 1$. If not, we have found a factor of M, and we are finished. This is pretty unlikely, but we know that a and M are coprime: they have no integer factors in common.
3. Find the nonzero order r of a mod M. This means that $a^r \equiv 1$ mod M. If r is odd, go back to step 1 and try again with a different a.
4. If r is even, we have

$$a^r \equiv 1 \bmod M \Rightarrow a^r - 1 \equiv 0 \bmod M$$
$$\Rightarrow \left(a^{r/2} - 1\right)\left(a^{r/2} + 1\right) \equiv 0 \bmod M.$$

5. Look at $\gcd(a^{\frac{r}{2}} - 1, M)$ and, if necessary, $\gcd(a^{\frac{r}{2}} + 1, M)$. If either of these does not equal 1, we have found a factor of M and succeeded.
6. If both of these greatest common divisors are 1, we repeat all the above from step 1 with another random a. We continue to do this until we find a factor.

To learn more

More advanced treatments go into this algorithm's full complexity analysis and number theory, starting with Shor's original paper. [202] [137, Chapter 11] [150, Chapter 3] [189, Chapter 5]

In 2001, scientists demonstrated factoring the number 15 via Shor's factoring algorithm on a 7-qubit NMR quantum computer. [221]

The Cirq developers provide detailed code for running Shor's algorithm. [43]

10.8   Summary

In this chapter, we did some hard math to understand how to factor integers much faster than we can classically. Along the way, we delved deeply into several nontrivial quantum algorithms used in other quantum applications. These algorithms include the Quantum Fourier Transform, phase estimation, and order finding. These form a sound basis for understanding other quantum algorithms and their circuits.

Next, we turn our attention to the connections between the slightly abstract concepts we have seen and the physical quantum computers we can build today.

To learn more

Although we have covered several of the most common quantum algorithms, there are many other quantum algorithms. Techniques such as order finding are part of advanced algorithms in addition to Shor's factorization. [116] [137] [153] [172] [117]

11

Getting Physical

*The non-physicist finds it hard to believe that really the
ordinary laws of physics, which he regards as the prototype
of inviolable precision, should be based on the statistical
tendency of matter to go over into disorder.*

– Erwin Schrödinger

It's time to discuss some considerations about how we go from theoretical mathematics and physics to the applied and experimental.

The qubits we make and use in the lab for research and those we will deploy for commercial applications involve physical hardware devices such as photonic and microwave controllers. They are subject to noise from the environment, their electronic components, and artifacts from manufacturing choices. Hardware improvements decrease the disturbances, but software and system ones can too. The long-term goal is to have fully fault-tolerant, error-corrected quantum computing devices.

This chapter concludes with a discussion of light and photons to illustrate how properties like superposition manifest themselves in the physical world. Though this book is a mathematical treatment of quantum computing, this section is a starting point for those who wish to see a physical approach.

Topics covered in this chapter

11.1 That's not logical

The qubits such as those in the last two chapters are examples of *logical qubits*. We can use them indefinitely, they never lose state when idle, and we can apply as many gates to them as we wish without errors.

When you build a quantum computer, the actual physical implementations of qubits aren't as perfect as logical qubits. Such a qubit, called a *physical qubit*, starts to lose its ability to hold onto a state after its *coherence time*. We also say that the qubit is *decohering*.

It's a goal of quantum computing researchers and engineers to delay the decay of a physical qubit's quantum state as long as possible. Since the decay is inevitable, a goal of fault tolerance and error correction is to handle and fix the effects of the qubits' decoherence throughout the execution of a circuit.

Is it possible to create objects that act like logical qubits from physical ones? Research today says "Yes," but it will require hundreds to thousands of physical qubits to make one logical qubit. When we get there, we will have *fault tolerance*, where errors are detected and corrected.

Small errors creep into the state when gates are applied. After too many gates, you pass the coherence time and the physical qubit becomes unreliable. The errors accumulate so much that further use and measurement are too inaccurate for practical computing.

Two simultaneous and connected goals when constructing a quantum computer are to increase coherence time and reduce errors.

You may see or hear the term "short-depth circuit." How many gates are in such a circuit? There is no hard and fast number, though expect it to increase over time. A reasonable working definition of a short-depth circuit is one you can run and from which you can get usable results before decoherence sets in and errors overwhelm the computation. When working with quantum computing hardware, ensure you can see the current operating statistics about coherence times and errors.

11.2   What does it take to be a qubit?

In his 2000 paper "The Physical Implementation of Quantum Computation," David P. DiVincenzo laid out five "requirements for the implementation of quantum computation." [69]

In his words, they are:

1. *A scalable physical system with well characterized qubits*
2. *The ability to initialize the state of the qubits to a simple fiducial state, such as $|000\ldots\rangle$*
3. *Long relevant decoherence times, much longer than the gate operation time*
4. *A "universal" set of quantum gates*
5. *A qubit-specific measurement capability*

Let's discuss what each of these means, following his lead.

Scalable physical system

In the physical system we manufacture for quantum computing, we need to create a qubit with two clearly delineated states, $|0\rangle$ and $|1\rangle$. Other states may be possible, but we must control the qubit to keep it at either $|0\rangle$ or $|1\rangle$.

The qubit must be able to move into a valid superposition of $|0\rangle$ and $|1\rangle$ that obeys the rules with amplitudes and probabilities. As we add more qubits, we must be able to entangle the qubits either directly by physical means or indirectly through a sequence of gates in a circuit.

It is not necessary to physically connect every qubit with every other qubit. The architecture determines the degree of connectivity so that overall performance and manufacturability are optimized. For example, Figure 11.1 is a connection map you might see for a quantum computer where each atom connects to its nearest horizontal or vertical neighbor.

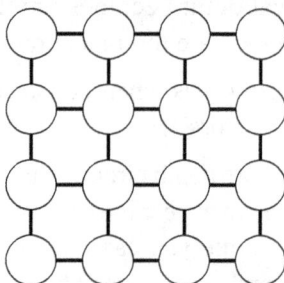

Figure 11.1: A 16-qubit quantum computer "nearest neighbor" connection map

Through the entanglement, starting with the physical connections, we must be able to see and use the doubling of the complex (Hilbert) vector space for every additional qubit added to the system.

Since one qubit is never enough, we should be able to add, over time, sufficient additional qubits to do nontrivial quantum calculations. The cost to add these qubits should not be prohibitive. We would not, for example, want the economic cost or the engineering complexity to scale exponentially as we increase the number of qubits.

Initializing qubits

With very high probability, we must be able to initialize a qubit to a known initial state. We call this "high-fidelity state preparation."

Since it is common for algorithms to begin with qubits in $|0\rangle$, this is a good choice. If $|1\rangle$ is a better choice for the technology, applying an **X** gate after initialization gives an equivalent effect.

Long decoherence

As we will see in section 11.4, decoherence causes a qubit to move from a desired quantum state to something else. If too much decoherence happens, the state is random and useless.

The qubit must have a long enough coherence time to execute enough quantum gates to implement an algorithm that does something useful. If you have a long coherence time, but your gates take a long time to run, that may be equivalent to a short coherence time but with fast gates. Therefore, these two factors are paired and will be critical for determining the total circuit execution time.

Here's a rough analogy to give you an idea about coherence time. Suppose I send you a photograph of a maple tree, and you are looking at it on your phone. Due to a hardware glitch, 100 pixels on the screen turn red every second. Despite this "noise" in the image, you can initially still tell the image is a maple tree, though the picture is becoming less and less coherent. At some point, you can no longer identify the tree as a maple; sometime later, you cannot even tell that you are looking at a tree. The coherence time is the length of time you had before that image became so chaotic that it lost its essential information.

Long coherence, fast enough gates, and low error rates will be the key to success with Noisy Intermediate Scale Quantum (NISQ) quantum computers.

Measurement capability

We must be able to force the qubit reliably into one or the other of two orthonormal basis states, often $|0\rangle$ and $|1\rangle$. We call this *high-fidelity measurement*. The error rate of this operation must be low enough to allow for effective computation. If we get the wrong measurement answer, we lose all the previous work on executing the circuit.

If we move the qubit to $|+\rangle = \frac{\sqrt{2}}{2}|0\rangle + \frac{\sqrt{2}}{2}|1\rangle$, it should measure to either $|0\rangle$ or $|1\rangle$ with 0.5 probability each. The same is true for quantum states with known probability amplitudes before measurement.

Universal set of gates

You can't build a house if you don't have the right tools. You can't make general quantum algorithms without a complete enough set of gates.

In section 9.3, we looked at how to construct a gate from other, more primitive ones. The gates native to a particular technology implementing qubits may not look like the ones we have seen in this book. Still, as long as they can be composed into a definitive collection, we can develop, implement, and deploy practical algorithms.

11.3   Quantum cores and interconnects

However you build or trap objects that behave like physical qubits, there is a maximum number of qubits that you can put in a device and reliably control. Even if you could put more, there may be other factors that put an upper bound on the qubit capacity. Larger semiconductor chips, for example, are difficult to manufacture, and any flaws could spoil the chips and decrease yield.

I call such a unit with a fixed number of qubits a *quantum core*. These units are analogous to the multiple cores in classical processing units. For example, my desktop computer has an AMD processor with 12 cores. Figure 11.2 is a diagram that helps us visualize a quantum core with 16 qubits.

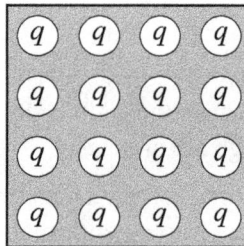

Figure 11.2: A single quantum core with 16 qubits

I chose 16 as a convenient number of qubits to illustrate the concepts in this section. Industry vendors have demonstrated cores with several dozen to several hundred qubits.

Practical quantum computers will need hundreds of thousands to millions of qubits upon which we can run circuits with millions of gates. Will a logical qubit extend beyond one physical core? How can we hope to do this scaling if our core size is limited to a few hundred?

Classical processor manufacturers added more cores to deal with the slowing of Moore's Law. If we can't make a processor with more transistors, make more processors, call them cores, and connect them. So, let's add three more quantum cores for a total of four, as in Figure 11.3.

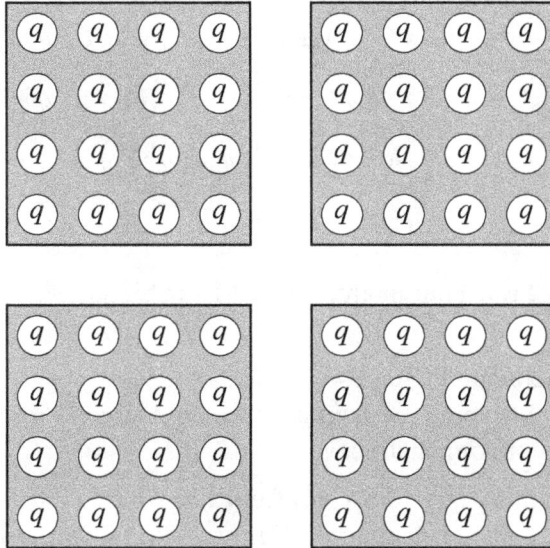

Figure 11.3: Four individual 16-qubit quantum cores

Do we now have a 64 = 4 × 16 qubit quantum computer? No, we have four 16-bit quantum computers. As shown, there are no connections between the cores. We cannot perform 2-qubit operations on qubits in different cores. In particular, we cannot entangle qubits across cores, so the quantum programming model fails for the system as a whole.

The connections we need must support these quantum operations with low enough error rates to make them useful. In Figure 11.4, I show *quantum interconnects* with double lines between each horizontally or vertically adjacent cores.

The simplest way to think of an interconnect is as an extension of how we connect qubits within a core to perform operations such as **SWAP** and **CNOT**. However, the situation is much more difficult unless we use very similar technology within the core and for the interconnects.

First, are we working with interconnects of quantum cores of the same modality, or, for example, are we trying to link a cold atom core with a superconducting one? Each technology has its pros and cons. Cold atom qubits have relatively slow gates but long coherence times.

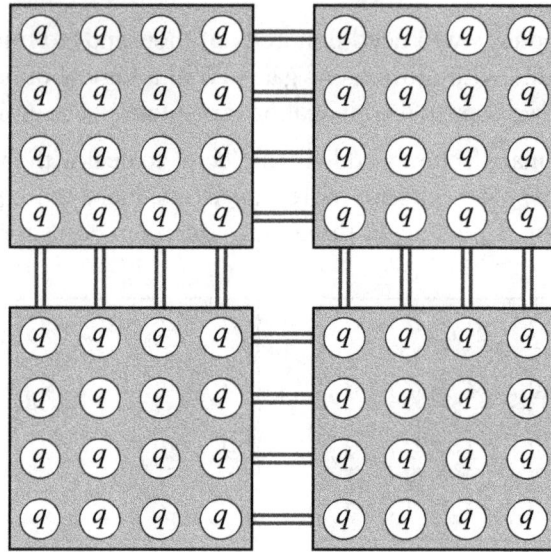

Figure 11.4: Four interconnected 16-qubit quantum cores

We can fabricate superconducting cores on chips allowing fast gates, but the qubits have short coherence times. We might be trying to use cold atoms for quantum memory and superconducting qubits for computation.

Second, how do we move quantum states from a core to the interconnect medium, such as a fiber optic cable, and into another core? This will likely involve *transduction*, where we might move the quantum state from an ion to a photon to a cold atom, for example. [133] Teleportation, as we discussed in section 9.3.5, is involved here.

Finally, must we perform error correction on the transmitted quantum states? We need more qubits to do error correction, so we need more cores. Adding more cores might increase the need for error correction, and hence, more qubits.

We will need quantum interconnects to:

- build large quantum computers from homogeneous cores
- build large quantum computers from heterogeneous cores
- build more modular quantum systems
- build quantum computers with redundant cores for greater reliability
- design specialized quantum cores for different algorithms and then combine them into larger systems
- connect quantum computers and quantum memory bi-directionally
- network quantum computers and transmit quantum-encoded data across a network
- connect quantum computers and memory to quantum sensors for positioning, navigation, timing, and radio-frequency reception

To learn more

I think it is likely that quantum computer providers will provide quantum interconnects between their homogeneous quantum cores. Nevertheless, within a qubit modality such as superconducting or neutral atoms, independent, commercial, and academic researchers are working together to address problems and their possible solutions. [6] [135]

Since quantum interconnects are more general than quantum computing, their design requirements and roadmaps are being studied by scientists and engineers in areas such as chemistry and communications. [8] [9]

11.4 Decoherence

There are three measurements that quantum computing researchers frequently use to measure coherence time: T_1, T_2, and its cousin T_2^*. They are single physical qubit measurements, so we can use the Bloch sphere to discuss them. Their use goes back to Felix Bloch's work on nuclear magnetic resonance (NMR) in the 1940s. [18]

Let's begin with T_1.

11.4.1 T_1

T_1 goes under several names, all of them connected to the physics of various underlying quantum processes:

- relaxation time,
- thermal relaxation,
- longitudinal relaxation,
- spontaneous emission time,
- amplitude damping, and
- longitudinal coherence time.

It is related to the energy loss as the quantum state decays from the higher energy $|1\rangle$ state to the $|0\rangle$ ground state. This energy is transmitted to, or leaked into, the environment and lost from the qubit. We measure T_1 in seconds or some fraction thereof, such as microseconds. A microsecond is one-millionth of a second, 10^{-6} seconds.

For the computation of T_1, an **X** gate moves the qubit state from $|0\rangle$ to $|1\rangle$. The decay toward the lower energy state $|0\rangle$ is exponential and follows the rule

$$e^{-\frac{t}{T_1}}$$

for some constant T_1. Informally, the larger the value of T_1, the longer the qubit stays closer to $|1\rangle$. Figure 11.5 shows the decay from $|1\rangle$.

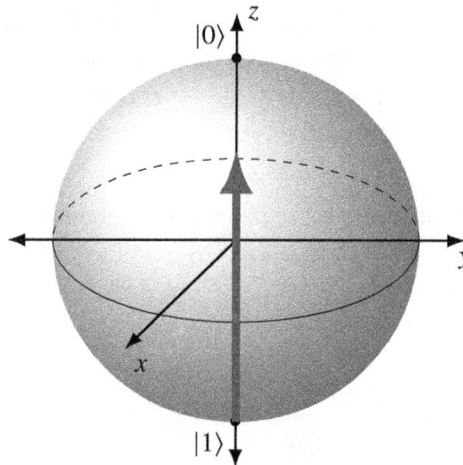

Figure 11.5: T_1 quantum state decay

In the following, we use the Greek letter Δ, "Delta," to indicate the incremental difference between some value and the next.

An outline of a scheme to compute T_1 looks like this:

1. Initialize a counter c in $\mathbf{Z}$ to 0. Initialize time t to 0. Initialize the number of shots (runs) per time increment to some integer n. For example, $n = 1024$ is reasonable. Choose some very small ϵ in $\mathbf{R}$.
2. Set the time increment between measurements to some small value Δt.
3. Add Δt to t.
4. Initialize the qubit to $|0\rangle$, apply $\mathbf{X}$, and wait t seconds.
5. Measure. If we see $|1\rangle$, add 1 to c.
6. Go back to step 4 and repeat $n - 1$ times. If we have done this already, go to the next step.
7. Compute $p_t = \frac{c}{n}$ as the percentage of times we have seen $|1\rangle$.
8. Save and plot the data (t, p_t).
9. Reset c to 0, go back to step 3, and repeat until $p_t < \epsilon$.

As t increases, we expect to see $|1\rangle$ less and less frequently.

The flowchart in Figure 11.6 shows an example process for computing T_1.

I show the decay of the quantum states for two qubits, q_1 and q_2, in Figure 11.7. T_1 is the value of t when $p_t = \frac{1}{e} \approx 0.368$. In this example, q_2 has a larger T_1 and *a larger longitudinal coherence time.*

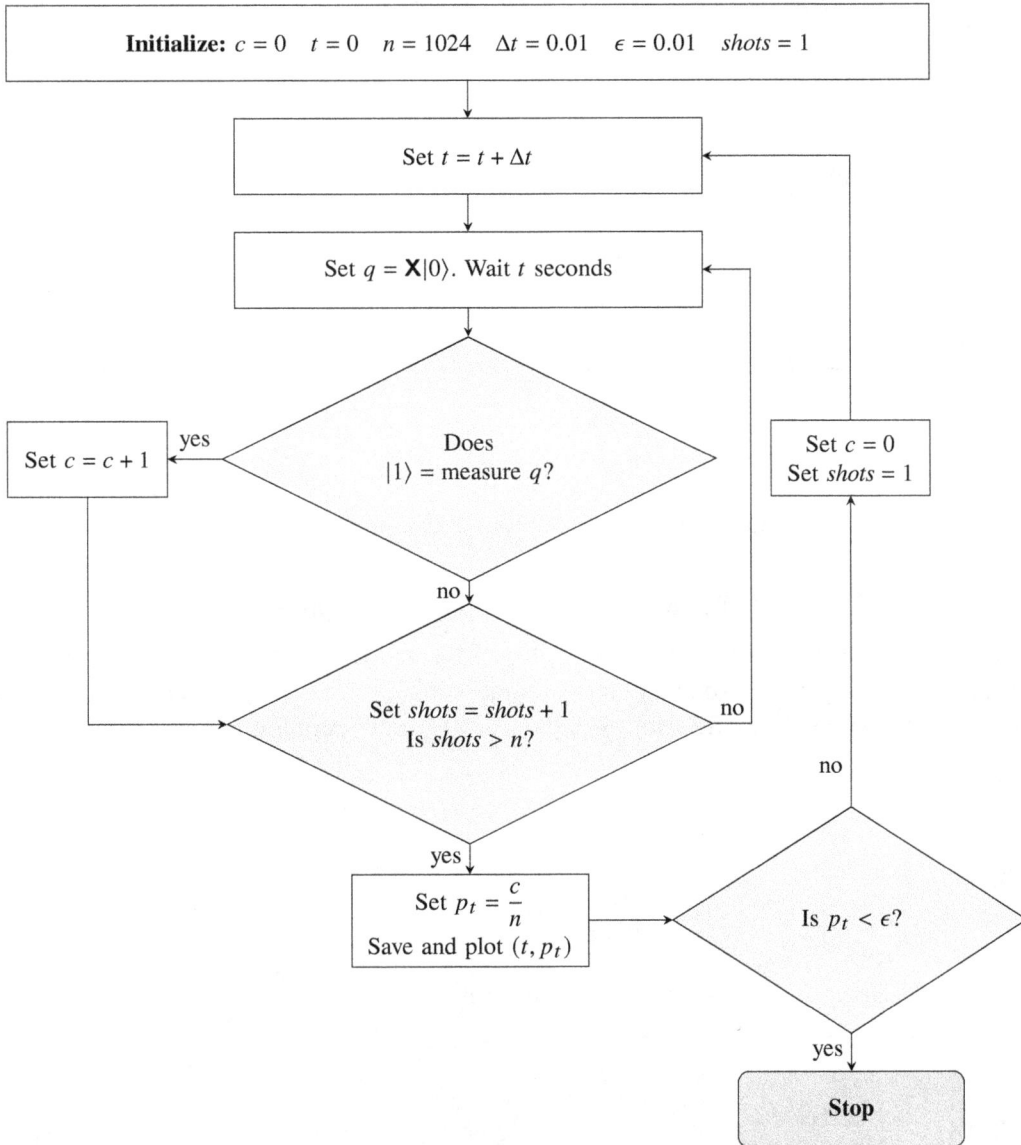

Figure 11.6: Flowchart for calculating T_1

It's interesting to ask at this point when my qubit is in state $|0\rangle$ due to the decay. If we wait long enough after T_1, will the qubit go entirely to the lower energy state? Theoretically, it is getting asymptotically closer, and the probability of seeing $|0\rangle$ is increasing to 0.9999+.

In practice, if you want the qubit back in an initial $|0\rangle$ state, you wait a time which is a few integer multiples of T_1. You now either assume that you statistically are at $|0\rangle$ or you do

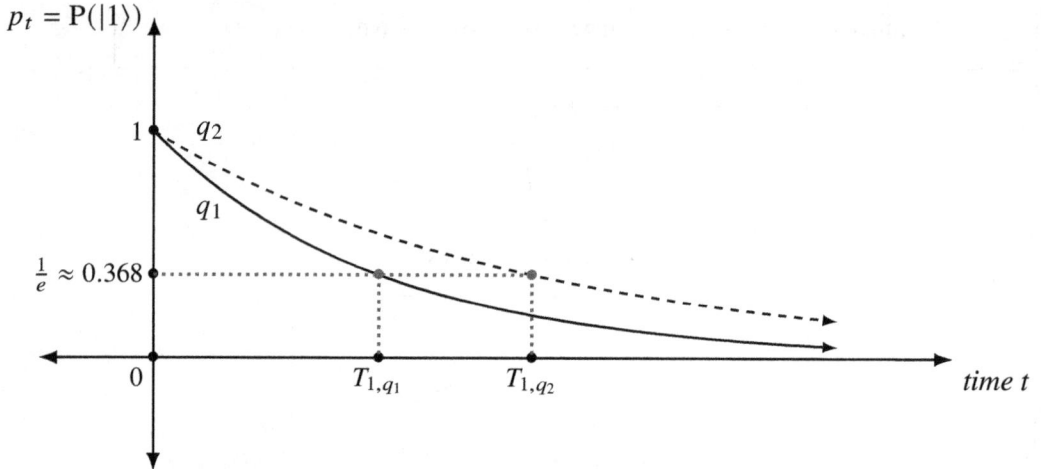

Figure 11.7: T_1 decay for two example qubits

a measurement. If you get $|0\rangle$, you are done. If you get $|1\rangle$, apply an **X**.

This last step depends on your ability to do such a conditional action in your hardware and control software. If you can, you don't have to wait past T_1; you can measure and conditionally move to $|0\rangle$ when you wish. See, for example, the $|0\rangle$ reset operation in section 7.6.14.

Given

$$P(|1\rangle) = e^{-t/T_1},$$

we have

$$P(|0\rangle) = 1 - e^{-t/T_1}.$$

If you wait $4T_1$ seconds, the probability of your getting $|0\rangle$ is $1 - e^{-4T_1/T_1} = 1 - e^{-4} \approx 0.98168$. If you wait $10T_1$ seconds, the probability is $1 - e^{-10} \approx 0.99995$.

11.4.2 T_2 and T_2^*

If T_1 concerns itself with going from the south pole to the north, T_2 adds the extra element of what is happening at the equator. As a reminder, when I say "the equator," I mean the intersection of the xy-plane with the Bloch sphere.

Like T_1, T_2 and its related metric T_2^* go by several names:

- dephasing time,
- elastic scattering time,
- phase coherence time,
- phase damping, and

- transverse coherence time.

Let's begin with T_2^*. In a perfect world, the circuit

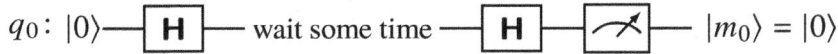

$$q_0: |0\rangle \boxed{H} \text{— wait some time —} \boxed{H} \boxed{\measuredangle} \quad |m_0\rangle = |0\rangle$$

would always return $|0\rangle$ with a probability of 1.0.

The circuit should bring us from $|0\rangle$ to $|+\rangle$ and back to $|0\rangle$. We move to the equator and then go back to $|0\rangle$. Note that neither $|0\rangle$ nor $|1\rangle$ has a phase component, so we need to experiment elsewhere, and the equator is the obvious choice.

This doesn't happen with a physical qubit. Instead, once we move to the equator, we begin drifting a little around the xy-plane.

In the example in Figure 11.8 on the Bloch sphere, once we get to $|+\rangle$, we move counterclockwise by some small angle φ in some small time increment. That is, the qubit state is not stable.

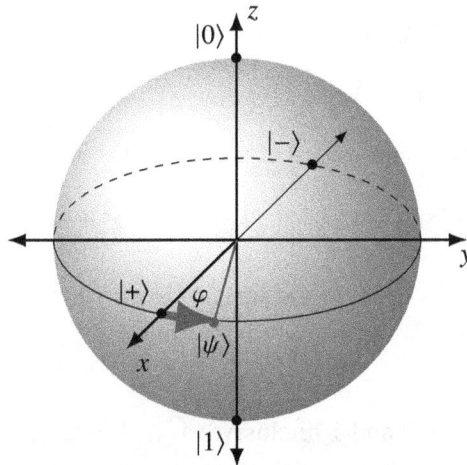

Figure 11.8: Phase drift of qubit state

We also expect the state to move toward lower energy, but we are focusing on what is happening with the phase. Similarly, when we look at T_1, there can be phase drift, but we are looking at the longitudinal decoherence.

This is an idealized and simplified version of the circuit where we see only the phase shift:

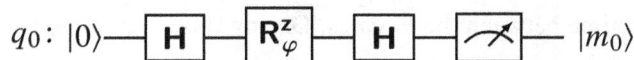

$$q_0: |0\rangle \boxed{H} \boxed{R_\varphi^z} \boxed{H} \boxed{\measuredangle} \quad |m_0\rangle$$

Consider the matrix version:

$$
\mathbf{H}\,\mathbf{R}^{\mathbf{z}}_{\varphi}\,\mathbf{H}\,|0\rangle =
\begin{bmatrix} \frac{\sqrt{2}}{2} & \frac{\sqrt{2}}{2} \\ \frac{\sqrt{2}}{2} & -\frac{\sqrt{2}}{2} \end{bmatrix}
\begin{bmatrix} 1 & 0 \\ 0 & e^{\varphi i} \end{bmatrix}
\begin{bmatrix} \frac{\sqrt{2}}{2} & \frac{\sqrt{2}}{2} \\ \frac{\sqrt{2}}{2} & -\frac{\sqrt{2}}{2} \end{bmatrix}
\begin{bmatrix} 1 \\ 0 \end{bmatrix}
$$

$$
= \begin{bmatrix} \frac{1}{2}+\frac{1}{2}e^{\varphi i} & \frac{1}{2}-\frac{1}{2}e^{\varphi i} \\ \frac{1}{2}-\frac{1}{2}e^{\varphi i} & \frac{1}{2}+\frac{1}{2}e^{\varphi i} \end{bmatrix}
\begin{bmatrix} 1 \\ 0 \end{bmatrix}
= \begin{bmatrix} \frac{1}{2}+\frac{1}{2}e^{i\varphi} \\ \frac{1}{2}-\frac{1}{2}e^{i\varphi} \end{bmatrix}
$$

$$
= \left(\frac{1}{2}+\frac{1}{2}e^{i\varphi}\right)|0\rangle + \left(\frac{1}{2}-\frac{1}{2}e^{i\varphi}\right)|1\rangle
$$

$$
= \frac{1}{2}\left((1+e^{i\varphi})\,|0\rangle + (1-e^{i\varphi})\,|1\rangle\right)
$$

When $\varphi = 0$, we get $|0\rangle$, as expected. When $\varphi = \pi$, $\mathbf{R}^{\mathbf{z}}_{\varphi} = \mathbf{R}^{\mathbf{z}}_{\pi} = \mathbf{Z}$, and the result is $|1\rangle$. When $0 < \varphi < \pi$, the two probability amplitudes are nonzero.

In particular, the amplitude of $|0\rangle$ is

$$
\frac{1}{2}\left(1+e^{i\varphi}\right) = \frac{1}{2}\left(1+\cos(\varphi)+i\sin(\varphi)\right).
$$

The probability of getting $|0\rangle$ is the square of the absolute value of that expression, which is

$$
\frac{1}{4}|1+\cos(\varphi)+i\sin(\varphi)|^2 = \frac{1}{4}\left((1+\cos(\varphi))^2 + \sin(\varphi)^2\right)
$$

$$
= \frac{1}{4}\left(\sin(\varphi)^2 + \cos(\varphi)^2 + 2\cos(\varphi) + 1\right)
$$

$$
= \frac{1+\cos(\varphi)}{2}.
$$

Note that this value is between 0 and 1, inclusive, as it should be.

If the phase change continued at a constant rate over time, you might expect the graph to look like Figure 11.9.

Instead, there is decay toward a probability of 0.5 but with the same short-term periodic behavior as in Figure 11.10.

It is only short term because, eventually, the quantum state will fully decay to $|0\rangle$, and the final $\mathbf{H}$ will place the state on the equator. At that point, the probability of getting $|0\rangle$ is exactly 0.5.

We call the measurement here T_2^*, and the circuit is a *Ramsey experiment*. We are considering the wait time between the $\mathbf{H}$ gates. During this time, some rotation φ around the z-axis occurs.

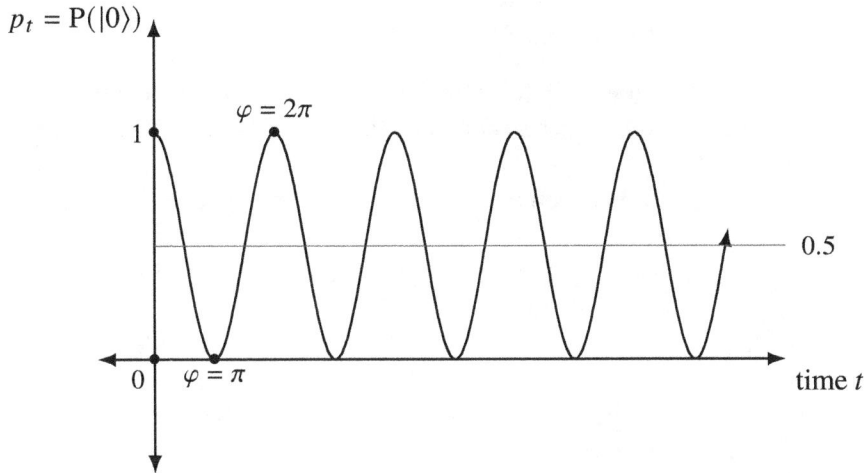

Figure 11.9: Constant phase change

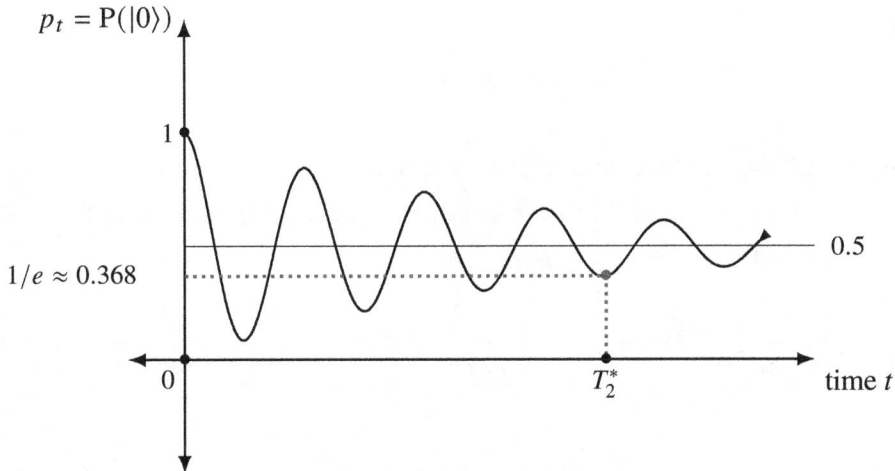

Figure 11.10: Phase change with decay

I want to emphasize again that what I have shown here assumed only one kind of noise, the phase drift, and even that was constant. In a real qubit, other noise and irregularities will affect the coherence, including longitudinal decoherence.

Moreover, by using $\mathbf{R}^{z}_{\varphi}$ to illustrate the phase drift, I've given the impression that the noise looks like a nice unitary transformation. It does not, as we see in the next section.

The high-level scheme to measure T_2^* is:

1. Initialize a counter c in $\mathbf{Z}$ to 0. Initialize time t to 0. Initialize the number of runs per time increment to some integer n. For example, $n = 1024$ is reasonable. Choose some very small ϵ in $\mathbf{R}$.
2. Set the time increment between measurements to some small value Δt.
3. Add Δt to t.
4. Initialize the qubit to $|0\rangle$, apply $\mathbf{H}$, and wait t seconds. Apply $\mathbf{H}$ again.
5. Measure. If we see $|1\rangle$, add 1 to c.
6. Go back to step 4 and repeat $n - 1$ times. If we have done this already, go to the next step.
7. Compute $p_t = \frac{c}{n}$ as the percentage of times we have seen $|1\rangle$.
8. Save and plot the data (t, p_t).
9. Reset c to 0, go back to step 3, and repeat until $0.5 - \epsilon < p_t < 0.5 + \epsilon$.

The circuit for step 4 is

$$q_0: |0\rangle \boxed{\mathbf{H}} \text{— wait } t \text{ seconds —} \boxed{\mathbf{H}} \boxed{\measuredangle} \ |m_0\rangle$$

For small enough Δt, T_2^* is the largest time t where $p_t \leq \frac{1}{e}$.

The flowchart in Figure 11.11 shows an example process for computing T_2^*.

We get a related metric T_2 via a *Hahn Echo* computed with a similar circuit:

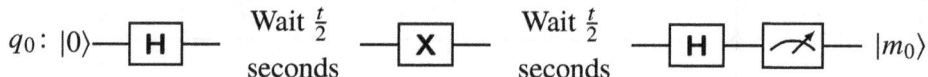

$$q_0: |0\rangle \boxed{\mathbf{H}} \text{— } \substack{\text{Wait } \frac{t}{2} \\ \text{seconds}} \text{ —} \boxed{\mathbf{X}} \text{— } \substack{\text{Wait } \frac{t}{2} \\ \text{seconds}} \text{ —} \boxed{\mathbf{H}} \boxed{\measuredangle} \ |m_0\rangle$$

The difference from T_2^* is that instead of waiting the full time t before the final $\mathbf{H}$, we wait half that long, do an $\mathbf{X}$, wait the remaining time, and then conclude with the $\mathbf{H}$ and measurement. By doing this, we are canceling some phase drift but keeping the effects of other noise. We call this technique ''refocusing.'' [197] This is related to the technique of *dynamical decoupling*, which helps ''decouple'' the qubit from the effects of noise from the surrounding environment. [223]

Generally, $T_2^* \leq T_2 \leq 2T_1$. [228]

11.4.3 Pure versus mixed states

Each of the quantum states we have considered so far is a *pure state*. These are single linear combinations of basis kets where the probability amplitudes are complex numbers. The sum

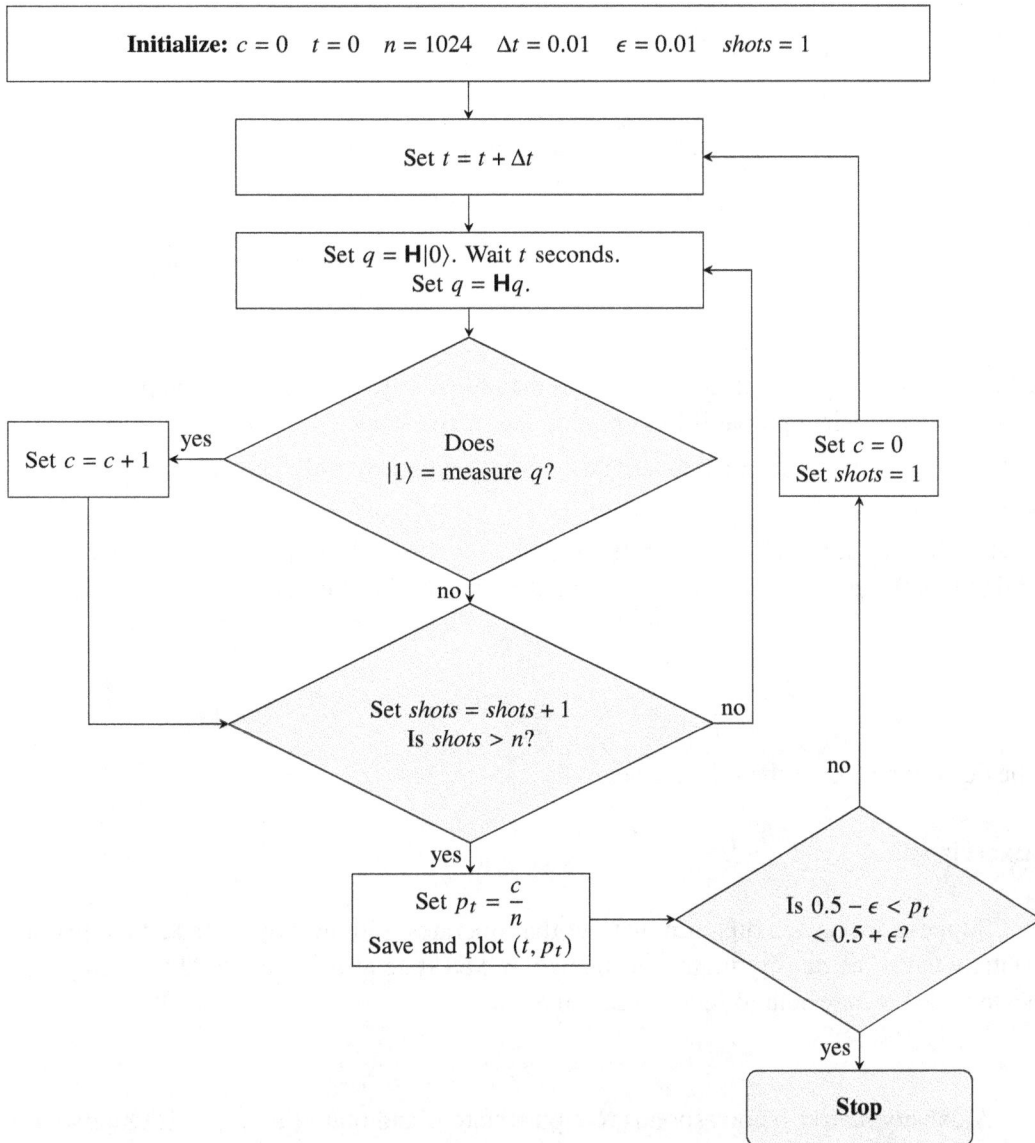

Figure 11.11: Flowchart for calculating T_2^*

of the squares of their absolute values adds up to 1. Each square of an absolute value is the probability that we will see the corresponding basis ket when we measure.

Sometimes we need to represent a collection, an *ensemble*, of pure states in which our quantum register may reside. This is different from a superposition, where we are looking at a quantum phenomenon related to the complex coefficients of the basis kets.

If $\{|\psi\rangle_1, \ldots, |\psi\rangle_k\}$ is a collection of pure quantum register states, we define a *mixed state M* as

$$M = \sum_{j=1}^{k} p_j |\psi\rangle_j \text{ for } 0 \le p_j \le 1$$

with p_j in $\mathbf{R}$ and

$$\sum_{j=1}^{k} p_j = 1 .$$

We have a double layer of probabilities with the probability amplitudes on the pure quantum states and the classical probabilities creating the mixed state.

A pure state is a special trivial case of a mixed state with only one quantum state in the ensemble with $p_1 = 1$.

The density matrix of a mixed state M is the sum of the density matrix of the pure states weighted by the p_j. If $\rho_j = |\psi_j\rangle\langle\psi_j|$ is the density matrix of a pure state in the ensemble, then

$$\rho = \sum_{j=1}^{k} p_j \rho_j$$

is the density matrix of the mixed state.

Exercise 11.1

Suppose we have a quantum gate $\mathbf{U}$ that operates with no errors. If M is a mixed state, what is the density matrix of the new mixed state after we apply $\mathbf{U}$ to each pure state in M? It may help to review section 8.2.3.

A density matrix ρ corresponds to a pure state if and only if $\mathrm{tr}(p^2) = 1$. Otherwise, $\mathrm{tr}(p^2) < 1$, and we have a nontrivial mixed state.

Consider the ensemble

$$\left\{ |\psi\rangle_1 = |+\rangle = \frac{\sqrt{2}}{2}(|0\rangle + |1\rangle), \ |\psi\rangle_2 = |-\rangle = \frac{\sqrt{2}}{2}(|0\rangle - |1\rangle) \right\} .$$

The sum $p|+\rangle + (1-p)|-\rangle$ is a nontrivial mixed state if $p \neq 0$ and $p \neq 1$. We might get such an ensemble if the computation is especially noisy and gets each result with the given probabilities.

We first compute the density matrices

$$\rho_1 = |+\rangle\langle+| = \begin{bmatrix} \frac{1}{2} & \frac{1}{2} \\ \frac{1}{2} & \frac{1}{2} \end{bmatrix} \quad \text{and} \quad \rho_2 = |-\rangle\langle-| = \begin{bmatrix} \frac{1}{2} & -\frac{1}{2} \\ -\frac{1}{2} & \frac{1}{2} \end{bmatrix}$$

and so

$$\rho = p \begin{bmatrix} \frac{1}{2} & \frac{1}{2} \\ \frac{1}{2} & \frac{1}{2} \end{bmatrix} + (1-p) \begin{bmatrix} \frac{1}{2} & -\frac{1}{2} \\ -\frac{1}{2} & \frac{1}{2} \end{bmatrix} = \begin{bmatrix} \frac{1}{2} & p-\frac{1}{2} \\ p-\frac{1}{2} & \frac{1}{2} \end{bmatrix}.$$

The square of ρ is

$$\begin{bmatrix} p^2 - p + \frac{1}{2} & p - \frac{1}{2} \\ p - \frac{1}{2} & p^2 - p + \frac{1}{2} \end{bmatrix},$$

with

$$\mathrm{tr}\left(\rho^2\right) = 2p^2 - 2p + 1.$$

If $p = 0$ or $p = 1$, this is a pure state. Plotting the graph for $0 \le p \le 1$ in Figure 11.12, we see that it is always less than 1 otherwise.

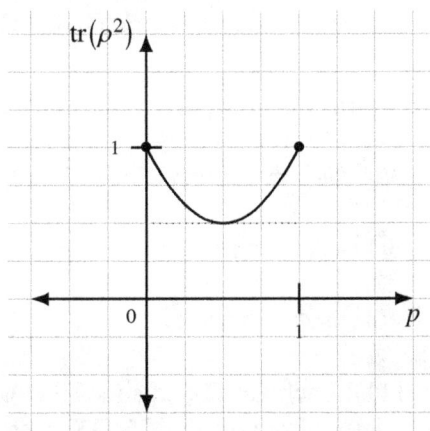

Figure 11.12: Plot showing values of p for pure and mixed states

Exercise 11.2

Prove algebraically that $2p^2 - 2p + 1 < 1$ when $0 < p < 1$.

11.5   Error correction for physical qubits

In section 2.1 and section 6.4, we looked at some basic ideas around classical repetition codes. If you want to send information, transmit multiple copies of it. If enough copies get through unscathed, the recipient can determine what you sent.

For the quantum situation, the No-Cloning Theorem (section 9.3.4) says that we can't copy the state of a qubit, so traditional repetition is not available.

We can do entanglement, and it turns out that this is powerful enough when combined with aspects of traditional error correction to give us quantum error correction, or *QEC*.

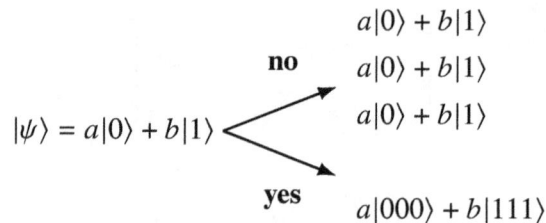

$$
|\psi\rangle = a|0\rangle + b|1\rangle
\begin{array}{l}
\textbf{no} \\
\\
\\
\textbf{yes}
\end{array}
\begin{array}{l}
a|0\rangle + b|1\rangle \\
a|0\rangle + b|1\rangle \\
a|0\rangle + b|1\rangle \\
\\
a|000\rangle + b|111\rangle
\end{array}
$$

How can we go from $|\psi\rangle = a|0\rangle + b|1\rangle$ to $a|000\rangle + b|111\rangle$? As you start thinking about such questions, there are two good starting points: ''Would applying an **H** change the situation into something I know how to handle?'' and ''How might a **CNOT** and entanglement affect things?''.

Since I already let on that entanglement is part of the solution, note that a simple

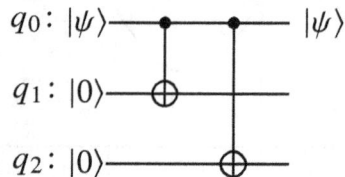

$$
\begin{array}{l}
q_0: |\psi\rangle \quad\bullet\quad\bullet\quad |\psi\rangle \\
q_1: |0\rangle \quad\oplus \\
q_2: |0\rangle \quad\quad\oplus
\end{array}
$$

takes $|\psi\rangle|0\rangle|0\rangle$ to $a|000\rangle + b|111\rangle$. Each **CNOT** changes the $|0\rangle$ in q_1 and q_2 to $|1\rangle$ if the amplitude b of $|1\rangle$ in $|\psi\rangle$ is nonzero. Similarly, the **CNOT** does nothing if the amplitude a of $|0\rangle$ in $|\psi\rangle$ is nonzero.

Given this, how can we fix bit flips?

11.5.1   Correcting bit flips

In the classical case of a bit, only one thing can go wrong: the value changes from **0** to **1**, or vice versa. Of course, noise may cause multiple bits to change, but for one bit, there is only one kind of error.

In the quantum case, a bit flip interchanges $|0\rangle$ and $|1\rangle$ so that a general state $a|0\rangle + b|1\rangle$ becomes $b|0\rangle + a|1\rangle$ instead. From section 7.6.2, this is what an **X** gate does, but when we think about noise and errors, we are saying that a bit flip *might* happen, not that it definitely does.

If we knew that an **X** was applied on purpose, we could do another one and fix the problem. If the bit flip happened because of an error, we need to get more clever. Consider the circuit in Figure 11.13.

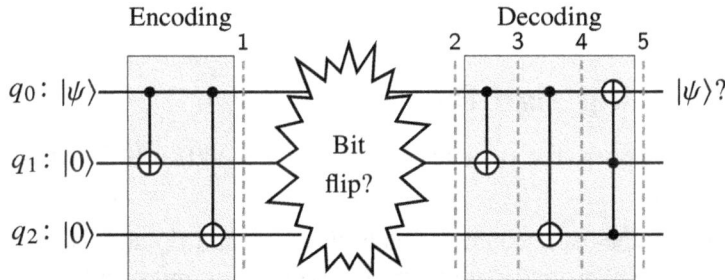

Figure 11.13: Circuit correcting a single bit flip

We start the analysis by looking at the possible quantum states at each numbered vertical line. We begin with $|\psi\rangle = |0\rangle$.

	Initial $|\psi\rangle$	Step 1	Step 2	Step 3	Step 4	Step 5	Final $|\psi\rangle$
No errors	$|0\rangle$	$|000\rangle$	$|000\rangle$	$|000\rangle$	$|000\rangle$	$|000\rangle$	$|0\rangle$
One error	$|0\rangle$	$|000\rangle$	$|001\rangle$	$|001\rangle$	$|001\rangle$	$|001\rangle$	$|0\rangle$
	$|0\rangle$	$|000\rangle$	$|010\rangle$	$|010\rangle$	$|010\rangle$	$|010\rangle$	$|0\rangle$
	$|0\rangle$	$|000\rangle$	$|100\rangle$	$|110\rangle$	$|111\rangle$	$|011\rangle$	$|0\rangle$
Two errors	$|0\rangle$	$|000\rangle$	$|011\rangle$	$|011\rangle$	$|011\rangle$	$|111\rangle$	$|1\rangle$
	$|0\rangle$	$|000\rangle$	$|101\rangle$	$|111\rangle$	$|110\rangle$	$|110\rangle$	$|1\rangle$
	$|0\rangle$	$|000\rangle$	$|110\rangle$	$|100\rangle$	$|101\rangle$	$|101\rangle$	$|1\rangle$
Three errors	$|0\rangle$	$|000\rangle$	$|111\rangle$	$|101\rangle$	$|100\rangle$	$|100\rangle$	$|1\rangle$

The circuit in Figure 11.13 corrects up to one bit flip error in q_0. When the error is not corrected, the result of the circuit is always a bit flip in q_0.

If the probability of getting a bit flip error is p, the probability of no error is $1 - p$. We previously worked through the full probability of our being able to fix at most a single error in section 6.4.

> ### Exercise 11.3
>
> What is the role of the Toffoli gate between vertical lines 4 and 5 in the circuit?

> ### Exercise 11.4
>
> Create the table for $|\psi\rangle$ having the initial state $|1\rangle$.

11.5.2   Correcting sign flips

A sign flip is a π phase error that switches $a|0\rangle + b|1\rangle$ and $a|0\rangle - b|1\rangle$. As we saw in section 7.6.3, a **Z** gate does this.

Changing between the usual computation basis of $|0\rangle$ and $|1\rangle$ and the Hadamard basis of $|+\rangle$ and $|-\rangle$ has the handy property of interchanging bit flips and sign flips. We only have to insert some **H** gates into the circuit in Figure 11.13 to fix possible sign flips, as shown in Figure 11.14. This is a consequence of **H** ∘ **X** ∘ **H** = **Z** and the equivalent **H** ∘ **Z** ∘ **H** = **X**.

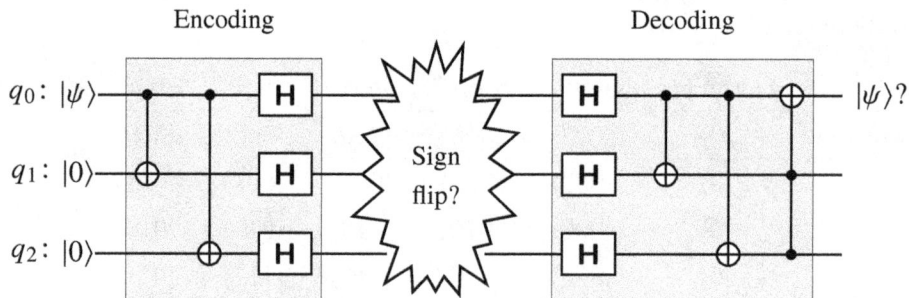

Figure 11.14: Circuit correcting a single sign flip

Can we combine these ideas to fix, at most, one bit, a sign flip, or both? This would be equivalent to fixing an errant **X**, **Z**, or **Y** gate.

11.5.3   The 9-qubit Shor code

To correct either one sign flip or one bit flip, we need eight additional qubits beyond the qubit we are trying to maintain. The circuit in Figure 11.15 is based on work published by Peter Shor in 1995, the same year he published his breakthrough factoring paper. [201] It combines the correction circuits from Figure 11.13 and Figure 11.14.

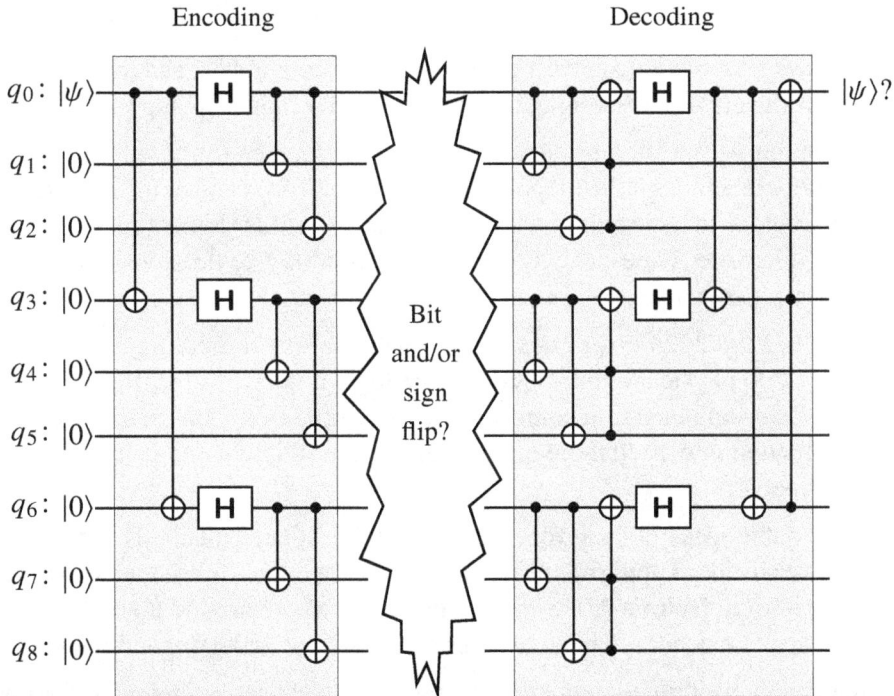

Figure 11.15: The 9-qubit Shor error-correcting code

As we saw earlier in section 7.7, we can write any 2-by-2 unitary matrix as a complex unit times a linear combination of I_2 and the three Pauli matrices. I_2, σ_x, σ_y, and σ_z are the matrices for the **ID**, **X**, **Y**, and **Z** gates, respectively. Since we can repair a single error for these gates (where **ID** is not an error), we can fix any single error that is a linear combination of them.

> The Shor 9-bit code can correct any single qubit error corresponding to a unitary gate.

If we have n qubits, we can use $9n$ qubits to duplicate the above circuit n times. Andrew Steane introduced a improved 7-qubit code in 1996 that can correct any single qubit error. [207] The best error-correcting code that can correct like the Shor code uses only 5 qubits, which is as good as possible using simple schemes. [130] [208]

What happens if an error occurs in one of the **CNOT** or Toffoli gates in the circuit? We need to either have exceptionally low error rates for them, or correct the correcting gates themselves.

11.5.4 Considerations for general fault tolerance

It appears we have a problem: to correct errors, we need more qubits, and then we need more qubits to correct the error-correcting qubits, and so on. Does it ever stop?

Yes, but we must use different methods such as *surface codes* based on group theory and a branch of mathematics called topology. In essence, if we can get the error rates of our qubits and gates close to a certain threshold, we can use entanglement and a lot of qubits to give us fault tolerance. We especially need our two-qubit gate fidelities to improve since those are usually much worse than for single gates.

How many? At the 2024 error rates of the best quantum computing systems, we need approximately 1,000 physical qubits to create one logical qubit. At the time of writing this book, the largest working quantum computer we know of is from IBM and has 1,121 qubits. [36] One logical qubit may need more qubits than we can fit into a *quantum core*, as we will define it in section 11.3.

One logical qubit does not do anyone much good. We'll need hundreds and thousands of these for the most advanced applications people foresee for quantum computers. For example, for Shor's algorithm to factor a 2,048-bit number, somewhere around 20 million = 2×10^7 physical qubits may be needed. This translates to $2 \times 10^4 = 20,000$ logical qubits. [91]

Other than being used in computation, we might also use fault-tolerant, error-corrected qubit technology for quantum memory and storage. Note, however, there is a twist to this. Unlike in classical computing, where you can copy data from memory into a working register for use, you cannot copy a qubit per the No-Cloning Theorem from section 9.3.4.

But you can use teleportation (section 9.3.5)! It's bizarre to imagine a computing system with teleportation but no data replication.

I believe that quantum computer providers will introduce error correction partially and incrementally. As we become better able to build quantum devices with lower qubit and gate error rates, we'll be able to perform some degree of limited error correction to at least extend coherence times for some qubits. We will use these ''improved qubits'' and the remaining physical qubits in algorithms that may not look quite so clean and elegant as what we saw in Chapter 9, ''Wiring Up the Circuits,'' and Chapter 10, ''From Circuits to Algorithms.''

By ''us,'' I really mean ''our optimizing quantum compilers,'' commonly called *transpilers*. As the architecture of quantum devices gets more sophisticated, we need compilers to smartly and optimally map our quantum circuit code to the number and kinds of qubits and available circuit depths. [34]

The formal description of single-qubit errors is in terms of density matrices, mixed states, and probabilities and gives rise to the same for two qubits and the gates that operate upon them. This theory is part of the machinery we will implement for large-scale quantum error correction. [162, Chapter 8]

> **To learn more**
>
> For an overview of error correction techniques and to see early qubit estimates for implementing Shor's factoring algorithm, see Fowler et al. [84] Over time, calculations for such estimates tighten up and improve.
>
> With what we have covered in this book, you can now read a "beginners guide" to advanced error correction. [64] There is significant current research on error correction and potential hardware implementations. [20] [87] [44]

11.6 Quantum benchmarks

How powerful is a gate- and circuit-based quantum computer? How much progress are we making with one qubit modality versus another? What does that mean when we say we can find a solution on a "powerful enough" quantum computer? When will we know we have arrived?

Benchmarks help us compare performance within a particular class of processors or across processors from competitive providers. For example, we can measure the coherence times among superconducting qubits from competitors or compare 2-qubit gate fidelities among all types of quantum computers to which we have access.

While knowing how well a given qubit is doing with coherence times and error rates is undoubtedly useful, it tells you nothing about the overall system and how well the components work together. You may have one or two spectacular, connected, and low-error-rate qubits, but other aspects of your system may make it unusable for executing practical algorithms.

Implementing hundreds of very bad qubits does not give you an advantage in the circuit model over having far fewer but excellent qubits with good control and measurement. We need whole-system, or "holistic," metrics that can tell us at a glance the relative performance of our quantum computer and individual metrics that give us information about individual performance factors.

11.6.1 Performance factors

The most valuable benchmarks test factors that account for many positive and negative behaviors. What are these factors?

Calibration errors

How well are the electronic controls calibrated for programming and measuring qubits to ensure accurate operation and error mitigation?

Circuit optimization

The theory and implementation of optimizing compilers for classical computers are well-known and have been studied for decades. Quantum *transpiling* (transformational compiling) is in its infancy, but computer scientists, quantum researchers, and software developers from academia and industry are making fast progress. [93]

How well does an optimizing quantum transpiler improve the layout and performance of a circuit across its depth and quantum register width?

> A well-performing optimizing quantum transpiler can improve performance by reducing the number of gates and rearranging how and when they operate on qubits. By avoiding qubits with shorter coherence times and greater 1- and 2-qubit error rates and using native gates on well-connected qubits, algorithm performance may be increased significantly by the transpiler.

I believe use of the words "transpiler" and "transpilation" will eventually stop and be replaced by the simpler words, "compiler" and "compilation."

Coherence time

How long does a qubit stay in a usable state, as we discussed in section 11.4? How does this vary among qubits?

Connectivity and coupling map

How are qubits connected to other qubits, and in what patterns?

Having qubits connected to more qubits can be an improvement if that coupling does not introduce additional errors across the connected qubits.

> I call a qubit not connected to any other qubit an *orphan*. A device with two orphan qubits is not a 2-qubit quantum computing system. It is two 1-qubit systems.

Crosstalk

How does changing the state of one qubit unintentionally and adversely affect the states of nearby qubits, either in gate operations or through more passive entanglement?

Gate fidelity

How accurately do gate operations move qubits from their current to new states? How does this vary among qubits?

As a metric, gate fidelity varies between 0.0 and 1.0, inclusively. A value of 1.0 says the gate perfectly implements the intended logical unitary transformation. Gate fidelity is equal to 1 minus the gate error rate. Two-qubit gates typically have much higher gate error rates than single-qubit gates, on the order of ten times worse.

Gate parallelism

How many gate operations can we run on qubits in parallel simultaneously? This concept is different from quantum parallelism. If we want to apply an **H** gate to each of a hundred qubits, does it take one hundred times longer than applying it to one qubit?

Gate speed

How fast are the single- and multi-qubit gates? How fast are the native gates versus the higher-level gates constructed from them?

Suppose you can execute an **H** gate in 1 second, but I can do it on my system in 200 milliseconds. If your coherence time is 5 seconds and mine is 1 second, we can each reasonably run five of these gates. But yours takes five times longer than mine! I win! That might not be the case if I have a lower gate fidelity. Running fast gates with many errors might not deliver practical results.

Initialization fidelity

How accurately can we set the initial qubit state to something known, usually $|0\rangle$? This capability is the second DiVincenzo requirement in section 11.2. Initialization fidelity is equal to 1 minus the initialization error rate. How does this vary among qubits?

We sometimes use the phrase *state preparation* to refer to setting the initial state of a qubit to $|0\rangle$, though we also use it, as in section 13.2, to set a collection of qubits to some specific quantum state.

Measurement fidelity

How accurately can we collapse a qubit state and read it out as $|0\rangle$ or $|1\rangle$? Measurement fidelity is equal to 1 minus the measurement error rate. How does this vary among qubits?

> *State preparation and measurement (SPAM)* refers to how well we can initialize our qubits to $|0\rangle$ before running a circuit and how accurately we can measure the results when we are done.

Number of qubits

How many operational, connected qubits do you have? More can be better, but not always. In any case, you need a sufficient number. It may be obvious, but you cannot count a qubit that does not work and cannot participate in 2-qubit gate operations for entanglement.

The number of qubits alone is a terrible and inaccurate metric of the quality and performance of a quantum computer.

Spectator errors

How much is a supposedly idle qubit affected during a 1- or 2-qubit gate operation on a physically connected qubit?

11.6.2 Performance benchmarks

By a "performance benchmark," I mean a test of a quantum computing system's fundamental and core software and hardware characteristics. Relative to the factors in section 11.6.1, these include

- T_1 (section 11.4.1) and T_2 (section 11.4.2) coherence times.
- Best, worst, and average 1- and 2-qubit gate fidelities and speeds. You should know which gates are tested and the results for individual or appropriate pairs of qubits.
- Number of qubits. It may seem odd to include this, but an industry analyst once asked me how we could prove that a quantum computer had the number of functional qubits we claimed.
- Gate parallelism and its effect on crosstalk, spectator errors, and use of available coherence time.
- The ratio of coherence times to gate speeds. How many operations can you execute on a qubit before it becomes statistically unusable?

> Benchmarks are not an issue of trust in vendors' claims: they must be independently verifiable by third parties.

It is also important to measure the ability of the quantum system to entangle two or more qubits. The circuit in Figure 11.16 creates the entangled Greenberger-Horne-Zeilinger (GHZ) state for n qubits. We first saw this in Exercise 9.8 after we discussed Bell states in section 9.3.3.

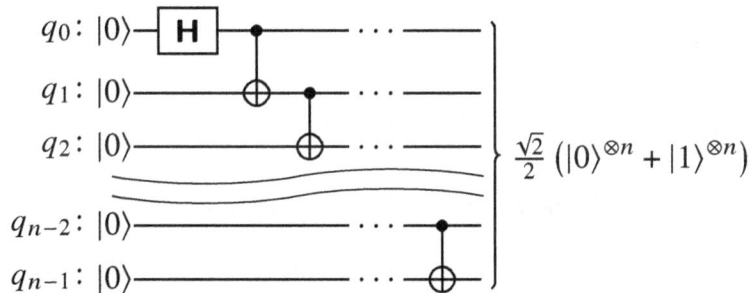

Figure 11.16: The n-qubit entangled GHZ state

Exercise 11.5

What well-known quantum state do we get with two qubits in Figure 11.16?

For enough executions of this circuit, we expect measurements with all **0**s and **1**s each showing up roughly half the time. If this ratio is significantly off or we see other combinations of **0**s and **1**s, we failed to entangle the qubits or we had noise caused by factors such as initialization or measurement errors.

A good way to gauge success is by using the Hellinger distance we saw in section 6.7. Suppose we have 10 qubits and execute the GHZ circuit 1,000 times. We expect to see **0000000000** 500 times, **1111111111** 500 times, and any other combination zero times. We compare this to what we actually measure on those 1,000 runs and compute the Hellinger distance on the two distributions. The closer we are to 0.0, the better we have successfully entangled the qubits. [217, IV.A]

11.6.3 Volumetric benchmarks

Quantum Volume (QV) is an architecture-independent metric devised by IBM Research scientists in 2017. It is an example of a *volumetric benchmark*. [19]

In such a benchmark, we run a set of circuits of depth d on a quantum register of n qubits. The benchmark rules specify the circuits, the number of times we run the circuits, and how to measure success. From this, we get a score. If the score is high enough, we have succeeded for the combination of d and n. Presumably, we then report this to the world.

Though the number of qubits n is a single number, we consider it as a two-dimensional "area" where we imagine each qubit being in a 1-by-1 square. The two-dimensional qubit area times the circuit depth gives us the "volume."

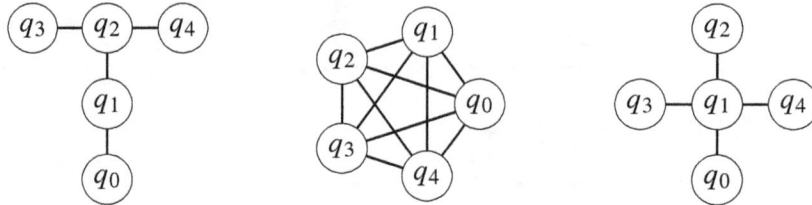

Figure 11.17: Three qubit connectivity configurations, each with "area" 5

Note the all-to-all connectivity in the middle configuration in Figure 11.17. Once the number of qubits gets much larger, connecting them directly and physically with some hardware implementations is impossible. For example, with 15 qubits, we have a beautiful, if impractical, connection topology in Figure 11.18 for hard-wiring the qubits.

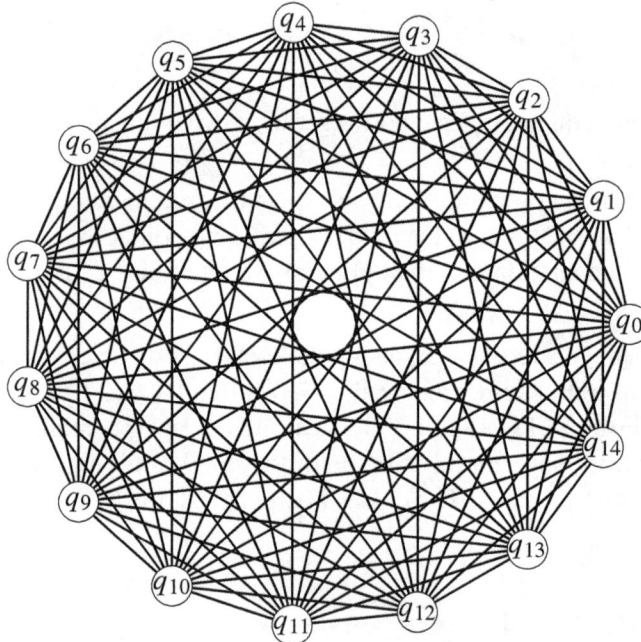

Figure 11.18: All-to-all connectivity for 15 qubits

If the quantum computer has more than n qubits, we want to find the subset of n qubits that gives us the best score. All the factors in section 11.6.1 can affect the score.

How do we compare results for two benchmark scores for systems with depths d_1 and d_2 and areas n_1 and n_2? If $d_1 = d_2$ and $n_1 = n_2$, we can look directly at one versus the other. When the numbers vary, it can be more difficult.

Exercise 11.6

Suppose two quantum processors, P_1 and p_2, have the same benchmark score. Which processor is better if $n_1 = n_2$ but $d_1 = d_2 + 1$? Which processor is better if $d_1 = d_2$ but $n_1 = n_2 + 1$?

A straightforward way to simplify this is to let $d = n$. System providers report QV as 2^n, where their best system performance is on a test circuit with area n qubits by depth n. Since this number can get large, it's not uncommon for people to refer to a "QV of n," though this is technically incorrect.

Let's look at the model of the circuits IBM defined for QV calculations. Figure 11.19 is my adaptation of the circuit template diagram from their paper. They also define their probabilistic *heavy output* criteria of success there. [58]

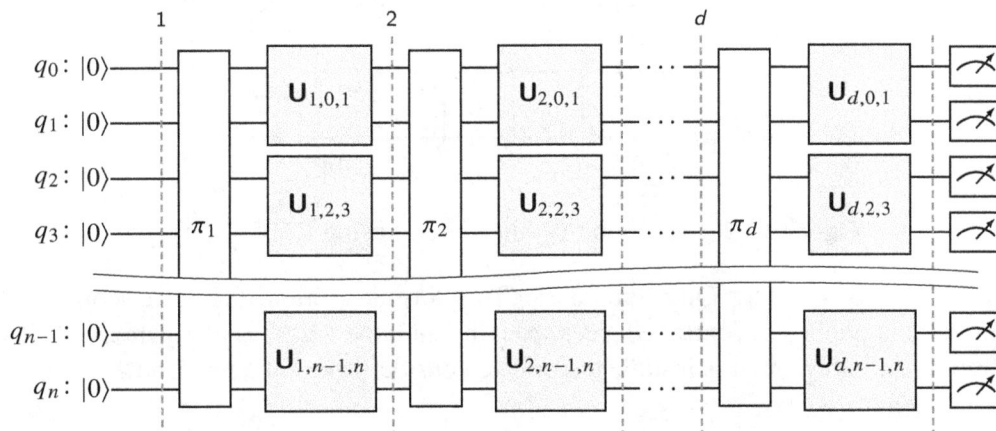

Figure 11.19: The model of a QV circuit

The vertical dotted lines separate each *layer* ℓ in the circuit. Each $\mathbf{U}_{\ell,j,k}$ is a 2-qubit gate, which we can think of as a 4-by-4 unitary matrix. In fact, since we can multiply the unitary matrix by a complex number of absolute value 1, we can assume the matrix is in $\mathbf{SU}(4, \mathbf{C})$. See section 5.8 for a reminder of the properties of unitary transformations and matrices.

We can consider any 2-by-2 unitary matrix U as a 4-by-4 unitary matrix via $U \otimes I_2$ or $I_2 \otimes U$. By the discussion of universality in section 9.3, we can construct any quantum algorithm by composing these 2-qubit gates, including **SWAP** gates.

By choosing a random and big enough collection of the $\mathbf{U}_{\ell,j,k}$, we can "stress" the quantum system to see how well it performs. What, though, are the π_ℓ gates at each layer, and why do we include them?

Let's start with a simple example of four layers with four qubits. The only 2-qubit gates we use are **CNOT**s. Because their determinants equal -1 and not 1, these gates are not in $\mathbf{SU}(4, \mathbf{C})$, but they will serve for illustrative purposes.

Exercise 11.7

Let M be the 4-by-4 matrix for **CNOT**. Find a real number c such that $\det(cM) = 1$.

The circuit in Figure 11.20 only tests gates involving qubits 0 and 1, and 2 and 3.

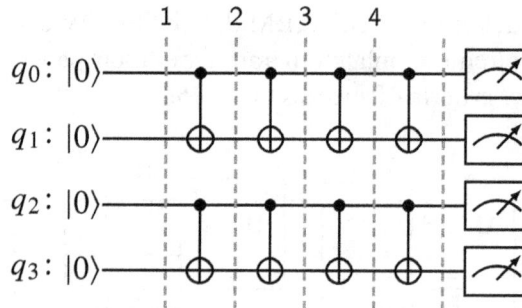

Figure 11.20: A 4-qubit QV-like circuit using **CNOT** gates

In our discussion of the Quantum Fourier Transform in section 10.1.3, we show that the circuit for four qubits has controlled gates spanning multiple wires, as in Figure 11.21. If we are testing our hardware, it is insufficient only to consider adjacent qubits and 2-qubit gates between them.

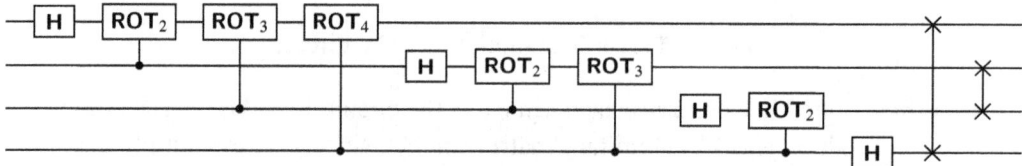

Figure 11.21: The Quantum Fourier Transform circuit for four qubits

The π_ℓ gates in Figure 11.19 are permutations of the qubits, which we then take two at a time. A better test circuit with **CNOT**s uses such random permutations.

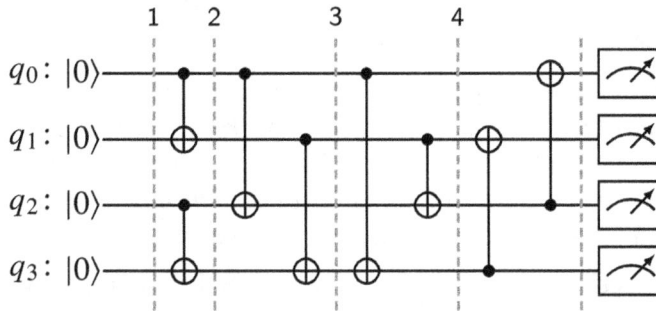

Figure 11.22: Testing using random **CNOT** gates across qubits

In the example in Figure 11.22, we use a **CNOT** for each $\mathbf{U}_{\ell,j,k}$, but a QV circuit would test over arbitrary gates in $\mathbf{SU}(4, \mathbf{C})$.

Exercise 11.8

The circuit in Figure 11.19 assumes we have an even number of qubits. What's a reasonable approach to take if we have an odd number?

If I have built a quantum system and report a QV of 2^n, I evidently cannot meet the success criteria for $n + 1$ qubits and layers. If your system has a higher QV than mine, you can execute circuits on more qubits more accurately.

QV results should be demonstrated on actual quantum computing hardware by system providers. Extrapolated results for QV beyond the number of implemented qubits are useless and misleading.

The QV benchmark tells us nothing about how fast the circuits run. To test that, IBM introduced another benchmark using QV circuits called *Circuit Layer Operations per Second*, abbreviated as *CLOPS*. [226] CLOPS is defined in terms of high-level gates, not the ones that end up running on specific hardware. In 2023, IBM introduced *CLOPS$_h$* to handle this variation. They also introduced the *Error Per Layered Gate (EPLG)* benchmark to look holistically at the performance of the entire process as well as groups of individual qubits. [225]

Though we define a QV circuit as in Figure 11.19, your quantum software development kit or software from a third party can optimize what ultimately runs on the hardware. QV and CLOPS scores can benefit significantly from your software toolchain. [93] [186]

11.6.4   Algorithmic and application benchmarks

Some quantum practitioners combine benchmarks not included in the categories in sections 11.6.2 and 11.6.3 into one they call *application benchmarks*. I prefer to split them into two categories: algorithmic and application benchmarks.

The distinction can be challenging to discern and somewhat arbitrary in some cases, but I informally say that an *algorithmic benchmark* tests the performance of the code for a quantum algorithm that you would not normally run on its own: it is part of a bigger and presumably more solution-oriented computation. An *application benchmark* tests performance for a complete solution to some problem or practical use case.

Such benchmarks show quickly and accurately whether quantum systems produce the correct result. Testing suites from the QED-C and Infleqtion include both kinds of benchmarks. [141] [140] [217]

Testing factoring via Shor's algorithm (section 10.7) is an application benchmark. Order and period finding (section 10.6) is part of Shor's factoring algorithm, but testing it independently is an algorithmic benchmark.

Exercise 11.9

Do you consider a test of Grover's search algorithm (section 9.7.1) an algorithmic or application benchmark? Why?

Algorithmic benchmarks

I consider tests of the performance and accuracy of the following to be algorithmic benchmarks:

- Amplitude amplification – section 9.6
- Grover's search algorithm – section 9.7.1
- The Deutsch-Jozsa algorithm – section 9.8
- The Bernstein-Vazirani algorithm – section 9.9
- Simon's algorithm – section 9.10
- Quantum Fourier Transform – section 10.1
- Phase estimation – section 10.5
- Order and period finding – section 10.6
- The Harrow-Hassidim-Lloyd (HHL) algorithm [104] [62]

Application benchmarks

I consider tests of the performance and accuracy of the following to be application benchmarks:

- Factoring via Shor's algorithm – section 10.7
- Quantum kernels for support vector machines – section 13.4
- Quantum neural networks – section 13.3
- Quantum approximate optimization algorithm – section 12.8

11.7   The software stack and access

One way of accessing a quantum computing system looks like this:

1. You download and install software development tools such as the Cirq or Qiskit open-source quantum computing framework to your laptop or workstation. [41] [179]
2. You develop your quantum code in a programmer's editor or a Jupyter™ notebook. [175]
3. When run, part of your application connects to a quantum simulator on your computer or remotely to a simulator or quantum hardware.
4. The remote connection is via the internet/cloud.
5. Your application invokes one or more processes that run on the quantum hardware or a simulator.
6. Ultimately, your application uses the results of the quantum computation and does something valuable within your use case.

There are at least two other similar scenarios:

- Instead of developing locally, you use a web browser-based environment where your Jupyter notebooks are edited, tested, stored, and executed on the cloud.
- You have runnable code that you place in a container in the cloud and access quantum computers close to or remote from classical cloud servers.

For developers, the software stack looks like the upper portion of the diagram in Figure 11.23.

On the bottom of the software stack is the **Quantum Hardware Control** level. Quantum computing systems might use photonic or microwave control systems, allowing direct definition and delivery of instructions configuring and executing quantum gates and operations.

Above that is the **Low-Level Quantum Circuits** level, which provides support for using built-in gates and creating new circuits. This allows implementing them within quantum registers and building out the algorithms discussed in Chapter 7, ''One Qubit,'' through Chapter 10, ''From Circuits to Algorithms.''

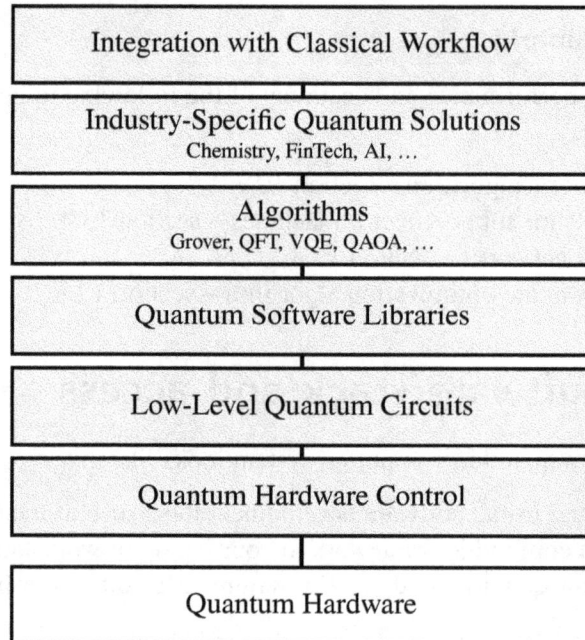

Figure 11.23: A quantum software and hardware stack

At the **Quantum Software Libraries** and **Algorithms** levels, the coder can reuse previously defined and optimized algorithms and circuits within their circuits or application code. When using these libraries, the developer mindset is still in terms of how quantum algorithms work but is well above anything we could describe as "assembly language."

Next, the **Industry-Specific Quantum Solutions** level provides high-level software libraries for use cases in specific industries or general applications such as AI. A developer might not know that a quantum computing system is involved here.

Finally, code running on quantum computing systems must fit in with classical applications and workflow, and this happens at the **Integration with Classical Workflow** level.

This stack representation gives you a rough idea of where functionality is provided from deep down, close to the quantum computer, and up to the most abstract access points. Any particular framework may structure its developer software stack with more or fewer levels.

Before we leave this topic, I want to give my opinion on whether we need new programming languages just for quantum computing or if we should embed the functionality within existing languages. For various scientific applications in the past, I've done both.

For many of us, it's fun to create new languages. That might not be *your* idea of fun, but so be it! It's very tempting to start building a quantum programming environment and then find you are spending too much time doing classical computer science engineering, most of which has likely been done before – and better.

Modern programming languages such as Python, Swift, Go, Java, Rust, and C++ are superb for software development. For me, it makes much more sense to build the quantum gate, circuit, and execution support within the type systems of these languages. This way, you can quickly use the entire toolchain and support for the established languages. You can then concentrate on quickly and comprehensively adding quantum software development.

Moreover, suppose your development framework is open-source. In that case, you have a much larger potential set of contributors who know the existing languages than if you need to teach them a new one.

For example, Qiskit and Cirq use Python as the primary developer language but provide extensive libraries at all levels of their software stacks. Engineers can implement low-level optimized code and provide Python library interfaces to developers working higher in the stack, if necessary.

If a low-level quantum "machine language" is required, its creators should use modern and consistent computer science principles, patterns, and best practices.

> A *full stack* is the complete software stack plus all the hardware on which it runs. Vendors use this phrase for marketing, so check carefully what they really provide.

11.8 Simulation

Is it possible to simulate a quantum computer on a classical computer? If we could do it, "quantum computing" would be only another technique for coding software on our current machines.

In this section, we look at what you must consider if you want to write a simulator for manipulating logical qubits. In particular, we look at *state vector simulation*. In section 11.8.6, we look at simulation using density matrices.

Simulation is good for experimentation, education, and debugging part of a quantum circuit. If you have a simulator handy, such as one that Qiskit or Cirq provides, you can use it for small problems.

We look at how you might build a simulator in general terms. I offer no complete code in any specific programming language but more of a list of what you need to consider.

11.8.1 Qubits

When thinking about building a quantum computing circuit simulator, your first decision is how you represent qubits. With this and your other choices, you can create a general model or specialize it. We're going for the general case. Once you complete this section, you can think about optimizing each interconnected part individually and together.

We want to work with more than one qubit, so we do not use a Bloch sphere. We hold the state of a qubit in two complex numbers, and we can store them in an ordered list, array, or similar structure. If your programming language or environment has a mathematical vector type, use it.

While we might use an exact value here, such as

$$\frac{\sqrt{2}}{2}|0\rangle + \frac{\sqrt{2}}{2}|1\rangle \,,$$

your language or environment probably uses floating point numbers for the real and imaginary parts of complex numbers. So, the above might be

$$0.7071067811865476|0\rangle + 0.7071067811865476|1\rangle$$

with

$$|0.7071067811865476|^2 + |0.7071067811865476|^2 = 1.0000000000000002 \,.$$

You must keep track of and possibly control this error if you use many qubits or gates.

You should consider using a symbolic mathematics library such as **SymPy** for a small circuit simulator, though the time and memory overhead might be too much. [212] Also, symbolic expressions can get complicated and messy quickly, so your system's ability to simplify these expressions is critical.

If you have an n-bit quantum register, you must represent a *state vector* of 2^n complex numbers. If $n = 10$, a list of 1,024 complex numbers uses 9,024 bytes. For 20 qubits, it is 8,697,464 bytes, or approximately 8.3MB. Just adding two more qubits brings this to 35,746,776, or 34MB.

Think about this: for a single state of a quantum register with 22 qubits, you need 34MB to represent it. It gets exponentially bigger and worse than this as we add more qubits. We are over a gigabyte per state at 27 qubits. It's not only storage that is increasing; the time required to manipulate all those values is getting big fast. Your choice of algorithms at every level is critical.

It gets even worse: the size of the matrix for a gate is the *square* of the number of entries in the qubit state ket.

General-purpose quantum computation state-vector simulation will get too big and time-impractical even for supercomputers somewhere in the mid-40 number of qubits. If you have a specific problem you are trying to simulate, you may be able to simplify the mathematical formulas representing the circuit. Just as $\sin^2(x) + \cos^2(x) = 1$ reduces to the much simpler 1, the math for your circuit may get smaller.

Consider using a sparse representation for qubits and ket vectors. Do you really need $2^{50} = 1,125,899,906,842,624$ numbers to represent the state $|0\rangle^{\otimes 50}$? After all, there are only two pieces of significant information there, 0 and 50. Add a little overhead to represent the sparse ket, and you can fit it into a few bytes.

11.8.2 Gates

If qubits are vectors, then gates are matrices. The most straightforward way of implementing multi-wire circuits is to construct the tensor product matrix for two gates. These matrices get large: if you have n qubits, your matrices will be 2^n-by-2^n in size.

For the subcircuit

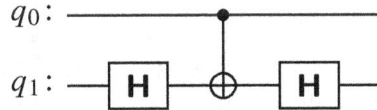

we have the product of the matrices corresponding to $\mathbf{ID} \otimes \mathbf{H}$:

$$\begin{bmatrix} 1 & 0 \\ 0 & 1 \end{bmatrix} \otimes \begin{bmatrix} \frac{\sqrt{2}}{2} & \frac{\sqrt{2}}{2} \\ \frac{\sqrt{2}}{2} & -\frac{\sqrt{2}}{2} \end{bmatrix} = \begin{bmatrix} \frac{\sqrt{2}}{2} & \frac{\sqrt{2}}{2} & 0 & 0 \\ \frac{\sqrt{2}}{2} & -\frac{\sqrt{2}}{2} & 0 & 0 \\ 0 & 0 & \frac{\sqrt{2}}{2} & \frac{\sqrt{2}}{2} \\ 0 & 0 & \frac{\sqrt{2}}{2} & -\frac{\sqrt{2}}{2} \end{bmatrix},$$

the **CNOT**:

$$\begin{bmatrix} 1 & 0 & 0 & 0 \\ 0 & 1 & 0 & 0 \\ 0 & 0 & 0 & 1 \\ 0 & 0 & 1 & 0 \end{bmatrix},$$

and then another $\mathbf{ID} \otimes \mathbf{H}$. This result is

$$\begin{bmatrix} 1 & 0 & 0 & 0 \\ 0 & 1 & 0 & 0 \\ 0 & 0 & 1 & 0 \\ 0 & 0 & 0 & -1 \end{bmatrix}.$$

As we know, it flips the sign of $|11\rangle$. We could have done less matrix manipulation if we had identified this as a standard pattern.

Exercise 11.10

How would you implement an **X** gate on a qubit represented as a pair of complex numbers without using matrix multiplication?

11.8.3 Measurement

Once you come up with a final 1-qubit quantum register state such as

$$\frac{\sqrt{2}}{2}|0\rangle - \frac{\sqrt{2}}{2}i\,|1\rangle\,,$$

or a 2-qubit quantum register state such as

$$0.3872983346207417\,i\,|00\rangle + 0.6082762530298219\,|01\rangle -$$
$$0.5099019513592785\,|10\rangle + 0.469041575982343\,i\,|11\rangle\,,$$

how do you simulate measurement? We use the simulated sampling method using random numbers from section 6.5.

If there is one ket with nonzero amplitude, then that must be the measurement result. We now assume there are two or more nonzero amplitudes.

Compute the probabilities corresponding to each standard basis ket, using the ket subscripting notation from section 8.2.2: if

$$|\psi\rangle = \sum_{j=0}^{2^n-1} a_j|j\rangle_n\,,$$

then let

$$p_j = \left|a_j\right|^2 = a_j\overline{a_j}\,.$$

Subject to a little round-off error,

$$1.0 = \sum_{j=0}^{2^n-1} p_j\,.$$

These are the *example probabilities* we use in Figure 6.3 in section 6.5.

Consider the output of the Python calculation:

```
sample_n_times([0.15, 0.37, 0.26, 0.22], 1000000)
```

```
Results for 1000000 simulated samples
```

Event	Actual Probability	Simulated Probability
0	0.15	0.1497
1	0.37	0.3704
2	0.26	0.2595
3	0.22	0.2205

Here, $E_0 = |00\rangle$, $E_1 = |01\rangle$, and so on.

As another example, we can look at simulated measurements for a balanced superposition of four qubits. In this case, each amplitude is 0.25, and its probability is 0.0625. Here is a sample run of 1,000,000 iterations:

```
sample_n_times([1.0/16 for _ in range(16)], 1000000)
```

```
Results for 1000000 simulated samples
```

Event	Actual Probability	Simulated Probability
0	0.0625	0.0624
1	0.0625	0.0624
2	0.0625	0.0625
3	0.0625	0.0625
4	0.0625	0.062
5	0.0625	0.0627
6	0.0625	0.0628
7	0.0625	0.0627
8	0.0625	0.0624
9	0.0625	0.0624
10	0.0625	0.0626
11	0.0625	0.0625
12	0.0625	0.0623
13	0.0625	0.0627
14	0.0625	0.0629
15	0.0625	0.0623

Again recall, for example, that getting E_7 means we are getting a result of $|7\rangle$ on measurement.

The sampling method in section 6.5 pre-computes a list of probability sums with length equal to two to the number of qubits. That is, the algorithm is exponential. When the number of qubits gets large, so does this list and the steps needed to traverse it. It may be more efficient to compute the probability sums and make the comparisons without creating the list first.

This method works, though it can be expensive for a general quantum state. To measure a quantum state generated by a specific circuit, it may be much more efficient to simulate measurement in other ways. [27]

11.8.4 Circuits

To simulate a circuit, you need to represent it in some way. Think about the wire model and the horizontal steps from left to right where you place and execute gates.

Multi-qubit gates span wires, so you must specify wire inputs and outputs. You must check for errors to ensure two gates in the same step do not involve the same input and output wires.

I recommend starting with an API, an application programming interface, to a collection of software routines that sits on top of your internal circuit representation. If you start by developing a new language to write circuits, you'll likely spend more early coding cycles on the language rather than the simulator itself.

11.8.5 Coding a simulator

Should you decide to code a quantum simulator, here is some advice:

- Don't bother unless you want to do it as an educational project, have a brilliant new idea, or can use specialized hardware. There are plenty of simulators out there, many of them open-source.
- Don't start by optimizing circuits. It can be difficult enough to debug code that is supposed to do the sequence of operations you originally wrote.
- When you start optimizing, look for the easy stuff, such as removing consecutive gates that do nothing. Three examples are **H H**, **X X**, and **Z Z**.
- Don't start tensoring matrices together until you have a wire-spanning operation such as **CNOT**.
- Don't do full matrix multiplication for simple gates on one or two qubits. Code them directly.
- Write efficient code that simulates standard gates and gate combinations. Do not, for example, build a **CNOT** from a Toffoli gate, but do provide the Toffoli gate in your collection.

- Go much deeper into how engineers implement quantum gates from more primitive gates. Learn about Clifford gates and how to simulate them, for example. This will require deeper knowledge of quantum computing and computer science. [26] [25]

To learn more

To re-emphasize my point about not necessarily coding your own, a web search of a "list of quantum simulators" will turn up dozens of simulators in multiple programming languages, many of them open-source.

11.8.6   Simulation using density matrices

Rather than simulate using a 2^n-by-2^n unitary matrix U for a gate and a state vector for $|\psi\rangle$ of length 2^n for n qubits, we can instead use U, its adjoint, and the density matrix ρ for $|\psi\rangle$:

$$U |\psi\rangle \mapsto U |\psi\rangle\langle\psi| U^\dagger = U\rho U^\dagger = U\rho U^{-1}.$$

This form has advantages because the density matrix can include an ensemble of quantum states with their probabilities, as we saw in section 8.2.3. In particular, we can simulate the effect of noise on the evaluation of the circuit. The states in an ensemble can represent the weighted possible outcomes of state preparation, gates, and measurement as we might see from actual runs of the quantum system we would like to simulate. [39]

While this is a significant capability compared to state vector simulation, it has its cost. Whereas $|\psi\rangle$ is $O(2^n)$ for the memory size of the state vector, ρ is

$$O(2^n \times 2^n) = O\left(2^{2n}\right) = O(4^n)$$

for the density matrix.

Exercise 11.11

For a fixed amount of memory, why can you only simulate one-half the number of qubits using density matrices as you can with state vectors?

An implementation using GPUs can provide significant performance improvements for a simulation involving matrices, vectors, and algebraic operations with them. [155]

11.9 Light and photons

Light illuminates the things around us. It can be as dim and small as a faraway star on a clear night or as harsh and bright as the sun or the output of welding equipment. Understanding the nature of light was a central research direction in physics in the nineteenth and early twentieth centuries.

The answers were far more complicated than anyone imagined, gave birth to quantum mechanics, and involved the electromagnetic spectrum well beyond visible light.

11.9.1 Photons

Does light behave like a wave, with *amplitude* A (height) and *wavelength* λ, as in Figure 11.24? λ is the distance between two wave crests or other corresponding points.

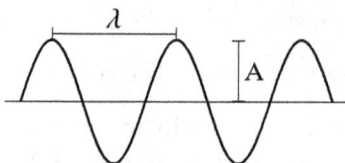

Figure 11.24: Metrics associated with waves

Or does light behave like a particle with a well-defined shape, shooting off in various directions, as in Figure 11.25? Can particles have different energies? Can particles have different colors?

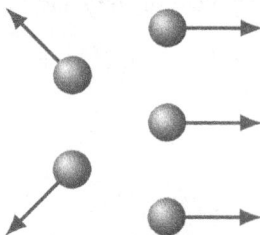

Figure 11.25: Particles moving in the same and different directions

Light has both wave-like and particle-like characteristics. The fundamental unit of light is called a *photon*. It has no charge, and, according to theory, it has no mass.

A photon never sits still. The *speed of light* is how fast a photon moves in a vacuum. We denote this speed by c, which is 299,792,458 meters per second, approximately 186,282 miles per second.

When two waves take up the same space simultaneously, we get *superposition*, as shown on the left-hand side of Figure 11.26.

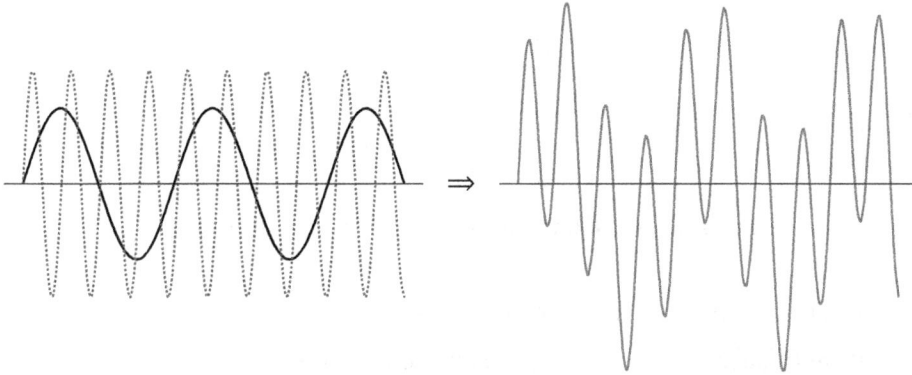

Figure 11.26: Superposition of waves

This leads to *interference*, shown on the right-hand side of Figure 11.26. At any point where the waves overlap, their amplitudes, positive or negative, add to give a new combined amplitude. If both amplitudes are the same sign, we get *constructive interference*. When they differ, we get *destructive interference*. We have *complete* destructive interference if the new amplitude is zero.

For a given wave with a repeating period, as shown in the example in Figure 11.27, we measure from the beginning of the period to the end and call this the *phase* φ. It takes on values from 0 to 2π in radians.

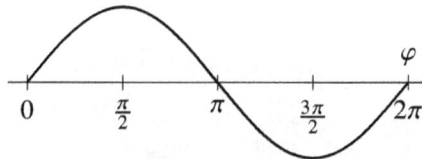

Figure 11.27: Wave with period 2π

We usually measure wavelengths in some variation of the meter such as the nanometer, **nm**. One nm = 10^{-9} meters or one-billionth of a meter.

A wave traveling at a constant speed s has frequency ν, equal to s divided by the wavelength λ. ν is the Greek letter "nu."

$$\nu = \text{frequency} = \frac{\text{speed}}{\text{wavelength}} = \frac{\text{speed}}{\lambda}$$

$$\lambda = \text{wavelength} = \frac{\text{speed}}{\text{frequency}} = \frac{\text{speed}}{\nu}$$

When two waves have the same shape, amplitude, and frequency but are possibly offset horizontally, we say the waves are *coherent*. The offset $\Delta\varphi$, pronounced "delta phi," is the *phase difference* or *phase offset*.

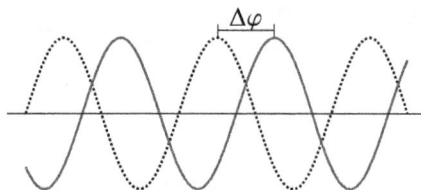

Figure 11.28: Coherent waves with phase difference

Some authors also call this phase difference φ, which is confusing.

We measure frequency in *hertz* (**Hz**) which is one complete cycle per second. The solid curve in Figure 11.29 has a frequency of 1 Hz, while the dotted curve has a frequency of 4 Hz.

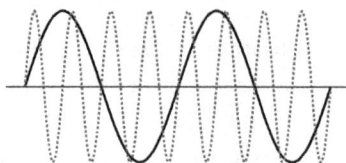

Figure 11.29: Waves with 1 Hz and 4 Hz frequencies

One *gigahertz* (**GHz**) is a frequency of one billion (10^9) cycles per second. A *terahertz* (**THz**) is 10^{12} cycles per second. The hertz unit is named after physicist Heinrich Rudolf Hertz (Figure 11.30).

Figure 11.30: Heinrich Rudolf Hertz

To finish our discussion of photons, we need to know about a fundamental value that appears to be essential to how our universe works. If we vary this number, our physics would be different or impossible. *Planck's constant*, h, is an exceptionally small number and is

$$h = 6.62607015 \times 10^{-34} \, \frac{m^2 kg}{s}$$

$$= 0.000000000000000000000000000000000662607015 \, \frac{m^2 kg}{s}.$$

The unit to the right is "meters squared kilograms per second." It is related to the *Joule* (J), a unit of energy, and is 1 meter squared kilograms per second squared, or $m^2 kg/s^2$. Given the abbreviations m = meter, s = second, kg = kilogram, and J = Joule, Planck's constant in these units is

$$h = 6.62607015 \times 10^{-34} \, J \, s.$$

Planck's reduced constant is

$$\hbar = \frac{h}{2\pi} = 1.054571817 \ldots \times 10^{-34} \, J \, s.$$

Thinking of a photon as a wave, let ν be its frequency measured in Hz. Its energy, E, measured in Joules, is

$$E = h\nu.$$

Exercise 11.12

What is the unit we used for Hz? Determine this from the units for E and ν. One Hz is equal to how many Joules?

The higher the frequency of the photon (or the smaller its wavelength), the greater its energy.

Visible light is only part of the electromagnetic spectrum. Infrared radiation, microwaves, and radio waves have wavelengths longer than visible light, with less energy. Ultraviolet radiation, x-rays, and gamma (γ) rays have shorter wavelengths than visible light, hence higher frequencies and more energy.

γ rays have frequencies above 10^{19} Hz and wavelengths less than 10^{-11} m. On the other side, microwaves have frequencies between 1 GHz and 300 GHz, and wavelengths from 0.30 m to 0.001 m. Note that the exact wavelength boundaries between different types of electromagnetic radiation vary quite a bit in books and articles, depending on which source you consult.

We define *coherent light* as above (same amplitude, same frequency), but we require that the waves are in phase with one another. Light that varies in frequency or phase is called *incoherent light*.

Coherent light can be produced via **L**ight **A**mplification by **S**timulated **E**mission of **R**adiation, which gives rise to the word "laser." We can focus a laser to send a beam of photons a great distance or for cutting materials. They are also used in scanners at stores to read bar codes and, historically, to read and write data to compact discs, DVDs, and Blu-ray discs. Lasers with specific frequencies can cool down atoms close to absolute zero, allowing us to create quantum computers and sensors.

11.9.2   The double-slit experiment

Let's consider an experiment to see how light behaves like a wave and a particle.

Suppose you have a device to shoot perfectly spherical pellets against a smooth, blank wall. The pellets are the same size and do not vary in their straight path or speed once they leave the device:

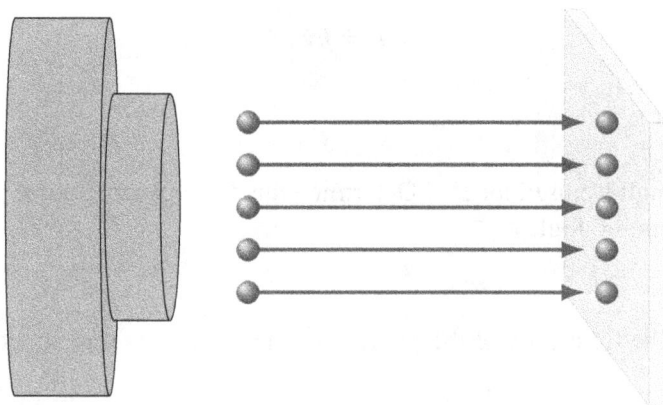

We can see where each pellet strikes the wall.

Let's insert a pellet-proof flat shield between the device and the wall. Also, we cut a horizontal slit that should allow only the center pellet to pass through:

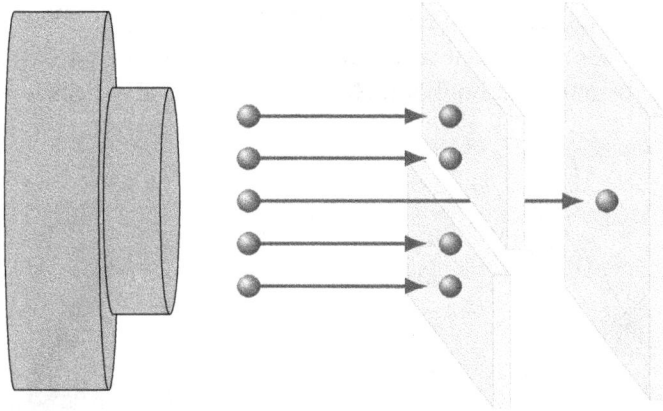

The shield blocks all the pellets except those lined up with the slit.

We can repeat this with two slits:

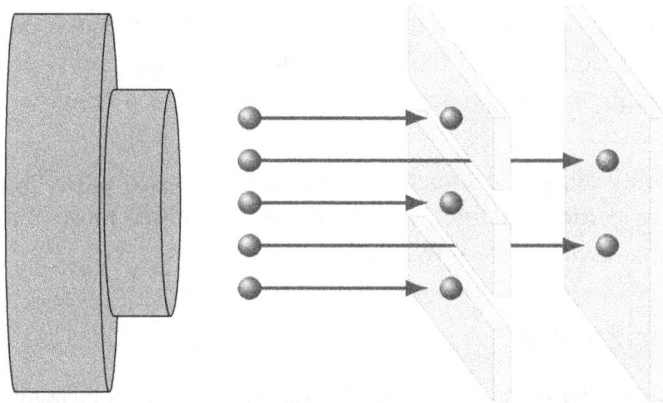

If we shoot many pellets and allow for horizontal scattering, the impact area on the wall, shown in dark gray, would look like the shape of the slits:

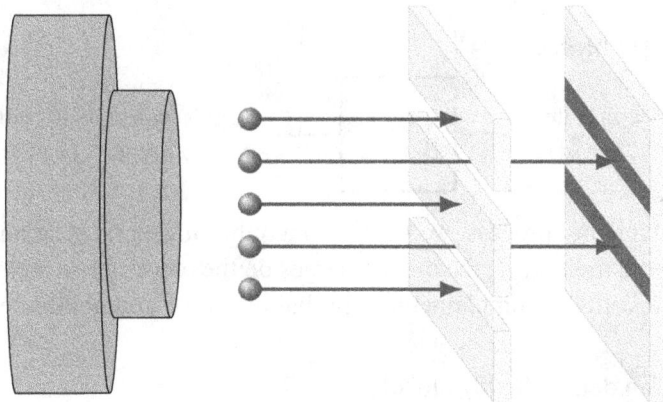

Instead of pellets, let's consider photons. Our "photon shooting" device is a laser, so the light is coherent with some constant wavelength. Thought of as a particle, a photon passes through one slot or the other but not both. However, photons also behave as waves:

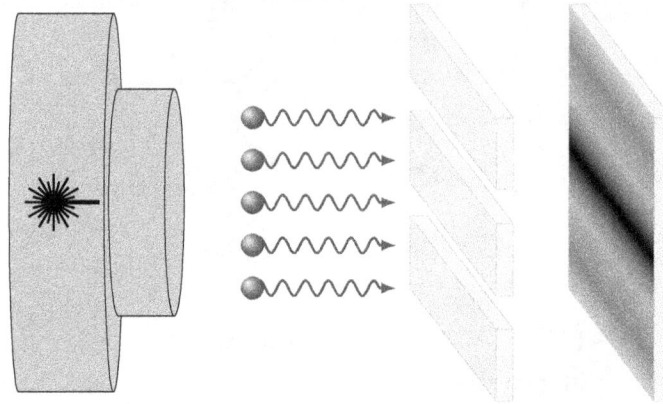

The light waves interfere with themselves after they pass through the slots. Instead of getting solid bands directly behind the slits, we get diffraction and strong bands between the slits and weakening bands to each side. This behavior is a result of constructive and destructive interference.

We call this ability of light to sometimes behave like a wave and sometimes behave like a particle the "wave-particle duality." However, it is considered more of a historic physical model than modern *quantum optics*. [83] [188]

11.9.3   Polarization

We now look at the mathematics behind the famous three-filter polarization experiment.

Consider a general quantum state for one qubit in the computational basis: $|\psi\rangle = a|0\rangle + b|1\rangle$. We will pass the qubit through a series of procedures and see what comes out the other end.

The first is the $|1\rangle$ blocker:

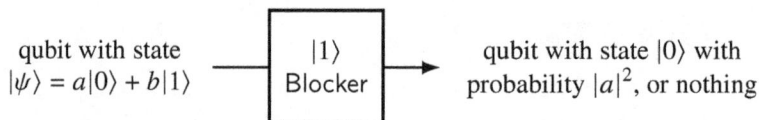

In this somewhat unnatural process, we start with a qubit in general state and pass it through the blocker. With probability $|a|^2$, the qubit emerges on the other side in state $|0\rangle$. The qubit is completely blocked with the complementary probability $|b|^2$, and nothing emerges. Bye-bye qubit.

Similarly, we can define the $|0\rangle$ blocker:

```
qubit with state          |0⟩         qubit with state |1⟩ with
|ψ⟩ = a|0⟩ + b|1⟩        Blocker      probability |b|², or nothing
```

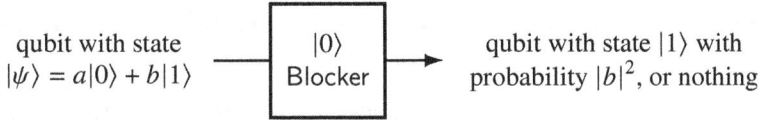

If we compose these, no qubit makes it through:

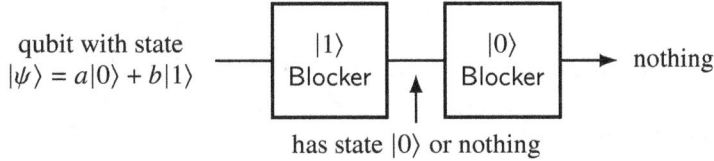

```
qubit with state        |1⟩        |0⟩
|ψ⟩ = a|0⟩ + b|1⟩    Blocker    Blocker      nothing
                                ↑
                     has state |0⟩ or nothing
```

Our final procedure is the $|+\rangle$ blocker:

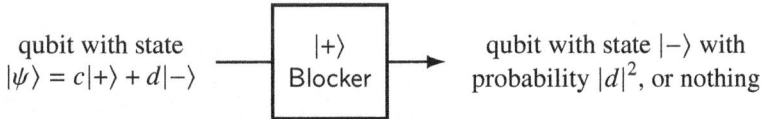

```
qubit with state          |+⟩         qubit with state |−⟩ with
|ψ⟩ = c|+⟩ + d|−⟩      Blocker      probability |d|², or nothing
```

What do we get if we do this?

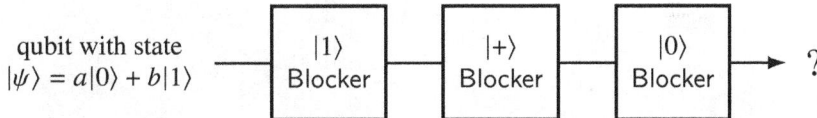

```
qubit with state      |1⟩       |+⟩       |0⟩
|ψ⟩ = a|0⟩ + b|1⟩  Blocker   Blocker   Blocker      ?
```

Recall that we have these fundamental equalities among basis kets:

$$|+\rangle = \tfrac{\sqrt{2}}{2}(|0\rangle + |1\rangle) \qquad |-\rangle = \tfrac{\sqrt{2}}{2}(|0\rangle - |1\rangle)$$

$$|0\rangle = \tfrac{\sqrt{2}}{2}(|+\rangle + |-\rangle) \qquad |1\rangle = \tfrac{\sqrt{2}}{2}(|+\rangle - |-\rangle)$$

After the $|1\rangle$ blocker, we have $|0\rangle$ with probability $|a|^2$, if anything. Assuming something is there, it is also equal to $\tfrac{\sqrt{2}}{2}(|+\rangle + |-\rangle)$. We run this through the $|+\rangle$ blocker, and with probability $\tfrac{1}{2} = (\tfrac{\sqrt{2}}{2})^2$, we get $|-\rangle$ or nothing. If anything, it also equals $\tfrac{\sqrt{2}}{2}(|0\rangle - |1\rangle)$.

We now pass it through the $|0\rangle$ blocker. With probability $\tfrac{1}{2} = (\tfrac{\sqrt{2}}{2})^2$, we get the qubit in state $|1\rangle$.

In the case where we used only the $|1\rangle$ and $|0\rangle$, no qubit in any state made it through. Oddly enough, if we inserted the $|+\rangle$ blocker between them, that qubit in the initial state $a|0\rangle + b|1\rangle$ made it through with probability $|a|^2 \times \tfrac{1}{2} \times \tfrac{1}{2} = \tfrac{|a|^2}{4}$.

When you think of a photon as a wave, the wave travels in one direction, but the crests and troughs of the waves are perpendicular to the direction. Consider a string on a musical instrument. If you pluck it by pulling it straight up and releasing it, the wave rises and falls vertically, ↑. If you pluck it directly on its side, the wave rises and falls from left to right, or horizontally, →.

A photon is a two-state quantum system, and we can use $\{|\uparrow\rangle, |\rightarrow\rangle\}$ as an orthonormal basis. Rather than thinking about a qubit making it through the above blocking processes, we consider a photon passing through or being absorbed by a polarization filter. We start with a photon in the general $a|\uparrow\rangle + b|\rightarrow\rangle$ state.

A $|\uparrow\rangle$ vertical polarization filter absorbs the photon with probability $|a|^2$ and passes it through with probability $|b|^2$. Similarly, a $|\rightarrow\rangle$ horizontal polarization filter absorbs the photon with probability $|b|^2$ and passes it through with probability $|a|^2$.

A $|\uparrow\rangle$ filter followed by a $|\rightarrow\rangle$ filter absorbs all photons. This behavior is similar to our $|1\rangle$ blocker followed by the $|0\rangle$ blocker:

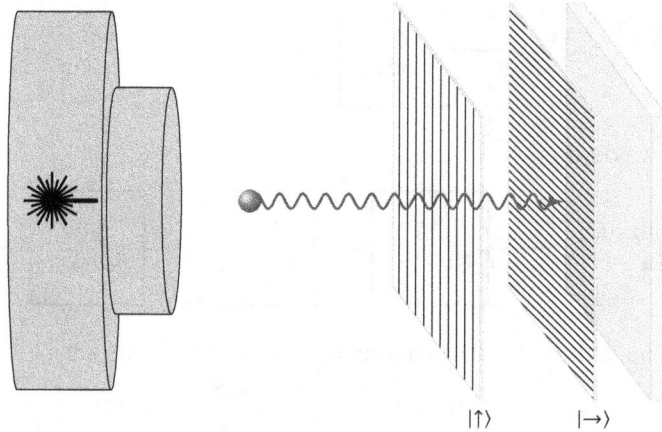

We define an additional orthonormal basis $\{|\nearrow\rangle, |\searrow\rangle\}$, where

$$|\nearrow\rangle = \frac{\sqrt{2}}{2}\,(|\rightarrow\rangle + |\uparrow\rangle) \quad \text{and} \quad |\searrow\rangle = \frac{\sqrt{2}}{2}\,(|\rightarrow\rangle - |\uparrow\rangle)\;.$$

If we add a middle filter for $|\nearrow\rangle$, the photon reaches the wall with probability $\frac{|a|^2}{4}$. The basis $\{|\nearrow\rangle, |\searrow\rangle\}$ plays the role of $\{|+\rangle, |-\rangle\}$ from above:

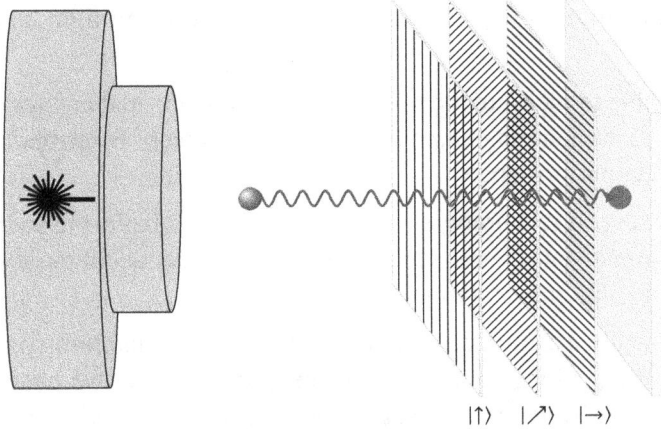

$|\uparrow\rangle \quad |\nearrow\rangle \quad |\rightarrow\rangle$

This experiment was first proposed in a 1930 textbook by Paul Dirac. [68] It demonstrates quantum states, superposition, and alternative sets of basis kets.

Exercise 11.13

Instead of having the middle filter at 45° to the others, imagine rotating it from the horizontal to the vertical. How does the probability of a photon reaching the wall change? Can you express this mathematically?

To learn more

Given the polarization of light as a two-state quantum system, you might think that you can use photons to implement qubits. You would be correct; this is the basis for significant academic research and several start-up companies.

To see how the techniques satisfy DiVincenzo's criteria from section 11.2, see the articles by Knill, O'Brien, and others. [125] [164] [165]

11.10   Summary

In this chapter, we connected the ''logical'' idea of qubits and circuits with the ''physical'' reality of how you might build a quantum computer.

Physical qubits don't survive forever, and decoherence explains the several ways in which quantum states wander over time. While we do not yet have large enough systems to implement fault tolerance, we examined what error correction might be able to do in the quantum realm.

We need to be able to measure the progress we are making and answer questions such as "How powerful is your quantum computer?". Our discussion of benchmarks looked at many factors that can affect performance.

We mentioned several technologies that researchers are exploring to implement qubits. According to their proponent scientists and engineers, superconducting transmon qubits, cold atoms, ion traps, and photonic techniques all hold promise.

We looked at the polarization of light to show a physical quantum system. We used our ket notation and superposition to understand the unusual effect we observed when using three filters. Through this, we could see that the theory of quantum mechanics does seem to provide a good model for what we experimentally observe, at least in this case. A reader who wishes to see the development of quantum computing from physics can start with this interpretation.

In the next chapter, we begin to look at advanced topics, starting with algorithms that do not require perfect logical qubits. These are the so-called "NISQ algorithms," and they attempt to solve problems in the presence of qubit and gate errors.

III

Advanced Topics

12

Considering NISQ Algorithms

Of all noises, I think music is the least disagreeable.

– Samuel Johnson

Noisy Intermediate-Scale Quantum (NISQ) computers have qubits that are not fully fault-tolerant and error-corrected. Decoherence and initialization, gate, and measurement errors make calculations even more unpredictable than normal quantum indeterminacy would indicate. At the time of writing, every available computer is NISQ.

Do we wait until we have perfect logical qubits to implement the routines in Chapter 10, "From Circuits to Algorithms"? Are there algorithms that use short-depth quantum circuits intermixed with classical methods to approximate solutions to problems that are otherwise exponentially hard?

In this chapter, we look at an algorithm for optimization that is an example of a quantum eigensolver that may produce practical results while we wait for full fault tolerance. Since many of the applications of NISQ methods are in physics and quantum chemistry, I include many references to articles that explore the science behind them in detail if you are interested or have the requisite background. These references include discussions of other NISQ algorithms, such as the Variational Quantum Eigensolver and its applications to quantum chemistry. Since this book is primarily a mathematical approach to quantum computing and is self-contained, I leave those discussions to others.

We work through or extend foundational concepts such as cost functions, graphs, heuristics, Hermitian matrices, expectation, time evolution, parameterized circuits, and Hamiltonians to provide the tools we need to understand the algorithm in this chapter.

> **To learn more**
>
> This chapter uses several concepts from machine learning that I cover in Chapter 15 of *Dancing with Python*. [211] We also use some concepts from calculus, such as continuity, derivatives, and partial derivatives. [205]

Topics covered in this chapter

12.1 Cost functions and optimization

Let's begin with an ad hoc definition of a concept we need when discussing many NISQ algorithms, the *cost function*, where we defined functions in section 4.1. As you would expect, such a function C computes the cost of something given one or more inputs. We might express the cost in money, work hours, resources consumed, relative health while undergoing a new medical treatment, or any measure of something used or lost. In machine learning, we employ a cost function to measure how close actual data values are to those predicted by a model we construct.

In all these examples, we are interested in minimizing the cost function. We want to find when something costs the least money, requires the fewest hours of work or resources, causes the most minor medical trauma or inconvenience, or produces an AI model closest to the training data. This is an optimization problem.

The examples in this section have continuous input parameters, such as all real numbers x such that $-1 \leq x \leq 1$. The parameters may also be discrete, such as an input x restricted to a finite set of integers. Of particular importance to us later in this chapter will be *binary* parameters, where the input value is either 0 or 1. We might then consider $C(\mathbf{x})$, where $\mathbf{x}$ is a bit string of some length n, such as **011010011** for $n = 9$.

12.1.1 One-variable functions

For the curve on the left-hand side of Figure 12.1, labeled "A," we can observe that there is one minimum. By adding coordinates and having an explicit equation for C, as shown in Figure 12.1 B, we can efficiently compute the minimum at the point $(x, y) = (1, 1)$. Since C has one variable, we call its graph the *cost curve*.

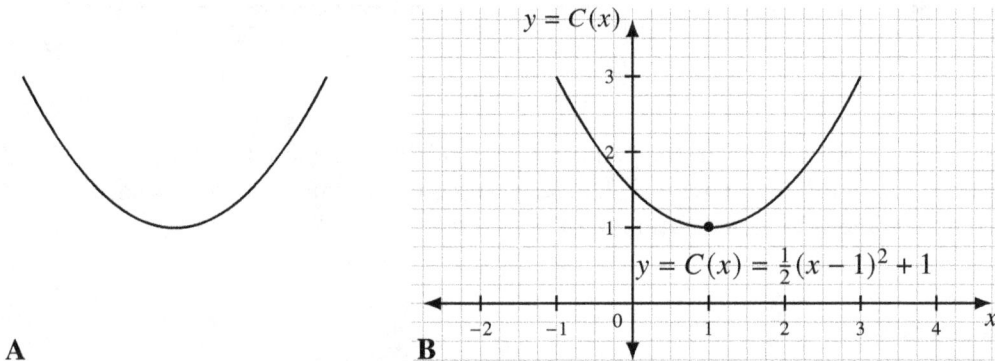

A   **B**

Figure 12.1: A simple cost function

Using calculus, we compute $C'(x)$, the derivative of $C(x)$, to be $x - 1$. We set this to 0 and solve for x, yielding $x = 1$. The y-value is $C(1) = 1$. We must check that this is a minimum, not a maximum or inflection point.

Alternatively, we can make an initial educated guess for the x-value of the minimum and then look at points a little to the left and a little to the right of x, say $x - \delta$ and $x + \delta$ for a small positive real value of δ. We use these to move in the direction where C is decreasing. That is, we look at the slopes of the lines connecting the points $P_1 = (x - \delta, C(x - \delta))$ and $P_2 = (x, C(x))$, and P_2 and $P_3 = (x + \delta, C(x + \delta))$. We move in the direction of the lesser slope. We repeat this process and decrease δ until we are at or sufficiently close to the minimum.

Exercise 12.1

In the following graph, we start with $x = 2$ and $\delta = 0.5$.

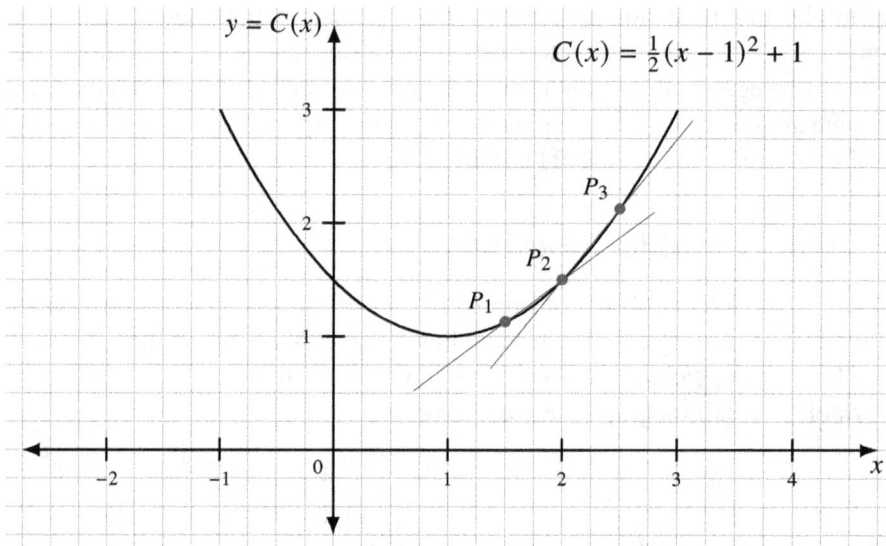

$$C(x) = \tfrac{1}{2}(x - 1)^2 + 1$$

What are the coordinates of the points P_1, P_2, and P_3? What are the slopes of the lines between P_1 and P_2, and P_2 and P_3? Stated in terms of this information, in what direction should you move toward the minimum of the cost function?

Exercise 12.2

What should we do if the slopes of the lines connecting P_1 and P_2, and P_2 and P_3 are equal?

Another word for slope is *gradient*, and we also use the word to refer to the derivative of a function from $\mathbf{R} \rightarrow \mathbf{R}$ and the vector of partial derivatives for a function from $\mathbf{R}^n \rightarrow \mathbf{R}$.

Cost functions arise when we perform *curve fitting* for observed data. Suppose we have n points of real-life data $(x_1, y_1) \ldots (x_n, y_n)$. Can we find a function f that models our data so that $y_j = f(x_j)$ for $1 \leq j \leq n$? Can we get as close as possible if we cannot have equality? If we constrain f to be a linear function, we are performing *linear regression,* which you may have seen in statistics or machine learning. [211, Section 15.7]

We define $e_j = y_j - f(x_j)$, the error between what we observe (y_j) and what our model ($f(x_j)$) tells us. The *Mean Squared Error*, MSE, is our cost function

$$C(x) = \frac{1}{n} \sum_{j=1}^{n} (y_j - f(x_j))^2 .$$

We want to minimize the sum of the squares of the errors divided by the number of observations.

For linear regression, $f(x) = y = mx + b$, which is the equation of a line. Let μ_x be the mean (average) of the x values and μ_y be the mean (average) of the y values. $C(x)$ is minimized when

$$m = \frac{\sum_{j=1}^{n} (x_j - \mu_x)(y_j - \mu_y)}{\sum_{j=1}^{n} (x_j - \mu_x)^2} \qquad b = \mu_y - m\mu_x .$$

This is an exact solution to the optimization problem. Figure 12.2 shows the optimal line fitted to 100 points by linear regression.

The situation is more complicated when we have multiple minima, as shown in Figure 12.3 A. We have a *local minimum* at $x \approx 1.3882$, but the *global minimum* is at $x \approx 3.9677$. We must ensure that we do not get trapped in a ''valley'' of a local minimum and miss the global minimum entirely.

If we measure error as a value between 0.0 and 1.0, where 0.0 means no error, then *fidelity* is $1-$ the error. We saw this in section 11.6.1 when we discussed metrics such as gate fidelity. If we find where the error is minimized, we also find where the fidelity is maximized. Therefore, we lose no generality when considering the minimum values of a function instead of maximums of a related function. The graph shown in Figure 12.3 B is the same as the one above, just inverted and pushed upward. A cost function is an example of an *objective function*, which is any function we want to minimize or maximize.

In business, the profit is an objective function

$$\text{profit}(x) = \text{revenue}(x) - \text{cost}(x) .$$

We can maximize profit by minimizing cost for fixed revenue. This is another example of a cost function minimization translated into a maximization problem. Even though we may think of ''C'' for ''cost,'' the literature often uses $C(x)$ as a cost function to be minimized or a profit function to be maximized.

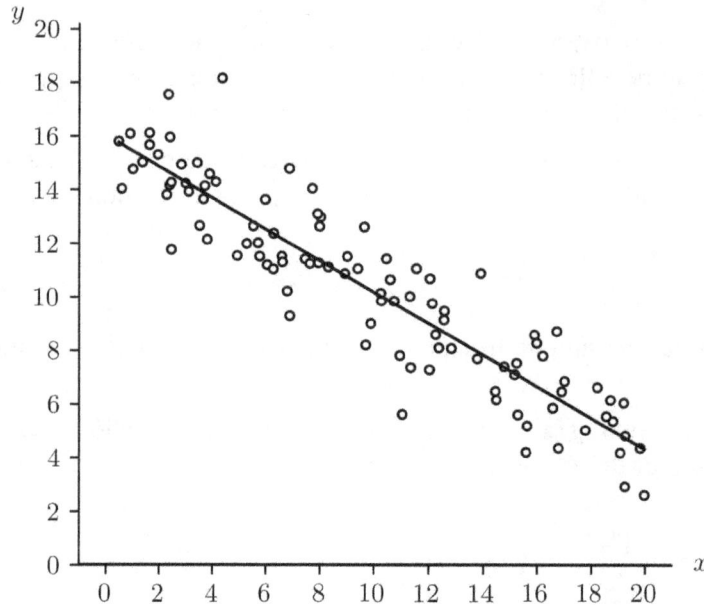

Figure 12.2: Linear regression on 100 points

A *barren plateau* is another situation we must avoid when seeking a minimum, as shown in Figure 12.4. When the x-coordinate is 3.5, the slope (gradient) of the curve is 0. Even if we move a little to the left or right, the slope remains 0, and we cannot determine in which direction to move to the minimum.

12.1.2 Multivariable functions and gradient descent

A cost function with one variable is neither very interesting nor difficult to optimize. Most cost functions have many inputs. For example, if you were determining the cost of manufacturing quantum computers, you might input

- the number of systems to build
- the cost of the components, such as refrigeration units, cryostats, lasers, and control hardware
- the cost of the people who build and ship the units, with all overhead, such as healthcare and insurance
- the cost of the machines used in manufacturing
- real estate expenses and property insurance

Even with only two variables, finding the minimum of a cost function may be tricky. The graphs shown in Figure 12.5 are extensions of the parabola in Figure 12.1 to three dimensions. On the left, in the graph labeled "A," the function only depends on one input. On the right,

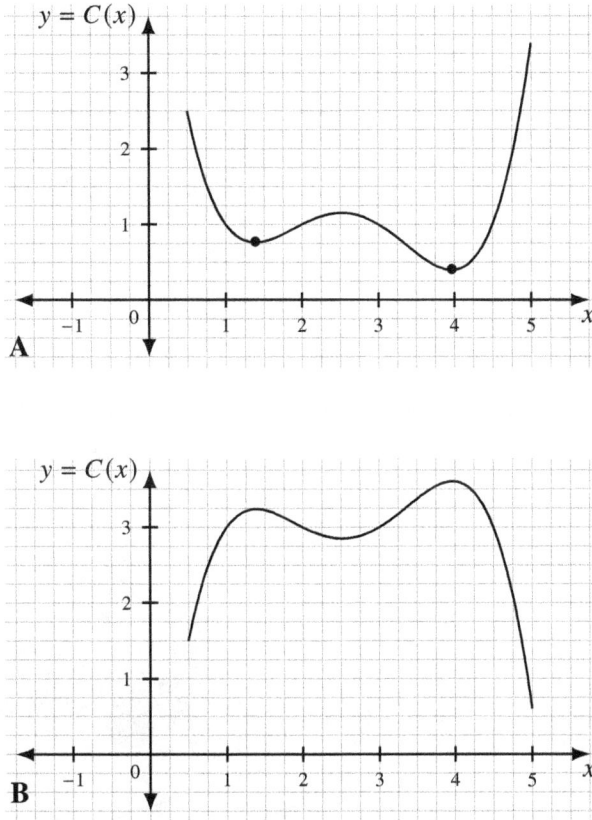

Figure 12.3: Local and global minimums, and inversion to find maximum values

in the graph labeled "B," the function uses both inputs symmetrically. They are each a *cost surface*.

In Figure 12.5 A, there is a line of minima. The minimum cost is independent of one of the variables. In Figure 12.5 B, there is a single minimum. If you start at any point, you should choose the direction where the cost decreases fastest to reach the minimum efficiently.

Let's use the gradient descent optimization technique, since we have the equations for these two graphs. We saw a version of this in Exercise 12.1 and the discussion preceding it.

We have two functions f and g that map from $\mathbf{R}^2 \to \mathbf{R}$. We graph these in three dimensions using points $(x, y, z) = (x, y, f(x, y))$ and $(x, y, z) = (x, y, g(x, y))$, respectively. Let's begin with Figure 12.5 A.

We first compute the gradient of $f(x, y) = (x - 1)^2 + 1$:

$$\text{grad } f = \nabla f = \left(\frac{\partial f}{\partial x}, \frac{\partial f}{\partial y}\right) = (2x - 2, 0) \ .$$

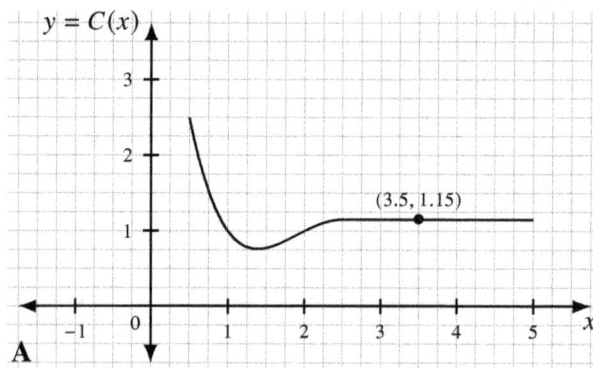

Figure 12.4: A function with a barren plateau

$$z = f(x,y) = (x-1)^2 + 1 \qquad z = g(x,y) = (x-1)^2 + (y-1)^2 + 1$$

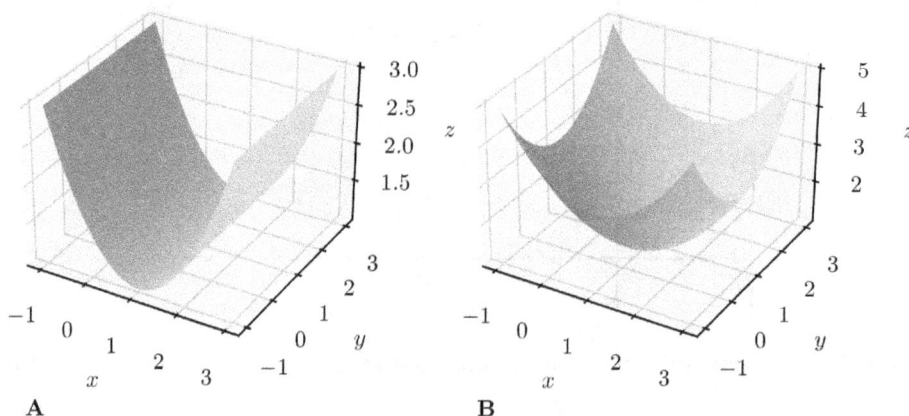

Figure 12.5: Parabolic minimums in three dimensions

This is an expression from multivariable calculus and says that the gradient of f is a vector composed of the partial derivative of f with respect to x and the partial derivative of f with respect to y. We use the "∇" symbol for the gradient, and we pronounce this "del." f does not depend on y, which is why the partial derivative with respect to y is 0. It is also why the graph looks like a parabola extruded along the y-axis.

We begin at the point $P_0 = (x,y) = (-1,0)$ and compute $\nabla f(-1,0)$. This is a vector in the xy-plane. If we move in this direction to $(-1,0) + (-4,0) = (-5,0)$, we head toward a **larger** value of f. Since we want to move toward a minimum, we use $-\nabla f$.

Given P_n, we compute a new point

$$P_{n+1} = P_n - \eta \nabla f(P_n),$$

where η is a small positive real number called the *learning rate* or the *step size*. η is the Greek letter "eta."

Figure 12.6 shows P_0 through P_6 going from left to right, with $\eta = 0.25$. If we compute $\nabla f(P_6)$, we get 0, meaning we have reached a *stable point*. This is a good candidate for a minimum, and we should check.

$$z = f(x, y) = (x - 1)^2 + 1$$

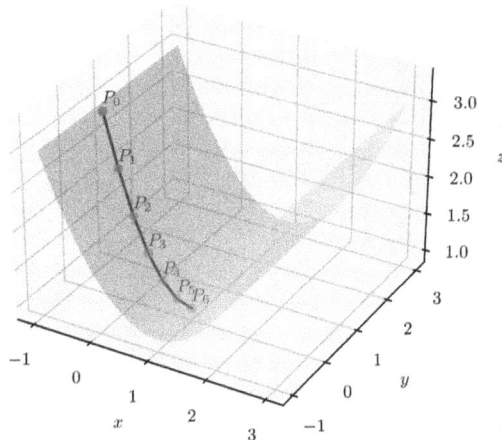

Figure 12.6: Gradient descent on a 3D surface that is independent of y

This is a simple and well-behaved example, and the flowchart in Figure 12.7 shows the algorithm's major steps. In practice, we would look at $|\nabla f(P_n)|$ and adjust the size of the learning rate. We might also find ourselves trapped in a local minimum or barren plateau. We can introduce *stochastic*, or probabilistic, variations to find good starting places and learning rates. We must have criteria for when we are close enough to a minimum: sometimes, an efficiently computed good approximation is better than an exact but expensive solution.

Exercise 12.3

Perform gradient descent to a minimum for the graph in Figure 12.5 B. In this case,

$$g(x, y) = (x - 1)^2 + (y - 1)^2 + 1$$

$$\text{grad } g = \nabla g = \left(\frac{\partial g}{\partial x}, \frac{\partial g}{\partial y} \right) = (2x - 2, 2y - 2) \ .$$

Use $\eta = 0.2$ and begin at $P_0 = (3, 2)$.

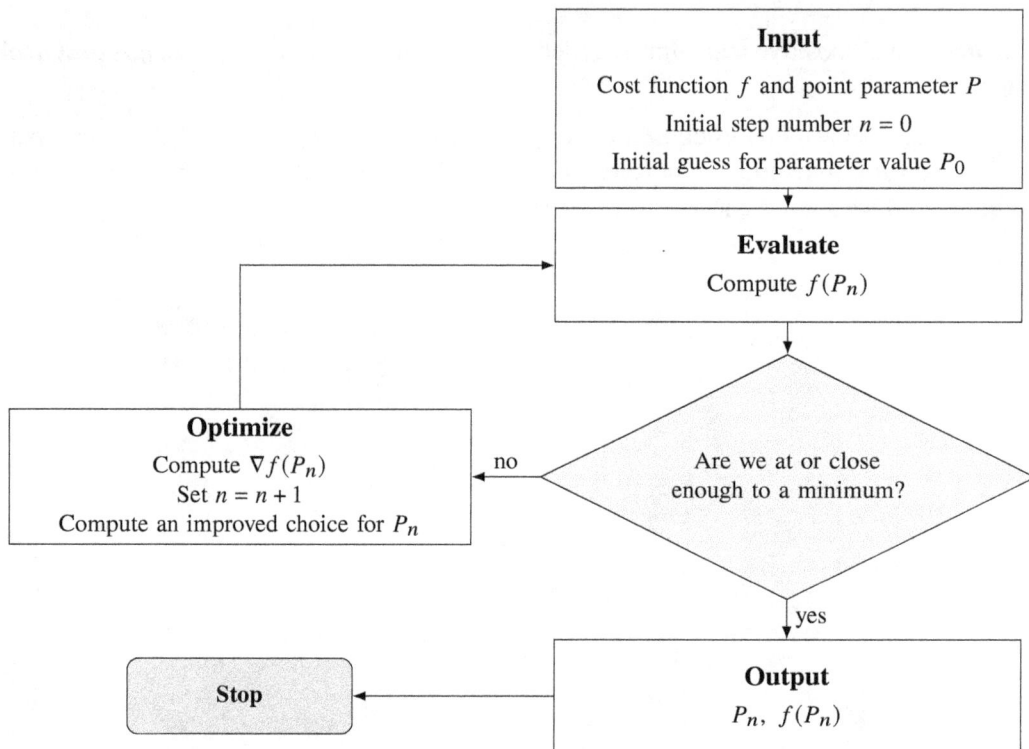

Figure 12.7: Flowchart showing a simple optimization loop

Figure 12.8 shows three interesting three-dimensional situations concerning minima. In Figure 12.8 A, we have two lines of minima, but only one contains the global minima. Compare this with the graph in Figure 12.5 A.

Figure 12.8 B shows a *saddle point*: a minimum in one direction and a maximum in the orthogonal direction. It is the graph of $z = x^2 - y^2$ Another name for a saddle point is a *minmax point*. It is neither a local minimum nor maximum.

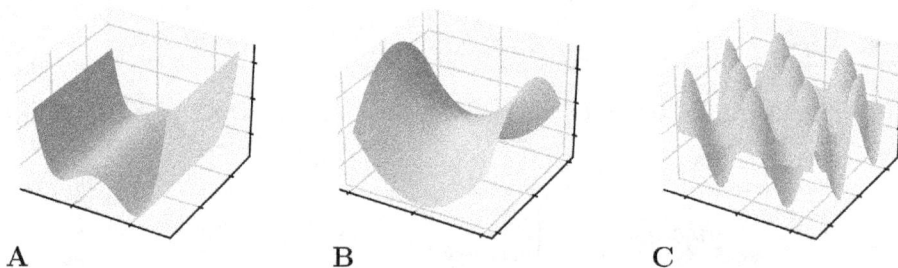

Figure 12.8: Minima examples in three dimensions

In Figure 12.8 C, we have multiple global minima that repeat periodically. It is the graph of $z = \cos(x)\sin(y)$.

When we have more than two inputs, we would need more than three dimensions to show the graph of the cost function, its *cost hyper-surface* or *cost landscape*. While geometric principles and thinking are part of optimization, we must employ more sophisticated techniques from linear algebra, probability, multivariable calculus, and numerical analysis. Optimization is an entire discipline of applied mathematics.

Given the complexity and the value of finding optimal or near-optimal solutions, it should not surprise you that researchers are trying to use quantum computers to find good answers quickly and cost-effectively. (Yes, that was a pun!) If we can efficiently evaluate the cost function or its gradients using classical computing techniques, there is no point in looking for a quantum solution. As with heuristics, which we will examine next, we may start by believing that one (quantum) method is best, only to discover that a better (classical) one already exists.

Exercise 12.4

Discuss how gradient methods can go wrong in the presence of a saddle point.

12.2 Heuristics

Is there a difference between an algorithm that provides an exact sequence of steps to follow to solve a problem and a quick-and-dirty solution with shortcuts that may work sometimes? This section discusses the latter, but, for contrast, note that we have seen many examples of *exact algorithms*:

- Addition in section 2.5
- Sorting in section 2.8.1
- Searching in section 2.8.2
- Euclid's algorithm in section 3.4.1
- The Gram-Schmidt orthonormalization process in section 5.7.6
- Quantum teleportation in section 9.3.5
- Amplitude amplification in section 9.6
- Grover's search algorithm in section 9.7.1
- The Deutsch-Jozsa algorithm in section 9.8
- The Bernstein-Vazirani algorithm in section 9.9
- Simon's algorithm in section 9.10
- The Quantum Fourier Transform in section 10.1

- Phase estimation in section 10.5
- Order and period finding in section 10.6
- Shor's factoring algorithm in section 10.7

In each of these, we follow a designated set of steps, such as a recipe, to get the exact answer. For some, we must repeat all or part of the algorithm to ensure the answer is correct. We can perform a probabilistic analysis to guide us on how many iterations are necessary. An algorithm may fail to find an exact solution, such as when we use a gradient method and discover a local minimum instead of a global one.

A *heuristic* is a technique or approach that takes shortcuts and may find an exact or good enough result. It may be faster than an exact algorithm, although it may not evaluate all possible solutions or find the most precise answer. A heuristic is all about **speed**.

> The terminology in the literature can be confusing because sometimes ''algorithm'' is used broadly and includes heuristics, and other times, it means ''exact algorithm.'' Similarly, a ''heuristic'' may be called a ''heuristic algorithm.''

Let's examine two problems that warrant heuristic approaches, but first, we need an introduction to graphs.

12.2.1 Graphs

A *graph* is a collection of objects called *vertices* and connections or relationships between pairs of vertices called *edges*. We sometimes call a vertex a *node*. Figure 12.9 is a graph with four vertices and four edges.

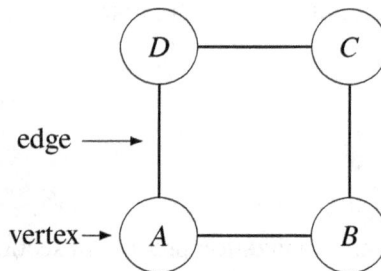

Figure 12.9: A graph with four vertices and four edges

Let **G** be a graph and **V** and **E** be its sets of vertices and edges, respectively. We write

$$\mathbf{G} = (\mathbf{V}, \mathbf{E}).$$

We denote by $|\mathbf{V}|$ the number of vertices and by $|\mathbf{E}|$ the number of edges in **G**.

We can assign a property to a vertex or edge, such as a label, cost, size, distance, or another named value. If an edge has a single numeric property, we usually call it a *weight*. Figure 12.10 is a graph with four vertices, six edges, and weights on the edges.

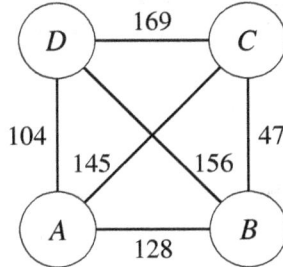

Figure 12.10: A graph with four vertices and six edges with weights

We label the edges with the labels of the vertices to which they are connected: *AB*, *BC*, *CD*, *AD*, *AC*, and *BD*. For example, we denote the weight of the edge *AB* by w_{AB}.

The table in Figure 12.11 shows the road distance in miles between four cities in Scotland. It is symmetric across the diagonal; the distance between two cities is the same in either direction.

	A = Aberdeen	*B* = Edinburgh	*C* = Glasgow	*D* = Inverness
A = Aberdeen	0	128	145	104
B = Edinburgh	128	0	47	156
C = Glasgow	145	47	0	169
D = Inverness	104	156	169	0

Figure 12.11: Distances among four cities in Scotland

The graph in Figure 12.10 shows this same data, with the edge weights being the inter-city distances. It is an *undirected graph* because we are not stating anything special about the order in which the edges connect the vertices. This implies that *AB* and *BA* are the same edge.

Suppose there is a traffic stoppage on the motorway going from Aberdeen to Edinburgh. The police send drivers on a detour that adds 10 miles to the trip in that direction. In this case, we can use a *directed graph*:

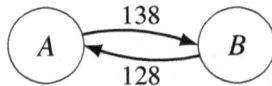

AB and *BA* are different edges because the graph is directed. In the following, all our graphs are undirected. We also assume that every vertex has at least one edge connected to it.

12.2.2 Max-Cut Problem

Let G be a graph and V and E be its sets of vertices and edges, respectively.

Let U be a proper nonempty subset of V. This means that U contains at least one vertex but not all vertices of V. We define U' as the *complement* of U: U' is the set of all vertices in V that are not in U.

Given U, we define $\delta(U)$ to be the set of all edges uu' for vertices u in U and u' in U'. We pronounce $\delta(U)$ as "delta U."

We call $\delta(U)$ a *cut* and denote by $|\delta(U)|$ the size of $\delta(U)$. $|\delta(U)|$ is the number of edges that connect vertices in U with vertices in its complement.

Exercise 12.5

Explain why this formula computes $|\delta(U)|$:

$$|\delta(U)| = \sum_{u \text{ in } U} \sum_{u' \text{ in } U'} 1, \text{ if } uu' \text{ is in } E$$

The *Maximum Cut* or *Max-Cut Problem* for V is to find a proper nonempty subset U of V so that $|\delta(U)|$ is as large as possible. U may not be unique. We call such a U a *maximum cut*. Per its name, Max-Cut is an optimization problem to maximize the objective function $|\delta(U)|$.

The Max-Cut Problem seems abstract. Why do we care about solutions to it? There are applications in theoretical physics, but this doesn't reduce the abstraction very much for most people. More practically, it is helpful in designing networks and classical integrated circuits for semiconductor chips involving millions of transistors. [11] Later in this chapter in section 12.8, we show a NISQ algorithm to solve the Max-Cut problem for certain types of graphs.

Figure 12.12: Two cuts of a graph with four vertices and four edges

Figure 12.12 shows two cuts of a simple graph that looks like a square. On the left, $U = \{A\}$ and $U' = \{B, C, D\}$. $\delta(U) = \{AB, AD\}$. $|\delta(U)| = 2$.

On the right, $\mathbf{U} = \{A, B\}$ and $\mathbf{U'} = \{C, D\}$. $\delta(\mathbf{U}) = \{BC, AD\}$. $|\delta(\mathbf{U})| = 2$ again. Can we do better?

Since we are trying to find the best solution among many possible combinations of vertices, Max-Cut is a *combinatorial optimization problem.*

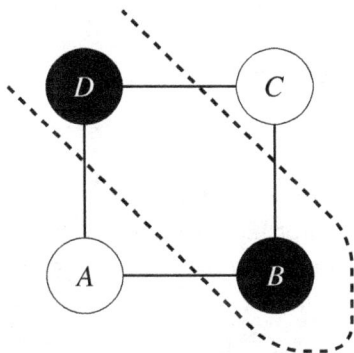

Figure 12.13: A maximum cut

Figure 12.13 shows a maximum cut $\delta(\mathbf{U}) = \{AB, BC, CD, AD\}$ where $\mathbf{U} = \{A, C\}$ and $\mathbf{U'} = \{B, D\}$. We know this is the maximum because there are four edges in $\mathbf{V}$, which is the cut's size. In other graphs, the Max-Cut size might be less than $|\mathbf{E}|$.

Well, that didn't seem so hard! Try to solve Max-Cut for the graph in Figure 12.14.

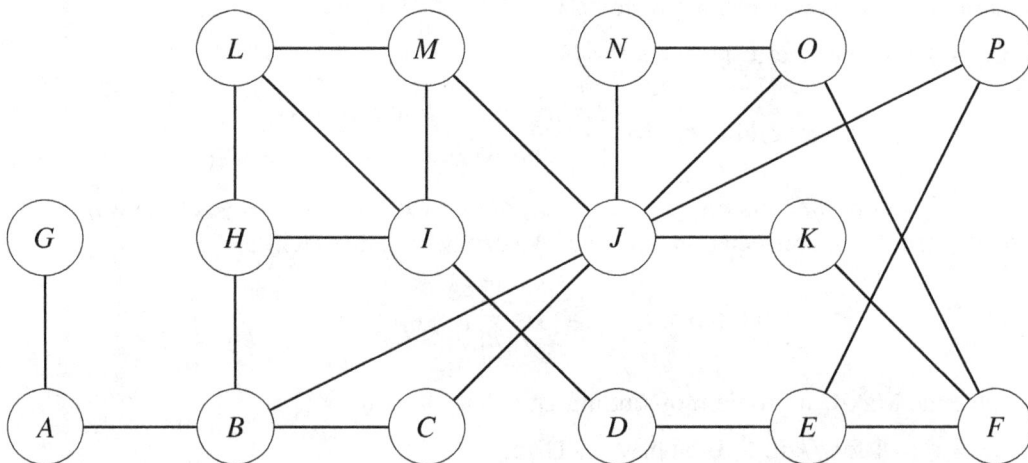

Figure 12.14: A large graph with a difficult Max-Cut calculation

Not so easy, right? In general, the Max-Cut Problem is NP-Hard, which we defined in section 10.3. [121] Thus, the problem cannot be solved using a deterministic algorithm in polynomial time, and it is among the hardest of such problems. For this reason, researchers have developed heuristics to attempt to find acceptable, if not optimal, solutions quickly.

[123] It is also why people are trying to use quantum computers to find better solutions faster than we can do classically.

We can extend the Max-Cut Problem by including weights:

$$|\delta(\mathbf{U})| = \sum_{u \text{ in } \mathbf{U}} \sum_{u' \text{ in } \mathbf{U}'} w_{uu'}, \text{ if } uu' \text{ is in } \mathbf{E}.$$

Henceforth, we will only use weights equal to 0 or 1.

Exercise 12.6

Suppose the edges in $\mathbf{E}$ do not have weights. What weights would you assign to the edges to use this extended definition for $|\delta(\mathbf{U})|$ instead of the simpler one that only counts edges?

Let's look at an alternative definition of $|\delta(\mathbf{U})|$. We number and label the $|\mathbf{V}|$ vertices in $\mathbf{V}$ by integers 1 through $|\mathbf{V}|$. Consider the bit string $\mathbf{x}$ consisting of $|\mathbf{V}|$ **0**s and **1**s. If x_k is the bit in position k in $\mathbf{x}$,

$$x_k = \begin{cases} 1 & \text{if vertex } k \text{ is in } \mathbf{U} \\ 0 & \text{if vertex } k \text{ is in } \mathbf{U}'. \end{cases}$$

For simplicity, we now shorten "vertex k is in $\mathbf{U}$" to "k is in $\mathbf{U}$."

Consider the product $x_j(1 - x_k)$ for jk in $\mathbf{E}$. We have

$$x_j(1 - x_k) = \begin{cases} 1 & \text{if } j \text{ is in } \mathbf{U} \text{ and } k \text{ is in } \mathbf{U}' \\ 0 & \text{otherwise.} \end{cases}$$

We only define weights for edges jk in $\mathbf{E}$, but we can extend this by setting $w_{jk} = 0$ for vertices j and k not connected by an edge. We can now define $C(\mathbf{x})$ and see that

$$|\delta(\mathbf{U})| = C(\mathbf{x}) = \sum_{j=1}^{|\mathbf{V}|} \sum_{k=1}^{|\mathbf{V}|} w_{jk} x_j(1 - x_k).$$

We solve the Max-Cut problem by finding an $\mathbf{x}$ that maximizes $C(\mathbf{x})$.

Set $w_{jk} = 1$ for jk in $\mathbf{E}$, 0 otherwise. Then,

$$\begin{aligned} C(\mathbf{x}) &= \sum_{j=1}^{|\mathbf{V}|} \sum_{k=1}^{|\mathbf{V}|} w_{jk} x_j(1 - x_k) \\ &= \sum_{jk \text{ in } \mathbf{E}} \left(x_j(1 - x_k) + x_k(1 - x_j) \right) \end{aligned}$$

$$= \sum_{jk \text{ in } \mathbf{E}} \left(x_j + x_k - 2x_j x_k\right).$$

Consider the substitution that maps x_j to $\frac{1}{2}\left(1 - z_j\right)$ for new integer variables z_j. Under this transformation, $z_j = 1$ corresponds to $x_j = \mathbf{0}$, and $z_j = -1$ corresponds to $x_j = \mathbf{1}$. $z_j = -1$ if j is in $\mathbf{U}$, and $z_j = 1$ if j is in $\mathbf{U}'$.

With these substitutions, we seek to maximize

$$C(\mathbf{z}) = \frac{1}{2} \sum_{j=1}^{|\mathbf{V}|} \sum_{k=1}^{|\mathbf{V}|} w_{jk}(1 - z_j z_k) = \frac{1}{2} \sum_{jk \text{ in } E} (1 - z_j z_k)$$

for $w_{jk} = 1$ for jk in $\mathbf{E}$, and 0 otherwise. If we define

$$C_{jk}(\mathbf{z}) = \frac{1}{2}(1 - z_j z_k),$$

then we can write the cost function as the sum

$$C(\mathbf{z}) = \frac{1}{2} \sum_{jk \text{ in } E} (1 - z_j z_k) = \sum_{jk \text{ in } E} C_{jk}(\mathbf{z}).$$

Exercise 12.7

Show that finding a $\mathbf{z}$ that maximizes $C(\mathbf{z})$ solves the Max-Cut problem.

Exercise 12.8

State the formulas for $C(\mathbf{x})$ and $C(\mathbf{z})$ for the following graph. Give values for $\mathbf{U}$, $\mathbf{U}'$, $\mathbf{x}$, and $\mathbf{z}$ that solve the graph's Max-Cut Problem.

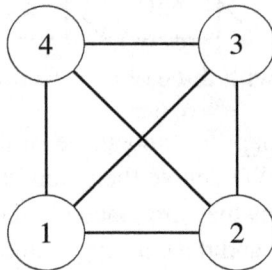

This is a *3-regular* graph since every vertex connects to three other vertices.

Exercise 12.9

How would minimizing

$$D(\mathbf{z}) = \frac{1}{2} \sum_{jk \text{ in } E} z_j z_k$$

help you maximize $C(\mathbf{z})$?

12.2.3   The Knapsack Problem

Suppose you are going on a trip and place everything you need in a knapsack. The objects you bring may vary by weight but also by value. There is a constraint: you can only carry so much total weight. You want to bring objects that maximize the total value but are within the weight limit. How do you choose which objects to bring?

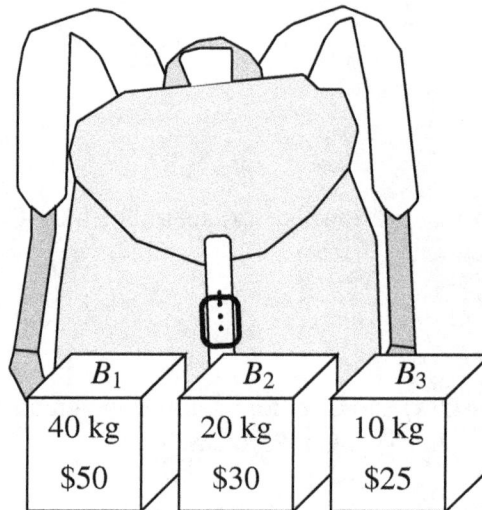

Figure 12.15: A knapsack with three objects of different weights and values

Let's do an analysis of the knapsack and three objects in Figure 12.15. The figure shows three boxes, B_1, B_2, and B_3. We denote their weights by $\{w_1, w_2, w_3\}$, their values by $\{v_1, v_2, v_3\}$, and the number of times they are placed in the box by $\{n_1, n_2, n_3\}$, respectively. The weight values are in kilograms, and the currency values are in United States dollars. You can use other units.

We first restrict ourselves to the *0–1 Knapsack Problem*. In this situation, we either do not include an object, so place it in the knapsack zero times, or put it once in the knapsack. Each n_k is 0 or 1. If we restrict the knapsack to holding at most N kilograms, the 0–1

Knapsack Problem on three objects is to find the values for the n_k that maximize the sum in the inequality

$$\sum_{k=1}^{3} n_k w_k = n_1 w_1 + n_2 w_2 + n_3 w_3 \leq N.$$

Though I chose three objects for this example, we can have as many objects as we wish for this kind of problem. We are ignoring the volume of the objects, but we can extend the problem with an additional constraint that limits how much room the objects take up in the knapsack. For example, we would need to consider weight and size if we were packing a truck or plane.

The brute-force algorithm when considering n objects for the Knapsack Problem has exponential complexity $O(2^n)$. Each object is either placed in or omitted from the knapsack, so we consider 2^n bit strings of length n.

Consider the case where the weight limit N is 5 kg. The smallest box weight is $w_1 = 10$, so we can place none of the boxes in the knapsack:

$$n_1 = n_2 = n_3 = 0.$$

Next, suppose the weight limit $N \geq 70$ kg. The sum of the box weights is 70, so we can put all the boxes in the knapsack:

$$n_1 = n_2 = n_3 = 1.$$

The problem only becomes interesting when $10 \leq N \leq 70$.

Let $N = 45$. If we adopt a *greedy* heuristic approach, we begin by choosing the heaviest box under this limit. This is B_1, with $w_1 = 40$. We only have 5 kg left in our weight budget, so we cannot place B_2 or B_3 in the knapsack. The total value of the objects in the knapsack is $v_1 = \$50$. Is this optimal?

If we place B_2 and B_3 in the knapsack, the total weight $w_2 + w_3 = 30 \leq N$. The value is $v_2 + v_3 = \$55$. No other combination of boxes produces a higher total value.

The exhaustive brute-force method looks at all eight $n_1 n_2 n_3$ combinations 000, 001, 010, 011, 100, 101, 110, and 111 and finds an optimal knapsack packing configuration.

If we replace the condition $0 \leq n_k \leq 1$ with $0 \leq n_k \leq c$ for some fixed nonnegative integer c, we have the "Bounded Knapsack Problem." If we can have as many objects as we wish, the problem is unbounded. Strangely, a "fractional" problem version allows us to break the objects into pieces before packing them. We can also have multiple knapsacks. In general, the Knapsack Problem is NP-Hard.

> ### Exercise 12.10
>
> Is the Knapsack Problem a minimization or maximization problem?

12.3   Hermitian matrices again

Recall that in section 5.4.1, we defined a square n-by-n complex matrix A on a vector space V to be Hermitian if $A = A^\dagger$: A is equal to its conjugate transpose and is self-adjoint. For the inner product $\langle \, , \rangle$,

$$\langle A\mathbf{v}_1, \mathbf{v}_2 \rangle = \langle \mathbf{v}_1, A^\dagger \mathbf{v}_2 \rangle = \langle \mathbf{v}_1, A\mathbf{v}_2 \rangle$$

for all vectors $\mathbf{v}_1$ and $\mathbf{v}_2$ in V. We now need some additional properties of Hermitian matrices for the consideration of NISQ algorithms.

It follows from the definition of a Hermitian matrix that:

- The diagonal elements of A are real.
- If c is a real number, cA is Hermitian.
- The eigenvalues λ_j of A are real. Some eigenvalues may appear more than once.
- The eigenvectors corresponding to distinct eigenvalues are orthogonal.
- By the Spectral Theorem in section 5.10, we can find $\{\mathbf{u}_1, \ldots, \mathbf{u}_n\}$ orthonormal eigenvectors of V with corresponding eigenvalues $\{\lambda_1, \ldots, \lambda_n\}$. Many proofs regarding A involve reducing applications of A to expressions involving the $\mathbf{u}_j$ and λ_j.
- Let U be the matrix with the jth column equal to $\mathbf{u}_j$. U is unitary, as you can see by considering $UU^\dagger = I_n = U^\dagger U$.
- Let D be the diagonal matrix with diagonal entries $\{\lambda_1, \ldots, \lambda_n\}$. We can transform A to D by a unitary change of basis because

$$A = UDU^\dagger = U \begin{bmatrix} \lambda_1 & 0 & 0 & \cdots & 0 & 0 & 0 \\ 0 & \lambda_2 & 0 & \cdots & 0 & 0 & 0 \\ \vdots & \vdots & \vdots & \ddots & \vdots & \vdots & \vdots \\ 0 & 0 & 0 & \cdots & 0 & \lambda_{n-1} & 0 \\ 0 & 0 & 0 & \cdots & 0 & 0 & \lambda_n \end{bmatrix} U^\dagger = \sum_{j=1}^n \lambda_j |u_j\rangle\langle u_j|$$

$$D = U^\dagger AU = U^\dagger AU$$

- If A has k distinct eigenvalues, we can decompose V into the direct sum (section 5.11) of *eigenspaces* $V_1, \ldots, V_k$, with each V_j spanned by orthonormal eigenvectors corresponding to λ_j:

$$V = V_1 \oplus \cdots \oplus V_k \,.$$

Exercise 12.11

Let M be an n-by-n complex matrix. Prove that the $2n$-by-$2n$ matrix

$$\begin{bmatrix} \mathbf{0} & M \\ M^\dagger & \mathbf{0} \end{bmatrix}$$

is Hermitian, where $\mathbf{0}$ is an n-by-n matrix of zeros.

12.3.1 Hermitian-unitary correspondence

If A is Hermitian with eigenvalues $\{\lambda_1, \ldots, \lambda_n\}$ and orthonormal eigenvectors $\{\mathbf{u}_1, \ldots, \mathbf{u}_n\}$, we define e^{iA} as

$$e^{iA} \stackrel{\text{def}}{=} \sum_{j=1}^{n} e^{i\lambda_j} |u_j\rangle\langle u_j| = U \begin{bmatrix} e^{i\lambda_1} & 0 & 0 & \cdots & 0 \\ 0 & e^{i\lambda_2} & 0 & \cdots & 0 \\ \vdots & \vdots & \ddots & \cdots & \vdots \\ 0 & 0 & 0 & \cdots & e^{i\lambda_n} \end{bmatrix} U^\dagger \,.$$

Each λ_j is a real number, possibly 0, but each

$$e^{i\lambda_j}$$

is *nonzero* and, in particular, a *complex unit*. Its conjugate is its inverse,

$$e^{-i\lambda_j} \,.$$

Let G and H be n-by-n complex matrices. By the general properties of matrices from section 5.5:

$$\overline{GH} = \overline{G}\,\overline{H} \qquad (GH)^\mathsf{T} = H^\mathsf{T} G^\mathsf{T} \qquad (GH)^\dagger = H^\dagger G^\dagger \,.$$

If G and H are invertible,

$$(GH)^{-1} = H^{-1} G^{-1} \,.$$

Thus,

$$\left(e^{iA}\right)^\dagger = U \begin{bmatrix} e^{-i\lambda_1} & 0 & 0 & \cdots & 0 \\ 0 & e^{-i\lambda_2} & 0 & \cdots & 0 \\ \vdots & \vdots & \ddots & \cdots & \vdots \\ 0 & 0 & 0 & \cdots & e^{-i\lambda_n} \end{bmatrix} U^\dagger$$

and

$$e^{iA}(e^{iA})^{\dagger} = U \begin{bmatrix} e^{i\lambda_1} & 0 & 0 & \cdots & 0 \\ 0 & e^{i\lambda_2} & 0 & \cdots & 0 \\ \vdots & \vdots & \ddots & \cdots & \vdots \\ 0 & 0 & 0 & \cdots & e^{i\lambda_n} \end{bmatrix} U^{\dagger} U \begin{bmatrix} e^{-i\lambda_1} & 0 & 0 & \cdots & 0 \\ 0 & e^{-i\lambda_2} & 0 & \cdots & 0 \\ \vdots & \vdots & \ddots & \cdots & \vdots \\ 0 & 0 & 0 & \cdots & e^{-i\lambda_n} \end{bmatrix} U^{\dagger}$$

$$= U \begin{bmatrix} e^{i\lambda_1} & 0 & 0 & \cdots & 0 \\ 0 & e^{i\lambda_2} & 0 & \cdots & 0 \\ \vdots & \vdots & \ddots & \cdots & \vdots \\ 0 & 0 & 0 & \cdots & e^{i\lambda_n} \end{bmatrix} \begin{bmatrix} e^{-i\lambda_1} & 0 & 0 & \cdots & 0 \\ 0 & e^{-i\lambda_2} & 0 & \cdots & 0 \\ \vdots & \vdots & \ddots & \cdots & \vdots \\ 0 & 0 & 0 & \cdots & e^{-i\lambda_n} \end{bmatrix} U^{\dagger}$$

$$= U I_n U^{\dagger} = I_n = U^{\dagger} I_n U .$$

> Let A be an n-by-n complex Hermitian matrix with eigenvalues $\{\lambda_1, \ldots, \lambda_n\}$ and orthonormal eigenvectors $\{\mathbf{u}_1, \ldots, \mathbf{u}_n\}$. The matrix e^{iA} is **unitary**. Its eigenvalues are
> $$\{e^{i\lambda_1}, \ldots, e^{i\lambda_n}\} ,$$
> corresponding to the same orthonormal eigenvectors $\{\mathbf{u}_1, \ldots, \mathbf{u}_n\}$.

What is perhaps astounding is that **every** complex unitary matrix U is e^{iA} for some complex Hermitian matrix A. [137, Theorem 18.1] We, therefore, have a correspondence

$$\text{Hermitian } A \leftrightarrow \text{Unitary } U = e^{iA} .$$

This relationship offers an important tool for solving problems involving Hermitian matrices, whereby we can shift to unitary matrices and, hence, quantum gates and circuits.

Exercise 12.12

Let A be the n-by-n zero matrix. Trivially, A is Hermitian. What is the unitary matrix e^{iA}?

Exercise 12.13

Let A be an n-by-n Hermitian matrix and M be a n-by-n unitary matrix. Show that
$$e^{iMAM^{\dagger}} = Me^{iA}M^{\dagger} .$$

To better understand the expression e^{iA}, we need some formulas from calculus. We can write the exponential, cosine, and sine functions for a real number x as the infinite sums:

$$e^x = \sum_{n=0}^{\infty} \frac{x^n}{n!} = 1 + x + \frac{x^2}{2!} + \frac{x^3}{3!} + \cdots$$

$$\cos(x) = \sum_{n=0}^{\infty} \frac{(-1)^n x^{2n}}{(2n)!} = 1 - \frac{x^2}{2!} + \frac{x^4}{4!} - \cdots$$

$$\sin(x) = \sum_{n=0}^{\infty} \frac{(-1)^n x^{2n+1}}{(2n+1)!} = x - \frac{x^3}{3!} + \frac{x^5}{5!} - \cdots$$

These infinite sums are examples of *power series*. "Series" means that we are computing a sum, "power" that we adding terms with increasing exponents, and "infinite" that we do not stop at some point.

Note that all exponents of x in the cosine are even, which is why it is an even function. A similar statement holds for sine being an odd function.

Let M be a square matrix such that $M^2 = I$, the identity matrix. Important examples of these are identity matrices, Pauli matrices, and the Hadamard matrices. This implies that $M^n = M$ if n is an odd integer and is I if n is even.

Let θ be a variable representing a real number, typically an angle measured in radians. Then,

$$
\begin{aligned}
e^{i\theta M} &= \sum_{n=0}^{\infty} \frac{i^n \theta^n M^n}{n!} \\[2mm]
&= \sum_{n=0}^{\infty} \frac{i^{2n} \theta^{2n} M^{2n}}{(2n)!} + \sum_{n=0}^{\infty} \frac{i^{2n+1} \theta^{2n+1} M^{2n+1}}{(2n+1)!} \quad \text{(separate into even and odd powers)} \\[2mm]
&= I \sum_{n=0}^{\infty} \frac{i^{2n} \theta^{2n}}{(2n)!} + M \sum_{n=0}^{\infty} \frac{i^{2n+1} \theta^{2n+1}}{(2n+1)!} \quad \text{(handle powers of } M) \\[2mm]
&= I \sum_{n=0}^{\infty} \frac{(-1)^n \theta^{2n}}{(2n)!} + iM \sum_{n=0}^{\infty} \frac{(-1)^n \theta^{2n+1}}{(2n+1)!} \quad \text{(handle powers of } i) \\[2mm]
&= I \cos(\theta) + iM \sin(\theta). \quad \text{(use power series definitions)}
\end{aligned}
$$

From this equation, we compute:

$$e^{i\frac{\pi}{2}\sigma_0} = e^{i\frac{\pi}{2}I_2} = iI_2 \qquad\qquad e^{i\frac{\pi}{2}\sigma_x} = e^{i\frac{\pi}{2}\mathbf{X}} = i\sigma_x$$

$$e^{i\frac{\pi}{2}\sigma_y} = e^{i\frac{\pi}{2}\mathbf{Y}} = i\sigma_y \qquad\qquad e^{i\frac{\pi}{2}\sigma_z} = e^{i\frac{\pi}{2}\mathbf{Z}} = i\sigma_z$$

Note, for example, that σ_z and $i\sigma_z$ are equivalent quantum operators up to a global phase. Similarly,

$$e^{-i\frac{\pi}{2}\sigma_0} = e^{-i\frac{\pi}{2}I_2} = e^{i\left(\frac{-\pi}{2}\right)I_2} = -iI_2$$

$$e^{-i\frac{\pi}{2}\sigma_x} = e^{-i\frac{\pi}{2}X} = e^{i\left(\frac{-\pi}{2}\right)X} = -i\sigma_x$$

$$e^{-i\frac{\pi}{2}\sigma_y} = e^{-i\frac{\pi}{2}Y} = e^{i\left(\frac{-\pi}{2}\right)Y} = -i\sigma_y$$

$$e^{-i\frac{\pi}{2}\sigma_z} = e^{-i\frac{\pi}{2}Z} = e^{i\left(\frac{-\pi}{2}\right)Z} = -i\sigma_z$$

Exercise 12.14

With M as above, show that

$$e^{-i\theta M} = I\cos(\theta) - iM\sin(\theta).$$

Exercise 12.15

Let A be the n-by-n matrix πI_n. What is the unitary matrix $U = e^{iA}$?

Exercise 12.16

Review section 10.5 on phase estimation, and state the value of that algorithm in light of what you now know about the correspondence between Hermitian and unitary matrices.

12.3.2 Pauli strings and sums

Recall that you proved in Exercise 7.39 that I_2 and the Pauli matrices σ_x σ_y, and σ_z are a basis of the 2-by-2 real vector space of complex Hermitian matrices. By looking at tensor products of bases, the *Pauli strings*

$$H_1 \otimes \cdots \otimes H_n \text{ with each } H_j \text{ in } \{I_2 = \sigma_0, \sigma_x, \sigma_y, \sigma_z\}$$

are a basis of the real vector space of 2^n-by-2^n complex Hermitian matrices. We can write any such Hermitian matrix H as a *Pauli sum*

$$H = \sum_{j=1}^{n} c_j P_j$$

for Pauli strings P_j and real numbers c_j.

Exercise 12.17

Why are Pauli strings and sums Hermitian?

Rather than using matrices, we can also specify Pauli strings using operators:

$$H_1 \otimes \cdots \otimes H_n \text{ with each } H_j \text{ in } \{\textbf{ID}, \textbf{X}, \textbf{Y}, \textbf{Z}\} .$$

In the literature, quantum practitioners often write Pauli strings by concatenating the letters I, X, Y, and Z. Therefore, for example,

$$\text{XIZZY} = \sigma_x \otimes I_2 \otimes \sigma_z \otimes \sigma_z \otimes \sigma_y$$

or

$$\text{XIZZY} = \textbf{X} \otimes \textbf{ID} \otimes \textbf{Z} \otimes \textbf{Z} \otimes \textbf{Y} .$$

Another notation you may see omits the identity matrices and uses subscripts for the positions of the Pauli matrices:

$$X_1 Z_3 Z_4 Y_5 = \sigma_x \otimes I_2 \otimes \sigma_z \otimes \sigma_z \otimes \sigma_y .$$

Exercise 12.18

The Pauli strings of length two are listed in appendix section A.4. How many nonzero entries are there in each row and column?

Exercise 12.19

Why is the square of a Pauli string, the Pauli string composed with itself, equal to the tensor product of copies of I_2?

12.4 Expectation and the variational principle

In section 6.6, we defined the concept of expectation. In section 7.3.4, we further related expectation to observables. Let's re-express some of those results in terms of eigenvectors $\mathbf{u}_j$ and eigenvalues λ_j of a Hermitian matrix A from the last section.

Let

$$|\psi\rangle = \sum_{j=1}^n a_j |\mathbf{u}_j\rangle \text{ with } 1 = \sum_{j=1}^n |a_j|^2$$

be a quantum state. Each $a_j = \langle \mathbf{u}_j | \psi \rangle$. Therefore,

$$|\psi\rangle = \sum_{j=1}^n \langle \mathbf{u}_j | \psi \rangle |\mathbf{u}_j\rangle \text{ with } 1 = \sum_{j=1}^n |\langle \mathbf{u}_j | \psi \rangle|^2 .$$

We define

$$M_j = |\mathbf{u}_j\rangle\langle \mathbf{u}_j| .$$

Each M_j is Hermitian and is a projector, meaning that $M_j \circ M_j = M_j^2 = M_j$. We have

$$\langle \psi | M_j | \psi \rangle = |a_j|^2$$

and this is the probability of measuring $|\mathbf{u}_j\rangle$. The eigenvectors of M_j are the $\mathbf{u}_k$ for $1 \le k \le n$. The eigenvalue of M_j corresponding to $\mathbf{u}_j$ is 1. All other eigenvalues are 0.

The M_j are observables since their eigenvectors form a basis for our quantum state vector space by construction.

The expected value, or expectation, $\langle A \rangle$ of A given the state $|\psi\rangle$ is

$$\langle A \rangle = \sum_{j=1}^n |\langle u_j | \psi \rangle|^2 \lambda_j = \langle \psi | A | \psi \rangle \text{ with } 1 = \sum_{j=1}^n |\langle u_j | \psi \rangle|^2 .$$

Let $\lambda_{\min}$ be the minimum eigenvalue. Then,

$$\langle A \rangle >= \sum_{j=1}^n |\langle u_j | \psi \rangle|^2 \lambda_j \ge \sum_{j=1}^n |\langle u_j | \psi \rangle|^2 \lambda_{\min} = \lambda_{\min} \sum_{j=1}^n |\langle u_j | \psi \rangle|^2 = \lambda_{\min} .$$

Minimizing $\langle A \rangle$ by varying $|\psi\rangle$ gives us a good approximation to the smallest eigenvalue of A. Conversely, the smallest eigenvalue of A is a lower bound to $\langle A \rangle$ over all values of $|\psi\rangle$. This inequality is an instance of the *variational principle*, and an algorithm or method based on it is called a *variational quantum algorithm* or, simply, a *variational algorithm*. QAOA in section 12.8 is an example of a variational algorithm.

Similarly, let $\lambda_{\max}$ be the maximum eigenvalue. Then

$$\langle A \rangle = \sum_{j=1}^n |\langle u_j | \psi \rangle|^2 \lambda_j \le \sum_{j=1}^n |\langle u_j | \psi \rangle|^2 \lambda_{\max} = \lambda_{\max} \sum_{j=1}^n |\langle u_j | \psi \rangle|^2 = \lambda_{\max} .$$

Maximizing $\langle A \rangle$ by varying $|\psi\rangle$ gives us a good approximation to the largest eigenvalue of A. Conversely, the largest eigenvalue of A is an upper bound to $\langle A \rangle$ over all values of $|\psi\rangle$.

Later in this chapter, we will seek to find a parameterized circuit that creates the quantum states $|\psi\rangle$ for a specific A that helps solve a problem we care about.

12.5 Time evolution

Another idea we need to understand for NISQ algorithms is *time evolution*. We begin with some results from single and multivariable calculus, complex analysis, differential equations, and linear algebra. While that is a formidable list of topics, the mathematical objects we manipulate are from Part I of this book.

Let g be a real-valued function of one real variable t. I chose t because I want you to think of it as the time variable. It is easiest to think of t having values in a continuous portion of $\mathbf{R}$, although it could exclude points where g is not defined. t might take values from a finite set of numbers or a discrete set such as $\mathbf{Z}$. In any case, for two values t_1 and t_2 in the domain of g, with $t_1 < t_2$, we can consider how g *evolves* when passing from t_1 to t_2. A common choice is $t_1 = 0$ and $t_2 = 1$.

For example, suppose you invest 500 units in some currency in an account that compounds interest continuously at 4% a year. Then,

$$g(t) = 500e^{0.4t} \, .$$

g defines the balance in the account. The account is a *system*, and $g(t)$ is the *state* of the system at time t. As t begins at 0 and increases, the change in $g(t)$ describes the *time evolution* of the system's state.

More generally, g might have other input variables in addition to t. The range of g could be complex numbers, vectors, matrices, kets, or other objects.

A real-valued function g of one real variable t is *continuous* at a value t_0 if $g(t_0)$ is defined, and if $g(t_0)$ is the *limit* of g as t approaches t_0 from the left and right. Informally, this means that the graph of g is not missing the point when $t = t_0$, and we can get as close to $g(t_0)$ as we like by making t sufficiently close to t_0 for $t > t_0$ and $t < t_0$. Intuitively, this means that the plot of g has no gaps or jumps. g is continuous if it is continuous at each point in its domain.

As we saw in section 4.2.3, a discontinuity is a point where a function is not continuous. Figure 12.16 shows four types of discontinuities. In plot **A**, the function $\left| \frac{1}{2t} \right|$ is not defined at $t_0 = 0$. Plot **B** shows the constant function $g(t) = 1.5$, except we omit the value when $t_0 = 1$. That is, $g(0)$ is not defined and is shown as an open circle.

In plot **C**, $g(1) = 0.5$ is defined and is the expected value when moving toward $t_0 = 1$ from the right. However, moving toward t_0 from the left, we would not get a function value of 1.5. Finally, plot **D** has g undefined when $t_0 = 1$, and the expected values from the left and right are different.

We can formalize and extend the notion of continuity for complex-valued functions of a single real or complex variable by using the absolute value to define concepts such as "as close as we would like."

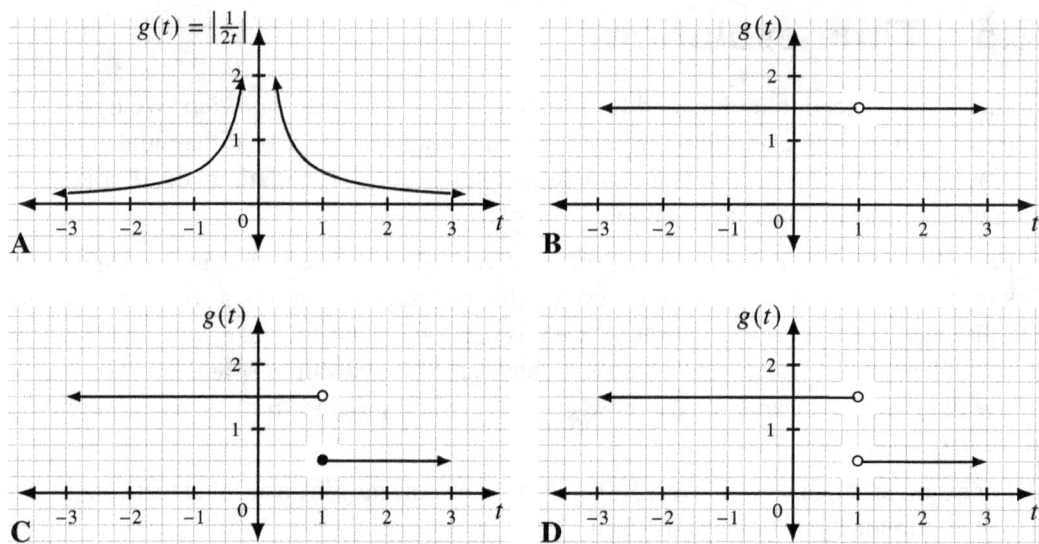

Figure 12.16: Discontinuities in functions of one real variable

Considerations of how g changes over time usually involve calculus or its generalization, analysis. If g is a function of the single variable t, we denote its *derivative* by

$$\frac{d}{dt}g(t) .$$

If g has multiple variables, we use "∂" instead of "d". Its first and second partial derivatives with respect to t are

$$\frac{\partial}{\partial t}g(t) \text{ and } \frac{\partial^2}{\partial t^2}g(t) .$$

Exercise 12.20

If you have learned calculus, consider $g(t) = |t|$. What is the derivative of g with respect to t? Is it continuous?

Examples

The continuous function

$$g : t \mapsto (\cos(t), \sin(t))$$

maps $\mathbf{R}$ to points on the unit circle in $\mathbf{R}^2$. The time evolution as t increases is a counterclockwise rotation.

The continuous function

$$g : t \mapsto \cos(t) + \sin(t)i = e^{ti}$$

maps **R** to units in **C**. The time evolution as t increases is a counterclockwise rotation in the complex plane (section 4.5).

The continuous function

$$g : t \mapsto U_t = \begin{bmatrix} \cos(t) & -\sin(t) \\ \sin(t) & \cos(t) \end{bmatrix}$$

maps **R** to 2-by-2 rotation matrices. As t increases, the system evolves with the rotations moving further counterclockwise. Each U_t is unitary, and if t_1 and t_2 are in **R**, then

$$U_{t_1 + t_2} = U_{t_1} U_{t_2} = U_{t_2} U_{t_1} .$$

We say a family of unitary matrices that has this property is *additive*.

The continuous function

$$g : t \mapsto |\psi(t)\rangle = \cos(\frac{\pi}{2}t)|0\rangle + \sin(\frac{\pi}{2}t)|1\rangle = \mathbf{R}^{y}_{t\pi}|0\rangle \text{ for } 0 \leq t \leq 1$$

for evolves a quantum state from $|0\rangle$ to $|1\rangle$. We define $\mathbf{R}^{y}_{t\pi}|0\rangle$ in section 7.6.12.

Exercise 12.21

Since $\mathbf{R}^{z}_{\varphi}$ is a parameterized gate (section 7.6.6), we can define a continuous function with the Hadamard gate **H**

$$g : t \mapsto \mathbf{R}^{z}_{t\frac{\pi}{2}} \mathbf{H} |0\rangle$$

as a time evolution of quantum states. What are the values of $g(0)$ and $g(1)$?

12.6   Parameterized circuits

The **Z** gate is fixed in the amount it rotates around the z-axis, while the general $\mathbf{R}^{z}_{\varphi}$ gate has the variable parameter φ. When we include such a gate in a circuit, we get a family of circuits that vary with φ. We need such circuits for NISQ algorithms, and we have seen examples of them before.

In section 10.1.3, we developed the circuit for the Quantum Fourier Transform on three qubits and denoted it $\mathbf{QFT}_3$.

The z-rotations follow a pattern, with angles equal to π divided by powers of 2.

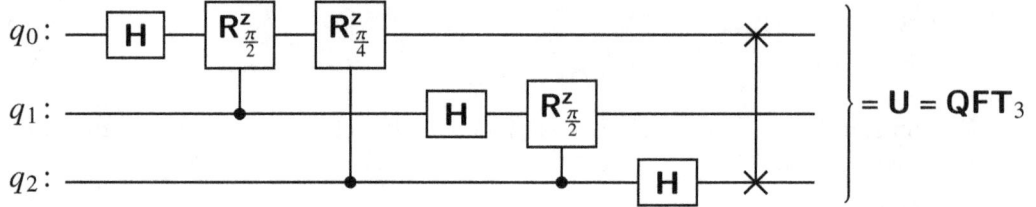

Figure 12.17: The Quantum Fourier Transform on three qubits

Let's add a parameter t to the rotation angle, as shown in Figure 12.18. When $t = 0$, each rotation gate is trivial and is the **ID** gate. When $t = 1$, we have **QFT**$_3$. We call this circuit with a single parameter **U**(t).

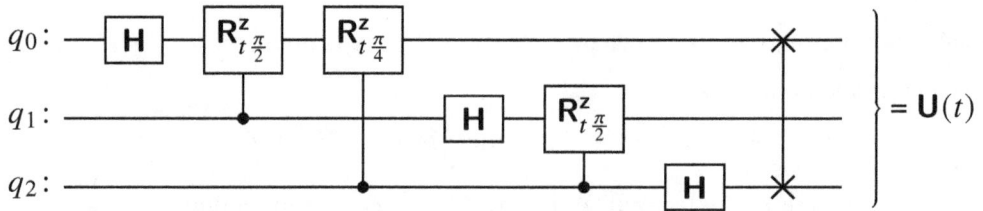

Figure 12.18: 1-Parameter Quantum Fourier Transform on three qubits

We can also add a parameter θ to replace the constant π. We denote this 2-parameter circuit as **U**(t, θ) as shown in Figure 12.19.

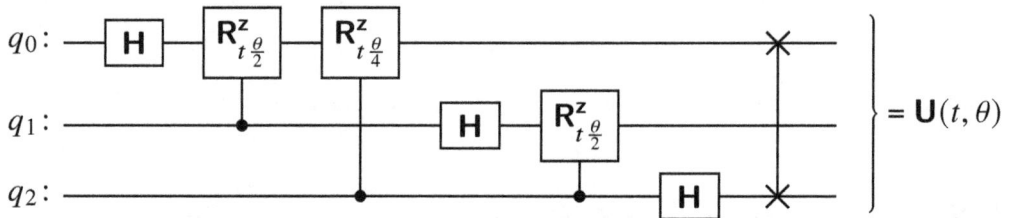

Figure 12.19: 2-Parameter Quantum Fourier Transform on three qubits

Exercise 12.22

Explicitly compute the 8-by-8 matrix for the entire **U**(t, θ) circuit. Use tensor products of the matrices for the 1- and 2-qubit gates.

Generally, we could have many angle parameters for x-, y-, and z-rotations. So, we can imagine a circuit named

$$\mathbf{U}(t, \theta_1, \theta_2, \theta_3, \theta_4, \theta_5).$$

In the literature, you may see each parameter, including what we have called t, named θ_j for some nonnegative integer j. When we want to refer to the collection of all θ_j, we use bold as we do with vectors: $\boldsymbol{\theta}$.

Parameterized circuits are functions that take one quantum state to another. For example,

$$\mathbf{U}(\theta_0, \theta_1, \theta_2, \theta_3, \theta_4, \theta_5) \, |0\rangle^{\otimes n}$$

takes $|0\rangle^{\otimes n}$ to another n-qubit quantum state. By varying the parameters, we might be able to compute a quantum state that has special significance, such as one representing the minimum of a cost function expressed in quantum terms.

In such a situation, we call such a circuit into which we substitute a specific choice for values of parameters an *ansatz*.

12.7 The Hamiltonian

Time evolution of a quantum system, represented as a sequence of quantum states, occurs via a continuous and additive family of unitary matrices U_t, where we often consider $0 \leq t \leq 1$. We define each family via

$$U_t = e^{-iHt} = \exp(-iHt)$$

for some Hermitian matrix H. Other constants that may appear in the numerator are absorbed into H. [189, Section 13.4.2]

We call the Hermitian matrix H the *Hamiltonian* of the quantum system after mathematician and physicist William Rowan Hamilton (Figure 12.20). Being Hermitian, we can write any Hamiltonian as a Pauli sum.

Given H in $U_t = e^{-iHt}$, the process of finding an approximate and suitable unitary U_t and related circuit within a given error is known as *Hamiltonian simulation*. [59] [62, Section 2.3]

At this point, those of you with a quantum physics background may ask yourselves, "Where's the definition of Hamiltonian in terms of the total energy of the system? Why didn't he start with that?" I believe that most people who use quantum computers will need to know less and less physics over time. For example, I can write an app for my smartphone today and know nothing about how transistors work.

On the other hand, we are in the early days of quantum computing, and understanding the physics helps, even if it is becoming less critical for coding. In this book, I explain the

Figure 12.20: William Rowan Hamilton (1805–1865)

mathematics behind the methods and leave it to you to go deeper into the physics if you wish. I believe many treatments of NISQ algorithms make deep assumptions about the math, including unitary and Hermitian matrices and topics such as tensor products and Pauli strings. The scope of this book is to give you a firm foundation to learn more and understand the fundamental concepts of quantum computing from a mathematical perspective.

We will return to the Hamiltonian several times in the remainder of this chapter and relate it to the problem at hand. To mollify those of you who want to see more physics, here is how the idea of a Hamiltonian comes up naturally.

In a quantum system such as an atom, we can describe the system's total energy as the sum of the kinetic (moving) and potential energy. If I hold a ball one meter above the ground, it has gravitational potential energy. When I drop the ball, that energy is translated to kinetic energy. If I draw back a rubber band on my thumb, it has elastic potential energy. When I release it, it has kinetic energy as it flies across the room.

In a hydrogen atom, the energy of the single electron is related to its negative charge and interactions with the single positive charge in the nucleus. For atoms and molecules with multiple electrons and protons, their interactions greatly complicate computing the energy of the whole system.

In any case, we can represent the total energy by a Hermitian matrix, the Hamiltonian. In physics, we usually write this as $\hat{H}$. Let $|\psi(t)\rangle$ be the quantum state of our system at time t. Via calculus, the *time-dependent* Schrödinger equation relates $\hat{H}$ and $|\psi(t)\rangle$ to describe the time evolution of the system:

$$i\hbar\frac{\partial}{\partial t}|\psi(t)\rangle = \hat{H}|\psi(t)\rangle,$$

where $\hbar$ is Planck's constant h divided by 2π. We can rewrite this differential equation as

$$\frac{\partial}{\partial t}|\psi(t)\rangle = -\frac{i}{\hbar}\hat{H}|\psi(t)\rangle\,,$$

which says the rate of change of the quantum state $|\psi(t)\rangle$ at time t is equal to that state, times -1, times the inverse of $\hbar$, times the constant Hermitian matrix $\hat{H}$. The solution to this equation is

$$|\psi(t)\rangle = e^{-i\hat{H}t/\hbar}|\psi(0)\rangle = \hat{U}(t)|\psi(0)\rangle\,.$$

$\hat{U}$ is unitary from our discussion in section 12.3 and describes the time evolution starting at the initial state $|\psi(0)\rangle$.

Exercise 12.23

For a fixed real value of t, why is $\frac{\hat{H}t}{\hbar}$ Hermitian?

Exercise 12.24

For a fixed positive real value of t, how are the eigenvalues and eigenvectors of $\frac{\hat{H}t}{\hbar}$ related to those of $\frac{\hat{H}}{\hbar}$?

The minimum energy of a system, which we call its *zero-point energy*, occurs when the system is in its *ground state*. We *define* the ground state as the eigenvector associated with the Hamiltonian's minimum eigenvalue (or eigenket). From section 12.4, we know that the expectation $\langle\hat{H}\rangle$ is greater than or equal to the smallest eigenvalue of $\hat{H}$.

For a Hamiltonian $\hat{H}$, we can approximate its ground state by minimizing its expectation $\langle\hat{H}\rangle$ as a cost function parameterized by a quantum state variable $|\psi\rangle$.

> **To learn more**
>
> Using a quantum computer and a classical computer, how could we do this minimization over all $|\psi\rangle$ on n qubits? A full description containing all the necessary background quantum mechanics and chemistry for the energy of an electron in the smallest atom, hydrogen, is well beyond the scope of this book, but I recommend you read other sources if you are interested. [98]
>
> Instead, with this motivation from physics, we focus on applying these ideas to optimization problems.

12.8 Quantum approximate optimization algorithm (QAOA)

The *quantum approximate optimization algorithm*, abbreviated as *QAOA*, is an example of a *variational quantum algorithm*. We can use it for combinatorial optimization problems such as the Max-Cut Problem we discussed in section 12.2.2, and we use this problem to illustrate the technique. [17] [37]

We begin by constructing the Hamiltonians, unitaries, and circuits we need to perform the optimization.

12.8.1 Encoding the problem

Recall from section 12.2.2 on the Max-Cut Problem that we use the integer vector **z** with $z_k = \pm 1$. $z_k = 1$ if k is in **U**, and $z_k = -1$ if k is in **U**'. We seek to maximize

$$C(\mathbf{z}) = \frac{1}{2} \sum_{jk \text{ in } E} (1 - z_j z_k) = \sum_{jk \text{ in } E} C_{jk}(\mathbf{z}).$$

We now map this general form with n vertices to Hermitian Pauli strings and a Pauli sum, which we defined in section 12.3 to get the maximization version of the *problem Hamiltonian*:

$$H_P = \frac{1}{2} \sum_{jk \text{ in } E} (I_{2^n} - Z_j Z_k) \qquad \text{(maximization version)}$$

$$Z_j Z_k = I_2 \otimes \cdots \otimes I_2 \otimes \underbrace{\sigma_z}_{j} \otimes I_2 \otimes \cdots \otimes I_2 \otimes \underbrace{\sigma_z}_{k} \otimes I_2 \otimes \cdots \otimes I_2$$

where $Z_j Z_k$ has σ_z in the jth and k^{th} positions, and I_2 in the remaining $n - 2$ positions. Because of the Z_j, the "*P*" in H_P sometimes stands for "phase," and H_P is the *phase Hamiltonian*.

We can rewrite this to include a constant diagonal matrix, where $|E|$ is the number of edges in E:

$$\frac{1}{2} \sum_{jk \text{ in } E} (I_{2^n} - Z_j Z_k) = \underbrace{\frac{|E|}{2} I_{2^n}}_{\text{constant}} - \frac{1}{2} \sum_{jk \text{ in } E} Z_j Z_k$$

We can ignore the constant in the optimization and add it back in at the end if necessary. Removing the negative sign in front of the $\frac{1}{2}$ on the right side of the equation changes the optimization from finding the maximum to finding the minimum. This gives us an alternative minimization version of the problem Hamiltonian:

$$H_P = \frac{1}{2} \sum_{jk \text{ in } E} Z_j Z_k \qquad \text{(minimization version)}$$

Exercise 12.25

In Exercise 12.8, I asked you to determine the $C(\mathbf{z})$ cost function for solving the Max-Cut Problem for the graph

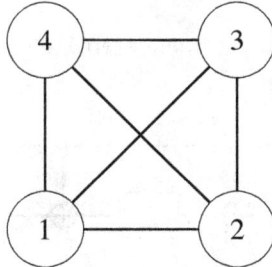

Find the corresponding minimization and maximization problem Hamiltonians.

We use the minimization problem Hamiltonian for the Max-Cut Problem, as do the Cirq and Qiskit QAOA tutorials. [42] [183] The original paper by Farhi et al. uses the maximization version. [78]

Finally, we define a parameterized unitary using the problem Hamiltonian:

$$U_P(\gamma) = e^{-i\gamma H_P} = \prod_{jk \text{ in } E} e^{-i\frac{\gamma}{2} Z_j Z_k} = \prod_{jk \text{ in } E} \exp\left(-i\frac{\gamma}{2} Z_j Z_k\right).$$

Since the square of a Pauli string is the identity matrix, $(Z_j Z_k)^2 = (Z_j \otimes Z_k)(Z_j \otimes Z_k) = I$. From section 12.3, we have

$$e^{-i\gamma \frac{1}{2} Z_j Z_k} = e^{i(\frac{-\gamma}{2}) Z_j Z_k} = \cos(\frac{-\gamma}{2}) I + i Z_j Z_k \sin(\frac{-\gamma}{2})$$

where $\theta = -\frac{1}{2}\gamma$.

Exercise 12.26

Let
$$U = \cos(\frac{-\gamma}{2})I + iZ_jZ_k\sin(\frac{-\gamma}{2}).$$

We know by construction that U is unitary, but show directly that $UU^\dagger = I$.

We also have the equality

$$e^{i\left(\frac{-\gamma}{2}\right)Z_jZ_k} = \left(e^{iZ_jZ_k}\right)^{\left(\frac{-\gamma}{2}\right)} = \exp\left(iZ_jZ_k\right)^{\left(\frac{-\gamma}{2}\right)}.$$

What does it mean to raise a **Z** gate to a real power? Since **Z** is a rotation,

$$\mathbf{Z} = \mathbf{R}^{\mathbf{z}}_\pi \quad \text{and} \quad \mathbf{Z}^r = \mathbf{R}^{\mathbf{z}}_{r\pi}.$$

Exercise 12.27

Show that the matrix for the unparameterized **ZZ** gate defined in section 8.3.5 is the same as the unitary for the circuit

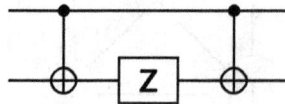

The circuit for $\mathbf{R}^{\mathbf{zz}}_\varphi$ on qubits j and k with $j < k$ is

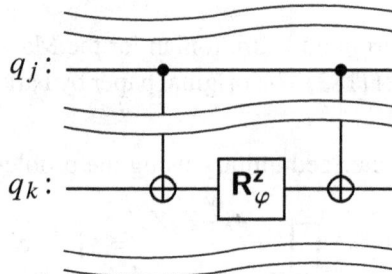

From section 7.6.6 and Exercise 12.14, we have

$$\mathbf{R}^{\mathbf{z}}_\varphi = \begin{bmatrix} e^{-\frac{\varphi i}{2}} & 0 \\ 0 & e^{\frac{\varphi i}{2}} \end{bmatrix} = e^{-i\frac{\varphi}{2}Z} = e^{-i\frac{\varphi}{2}\sigma_z}.$$

Putting this together, we can implement the required unitary exponentiation in a circuit using $\varphi = 2\gamma$ and the parameterized $\mathbf{R}_{2\gamma}^{\mathbf{zz}}$ gate.

12.8.2   Mixing things up

The second Hamiltonian we need is the *mixing Hamiltonian*, which we define as the Pauli sum

$$H_M = \sum_{j=1}^{n} X_j \, .$$

with the corresponding parameterized unitary

$$U_M(\beta) = e^{-i\beta H_M}$$

$$= e^{-i\beta\left(\sum_{j=1}^{n} X_j\right)} = e^{-i\beta(X_1 + X_2 + \cdots + X_n)}$$

$$= e^{-i\beta X_1} e^{-i\beta X_2} \cdots e^{-i\beta X_n} = \prod_{j=1}^{n} e^{-i\beta X_j} \, .$$

The mixing Hamiltonian ensures that we move closer to an optimal state and don't get stuck on an eigenvector of the problem Hamiltonian. β is the Greek letter "beta."

From section 7.6.12 and Exercise 12.14, we have

$$\mathbf{R}_{\varphi}^{\mathbf{x}} = \begin{bmatrix} \cos\left(\frac{\varphi}{2}\right) & -\sin\left(\frac{\varphi}{2}\right)i \\ -\sin\left(\frac{\varphi}{2}\right)i & \cos\left(\frac{\varphi}{2}\right) \end{bmatrix} = e^{-i\frac{\varphi}{2}X} = e^{-i\frac{\varphi}{2}\sigma_x} \, .$$

Therefore, $U_M(\beta)$ corresponds to the circuit

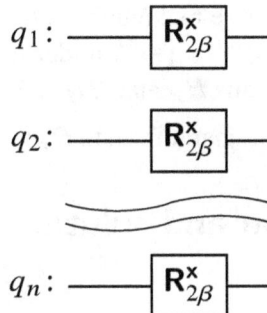

$$q_1: \quad -\boxed{\mathbf{R}_{2\beta}^{\mathbf{x}}}-$$

$$q_2: \quad -\boxed{\mathbf{R}_{2\beta}^{\mathbf{x}}}-$$

$$q_n: \quad -\boxed{\mathbf{R}_{2\beta}^{\mathbf{x}}}-$$

where I started the qubit numbering at 1 instead of 0.

We call γ and β *variational parameters*.

12.8.3 The ansatz and initial state

Given the unitary operators $U_P(\gamma)$ and $U_M(\beta)$, we can now construct the *ansatz* variational circuit in Figure 12.21 with p steps that alternate the operators. The initial state is a balanced superposition of the n qubits.

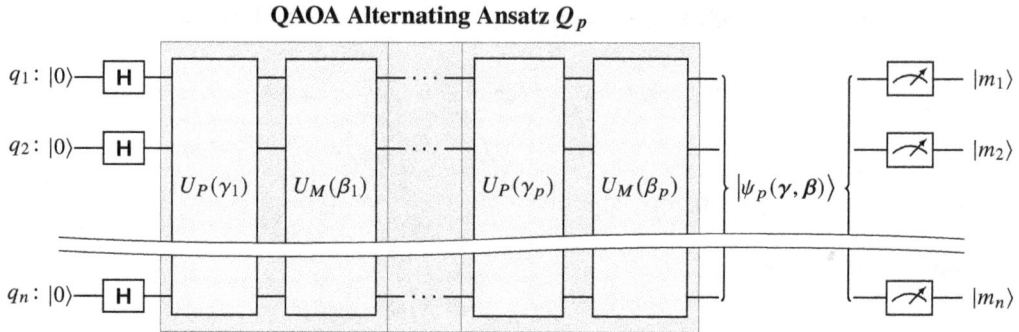

Figure 12.21: The QAOA alternating ansatz

We have built the Q_p ansatz by alternating U_P and U_M p times. We need the $2p$ real variational parameters γ_1 through γ_p and β_1 through β_p. In other words, we need two vectors in $\mathbf{R}^p$, γ and β. In practice, p often equals 1, but the approximation to the optimal value of the cost function gets closer as we increase p.

Exercise 12.28

Why can we assume $0 \le \beta_j, \gamma_j < 2\pi$ for all $1 \le j \le n$?

Since the β_j and γ_j are nonnegative real numbers, the circuit in Figure 12.21 is the time evolution of the initial state $\mathbf{H}^{\otimes n} |0\rangle^{\otimes n} = |+\rangle^{\otimes n}$ under the effect of the individual U_P and U_M corresponding to the Hamiltonians H_P and H_M.

We denote the pre-measurement quantum state $Q_p(|+\rangle^{\otimes n})$ by $|\psi_p(\gamma, \beta)\rangle$.

12.8.4 The expectation and solution

We now define the expectation

$$F_p(\gamma, \beta) = \langle \psi_p(\gamma, \beta) | H_P | \psi_p(\gamma, \beta) \rangle .$$

We compute F_p in the standard computational basis. F_p is a real-valued function, and we use classical optimization methods such as gradient descent to find a minimal value for F_p over the parameters γ and β. That is, we find $|\psi_p(\gamma, \beta)\rangle$, use classical optimization to find

---

better values for γ and β, and continue until we are satisfied we have a good approximation to a minimum for F_p. We might also stop after a given number of runs if the computation takes too long or is too expensive. This might happen, for example, if we land on a barren plateau.

For each particular set of values of γ and β, we run the circuit multiple times, the so-called number of shots. This value differs from p and the number of times we choose values for γ and β. Especially on NISQ machines, we need a large enough shot count to ensure a good distribution of results, with the likely solution appearing frequently.

Once we have reached an exact or good enough approximate minimum, we read off the **1**s and **0**s from the measurements $|m_1\rangle$ through $|m_n\rangle$. These correspond to the string **x** that defines the subsets **U** and **U'** as the solution to the Max-Cut Problem, as we originally defined in section 12.2.2.

For example, given the graph in Figure 12.22, we would expect to see the bit strings **1010** and **0101** computed the most times with many shots.

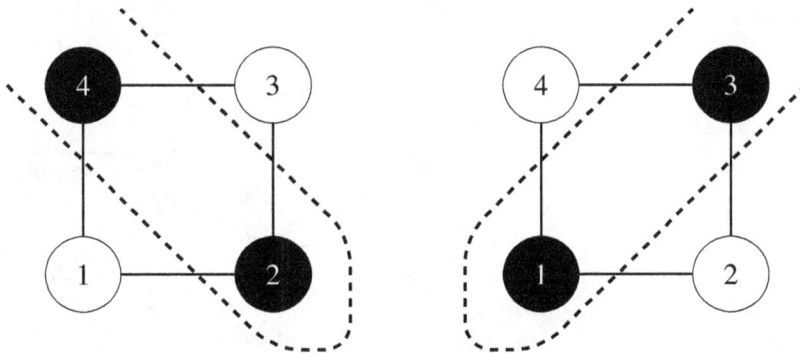

Figure 12.22: Two equivalent maximum cuts

Figure 12.23 shows the overall flow of the QAOA process.

Our sketch of the variational QAOA leaves open several important questions.

- The role of H_M is to prevent the time evolution from getting stuck on an eigenvalue, but how do H_P and H_M interact algebraically to permit our construction?
- Are there other choices for H_P and H_M that produce more efficient circuits on particular hardware?
- Are there better choices for the initial values of the γ_j and β_j other than setting them all to 0?
- Is QAOA more efficient and accurate than classical approaches, even when $p = 1$?
- What is the best choice for the classical optimizer?
- Can today's quantum computers handle large enough problems for big enough p to make QAOA practical?

- How large does p need to be to beat classical approaches?

There is much literature and research that attempt to answer these queries. [40] [46] [144] [242]

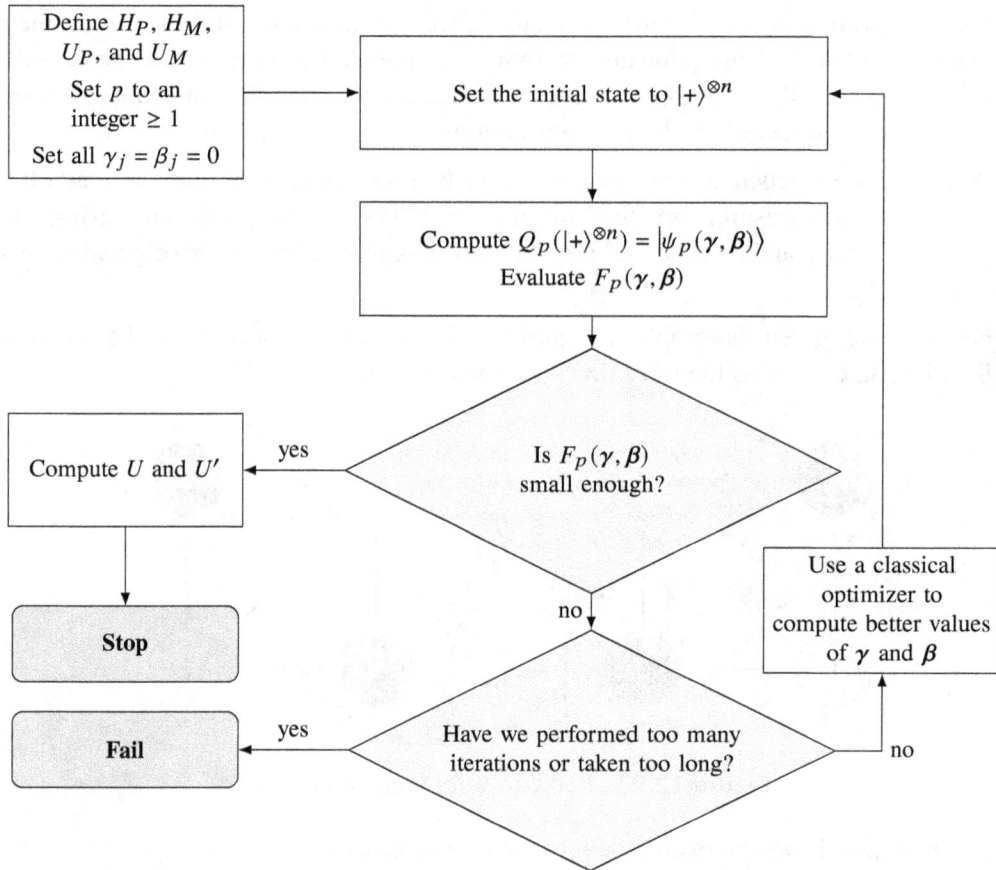

Figure 12.23: Flowchart for solving the Max-Cut Problem with QAOA

To learn more

Variants of QAOA have been developed for the Knapsack Problem. [193] We can often encode graph-based problems such as these in Hamiltonians in similar ways to what we have done for Max-Cut. Like QAOA for the Max-Cut Problem, the ultimate utility of these approaches is yet to be proven, though the Recursive QAOA (RQAOA) shows promise. [28]

12.8.5   Relationship to VQE

QAOA is a restricted version of the *Variational Quantum Eigensolver* or *VQE* quantum NISQ algorithm. [171] [216] VQE is used in finance and for physics and chemistry problems, such as finding a molecule's ground state energy, as outlined in section 12.7.

As you can see in Figure 12.24, most of the concepts are the same as for QAOA: an initial state, an ansatz, time evolution, classical optimization of parameters, and quantum-classical iteration until we find a suitable approximation.

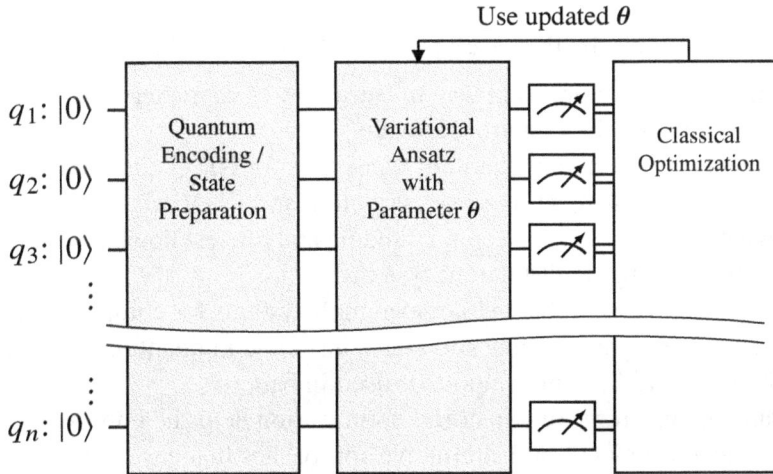

Figure 12.24: The general variational quantum eigensolver circuit

The double horizontal lines to the right of the qubit measurements in Figure 12.24 mean that we are transmitting classical bits, **0** and **1**, to the optimizer.

In the QAOA circuit for Max-Cut, the state preparation for the nodes and edges is encoded with the Problem Hamiltonian and ansatz, while the general VQE circuit calls them out separately. We discuss quantum encoding of classical data and state preparation in section 13.2. We will see a circuit like this again in section 13.3 when we discuss quantum neural networks.

To learn more

See the following example references for applications of VQE in specialized domains:

- General optimization: [2] [146]
- Finance: [74] [33] [178]
- Quantum chemistry: [120] [80] [196] [241]

12.9 Is NISQ worth it?

The bulk of this book covers algorithms using logical qubits, such as those by Grover (section 9.7.1) and Shor (section 10.7). Since we do not yet have logical qubits, we must make do with physical qubits with their noise and finite (and often short) coherence times. Unlike logical qubit algorithms that may have circuit depths and qubit counts in the thousands or millions, we must make do with a few dozen gates on a few dozen to a few hundred qubits. This situation defines the NISQ era as a prelude to the "Fault-Tolerant Quantum Computing" or "FTQC" era.

Here are some reasons why the development of NISQ algorithms is a good idea:

- NISQ algorithms are a practical way to learn how to characterize quantum hardware systems and improve their control software.
- Improvements in optimizing quantum transpilers for NISQ quantum algorithms will be applicable for implementing error correction and FTQC algorithms. [34]
- Any progress made may help keep the funding and interest flowing while we build the infrastructure for large fault-tolerant systems.
- While we are not close to having large enough systems for computation for big molecules such as proteins, we may soon have just enough quantum scale and power to work with the small lithium compounds used in batteries.
- Understanding quantum combinatorial optimization helps us improve our knowledge about classical techniques and alternative approaches in areas such as finance. [108]

Here are some reasons to be pessimistic about the value of NISQ algorithms:

- We may still not have enough qubits to do better than what we can do classically. [21, Section 3.3.2] [16] [79] [119] [121] [220]
- Decoherence limits our circuit depths, forcing us to use short-depth ansatzes. In QAOA, the alternating iteration count p must be small and often equal to 1.
- The approximations we get using variational methods may not be accurate enough for practical use because of gate noise and low measurement fidelity.
- A NISQ algorithm developer may need to understand too much physics versus computer science. We do not expect software developers for smartphones or laptops to know electronics to code. Yes, we are early with quantum computing, but it is hard to maintain training and educational enthusiasm when the prerequisites are severe.
- Any successful use of NISQ algorithms to gain advantages over classical techniques may be too esoteric and specific for application across industries.
- For problems that require up to 56 logical qubits, today's very large GPU-based systems can classically simulate quantum circuits. [142] Circuits needing up to about 35 to 40 logical qubits can be simulated using much smaller and less specialized classical systems. For many, these may provide sufficient learning, experimental, and validation platforms for quantum algorithm development.

At the time of writing, there seems to be increasing pessimism among many researchers about the ultimate value of NISQ for commercial or production use of quantum computing. [77] Most for-profit quantum computing vendors are outwardly optimistic about NISQ even if they do not yet provide large enough systems with good fidelities. Skeptics assert that extrapolating from past progress does not give us the confidence we will be able to meet the requirements for practical NISQ applications. Some argue we should focus nearly entirely on error correction and skip NISQ altogether. Such efforts must show frequent and significant milestones to maintain support.

An excellent 2023 survey of the state of NISQ algorithms for optimization is Abbas et al. [2]

If we achieve large-scale fault tolerant systems, this NISQ era will appear short-lived retrospectively. I think its effective lifetime will end between 2030 and 2035.

12.10   Summary

In this chapter, we looked at QAOA as an example of a quantum technique that does not require fault-tolerant, error-corrected qubits. QAOA is an example of a variational quantum eigensolver that uses the variational principle from physics to find solutions to combinatorial optimization problems, such as Max-Cut.

Variational algorithms have potential value because they can use relatively short-depth circuits in conjunction with classical optimization techniques, such as gradient descent. We introduced the concepts of Hamiltonian and ansatz and showed how expectation allows us to compute an upper bound for eigenvalues.

The chapter concluded with a sober look at the perceived versus actual value of NISQ algorithms. Do you think we should bother, or should we focus our efforts on fault-tolerant, error-corrected qubits?

13

Introduction to Quantum Machine Learning

Learning is the only thing the mind never exhausts, never fears, and never regrets.

– Leonardo da Vinci

It's hard to imagine an area of computer science and data analysis that has gotten more attention and investment in recent years than AI and machine learning. While quantum computers are still not "big data" machines because of their relatively short coherence times and numbers of qubits, it is still reasonable to ask if we can extend or replace existing machine learning algorithms or computational components with quantum versions. This is the field of *quantum machine learning*, or *QML*.

This chapter surveys and summarizes several techniques where quantum computing might improve the performance or accuracy of neural networks and support vector machines for classification. The chapter builds on the discussion in section 1.4.

The classical machine learning background for this chapter is beyond the scope of this book, but I provide references for each section. In particular, Chapter 15 of my *Dancing with Python* book reviews the machine learning topics covered here. [211] Similarly, there are now several book-length treatments of quantum machine learning for which this chapter introduces the concepts. [46]

Topics covered in this chapter

13.1   What is machine learning?

Consider my complete product browsing and purchase history with an online retailer. This data represents my experience of buying from the seller and their experience selling to me. How can the data and my new purchases help the retailer learn how to recommend and sell me additional products and services?

Machine learning is a large set of techniques where computer algorithms learn from existing data rather than having hardcoded decisions built into them. We create a *model* and *train* it from a subset of our data. If we have done a good job, this model predicts what we should do next to accomplish a goal, such as selling someone new clothes, books, or music.

Such algorithms and models improve their accuracy as they receive new data. They might also improve when humans or processes intervene to judge the correctness and quality of predictions and results.

In *unsupervised learning*, an algorithm looks for patterns in the data that may help users gain insight. An unsupervised algorithm may help the retailer see that I have increased interest in cooking, travel, or home repair during certain seasons. The seller can then preemptively give me product recommendations several weeks before I would typically purchase them.

In *supervised learning*, the training data has among its features the ''answer'' to a question we might ask about it. Suppose the online retailer has a travel bureau, and I book a vacation trip. Afterward, I buy books and clothes. The retailer labels the book and clothes data as possible travel accessories. If you then buy similar books or clothing, the retailer's machine learning algorithm might decide that you are likely looking to take a vacation and suggest possible flights and hotels.

In *reinforcement learning,* the algorithm adds some reward or penalty based on the outcome. If I purchase but then return a product, the algorithm might insert a negative score as a feature in the data associated with the deduced result. This feature could help the algorithm make a better future choice among actions. Perhaps I am taking a trip and want to buy new shirts. If I purchase and return some of them, the retailer can use my stated reason to update the data to note that the clothes might not be suitable for that kind of travel.

The information a machine learning algorithm uses to learn is called the *training set.* For supervised learning, the training set has one or more *label* features. When we get new unlabeled data, we run the algorithm and hope it matches the expected results. We create a machining learning model when we *fit* the training data with an algorithm to make predictions.

A *binary classification* problem takes input and determines if it is an example of one of two possibilities. For example, a photo classification machine learning model could accept an image of a dog or cat and tell you with high probability which kind of animal the photo depicts. In a classical model, the computation could output **0** to mean ''dog'' and **1** to mean ''cat.'' In a quantum model, we would first encode the photo in a multi-qubit quantum state. We could then run a quantum circuit to predict the type of animal in the image. If we measure one particular qubit at the end of the circuit and get $|0\rangle$, the animal is a dog. If we get $|0\rangle$, we have a cat.

Why bother using a quantum machine learning method instead of a classical one? There are several possible reasons:

- When done classically, the computation takes too long or uses too much memory or storage.
- Since the theory of quantum computing relies on linear algebra, we can use quantum computers in some circumstances as ''linear algebra calculators.'' Machine learning uses linear algebra extensively.
- Quantum kernel methods may speed up or provide better classification than their classical counterparts. Our machine learning workflow then becomes a hybrid of classical and quantum computation.
- Superposition, entanglement, and interference are part of the quantum computing programming model but not the classical model. They may allow us to find patterns not otherwise discoverable using traditional techniques.
- If search is an element of a machine learning model and the data is already encoded in quantum states, Grover's search algorithm (section 9.7.1) may provide a quadratic speedup.

In this chapter, we look at the basics of quantum neural networks and quantum kernels, along with the mathematical tools they employ. There are many other areas of machine learning where researchers are trying to apply quantum computing and determine if there are practical advantages over classical means. I list several of these with references at the end of the chapter.

Data is key to machine learning, and if we want to use data in a quantum computing algorithm, it must be in a usable form. Quantum computers do not operate directly on classical data such as bits, numbers, strings, or lists. We must convert such data into multi-qubit quantum states that we can manipulate with gates in circuits. In particular, data for machine learning must be encoded in quantum states, and the next section covers several techniques for doing this.

13.2   Methods for encoding data

If classical computers use bits **0** and **1**, but quantum computers use qubits represented as

$$a|0\rangle + b|1\rangle$$

for complex a and b, where $|a|^2 + |b|^2 = 1$, how do we efficiently map classical data into a multi-qubit quantum representation? We must *quantum encode* classical data so a quantum computer can use it.

In some instances, it may make sense to encode $\mathbf{0} \mapsto |0\rangle$ and $\mathbf{1} \mapsto |1\rangle$, but this would not be practical if our application involves the huge amount of information typically used in machine learning, for example. In this section, we look at several techniques for quantum-encoding classical data. There is a trade-off between being efficient with time spent encoding and decoding versus the number of qubits needed to store the information.

Suppose we have a real n-dimensional vector $\mathbf{x}$. We want to represent $\mathbf{x}$ in an N-qubit state $|\psi\rangle$ with $N \leq n$. We do this via an encoding circuit or unitary operator

$$U_\mathbf{x} : |0\rangle^{\otimes N} \mapsto |\psi\rangle \quad \text{so that} \quad U_\mathbf{x}|0\rangle^{\otimes N} = |\psi\rangle .$$

We call this process quantum *state preparation*. It may be computationally difficult to find a suitable $U_\mathbf{x}$, or the circuit implementing $U_\mathbf{x}$ may be very deep.

Since $U_\mathbf{x}$ is invertible, it may be easier to compute the inverse mapping

$$U_\mathbf{x}^{-1} : |\psi\rangle \mapsto |0\rangle^{\otimes N} \quad \text{so that} \quad U_\mathbf{x}^{-1}|\psi\rangle = |0\rangle^{\otimes N} .$$

If we want to parameterize the encoding circuit by some θ, we use the notation

$$U_{\mathbf{x},\theta} : |0\rangle^{\otimes N} \mapsto |\psi\rangle .$$

13.2.1 Basis encoding

The idea behind basis encoding is simple: represent data using bits and then use a qubit for each bit.

Let's begin with a byte. A byte is eight bits, so we need eight qubits. Suppose we have the value **01101011**. A circuit to encode this data with q_0 holding the left-most bit value is shown in Figure 13.1.

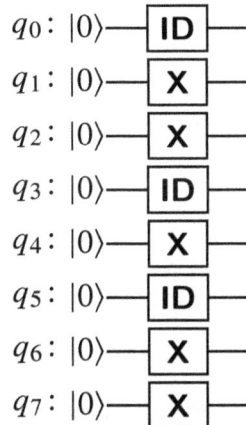

Figure 13.1: A quantum circuit for a bit encoding

I included the explicit **ID** gates for clarity, but you can omit them.

> **Exercise 13.1**
>
> What quantum state does this circuit produce?

You can code the **X** gates manually if you want to use this particular byte, or you can write some Python code for an arbitrary byte to generate this part of the circuit.

```
# Construct a circuit from a byte using Cirq
import cirq

circuit = cirq.Circuit()
qubits = cirq.LineQubit.range(8)

def build_circuit_from_byte(byte):
    # Iterate at most 8 times over the input
    for n in reversed(range(8)):
```

```
        if byte % 2:
            # Insert an X gate to get |1>
            circuit.append(cirq.X(qubits[n]))
        else:
            # Insert an identity gate to keep |0>
            circuit.append(cirq.I(qubits[n]))
        byte //= 2

build_circuit_from_byte(0b01101011)

print(circuit)

    0: ---I---

    1: ---X---

    2: ---X---

    3: ---I---

    4: ---X---

    5: ---I---

    6: ---X---

    7: ---X---
```

We use Python's remainder operation % in the code to test whether the byte represents an odd or even number. If it is odd, we insert an **X** gate to change the initial $|0\rangle$ to $|1\rangle$. In the even case, we insert the do-nothing identity gate **ID**. Next, we perform integer division by two to look at the next bit to the left. We repeat this process to handle all eight bits.

For a nonnegative integer n represented using b bits, we need at most b **X** gates to convert $|0\rangle^{\otimes b}$ to the quantum basis encoding for n. The storage complexity is also linear in b, since we need one qubit per bit.

This method easily extends to 32- or 64-bit integers, though you may need to handle a sign bit. You can also encode ASCII or multi-byte Unicode characters in this way.

If you wish to encode two 64-bit integers, you can put the first in qubits 0 to 63 and the second in qubits 64 to 127. For variable sequences of bytes or other data, you can first encode the number of entries and then consecutively encode the individual items in consecutive qubits.

You can convert a floating-point number to a binary form, as discussed in section 3.5.3. You will likely need to fix the number of bits to represent the fractional portion or encode how many there are.

> **To learn more**
>
> I introduce these arithmetic operators in Section 2.6 of *Dancing with Python*. [211]

13.2.2 Amplitude encoding

Suppose we have the data about five households shown in Figure 13.2. We know the number of adults, children, cats, and dogs for each household.

Household Id	Adults	Children	Cats	Dogs
1	2	2	0	1
2	1	0	2	0
3	3	1	0	0
4	2	4	3	2
5	1	2	1	1

Figure 13.2: Household information with adults, children, cats, and dogs

Look at the five values for the number of adults in the households in Figure 13.2. They are: 2, 1, 3, 2, 1. These could represent a *feature* for data analysis or machine learning. We want to map this information to the amplitudes of a multi-qubit quantum state.

We know that the sum of the squares of the absolute values of amplitudes must be 1, so we first normalize the **Adults** vector containing the data to create a new vector **a**:

$$\mathbf{Adults} = (2, 1, 3, 2, 1)$$

$$\|\mathbf{Adults}\| = \sqrt{2^2 + 1^2 + 3^2 + 2^2 + 1^2} = \sqrt{19}$$

$$\mathbf{a} = (a_0, a_1, a_2, a_3, a_4)$$

$$= \left(\frac{2}{\sqrt{19}}, \frac{1}{\sqrt{19}}, \frac{3}{\sqrt{19}}, \frac{2}{\sqrt{19}}, \frac{1}{\sqrt{19}} \right)$$

$$\approx (0.4588, 0.2294, 0.6882, 0.4588, 0.2294).$$

Since we have five data items, we need at least three qubits to hold these amplitudes because $2^2 < 5 < 2^3$. We define the quantum state

$$|\psi\rangle = a_0|000\rangle + a_1|001\rangle + a_2|010\rangle + a_3|011\rangle + a_4|100\rangle$$
$$+ 0|101\rangle + 0|110\rangle + 0|111\rangle$$
$$= 0.4588\,|000\rangle + 0.2294\,|001\rangle + 0.6882\,|010\rangle + 0.4588\,|011\rangle + 0.2294\,|100\rangle$$

with the amplitudes of the kets $|101\rangle$, $|110\rangle$, and $|111\rangle$ each equal to 0. We pad the quantum state with 0s for amplitudes beyond those we need to represent the data. In this case, we set the last three amplitudes to 0, but we could have used the first three.

In general, for $m > 0$ data items, we choose the smallest positive n in $\mathbf{Z}$ such that $m \leq 2^n$. Equivalently, $\log_2(m) \leq n$. We need n qubits to encode the data.

Exercise 13.2

What is the qubit storage O() complexity for $m > 0$ date items?

We next normalize the data to get a vector of length 1. For machine learning applications, we may have previously used min-max normalization, standardization, or mean normalization to scale the data.

We now assume that our vector **a** has 2^n entries. The sum of the squares of the first m entries is equal to 1. The remaining $2^n - m$ entries are each 0. This gives us

$$|\psi\rangle = \sum_{j=0}^{2^{n-1}} a_j|j\rangle_n$$

where we use the ket subscripting notation from section 8.2.2. This expression is the *amplitude encoding* of our data. Though we started with real-value data, the amplitudes in $|\psi\rangle$ can be in $\mathbf{C}$. Our construction of $|\psi\rangle$ from $|0\rangle$ is an example of quantum state preparation.

Encoding one record or column from a database for machine learning is probably not that useful. If we want to access the entire database in our quantum system, we can concatenate the records or columns to make one long vector, normalize it, and then use amplitude encoding.

If C is the number of columns and R is the number of rows in our database, we need $C \times R$ amplitudes and approximately $\log_2(C \times R)$ qubits.

The general problem of finding a unitary transformation or a quantum circuit that converts $|0\rangle^{\otimes n}$ to an arbitrary quantum state $|\psi\rangle$ on n qubits

$$|0\rangle^{\otimes n} - \boxed{\mathbf{U}} - |\psi\rangle$$

is equivalent to its inverse

$$|\psi\rangle - \boxed{\mathsf{U}^\dagger = \mathsf{U}^{-1}} - |0\rangle^{\otimes n}$$

because we can run the reversible circuit backward. For this reason, you will sometimes see the state preparation problem given as its "inverse" $|\psi\rangle \mapsto |0\rangle^{\otimes n}$.

We can generalize to mapping $|\psi\rangle_1$ to $|\psi\rangle_2$ on n qubits by passing through $|0\rangle^{\otimes n}$ as an intermediary:

$$|\psi\rangle_1 \mapsto |0\rangle^{\otimes n} \mapsto |\psi\rangle_2 .$$

We call this a *general quantum state transformation*.

> **To learn more**
>
> I cover data normalization methods in section 15.3 of *Dancing with Python*. [211]

1-qubit encoding

Let's look at an example that encodes the vector $(1, \sqrt{3})$ in the amplitudes of one qubit. We normalize the vector to get

$$\mathbf{a} = (a_0, a_1) = \left(\frac{1}{2}, \frac{\sqrt{3}}{2} \right) .$$

What gates can we use to produce the state

$$a_0|0\rangle + a_1|1\rangle = \frac{1}{2}|0\rangle + \frac{\sqrt{3}}{2}|1\rangle = \cos\left(\frac{\pi}{3}\right)|0\rangle + \sin\left(\frac{\pi}{3}\right)|1\rangle ?$$

Consider the linear transformation U_θ

$$U_\theta : (x, y) \mapsto (x\cos(\theta) - y\sin(\theta), x\sin(\theta) + y\cos(\theta))$$

$$U_\theta \begin{bmatrix} x \\ y \end{bmatrix} = \begin{bmatrix} \cos(\theta) & -\sin(\theta) \\ \sin(\theta) & \cos(\theta) \end{bmatrix} \begin{bmatrix} x \\ y \end{bmatrix} = \begin{bmatrix} x\cos(\theta) - y\sin(\theta) & x\sin(\theta) + y\cos(\theta) \end{bmatrix} .$$

For $\theta = \frac{\pi}{3}$,

$$U_{\frac{\pi}{3}}|0\rangle = U_{\frac{\pi}{3}}\begin{bmatrix}1\\0\end{bmatrix} = \begin{bmatrix}\cos\left(\frac{\pi}{3}\right) & -\sin\left(\frac{\pi}{3}\right)\\ \sin\left(\frac{\pi}{3}\right) & \cos\left(\frac{\pi}{3}\right)\end{bmatrix}\begin{bmatrix}1\\0\end{bmatrix}$$

$$= \begin{bmatrix}\cos\left(\frac{\pi}{3}\right) & \sin\left(\frac{\pi}{3}\right)\end{bmatrix}$$

$$= \cos\left(\frac{\pi}{3}\right)|0\rangle + \sin\left(\frac{\pi}{3}\right)|1\rangle$$

$$= \frac{1}{2}|0\rangle + \frac{\sqrt{3}}{2}|1\rangle.$$

We are looking for a sequence of one or more gates, $\mathbf{U}_{\frac{\pi}{3}}$, implementing the action of the unitary matrix $U_{\frac{\pi}{3}}$.

$$q_0: |0\rangle\!-\!\boxed{\mathbf{U}_{\frac{\pi}{3}}}\!-\!\tfrac{1}{2}|0\rangle + \tfrac{\sqrt{3}}{2}|1\rangle$$

The $\mathbf{R}_{\varphi}^{\mathsf{y}}$ y-rotation gate from section 7.6.12 with $\varphi = \frac{2\pi}{3}$ is exactly what we need. We have

$$\mathbf{R}_{\varphi}^{\mathsf{y}} = \begin{bmatrix}\cos\left(\frac{\varphi}{2}\right) & -\sin\left(\frac{\varphi}{2}\right)\\ \sin\left(\frac{\varphi}{2}\right) & \cos\left(\frac{\varphi}{2}\right)\end{bmatrix}$$

$$\mathbf{R}_{\varphi}^{\mathsf{y}}|0\rangle = \begin{bmatrix}\cos\left(\frac{\varphi}{2}\right)\\ \sin\left(\frac{\varphi}{2}\right)\end{bmatrix} = \cos\left(\frac{\varphi}{2}\right)|0\rangle + \sin\left(\frac{\varphi}{2}\right)|1\rangle$$

$$\mathbf{U}_{\frac{\pi}{3}} = \mathbf{R}_{\frac{2\pi}{3}}^{\mathsf{y}} = \begin{bmatrix}\cos\left(\frac{\pi}{3}\right) & -\sin\left(\frac{\pi}{3}\right)\\ \sin\left(\frac{\pi}{3}\right) & \cos\left(\frac{\pi}{3}\right)\end{bmatrix}$$

$$\mathbf{R}_{\frac{2\pi}{3}}^{\mathsf{y}}|0\rangle = \begin{bmatrix}\cos\left(\frac{\pi}{3}\right)\\ \sin\left(\frac{\pi}{3}\right)\end{bmatrix} = \begin{bmatrix}\frac{1}{2}\\ \frac{\sqrt{3}}{2}\end{bmatrix} = \frac{1}{2}|0\rangle + \frac{\sqrt{3}}{2}|1\rangle$$

with circuit

$$q_0 : |0\rangle - \boxed{\mathbf{R}^{\mathbf{y}}_{\frac{2\pi}{3}}} - \tfrac{1}{2}|0\rangle + \tfrac{\sqrt{3}}{2}|1\rangle$$

How can we extend this 1-qubit state preparation to a general quantum state

$$|\psi\rangle = a|0\rangle + b|1\rangle$$

when a and b are in $\mathbf{C}$?

From the discussions in sections 7.3.1 and 7.3.2, we know that, up to a global phase, we can represent this general quantum state $|\psi\rangle$ as

$$|\psi\rangle = \cos\left(\frac{\theta}{2}\right)|0\rangle + \sin\left(\frac{\theta}{2}\right)e^{\varphi i}|1\rangle.$$

This is very close to what we obtained with the $\mathbf{U}_{\frac{\theta}{2}}$ and y-rotation gate above:

$$\mathbf{U}_{\frac{\theta}{2}} = \mathbf{R}^{\mathbf{y}}_{\theta}|0\rangle = \begin{bmatrix} \cos\left(\frac{\theta}{2}\right) \\ \sin\left(\frac{\theta}{2}\right) \end{bmatrix} = \cos\left(\frac{\theta}{2}\right)|0\rangle + \sin\left(\frac{\theta}{2}\right)|1\rangle,$$

except that we are missing the local phase $e^{\varphi i}$ on $|1\rangle$. We can remedy this with a z-rotation gate:

$$\mathbf{R}^{\mathbf{z}}_{\varphi}\mathbf{R}^{\mathbf{y}}_{\theta}|0\rangle = \begin{bmatrix} 1 & 0 \\ 0 & e^{\varphi i} \end{bmatrix} \begin{bmatrix} \cos\left(\frac{\theta}{2}\right) \\ \sin\left(\frac{\theta}{2}\right) \end{bmatrix} = \cos\left(\frac{\theta}{2}\right)|0\rangle + \sin\left(\frac{\theta}{2}\right)e^{\varphi i}|1\rangle.$$

The circuit that implements the 1-qubit state preparation for

$$|\psi\rangle = \cos\left(\frac{\theta}{2}\right)|0\rangle + \sin\left(\frac{\theta}{2}\right)e^{\varphi i}|1\rangle$$

from $|0\rangle$ is

$$q_0 : |0\rangle - \boxed{\mathbf{R}^{\mathbf{y}}_{\theta}} - \boxed{\mathbf{R}^{\mathbf{z}}_{\varphi}} - |\psi\rangle = \cos\left(\frac{\theta}{2}\right)|0\rangle + \sin\left(\frac{\theta}{2}\right)e^{\varphi i}$$

Exercise 13.3

Under what conditions for the value of b can we skip using the z-rotation?

Exercise 13.4

What is the circuit that maps $|\psi\rangle$ to $|0\rangle$?

2-qubit encoding

We next consider the problem of mapping

$$|00\rangle \mapsto |\psi\rangle = a_{00}|00\rangle + a_{01}|01\rangle + a_{10}|10\rangle + a_{11}|11\rangle$$

for complex numbers a_{00}, a_{01}, a_{10}, and a_{11}.

Since this is a quantum state,

$$|a_{00}|^2 + |a_{01}|^2 + |a_{10}|^2 + |a_{11}|^2 = 1$$

and not all a_{jk} can equal 0.

Let's begin with some special cases. Suppose three of the amplitudes are 0. The nonzero amplitude has absolute value 1. For example, we might want to map

$$|00\rangle \mapsto |\psi\rangle = e^{\varphi i}|11\rangle$$
$$= \left(\mathbf{R}_\varphi^z \otimes \mathbf{ID}\right)\left(\mathbf{X} \otimes \mathbf{X}\right)\left(|0\rangle \otimes |0\rangle\right).$$

We can do this with the circuit

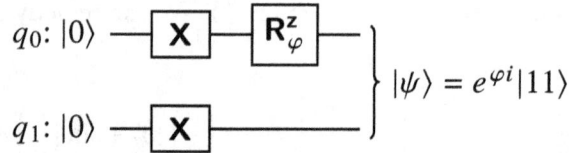

$$q_0: |0\rangle \quad\boxed{\mathbf{X}}\quad\boxed{\mathbf{R}_\varphi^z}$$
$$q_1: |0\rangle \quad\boxed{\mathbf{X}}$$
$$\left.\right\} |\psi\rangle = e^{\varphi i}|11\rangle$$

Exercise 13.5

What are the circuits that map $|00\rangle$ to $e^{\varphi i}|00\rangle$, $e^{\varphi i}|01\rangle$, and $e^{\varphi i}|10\rangle$?

Next, suppose precisely two of the amplitudes are 0. If they are the last two, then we wish to map

$$|00\rangle = |0\rangle \otimes |0\rangle \mapsto |\psi\rangle = a_{00}|00\rangle + a_{01}|01\rangle$$
$$= |0\rangle \otimes (a_{00}|0\rangle + a_{01}|1\rangle) .$$

This is simply the 1-qubit encoding problem on the second qubit. Similarly, if the first two amplitudes are 0, we have the 1-qubit encoding problem on the first qubit.

We can now consider the general 2-qubit case where

$$|a_{00}|^2 + |a_{01}|^2 \neq 0 \quad \text{and} \quad |a_{10}|^2 + |a_{11}|^2 \neq 0 .$$

We rewrite the target encoding as

$$|\psi\rangle = a_{00}|00\rangle + a_{01}|01\rangle + a_{10}|10\rangle + a_{11}|11\rangle$$

$$= \sqrt{|a_{00}|^2 + |a_{01}|^2}\, \frac{a_{00}|00\rangle + a_{01}|01\rangle}{\sqrt{|a_{00}|^2 + |a_{01}|^2}} + \sqrt{|a_{10}|^2 + |a_{11}|^2}\, \frac{a_{10}|00\rangle + a_{11}|01\rangle}{\sqrt{|a_{10}|^2 + |a_{11}|^2}}\,.$$

We can create this quantum state from $|00\rangle$ by 1-qubit encodings $\mathbf{U}_0$ and $\mathbf{U}_1$ on the first and second qubits, respectively, and a controlled general quantum state transformation $\mathbf{U}_{0,1}$ from the first to the second qubit: [60]

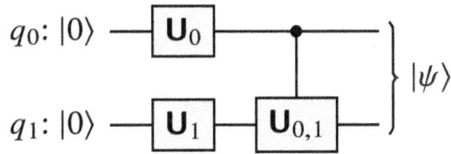

$$q_0: |0\rangle \;-\!\boxed{\mathbf{U}_0}\!-\!\bullet\!-$$
$$\left.\begin{array}{c} \\ \\ \end{array}\right\} |\psi\rangle$$
$$q_1: |0\rangle \;-\!\boxed{\mathbf{U}_1}\!-\!\boxed{\mathbf{U}_{0,1}}\!-$$

where

$$\mathbf{U}_0 : |0\rangle \mapsto \sqrt{|a_{00}|^2 + |a_{01}|^2}\,|0\rangle + \sqrt{|a_{10}|^2 + |a_{11}|^2}\,|1\rangle$$

$$\mathbf{U}_1 : |0\rangle \mapsto \frac{a_{00}}{\sqrt{|a_{00}|^2 + |a_{01}|^2}}\,|0\rangle + \frac{a_{01}}{\sqrt{|a_{00}|^2 + |a_{01}|^2}}\,|1\rangle$$

and

$$\mathbf{U}_{0,1} : \frac{a_{00}}{\sqrt{|a_{00}|^2 + |a_{01}|^2}}\,|00\rangle + \frac{a_{01}}{\sqrt{|a_{00}|^2 + |a_{01}|^2}}\,|01\rangle$$

$$\mapsto |00\rangle$$

$$\mapsto \frac{a_{10}}{\sqrt{|a_{10}|^2 + |a_{11}|^2}}\,|00\rangle + \frac{a_{11}}{\sqrt{|a_{10}|^2 + |a_{11}|^2}}\,|01\rangle\,.$$

Exercise 13.6

Using the techniques in this section, show how to perform the three encodings

$$|00\rangle \mapsto \frac{1}{2}|01\rangle + \frac{\sqrt{3}}{2}|10\rangle$$

$$|00\rangle \mapsto \sqrt{0.1}\,|00\rangle + \sqrt{0.6}\,|10\rangle + \sqrt{0.3}\,|11\rangle$$

$$|00\rangle \mapsto \frac{1}{2}\sum_{j=0}^{3}|j\rangle_2$$

For each, state how many 1- and 2-qubit gates you need.

---

n-qubit encoding

The general case for complex amplitudes and $n > 2$ qubits is much more complicated than that for one or two qubits, and I refer you to the literature for the details. The number of operations needed is exponential in the number of data values, rounded up to the next power of 2. [158] [198, section 4.2] The method involves a sequence of multi-controlled z-rotations followed by multi-controlled y-rotations, where the number of gates is exponential in the number of qubits. The controlled z-rotations transform the amplitudes to real numbers, and the controlled y-rotations then successively transform the quantum state to $|0\rangle^{\otimes n}$.

The Harrow-Hassidim-Loyd (HHL) algorithm for solving systems of linear equations uses amplitude encoding. [104]

13.2.3 Angle encoding

Suppose we have a number φ in $\mathbf{R}$, with $0 \le \varphi \le \frac{\pi}{2}$. We can encode φ, an angle, as a quantum state via

$$\cos(\varphi)|0\rangle + \sin(\varphi)|1\rangle\,.$$

We create this state as we did for 1-qubit amplitude encoding. That is, the 1-qubit angle encoding for φ is the 1-qubit amplitude encoding for $(\cos(\varphi), \sin(\varphi))$.

Suppose we know that someone or something created the state $a|0\rangle + b|1\rangle$ from an angle encoding. For example, assume a and b are real numbers between 0 and 1, inclusive. If $a = 0$, then $\varphi = \frac{\pi}{2}$. Otherwise, $\varphi = \arctan(b, a)$, where arctan is the inverse tangent function from section 4.3.2.

Exercise 13.7

Suppose I tell you I have a secret real number φ between 0 and $\frac{\pi}{2}$, inclusive. I run the circuit

$$q_0: |0\rangle - \boxed{R^y_{2\varphi}} - \boxed{\measuredangle} - |m_0\rangle$$

1,000 times. When I measure the result, I get **0** 95 times and **1** 905 times. What is φ?

If we have multiple real numbers $\varphi_1, \ldots, \varphi_n$, each between 0 and $\frac{\pi}{2}$, inclusive, we can encode these using the tensor product

$$
\begin{aligned}
(\varphi_1, \ldots, \varphi_n) &\mapsto R^y_{2\varphi_1} \otimes \cdots \otimes R^y_{2\varphi_n} |0\rangle^{\otimes n} \\
&= (\cos(\varphi_1)|0\rangle + \sin(\varphi_1)|1\rangle) \otimes \cdots \otimes (\cos(\varphi_n)|0\rangle + \sin(\varphi_n)|1\rangle) \\
&= \bigotimes_{i=1}^{n} (\cos(\varphi_i)|0\rangle + \sin(\varphi_i)|1\rangle) .
\end{aligned}
$$

Instead of using R^y_φ, we could have used R^x_φ or R^z_φ.

For n data items, we need n qubits and n quantum operations to perform the angle encoding. Therefore, the storage and execution time complexity is linear in n.

Exercise 13.8

Why do we restrict $0 \leq \varphi \leq \frac{\pi}{2}$? Why don't we make the upper limit π or 2π? Could we have used the atan2 function instead of atan to resolve any difficulties? (You should look up atan2 and its behavior in a programming language such as Python.)

To learn more

Adjusting the numeric range of a group of numbers (in this case, between 0 and $\frac{\pi}{2}$) is called *feature scaling* or *normalization*. I cover this in Section 15.3 of *Dancing with Python*. [211]

13.2.4 Dense angle encoding

In section 13.2.3, we used angle encoding to map n real numbers, normalized to be between 0 and $\frac{\pi}{2}$, to n qubits. We can do a little better and only use $\frac{n}{2}$ qubits. [132]

Given two numbers φ_1 and φ_2 in **R**, we can encode both values in a single quantum state via

$$\cos(\pi\varphi_1)\,|0\rangle + e^{2\pi i \varphi_2}\sin(\pi\varphi_1)\,|1\rangle .$$

We have used φ_2 to add a relative phase. Given the trigonometric periodicity in the expression, we have effectively scaled the inputs so that $0 \leq \varphi_1 \leq 2$ and $0 \leq \varphi_2 \leq 1$.

If n is even, we can use $\frac{n}{2}$ qubits to encode φ_1 through φ_n:

$$\bigotimes_{i=1}^{n/2} \left(\cos(\pi\varphi_{2i-1})\,|0\rangle + e^{2\pi i \varphi_{2i}}\sin(\pi\varphi_{2i-1})\,|1\rangle \right) .$$

If n is odd and greater than 2, we can either decide to drop φ_n or, more likely, increase n by 1 and set φ_n equal to 0.

While we have halved the number of qubits needed for dense angle encoding versus regular angle encoding, we have doubled the number of operations. The storage and execution time complexities are still linear, but these factors of 2 may affect which encoding you use. For example, you would likely choose the dense version if you have a quantum system with relatively few qubits but deep circuit depth.

Exercise 13.9

Show the y and z angle rotation gates from sections 7.6.12 and 7.6.6 for creating the dense angle encoding of φ_1 and φ_2 from $|0\rangle$.

Exercise 13.10

Suppose we know that someone or something created the state $a|0\rangle + b|1\rangle$ from a dense angle encoding. For example, a is in **R** with $0 \leq a \leq 1$, and b is in **C**. How can we recover φ_1 and φ_2?

Exercise 13.11

Show the y and z angle rotation gates from sections 7.6.12 and 7.6.6 for creating the tensor product dense angle encoding of φ_1 to φ_n from $|0\rangle^{\otimes n}$.

13.3 Quantum neural networks

Let's recall some definitions regarding neural networks from my book *Dancing with Python*. [211, Section 15.8]

Figure 13.3 shows a *neural network* with three input *nodes*, four nodes in the hidden layer, and two output nodes. Another name for a node is a *neuron*. I've shown *weights w* in the network on the connections from the input nodes going to the hidden nodes, and from the hidden nodes to the output nodes. Note how the network sends the value of each node to every node in the next layer.

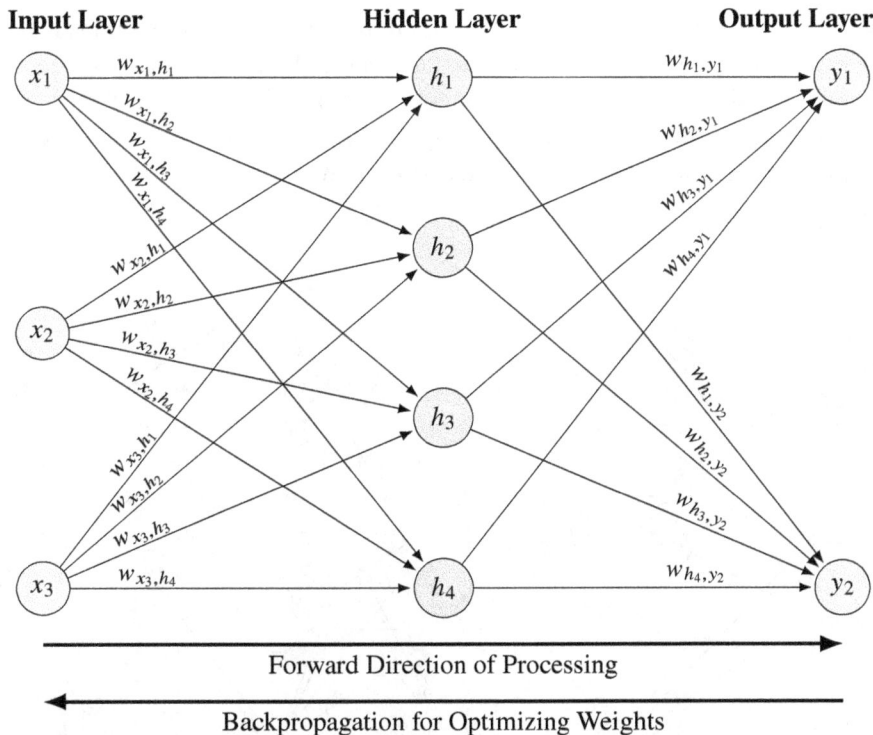

Figure 13.3: Neural network with 3 inputs, 4 hidden nodes, and 2 outputs

We compute a value from the input values and weights for each node in the hidden layers. These are real numbers that we may restrict to the binary values **0** and **1**. We also have an associated *activation function* for each node in the hidden layer, determining what value to send to each node in the output layer. Activation functions are often nonlinear.

In this general model of a simple neural network, we know nothing about the inputs $\{x_j\}$ and outputs $\{y_k\}$. The $\{x_j\}$ are all data and may have been prepared from a data set or live information as it became available. The $\{y_k\}$ somehow represent the answer or result we are seeking.

In the case of *supervised machine learning*, we know the "right" answer $\{z_k\}$ from a given set of inputs. We can construct an error or *loss* function as a cost function to see how far off the $\{y_k\}$ are from the $\{z_k\}$. We want to minimize the errors across a broad collection of $\{x_j\}$ from a *training data set*.

Kaggle is an excellent online source of machine learning data sets. [118]

Reducing the error or loss involves optimizing the weights between nodes. We do this through *backpropagation*, where we tune the network and the weights using the activation functions and a classical optimization technique such as gradient descent. We use a *test data set*, different from the training data set, to verify that our model performs as expected. After that, we deploy the neural network in production on new data.

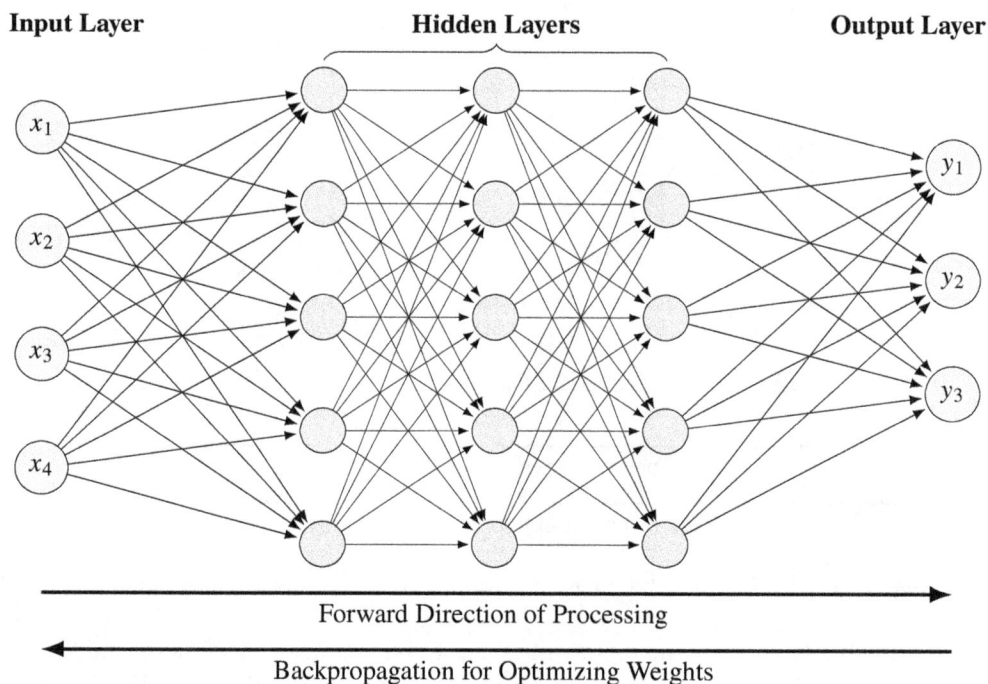

Figure 13.4: Deep neural network with 4 inputs, 3 hidden layers, and 3 outputs

Having only one hidden layer limits our ability to create sophisticated enough models to recognize patterns in complicated data. We create multiple hidden layers to build a *deep neural network*, as in Figure 13.4. Every arrow connecting nodes has an associated weight, though I do not show them. Each hidden node has an activation function determining the value sent to each node in the next layer.

A note for machine learners: For simplicity, I am not showing the *bias* values for the hidden nodes. The bias values allow you to adjust the network to fit your data better. I am assuming the model incorporates them into the nodes and weight structure.

We also use backpropagation to tune deep neural networks. Thinking of the neural network as a function, we can treat the weights as parameters to be optimized. We might use θ instead of w to represent a parameter under that interpretation.

Exercise 13.12

Draw a flow chart of neural network training that includes the following steps:

1. Standardization or normalization of classical data
2. Input of data to the neural network
3. Forward processing
4. Creation of output and evaluation of the error function
5. Iterative optimization of the weights through backpropagation
6. Final selection of weights and process termination

Exercise 13.13

Where might a barren plateau show itself in training a neural network?

Suppose we want to create a *quantum neural network* (QNN) by replacing the nodes with qubits and the values in **R** with quantum states. This direct translative approach has several difficulties, including the reversibility and nonlinearity of activation functions. [227]

Another possibility for a quantum version involves taking the input data and quantum-encoding it using a technique such as those shown in section 13.2. We then iteratively optimize and minimize an error (cost) function by changing the weights (parameters) and using the result.

Exercise 13.14

What are the implications of the No-Cloning Theorem from section 9.3.4 for sending the quantum state of a node to every node in the next layer? For what values of $|x\rangle$ will the circuit

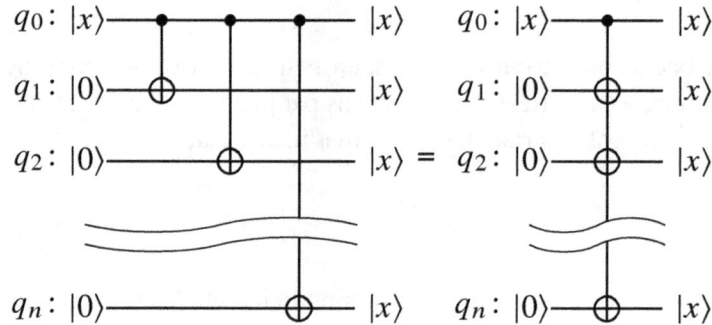

make n copies of $|x\rangle$?

In Figure 13.5, we compare the variational quantum and classical approaches to neural networks. The upper portion is very similar to what we saw in the QAOA circuit in Figure 12.21 and is the general VQE circuit in Figure 12.24. The ansatz we use depends on the machine learning task and the input data set, so is not shown in more detail here. Chapter 5 of Schuld and Petruccione provides examples. [198]

The quantum neural network flowchart in Figure 13.6 is also similar to the QAOA flowchart in Figure 12.23 in section 12.8.

Figure 13.6 shows an outline of the processing of a quantum neural network. We begin with already quantum-encoded data, such as output from a quantum sensor or a quantum computation, or we take classical data and encode it using one of the methods in section 13.2.

The critical questions regarding using variational methods as neural networks are:

- Do we lose any possible quantum advantage by having to expensively quantum encode classical data?
- Can we solve big enough problems with today's small quantum computers to make it worthwhile?
- Can NISQ quantum computers with low enough error rates produce useful results from quantum neural networks?

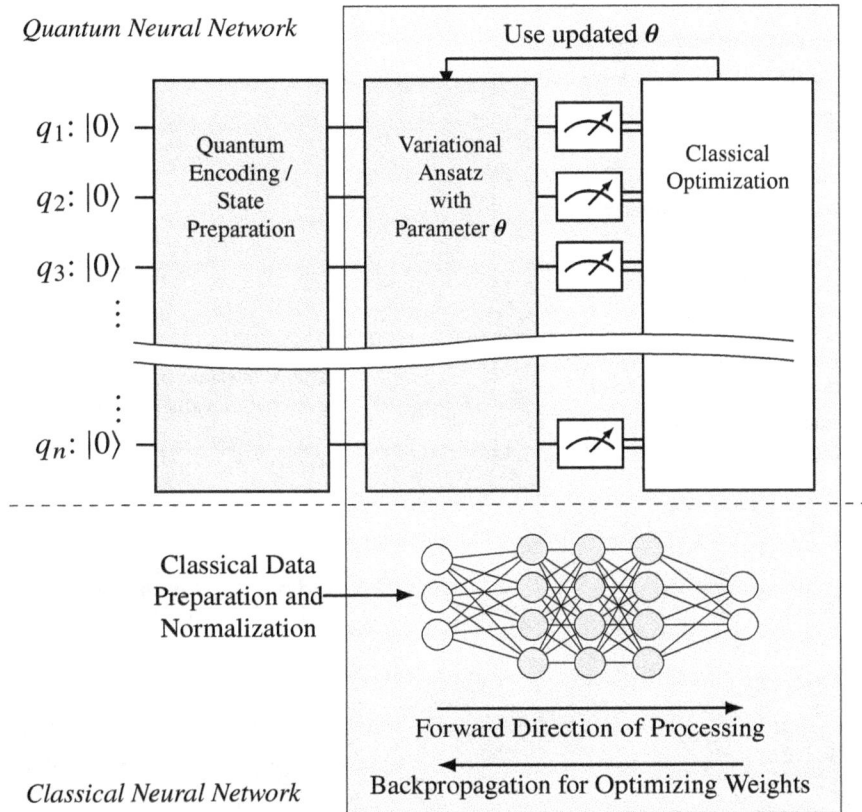

Figure 13.5: Comparison of quantum and classical neural networks

---

To learn more

For classical deep neural networks, see Goodfellow et al. [94]

The work by Schuld and Petruccione is among the best book references for quantum neural networks. [198] Abbas et al. look at metrics for the trainability of quantum neural networks compared to classical methods to see if there might be a possible quantum advantage. [3] The Qiskit documentation describes how to define and execute quantum neural networks as variational circuits. [181]

Barren plateaus in quantum neural networks can increase exponentially with the number of qubits and are an area of active study. [147] [176]

nontrivial examples of neural networks, classical or quantum, require data and a fair amount of machinery. I encourage you to work through the Qiskit quantum neural network tutorial. [182]

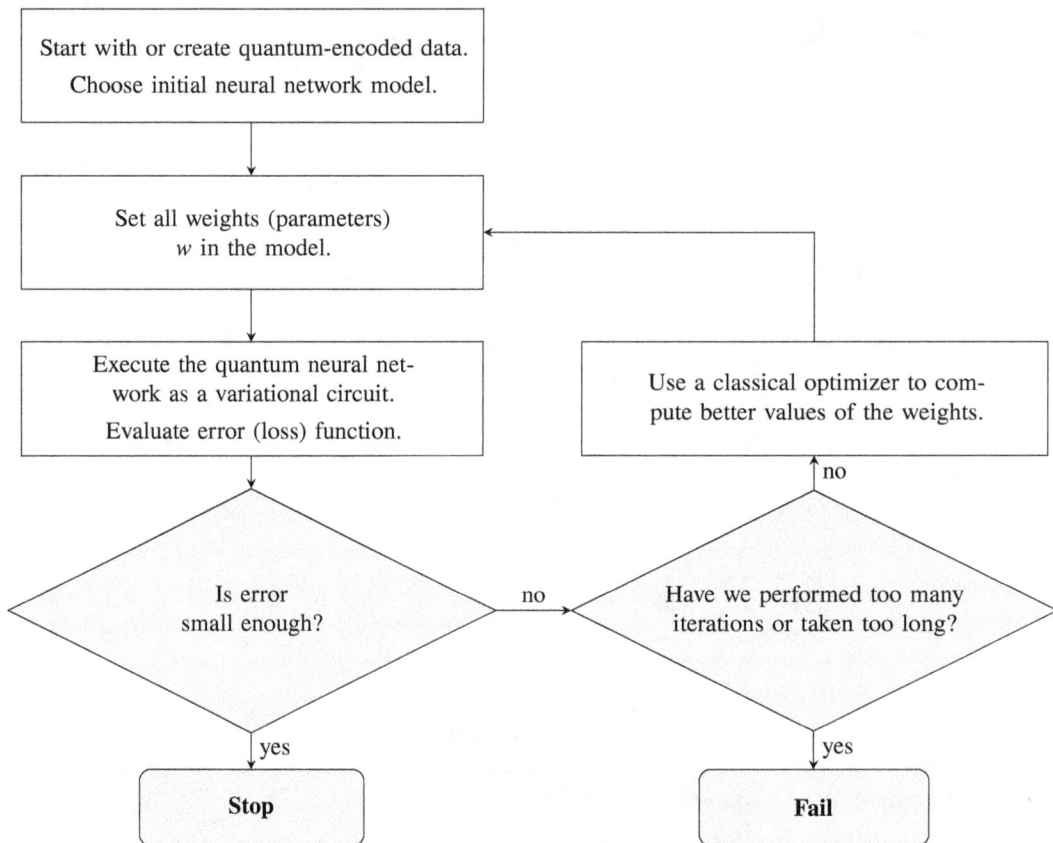

Figure 13.6: Flowchart for a quantum neural network

13.4 Quantum kernels for SVMs

In section 1.4, we saw the concept of a support vector machine, or SVM, for binary classification. We mentioned kernel functions and the kernel trick to move points to a higher dimension where we can separate them with a hyperplane. An SVM is an example of a *kernel machine*. Let's clarify their definitions and see where quantum may help.

13.4.1 Hyperplanes and feature maps

A *hyperplane* is an $n-1$ dimension linear object within an n-dimensional vector space. We assume the vector space is over $\mathbf{R}$ in this section. For example, a line is a hyperplane in $\mathbf{R}^2$, and a plane is a hyperplane in $\mathbf{R}^3$. Though harder to visualize, the 3-dimensional object defined with coordinates (x_1, x_2, x_3, x_4) in $\mathbf{R}^4$ by the equation

$$x_1 - 5x_2 + 2x_3 - 4x_4 = 1$$

is a hyperplane. Hyperplanes can be subspaces, but they need not be.

We call the function φ that transforms the original data points to the larger dimension *feature space* a *feature map*. The feature map is usually nonlinear. While there are standard candidates for use as feature maps, your choice will vary by the characteristics of the data you are trying to classify.

13.4.2 Norms

We group similar points once we map the original data to the feature space. In the case of binary classification, we group them into two categories: those on one side of the hyperplane and those on the other. The hyperplane is a *decision boundary* that we use for *linear classification*.

For example, we might use the Euclidean norm from section 5.7.3 to group points that are closest together and to calculate the equation for the hyperplane. Our choice of feature map will determine if this is a suitable distance method to measure similarity. We can often simplify the computation by using the square of the Euclidean norm, which is the dot product.

For vectors $\mathbf{v}$ and $\mathbf{w}$ in $\mathbf{R}^n$, we have

$$
\begin{aligned}
\|\mathbf{v}\| &= \sqrt{\mathbf{v} \cdot \mathbf{v}} && \text{Euclidean norm} \\
\|\mathbf{v}\|^2 &= \mathbf{v} \cdot \mathbf{v} && \text{Squared Euclidean norm} \\
\|\mathbf{v} - \mathbf{w}\| &= \sqrt{(\mathbf{v} - \mathbf{w}) \cdot (\mathbf{v} - \mathbf{w})} && \text{Euclidean distance} \\
\|\mathbf{v} - \mathbf{w}\|^2 &= (\mathbf{v} - \mathbf{w}) \cdot (\mathbf{v} - \mathbf{w}) && \text{Squared Euclidean distance}
\end{aligned}
$$

In general, a *norm* on a real or complex vector space V is a function

$$ N : V \to \mathbf{R} $$

such that the following hold for all $\mathbf{v}$ and $\mathbf{w}$ in V:

- $N(\mathbf{v} + \mathbf{w}) \leq N(\mathbf{v}) + N(\mathbf{w})$ (Triangle inequality),
- $N(a\mathbf{v}) = |a| N(\mathbf{v})$ for all scalars a, and
- $N(\mathbf{v}) = 0$ if and only if $\mathbf{v} = 0$.

Exercise 13.15

Show that the Euclidean norm is, in fact, a norm.

We also call the Euclidean norm the L^2 norm. For $\mathbf{v} = (v_1, \ldots, v_n)$,

$$ \|\mathbf{v}\| = \|\mathbf{v}\|_2 = L^2(\mathbf{v}) = \sqrt{\sum_{j=1}^{n} v_j^2}. $$

The L^1 norm is the sum of the absolute values of the vector entries:

$$\|\mathbf{v}\|_1 = L^1(\mathbf{v}) = \sum_{j=1}^{n} |v_j|.$$

Exercise 13.16

Suppose you are in a city, and you need to get from the location marked with the square ■ to the point marked with the star ★ in this diagram:

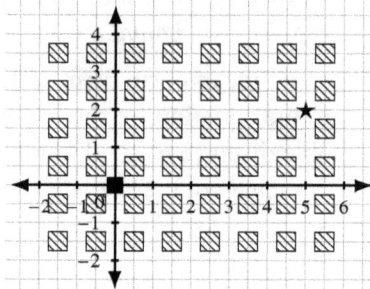

Using the L^1 and L^2 norms, compute the distances between the locations. Which norm is more useful if you are walking?

The L^1 and L^2 norms are special cases of the L^p norm

$$\|\mathbf{v}\|_p = L^p(\mathbf{v}) = \left(\sum_{j=1}^{n} |v_j|^p\right)^{\frac{1}{p}}.$$

We can define a function Lp in Python to compute the L^p norm.

```
def Lp(v, p):
  assert isinstance(v, list) and isinstance(p, int) and p > 0
  sum = 0
  for entry in v:
    sum += pow(abs(entry), p)
  return pow(sum, 1/p)
```

For a vector $\mathbf{v} = (3, 7)$ in $\mathbf{R}^2$, we can now compute $L^2(\mathbf{v})$.

```
v = [3,7]
Lp(v, 2)
```

```
7.615773105863909
```

We now compute $L^p(\mathbf{v})$ for increasing values of p:

```
for p in [1, 2, 10, 25, 50, 100]:
    print(f"{p}: {Lp(v, p)}")
```

```
1: 10.0
2: 7.615773105863909
10: 7.000146315163547
25: 7.000000000176905
50: 7.0
100: 7.0
```

Exercise 13.17

Is 7.0 really the value of $L^p(\mathbf{v})$ for $p = 50$ and $p = 100$? Why or why not?

The L^∞ norm is the maximum of the absolute values of the vector entries:

$$\|\mathbf{v}\|_\infty = L^\infty(\mathbf{v}) = \max_{1 \le j \le n} |v_j| \,.$$

It is also the limit of L^p as p approaches $+\infty$.

$$L^\infty(\mathbf{v}) = \lim_{p \to +\infty} L^p(\mathbf{v}) \,.$$

Exercise 13.18

Graph the vectors in $\mathbf{R}^2$ whose L^∞ norms equal 5.

13.4.3   Kernels

Given some choice of norm, two vectors are *similar* if the distance between them or the norm of their difference is less than some threshold. In the case of the Euclidean L^2 norm, we can use the dot (inner) product without taking the square root. For two original data points $\mathbf{x}$ and $\mathbf{y}$, we can define their being similar via the process:

- Use the feature map φ to map $\mathbf{x}$ and $\mathbf{y}$ to the feature space, producing $\varphi(\mathbf{x})$ and $\varphi(\mathbf{y})$.
- Use the dot product to compute the square of the distance between $\varphi(\mathbf{x})$ and $\varphi(\mathbf{y})$ represented as column vectors:

$$k(\mathbf{x}, \mathbf{y}) = (\varphi(\mathbf{x}) - \varphi(\mathbf{y})) \cdot (\varphi(\mathbf{x}) - \varphi(\mathbf{y}))$$
$$= (\varphi(\mathbf{x}) - \varphi(\mathbf{y}))^\mathsf{T} (\varphi(\mathbf{x}) - \varphi(\mathbf{y})).$$

- Declare $\mathbf{x}$ and $\mathbf{y}$ similar if $k(\mathbf{x}, \mathbf{y}) < \epsilon$ for some small ϵ in $\mathbf{R}$.

The function k is an example of a kernel. It appears to be a function on the original data, but its implementation involves finding an appropriate φ and feature space and then computing a dot product. This might not appear onerous for an original data point vector with two or three coordinates. However, calculating the nonlinear φ and the dot products can be computationally expensive when we have thousands of data points with many coordinates.

A kernel k must be an $\mathbf{R}$-valued symmetric function: $k(\mathbf{x}, \mathbf{y}) = k(\mathbf{y}, \mathbf{x})$. It must also be positive semi-definite: $k(\mathbf{x}, \mathbf{y}) \geq 0$. [200]

In general, we must base the behavior of a kernel k on that of an inner product $\langle, \rangle$ as we define it in section 5.7.2. Said otherwise, the feature space must be an inner product space. We need not have an explicit formula for φ. A kernel avoids the explicit computation of the coordinates in the feature space.

The *kernel trick* is finding and using a suitable kernel k that measures similarity efficiently. The best, or at least a good, kernel to use is very dependent on the original data. Machine learners experiment with standard kernel models in the hope of finding a useful kernel for classification. There are no guarantees for a given data set that any classical kernel function will classify the values: the information may be just noise.

Given a kernel k operating on d data vectors $\mathbf{x}_1, \ldots, \mathbf{x}_d$, we define the *Gram matrix*

$$K = \begin{bmatrix} k(\mathbf{x}_1, \mathbf{x}_1) & \cdots & k(\mathbf{x}_1, \mathbf{x}_d) \\ \vdots & \ddots & \vdots \\ k(\mathbf{x}_d, \mathbf{x}_1) & \cdots & k(\mathbf{x}_d, \mathbf{x}_d) \end{bmatrix}.$$

The (i, j) entry of K is $K_{i,j} = k(\mathbf{x}_i, \mathbf{x}_j)$. As such, the Gram matrix acts as a convenient lookup method to avoid repeated recalculation of kernels. You can pre-compute all the $K_{i,j}$ or compute and store them as you proceed.

Exercise 13.19

How many entries does a Gram matrix have if the original data set has one million vectors?

Example kernels

The function

$$k(\mathbf{x}, \mathbf{y}) = \mathbf{x} \cdot \mathbf{y} = \mathbf{x}^\mathsf{T} \mathbf{y} = \langle \mathbf{x}, \mathbf{y} \rangle$$

is a linear kernel with $\varphi(\mathbf{x}) = \mathbf{x}$.

Exercise 13.20

What is the dimension of the feature space for this linear kernel?

The function

$$k(\mathbf{x}, \mathbf{y}) = (\mathbf{x} \cdot \mathbf{y} + c)^2 = \left(\mathbf{x}^\mathsf{T}\mathbf{y} + c\right)^2 = (\langle \mathbf{x}, \mathbf{y} \rangle + c)^2$$

for $c \geq 0$ in $\mathbf{R}$ is a quadratic kernel. However, it does not appear to be of the form $\langle \varphi(\mathbf{x}), \varphi(\mathbf{y}) \rangle$. Let's do some math for the special case when $\mathbf{x}$ and $\mathbf{y}$ are 2-dimensional.

$$\mathbf{x} = \begin{bmatrix} x_1 \\ x_2 \end{bmatrix} \qquad \mathbf{y} = \begin{bmatrix} y_1 \\ y_2 \end{bmatrix}$$

We expand k:

$$\begin{aligned} k(\mathbf{x}, \mathbf{y}) &= (\langle \mathbf{x}, \mathbf{y} \rangle + c)^2 = (x_1 y_1 + x_2 y_2 + c)^2 \\ &= x_1{}^2 y_1{}^2 + x_2{}^2 y_2{}^2 + 2x_1 x_2 y_1 y_2 + (2x_1 y_1 + 2x_2 y_2)c + c^2 \\ &= x_1{}^2 y_1{}^2 + x_2{}^2 y_2{}^2 + \left(\sqrt{2}x_1 x_2\right)\left(\sqrt{2}y_1 y_2\right) \\ &\quad + \left(\sqrt{2c}x_1\right)\left(\sqrt{2c}y_1\right) + \left(\sqrt{2c}x_2\right)\left(\sqrt{2c}y_2\right) + c^2 \end{aligned}$$

and then define

$$\varphi(\mathbf{x}) = \begin{bmatrix} x_1^2 & x_2^2 & \sqrt{2}x_1 x_2 & \sqrt{2c}x_1 & \sqrt{2c}x_2 & c \end{bmatrix}^\mathsf{T}.$$

Exercise 13.21

With the definitions as above, show that $k(\mathbf{x}, \mathbf{y}) = \langle \varphi(\mathbf{x}), \varphi(\mathbf{y}) \rangle$.

Are there other choices for the definition of φ?

Exercise 13.22

What is the dimension of the feature space if $c > 0$? If $c = 0$?

Exercise 13.23

Now, assume that $\mathbf{x}$ and $\mathbf{y}$ are n-dimensional for $n \geq 2$ in $\mathbf{Z}$. Show the expansion of k using Σ summation notation and provide a definition for φ. What is the dimension of the feature space?

The function

$$k(\mathbf{x}, \mathbf{y}) = (\mathbf{x} \cdot \mathbf{y} + c)^n = \left(\mathbf{x}^{\mathsf{T}}\mathbf{y} + c\right)^n = (\langle \mathbf{x}, \mathbf{y} \rangle + c)^n$$

for $c \geq 0$ in $\mathbf{R}$ and $n > 2$ in $\mathbf{Z}$ is a polynomial kernel. When $n = 2$, we have a quadratic kernel.

The function

$$k(\mathbf{x}, \mathbf{y}) = \exp\left(-\frac{\|\mathbf{x} - \mathbf{y}\|_2^2}{2\sigma^2}\right)$$

$$= \exp\left(-\gamma\|\mathbf{x} - \mathbf{y}\|_2^2\right) \text{ with } \gamma = \frac{1}{2\sigma^2}$$

for σ a nonzero real number and $\|\mathbf{x} - \mathbf{y}\|_2$ the Euclidean norm, is a *radial basis function* (RBF) kernel.

Exercise 13.24

What is the maximum value of an RBF kernel? What is the minimum value?

Suppose we expand exp as an infinite power series (section 12.3.1), and perform a calculation similar to what we did for a quadratic kernel. We would then see that the feature space is infinite-dimensional. For this book, this statement is merely an observation but shows some of the complexity of machine learning and practical computation. While we may have formulas for them, we cannot calculate infinite feature space coordinates. Using a kernel avoids this problem.

Now that we have seen several classical kernels, we consider how quantum approaches might do better.

13.4.4 Quantum kernels

For use with SVM, we now introduce quantum kernels. The only aspect of the classification that is quantum is the kernel calculation on a quantum computer. All other components of the SVM machine learning process are classical.

In the quantum case, we associate a feature map φ with a unitary operator $U_{\varphi(\mathbf{x})}$, and we define

$$|\varphi(\mathbf{x})\rangle = U_{\varphi(\mathbf{x})}|0\rangle^{\otimes n}$$

and

$$k(\mathbf{x}, \mathbf{y}) = |\langle\varphi(\mathbf{y})| \, |\varphi(\mathbf{x})\rangle|^2 = |\langle\varphi(\mathbf{y})|\varphi(\mathbf{x})\rangle|^2 = \left|\langle 0|^{\otimes n} U_{\varphi(\mathbf{y})}^\dagger U_{\varphi(\mathbf{x})}|0\rangle^{\otimes n}\right|^2.$$

$k(\mathbf{x}, \mathbf{y})$ measures the *fidelity* or *transition amplitude* between the two quantum states $|\varphi(\mathbf{x})\rangle$ and $|\varphi(\mathbf{y})\rangle$. When $\mathbf{x} = \mathbf{y}$, $k(\mathbf{x}, \mathbf{y}) = 1$. We begin with an initial state and do something to it based on $\mathbf{x}$. We then do the inverse operation, but based on $\mathbf{y}$. k measures how close we return to the initial state. We use this "closeness" to measure how similar $\mathbf{x}$ is to $\mathbf{y}$ and classify based on that. [239]

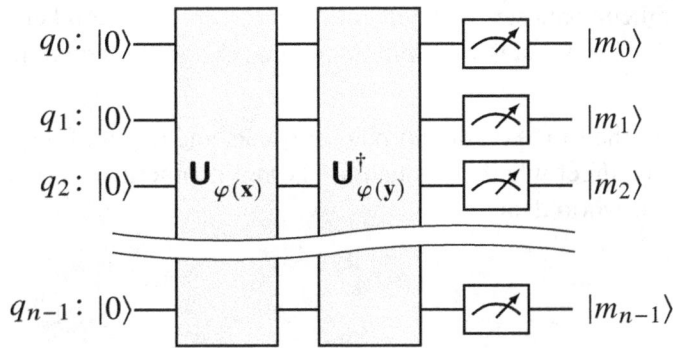

Figure 13.7: Quantum circuit for computing $k(\mathbf{x}, \mathbf{y})$

We can estimate $k(\mathbf{x}, \mathbf{y})$ by running N shots of the circuit in Figure 13.7, where you choose N to be as large as is reasonable based on your quantum computer's circuit and shots per second speed. For example, N could be 512 or 1,024. If we define

$$C = \text{number of times } |m_0 m_1 m_2 \ldots m_{n-1}\rangle = |0\rangle^{\otimes n},$$

then $k(\mathbf{x}, \mathbf{y}) \approx \frac{C}{N}$.

A *Z feature map* encodes the n coordinates of a real-valued vector $\mathbf{x} = (x_1, x_2, \ldots, x_n)$ to n qubits via

$$U_{\varphi(\mathbf{x})} = \exp\left(i \sum_{j=1}^n x_j Z_j\right) \mathbf{H}^{\otimes n} \quad \text{and} \quad |\varphi(\mathbf{x})\rangle = \exp\left(i \sum_{j=1}^n x_j Z_j\right) \mathbf{H}^{\otimes n}|0\rangle^{\otimes n}$$

where Z_j is the Pauli matrix σ_z operating in the jth position as in section 12.3.2. [185]

We can similarly define I, X, and Y feature maps by substituting I_j, X_j, and Y_j for Z_j. We can generally substitute Pauli strings for Z_j to get a *Pauli feature map*. [177] For each, note that the feature space is $\mathbf{C}^{2^n}$, with dimension 2^n as a complex vector space and 4^n as a real one. Though we call these feature maps, they also work as quantum encodings of classical data.

Starting with classical data, can one find a quantum kernel that outperforms any classical kernel? The answer is "yes," but there is a catch. We cannot show this is true for an arbitrary original data set, but it is possible to construct a quantum kernel *and then create data* for which the kernel outperforms any classical version. [113] [138] Finding a well-performing classical or quantum kernel is a combination of science and art. This should guarantee employment for kernel-method machine learning specialists for at least a bit longer.

If a classical kernel is easy to compute, there is no need to resort to a quantum kernel. Does the quantum kernel provide a significant computational advantage and classification power? A fundamental problem is showing that a quantum approach is better than any classical kernel for a given, nonsynthetic data set. A statement such as "this quantum kernel we invented is better than a few classical kernels we tried" is not general proof, though it may qualify as a heuristic.

In the NISQ era, the limits on the number of qubits and depth of high-fidelity gates in circuits will strongly affect whether a quantum kernel is practical in production use with large amounts of real-world data.

To learn more

Researchers are experimenting with quantum kernels for many applications:

- Electronic health records [129]
- High energy physics [240]
- Natural language processing (NLP) [239]
- Neurobiology [222]
- Phases of quantum matter [195]

In addition, several are looking beyond the theory to see how well quantum kernel approaches work on NISQ systems. [110]

For a nontrivial example and implementation of a quantum kernel, see the Qiskit documentation. [180]

13.5 Other quantum machine learning research areas

In addition to quantum neural networks and kernels, researchers are investigating several other techniques. These include:

- Quantum Born machines [52] [92]
- Quantum Boltzman machines [5] [156]
- Quantum convolution neural networks [47] [166]
- Quantum generative adversarial networks [139] [243]
- Relationships between deep learning models and kernel machines [71]

13.6 Summary

This chapter introduced two quantum alternatives to classical machine learning methods: quantum neural networks and kernels. We also looked at several ways to represent classical data in quantum states.

Throughout the discussions, we returned to the same question several times: Can we show that quantum machine learning offers a significant quantum advantage compared to classical methods? The answer is a definite "maybe ... one day ... possibly"! In any case, "not yet" is the consensus at the time of writing. I encourage you to track the progress of quantum machine learning as quantum computers increase in size, performance, and quality. To avoid the hype, you should keep an open mind but always ask yourself honest questions about what you are trying to accomplish with what tools. [232]

14

Questions about the Future

We can only see a short distance ahead, but we can see
plenty there that needs to be done.

– Alan Turing [220]

How will quantum computing evolve over the coming years and decades? It's critical not to say that quantum computing **will** do this or that, but rather **may**. Until someone does this or that, it's speculation, hype, or a work in progress.

Via a series of motivating questions, I give you a framework to check the progress of the full software, hardware, and systems stack shown in Figure 14.1. These questions also deal with how, where, and when you might start using, teaching, or learning about quantum computing.

The state of the art will be changing rapidly. Returning to these questions and their answers every few months will help you gauge what academia and the industry have done and why it is significant. They will allow you to understand whether quantum is ready for you and if you are ready for quantum.

Topics covered in this chapter

[585]

14.1 Ecosystem and community

''Ecosystem'' is an overused and often vague word regarding groups of individuals who have some connection to an activity. I will now try to be more precise in describing the breadth of the quantum computing ecosystem.

The goal of the ecosystem is to reach *Practical Quantum Advantage*, where quantum computing with classical computing can do **significantly** better than classical computing alone on significant problems for business, science, and government. I do not consider a slight improvement over classical methods true Quantum Advantage. I am also suspicious of announcements of advantages that do not apply to the problems of societal or commercial value.

For the following sections, think about what role or roles you have or want to have in the quantum computing ecosystem, and then answer those questions relevant to you.

What role or roles do you play in the quantum computing ecosystem?

- Algorithm developer
- Business development or sales-person
- Business or technology executive
- Business partner
- Cloud access provider
- Communications
- Community leader or participant
- Consultant
- Development tools provider
- Educator
- Full stack provider
- Hardware provider
- Industry analyst
- Industry use case expert
- Journalist
- Marketing
- Quantum application software provider
- Quantum hardware engineer
- Quantum software engineer

- Quantum software platform provider
- Scientist or researcher
- Software development tools provider
- Student
- Support
- Systems integrator
- Venture capitalist or other investor
- Other

To clarify some of these role definitions:

- Hardware provider – supplies the quantum computing hardware
- Quantum software platform provider – supplies the runtime software
- Software development tools provider – supplies the tools needed to create quantum circuits and applications
- Quantum application software provider – supplies the top-level applications that implement industry use cases
- Cloud access provider – supplies the cloud services that allow you to use remote quantum computers
- Full stack provider – supplies all of the above

Considering community and team engagement:

- How do you interact with other members of the quantum computing ecosystem doing similar work?
- How do you interact with other parts of the ecosystem that do complementary work?
- How could these interactions get started or be made more productive?
- How *must* these interactions become broader and richer as quantum computing develops?
- Are you part of an open-source community developing quantum computing software?
- What are you doing personally to improve the quality and reach of the quantum computing community?
- If you are part of a start-up, how can vendors better support you?
- If you are an analyst or a consultant, how can you best get the information you need to advise your clients?
- How should we all work together to achieve Quantum Advantage faster?

14.2   Applications and strategy

What do we mean by a ''quantum application''? It's not software where the only computer used is a quantum one. That is not possible today, nor will it be necessary or possible for many decades or even centuries. A quantum application is a hybrid classical-quantum solution that uses both kinds of hardware and software.

Industry use cases, as I touched upon briefly in Chapter 1, "Why Quantum Computing," will drive the creation of these applications. Over the years, the definition of the use cases will change as we better understand how quantum computing systems can and can't help us.

Together with those in the other sections, these questions will help you think about use cases for quantum computing and your plan for matching them to quantum solutions:

- Where is your classical computing taking too long or using too many resources?
- Where is your classical computing too inaccurate?
- Where is your classical computing too expensive?
- Do you currently use High-Performance Computing (HPC)? If so, what are the bottlenecks in your solutions?
- Can you pinpoint areas with exponential growth of memory use or computation time?
- Is your application data- or computation-intensive?
- In what ways do you want to scale the computation in your system?
- Do you want to do what you are doing now faster, or do you want greater computing capacity to examine more possibilities and scenarios?
- Are there use cases in industries similar to yours looking at pathways to quantum computing?
- Are there proposed NISQ quantum solutions for your use cases, or will you need fault tolerance? A "NISQ quantum solution" can operate with noisy qubits and short-depth circuits (section 11.1).
- How will quantum computing fit into your existing workflow?
- Do you understand your quantum strategy well enough to know which applications will be possible in the short, medium, and long terms?
- Do you work with vendors, industry analysts, management consultants, and system integrators to hone your quantum strategy?
- What is their expertise in understanding the current state of quantum hardware and software?
- Have you established your quantum education, experimentation, and implementation roadmap?

These questions are only relevant if you can use the quantum computing systems you need. In the next section, we look at the different kinds of system access and what you must consider to use them effectively.

14.3   Computing system access

''Access'' refers to how you connect to a quantum computing system. Connecting via the cloud can give you all the benefits of cloud computing regarding security, elastic resources, and software and hardware upgrades.

You must ensure you have all the access you need to succeed in your quantum computing program, whether for education, experimentation, development, or eventual production deployment.

- Can you get the quantum computing capacity you need through the cloud?
- What are your security requirements for such remote access?
- Do you require a special hosted quantum cloud data center for legislative, national, or military reasons?
- Can you use a remote quantum computer in another country?
- From which countries *can you* and *can you not* access quantum computers?
- What are your quality of service requirements for quantum computing, including uptime, prioritization, and scheduling?
- Will you need access to more than one quantum computer at a time?
- Regarding system measurements and benchmarks such as those we discussed in section 11.6, how powerful a machine, or machines, do you need?
- Does your quantum computing provider have a roadmap to provide you access to their newest and most powerful systems?
- Can you access quantum computers on the same vendor cloud where you run your classical applications?
- Do you anticipate a need to own a quantum computer versus accessing one via the cloud?
- If you purchase a quantum computer, when will it become obsolete compared to newer models?

14.4   Software

If a quantum computer is to be programmable, it must have software, as discussed in section 11.7. More than that, your chosen system must have a complete software stack of runtime facilities and development tools, as shown in the upper portion of Figure 14.1.

Note: this is the same stack shown in Figure 11.23.

- Do you prefer working with new, semi-proprietary languages for quantum computing, or would you reuse existing skills in popular languages such as Python instead?
- Does your staff already have software engineering skills in Python?

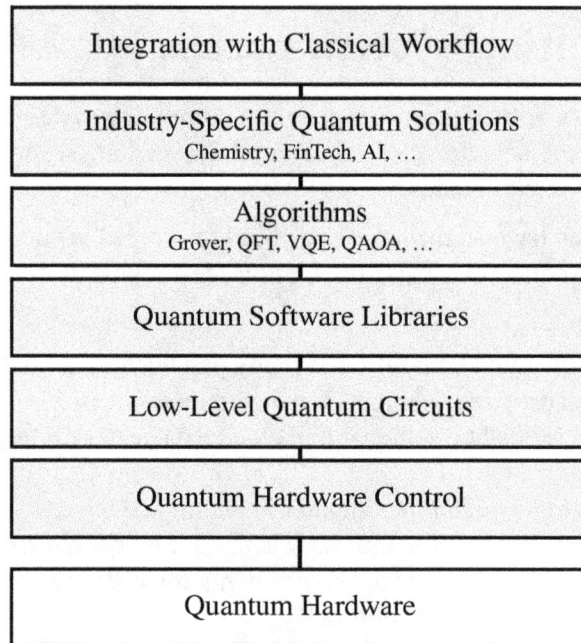

Figure 14.1: A quantum software and hardware stack

- Have you surveyed the current development platforms for quantum computing? Does your staff have expertise in Cirq or Qiskit?
- Have you assessed the breadth of functionality and algorithms implemented in the stack's Quantum Software Libraries and Algorithms levels?
- Do you need ready-made optimized circuits at the stack's Low-Level Quantum Circuits and Quantum Software Libraries levels?
- Will you be implementing new circuits?
- What is the level of abstraction with which you can create circuits?
- Does the programming environment offer direct access to the operating characteristics of the hardware?
- Can you design new gates and directly control the qubit hardware in the stack's Low-Level Quantum Circuits or Quantum Hardware Control levels?
- Do the development environment and programming language only target quantum simulators?
- Can you write code and run it on quantum hardware and simulators?
- Is your quantum software development platform open-source? Is everything open-source, or only part of the platform?
- If so, is the open-source software supported by a large, vibrant, multidisciplinary group of developers?

- What open-source license does it use? Is this consistent with your commercialization plans? Have you talked to your intellectual property attorney recently?
- What documentation and media support are available to help you start developing? Are there books available to help you learn?
- For how long has the software platform been under development?
- Is there a public roadmap for planned future development?
- What is the software development toolchain in your quantum platform?
- Does your platform contain an optimizing quantum transpiler to get the best application performance on the hardware? Are there third-party optimizers that work on your platform?
- What facilities are there for debugging your code?
- How easily and graphically can you see and understand the results of your circuits?

14.5   Hardware

A quantum computing system needs real quantum computing hardware. While simulators may be helpful for learning, experimenting, and debugging small problems, the sooner you use actual hardware, the quicker you'll take advantage of its potential. You are not doing quantum computing if you are solely using classical hardware.

- Are you sure your vendor provides access to real quantum hardware, or is it only a simulator?
- Is the quantum hardware general purpose (also known as *universal*), or is it designed to solve only one kind of problem?
- Can your quantum hardware be used to solve problems significantly better than classical technologies? If not, when will this happen?
- Does the choice of qubit modality make a difference to you?
- What qubit modality produces systems with the best benchmark scores for your intended applications?
- How are the number of high-quality qubits scaling for the technology you choose?
- Can you use the same quantum software development environment to target different quantum hardware?
- Does your quantum computing system offer physical qubits, logical qubits, or both?
- Can your quantum hardware, with its associated software, be used to entangle many qubits?
- Are you confident that your quantum computing hardware provider will provide you with long-term support and continue to enhance the technology?

14.6 Education

I split the questions about education for quantum computing and coding between teaching and learning.

Teaching

- Do you currently teach or plan to teach a class involving quantum computing?
- Do you teach a single class on the topic or parts of the subject in different courses?
- Where would you augment the following courses with quantum computing: Artificial Intelligence, Chemistry, Computer Science, Engineering, Materials Science, Philosophy, Physics, Pure and Applied Mathematics, and Quantitative Economics and Finance?
- Do you supplement the material with hands-on homework or labs using a software development environment?
- Do your students download the development environment or use it on the cloud through a browser?
- Do you use a textbook, your own material, or both?
- Do you supplement your material with online content, videos, and exercises?
- Are you part of a community developing teaching materials?
- How do you augment student activities in quantum computing outside the classroom?
- Do you take online quantum computing classes to learn how to teach the subject better?

Learning

- Have you taken a class on quantum computing in school, through your organization, or online?
- What classes have you taken that could have been extended with quantum computing content?
- Have you asked your teachers or professors to include that content?
- Are you willing to learn about quantum computing outside the classroom?
- Have you participated in a quantum computing hackathon at your school or in your organization?

- Are you willing to host such a hackathon with help from a quantum computing vendor?
- Have you visited an exhibit about quantum computing at a science museum?
- How important is it to you to get badges for your résumé that show your proficiency in quantum computing?
- Do you know how to code, specifically Python? Python is one of the most commonly used programming languages for scientific and AI applications.

Figure 14.2: The author speaking at the Boston Museum of Science in 2019

- Do you plan to do quantum computing research or software engineering, or is this just an interest of yours?
- If you call yourself an ''quantum enthusiast,'' how do you plan to become a quantum practitioner?

14.7 Workforce

You can't build a quantum computing program without people, and they must have the right skills and education for your part in the ecosystem.

- Does your organization have staff to guide you in your quantum business and technical strategy?
- Is ''quantum computing'' part of the skills profile for your employees?
- What is your recruiting plan to build quantum expertise in your organization?
- Have you targeted colleges and universities that include quantum computing in their curricula for recruiting?
- Do you attend quantum computing conferences to recruit?
- Do you look for badges showing your employees' and job applicants' quantum computing proficiency?
- Will you reimburse employees who take quantum computing classes or training programs?
- Are quantum computing conferences on the list of approved employee expenses, including management?

- What new jobs will be created in your organization when we reach Quantum Advantage?
- Do you have staff with graduate degrees in physics who can code?
- Do you have staff with graduate degrees in computer science who can understand the physics of quantum computing hardware?
- If you sell quantum hardware, do you have innovative manufacturing technicians who can create your products?
- Do you recruit from foreign countries?
- Do you need help building out your skills and recruiting strategy?
- Is your Chief Technical Officer (CTO) ''quantum computing savvy''?

14.8 Summary

In this book's final chapter, we examined questions that allow you to think about the development of quantum computing and how you can use it. The answers will help you gauge progress in the field. This progress will likely be uneven as temporary scientific and engineering roadblocks are discovered and then bypassed or overcome.

Afterword

The computing capacity and performance of quantum systems must increase dramatically until we have full fault tolerance and hundreds of thousands of qubits. These metrics may not increase smoothly over the next few years and decades, but might instead jump like a step function as we improve this or that part of the hardware, software, or system engineering.

Quantum computing is not a niche: I predict it will first be used to complement classical computing systems and then grow in power and importance as the 21st century progresses. It could very well become the most important computing technology of our lifetimes.

In this book, I have tried to give you a solid foundation for understanding quantum computing. Mathematics is needed to see what is really going on, but I have provided what you need to get well into the subject. In various places, I have pointed out how you can learn more about a topic. I encourage you to do so, and you are now equipped for independent study. You have the basis to read more advanced texts on the subject as well as research papers. You may need to supplement what we have discussed here through other reading.

Quantum computing has something for everyone, no matter what your scientific or technical background. I hope you go forth and help shape the future of computing.

Appendices

A

Quick Reference

Topics covered in this appendix

A.1 One qubit kets

Computational basis (Z)

$$|0\rangle = \begin{bmatrix} 1 \\ 0 \end{bmatrix} \qquad |1\rangle = \begin{bmatrix} 0 \\ 1 \end{bmatrix}$$

Hadamard basis (X)

$$|+\rangle = \frac{\sqrt{2}}{2} \begin{bmatrix} 1 \\ 1 \end{bmatrix} \qquad |-\rangle = \frac{\sqrt{2}}{2} \begin{bmatrix} 1 \\ -1 \end{bmatrix}$$

Circular basis (Y)

$$|i\rangle = |\circlearrowleft\rangle = \frac{\sqrt{2}}{2}(|0\rangle + i|1\rangle) = \frac{\sqrt{2}}{2}\begin{bmatrix} 1 \\ i \end{bmatrix}$$

$$|-i\rangle = |\circlearrowright\rangle = \frac{\sqrt{2}}{2}(|0\rangle - i|1\rangle) = \frac{\sqrt{2}}{2}\begin{bmatrix} 1 \\ -i \end{bmatrix}$$

A.2   Two qubit kets

Computational basis

$$|00\rangle = \begin{bmatrix} 1 \\ 0 \\ 0 \\ 0 \end{bmatrix} \quad |01\rangle = \begin{bmatrix} 0 \\ 1 \\ 0 \\ 0 \end{bmatrix} \quad |10\rangle = \begin{bmatrix} 0 \\ 0 \\ 1 \\ 0 \end{bmatrix} \quad |11\rangle = \begin{bmatrix} 0 \\ 0 \\ 0 \\ 1 \end{bmatrix}$$

Bell state basis

$$|\Phi^+\rangle = \frac{\sqrt{2}}{2}|00\rangle + \frac{\sqrt{2}}{2}|11\rangle \qquad |\Psi^+\rangle = \frac{\sqrt{2}}{2}|01\rangle + \frac{\sqrt{2}}{2}|10\rangle$$

$$|\Phi^-\rangle = \frac{\sqrt{2}}{2}|00\rangle - \frac{\sqrt{2}}{2}|11\rangle \qquad |\Psi^-\rangle = \frac{\sqrt{2}}{2}|01\rangle - \frac{\sqrt{2}}{2}|10\rangle$$

A.3   Pauli gates and matrices

$$I_2 = \sigma_0 = \begin{bmatrix} 1 & 0 \\ 0 & 1 \end{bmatrix} \quad \sigma_x = \begin{bmatrix} 0 & 1 \\ 1 & 0 \end{bmatrix} \quad \sigma_y = \begin{bmatrix} 0 & -i \\ i & 0 \end{bmatrix} \quad \sigma_z = \begin{bmatrix} 1 & 0 \\ 0 & -1 \end{bmatrix}$$

A.4 Pauli strings of length 2

This section lists the Pauli strings of length 2 as defined in section 12.7.

$$I_2 \otimes I_2 = \mathrm{II} = \begin{bmatrix} 1 & 0 & 0 & 0 \\ 0 & 1 & 0 & 0 \\ 0 & 0 & 1 & 0 \\ 0 & 0 & 0 & 1 \end{bmatrix} \qquad I_2 \otimes \sigma_x = \mathrm{IX} = \begin{bmatrix} 0 & 1 & 0 & 0 \\ 1 & 0 & 0 & 0 \\ 0 & 0 & 0 & 1 \\ 0 & 0 & 1 & 0 \end{bmatrix}$$

$$I_2 \otimes \sigma_y = \mathrm{IY} = \begin{bmatrix} 0 & i & 0 & 0 \\ -i & 0 & 0 & 0 \\ 0 & 0 & 0 & i \\ 0 & 0 & -i & 0 \end{bmatrix} \qquad I_2 \otimes \sigma_z = \mathrm{IZ} = \begin{bmatrix} 1 & 0 & 0 & 0 \\ 0 & -1 & 0 & 0 \\ 0 & 0 & 1 & 0 \\ 0 & 0 & 0 & -1 \end{bmatrix}$$

$$\sigma_x \otimes I_2 = \mathrm{XI} = \begin{bmatrix} 0 & 0 & 1 & 0 \\ 0 & 0 & 0 & 1 \\ 1 & 0 & 0 & 0 \\ 0 & 1 & 0 & 0 \end{bmatrix} \qquad \sigma_x \otimes \sigma_x = \mathrm{XX} = \begin{bmatrix} 0 & 0 & 0 & 1 \\ 0 & 0 & 1 & 0 \\ 0 & 1 & 0 & 0 \\ 1 & 0 & 0 & 0 \end{bmatrix}$$

$$\sigma_x \otimes \sigma_y = \mathrm{XY} = \begin{bmatrix} 0 & 0 & 0 & i \\ 0 & 0 & -i & 0 \\ 0 & i & 0 & 0 \\ -i & 0 & 0 & 0 \end{bmatrix} \qquad \sigma_x \otimes \sigma_z = \mathrm{XZ} = \begin{bmatrix} 0 & 0 & 1 & 0 \\ 0 & 0 & 0 & -1 \\ 1 & 0 & 0 & 0 \\ 0 & -1 & 0 & 0 \end{bmatrix}$$

$$\sigma_y \otimes I_2 = \mathrm{YI} = \begin{bmatrix} 0 & 0 & i & 0 \\ 0 & 0 & 0 & i \\ -i & 0 & 0 & 0 \\ 0 & -i & 0 & 0 \end{bmatrix} \qquad \sigma_y \otimes \sigma_x = \mathrm{YX} = \begin{bmatrix} 0 & 0 & 0 & i \\ 0 & 0 & i & 0 \\ 0 & -i & 0 & 0 \\ -i & 0 & 0 & 0 \end{bmatrix}$$

$$\sigma_y \otimes \sigma_y = \mathrm{YY} = \begin{bmatrix} 0 & 0 & 0 & -1 \\ 0 & 0 & 1 & 0 \\ 0 & 1 & 0 & 0 \\ -1 & 0 & 0 & 0 \end{bmatrix} \qquad \sigma_y \otimes \sigma_z = \mathrm{YZ} = \begin{bmatrix} 0 & 0 & i & 0 \\ 0 & 0 & 0 & -i \\ -i & 0 & 0 & 0 \\ 0 & i & 0 & 0 \end{bmatrix}$$

$$\sigma_z \otimes I_2 = ZI = \begin{bmatrix} 1 & 0 & 0 & 0 \\ 0 & 1 & 0 & 0 \\ 0 & 0 & -1 & 0 \\ 0 & 0 & 0 & -1 \end{bmatrix} \qquad \sigma_z \otimes \sigma_x = ZX = \begin{bmatrix} 0 & 1 & 0 & 0 \\ 1 & 0 & 0 & 0 \\ 0 & 0 & 0 & -1 \\ 0 & 0 & -1 & 0 \end{bmatrix}$$

$$\sigma_z \otimes \sigma_y = ZY = \begin{bmatrix} 0 & i & 0 & 0 \\ -i & 0 & 0 & 0 \\ 0 & 0 & 0 & -i \\ 0 & 0 & i & 0 \end{bmatrix} \qquad \sigma_z \otimes \sigma_z = ZZ = \begin{bmatrix} 1 & 0 & 0 & 0 \\ 0 & -1 & 0 & 0 \\ 0 & 0 & -1 & 0 \\ 0 & 0 & 0 & 1 \end{bmatrix}$$

A.5 Greek letters

Name	Lowercase	Uppercase	Name	Lowercase	Uppercase
alpha	α	A	nu	ν	N
beta	β	B	xi	ξ	Ξ
gamma	γ	Γ	omicron	o	O
delta	δ	Δ	pi	π	Π
epsilon	ϵ	E	rho	ρ	P
zeta	ζ	Z	sigma	σ	Σ
eta	η	H	tau	τ	T
theta	θ	Θ	upsilon	υ	Y
iota	ι	I	phi	φ	Φ
kappa	κ	K	chi	χ	X
lambda	λ	Λ	psi	ψ	Ψ
mu	μ	M	omega	ω	Ω

B

Notices

In this appendix, we document the trademarks and legal notices associated with the software we mention in the book.

Topics covered in this appendix

B.1 Photos, images, and diagrams

Unless otherwise noted, all photographs, images, and diagrams were created by the author, Robert S. Sutor. They share the same copyright as the book itself.

- The photo of Richard Feynman in section 1.2 is in the public domain.
- The image of the 74181 four-bit ALU in section 2.5 is subject to use under the Creative Commons Attribution-ShareAlike 3.0 Unported license and was obtained from `https://en.wikipedia.org/wiki/Arithmetic_logic_unit#/media/File:74181aluschematic.png`.

- The photo of John von Neumann in section 2.8.1 is subject to use via the Los Alamos National Laboratory notice.
- The photo of Niels Henrik Abel in section 3.6.1 is in the public domain.
- The photo of Charles Hermite in section 5.4.1 is in the public domain.
- The image of Carl Friedrich Gauss immediately before section 5.6 is in the public domain.
- The photo of David Hilbert in section 5.7.3 is in the public domain.
- The photo of Andrey Markov in section 6.8 is in the public domain.
- The portrait of Pafnuty Chebyshev in section 6.8 is in the public domain.
- The photo of Felix Bloch in section 7.5 is subject to use under the Creative Commons Attribution 3.0 Unported license.
- The photo of Wolfgang Pauli in section 7.6.2 is in the public domain.
- The photo of Jacques Hadamard in section 7.6.5 is in the public domain.
- The photo of Erwin Schrödinger in section 8.4 is in the public domain.
- The photo of Niels Bohr in section 8.4 is in the public domain.
- The photo of David Deutsch in section 9.8 is is subject to use under the Creative Commons Attribution 3.0 Unported license.
- The photo of Leopold Kronecker in section 10.1.1 is in the public domain.
- The photo of Peter Shor in section 10.2 is subject to use under the Creative Commons Attribution 3.0 Unported license.
- The portrait of Pierre de Fermat in section 10.2.3 is in the public domain.
- The diagram in Figure 11.23 is based on a similar diagram developed by the author for the Infleqtion company. Used with permission.
- The photo of Heinrich Rudolf Hertz in section 11.9.1 is in the public domain.
- The portrait of William Rowan Hamilton in section 12.7 is in the public domain.
- The portrait of Max Born in section 13.4.4 is in the public domain.
- The photo of Robert S. Sutor at the Boston Museum of Science in Chapter 14, ''Questions about the Future,'' was taken by Carol Lynn Alpert. Used with permission.

B.2   Marks

- IBM® and Qiskit®, are registered trademarks of IBM Corporation.
- The Jupyter Trademark is registered with the U.S. Patent and Trademark Office.
- ''Major League Baseball'' is a service mark of Major League Baseball Properties, Inc.
- MATLAB® is a registered trademark of The MathWorks, Inc.
- Mathematica® is a registered trademark of Wolfram Research, Inc.
- Pennylane® is a registered trademark of Xanadu Quantum Technologies Inc.
- Polaroid® is a registered trademark of Polaroid Corporation.
- Python® is a registered trademark of the Python Software Foundation. Python is

copyright © 2001–2024 Python Software Foundation.

- The Python logo is a trademark of the Python Software Foundation: `https://www.python.org/community/logos/`.
- Pytorch® is a registered trademark of Facebook, Inc.
- STAR TREK® is the registered trademark of CBS Studios Inc.
- SuperstaQ and SupermarQ are trademarks of Super.tech and Infleqtion, Inc.
- Wikipedia® is a registered trademark of the Wikimedia Foundation, Inc.
- YouTube® is a registered trademark of Google Inc.

B.3 Creative Commons Attribution-NoDerivs 2.0 Generic

You are free to:

- **Share** – copy and redistribute the material in any medium or format for any purpose, even commercially.

The licensor cannot revoke these freedoms as long as you follow the license terms.

Under the following terms:

- **Attribution** – You must give appropriate credit, provide a link to the license, and indicate if changes were made. You may do so in any reasonable manner, but not in any way that suggests the licensor endorses you or your use.
- **NoDerivatives** – If you remix, transform, or build upon the material, you may not distribute the modified material.
- **No additional restrictions** – You may not apply legal terms or technological measures that legally restrict others from doing anything the license permits. [55]

    `https://creativecommons.org/licenses/by-nd/2.0/legalcode`

B.4 Creative Commons Attribution-ShareAlike 2.0 Germany

You are free to:

- **Share** – copy and redistribute the material in any medium or format.
- **Adapt** – remix, transform, and build upon the material for any purpose, even commercially.

The licensor cannot revoke these freedoms as long as you follow the license terms.

Under the following terms:

- **Attribution** – You must give appropriate credit, provide a link to the license, and indicate if changes were made. You may do so in any reasonable manner, but not in any way that suggests the licensor endorses you or your use.
- **ShareAlike** – If you remix, transform, or build upon the material, you must distribute your contributions under the same license as the original.
- **No additional restrictions** – You may not apply legal terms or technological measures that legally restrict others from doing anything the license permits. [56]

  `https://creativecommons.org/licenses/by-sa/2.0/de/deed.en`

B.5 Creative Commons Attribution 3.0 Unported

You are free to:

- **Share** – copy and redistribute the material in any medium or format.
- **Adapt** – remix, transform, and build upon the material for any purpose, even commercially.

The licensor cannot revoke these freedoms as long as you follow the license terms.

Under the following terms:

- **Attribution** – You must give appropriate credit, provide a link to the license, and indicate if changes were made. You may do so in any reasonable manner, but not in any way that suggests the licensor endorses you or your use.
- **No additional restrictions** – You may not apply legal terms or technological measures that legally restrict others from doing anything the license permits. [54]

  `https://creativecommons.org/licenses/by/3.0/legalcode`

B.6 Creative Commons Attribution-ShareAlike 3.0 Unported

You are free to:

- **Share** – copy and redistribute the material in any medium or format for any purpose, even commercially.
- **Adapt** – remix, transform, and build upon the material for any purpose, even commercially.

The licensor cannot revoke these freedoms as long as you follow the license terms.

Under the following terms:

- **Attribution** – You must give appropriate credit , provide a link to the license, and indicate if changes were made . You may do so in any reasonable manner, but not in any way that suggests the licensor endorses you or your use.
- **ShareAlike** – If you remix, transform, or build upon the material, you must distribute your contributions under the same license as the original.
- **No additional restrictions** – You may not apply legal terms or technological measures that legally restrict others from doing anything the license permits. [57]

Notices:

You do not have to comply with the license for elements of the material in the public domain or where your use is permitted by an applicable exception or limitation .

No warranties are given. The license may not give you all of the permissions necessary for your intended use. For example, other rights such as publicity, privacy, or moral rights may limit how you use the material.

> https://creativecommons.org/licenses/by-sa/3.0/deed.en

B.7   Los Alamos National Laboratory

''Unless otherwise indicated, this information has been authored by an employee or employees of the Los Alamos National Security, LLC (LANS), operator of the Los Alamos National Laboratory under Contract No. DE-AC52-06NA25396 with the U.S. Department of Energy. The U.S. Government has rights to use, reproduce, and distribute this information. The public may copy and use this information without charge, provided that this Notice and any statement of authorship are reproduced on all copies. Neither the Government nor LANS makes any warranty, express or implied, or assumes any liability or responsibility for the use of this information.''

B.8   Python 3 license

Python 3 is made available under the license at

> https://docs.python.org/3/license.html .

At the time of writing this book, the license was for version 3.11.8:

1. This LICENSE AGREEMENT is between the Python Software Foundation (''PSF''), and the Individual or Organization (''Licensee'') accessing and otherwise using Python 3.11.8 software in source or binary form and its associated documentation.

2. Subject to the terms and conditions of this License Agreement, PSF hereby grants Licensee a nonexclusive, royalty-free, world-wide license to reproduce, analyze, test, perform and/or display publicly, prepare derivative works, distribute, and otherwise use Python 3.11.8 alone or in any derivative version, provided, however, that PSF's License Agreement and PSF's notice of copyright, i.e., "Copyright © 2001-2024 Python Software Foundation; All Rights Reserved" are retained in Python 3.11.8 alone or in any derivative version prepared by Licensee.

3. In the event Licensee prepares a derivative work that is based on or incorporates Python 3.11.8 or any part thereof, and wants to make the derivative work available to others as provided herein, then Licensee hereby agrees to include in any such work a brief summary of the changes made to Python 3.11.8.

4. PSF is making Python 3.11.8 available to Licensee on an "AS IS" basis. PSF MAKES NO REPRESENTATIONS OR WARRANTIES, EXPRESS OR IMPLIED. BY WAY OF EXAMPLE, BUT NOT LIMITATION, PSF MAKES NO AND DISCLAIMS ANY REPRESENTATION OR WARRANTY OF MERCHANTABILITY OR FITNESS FOR ANY PARTICULAR PURPOSE OR THAT THE USE OF PYTHON 3.11.8 WILL NOT INFRINGE ANY THIRD PARTY RIGHTS.

5. PSF SHALL NOT BE LIABLE TO LICENSEE OR ANY OTHER USERS OF PYTHON 3.11.8 FOR ANY INCIDENTAL, SPECIAL, OR CONSEQUENTIAL DAMAGES OR LOSS AS A RESULT OF MODIFYING, DISTRIBUTING, OR OTHERWISE USING PYTHON 3.11.8, OR ANY DERIVATIVE THEREOF, EVEN IF ADVISED OF THE POSSIBILITY THEREOF.

6. This License Agreement will automatically terminate upon a material breach of its terms and conditions.

7. Nothing in this License Agreement shall be deemed to create any relationship of agency, partnership, or joint venture between PSF and Licensee. This License Agreement does not grant permission to use PSF trademarks or trade name in a trademark sense to endorse or promote products or services of Licensee, or any third party.

8. By copying, installing or otherwise using Python 3.11.8, Licensee agrees to be bound by the terms and conditions of this License Agreement.

C

Production Notes

Topics covered in this appendix

C.1   How this book was built

I wrote the content for this book primarily in HTML, augmented with LaTeX in tag attributes. Additional content included:

- Static JPG images.
- LaTeX files using packages including `tikz`, `circuitikz`, and `quantikz`. I processed these with *pdflatex* and then the *convert* utility from *ImageMagick* to create JPG images.
- Python files using **matplotlib** for plots and charts. I ran these in batch mode to generate JPG images.

For many images, especially those I generated, I used *convert* from *ImageMagick* to remove extra surrounding whitespace.

I wrote several Python scripts to generate the book and features within it, such as index marking. For example, one script processed HTML chapter files and extracted the Python code. The script then ran the code through *Jupyter* in noninteractive mode to capture all Python output.

I used Python and the package **python-docx** to create a Microsoft Word docx file for editing and reviewing. I especially want to thank the developers of **python-docx** along with those who published fixes and extensions on the web.

C.2   Citing this book

If you cite this book with BibTeX, please use

```
@BOOK{Sutor:2024:DwQ,
    AUTHOR = {Sutor, Robert S.},
    PUBLISHER = {Packt Publishing},
    DATE = {2024},
    EDITION = {2},
    ISBN = {978-1-83763-675-4},
    TITLE = {Dancing with Qubits, Second Edition},
    SUBTITLE = {From qubits to algorithms, embark
        on the quantum computing journey shaping our future
    }
}
```

The following sections list the details of my Python and LaTeX development environment during the book creation.

C.3   Python version

Python 3.11.8 (tags/v3.11.8:db85d51, Feb 6 2024, 22:03:32)
[MSC v.1937 64 bit (AMD64)]

C.4   LaTeX environment

pdfTeX 3.141592653-2.6-1.40.25 (TeX Live 2023)
kpathsea version 6.3.5
Copyright 2023 Han The Thanh (pdfTeX) et al.
There is NO warranty. Redistribution of this software is
covered by the terms of both the pdfTeX copyright and
the Lesser GNU General Public License.
For more information about these matters, see the file
named COPYING and the pdfTeX source.
Primary author of pdfTeX: Han The Thanh (pdfTeX) et al.

Compiled with libpng 1.6.39; using libpng 1.6.39
Compiled with zlib 1.2.13; using zlib 1.2.13
Compiled with xpdf version 4.04

Other Books You May Enjoy

If you enjoyed this book, you may be interested in these other books by Packt:

Dancing with Python
Robert S. Sutor
ISBN: 978-1-80107-785-9

- Explore different quantum gates and build quantum circuits with Qiskit and Python
- Write succinct code the Pythonic way using magic methods, iterators, and generators
- Analyze data, build basic machine learning models, and plot the results
- Search for information using the quantum Grover Search Algorithm
- Optimize and test your code to run efficiently

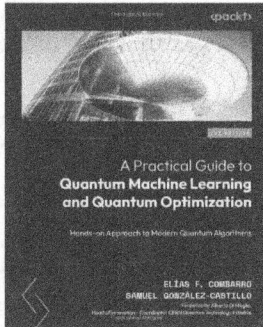

A Practical Guide to Quantum Machine Learning and Quantum Optimization
Elías F. Combarro and Samuel González-Castillo
ISBN: 978-1-80461-383-2

- Review the basics of quantum computing
- Gain a solid understanding of modern quantum algorithms
- Understand how to formulate optimization problems with QUBO
- Solve optimization problems with quantum annealing, QAOA, GAS, and VQE
- Find out how to create quantum machine learning models
- Explore how quantum support vector machines and quantum neural networks work using Qiskit® and PennyLane®
- Discover how to implement hybrid architectures using Qiskit and PennyLane and its PyTorch® interface

Leave a review – let other readers know what you think

Please share your thoughts on this book with others by leaving a review on the site that you bought it from. If you purchased the book from Amazon, please leave us an honest review on this book's Amazon page. This is vital so that other potential readers can see and use your unbiased opinion to make purchasing decisions, we can understand what our customers think about our products, and our authors can see your feedback on the title that they have worked with Packt to create. It will only take a few minutes of your time, but is valuable to other potential customers, our authors, and Packt. Thank you!

References

[1] Aaronson, Scott and Rall, Patrick. "Quantum Approximate Counting, Simplified". In: *Symposium on Simplicity in Algorithms (SOSA)*. Jan. 2020, pp. 24–32. URL: https://epubs.siam.org/doi/abs/10.1137/1.9781611976014.5.

[2] Abbas, Amira, Ambainis, Andris, Augustino, Brandon, Bärtschi, Andreas, Buhrman, Harry, Coffrin, Carleton, Cortiana, Giorgio, Dunjko, Vedran, Egger, Daniel J., Elmegreen, Bruce G., Franco, Nicola, Fratini, Filippo, Fuller, Bryce, Gacon, Julien, Gonciulea, Constantin, Gribling, Sander, Gupta, Swati, Hadfield, Stuart, Heese, Raoul, Kircher, Gerhard, Kleinert, Thomas, Koch, Thorsten, Korpas, Georgios, Lenk, Steve, Marecek, Jakub, Markov, Vanio, Mazzola, Guglielmo, Mensa, Stefano, Mohseni, Naeimeh, Nannicini, Giacomo, O'Meara, Corey, Tapia, Elena Peña, Pokutta, Sebastian, Proissl, Manuel, Rebentrost, Patrick, Sahin, Emre, Symons, Benjamin C. B., Tornow, Sabine, Valls, Victor, Woerner, Stefan, Wolf-Bauwens, Mira L., Yard, Jon, Yarkoni, Sheir, Zechiel, Dirk, Zhuk, Sergiy, and Zoufal, Christa. *Quantum Optimization: Potential, Challenges, and the Path Forward*. Dec. 4, 2023. URL: https://arxiv.org/abs/2312.02279.

[3] Abbas, Amira, Sutter, David, Zoufal, Christa, Lucchi, Aurelien, Figalli, Alessio, and Woerner, Stefan. "The power of quantum neural networks". In: *Nature Computational Science* 1.6 (June 2021), pp. 403–409.

[4] Ahlfors, L. V. *Complex Analysis. An introduction to the theory of analytic functions of one complex variable*. 3rd ed. International Series in Pure and Applied Mathematics 7. McGraw-Hill Education, 1979.

[5] Amin, Mohammad H., Andriyash, Evgeny, Rolfe, Jason, Kulchytskyy, Bohdan, and Melko, Roger. "Quantum Boltzmann Machine". In: *Physical Review X* 8.2 (May 2018). URL: http://dx.doi.org/10.1103/PhysRevX.8.021050.

[6] Ang, James, Carini, Gabriella, Chen, Yanzhu, Chuang, Isaac, DeMarco, Michael Austin, Economou, Sophia E., Eickbusch, Alec, Faraon, Andrei, Fu, Kai-Mei, Girvin, Steven M., Hatridge, Michael, Houck, Andrew, Hilaire, Paul, Krsulich, Kevin, Li, Ang, Liu, Chenxu, Liu, Yuan, Martonosi, Margaret, McKay, David C., Misewich,

James, Ritter, Mark, Schoelkopf, Robert J., Stein, Samuel A., Sussman, Sara, Tang, Hong X., Tang, Wei, Tomesh, Teague, Tubman, Norm M., Wang, Chen, Wiebe, Nathan, Yao, Yong-Xin, Yost, Dillon C., and Zhou, Yiyu. *Architectures for Multinode Superconducting Quantum Computers*. 2022. URL: https://arxiv.org/abs/221 2.06167.

[7] Artzy, R. *Linear Geometry*. Addison-Wesley series in mathematics. Addison-Wesley Publishing Company, 1974.

[8] Awschalom, David, Berggren, Karl K., Bernien, Hannes, Bhave, Sunil, Carr, Lincoln D., Davids, Paul, Economou, Sophia E., Englund, Dirk, Faraon, Andrei, Fejer, Martin, Guha, Saikat, Gustafsson, Martin V., Hu, Evelyn, Jiang, Liang, Kim, Jungsang, Korzh, Boris, Kumar, Prem, Kwiat, Paul G., Lončar, Marko, Lukin, Mikhail D., Miller, David A.B., Monroe, Christopher, Nam, Sae Woo, Narang, Prineha, Orcutt, Jason S., Raymer, Michael G., Safavi-Naeini, Amir H., Spiropulu, Maria, Srinivasan, Kartik, Sun, Shuo, Vučković, Jelena, Waks, Edo, Walsworth, Ronald, Weiner, Andrew M., and Zhang, Zheshen. "Development of Quantum Interconnects (QuICs) for Next-Generation Information Technologies". In: *PRX Quantum* 2 (1 Feb. 2021), p. 017002. URL: https://link.aps.org/doi/10.1103/PRXQuantum.2.017002.

[9] Awschalom, David D., Bernien, Hannes, Brown, Rex, Clerk, Aashish, Chitambar, Eric, Dibos, Alan, Dionne, Jennifer, Eriksson, Mark, Fefferman, Bill, Fuchs, Greg David, Gambetta, Jay, Goldschmidt, Elizabeth, Guha, Supratik, Heremans, F. Joseph, Irwin, Kent David, Jayich, Ania Bleszynski, Jiang, Liang, Karsch, Jonathan, Kasevich, Mark, Kolkowitz, Shimon, Kwiat, Paul G., Ladd, Thaddeus, Lowell, Jay, Maslov, Dmitri, Mason, Nadya, Matsuura, Anne Y., McDermott, Robert, Meter, Rod van, Miller, Aaron, Orcutt, Jason, Saffman, Mark, Schleier-Smith, Monika, Singh, Manish Kumar, Smith, Phil, Suchara, Martin, Goudeh-Fallah, Farzam, Turlington, Matt, Woods, Benjamin, and Zhong, Tian. "A Roadmap for Quantum Interconnects". In: (July 2022). URL: https://www.osti.gov/biblio/1900586.

[10] Barad, Karen. *Meeting the Universe Halfway. Quantum Physics and the Entanglement of Matter and Meaning*. 2nd ed. Duke University Press Books, 2007.

[11] Barahona, Francisco, Grötschel, Martin, Jünger, Michael, and Reinelt, Gerhard. "An Application of Combinatorial Optimization to Statistical Physics and Circuit Layout Design". In: *Operations Research* 36.3 (1988), pp. 493–513.

[12] Bennett, Charles H., Brassard, Gilles, Crepeau, Claude, Jozsa, Richard, Peres, Asher, and Wootters, William K. "Teleporting an unknown quantum state via dual classical and Einstein-Podolsky-Rosen channels". In: *Physical Review Letters* 70 (1993), pp. 1895–1899.

[13] Bernstein, Daniel J. "Detecting Perfect Powers in Essentially Linear Time". In: *Mathematics of Computation* 67.223 (July 1998), pp. 1253–1283.

[14] Bernstein, Ethan and Vazirani, Umesh. "Quantum Complexity Theory". In: *Proceedings of the Twenty-Fifth Annual ACM Symposium on Theory of Computing*. STOC '93. San Diego, California, USA: Association for Computing Machinery, 1993, pp. 11–20.

[15] Bertsekas, D.P. and Tsitsiklis, J.N. *Introduction to Probability*. 2nd ed. Athena Scientific optimization and computation series. Athena Scientific, 2008.

[16] Beverland, Michael E., Murali, Prakash, Troyer, Matthias, Svore, Krysta M., Hoefler, Torsten, Kliuchnikov, Vadym, Low, Guang Hao, Soeken, Mathias, Sundaram, Aarthi, and Vaschillo, Alexander. *Assessing requirements to scale to practical quantum advantage*. 2022. URL: https://arxiv.org/abs/2211.07629.

[17] Bharti, Kishor, Cervera-Lierta, Alba, Kyaw, Thi Ha, Haug, Tobias, Alperin-Lea, Sumner, Anand, Abhinav, Degroote, Matthias, Heimonen, Hermanni, Kottmann, Jakob S., Menke, Tim, Mok, Wai-Keong, Sim, Sukin, Kwek, Leong-Chuan, and Aspuru-Guzik, Alán. "Noisy intermediate-scale quantum algorithms". In: *Rev. Mod. Phys.* 94 (1 Feb. 2022), p. 015004. URL: https://link.aps.org/doi/10.1103/RevModPhys.94.015004.

[18] Bloch, F. "Nuclear Induction". In: *Physical Review* 70 (7-8 Oct. 1946), pp. 460–474.

[19] Blume-Kohout, Robin and Young, Kevin C. "A volumetric framework for quantum computer benchmarks". In: *Quantum* 4 (Nov. 2020).

[20] Bombin, H. and Martin-Delgado, M. A. "Optimal resources for topological two-dimensional stabilizer codes: Comparative study". In: *Physical Review A* 76 (1 July 2007), p. 012305.

[21] Bouland, Adam, van Dam, Wim, Joorati, Hamed, Kerenidis, Iordanis, and Prakash, Anupam. *Prospects and challenges of quantum finance*. 2020. URL: https://arxiv.org/abs/2011.06492.

[22] Braine, Lee, Egger, Daniel J., Glick, Jennifer, and Woerner, Stefan. "Quantum Algorithms for Mixed Binary Optimization Applied to Transaction Settlement". In: *IEEE Transactions on Quantum Engineering* 2 (2021), pp. 1–8.

[23] Brassard, Gilles and Hoyer, Peter F. "An Exact Quantum Polynomial-Time Algorithm for Simon's Problem". In: *Proceedings of the Fifth Israel Symposium on the Theory of Computing Systems (ISTCS '97)*. ISTCS '97. IEEE Computer Society, 1997.

[24] Brassard, Gilles, Hoyer, Peter F., Mosca, Michele, and Tapp, Alain. "Quantum Amplitude Amplification and Estimation". In: *Quantum Computation and Information*. Ed. by S. J. Lomonaco and H. E. Brandt. Contemporary Mathematics Series. AMS, 2000.

[25] Bravyi, Sergey, Browne, Dan, Calpin, Padraic, Campbell, Earl, Gosset, David, and Howard, Mark. "Simulation of quantum circuits by low-rank stabilizer decompositions". In: *Quantum* 3 (Sept. 2019), p. 181.

[26] Bravyi, Sergey and Gosset, David. "Improved Classical Simulation of Quantum Circuits Dominated by Clifford Gates". In: *Physical Review Letters* 116.25, 250501 (June 2016), p. 250501.

[27] Bravyi, Sergey, Gosset, David, and Liu, Yinchen. "How to Simulate Quantum Measurement without Computing Marginals". In: *Phys. Rev. Lett.* 128 (22 June 2022), p. 220503. URL: https://link.aps.org/doi/10.1103/PhysRevLett.128.2 20503.

[28] Bravyi, Sergey, Kliesch, Alexander, Koenig, Robert, and Tang, Eugene. "Hybrid quantum-classical algorithms for approximate graph coloring". In: *Quantum* 6 (Mar. 2022), p. 678. URL: http://dx.doi.org/10.22331/q-2022-03-30-678.

[29] Bressoud, David M. *Factorization and primality testing*. Undergraduate Texts in Mathematics. Springer-Verlag New York, 1989.

[30] Brubaker, Ben. *Versatile neutral atoms emerge as an intriguing quantum computing platform*. Aug. 24, 2022. URL: https://physicstoday.scitation.org/do/10 .1063/PT.6.1.20220824a/full/.

[31] Brunacini, Sam. *Parametric flowers*. Dec. 27, 2023. URL: http://sambrunacini .com/parametric-flowers/.

[32] Bruzewicz, Colin D., Chiaverini, John, McConnell, Robert, and Sage, Jeremy M. "Trapped-ion quantum computing: Progress and challenges". In: *Applied Physics Reviews* 6.2 (2019), p. 021314.

[33] Buonaiuto, Giuseppe, Gargiulo, Francesco, De Pietro, Giuseppe, Esposito, Massimo, and Pota, Marco. "Best practices for portfolio optimization by quantum computing, experimented on real quantum devices". In: *Scientific Reports* 13.1 (Nov. 8, 2023), p. 19434. URL: https://doi.org/10.1038/s41598-023-45392-w.

[34] Campbell, Colin, Chong, Frederic T., Dahl, Denny, Frederick, Paige, Goiporia, Palash, Gokhale, Pranav, Hall, Benjamin, Issa, Salahedeen, Jones, Eric, Lee, Stephanie, Litteken, Andrew, Omole, Victory, Owusu-Antwi, David, Perlin, Michael A., Rines, Rich, Smith, Kaitlin N., Goss, Noah, Hashim, Akel, Naik, Ravi, Younis, Ed, Lobser, Daniel, Yale, Christopher G., Huang, Benchen, and Liu, Ji. *Superstaq: Deep Optimization of Quantum Programs*. 2023. URL: https://arxiv.org/abs/2309.05157.

[35] Cao, Yudong, Romero, Jonathan, Olson, Jonathan P., Degroote, Matthias, Johnson, Peter D., Kieferová, Mária, Kivlichan, Ian D., Menke, Tim, Peropadre, Borja, Sawaya, Nicolas P. D., Sim, Sukin, Veis, Libor, and Aspuru-Guzik, Alán. "Quantum Chemistry in the Age of Quantum Computing". In: *Chemical Reviews* 119 (19 2019).

[36] Castelvecchi, Davide. "IBM releases first-ever 1,000-qubit quantum chip". In: *Nature* (Dec. 4, 2023). URL: https://www.nature.com/articles/d41586-023-0385 4-1.

[37] Cerezo, M., Arrasmith, Andrew, Babbush, Ryan, Benjamin, Simon C., Endo, Suguru, Fujii, Keisuke, McClean, Jarrod R., Mitarai, Kosuke, Yuan, Xiao, Cincio, Lukasz, and Coles, Patrick J. "Variational quantum algorithms". In: *Nature Reviews Physics* 3.9 (Sept. 1, 2021), pp. 625–644.

[38] Chatterjee, Anasua, Stevenson, Paul, De Franceschi, Silvano, Morello, Andrea, Leon, Nathalie P. de, and Kuemmeth, Ferdinand. "Semiconductor qubits in practice". In: *Nature Reviews Physics* 3.3 (Mar. 1, 2021), pp. 157–177.

[39] Chaudhary, Himanshu, Mahato, Biplab, Priyadarshi, Lakshya, Roshan, Naman, Utkarsh, and Patel, Apoorva D. *A Software Simulator for Noisy Quantum Circuits.* Dec. 25, 2021. URL: https://arxiv.org/abs/1908.05154.

[40] Choi, Jaeho and Kim, Joongheon. "A Tutorial on Quantum Approximate Optimization Algorithm (QAOA): Fundamentals and Applications". In: *2019 International Conference on Information and Communication Technology Convergence (ICTC)*. 2019, pp. 138–142.

[41] Cirq Developers. *Cirq.* Sept. 2022.

[42] Cirq Developers. *QAOA.* URL: https://quantumai.google/cirq/experiment s/qaoa.

[43] Cirq Developers. *Shor's algorithm.* URL: https://quantumai.google/cirq/ex periments/shor.

[44] Cleland, Andrew N. "An introduction to the surface code". In: *SciPost Phys. Lect. Notes* (2022), p. 49. URL: https://scipost.org/10.21468/SciPostPhysLect Notes.49.

[45] Cleve, R., Ekert, A., Macchiavello, C., and Mosca, M. "Quantum algorithms revisited". In: *Proceedings of the Royal Society of London. Series A: Mathematical, Physical and Engineering Sciences* 454.1969 (Jan. 1998), pp. 339–354. URL: http://dx.doi.org/10.1098/rspa.1998.0164.

[46] Combarro, Elías F. and Samuel, González-Castillo. *A Practical Guide to Quantum Machine Learning and Quantum Optimization.* Packt Publishing, 2023.

[47] Cong, Iris, Choi, Soonwon, and Lukin, Mikhail D. "Quantum convolutional neural networks". In: *Nature Physics* 15.12 (Dec. 1, 2019), pp. 1273–1278. URL: https://doi.org/10.1038/s41567-019-0648-8.

[48] Conway, J. B. *Functions of One Complex Variable.* 2nd ed. Graduate Texts in Mathematics 11. Springer-Verlag, 1978.

[49] Coppersmith, D. and Winograd, S. "Matrix Multiplication via Arithmetic Progressions". In: *Proceedings of the Nineteenth Annual ACM Symposium on Theory of Computing*. STOC '87. New York, New York, USA: ACM, 1987, pp. 1–6.

[50] Cormen, Thomas H., Leiserson, Charles E., Rivest, Ronald L., and Stein, Clifford. *Introduction to Algorithms*. 3rd ed. The MIT Press, 2009.

[51] Coxeter, H. S. M. *Introduction to geometry*. 2nd ed. Wiley classics library. John Wiley and Sons, 1999.

[52] Coyle, Brian, Mills, Daniel, Danos, Vincent, and Kashefi, Elham. "The Born supremacy: quantum advantage and training of an Ising Born machine". In: *npj Quantum Information* 6.1 (July 2020), p. 60. URL: https://doi.org/10.1038/s41534-020-00288-9.

[53] Crandall, R. and Pomerance, C. *Prime Numbers: a Computational Approach*. 2nd ed. Springer, 2005.

[54] Creative Commons. *Attribution 3.0 Unported (CC BY 3.0)*. URL: https://creativecommons.org/licenses/by/3.0/legalcode.

[55] Creative Commons. *Attribution-NoDerivs 2.0 Generic (CC BY-ND 2.0)*. URL: https://creativecommons.org/licenses/by-nd/2.0/legalcode.

[56] Creative Commons. *Attribution-ShareAlike 2.0 Germany (CC BY-SA 2.0 DE)*. URL: https://creativecommons.org/licenses/by-sa/2.0/de/legalcode.

[57] Creative Commons. *Attribution-ShareAlike 3.0 Unported (CC BY-SA 3.0 DEED)*. URL: https://creativecommons.org/licenses/by-sa/3.0/.

[58] Cross, Andrew W., Bishop, Lev S., Sheldon, Sarah, Nation, Paul D., and Gambetta, Jay M. "Validating quantum computers using randomized model circuits". In: *Phys. Rev. A* 100 (3 Sept. 2019), p. 032328. URL: https://link.aps.org/doi/10.1103/PhysRevA.100.032328.

[59] Cubitt, Toby S., Montanaro, Ashley, and Piddock, Stephen. "Universal quantum Hamiltonians". In: *Proceedings of the National Academy of Sciences* 115.38 (Aug. 2018), pp. 9497–9502.

[60] DaftWullie. *How to prepare an arbitrary two-qubit state?* 2022. URL: https://quantumcomputing.stackexchange.com/questions/12540/how-to-prepare-an-arbitrary-two-qubit-state.

[61] Dasgupta, Sanjoy, Papadimitriou, Christos H., and Vazirani, Umesh. *Algorithms*. McGraw-Hill, Inc., 2008.

[62] Dervovic, Danial, Herbster, Mark, Mountney, Peter, Severini, Simone, Usher, Naïri, and Wossnig, Leonard. *Quantum linear systems algorithms: a primer*. Feb. 22, 2018. URL: https://arxiv.org/abs/1802.08227.

[63]   Deutsch, D. and Jozsa, R. "Rapid Solution of Problems by Quantum Computation". English. In: *Proceedings of the Royal Society A: Mathematical, Physical and Engineering Sciences* 439 (1992), pp. 553–558.

[64]   Devitt, Simon J., Munro, William J., and Nemoto, Kae. "Quantum error correction for beginners". In: *Reports on Progress in Physics* 76.7, 076001 (July 2013), p. 076001.

[65]   Devoret, M. H. and Schoelkopf, R. J. "Superconducting Circuits for Quantum Information: An Outlook". In: *Science* 339.6124 (2013), pp. 1169–1174.

[66]   Diebel, James. "Representing Attitude: Euler Angles, Unit Quaternions, and Rotation Vectors". In: *Matrix* 58 (Jan. 2006), pp. 1–35. URL: https://www.astro.rug.nl /software/kapteyn-beta/_downloads/attitude.pdf.

[67]   Dieks, D. "Communication by EPR devices". In: *Physics Letters A* 92.6 (1982), pp. 271–272. URL: https://www.sciencedirect.com/science/article/pii /0375960182900846.

[68]   Dirac, P. A. M. "The Principles of Quantum Mechanics". In: *Nature* 136.3437 (Sept. 1, 1935), pp. 411–412.

[69]   DiVincenzo, David P. "The physical implementation of quantum computation". In: *Fortschritte der Physik* 48.9-11 (2000), pp. 771–783.

[70]   DiVincenzo, David P. *Looking back at the DiVincenzo criteria*. 2018. URL: https: //blog.qutech.nl/index.php/2018/02/22/looking-back-at-the-divin cenzo-criteria/.

[71]   Domingos, Pedro. "Every Model Learned by Gradient Descent Is Approximately a Kernel Machine". In: (2020).

[72]   Draper, Thomas G. *Addition on a Quantum Computer*. 2000. URL: https://arxiv .org/abs/quant-ph/0008033.

[73]   Dummit, D. S. and Foote, R. M. *Abstract Algebra*. 3rd ed. Wiley, 2004.

[74]   Egger, Daniel J., Gambella, Claudio, Marecek, Jakub, McFaddin, Scott, Mevissen, Martin, Raymond, Rudy, Simonetto, Andrea, Woerner, Stefan, and Yndurain, Elena. "Quantum Computing for Finance: State-of-the-Art and Future Prospects". In: *IEEE Transactions on Quantum Engineering* 1 (2020), pp. 1–24. URL: http://dx.doi.o rg/10.1109/TQE.2020.3030314.

[75]   Egger, Daniel J., García Gutiérrez, Ricardo, Mestre, Jordi Cahué, and Woerner, Stefan. "Credit Risk Analysis Using Quantum Computers". In: *IEEE Transactions on Computers* 70.12 (2021), pp. 2136–2145.

[76] Endo, Katsuhiro, Nakamura, Taichi, Fujii, Keisuke, and Yamamoto, Naoki. "Quantum self-learning Monte Carlo and quantum-inspired Fourier transform sampler". In: *Physical Review Research* 2.4 (Dec. 2020). URL: http://dx.doi.org/10.1103/PhysRevResearch.2.043442.

[77] Ezratty, Olivier. *Where are we heading with NISQ?* 2023. URL: https://arxiv.org/abs/2305.09518.

[78] Farhi, Edward, Goldstone, Jeffrey, and Gutmann, Sam. *A Quantum Approximate Optimization Algorithm*. 2014. URL: https://arxiv.org/abs/1411.4028.

[79] Faye, Jan. "Copenhagen Interpretation of Quantum Mechanics". In: *The Stanford Encyclopedia of Philosophy*. Ed. by Edward N. Zalta. Winter 2019 Edition. Metaphysics Research Lab, Stanford University, Dec. 6, 2019. URL: https://plato.stanford.edu/archives/win2019/entries/qm-copenhagen/.

[80] Fedorov, Dmitry A., Peng, Bo, Govind, Niranjan, and Alexeev, Yuri. "VQE method: a short survey and recent developments". In: *Materials Theory* 6.1 (Jan. 6, 2022), p. 2. URL: https://doi.org/10.1186/s41313-021-00032-6.

[81] FermiLab. *What is the number of atoms in the world?* 2014. URL: https://www.fnal.gov/pub/science/inquiring/questions/atoms.html.

[82] Feynman, Richard P. "Simulating Physics with Computers". In: *International Journal of Theoretical Physics* 21.6 (June 1, 1982), pp. 467–488.

[83] Feynman, Richard P. *QED: The Strange Theory of Light and Matter*. Princeton Science Library 33. Princeton University Press, 2014.

[84] Fowler, Austin G., Mariantoni, Matteo, Martinis, John M., and Cleland, Andrew N. "Surface codes: Towards practical large-scale quantum computation". In: *Phys. Rev. A* 86 (3 Sept. 2012), p. 032324.

[85] Free Software Foundation. *The GNU Multiple Precision Arithmetic Library*. URL: https://gmplib.org/.

[86] Furness, Peter. "Applications of Monte Carlo Simulation in marketing analytics". In: *Journal of Direct, Data and Digital Marketing Practice* 13 (2 Oct. 27, 2011).

[87] Gambetta, Jay M., Chow, Jerry M., and Steffen, Matthias. "Building logical qubits in a superconducting quantum computing system". In: *npj Quantum Information* 3.1 (2017). URL: https://www.nature.com/articles/s41534-016-0004-0.

[88] Garca Ripoll, Juan José. *Quantum Information and Quantum Optics with Superconducting Circuits*. Cambridge University Press, 2022.

[89] Gidney, Craig. "Halving the cost of quantum addition". In: *Quantum* 2 (June 2018), p. 74.

[90]   Gidney, Craig. *Asymptotically Efficient Quantum Karatsuba Multiplication*. 2019. URL: https://arxiv.org/abs/1904.07356.

[91]   Gidney, Craig and Ekerå, Martin. "How to factor 2048 bit RSA integers in 8 hours using 20 million noisy qubits". In: *Quantum* 5 (Apr. 2021), p. 433.

[92]   Gili, Kaitlin, Hibat-Allah, Mohamed, Mauri, Marta, Ballance, Chris, and Perdomo-Ortiz, Alejandro. *Do Quantum Circuit Born Machines Generalize?* 2023.

[93]   Gokhale, Pranav, Javadi-Abhari, Ali, Earnest, Nathan, Shi, Yunong, and Chong, Frederic T. "Optimized Quantum Compilation for Near-Term Algorithms with Open-Pulse". In: *2020 53rd Annual IEEE/ACM International Symposium on Microarchitecture (MICRO)*. 2020, pp. 186–200.

[94]   Goodfellow, Ian J., Bengio, Yoshua, and Courville, Aaron. *Deep Learning*. http://www.deeplearningbook.org. Cambridge, MA, USA: MIT Press, 2016.

[95]   Gossett, Phil. *Quantum Carry-Save Arithmetic*. 1998. URL: https://arxiv.org/abs/quant-ph/9808061.

[96]   Graham, T. M., Song, Y., Scott, J., Poole, C., Phuttitarn, L., Jooya, K., Eichler, P., Jiang, X., Marra, A., Grinkemeyer, B., Kwon, M., Ebert, M., Cherek, J., Lichtman, M. T., Gillette, M., Gilbert, J., Bowman, D., Ballance, T., Campbell, C., Dahl, E. D., Crawford, O., Blunt, N. S., Rogers, B., Noel, T., and Saffman, M. "Multi-qubit entanglement and algorithms on a neutral-atom quantum computer". In: *Nature* 604.7906 (Apr. 1, 2022), pp. 457–462.

[97]   Gribbin, John. *The Many-Worlds Theory, Explained*. May 2020. URL: https://thereader.mitpress.mit.edu/the-many-worlds-theory/.

[98]   Griffiths, David J. and Schroeter, Darrell F. *Introduction to Quantum Mechanics*. 3rd ed. Cambridge University Press, 2018.

[99]   Grover, Lov K. "A Fast Quantum Mechanical Algorithm for Database Search". In: *Proceedings of the Twenty-Eighth Annual ACM Symposium on the Theory of Computing*. Philadelphia, Pennsylvania, USA, 1996, pp. 212–219.

[100]   Gulka, Michal, Wirtitsch, Daniel, Ivády, Viktor, Vodnik, Jelle, Hruby, Jaroslav, Magchiels, Goele, Bourgeois, Emilie, Gali, Adam, Trupke, Michael, and Nesladek, Milos. "Room-temperature control and electrical readout of individual nitrogen-vacancy nuclear spins". In: *Nature Communications* 12.1 (July 20, 2021), p. 4421.

[101]   Halmos, Paul R. *Finite-Dimensional Vector Spaces*. Undergraduate Texts in Mathematics. Springer Publishing Company, Incorporated, 1993.

[102]   Hamming, R.W. "Error Detecting and Error Correcting Codes". In: *Bell System Technical Journal* 29.2 (1950).

[103]   Hamming, R.W. *Numerical Methods for Scientists and Engineers*. Dover Books on Engineering. Dover, 1986.

[104]   Harrow, Aram W., Hassidim, Avinatan, and Lloyd, Seth. "Quantum Algorithm for Linear Systems of Equations". In: *Physical Review Letters* 103 (15 Oct. 2009), p. 150502.

[105]   Havlíček, Vojtěch, Córcoles, Antonio D., Temme, Kristan, Harrow, Aram W., Kandala, Abhinav, Chow, Jerry M., and Gambetta, Jay M. "Supervised learning with quantum-enhanced feature spaces". In: *Nature* 567.7747 (Mar. 1, 2019), pp. 209–212.

[106]   Heisenberg, W. *Across the frontiers*. Ox Bow Press, 1990.

[107]   Henriet, Loïc, Beguin, Lucas, Signoles, Adrien, Lahaye, Thierry, Browaeys, Antoine, Reymond, Georges-Olivier, and Jurczak, Christophe. "Quantum computing with neutral atoms". In: *Quantum* 4 (Sept. 2020), p. 327.

[108]   Herman, Dylan, Googin, Cody, Liu, Xiaoyuan, Galda, Alexey, Safro, Ilya, Sun, Yue, Pistoia, Marco, and Alexeev, Yuri. *A Survey of Quantum Computing for Finance*. 2022. URL: https://arxiv.org/abs/2201.02773.

[109]   Hertz, David B. "Risk Analysis in Capital Investment". In: *Harvard Business Review* (Sept. 1979).

[110]   Heyraud, Valentin, Li, Zejian, Denis, Zakari, Boité, Alexandre, and Ciuti, Cristiano. "Noisy quantum kernel machines". In: *Physical Review A* 106.5 (Nov. 2022).

[111]   Hill, R. *A First Course in Coding Theory*. Oxford Applied Linguistics. Clarendon Press, 1986.

[112]   Hoffstein, Jeffrey, Pipher, Jill, and Silverman, Joseph H. *An Introduction to Mathematical Cryptography*. 2nd ed. Undergraduate Texts in Mathematics 152. Springer Publishing Company, Incorporated, 2014.

[113]   Huang, Hsin-Yuan, Broughton, Michael, Mohseni, Masoud, Babbush, Ryan, Boixo, Sergio, Neven, Hartmut, and McClean, Jarrod R. "Power of data in quantum machine learning". In: *Nature Communications* 12.1 (May 2021). URL: http://dx.doi.org/10.1038/s41467-021-22539-9.

[114]   Institute for Advanced Study. *John von Neumann: Life, Work, and Legacy*. URL: https://www.ias.edu/von-neumann.

[115]   Ireland, Kenneth and Rosen, Michael. *A Classical Introduction to Modern Number Theory*. 2nd ed. Graduate Texts in Mathematics 84. Springer-Verlag New York, 1990.

[116] J., Abhijith, Adedoyin, Adetokunbo, Ambrosiano, John, Anisimov, Petr, Casper, William, Chennupati, Gopinath, Coffrin, Carleton, Djidjev, Hristo, Gunter, David, Karra, Satish, Lemons, Nathan, Lin, Shizeng, Malyzhenkov, Alexander, Mascarenas, David, Mniszewski, Susan, Nadiga, Balu, O'malley, Daniel, Oyen, Diane, Pakin, Scott, Prasad, Lakshman, Roberts, Randy, Romero, Phillip, Santhi, Nandakishore, Sinitsyn, Nikolai, Swart, Pieter J., Wendelberger, James G., Yoon, Boram, Zamora, Richard, Zhu, Wei, Eidenbenz, Stephan, Bärtschi, Andreas, Coles, Patrick J., Vuffray, Marc, and Lokhov, Andrey Y. "Quantum Algorithm Implementations for Beginners". In: *ACM Transactions on Quantum Computing* 3.4 (July 22, 2022).

[117] Jordan, Stephen. *Quantum Algorithm Zoo*. URL: `https://Jordan:QuantumAlgor ithmZoo.org/`.

[118] *Kaggle*. URL: `https://www.kaggle.com/`.

[119] Kaliski, Burt. "Subexponential Time". In: *Encyclopedia of Cryptography and Security*. Ed. by Henk C. A. van Tilborg and Sushil Jajodia. Springer US, 2011, pp. 1267–1267.

[120] Kandala, Abhinav, Mezzacapo, Antonio, Temme, Kristan, Takita, Maika, Brink, Markus, Chow, Jerry M., and Gambetta, Jay M. "Hardware-efficient variational quantum eigensolver for small molecules and quantum magnets". In: *Nature* 549 (Sept. 13, 2017), pp. 242–247.

[121] Karp, Richard M. "Reducibility among Combinatorial Problems". In: *Complexity of Computer Computations: Proceedings of a symposium on the Complexity of Computer Computations, held March 20–22, 1972, at the IBM Thomas J. Watson Research Center, Yorktown Heights, New York, and sponsored by the Office of Naval Research, Mathematics Program, IBM World Trade Corporation, and the IBM Research Mathematical Sciences Department*. Ed. by Raymond E. Miller, James W. Thatcher, and Jean D. Bohlinger. Boston, MA, USA: Springer US, 1972, pp. 85–103.

[122] Khinchin, A. Ya. *Continued Fractions*. Revised Edition. Dover Books on Mathematics. Dover Publications, 1997.

[123] Khot, Subhash, Kindler, Guy, Mossel, Elchanan, and O'Donnell, Ryan. "Optimal Inapproximability Results for MAX-CUT and Other 2-Variable CSPs?" In: *SIAM Journal on Computing* 37.1 (2007), pp. 319–357.

[124] Kitaev, A. Yu., Shen, A. H., and Vyalyi, M. N. *Classical and Quantum Computation*. American Mathematical Society, 2002.

[125] Knill, E., Laflamme, R., and Milburn, G. J. "A scheme for efficient quantum computation with linear optics". In: *Nature* 409.6816 (2001), pp. 46–52.

[126] Knuth, Donald E. *The Art of Computer Programming, Volume 2: Seminumerical Algorithms*. 3rd ed. Addison Wesley Longman Publishing Co., Inc., 1998.

[127] Knuth, Donald E. *The Art of Computer Programming, Volume 3: Sorting and Searching*. 2nd ed. Addison Wesley Longman Publishing Co., Inc., 1998.

[128] Koblitz, Neal. *A Course in Number Theory and Cryptography*. 2nd ed. Graduate Texts in Mathematics 114. Springer-Verlag, 1994.

[129] Krunic, Zoran, Flother, Frederik, Seegan, George, Earnest-Noble, Nate, and Omar, Shehab. "Quantum Kernels for Real-World Predictions Based on Electronic Health Records". In: *IEEE Transactions on Quantum Engineering* 3 (2022), pp. 1–11.

[130] Laflamme, Raymond, Miquel, Cesar, Paz, Juan Pablo, and Zurek, Wojciech Hubert. "Perfect Quantum Error Correcting Code". In: *Physical Review Letters* 77 (1 July 1996), pp. 198–201.

[131] Lang, S. *Algebra*. 3rd ed. Graduate Texts in Mathematics 211. Springer-Verlag, 2002.

[132] LaRose, Ryan and Coyle, Brian. "Robust data encodings for quantum classifiers". In: *Physical Review A* 102.3 (Sept. 2020).

[133] Lauk, Nikolai, Sinclair, Neil, Barzanjeh, Shabir, Covey, Jacob P., Saffman, Mark, Spiropulu, Maria, and Simon, Christoph. "Perspectives on quantum transduction". In: *Quantum Science and Technology* 5.2 (Mar. 2020), p. 020501.

[134] Lewis, Peter J. *Interpretations of Quantum Mechanics*. URL: https://iep.utm.edu/int-qm/.

[135] Li, Yiyi and Thompson, Jeff. *High-rate and high-fidelity modular interconnects between neutral atom quantum processors*. Jan. 8, 2024. URL: https://arxiv.org/abs/2401.04075.

[136] Link, Rachel. *How Much Caffeine Do Coke and Diet Coke Contain?* 2018. URL: https://www.healthline.com/nutrition/caffeine-in-coke.

[137] Lipton, Richard J. and Regan, Kenneth W. *Quantum Algorithms via Linear Algebra*. 2nd ed. The MIT Press, Apr. 6, 2021.

[138] Liu, Yunchao, Arunachalam, Srinivasan, and Temme, Kristan. "A rigorous and robust quantum speed-up in supervised machine learning". In: *Nature Physics* 17.9 (Sept. 1, 2021), pp. 1013–1017.

[139] Lloyd, Seth and Weedbrook, Christian. "Quantum Generative Adversarial Learning". In: *Physical Review Letters* 121.4 (July 2018). URL: http://dx.doi.org/10.1103/PhysRevLett.121.040502.

[140] Lubinski, Thomas, Goings, Joshua J., Mayer, Karl, Johri, Sonika, Reddy, Nithin, Mehta, Aman, Bhatia, Niranjan, Rappaport, Sonny, Mills, Daniel, Baldwin, Charles H., Zhao, Luning, Barbosa, Aaron, Maity, Smarak, and Mundada, Pranav S. *Quantum Algorithm Exploration using Application-Oriented Performance Benchmarks*. 2024. URL: https://arxiv.org/abs/2402.08985.

[141] Lubinski, Thomas, Johri, Sonika, Varosy, Paul, Coleman, Jeremiah, Zhao, Luning, Necaise, Jason, Baldwin, Charles H., Mayer, Karl, and Proctor, Timothy. *Application-Oriented Performance Benchmarks for Quantum Computing*. 2023. URL: https://arxiv.org/abs/2110.03137.

[142] Lubowe, Tom, Yamaguchi, Takuma, and Morino, Shinya. *Achieving Supercomputing-Scale Quantum Circuit Simulation with the NVIDIA cuQuantum Appliance*. Sept. 22, 2022. URL: https://developer.nvidia.com/blog/achieving-supercomputing-scale-quantum-circuit-simulation-with-the-cuquantum-appliance/.

[143] Lutz, Mark. *Learning Python*. 5th ed. O'Reilly Media, 2013.

[144] Lykov, Danylo, Wurtz, Jonathan, Poole, Cody, Saffman, Mark, Noel, Tom, and Alexeev, Yuri. "Sampling frequency thresholds for the quantum advantage of the quantum approximate optimization algorithm". In: *npj Quantum Information* 9.1 (July 25, 2023), p. 73.

[145] Mac Lane, Saunders. *Categories for the Working Mathematician*. 2nd ed. Graduate Texts in Mathematics 5. Springer New York, 1998.

[146] Matsuo, Atsushi, Suzuki, Yudai, Hamamura, Ikko, and Yamashita, Shigeru. "Enhancing VQE Convergence for Optimization Problems with Problem-Specific Parameterized Quantum Circuits". In: *IEICE Transactions on Information and Systems* E106.D.11 (Nov. 2023), pp. 1772–1782. URL: http://dx.doi.org/10.1587/transinf.2023EDP7071.

[147] McClean, Jarrod R., Boixo, Sergio, Smelyanskiy, Vadim N., Babbush, Ryan, and Neven, Hartmut. "Barren plateaus in quantum neural network training landscapes". In: *Nature Communications* 9.1 (Nov. 16, 2018), p. 4812. URL: https://doi.org/10.1038/s41467-018-07090-4.

[148] McEliece, Robert J. *Finite Fields for Computer Scientists and Engineers*. 10th ed. The Springer International Series in Engineering and Computer Science 23. Springer US, 1987.

[149] Meckes, Elizabeth S. and Meckes, Mark W. *Linear Algebra*. Cambridge Mathematical Textbooks. Cambridge University Press, 2018.

[150] Mermin, N. David. *Quantum Computer Science: An Introduction*. Cambridge University Press, 2007.

[151] Miller, Steven J. and Takloo-Bighash, Ramin. *An Invitation to Modern Number Theory*. Princeton University Press, Mar. 26, 2006.

[152] Montanaro, Ashley. "Quantum speedup of Monte Carlo methods". In: *Proceedings of the Royal Society A: Mathematical, Physical and Engineering Sciences* 471.2181 (2015), p. 20150301.

[153] Montanaro, Ashley. "Quantum algorithms: an overview". In: *npj Quantum Information* 2.1 (Jan. 12, 2016), p. 15023.

[154] Moore, Gordon E. "Cramming more components onto integrated circuits". In: *Electronics* 38.8 (1965), p. 114.

[155] Morino, Shinya, Hehn, Andreas, and Fang, Leo. *Accelerating Quantum Circuit Simulation with NVIDIA cuStateVec*. Mar. 9, 2022. URL: https://developer.nvidia.com/blog/accelerating-quantum-circuit-simulation-with-nvidia-custatevec/.

[156] Moro, Lorenzo and Prati, Enrico. "Anomaly detection speed-up by quantum restricted Boltzmann machines". In: *Communications Physics* 6.1 (Sept. 23, 2023), p. 269. URL: https://doi.org/10.1038/s42005-023-01390-y.

[157] Mosca, Michele and Piani, Marco. *2022 Quantum Threat Timeline Report*. 2022. URL: https://evolutionq.com/quantum-threat-timeline-2022.html.

[158] Möttönen, Mikko, Vartiainen, Juha J., Bergholm, Ville, and Salomaa, Martti M. "Transformation of Quantum States Using Uniformly Controlled Rotations". In: *Quantum Info. Comput.* 5.6 (Sept. 2005), pp. 467–473.

[159] Muthukrishnan, Ashok. *Classical and Quantum Logic Gates: An Introduction to Quantum Computing*. URL: http://www2.optics.rochester.edu/users/stroud/presentations/muthukrishnan991/LogicGates.pdf.

[160] Needham, T. and Penrose, R. *Visual Complex Analysis*. 25th Anniversary Edition. OUP Oxford, 2023. URL: https://books.google.com/books?id=GoCsEAAAQBAJ.

[161] Neri, Ferrante. *Linear Algebra for Computational Sciences and Engineering*. 2nd ed. Springer, 2019.

[162] Nielsen, Michael A. and Chuang, Isaac L. *Quantum Computation and Quantum Information*. 10th Anniversary Edition. Cambridge University Press, 2011.

[163] Nikulin, M. S. *Hellinger distance*. June 5, 2020. URL: https://encyclopediaofmath.org/index.php?title=Hellinger_distance.

[164] O'Brien, Jeremy L. "Optical Quantum Computing". In: *Science* 318.5856 (2007), pp. 1567–1570.

[165] O'Brien, Jeremy L., Furusawa, Akira, and Vučković, Jelena. "Photonic quantum technologies". In: *Nature Photonics* 12.3 (2009), pp. 687–695.

[166] Oh, Seunghyeok, Choi, Jaeho, and Kim, Joongheon. "A Tutorial on Quantum Convolutional Neural Networks (QCNN)". In: *2020 International Conference on Information and Communication Technology Convergence (ICTC)*. 2020, pp. 236–239.

[167] Olds, C. D. *Continued Fractions*. Mathematical Association of America, 1963.

[168] Oppenheim, Alan V., Willsky, Alan S., and Nawab, S. Hamid. *Signals & Systems*. 2nd ed. Prentice-Hall, Inc., 1996.

[169] Palca, Joe. *The World Has A New Largest-Known Prime Number*. URL: https://www.npr.org/2018/12/21/679207604/the-world-has-a-new-largest-known-prime-number.

[170] Park, James L. "The concept of transition in quantum mechanics". In: *Foundations of Physics* 1.1 (Mar. 1, 1970), pp. 23–33.

[171] Peruzzo, Alberto, McClean, Jarrod, Shadbolt, Peter, Yung, Man-Hong, Zhou, Xiao-Qi, Love, Peter J., Aspuru-Guzik, Alán, and O'Brien, Jeremy L. "A variational eigenvalue solver on a photonic quantum processor". In: *Nature Communications* 5.1 (July 23, 2014), p. 4213.

[172] Pittenger, A.O. *An Introduction to Quantum Computing Algorithms*. Progress in Computer Science and Applied Logic. Birkhäuser Boston, 2012.

[173] Preskill, John. "Quantum Computing in the NISQ era and beyond". In: *Quantum* 2 (Aug. 2018), p. 79.

[174] Pretzel, Oliver. *Error-correcting Codes and Finite Fields*. Student Edition. Oxford University Press, Inc., 1996.

[175] Project Jupyter. *Project Jupyter*. 2024. URL: https://jupyter.org/.

[176] Qi, Han, Wang, Lei, Zhu, Hongsheng, Gani, Abdullah, and Gong, Changqing. "The barren plateaus of quantum neural networks: review, taxonomy and trends". In: *Quantum Information Processing* 22.12 (Dec. 11, 2023), p. 435. URL: https://doi.org/10.1007/s11128-023-04188-7.

[177] Qiskit contributors. *PauliFeatureMap*. 2023. URL: https://qiskit.org/documentation/stubs/qiskit.circuit.library.PauliFeatureMap.html.

[178] Qiskit contributors. *Qiskit Finance Tutorials*. 2023. URL: https://qiskit.org/ecosystem/finance/tutorials/index.html.

[179] Qiskit contributors. *Qiskit: An Open-source Framework for Quantum Computing*. 2023.

[180] Qiskit contributors. *Quantum Kernel Machine Learning*. 2023. URL: https://qiskit.org/ecosystem/machine-learning/tutorials/03_quantum_kernel.html#.

[181] Qiskit contributors. *Quantum Neural Networks*. 2023. URL: https://qiskit.org/ecosystem/machine-learning/tutorials/01_neural_networks.html.

[182] Qiskit contributors. *Quantum Neural Networks*. 2023. URL: https://qiskit.org
/ecosystem/machine-learning/tutorials/01_neural_networks.html.

[183] Qiskit contributors. *Solving combinatorial optimization problems using QAOA*. 2023.
URL: https://learn.qiskit.org/course/ch-applications/solving-com
binatorial-optimization-problems-using-qaoa.

[184] Qiskit contributors. *UGate*. 2023. URL: https://qiskit.org/documentation
/stubs/qiskit.circuit.library.UGate.html.

[185] Qiskit contributors. *ZFeatureMap*. 2023. URL: https://qiskit.org/documenta
tion/stubs/qiskit.circuit.library.ZFeatureMap.html.

[186] Quantinuum. *TKET*. URL: https://www.quantinuum.com/developers/tket.

[187] Rabeau, J. R., Stacey, A., Rabeau, A., Prawer, S., Jelezko, F., Mirza, I., and
Wrachtrup, J. "Single Nitrogen Vacancy Centers in Chemical Vapor Deposited
Diamond Nanocrystals". In: *Nano Letters* 7 (Sept. 29, 2007), pp. 3433–3437.

[188] Rae, A.I.M. *Quantum physics: Illusion or reality?* 2nd ed. Canto Classics. Cambridge
University Press, Mar. 2012.

[189] Rieffel, Eleanor and Polak, Wolfgang. *Quantum Computing: A Gentle Introduction*.
The MIT Press, 2014.

[190] Rivest, R. L., Shamir, A., and Adleman, L. "A Method for Obtaining Digital Signa-
tures and Public-key Cryptosystems". In: *Commun. ACM* 21.2 (Feb. 1978), pp. 120–
126.

[191] Romano, Fabrizio. *Learn Python Programming*. 2nd ed. Packt Publishing, 2018.

[192] Rotman, J. *An Introduction to the Theory of Groups*. 4th ed. Graduate Texts in
Mathematics 148. Springer New York, 1995.

[193] Ruan, Yue, Marsh, Samuel, Xue, Xilin, Liu, Zhihao Liu, and Wang, Jingbo. "The
Quantum Approximate Algorithm for Solving Traveling Salesman Problem". In:
Computers, Materials & Continua 63.3 (2020), pp. 1237–1247. URL: http://www
.techscience.com/cmc/v63n3/38872.

[194] Ruiz-Perez, Lidia and Garcia-Escartin, Juan Carlos. "Quantum arithmetic with the
Quantum Fourier Transform". In: *Quantum Information Processing* 16.6 (2017).

[195] Sancho-Lorente, Teresa, Román-Roche, Juan, and Zueco, David. "Quantum kernels
to learn the phases of quantum matter". In: *Phys. Rev. A* 105 (4 Apr. 2022), p. 042432.
URL: https://link.aps.org/doi/10.1103/PhysRevA.105.042432.

[196] Sapova, Mariia D. and Fedorov, Aleksey K. "Variational quantum eigensolver techniques for simulating carbon monoxide oxidation". In: *Communications Physics* 5.1
(Aug. 6, 2022), p. 199. URL: https://doi.org/10.1038/s42005-022-00982-4.

[197]   Sardharwalla, Imdad S. B., Cubitt, Toby S., Harrow, Aram W., and Linden, Noah. *Universal Refocusing of Systematic Quantum Noise*. 2016. URL: https://arxiv.org/abs/1602.07963.

[198]   Schuld, M. and Petruccione, F. *Machine Learning with Quantum Computers*. Quantum Science and Technology. Springer International Publishing, 2021.

[199]   Sedgewick, Robert and Wayne, Kevin. *Algorithms*. 4th ed. Addison-Wesley Professional, 2011.

[200]   Shawe-Taylor, John and Cristianini, Nello. *Kernel Methods for Pattern Analysis*. Cambridge University Press, 2004.

[201]   Shor, Peter W. "Scheme for reducing decoherence in quantum computer memory". In: *Physical Review A* 52 (4 Oct. 1995), R2493–R2496.

[202]   Shor, Peter W. "Polynomial-Time Algorithms for Prime Factorization and Discrete Logarithms on a Quantum Computer". In: *SIAM J. Comput.* 26.5 (Oct. 1997), pp. 1484–1509.

[203]   Shores, Thomas S. *Applied Linear Algebra and Matrix Analysis*. 2nd ed. Undergraduate Texts in Mathematics. Springer, 2018.

[204]   Smith, Belinda. *Prime numbers keep your encrypted messages safe – here's how*. 2018. URL: https://www.abc.net.au/news/science/2018-01-20/how-prime-numbers-rsa-encryption-works/9338876.

[205]   Spivak, Michael. *Calculus*. 4th ed. Publish or Perish, 2008.

[206]   Stamatopoulos, Nikitas, Egger, Daniel J., Sun, Yue, Zoufal, Christa, Iten, Raban, Shen, Ning, and Woerner, Stefan. "Option Pricing using Quantum Computers". In: *Quantum* 4 (July 2020), p. 291.

[207]   Steane, Andrew M. "Multiple-particle interference and quantum error correction". In: *Proceedings of the Royal Society of London. Series A: Mathematical, Physical and Engineering Sciences* 452.1954 (Nov. 1996), pp. 2551–2577.

[208]   Steane, Andrew M. "A Tutorial on Quantum Error Correction". In: *Proceedings of the International School of Physics "Enrico Fermi"*. Amsterdam: IOS Press, 2006, pp. 1–32. URL: https://www2.physics.ox.ac.uk/sites/default/files/ErrorCorrectionSteane06.pdf.

[209]   Strang, Gilbert. *Linear algebra and its applications*. 4th ed. Belmont, CA: Thomson, Brooks/Cole, 2006. URL: http://www.amazon.com/Linear-Algebra-Its-Applications-Edition/dp/0030105676.

[210]   Strang, Gilbert. *Introduction to Linear Algebra*. 6th ed. Philadelphia, PA: Wellesley-Cambridge Press, 2022. URL: https://epubs.siam.org/doi/abs/10.1137/1.9781733146678.

[211] Sutor, Robert S. *Dancing with Python. Learn to code with Python and Quantum Computing*. Packt Publishing, 2021.

[212] SymPy Development Team. *SymPy symbolic mathematics library*. 2021. URL: http s://www.sympy.org/en/index.html.

[213] Tang, Ewin. "A Quantum-Inspired Classical Algorithm for Recommendation Systems". In: *Proceedings of the 51st Annual ACM SIGACT Symposium on Theory of Computing*. STOC 2019. Phoenix, AZ, USA: Association for Computing Machinery, 2019, pp. 217–228.

[214] The Python Software Foundation. *Python.org*. URL: https://www.python.org/.

[215] The Unicode Consortium. *About the Unicode® Standard*. 2017. URL: http://www .unicode.org/standard/standard.html.

[216] Tilly, Jules, Chen, Hongxiang, Cao, Shuxiang, Picozzi, Dario, Setia, Kanav, Li, Ying, Grant, Edward, Wossnig, Leonard, Rungger, Ivan, Booth, George H., and Tennyson, Jonathan. "The Variational Quantum Eigensolver: A review of methods and best practices". In: *Physics Reports* 986 (Nov. 2022), pp. 1–128.

[217] Tomesh, Teague, Gokhale, Pranav, Omole, Victory, Ravi, Gokul Subramanian, Smith, Kaitlin N., Viszlai, Joshua, Wu, Xin-Chuan, Hardavellas, Nikos, Martonosi, Margaret R., and Chong, Frederic T. "SupermarQ: A Scalable Quantum Benchmark Suite". In: *2022 IEEE International Symposium on High-Performance Computer Architecture (HPCA)*. 2022, pp. 587–603.

[218] Torlai, Giacomo, Mazzola, Guglielmo, Carleo, Giuseppe, and Mezzacapo, Antonio. "Precise measurement of quantum observables with neural-network estimators". In: *Phys. Rev. Research* 2 (2 June 2020), p. 022060. URL: https://link.aps.org/d oi/10.1103/PhysRevResearch.2.022060.

[219] Tuomanen, B. *Explore high-performance parallel computing with CUDA*. Packt Publishing, 2018.

[220] Turing, A. M. "Computing Machinery and Intelligence". In: *Computers and Thought*. Ed. by Edward A. Feigenbaum and Julian Feldman. MIT Press, 1995, pp. 11–35.

[221] Vandersypen, Lieven M. K., Steffen, Matthias, Breyta, Gregory, Yannoni, Costantino S., Sherwood, Mark H., and Chuang, Isaac L. "Experimental realization of Shor's quantum factoring algorithm using nuclear magnetic resonance". In: *Nature* 414.6866 (2001), pp. 883–887.

[222] Vasques, Xavier, Paik, Hanhee, and Cif, Laura. "Application of quantum machine learning using quantum kernel algorithms on multiclass neuron M-type classification". In: *Scientific Reports* 13.1 (July 17, 2023), p. 11541.

[223] Viola, Lorenza and Lloyd, Seth. "Dynamical suppression of decoherence in two-state quantum systems". In: *Physical Review A* 58.4 (Oct. 1998), pp. 2733–2744.

[224] von Neumann, John. "Various techniques used in connection with random digits". In: *Monte Carlo Method.* Ed. by A.S. Householder, G.E. Forsythe, and H.H. Germond. National Bureau of Standards Applied Mathematics Series, 12, 1951, pp. 36–38.

[225] Wack, Andrew and McKay, David. *Updating how we measure quantum quality and speed.* Nov. 20, 2023. URL: `https://research.ibm.com/blog/quantum-metric-layer-fidelity`.

[226] Wack, Andrew, Paik, Hanhee, Javadi-Abhari, Ali, Jurcevic, Petar, Faro, Ismael, Gambetta, Jay M., and Johnson, Blake R. *Quality, Speed, and Scale: three key attributes to measure the performance of near-term quantum computers.* 2021.

[227] Wan, Kwok Ho, Dahlsten, Oscar, Kristjánsson, Hlér, Gardner, Robert, and Kim, M.S. "Quantum generalisation of feedforward neural networks". In: *npj Quantum Information* 3.1 (Sept. 2017).

[228] Wang, X. R., Zheng, Y. S., and Yin, Sun. "Spin relaxation and decoherence of two-level systems". In: *Phys. Rev. B* 72 (12 Sept. 2005), p. 121303.

[229] Watrous, John. *Quantum Computational Complexity.* 2008. URL: `https://arxiv.org/abs/0804.3401`.

[230] Watrous, John. *The Theory of Quantum Information.* Cambridge University Press, 2018.

[231] Watrous, John. *CPSC 519/619: Introduction to Quantum Computing.* URL: `https://cs.uwaterloo.ca/~watrous/LectureNotes/CPSC519.Winter2006/all.pdf`.

[232] Wiebe, Nathan. "Key questions for the quantum machine learner to ask themselves". In: *New Journal of Physics* 22 (Sept. 2020).

[233] Wikipedia. *Abuse of notation.* Dec. 24, 2023. URL: `https://en.wikipedia.org/wiki/Abuse_of_notation`.

[234] Wikipedia. *Polynomial-time reduction.* June 6, 2023. URL: `https://en.wikipedia.org/wiki/Polynomial-time_reduction`.

[235] Wikipedia. *Approximations of π.* Jan. 10, 2024. URL: `https://en.wikipedia.org/wiki/Approximations_of_%CF%80`.

[236] Wittek, P. *Quantum Machine Learning. What quantum computing means to data mining.* Elsevier Science, 2016.

[237] Woerner, Stefan and Egger, Daniel J. "Quantum risk analysis". In: *npj Quantum Information* 5 (1 Feb. 8, 2019), pp. 198–201.

[238] Wootters, W. K. and Zurek, W. H. "A single quantum cannot be cloned". In: *Nature* 299.5886 (Oct. 1, 1982), pp. 802–803.

[239] Wright, Matt. *Design and Implementation of a Quantum Kernel for Natural Language Processing.* 2022. URL: https://arxiv.org/abs/2205.06409.

[240] Wu, Sau Lan, Sun, Shaojun, Guan, Wen, Zhou, Chen, Chan, Jay, Cheng, Chi Lung, Pham, Tuan, Qian, Yan, Wang, Alex Zeng, Zhang, Rui, Livny, Miron, Glick, Jennifer, Barkoutsos, Panagiotis Kl., Woerner, Stefan, Tavernelli, Ivano, Carminati, Federico, Di Meglio, Alberto, Li, Andy C. Y., Lykken, Joseph, Spentzouris, Panagiotis, Chen, Samuel Yen-Chi, Yoo, Shinjae, and Wei, Tzu-Chieh. "Application of quantum machine learning using the quantum kernel algorithm on high energy physics analysis at the LHC". In: *Physical Review Research* 3.3 (Sept. 2021).

[241] Zhang, Yu, Cincio, Lukasz, Negre, Christian F. A., Czarnik, Piotr, Coles, Patrick J., Anisimov, Petr M., Mniszewski, Susan M., Tretiak, Sergei, and Dub, Pavel A. "Variational quantum eigensolver with reduced circuit complexity". In: *npj Quantum Information* 8.1 (Aug. 12, 2022), p. 96. URL: https://doi.org/10.1038/s41534-022-00599-z.

[242] Zhou, Leo, Wang, Sheng-Tao, Choi, Soonwon, Pichler, Hannes, and Lukin, Mikhail D. "Quantum Approximate Optimization Algorithm: Performance, Mechanism, and Implementation on Near-Term Devices". In: *Phys. Rev. X* 10 (2 June 2020), p. 021067. URL: https://link.aps.org/doi/10.1103/PhysRevX.10.021067.

[243] Zoufal, Christa, Lucchi, Aurélien, and Woerner, Stefan. "Quantum Generative Adversarial Networks for learning and loading random distributions". In: *npj Quantum Information* 5.1 (Nov. 22, 2019), p. 103. URL: https://doi.org/10.1038/s41534-019-0223-2.

[244] Zwerver, A. M. J., Krähenmann, T., Watson, T. F., Lampert, L., George, H. C., Pillarisetty, R., Bojarski, S. A., Amin, P., Amitonov, S. V., Boter, J. M., Caudillo, R., Correas-Serrano, D., Dehollain, J. P., Droulers, G., Henry, E. M., Kotlyar, R., Lodari, M., Lüthi, F., Michalak, D. J., Mueller, B. K., Neyens, S., Roberts, J., Samkharadze, N., Zheng, G., Zietz, O. K., Scappucci, G., Veldhorst, M., Vandersypen, L. M. K., and Clarke, J. S. "Qubits made by advanced semiconductor manufacturing". In: *Nature Electronics* 5.3 (Mar. 1, 2022), pp. 184–190.

Index

S

T

W

X

Y

Z

Share your thoughts

Now that you've finished *Dancing with Qubits, Second Edition*, we'd love to hear your thoughts! Scan the QR code below to go straight to the Amazon review page for this book and share your feedback.

https://packt.link/r/1837636753

Your review is important to us and the tech community and will help us make sure we're delivering excellent quality content.

Learn more on Discord

Join the Discord community for this book, where you can share feedback, ask questions to the author, and learn about new releases:

https://discord.com/invite/9sJCQvCAAD.

Download a free PDF copy of this book

Thanks for purchasing this book!

Do you like to read on the go but are unable to carry your print books everywhere?

Is your eBook purchase not compatible with the device of your choice?

Don't worry, now with every Packt book you get a DRM-free PDF version of that book at no cost.

Read anywhere, any place, on any device. Search, copy, and paste code from your favorite technical books directly into your application.

The perks don't stop there, you can get exclusive access to discounts, newsletters, and great free content in your inbox daily.

Follow these simple steps to get the benefits:

- Scan the QR code or visit the link below:

https://packt.link/free-ebook/9781837636754

- Submit your proof of purchase
- That's it! We'll send your free PDF and other benefits to your email directly